The social world of early mode...

Manchester University Press

Politics, culture and society in early modern Britain

General Editors

PROFESSOR ANN HUGHES
PROFESSOR ANTHONY MILTON
PROFESSOR PETER LAKE

This important series publishes monographs that take a fresh and challenging look at the interactions between politics, culture and society in Britain between 1500 and the mid-eighteenth century. It counteracts the fragmentation of current historiography through encouraging a variety of approaches which attempt to redefine the political, social and cultural worlds, and to explore their interconnection in a flexible and creative fashion. All the volumes in the series question and transcend traditional interdisciplinary boundaries, such as those between political history and literary studies, social history and divinity, urban history and anthropology. They thus contribute to a broader understanding of crucial developments in early modern Britain.

The social world
of early modern Westminster

Abbey, court and community
1525–1640

J. F. MERRITT

Manchester
University Press
Manchester and New York

distributed exclusively in the USA by Palgrave

Published by Manchester University Press
Oxford Road, Manchester M13 9NR, UK
and Room 400, 175 Fifth Avenue, New York, NY 10010, USA
www.manchesteruniversitypress.co.uk

Distributed in the United States exclusively by
Palgrave Macmillan, 175 Fifth Avenue,
New York, NY 10010, USA

Distributed in Canada exclusively by
UBC Press, University of British Columbia, 2029 West Mall,
Vancouver, BC, Canada V6T 1Z2

British Library Cataloguing-in-Publication Data is available

Library of Congress Cataloging-in-Publication Data is available

ISBN 978 0 7190 8773 8 paperback

First published by Manchester University Press in hardback 2005

This paperback edition first published 2012

Printed by Lightning Source

Contents

Contents

Contents

Illustrations

All illustrations are reproduced by kind permission of the Guildhall Library,
Corporation of London

Acknowledgements

The pleasure of finally reaching the end of a work of this kind is matched only by that of being able to use the opportunity to thank those who have helped on the journey. But I must first acknowledge the good fortune of a Fullbright-Hays award and the generosity of my parents, which enabled me to come to England in the first place, to develop a fascination with the history of London and ultimately to pursue a Ph.D. at the University of London. This book has emerged from my original Ph.D. thesis, but over a number of years it has been substantially recast and extended to include some entirely new themes and an expanded chronology. I would therefore like to thank those who have helped me at various stages along the way.

I am especially grateful to those who have read over parts of the initial thesis or subsequently provided help and guidance. Pride of place here goes to Professor Caroline Barron, an exemplary supervisor and friend, whose blend of intellectual curiosity and shrewd critical insights has so often encouraged me. I would especially like to thank her for reading the entire typescript and for sharing her expertise on medieval London over many years. The high scholarly standards set by the work of Ian Archer and Gervase Rosser have proved an inspiration and I would like to thank them both for their encouragement and generosity, especially during my time as a postgraduate student. Others offered invaluable guidance during my postgraduate years, especially Dan Beaver, Pauline Croft, Vanessa Harding, Michael Power, Conrad Russell, Bob Tittler and Tim Wales. I have also benefited from the community of scholars attached to two very different seminars at the Institute of Historical Research: the Medieval and Tudor London seminar and the Tudor–Stuart seminar. Peter Lake gave kind support and encouragement when I was first contemplating how to turn my thesis into the broader study that I knew was required, and has offered valuable advice thereafter. At different moments many friends and colleagues have, sometimes unknowingly, provided much-appreciated thoughts, references and encouragement (and sometimes all three): I am very grateful to Lynn Hulse, Ken Fincham, Andrew Foster, Martin Ingram, Jeremy Boulton, Andrew Thrush, Nigel Ramsay, Diarmaid MacCulloch, Mark Goldie, Martha Carlin, Stephen O'Connor, Helen Bradley and Marian Campbell. I would particularly like to thank Patricia Croot of the Victoria County History for sharing her thoughts about Westminster's jurisdictional boundaries at very short notice.

I should also like to acknowledge the support I have received over the years from various funding bodies. As a postgraduate I benefited from a Clay Memorial Scholarship, an Overseas Research Studentship and a Central Research Fund grant from the University of London. A grant from the Leverhulme Trust has subsequently allowed me to pursue further research and writing connected to the book.

While undertaking research for this project, I have spent many fruitful hours at that invaluable archive repository, now renamed the Westminster Archives Centre, where Ms Alison Kenny has always been especially helpful. I have also been fortunate to have worked in the atmospheric environs of the Muniment Room at Westminster Abbey, and am indebted to Miss Christine Reynolds and Dr Richard Mortimer, Keeper of the Muniments, for their assistance and encouragement. Thanks are also due to the staff at the Guildhall Library, London Metropolitan Archives and the National Archives. I must also acknowledge the generosity of the Marquis of Salisbury for permitting me to consult the manuscripts at Hatfield House, and the Trustees of the Chatsworth Settlement and Olive, Countess Fitzwilliam and the Wentworth Woodhouse Settled Estates for permitting access to their manuscript collections. I would also like to thank the Dean and Chapter of Westminster for allowing me to read their chapter act books.

At Manchester University Press Alison Welsby has been an extremely understanding and patient editor, while Jonathan Bevan has filled her shoes with efficiency and good cheer, and I am very grateful to both of them.

Finally, my husband Anthony, who has lived with the assorted characters and themes of this book for many years, deserves far more credit than a few sentences can easily convey. His unfailing good humour, tact, enthusiasm and advice has not only made possible the completion of this book, but also made it (or at least certain phases of it) a pleasure.

JFM
March 2004

Abbreviations

London P&P	*London Past & Present*, ed. H.B. Wheatley (3 vols., 1891)
London VCH	*Victoria County History of London*, ed. W. Page (1909)
Manchée	W.H. Manchée, *The Westminster City Fathers* (1924)
Merritt thesis	J.F. Merritt, 'Religion, Government and Society in Early Modern Westminster, 1525–1625' (London Ph.D., 1992)
P&P	*Past & Present*
PCW	Peculiar Court of Westminster
Rosser	G. Rosser, *Medieval Westminster* (Oxford, 1989)
SL	*Survey of London* (London County Council, 1900–63; Greater London Council, 1966–83; Royal Commission on Historical Monuments, 1985–)
Stow	J. Stow, *A Survey of London*, ed. C.L. Kingsford (2 vols., Oxford, 1908)
Strype	J. Strype, *A Survey of the Cities of London and Westminster* (2 vols., 1720)
TNA	The National Archives, London
WAC	Westminster Archives Centre
WAM	Westminster Abbey Muniments
Webbs, *Parish and County*	S. Webb and B. Webb, *English Local Government (The Parish and the County)* (1906, rpt 1924)
Webbs, *Manor and Borough*	S. Webb and B. Webb, *English Local Government (The Manor and the Borough)* (1908, rpt 1924)

For printed works the place of publication is London unless otherwise stated

Introduction

Rediscovering early modern
Westminster

Westminster is the greatest City in England next London, not onely in Position, but
by the Dimensions thereof . . . it filleth as much ground (not to say containeth more
reasonable souls) then any City in the Land. But as a proper man seemeth a Dwarfe,
when placed next to a Giant; such the infelicity of Westminster, whose due greatness,
devoured by the vicinity of London, is insensible in the eyes of the Beholders.[1]

SO wrote Thomas Fuller in 1662. These words were also prophetic of the later
study of early modern Westminster: it has been 'insensible' in the eyes of historians too. This is all the more surprising because the medieval town and its abbey
have received significant attention from historians in recent years.[2] Indeed the
groundbreaking work of Gervase Rosser has used the complex medieval community
surrounding Westminster Abbey as a springboard for rethinking urban identity in the
country as a whole. For the early modern period, however, Westminster as a subject of
study has remained virtually untouched. This has left a peculiar void in the urban history
of the capital.[3] While medieval historians have explored how a town of Westminster
emerged and acquired a distinctive urban identity in the period before 1540, these
themes have not been investigated for the early modern period. And yet the Reformation
and the construction of the royal palace of Whitehall would clearly come to have an
enormous impact on this dynamic urban centre.

Not only does the early modern period disappear from histories of Westminster,
but Westminster itself seems almost entirely to disappear in works of sixteenth- and

---

1 Thomas Fuller, *History of the Worthies of England* (1662), pt ii, 235.

2 Rosser; B. Harvey, *Westminster Abbey and its Estates in the Middle Ages* (Oxford, 1977); Harvey,
   Living and Dying in England 1100–1540 (Oxford, 1993).

3 For example in P. Hunting, *Royal Westminster* (1981), the only detailed history of Westminster
   published in the twentieth century, the chapter on 'The medieval suburb' is immediately followed
   by another on 'Georgian Westminster'.

seventeenth-century history.[4] And this despite the fact that, by the eve of the Civil War, as one recent historian has noted, 'had they been independent settlements the three Westminster parishes of St Margaret's, St Clement Danes and St Martin in the Fields would have ranked among the half dozen largest English provincial cities'.[5] Given that Westminster was also, of course, the seat of national government – playing host to Whitehall Palace, the royal courts of justice and parliament – it is evident that this is a rather substantial town to have become 'insensible' in the history of the period.

Fuller rightly saw the proximity of London as the main reason why Westminster was so overshadowed, despite what he felt to be the area's significance. It is certainly true that the separate urban centres of London and Westminster became increasingly linked by the continuous development of buildings and streets in the early modern period. 'The little citie Westminster . . . is now by faire buildings joyned to London' as James Howell explained in 1657, while others wrote of how the two cities had become 'by insensible coalition . . . incorporated into one continued peece in point of posture, though not of Government'.[6] But it is important to recognize that there are other reasons behind the neglect of Westminster as an early modern subject for study. At the most basic level, this neglect can partly be explained by the nature of surviving sources. There is no consolidated archive of relevant source material. In terms of jurisdiction, Westminster lay outside the City of London, and therefore did not possess bodies such as the Court of Aldermen, Common Council or livery companies – nor did it normally interact with these London organizations. Accordingly, many of the institutional records used by historians to construct the bare bones of a town's history were therefore never produced in Westminster in the first place. For the medieval period the records of Westminster Abbey have partly allowed historians to reconstruct the complex society beyond the cloisters, but its records are less informative for the post-Reformation period. The records of the individual Westminster parishes do constitute a very rich and largely unexploited source, and local sessions materials also shed much light on local society. But many issues of interest for the early modern period require us to look beyond administrative sources to more scattered materials, including contemporary printed material and private family papers located in various parts of the country. More generally, the absence of a large body of civic records has made it difficult for historians to come to grips with how Tudor and Stuart Westminster functioned, and indeed its larger significance. Of course, the very *absence* of a body of civic records – the lack of a Westminster equivalent to the Corporation of London Record

---

4 It is entirely absent from two important recent surveys of urban patronage and urban government in this period: C.F. Patterson, *Urban Patronage in Early Modern England* (Stanford, 1999); R. Tittler, *The Reformation and the Towns in England: Politics and Political Culture c.1540–1640* (Oxford, 1998).

5 R.M. Smuts, 'The Court and its neighbourhood: royal policy and urban growth in the early Stuart West End', *Journal of British Studies* 30 (1991), p. 118.

6 James Howell, *Londinopolis* (1657), p. 346; Fynes Moryson, *An Itinerary Containing His Ten Yeeres Travell* (4 vols., 1907–8), IV, 149.

Office – itself tells us something important about the amorphous character of early modern Westminster.

There is also another significant reason why 'Westminster' as an organizing principle in historical scholarship apparently fades from view in the early modern period, and this is an historiographical one. Essentially, Westminster 'disappears' because it is subsumed within several different historiographies. For the early modern period, one of the key issues for historians is the emergence of London as a metropolis. If one focuses on this aspect of the capital's history, Westminster has a less clear identity – it may be seen as part of London's western suburbs, as a portion of urban Middlesex or simply as one of the many parts of the modern metropolis that fell outside the jurisdiction of the City of London. Indeed, there is surprising variation in how historians have used the terms 'western suburbs', 'Westminster' and 'West End', even when producing tables of statistics. In the process, we often find that Westminster's constituent parts are prised apart and divided up among different categories.[7] There is also, perhaps, a certain teleology at work. Because we know that Westminster will ultimately be absorbed by metropolitan London, the need to look at Westminster in its own right in the early modern period has, perhaps, seemed less vital. But looking at Westminster more closely, as we will see, actually helps us to understand more fully the complex process of metropolitan development – and not to take its final outcome as given.

Another historiographical reason why 'Westminster' has figured less as an organizing concept in the Tudor–Stuart period has been its virtual replacement by another important theme – the rise of London's West End. This subject has attracted the attention of a range of notable historians, whose work, although springing out of different preoccupations, has sought to explore the impact of Court and aristocracy as consumers and patrons on the westward development of the metropolis.[8] Despite the fact that many of the most important developments associated with this process, such as the building of Covent Garden and Britain's Burse, took place within the boundaries of Westminster, the town has tended to fade into the background of this historical analysis, largely passed over in a broader discussion of cultural phenomena. In the work of Lawrence Stone and other historians of the peerage, the area tends to appear as a *tabula rasa* upon which aristocratic figures effortlessly imprinted themselves and their cultural preoccupations. This is not of course to underestimate the value of scholarship which has as its focus the social and cultural history of the aristocracy. Nevertheless,

7   E.g. M.J. Power, 'The east and the west in early-modern London' in E.W. Ives, R.J. Knecht and J.J. Scarisbrick (eds.), *Wealth and Power in Tudor England* (1978), pp. 167–85; Thomas G. Barnes, 'The prerogative and environmental control of London building in the early seventeenth century: the lost opportunity', *California Law Review* 58 (1970), *passim*, esp. p. 1338, n.20; R.B. Shoemaker, *Prosecution and Punishment* (Cambridge, 1991), p. 276.

8   F.J. Fisher, 'The development of London as a centre of conspicuous consumption in the sixteenth and seventeenth centuries', *Transactions of the Royal Historical Society* 4th ser. 30 (1948), pp. 37–50; L. Stone, *Family and Fortune* (Oxford, 1973). For some important qualifications see Smuts, 'The Court'.

the very use of the jurisdictionally neutral term 'West End' (which was not current in the pre-1640 period) may have helped to encourage this tendency to write as if these developments occurred in a new area with no past history or institutions.[9]

Other portions of the Westminster landscape have been broken off and analysed by other specialist historiographies. Westminster Abbey, for example, has tended to be studied within what might be termed a 'cathedral history' school of study, where the focus remains very much on the internal workings of the institution. Similarly, Court historians have studied Whitehall Palace, substantially advancing our understanding of the royal Court and its topography, but this scholarship seldom examines what happened outside its precincts, nor has it studied the interaction of the Court and local society.[10]

There is an obvious value in uniting these different historiographies via an integrated study of the common Westminster dimension in which they occurred. A history of the emergent West End, for example, is enriched by a greater appreciation of the range of social groups interacting in the neighbourhood. As we will see, the temporary nature of much gentry residence, and the transitory nature of servant employment, helped to create a complex society, where (rather than the relatively stable and self-evident hierarchies of rural life) status, reputation and deference were negotiated and re-negotiated in often tense and acrimonious ways. The application of a Westminster dimension to the study of Whitehall Palace can also (as we will see) offer a very different view of Court history, with the palace embedded in the heart of an ancient busy urban centre, thronged by beggars, poor street-traders and would-be servants, and fearful of disease and disorder. In addition, while recent work on the expansion of the metropolis has usefully questioned assumptions of a binary and mutually antagonistic opposition between city and suburbs, this rejection of binary models can further benefit from a study of a single suburb such as Westminster, whose distinctive institutions and traditions help to question whether we can write of a single, uniform suburban experience in this period.[11]

But a Westminster perspective also makes sense as an organizing principle because it did have meaning for contemporaries. From the elites who organized a seventy-foot-high triumphal arch at Temple Bar to represent Westminster at the 1603 coronation to the thousands who signed a peace petition from the inhabitants of Westminster in 1642, men and women would have been quite aware of the town's

---

9 E. Jones, 'The first West End comedy', *Proceedings of the British Academy* 68 (1982), pp. 225–6, notes some of the first seventeenth-century usages of the term.

10 E. Carpenter (ed.), *A House of Kings: The History of Westminster Abbey* (1966); *Acts*; S. Thurley, *The Royal Palaces of Tudor England* (New Haven, 1993); D. Starkey (ed.), *The English Court: from the Wars of the Roses to the Civil War* (1987). Historians of parliament are now recognizing more fully the importance of parliament's Westminster context, although thus far they have focused on the institution's physical setting rather than its relationship with the local town: C.R. Kyle, 'Parliament and the Palace of Westminster: An exploration of public space in the early seventeenth century', *Parliamentary History* 21 (2002); C.R. Kyle and J. Peacey, '"Under cover of so much coming and going": Public access to parliament and the political process in early modern England' in C.R. Kyle and J. Peacey (eds.), *Parliament at Work* (Woodbridge, 2002).

11 J.P. Ward, *Metropolitan Communities* (Stanford, 1997).

4

separate status from London. Indeed, from 1601 Westminster could even boast its own coat of arms.[12]

It seems likely that such evidence has been neglected owing to an often unspoken assumption that the early modern town was essentially part of London, and that jurisdictional distinctions were curious but largely irrelevant anomalies. Yet as these chapters will show, such legal and administrative distinctions directly affected the daily life of inhabitants. Chief among these distinctions was the simple fact that the jurisdiction of the lord mayor and aldermen of London did not extend into Westminster. In particular, the City's powerful livery companies did not shape the structures of economic life in the town, and the desire to escape livery company jurisdiction clearly provided an incentive to live in Westminster (as was also true of other suburban areas). Equally, Westminster inhabitants would also have encountered the town's own legal institutions, for example the Court of Burgesses and (by the seventeenth century) its own Westminster sessions of the peace. Local inhabitants were also involved in the election of two MPs to sit for Westminster in parliament. As ratepayers, Westminster inhabitants would also have been aware that poor relief and plague regulations were organized differently (and separately) from those known to their London neighbours. As we will see, even religious authority in the area was distinctive, with parishioners of St Margaret's under the jurisdiction of the dean of Westminster, a figure who still wielded substantial secular authority in the town.

It is equally striking that the early modern period witnessed a series of initiatives to place Westminster's jurisdictional independence on a more secure and permanent footing. As we will see, there were no fewer than three serious attempts within a fifty-year period (1585–1633) to establish Westminster as an incorporated and independent city, with the full range of civic powers. These attempts have hitherto escaped the attention of historians, who have partly been more preoccupied with other issues of suburban expansion. Yet it is important to recognize that the growth of the metropolis more generally was accompanied by determined attempts to protect Westminster's distinctiveness, and to create a new separate city. The fact that early modern history has lacked a Westminster dimension may reflect the later, ultimate failure of Westminster's attempts to carve out a distinctive corporate identity for itself, but it should not detract from the importance and unresolved nature of these issues at the time. This makes it all the more important to reconstruct the history of this curious and anomalous locality.

Before proceeding to a full study of early modern Westminster, it will be useful to identify the most distinctive topographical features of the area in this period.

---

12 Manchée, pp. 209–10; C.H. Herford, P. Simpson and E.M.S. Simpson (eds.), *The Works of Ben Jonson* (11 vols., Oxford, 1925–52), VIII, 106–8; *LJ*, V, p. 507; *A Petition of the Citie of Westminster* (1643). The original Westminster peace petition to parliament survives as HLRO, MP 20 December 1642, but does not appear in V. Pearl, *London and the Outbreak of the Puritan Revolution* (Oxford, 1961) or K. Lindley, *Popular Politics and Religion in Civil War London* (Aldershot, 1997). I plan to discuss it in more detail elsewhere.

An urban centre had originally developed around Westminster Abbey and the adjacent Westminster Palace in the medieval period, when the twin poles of London and Westminster were physically separate. These were linked, however, by a main road running from King Street and along the Strand, towards London. Not surprisingly, most urban development initially clustered along these thoroughfares.

For the purposes of this book, 'Westminster' has been taken to cover the area referred to by contemporaries as the city and liberties of Westminster.[13] This consisted, by Elizabeth's reign, of three parishes – those of St Margaret's, St Martin in the Fields and St Clement Danes, an area illustrated on Norden's map of 1593, although the map excludes undeveloped portions to the west (fig. 1).[14] It was the parishes, rather than the manor, which increasingly constituted the most important local institutions and source of identity in our period. Accordingly, the two largest and best-documented of these parishes – St Margaret's and St Martin in the Fields – will provide the chief focus for many issues explored in this book.

In terms of the overall development of the area, however, it may be helpful to think of Westminster as divided into three general areas. The first of these was the Strand, which ran from the ancient Charing Cross (location of the Royal Mews) to Temple Bar in the east. It was Temple Bar that marked the boundary between Westminster and London. The Strand was especially noteworthy in our period for the townhouses of the aristocracy, many of them with gardens running down to the Thames. At the Charing Cross end of the Strand was St Martin's Lane – a fashionable address by the seventeenth century – and it was here that St Martin's church stood. More generally, the Strand was the site of many inns and taverns, as befitted such a busy thoroughfare. The highway ran through the parishes of St Martin in the Fields and St Clement Danes, and the church of St Clement's itself was situated in what was already a built-up area at the start of our period.

The most densely populated part of Westminster was the parish of St Margaret's, the ancient 'vill' of Westminster. Even in the seventeenth century, contemporaries might refer to 'Westminster' or the 'City of Westminster' when actually referring only to the parish of St Margaret's, with the other parts of Westminster referred to as its 'liberties'.[15] At the heart of the parish in the sixteenth century lay a complex of medieval and early Tudor buildings of national importance – Westminster Abbey, Whitehall Palace and Westminster Hall. All three stood in close proximity, with the parish church of St Margaret's located in the shadow of the Abbey church. Whitehall Palace itself

---

13 E.g. WAM 5299A; Surrey History Centre, LM/1989. The precise extent of the manor of Westminster continues to be an area of considerable scholarly controversy: see the forthcoming *VCH Westminster*.

14 The parish of St Mary le Strand ceased to exist in ecclesiastical terms after the Reformation, although it continued to be used in some circumstances as a unit for civil administration – see R. Sommerville, *The Savoy, Manor: Hospital: Chapel* (1960), pp. 48–9.

15 See below pp. 72, 129n, 305.

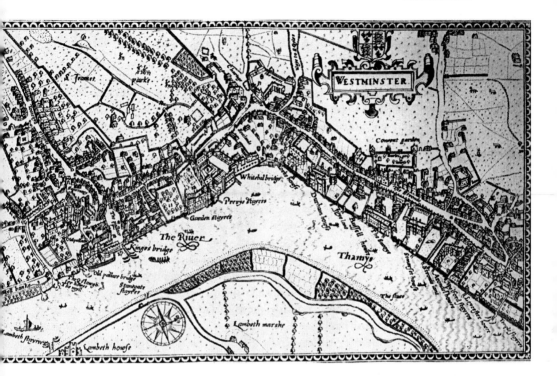

John Norden's 1593 bird's – eye view of Westminster. From left to right, note the Abbey (A), St Margaret Westminster (immediately to the right), St Martin in the Fields (O, opposite the Mews at Charing Cross) and St Clement Danes (R, in the middle of the Strand).

was a maze of rambling buildings which straddled King Street and fronted the river Thames. Nearby was New Palace Yard, with its public fountain, the largest open area in this constricted location by the Palace. Aside from King Street, the other main artery in this area was Tothill Street, another popular location for the inns and taverns that serviced the courtiers and government bureaucrats who flocked to the area.

But aside from these more built-areas of the town, large swathes of Westminster remained undeveloped land. Substantial portions of both St Margaret's and St Martin in the Fields contained land of this nature and it effectively formed an arc running from Knightsbridge and St James Park in the west to Covent Garden in the east. Areas to the north of the Strand contained a patchwork of garden plots and undistinguished houses. These came under increasing pressure in the early seventeenth century and it was here that the earl of Bedford's handsome, classically-inspired development of Covent Garden would take place in the 1630s. But it was the western portions of Westminster that were most characterized by open fields. Here, on the very edge of the metropolis were grazing lands, market gardens and royal parkland, all of which edged quite close to Whitehall Palace itself. From royal palace to garden plots, Westminster encompassed a remarkable range of contrasting landscapes and land usage.

Of course, buildings of national importance inevitably loom large in any description of Westminster. But this book particularly seeks to avoid a perspective whereby the heart of Westminster is treated as exclusively 'national space'. Rather, the same areas – sometimes even the same space and buildings – that played host to events of national importance might be appropriated by Westminster's inhabitants to perform very different functions. Westminster Hall may have housed the nation's law courts, but it was also the site of local parliamentary elections and the meeting place of Westminster's Sessions of the peace (from 1618), and by the 1650s was playing host to another civic event in the shape of the 'Westminster feast', a celebration of those inhabitants actually born in Westminster.[16] The Hall was also a space thronged by booksellers, law stationers and dealers in small wares and toys, as well as being a popular haunt of cutpurses.[17] Similarly, Westminster Abbey may have acted as a religious and ritual centre associated with the monarchy – the venue of royal burials and coronations – but it was also a dominant political and economic power in the locality. Within its doors local people – as well as tourists – would meet and converse, do business or (notoriously) receive stolen goods. It was here too that alms in the form of meat and bread were distributed to selected local poor on a weekly basis, while its large porch was also noted as a place for sellers of books and linen.[18] Similarly, the royal Tilt-yard may have been the stage for courtly tournaments, but it was also a rendezvous of prostitutes and their clients, as cases in the Westminster Sessions verify.[19] Equally, the same streets that witnessed royal processions at other times served as a punishment trail along which malefactors were whipped from Westminster Gatehouse (near the Abbey) right through to Temple Bar, where the bleeding unfortunates were formally ejected from the town.[20]

Early modern Westminster was almost uniquely a place where the national and the local collided, and which played home simultaneously to some of the richest and poorest people in England. We can do justice to its history only by exploring the interaction of all of the constituent elements of this remarkable locality.

---

16 Surrey History Centre, LM/1989; Sheffield City Archives, Elmhirst Pye Papers, MS 1287(c).

17 *London P&P*, III, 484; LMA, WJ/SR (NS), 21/142; TNA, E163/13/18, pp. 17–18.

18 E.g. LMA, WJ/SR (NS) 41/3, 4, 4a; P. Razzell (ed.), *The Journals of Two Travellers in Elizabethan and Early Stuart England* (1995), p. 41.

19 E.g. LMA, WJ/SR (NS) 39/88.

20 WAC, WCB1, p. 35; WCB2, p. 117.

Chapter 1

Henrician Westminster:
corporate life in a time of change
1525–47

THE decade of the 1530s was a tumultuous period for all of England. But for the town of Westminster and its parishes, in particular, this decade marked a decisive turning-point for many of its medieval institutions. A new and sumptuous royal residence was constructed in the very heart of the old vill of Westminster, and as the new Palace of Whitehall emerged, old buildings were demolished, parish boundaries were altered and forced royal purchases resulted in the seizure of large tracts of undeveloped land in the surrounding area. The 1530s were also, of course, a time of Reformation. This meant not only significant reforms of local religious culture but also the eclipse of an institution that stood at the heart of medieval Westminster. As the Crown dissolved religious houses across the nation, the once great and powerful Abbey at Westminster could not escape a similar fate. The dissolution of Westminster Abbey led to the disappearance of a pilgrimage centre and threatened its raison d'être as a source of prayers for the royal dead, while the institution's religious and economic influence in the town was substantially curtailed and redefined.

The dissolution of the monasteries was also, of course, simply one aspect of the wider changes introduced by the Henrician Reformation. The lives of men and women were further disrupted by a transformation in parish religion. Although the reigns of Edward VI and Mary would have their own unsettling affects on the town of Westminster, some of the most important structural changes to affect the town took place under Henry VIII, and it is impossible to understand much of the later history of Westminster without them. In this chapter, we will investigate precisely what these wide-ranging Henrician developments meant for the inhabitants of Westminster.

To address these issues, we first need to examine the nature of local identity in Westminster before and during the early Reformation period. How strong were corporate bonds among townspeople, and in what corporate activities did they engage? As many of the local rituals and communal festivities were of a religious nature, it will also be important to assess their nature in the light of the early Reformation. How did Henrician religious changes affect the corporate lives of these local men and women?

Finally, we need to consider the extent to which this religious impact was itself shaped by the important social, topographical and administrative changes in Westminster that ran parallel to the Henrician Reformation.

These questions are best explored by examining the parishes which constituted Westminster – how they operated in the pre-Reformation period, and especially the role played by the religious organizations which bore the brunt of the religious changes implemented by Henry and his immediate successors. In contrast to the City of London, there was no formal town government in Westminster, and local identities were therefore necessarily centred on parochial institutions and loyalties.[1] Medieval Londoners had their parish-based organizations, of course, but they could also participate in a number of organizations which extended beyond the parish. Individuals might belong to a livery company, hold office in City government and join not only a parish fraternity but also one of the fraternities based on the five orders of friars in London. Even taxation in London was based not on the parish but on the larger unit of the ward, and City parishes sometimes even straddled more than one ward.[2] In Westminster, by contrast, the parish provided an organizing principle for its inhabitants in a more exclusive way. Local government was less complex, without a lord mayor or court of aldermen, livery companies did not exist, taxation was based upon the parish and parish-based fraternities were the rule. While the manor of Westminster existed as a unit of administration, it is difficult to assess its impact on social relationships: not only is it poorly documented for our period, but the infrequency of its meetings made it a less likely vehicle for local initiatives than the parish.[3]

There were four parishes in Westminster at the turn of the sixteenth century. By far the most important of these was the parish of St Margaret's. Not only was St Margaret's the most populous and most significant parish in the town, it was intimately linked both spatially and administratively to Westminster Abbey itself. The other three parishes – St Clement Danes, St Martin in the Fields and St Mary le Strand – were all far less populous and less economically important than St Margaret's during the medieval period. The dissolution of the tiny parish of St Mary's in the 1540s, along with the dearth of records for the parish of St Clement's, makes a study of the two largest parishes, St Margaret Westminster and St Martin in the Fields, the best means of analysing the complex ties between social organization, local identity and religious life in this area.[4] In addition, the parishes of St Martin's and St Margaret's have been identified as two of

---

1 See Rosser, pp. 228–9, 289–93; Merritt thesis, pp. 18–19; and below, ch. 4.

2 C.M. Barron, 'London 1300–1540' in D.M. Palliser (ed.), *The Cambridge Urban History of Britain, vol. I 600–1540* (Cambridge, 2000), pp. 407, 428–32; C. Barron, 'The parish fraternities of Medieval London' in C.M. Barron and C. Harper-Bill (eds.), *The Church in Pre-Reformation Society* (Woodbridge, 1985), pp. 14–16, 23; S. Brigden, 'Religion and social obligation in Early sixteenth-century London', *P&P* 103 (1984), p. 95.

3 The surviving series of manorial court rolls ends in 1514 (Rosser, p. 5), at which time its activities seem to have focused on the parish of St Margaret. For the manor see also below, pp. 102n, 227.

4 The church of St Mary le Strand was torn down at the command of the Lord Protector around

only eighteen English parishes for which continuous and detailed parish records survive for the turbulent period 1535 to 1570.[5] This in itself makes a comparison of the two parishes particularly valuable. As we shall see, however, despite their proximity, these two parishes were to experience very different patterns of development over the succeeding century. Differences in social organization, administrative structure and corporate life in the two parishes also provide a study in contrasts. These crucial differences, as we shall see, partly shaped forms of lay piety in each parish as well as their very different responses to the religious reformations of Henry VIII and his children.

THE WESTMINSTER PARISHES BEFORE THE 1530S

ST MARGARET WESTMINSTER

Standing at the heart of Westminster, St Margaret's was arguably one of the most important parishes in the country. In the medieval period, the presence of Westminster Abbey and Westminster Palace had stimulated extensive urban development in the parish, which was also co-terminous with a 'vill' of Westminster. Most of this medieval building stretched along the axis of Tothill Street and King Street, the latter forming part of the highway linking Westminster to London. It was traditionally claimed that the laymen and women of the vill had originally worshipped in part of the Abbey church, but by the late eleventh century it seems that a separate parish church, dedicated to St Margaret, had been erected for the townspeople. By the sixteenth century, St Margaret's had for many years been one of the wealthiest and most established parishes in the capital, serving a varied community which not only included large numbers of brewers, butchers, innkeepers and royal officials but also a sprinkling of printers and luxury retailers. The parish and its officials still maintained close links with the Abbey, which owned most of the property in the locality, but the size and wealth of the parish had led it to develop a substantial amount of independence and self-confidence.[6]

1548 to make way for the building of Somerset House. The parish itself was already described as dissolved in a report of the chantry commissioners in 1547, and for most purposes was absorbed by St Clement Danes: R. Sommerville, *The Savoy, Manor: Hospital: Chapel* (1960), pp. 48–9. Records are sparse for the medieval period and pre-Reformation period, but for urban development see P. Croot, 'Before and after Drury House: Development of a Suburban Town House 1250–1800', *London Topographical Record*, 18 (2001). The parish of St Clement Danes is also poorly documented before the mid-seventeenth century, but see below. For both parishes see also Merritt thesis, pp. 19–23, and the overview account provided in the forthcoming Westminster volume of the *VCH Middlesex*.

5   R. Hutton, 'The Local Impact of the Tudor Reformations' in C. Haigh (ed.), *The English Reformation Revised* (Cambridge, 1987), p. 115.

6   Rosser, pp. 67, 122–43, 158–60, 210–15, 251–2.

St Margaret's was easily the wealthiest, most populous and most urbanized of the Westminster parishes, with 2,500 communicants recorded there in 1548.[7] The contrast between the more urbanized St Margaret's and the less settled St Martin's is perhaps best encapsulated by the titles adopted by successive sets of sixteenth-century churchwardens. Those of St Margaret's described themselves in their accounts as the 'Keper of the goodyes Juellis and ornaments' of the church, while those of St Martin's styled themselves more simply as 'churchwardens'. Henrician churchwardens at St Margaret's also benefited from a long tradition of parish government, with formalized procedures regulating parish finance and record keeping. The very presentation of parochial documents, carefully itemized in the hand of a professional scribe, with consistent categories of expenditure and income, speaks of the financial sophistication needed to manage the affairs of a large community. The fact that churchwardens were paid for their attendance and also for keeping a particular book suggests the business-like approach they brought to office-holding. Parish records also refer to the 'worshipful' of the parish who 'allowed' parish accounts and 'the olde laudable custome' of holding a supper when the accounts were audited and two new churchwardens selected from among their number.[8]

The accounts also reveal a larger, more sophisticated parish administration than that found in other Westminster parishes, employing a permanent staff of approximately thirteen men in the early sixteenth century. The composition of this staff reflects the size and wealth of the parish, its success in attracting bequests and, significantly, its links with the Abbey in the celebration of the ritual year. As befitted the close relations between Abbey and parish church, the curate was actually supplied by Westminster Abbey (specifically by the sacrist), and the parish employed at least two clerks, a sexton, a 'conduct' who led the choir, and a man solely responsible for maintaining the rood lights. On more important feast days, members of the Abbey choir or that of the Chapel Royal added their voices to those of the regular St Margaret's establishment – a clear indication that the elaborate polyphonic music that accompanied services in the church was in touch with the latest developments in musical taste. In addition, one of St Margaret's clerks received an extra 40s a year for teaching the 'Synging Children', who would have participated in services in the church. In 1548 the parish also reported to chantry commissioners that no fewer than six chantry priests served in the church.[9]

---

7 Kitching, pp. 64–5. If one adds two-fifths to account for children under fourteen, this roughly equates to a population of 3,500.

8 WAC, E2 (1530–32). Parish government in St Margaret's is examined more closely in ch. 4. For a snapshot of the richness of church goods at St Margaret's see the 1511 parish inventory printed in J.E. Smith (ed.), *A Catalogue of Westminster Records* (1900), pp. 235–7.

9 WAC, E3 (1530–32); Kitching, p. 65; Rosser, p. 254. A number of the members of the Chapel Royal were also parishioners of St Margaret's: see F. Kisby, 'Music and musicians of early Tudor Westminster', *Early Music* 23 (1995), pp. 223–41.

It seems likely that a taste for highly elaborate images, ceremonial and music at St Margaret's had developed at least partly because of the proximity of the Abbey church – and such taste could be maintained because of the support of the substantial numbers of wealthy laymen based in the parish. The association between Abbey and parish was further encouraged by their joint celebration of certain holy days – a custom that was preserved even after the Abbey's reconstitution as a collegiate church under a dean and chapter. These holy day processions would inevitably have been more elaborate and solemn than those undertaken by the parish on its own. The cult of saints in St Margaret's may also have received indirect encouragement from the Abbey. It should be remembered that, until its dissolution, the Abbey was a major pilgrimage centre, housing the shrine of Edward the Confessor, among other relics, and that St Margaret's itself claimed possession of relics of St Margaret and St George.[10]

The vigour of corporate life within St Margaret's is underlined by the sheer number of fraternities that the parish supported. The relationship between these fraternities and the parish is an intriguing one, especially in the light of changes inaugurated during the Henrician Reformation. Work by Gervase Rosser has emphasized the significant role that St Margaret's fraternities played in the secular government of the town by the late medieval period. The most wealthy and powerful of these fraternities was dedicated to the Assumption of the Virgin Mary, but no fewer than eight fraternities are recorded at St Margaret's, the earliest dating from 1385. Other fraternities were dedicated to St Cornelius, St John the Baptist, St George, St Christopher, Corpus Christi, St Mary Rounceval and the Holy Trinity. The number of fraternities and the populousness of St Margaret's itself may well reflect parishioners' desire to create smaller units within the parish, an interpretation given weight by the finding that the most successful and properous fraternities in the capital were actually located in the capital's large extra-mural parishes.[11]

St Margaret's fraternities were organizations of long standing, and their activities overlapped and augmented those of the parish in a number of ways. Nevertheless they operated in an independent fashion, electing their own officials, keeping their own accounts, holding their own special feasts, purchasing banners and other items necessary for processions and employing their own priests. Their primary function, of course, was to ensure that members received a good funeral and to pray for the souls of deceased members. In this sense they may rightly be considered exclusive organizations, yet there is no evidence that members withdrew in any way from the wider parish. Most churchwardens, for example, also belonged to one or more of the fraternities, while parochial and guild office normally went hand in hand. The wealth and organizing power of the fraternities also benefited the parish as whole, and the responsibilities assumed by the wealthiest of these paralleled the role played elsewhere in the

---

10 WAC, E3 (1530–32), E4 (1553–54); Rosser, pp. 35–6, 271, 284, 296.

11 Rosser, pp. 281–93; Kitching, p. xxxii.

country by a formally constituted town government. Given that Westminster, under the secular authority of its abbot, had no formal town government, it has been argued that these activities were crucial in enabling the 'vill' to cope with the economic dislocation of the late medieval period.[12]

Guilds contributed to parish life in the early sixteenth century in a number of ways. The guild of the Virgin's Assumption, for example, did not restrict its charity to its own members, but also maintained almshouses for the parish poor in Our Lady Alley. St Margaret's guilds also played a role in maintaining the fabric of the parish church, with the Assumption guild, for example, donating a bell to the parish church in 1522–23.[13] In the 1530s, when St Margaret's churchwardens evidently found that the expense of both a new rood loft and other building work exceeded what the parish could afford, help came in the form of loans supplied by the various fraternities. In 1534–35, the master and wardens of both the St Cornelius and Rounceval fraternities each gave £10 upon the receipt of 'Certayn plate' to further work upon the rood loft. A little more than a year later, additional loans were forthcoming, including £10 from the fraternity of the Virgin's Assumption, loaned 'upon the best Crosse'. The considerable assets of these fraternities put them in a position to act as bankers for the wider parish, a service which they were clearly happy to perform.[14]

The church of St Margaret's, of course, was the focal point of activities for the wider body of parishioners as well as for guild members. Not surprisingly, the elaborately decorated church of St Margaret's reflected the populous and long-established neighbourhood it served, where the proximity of the royal Court and Abbey meant that parishioners included both Crown and Abbey officials. By the early sixteenth century, however, the edifice of St Margaret's church had been much altered. An ambitious building programme had been undertaken between c.1487 and 1523, leaving the church largely as it stands today.[15] As a consequence, funds were not diverted into costly building programmes after 1523, as happened several times during the sixteenth century at St Martin in the Fields. Instead church revenues and the generous impulses of parishioners could be directed towards the provision of church furniture and ornaments, keeping the structure in good repair and maintaining the lights in the church. This rich environment for worship was complemented by the magnificent attire of those who served in the church and by the adornment of various altars. By the end of Henry VIII's reign, the parish owned no fewer than seventeen suits of vestments – each consisting of a set of hangings for the altar together with a

---

12 Merritt thesis, pp. 23–6; G. Rosser, 'The essence of medieval urban communities: the vill of Westminster, 1200–1540', *Transactions of the Royal Historical Society* 5th ser. 34 (1984), pp. 91–112.

13 For the details of these fraternities see Rosser, pp. 281–93, 310–20.

14 WAC, E3 (1534–35, 1535–36). Fraternities did, of course, make outright donations to the parish. Rosser rejects the suggestion that parishes and guilds represented alternative or mutually hostile foci of religious activity: A.G. Rosser, 'Communities of parish and guild in the late Middle Ages' in S.J. Wright (ed.), *Parish, Church and People* (1988), p. 42.

15 Rosser, p. 210; Rosser, 'Essence', p. 102.

suit of robes for the priest – as well as twenty-one copes, including three copes for children and thirteen corporas cloths.[16]

The church itself was well provided with lights, altars and images – all objects of devotion.[17] By the early sixteenth century the most striking of these must surely have been the two statues of St Catherine and St Margaret, both placed within highly ornate 'tabernacles' or wooden frames and situated in the chancel. The numerous chapels in the church would also have been lit with candles and accounts refer to chapels dedicated to St George, St Cornelius, St Erasmus, the Trinity, St John, St Mary and St Nicholas. Most of these saints also had fraternities associated with them in the parish, while other aspects of the church reflected the popularity of the cult of saints. A particular treasure was 'a piece of the head of St George, set in silver gilt', that was housed in the church and an object of special veneration to the members of the guild of St George, some of whom may have worn badges depicting an image of the saint on festive occasions. From 1535, parishioners could also rent 'St George's cloth' for use as a hearse cloth at funerals. St George, of course, was a popular saint nationally and associated with the Crown since the fourteenth century, but his association with a dragon may also have linked him in the minds of parishioners with their popular patron saint, St Margaret.[18]

St Margaret's parishioners displayed special devotion to their patron saint, and her cult held both religious and civic associations. The parish possessed a relic of the saint's finger and her image stood prominently in the chancel. The tabernacle holding this statue was an elaborate piece of workmanship, which seems to have depicted scenes from the life of the saint, St Margaret of Antioch, whose fame derived from her dramatic slaying of a dragon. Suspended over the statue was a crown of martyrs, while a coral rosary, on a silver chain with a pearl clasp, had been donated to the parish around 1500, to be hung upon the figure on appropriate occasions. In 1531–32, parishioners banded together to contribute towards the costs of the 'gylding' of St Margaret's tabernacle. The 'benevolence of good People' raised over £13 and donations were recorded from sixty-eight individuals, and 40s from 'our grett lady Brotherhed'. The latter donation is particularly worth noting, as it suggests how devotion to the saint drew all members of the parish together, as individuals or as member of smaller corporate communities.[19]

Religious devotion also expressed itself in St Margaret's through the celebration

---

16 M.E.C. Walcott, *The History of St Margaret Westminster* (1847), pp. 68–72, prints a complete inventory of church goods dating from early 1547. In 1528–29, a single suit of vestments purchased for the parish of Ashburton cost £32 13s 4d, which gives some sense of the cost involved: J.A.F. Thomson, *The Early Tudor Church and Society, 1485–1529* (1993), p. 282.

17 In addition to the rood lights, a 'lampe in the quyre' was funded from the sale of wood from a property in Hendon owned by the parish, which yielded 33s 4d a year. WAC, E3 (1538–39, 1546–47).

18 Rosser, pp. 283–4; WAC, E4 (1550–51).

19 Rosser, pp. 271–2; WAC, E3 (1531–32).

of the various holidays of the liturgical year. Certain holidays were celebrated with great pomp and display, when the participation of the entire parish was expected. These occasions, which doubtless attracted great numbers to the church, were also used to hold collections. The days of 'Common Gatherings' at St Margaret's were Whit Sunday, St Margaret's Day (not surprisingly), All Hallows Day, Christmas and Good Friday. The expenses associated with Easter also meant that additional gatherings were held for the sepulchre light and the 'paschal money' – the latter presumably to pay for the great paschal candle that burned throughout all the service of Easter, being lit for the last time on Ascension Day, six weeks later. The Easter practice of 'hocking' also served as a means of fund-raising. The custom involved a mock battle of the sexes on two consecutive days. On Hock Monday, the men of the parish pursued and caught the women of the parish, freeing them only upon payment of a 'ransom', the sum paid then being turned over to the parish. On Hock Tuesday, the role of sexes was reversed, as the wives of the parish bound the men before releasing them upon due payment. Hocktide was primarily an urban phenomenon in England, and was also observed at the adjacent parish of St Martin's, as well as in some other London parishes. The custom actually seems to have been an early fifteenth-century invention, and in the case of St Margaret's the activity appears to have been introduced in 1497 as a fund-raising activity connected with the rebuilding of the parish church.[20]

Most feast days gave rise to some form of corporate activity, and the most striking of these would have been public processions. The banners in the possession of St George's guild or those belonging to the fraternity of the Holy Trinity shed only a flicker of light on what must have been dramatic occasions, with members of the parish taking part in a single procession, but divided according to their special association with one grouping or another.[21] On Palm Sunday the parish usually paid for bread and ale, but this was probably restricted to the 'worshipful' of the parish, who read out the Passion gospel in church. There is no record, however, of any of the plays or more elaborate processions which took place on Palm Sundays at other churches in the capital, including St Martin's. The feast of Corpus Christi, of course, traditionally included an elaborate procession, probably led by the Corpus Christi brotherhood, while the church was decorated with red roses. References in parish documents from the 1510s and 1520s indicate that the procession included ministrels who played in the town, while the sacrament itself was carried under a canopy of cloth of gold. The symbolic importance of the Corpus Christi procession as a living representation of the community as a whole has been emphasized by a range of historians. Nevertheless, by the 1530s these festivities appear to have become less elaborate at St Margaret's.

---

20 E.g. WAC, E3 (1531–32), R. Hutton, *The Rise and Fall of Merry England: The Ritual Year 1400–1700* (Oxford, 1994), pp. 26, 36, 59–60. For the social implications of Hocktide and its celebration at Coventry in the form of a Hock Tuesday play see C. Phythian-Adams, 'Ceremony and the citizen: the communal year at Coventry 1450–1550' in P. Clark and P. Slack (eds.), *Crisis and Order in English Towns 1500–1700* (1972).

21 Rosser, pp. 283–4.

Accounts itemize payments to torch-bearers and for bread, ale and wine, but in 1531 these costs totalled only 2s 9d. Some subsequent years barely recorded any Corpus Christi expenses, although as late as 1547 the parish paid for torches, garlands and crosses on Corpus Christi Day.[22]

By contrast, parishioners always prepared elaborately for the feast of their patron saint, St Margaret, on 20 July. The very nature of preparations for St Margaret's Day speaks of its popularity, with the parish calling upon the resources of the Abbey and neighbouring notables to ensure its lavish celebration. The church itself was decorated with garlands of flowers and draped with rich silk or Arras hangings. The easy ties between the parish and members of the royal establishment are suggested by the fact that these costly hangings were often borrowed or hired from one of the royal palaces near London. In 1530, for example, the parish paid for 'Caryage of Clothes from Yorke place' in connection with the St Margaret's Day festivities. Members of the Chapel Royal also participated at the mass with which the day began. The neighbouring Abbey was also involved in the celebrations, with the choir of Westminster Abbey assisting at the festive mass in some years, while on at least one occasion St Margaret's churchwardens paid for the 'the Clothes of the Abbey'.[23] The celebrations included a procession of the parish virgins through the town, while the singing that such services would have entailed was supplemented by the brass instruments of 'the Wayttes . . . goying Aprocessyon'. The culmination of these activities involved a re-enactment of the legend of St Margaret, complete with dragon and bonfire. More music accompanied this stage in the proceedings, and churchwardens' accounts regularly list payments to 'the mynstrell for playing before the virgyne', clearly one of the highlights of the play. As on other feast days, the parish supplied bread, wine and ale for at least some of the large number of parishioners who must have attended the festivities.[24]

St Margaret's thus appears on the eve of the 1530s as a parish which enjoyed a strikingly rich ceremonial life, especially notable for the strength of lay devotion to patron saints and the important role played by the lay fraternities in parish life. This was a parish where the Henrician and Edwardian reformations could not fail to have a devastating impact.

---

22 WAC, E3 (1531–32 ff.); Rosser, p. 199. For a description of the activities associated with Passiontide and Palm Sunday see Hutton, *Merry England*, pp. 20–1. For the celebration of Corpus Christi see E. Duffy, *The Stripping of the Altars* (New Haven, 1992), pp. 43–4; M. Rubin, *Charity and Community in Medieval Cambridge* (Cambridge, 1987), pp. 243–71; Rubin, *Corpus Christi* (Cambridge, 1991), pp. 213–87; Rosser, 'Myth, image and social procession in the English medieval town', *Urban History* 23 (1996), pp. 18–19, 21. St Margaret's declining enthusiasm for the festival may reflect a broader metropolitan trend: there is no evidence that the famed Corpus Christi pageants, found in towns such as Coventry and York, took place in London or in a number of substantial provincial towns. In London, craft guilds lavished their attention upon the Midsummer Watch rather than Corpus Christi (Hutton, *Merry England*, pp. 40–4).

23 WAC, E3 (1530–32); Rosser, pp. 272–4.

24 In 1530, the waits were paid 5s 4d, while their breakfast cost the parish another 7d. WAC, E3 (1530–32, 1533–34).

ST MARTIN IN THE FIELDS

Although a church of St Martin in the Fields was in existence before the death of Henry II in 1189, the parish of St Martin's was originally subsumed within the larger parish of St Margaret's. In 1222, a decree concerning disputed jurisdiction between the bishop of London and the abbot of Westminster exempted St Martin's church and churchyard from the bishop's jurisdiction – but this was as part of St Margaret's parish. By 1300, however, St Martin's parish had come into existence, with the prior of Westminster as rector. These early relations do much to explain certain informal ties between the mother and daughter parish that lingered on into the sixteenth and even the seventeenth century, such as the sharing of parish commons.[25] The less established and relatively rural character of St Martin's parish is apparent from maps of the capital dating from the mid-sixteenth century. These show built-up areas around Charing Cross, the location of the Royal Mews and along the Strand, where episcopal palaces fronted the Thames. But aside from St Martin's church – itself very near Charing Cross – only fields are shown, while the westernmost parts of this enormous parish, extending as far as Knightsbridge – were sufficiently undeveloped not even to warrant inclusion. It was not until the mid-seventeenth century that maps of the capital actually depicted these western portions of St Martin's parish, not long before urban development led to these areas being redesignated as part of entirely new parishes.[26]

In the first half of the sixteenth century, St Martin in the Fields was very much a parish of contrasts. The parish contained large tracts of undeveloped fields, owned by a number of different religious houses, which were mostly used as pasture, but its built-up areas along Charing Cross and the Strand had held some noble and royal associations since the medieval period. The identity of the Henrician parish itself appears less formal and well-established in comparison with the more urbanized St Margaret's. Nor was there the large contingent of well-to-do laymen who jostled shoulders at St Margaret's. It is likely that the handful of prosperous benefactors to the church stood out from their fellow parishioners. The more informal character of early parish government clearly reflects St Martin's smaller and less wealthy population, but it was also related to the long-standing ties which bound it to the 'mother' parish of St Margaret's. In a matter of a few decades, however, structural and religious changes in the parish would require St Martin's to forge a new and more distinctive identity.[27]

The first churchwardens' accounts to survive for St Martin's provide the best evidence of its still-evolving forms of financial procedure and relatively ad hoc parochial government in the early sixteenth century. The accounts themselves initially vary

---

25 *SL*, XX, pt 3, p. 13; *London VCH*, p. 584.

26 For earlier see S. Prockter and A. Taylor (eds.), *A to Z of Elizabethan London* (Lympne Castle, 1979) and John Norden's 1593 bird's-eye view of Westminster.

27 Before 1500 only eleven wills survive for St Martin's, although the appropriate will registers date back to the fourteenth century: Merritt thesis, p. 34. This paucity of wills would suggest that St Martin's was not only less populous but less prosperous than the neighbouring St Margaret's.

in presentation, with the first set of accounts covering a five-year period from 1525 to 1530, and expenses not always fully itemized. From 1530 onwards, however, the accounts cover regular two-year terms, as was then customary at St Margaret's and many London churches.[28] Parish administration at St Martin's appears to have been less formally organized than at St Margaret's and to have employed fewer people. The parish had a vicar, appointed by Westminster Abbey, one clerk and one sexton. Rather than permanently employing a large staff, the parish made single payments as required. The clerk was paid 4s a year for keeping a book of burials, among his other duties, although this sum was evidently supplemented by the quarterly collections made for his wages throughout the parish. During the 1520s and 1530s, the wife of one Nicholas Clerk took on an array of tasks which at St Margaret's were allocated to the appropriate professional person and paid for on a yearly basis, including making surplices, scouring candlesticks and washing vestments.[29]

Although the less populous St Martin's was organized along simpler lines than St Margaret's, there are signs of significant corporate activity from at least the late fifteenth century. It seems likely that the building of a tower at St Martin's church dates from this period and two wills of the 1490s contain bequests to 'the church werkes'. In 1493, Edward Johnson, beer-brewer, left 20s for these works at St Martin's, 'to thentent [intent] that the parisshoners there the moore specially shall have my soule in ther speciall recomendations and prayers'. Other St Martin's men left bequests designed to benefit the community as a whole and to secure the testator's place in the memory and prayers of parishioners. In 1509, Richard Canryngham, serjeant farrier to the King (and therefore probably employed at the Royal Mews at Charing Cross, one of the most significant institutions in the parish at this time), left his best piece of silver to the church. He ordered his executors to use this silver to make a chalice, and directed that 'my name and my wiffes name to be sett in the foote and so the said chalice to remayn and abide in the same church for ever'.[30] The quarterly collections for the clerk's wages of the early sixteenth century also provide further evidence of co-operation among parishioners. Clearly the men and women of St Martin's were capable of taking collective action, but the overall impression remains that such activity was generally on a small scale and arose in response to particular needs.

This impression is also confirmed when one examines the employment of priests and clerks in the parish during the early sixteenth century. Most priests and clerks were employed on an ad hoc basis. In 1543–44, for example, St Martin's paid 12d

---

28 Kitto, pp. 1, 32.

29 *Ibid.*, pp. 13, 16–17. For St Martin's choir see below. The Abbey and Convent of Westminster was patron of the living throughout the medieval period, except for a brief time under Richard II, when the Crown made appointments. The Abbey lost the living to the bishop of London during the Reformation. The bishop of London's first appointment was Thomas Welles, who was made vicar in 1554: Hennessey, pp. 293–4.

30 TNA, PCC, Prob. 11/9/25; Prob. 11/16/18.

'to georg ye syngeng man for helping ye quyer the holy dayes'. Other passing references in St Martin's accounts mention priests who may occasionally have helped out in the parish, such as the payments to 'Sir' John Muckell, who was paid for 'for mendyng and byndyng' five books. A more regular figure in the parish was Thomas Sprynt, 'Sumtymes owr morrowmas prest', whose employment underlines the small-scale of operations at St Martin's.[31]

Sprynt probably derived his employment as a morrow mass priest from a bequest made to the parish by the King's master carpenter, Humphrey Cooke. The handling of Cooke's bequests highlights the uncertainty attached to the provision of services at St Martin's more generally. In 1530, among other bequests, Cooke left £1 6s 8d a year to maintain 'the morrowe mase kept in the saide churche' – an income stemming from his tenement 'The Bell' in St Martin's parish.[32] Many such foundations were intended to increase the number of masses available to the parish at large, but this was particularly true of donations left to support a morrow mass.[33] It seems likely that Cooke hoped to ensure the regularity of this particular provision. By 1534, however, St Martin's churchwardens had diverted 6s 8d from Cooke's bequest 'towardes the Mayten'nce of the Chirche Ornamentes'.[34] This diversion is perhaps a surprising one, but it suggests the financial constraints under which the parish operated. That this diversion may not have represented a mere one-off payment occasioned by unusual circumstances is confirmed by later costs of litigation generated by Cooke's bequest. In 1545, St Martin's churchwardens recorded their expenses in the Court of Common Pleas for the 'sewt of . . . owr morowmas prest'. The details of this suit remain unclear, but the following year, the wardens made their first gathering among St Martin's parishioners 'towarde the payment of the Morowmas prests wages', which yielded 14s 3d – a significant example of lay initiative and one perhaps related to an influx of new parishioners, which will be discussed below.[35]

Services at St Martin's may not have been as elaborate or as varied as those at St Margaret's, but, as we shall see, St Martin's parishioners did display an awareness of current religious fashion possibly related to the proximity of St Margaret's church and Westminster Abbey itself. On an everyday basis the clerk would have chanted parts of the mass. The parish also possessed an organ and on at least some occasions a choir took part in services. The first regular payments to an organ player date from 1527, although such payments are not uninterrupted during the rest of the Henrician period – unlike payments for maintaining the organ itself. This suggests that the clerk or a

31 Kitto, pp. 91, 104.

32 *Ibid.*, p. 108; TNA, PCC, Prob. 11/24/5.

33 Kitching, p. xxvi.

34 Kitto, p. 34.

35 *Ibid.*, pp. 108–9, 121. St Martin's chantry certificate lists Cooke's bequest for a morrow mass priest as 'detained' by one 'Master Bassell'. In 1555, the parish paid for a copy of Cooke's will as part of their expenditure on 'the Sute for the church goodes', Kitching, p. 64, Kitto, p. 157.

member of the choir may sometimes have played. On two occasions in the 1520s, the parish paid the sizeable sum of 16s 8d 'to Mr Watts for his Child to pley at Organs' and it seems likely that this was Robert Wattes, described as beadle of the fraternity of the Virgin's Assumption at St Margaret's by 1547.[36] Children would also have formed part of the choir – a body only fleetingly mentioned in surviving records – and accounts include payments for children's surplices. The choir and organ together would have supplied polyphonic music for at least some church services. The type of music performed is referred to only in an entry of 1526–27, when the wardens paid 2s for two 'playne Songebooks for the ffests of J'hc [Jesus] & of the Visitation of or lady'.[37]

Both the feasts of the name of Jesus and the Visitation of the Virgin were among the 'new' feasts of the church introduced into England in the late fifteenth and early sixteenth centuries. These feasts were particularly notable for the emphasis placed upon the suffering and humanity of Christ and the saints. Their celebration became very fashionable in London and took place at St Margaret Westminster from about 1500, although it seems likely that St Margaret's itself followed in the footsteps of Westminster Abbey. In keeping with this up-to-date liturgical fashion, it is notable that St Martin's also possessed an altar dedicated to Our Lady of Pity. This devotional subject – the Virgin supporting the corpse of Christ after his descent from the Cross – was yet another recognized by the new feasts. The celebration of the new feasts at St Martin's may partly derive from the example of St Margaret's, but also from an awareness of changing styles of lay piety among some of St Martin's more prosperous parishioners. This is clearly the case with Humphrey Cooke, whose gifts to the church went beyond provision of a morrow mass priest. Cooke also donated altar cloths for the Our Lady of Pity altar and left £1 6s 8d a year in his will 'to the maytenyning of Jhus masse to be song with note [i.e. polyphonically sung from part-books] every fryday within the parrishe churche . . . during the term of twenty yeres'.[38] In the key position of King's Master Carpenter, Cooke would doubtless have been aware of changing religious fashions, especially since his commissions had included the building of the Savoy Hospital and chapel as well as such prestigious projects such as the design and building of Corpus Christi College, Oxford.[39] If Cooke's bequest signalled an interest in new religious trends, its focus was once again on ensuring that the parish was actually in a

36 Kitto, pp. 10, 11, 14, 16, 32, 53, 91; Kitching, pp. 64–5. Robert Wattes is mentioned as the conduct at St Margaret's in WAC, E3 (1549–50), E4 (1550–51).

37 Kitto, pp. 10, 13, 14, 14n, 91. The feast of the name of Jesus fell on 7 August, while 2 July marked the Virgin's visit to Elizabeth.

38 R.W. Pfaff, *New Liturgical Feasts in Later Medieval England* (Oxford, 1970), pp. 54, 59, 78–83, 99; Rosser, p. 274; TNA, PCC, Prob. 11/24/5; Kitto, p. 20; *KW*, III, pt I, 30, 202–4.

39 Cooke was known personally to the founder of Corpus Christi, the humanist bishop Richard Foxe, who recommended his talents and trustworthiness. As a carpenter, however, Cooke's efforts at what later became Christ Church, Oxford, have been described as 'the last great work of medieval carpentry uncontaminated by Renaissance influence': J. Harvey, *English Medieval Architects* (Gloucester, 1984), pp. 64–5.

financial position to support services, such as the Jesus mass, which were clearly not entirely new to the parish.

The small-scale character of religious activity at St Martin's during the Henrician period also emerges from the fact that it was one of only three parishes in the suburbs of London that did *not* list a chantry priest in its chantry certificate at the beginning of Edward VI's reign – a pattern more characteristic of the smaller rural outparishes of Middlesex.[40] The parish also seems to have supported only one fraternity.[41] The paucity of landed endowments at St Martin's is especially striking when compared with the substantial income that bequests of various kinds had generated at St Margaret's.[42] It is at least possible that St Martin's suffered from its close proximity to St Margaret's and Westminster Abbey, which may well have drawn the benefactions of wealthy parishioners away from the smaller parish. The extent of these ties will be discussed below, but the overall picture remains of small-scale parochial activity dwarfed in comparison with the more organized, well-funded and elaborate activities at the neighbouring St Margaret's.[43]

St Martin's church also appears to have been a relatively simple building. During the first part of the sixteenth century, it remained a tiny medieval edifice, although a tower had been erected, probably during the late fifteenth century. The pre-Reformation church contained two, possibly three chapels, but information about the physical structure of the church is limited.[44] As with any pre-Reformation church, St Martin's church would also have been decorated with various images and illuminated by an ever-changing display of candles.

40 The chantry commission was created to report on landed income supporting chantries prior to their dissolution by the Crown. Those parishes in the county of Middlesex that did report a chantry priest were mostly large suburban parishes on the fringe of London, like St Martin's, rather than the rural out-parishes of the county: Kitching, p. xxxii.

41 The parish did not list a single fraternity on its chantry return, but surviving wills make it clear that a fraternity of St John Baptist was in existence at St Martin's as early as 1475 and as late as the 1520s: TNA, PCC, Prob. 11/21/38; GL, MS 9171, reg. 6/254v. There is no reason to suppose that it had disappeared by the 1540s. Its absence from the chantry certificate may have been because it was supported by quarterage dues rather than landed income – a form of funding more likely in a less prosperous parish such as St Martin's: Kitching, p. xxxii.

42 The chantry certificate did mention the 'detained' bequest of Humphrey Cooke and also one obit, left by Christian Norrice for twenty years, worth 10s a year: Kitching, pp. xiv, 64.

43 For a similar suggestion that the dearth of chantry priests and varied obits in the smaller rural outparishes of Middlesex outparishes resulted from their very proximity to London see Barron, 'Parish fraternities', p. 31.

44 References in 1532–33 to soldering and mending 'the gutter of saynt Johan's Chapell' and in 1540 to making pews in 'saint Johan's aisle' suggest that St John's chapel may have formed a structural division within the church rather than merely referring to an altar (Kitto, pp. 28, 72; *SL*, XX, pt 3, p. 20). This is confirmed by the request of Henry Lucas, a priest, asking to be buried in St John's chapel in 1494. In 1521, one Henry Went left 40d to the altar of St John the Baptist, which undoubtedly was located within the chapel (TNA, PCC, Prob. 11/10/14, Prob. 11/20/14, Prob. 11/16/18, Prob. 11/21/38). St Cuthbert's chapel may also have been structurally distinct from the main body of the church. A 1538 entry refers to a pew 'at seynt Cutberts Chapel dore', while in 1540, the wardens paid for materials and workmanship 'of the staires and ii pues in saynt Cuthberdes Chappell' (Kitto, pp. 61, 72). For the Our Lady of Pity altar see Merritt thesis, pp. 39–40.

The first year of surviving churchwardens' accounts records nearly £4 spent in 1525 on 'Carvying and garnysshyng of the Rode looft' and for making images of Jesus, the Virgin and the twelve prophets.[45] Overall though, while information is sparse, it seems clear that there was not the same degree of visual display that was evident at St Margaret's, nor the groups of parishioners or fraternities to support many different lights.[46]

Corporate activity at St Martin's also manifested itself in gifts presented to the parish church. Once again, St Martin's exhibited patterns distinct from those of St Margaret's. Of course, the social contours of the parish were significant here: gift-giving was partly determined by the wealth of the surrounding community and by the social prestige that attached to large donations and eye-catching gifts. During the period 1500–47, St Martin's church most often received gifts from single individuals, in contrast to the pattern of corporate gift-giving at St Margaret's. Clearly a splendid gift would have attracted greater attention at the less richly furnished St Martin's. The parish also had access to a few very important and wealthy potential donors, who fell outside the ambit of things parochial. It may even have solicited gifts from the episcopal townhouses located within its bounds. Between 1525 and 1530, for example, the bishop of Norwich and the former bishop of Durham (the townhouses of both sees were in St Martin's) donated expensive suits of vestments to the church.[47] Henry VIII himself also presented the parish with costly gifts of vestments some time between 1532 and 1534, although the churchwardens described this as being at the 'instance' of Thomas Alvard, the paymaster for the rebuilding of Whitehall Palace and (the accounts noted) 'gentilman and one of the counsaill of or Sou'aigne lorde the Kyng'. In this sense, St Martin's lack of resources was only relative, since there was always the possibility of donations from the Crown and its officials. Gifts from great men may have reflected their recognition that a less populous and settled parish, such as St Martin's, commanded fewer resources than the more urban St Margaret's. But most gifts to St Martin's were from men who worshipped there and were not on such a grand scale.[48]

St Martin's ceremonial life was also likely to have been correspondingly less rich than that of its neighbour, although parishioners enjoyed plays, processions and

---

45 Presumably some of this expenditure represented an improvement or replacement of what had pre-viously been there. A candlestick set before Our Lady of Pity (Kitto, p. 30) may refer to either a picture or a figure, while sums received under Edward for 'Images of Alybaster' (*ibid.*, p. 129) points to other figures that were the object of devotion. The church would appear to have contained a window depicting the Trinity, but our evidence derives from its later Edwardian removal (*ibid.*, p. 125).

46 In addition to lights hanging before the rood itself, accounts mention candles at All Hallows day, eight pounds of candles 'to sett Abowte the Churche on Cristmas Day in the Mornying', the sepulchre light (whose cost was met through a collection among parishioners), the great Paschal candle, the Tenebrae candle, the Judas candle and the twenty-four small tapers on the Lenten hearse or 'Judas crosse'. St Martin's also appears to have followed the peculiarly London fashion of hanging a basin from the roof for a Paschal candle, Kitto, pp. 64, 74, 83; H.B. Walters, *London Churches at the Reformation* (1939), pp. 52–3; *London VCH*, p. 239.

47 Kitto, p. 20.

48 *Ibid.*, p. 31; *KW*, IV, pt. II, 306; Merritt thesis, pp. 53–4.

Hocktide, and (as we shall see) celebrated Corpus Christi in an increasingly elaborate manner.[49] Overall though St Martin's and St Margaret's parishes present a study in contrasts, and partly as a consequence they were destined to experience the coming years of religious and political upheaval in significantly different ways. Nevertheless, it is important to note that the members of the parishes could and did intermingle in corporate affairs. It seems likely that pre-Reformation parishioners at St Martin's resorted to St Margaret Westminster for at least some of their devotional needs. Certainly the opportunites to display religious devotion and to participate in commemorative activities for the dead would have existed on a scale not available at St Martin's church.

There is clear evidence that parishioners of St Martin's joined the fraternities of St Margaret's, even if it is impossible to calculate precise numbers. In 1475, for example, the vicar of St Martin's himself was recorded as a member of the guild of the Virgin's Assumption. By the 1520s and 1530s it has been estimated that this fraternity had about two hundred members, and some of these clearly came from St Martin's parish.[50]

Probably the most important guild in which members of the different parishes came together was that of St Mary Rounceval, the chapel of which lay in St Margaret's parish. Henry Romayn, a St Martin's parishioner and member of the Assumption guild, who was generous in his donations to St Martin's church and contributed to the rebuilding costs in 1542, went on to serve as warden of the Rounceval guild from 1539 to 1541. At about the same time, Henry Russell, a carpenter and later a churchwarden at St Martin's, was among those signing the Rounceval guild accounts. Because the Rounceval hospital and chapel were located at Charing Cross and therefore not far from St Martin's church, this fraternity may have held a special attraction for St Martin's parishioners.[51] That the Rounceval accounts for 1522–23 contain a payment in reward to 'the Clerkes of Saynt Martyns' suggests at least occasional links between the two establishments.[52] Guild membership must presumably have helped to reinforce existing ties between the two parishes. It also seems that the Rounceval guild particularly attracted members from that part of St Margaret's parish nearest to Charing Cross and so nearest to the hospital. Membership in the guild may well have

49 Kitto, pp. 1, 9–11, 26–7, 31, 37–8, 50.

50 H.F. Westlake, *St Margaret's Westminster* (1914), p. 51. E.g. Henry Romayn, later the King's Locksmith, joined the Assumption guild in the 1510s, when he was described as living in Durham Rents, located in St Martin's parish: WAM, Guild of the Virgin's Assumption, accounts: 7–10 Hen. VIII, f. 5.

51 Kitto, pp. 57, 83; Rosser, p. 315; WAM, Rounceval guild accounts, 30–2 Hen. VIII, n.f. Men from St Margaret's parish filled most Rounceval guild offices, and many of these also served as St Margaret's churchwardens, such as William Jennyings, John Knight, Philip Lentall, George Lorde, William Phillips, William Russell, Richard Shelley, Robert Smallwood, Edward Stockwood and John Wright: Rosser, Appendix VIII.

52 WAM, Rounceval guild accounts, 12–13 Hen. VIII, n.f.

meant that these St Margaret's parishioners were in a position to judge the needs of their brothers in the neighbouring St Martin's. A case in point is that of John Wright, a baker from St Margaret's parish. Wright, who rented three tenements and a garden near Charing Cross, served as Master of the Rounceval guild in 1522–24 and as St Margaret's churchwarden 1534–36. In 1530, he presented St Martin's parish with a gift of candlesticks, and in 1541 St Martin's accounts records his bequest of 6s 8d and a 'Chales of Silver parcell gylte'.[53] Other Rounceval wardens from St Margaret's also donated small sums to St Martin's in the 1530s.[54]

For all their contrasts, then, Westminster's pre-Reformation parishes did not prevent their parishioners coming together in broader supra-parochial organizations. Overall, they present a picture of lively and interlocking corporate activities, where parishes, guilds and religious festivals fostered energetic social and religious contacts.

THE HENRICIAN REVOLUTION IN WESTMINSTER

As we have suggested, the decade of the 1530s was a time when the Crown made its presence felt in the locality in a manner both dramatic and intrusive. This intervention took many forms, but central here was the construction of the vast new complex of Whitehall Palace. In 1529 Henry VIII took possession of York Place and vastly expanded and redeveloped the former townhouse of the now-disgraced Cardinal Wolsey. The years 1530–32 then witnessed 'the largest and most ambitious building programme ever completed by an English king' as the new palace of Whitehall was created as a replacement for the old Westminster Palace, which had been destroyed by fire in 1512. By September of 1531 over nine hundred craftsmen and labourers were at work on the site, and more than three thousand cartloads of 'olde stone, bricks and chaulke' from the old Palace of Westminster trundled along King Street simply to provide rubble for the walls of the new palace.[55]

But if the old Palace of Westminster provided some of the building materials, it was the town of Westminster that was called upon to provide some of the land. Part of its main artery, King Street, was taken over and absorbed within the new palace, with the street broken up by the Holbein Gate, symbolically marking the entrance to the

---

53 Rosser, Appendix VIII; Kitto, pp. 20, 72.

54 Rosser, Appendix VIII (Richard Shelley and Robert Smallwood); Kitto, p. 57; Merritt thesis, pp. 47–8.

55 S. Thurley, *The Whitehall Palace Plan of 1670* (London Topographical Society, 1998), p. 1; G. Rosser and S. Thurley, 'Whitehall Palace and King Street, Westminster: the urban cost of princely magnificence', *London Topographical Record* 26 (1990), pp. 57–77; *KW*, IV, pt II, 287–8, 306–7. There was a further spate of relatively less substantial building work in the 1540s: S. Thurley, *Whitehall Palace: An Architectural History of the Royal Apartments, 1240–1698* (New Haven, 1999), pp. 52–9.

royal enclave of Whitehall and Westminster, and forming with the King Street Gate a royal processional route from Whitehall to the Abbey.[56] But it was not just the inhabitants of King Street who were affected. Other major buildings that stood in the way were removed, including the hospital of St James and the hospital and chapel of St Mary Rounceval. The creation of the new palace also prompted a sustained campaign by the Crown to take over huge swathes of land in the surrounding area, which were required for hunting, leisure and water supply for the sprawling new palace. An extensive series of land transfers in the 1530s – achieved by a series of forced purchases of land owned by religious foundations – carved out an enormous new royal domain of several thousand acres, comprising almost all the land from St Martin's Lane in the east to Ebury Bridge in the west and modern-day Oxford Street in the north. A further wave of forced land exchanges in the 1540s secured substantial lands to the north, including Marylebone Park, by which time the Crown had effectively replaced the abbot of Westminster as the principal landowner in the area.[57]

Much of this land was acquired from the Abbey, and the 1530s generally witnessed a significant change in the balance of power between Crown and Abbey in the locality. The Abbey had already shown itself ready to accede to the Crown's demands for land exchanges in 1530–1, but after the death of Abbot Islip the institution rapidly fell into the hands of the government. After a year's intermission the abbot was finally replaced – for the first time in three hundred years – by someone who was not chosen by the chapter from among themselves, but who was an outsider imposed upon them by the Crown. This was William Benson – a supporter of the Boleyn faction (indeed, he officiated at Anne Boleyn's coronation, and oversaw Abbey presentations to the Boleyn family) and a humanist friend of Cranmer who was sympathetic to the new religious reforms.[58] Benson ensured that the Abbey would comply with Crown policy, but in this matter he was primarily the lieutenant of the crucial figure in Westminster in the 1530s – the King's right-hand man, Thomas Cromwell. Cromwell was in receipt of an annual 'gift' from the Abbey from 1531 onwards and accepted a succession of posts in it. In a list of what he had achieved in the King's service (probably dating from 1536) Cromwell proudly listed the acquisition of land in Westminster for the palace.[59]

The Abbey was thus securely in Cromwell's pocket during the reforms of the 1530s, but this did not save it from dissolution along with the other remaining abbeys in 1540. The dissolution heralded yet more radical change for the area as the former Abbey now became the cathedral church of a newly formed diocese of Westminster

56 Thurley, *Whitehall Palace*, pp. 43–5, 60–1.

57 S. Thurley, 'Whitehall Palace and Westminster 1400–1600: a royal seat in transition' in D. Gaimster and P. Stamper (eds.), *The Age of Transition* (1997), pp. 98–101.

58 D. MacCulloch, *Thomas Cranmer* (New Haven, 1996), pp. 94, 246, 369, 422; H.F. Westlake, *Westminster Abbey* (2 vols., 1923), I, 198–9; E. Carpenter, *A House of Kings* (1966), pp. 107–9.

59 *L&P* xx, 1231.

(formally established on 17 December 1540). The Crown's continuing role in the institution is readily apparent. The very act that established the new bishopric explained that the Abbey was an appropriate cathedral seat because it housed the monuments of Henry's royal progenitors.[60] And the first (and, as events would prove, only) bishop of Westminster was the dean of the Chapel Royal, Thomas Thirlby, a trusted royal servant and diplomat.[61]

The creation of a new bishopric of Westminster boosted the profile of the area in other ways. The 1540 Act also formally granted to Westminster the title of 'city', and subsequently the locality began to send its own MPs to parliament. But given the dominant role of the Crown in the area, this appeared very much as a 'city' under royal control. A statute of 1536 had formally declared the extent of the King's new Palace of Westminster, declaring St James's parkland and King Street to be forever the property of the King's new Palace of Westminster.[62] Further legislation recognized the King's authority within his newly acquired lands by erecting an honour 'within his Grace's Citie of Westminster', and defining his exclusive hunting rights throughout the honour as encompassing much of Middlesex.[63]

On top of all of these radical institutional and jurisdictional reforms, the 1530s and 1540s also witnessed the Henrician Reformation of parish religion. In royal injunctions of 1536 and 1538 some aspects of traditional theology were condemned, the celebration of 'superfluous' saints' days was forbidden, images that had been 'abused with pilgrimages or offerings' were abolished and the maintaining of lights before such images condemned, and the veneration of holy relics was outlawed. Not the least dramatic manifestation of these changes occurred in Westminster Abbey itself, where the shrine of Edward the Confessor was plundered.[64]

THE IMPACT ON THE PARISHES

The revolution of the 1530s had transformed government and jurisdictional authority in Westminster. These changes would have profound long-term implications for the nature of the locality and its governance. But while the disappearance of the monks was an immediate and obvious alteration, the broader implications of the changed

---

60 GL, MS 9531/12 pt I, f. 248r; *L&P* xvi, 379 (30).

61 For whom see T. Shirley, *Thomas Thirlby* (1964). It is also notable that the properties of the new dean and chapter were controlled directly (and exceptionally among the new foundations) by the Court of Augmentations until 1542, when the chapter was finally properly endowed: C.S. Knighton, 'Collegiate foundations, 1540 to 1570, with special reference to St Peter Westminster' (Cambridge Ph.D., 1975), pp. 32–4.

62 28 Hen. VIII c. 12 (*Statutes of the Realm*, III, 668).

63 37 Hen. VIII c. 18 (*Statutes of the Realm*, III, 1009–10); *L&P* xx (ii), 850 (24); *L&P* xx (i), 1129; P.L. Hughes and J.F. Larkin (eds.), *Tudor Royal Proclamations* (New Haven, 3 vols., 1964–69), I, 356; Thurley, 'Whitehall and Westminster', p. 101.

64 For the later restoration of the shrine see Carpenter, *House*, pp. 110, 124–5.

role of the Abbey and the greatly enhanced royal presence in the area would take time to emerge.[65] Sometimes, the short-term impact on local inhabitants is difficult to trace – such as the possible changes in the conduct of the abbey's manorial jurisdiction.[66] In some areas, too, radical change was partly cloaked by a certain continuity of personnel. For example, the last abbot of Westminster had become the first dean of the new cathedral, while the prior and five of the monks became members of the new chapter. Some of the old abbey's powers of jurisdiction were also inherited by the new dean and chapter, after an initial hiatus.[67] More immediately significant, and potentially devastating in their effects, were the changes to the urban environment prompted by the creation of Whitehall Palace, and the reforms of parish religion in the 1530s.

SPATIAL CHANGE

The most immediate and devastating result of the building of Whitehall Palace came from the Crown's takeover of part of King Street – the main throughfare of the old vill, and the very heart of St Margaret's parish. This required the forced purchase of a number of important properties and tenements. The wealthier tenants were bought out, but the poorer tenants were simply ejected from their houses. After purchase of the leases, tenements in King Street were immediately demolished, the site cleared and levelled and enclosed by new walls. The Crown also procured 100 acres of pasture on other side of the street (which would soon be transformed into St James's Park).[68]

This sudden destruction of a whole neighbourhood was dramatic enough in itself. But it necessitated other changes, too, that were no less damaging. The new arrangement immediately created a problem for those St Margaret's parishioners living north of Whitehall Palace. They now had to pass through the Court gate whenever they wished to attend St Margaret's church, including when it was necessary to bring the bodies of their dead to church for burial. This created fears of infection in a period when the Crown had shown an increasing sensitivity to issues of disease in the capital.[69] The king wrote urgently to the abbot of Westminster in November 1534, and to the vicar of St Martin's three months later, ordering that those inhabitants living in the northern portion of St Margaret's were to be considered parishioners of St Martin's,

---

65 For the monks of Westminster before the Dissolution see B. Harvey, *Living and Dying in England 1100–1540* (Oxford, 1993); E.H. Pearce, *The Monks of Westminster Abbey* (Cambridge, 1916); Rosser, pp. 255–62, 298–300.

66 See below, ch. 3.

67 Knighton, 'Collegiate foundations', pp. 28, 178.

68 Thurley, *Whitehall Palace*, pp. 37–41; Rosser and Thurley, 'Whitehall Palace and King Street'. A 1532 act of parliament confirmed the exchange: 23 Hen. VIII c. 21 (*Statutes*, III, 388–92).

69 P. Griffiths, J. Landers, M. Pelling and R. Tyson, 'Population and disease, estrangement and belonging 1540–1700' in P. Clark (ed.), *The Cambridge Urban History of Britain Vol. II 1540–1840* (Cambridge, 2000), p. 213.

where they were to receive the sacraments, to pay tithes and – most important of all – to be buried.[70] It was not until 1542, however, that this direction was formalized as a change of parish boundaries, explicitly made 'for avoiding the danger of infection which might happen to our court by the carrying of dead bodies past our royal palace'.[71]

The delay may partly have been due to the reluctance of St Margaret's parishioners to transfer their allegiance. It was certainly true that the act had effectively sliced off one of the more densely populated portions of St Margaret's and placed it under the parochial jurisdiction of St Martin's. The granting of this land to St Martin's was justified also by the fact that the latter parish had itself been a significant loser from Henry's building programme in the area. Henry VIII had built St James's Palace upon the site of the former leper hospital of St James, pensioning off the remaining almswomen who still lived there, but, in doing so, he had also imparked arable land in St Martin's to form St James's Park, walling in the land 'with a sumptuous wall' and building courts for 'the tennis plays and cockfight'. The grant of a portion of St Margaret's parish to St Martin's in 1542 was therefore explained as partial compensation to St Martin's for land 'for ever lost by the imparking of certain farms and other titheable places . . . now inclosed for the support and preservation of our deer'.[72]

The fact that St Martin's acquired an urbanized area at much the same time that it also experienced a diminution of the open green spaces available to parishioners in the westernmost part of the parish presented a number of serious challenges to the structure and coherence of the parish. One of the most obvious consequences was the acquisition of many new parishioners. St Martin's population appears to have been on the increase in any case, but the redrawing of parish boundaries inevitably resulted in a sudden increase. It was still not a populous parish given its size, but in 1548 it recorded seven hundred communicants – less than a third of the number of communicants at the neighbouring St Margaret's, but still a sizeable number given the previously ad hoc nature of parochial organization.[73] Doubtless as a result of these pressures, a rebuilding of St Martin's church took place in 1542 – immediately after the boundary change was more formally confirmed. This was a remarkable event in late Henrician England. The recent dissolution of monasteries and hospitals meant that church-building as an activity had largely ground to a halt in England. Indeed in Westminster itself, the hospital and chapel of St Mary Rounceval, located at Charing Cross, had only recently fallen victim to the royal building programme at Whitehall. At St Martin's, however, population increase must have put tremendous pressure on the small medieval church. Certainly the scale of work on the church walls suggests that they were

---

70 *SL*, XX, pt 3, p. 1; J. McMaster, *A Short History of St Martin-in-the-Fields* (1916), pp. 14, 21–2; Private Act 23 Hen. VIII c. 33; *L&P*, vii, 1423; viii, 228; xvii, 220 (77).

71 *L&P*, xvii, 220 (77).

72 *Ibid.* For the earlier history of St James's Hospital see Rosser, pp. 300–10. On emparkment and the leasing of former church property in the area see below, ch. 6.

73 Kitching, pp. 64–5.

rebuilt, while aisles may have been built or extended, presumably to enlarge the building overall.[74]

This rebuilding shows a remarkable degree of corporate endeavour on the part of the parish: it was St Martin's own smaller version of the much celebrated communal mobilization that had paid for the rebuilding of St Margaret's at the start of the sixteenth century.[75] The amount of local support that this work commanded is certainly impressive. The parish received no fewer than eighty-seven donations to fund the work, representing about twelve per cent of the communicants recorded in 1548 or about a quarter of the adult male population. The sums donated ranged from 12d from one 'kyng the porter' to 40s, but, not surprisingly, the parish elite dominated, with fifteen of those contributing to the works having served or later serving as churchwarden.[76]

The willingness of St Martin's parishioners to spend money on items connected with the church and church services appears also from another fund-raising campaign organized in 1544–45. During this period forty-four donors contributed over £5 'toward the byeing of the Organes' – an impressive sum in light of the amounts that had already been solicited so recently for rebuilding the church.[77] The emergence of such parochial enthusiasm in St Martin's is all the more significant because it came at a time when boundary changes meant that the precise extent of the parish, and its relationship with the neighbouring parish of St Margaret's, were more confused and problematic than ever.

Boundary changes potentially drew the personnel of the different parishes even more closely together. After boundaries were redrawn, the site of St Mary Rounceval suddenly found itself within the limits of St Martin's parish. Nevertheless, the Rounceval guild seems still to have considered itself to be associated with St Margaret's parish, and its priests and endowments were listed on the chantry certificate provided by St Margaret's in 1547.[78] Given that the boundary change between the two parishes

---

74 Population pressure is also suggested by the introduction of pews into various parts of the church: Merritt thesis, pp. 39–40, 225–6. Only three churches in the capital (one of them St Martin's) are listed by W.K. Jordan as undergoing major repairs or building work between 1536 and 1551 (and one of them, St Giles Cripplegate, had been destroyed by fire): W.K. Jordan, *The Charities of London 1480–1600* (1960, rpt, Hamden, Conn., 1974), pp. 300–1. There is no evidence to support Jordan's assertion that St Martin's was rebuilt at the King's expense. Jordan also incorrectly dates the rebuilding to 1544.

75 For Rosser's discussion of the rebuilding of St Margaret's and its social significance see Rosser, pp. 266–71; Rosser, 'Essence'.

76 Kitto, pp. 78–9; Merritt thesis, pp. 225–7.

77 There is no clear record that a new organ was purchased. If not, the parish either relied on the old one or did without until Queen Mary donated 'A payre off Regalls' in 1554. If the purchase never took place, it is possible that some may have objected to the polyphonic music that an organ could have encouraged, but the significance of this gathering seems far more related to the willingness to make such donations during a period when many parishioners in England clearly hesitated to invest in their local church: Kitto, pp. 102–3, 158; R. Whiting, 'Abominable idols: images and image-breaking under Henry VIII', *JEH* 33 (1982), pp. 44–5.

78 Kitching, pp. 64–5. St Margaret's reported that the Court of Augmentations already paid £6 13s 4d a year to Richard Kylgo, priest and £1 6s 8d to Henry Elwoode, clerk, the income deriving from the endowments of the dissolved Rounceval hospital.

was not an entirely straightforward process, the Henrician alterations may actually have furthered existing links between the two parishes.

By 1542, however, the Rounceval chapel had ceased to function. Significantly, both parishes received goods out of the dissolved chapel, suggesting that each regarded itself as in some way affiliated with the hospital and guild. The same year, St Margaret's churchwardens paid 13s 4d 'for the takyng downe of or Lady Tabernakill at Rouncyvall & for settyng up therof in the Trinitie Ile'. When the hospital was officially dissolved in 1544, St Martin's then received a green satin cope 'wt flower' and a 'Redd Crosse of the same Satten out of the Rowncevall'. Also included in the Rounceval plunder were a censer, a lamp and a corporas case. These items were said to have come from the church 'by th'gyfte of master Northe Chancellor of the Augmentacyon', but specifically at the request of one Edward Myllet.[79] The dissolution of the Rounceval hospital and chapel might well be seen as a dress rehearsal for the Edwardian dissolution of the chantries, and in this respect it is interesting to note that local men used their influence to ensure that its vestments and liturgical vessels were transferred to neighbouring churches rather than being converted to secular use. Although both parishes received church goods out of the Rounceval chapel, the more valuable objects appear to have gone to the better-equipped St Margaret's church, while St Martin's acquired those more likely to be used in daily services. While it existed, the Rounceval guild was clearly a significant institution that brought the members of the two parishes together. Ironically, the dissolution of the hospital and chapel removed a focus for the guild at precisely the time when it might have played a far more important extra-parochial role in the locality.

Links between the parishes were further strengthened by immigration from St Margaret's into St Martin's. While the alteration of parish boundaries effectively achieved this at one stroke, it is clear that certain St Margaret's parishioners had already been moving into the less urban St Martin's during the early sixteenth century, although possibly retaining property in the former. Some of these individuals were craftsmen in the building trades and men associated with the King's Works, the body reponsible for the building and repair of royal palaces. It is possible that they found that St Martin's afforded more space and cheaper rents. This movement between parishes can be demonstrated by looking at the fortunes of the Russells, a prominent family of Westminster carpenters. Richard Russell was the foremost carpenter in fifteenth-century England. He lived in St Margaret's parish, where he worked for the Crown as well as supervising all building carried out by Westminster Abbey. His eldest son, William Russell, became a wealthy waxchandler and he remained in St Margaret's parish where the candles he supplied lit the churches of St Margaret (where he was warden 1530–32), St Martin in the Fields and Westminster Abbey itself.[80] Another

---

79 WAC, E3 (1541–42); Kitto, p. 103. Myllet was a member of Henry VIII's household and received land grants from the Crown, *L&P*, xv, g. 1032 (40b), xvi, g. 305 (7).

80 Rosser, p. 397; Kitto, p. 65. William Russell also acted as clerk of the works at Westminster Abbey. One of his daughters subsequently married Nicholas Ellys, the King's Master Mason, and St Margaret's churchwarden from 1546 to 1548, *KW*, III, pt I, 42.

son, John Russell, stepped into his father's shoes, becoming Master Carpenter of the King's Works and Surveyor of the Works at Westminster Abbey. John Russell moved into St Martin's parish, probably sometime after 1531, when he inherited property belonging to his father-in-law, the previous Master Carpenter, Humphrey Cooke. Thereafter, John Russell became a churchwarden at St Martin's in 1534 and was among its most influential parishioners – an influence that culminated in his selection as parliamentary representative for Westminster in 1545.[81]

Men of other backgrounds also moved into St Martin's, such as Edward Stockwood, gentleman. Stockwood had acted as a churchwarden at St Margaret's from 1518 to 1520 and as a warden of the Rounceval fraternity from 1520 to 1522. By 1525, however, he was serving as churchwarden of St Martin's, and from then on appears as an active parishioner there, until his death in 1537 when he was buried in St Martin's church.[82]

It is sometimes difficult to disentangle the impact of boundary changes with some undoubted immigration from St Margaret's into St Martin's. It is clear, however, that both circumstances brought St Margaret's men into St Martin's by the early 1540s. We have seen that the population increase partly associated with the boundary change stimulated new collective projects, but it is also notable that parish-based religious activity increased during the 1530s and 1540s. It is tempting to suggest that some of the wealthy men of King Street (from that portion of St Margaret's annexed to St Martin's) were responsible for this rise in parochial activity. Men with experience of St Margaret's more sophisticated parochial organization and vigorous corporate traditions may well have had a decisive influence over the increasing formalization of St Martin's parish records and organization. Nevertheless, the process should not be seen as a straightforward imposition of St Margaret's ways upon the less developed St Martin's. Those holy days upon which the parish chose to lavish great attention are particularly worth noting, especially since (as we shall see) the pattern differs considerably from that observed at St Margaret's.

RELIGIOUS CHANGE

The religious changes introduced during the 1530s had a profound impact on parish life in Westminster. Attacks on pilgrimages and monasteries obviously spelt doom for the Abbey, and must also have affected those parishes which benefited from serving the institution and the pilgrims that it attracted. It is possible, however, that the

81 *KW*, III, pt I, 23; Kitto, p. 32; Bindoff, *House of Commons*, s.n. John Russell. For further information on the Russell family see D.R. Ransome, 'Artisan dynasties in London and Westminster in the sixteenth century', *Guildhall Miscellany* 2, no. 6 (1964).

82 For Stockwood as a St Margaret's parishioner see Rosser, Appendix VIII; Kitto, pp. 1, 44. Other St Martin's churchwardens who appear first in the records of St Margaret's included the carpenter Robert Pennythorne, the baker Thurston Mayer and the glazier William Delahay: Kitto, pp. 56, 72, 78, 79, 158. For a discussion of parish office-holding and the importance of the network provided by the King's Works see below, ch. 4.

economic losses that the locality sustained from the dissolution may have been more than compensated for by the new development of Whitehall Palace. But attacks on the cult of saints, images and purgatory had direct implications for the religious and corporate life of the parishes, while the new intensity of royal involvement in the locality made the penalties for disobedience seem all the more threatening.

Attacks on saints' days posed an obvious threat to the corporate life of St Margaret's. The ban was not entirely unprecedented. In 1523, London's Court of Common Council had limited all feasts of dedication to 3 October, with the support of Archbishop Warham and Bishop Cuthbert Tunstall, who considered that such feasts of dedication were abused by the young and led to disorder. This earlier restriction had not affected St Margaret's, which was not under the ecclesiastical jurisdiction of London's bishop. Although the festive side of St Margaret's Day was clearly prominent, authorities in Westminster evidently felt no need to follow the example set by the capital. The strong identification of the town with the cult of St Margaret undoubtedly provides one explanation for this.[83] The royal injunctions of 1536, however, could not be ignored. They forbade the celebration of 'superfluous' holy days. Parishes were prohibited from celebrating the feast of their patron saint unless it was one of the few saints' days universally observed. Otherwise, feasts of dedication were restricted to the first Sunday in October. Despite the wide-reaching impact of such restrictions, the King ordered that priests were not to mention the abrogated feasts. Rather than giving the people a chance to 'murmur' about the changes, priests were to 'pass over the same with such secret silence as will fall into disuse'.[84]

In the face of these injunctions, St Margaret's proceeded cautiously. In 1537 her churchwardens did not record payments of any kind relating to St Margaret. The parish did collect 7s on 'Dedication Day' (i.e. the first Sunday in October) to replace the collection normally held on St Margaret's Day, but the amount collected was half the usual sum. From 1538 to 1542, expenses for 'Dedication Day' replace those normally listed for St Margaret's Day. These payments, however, were limited to those for rushes, bread and ale. In 1542, singing men received bread, wine and ale, but their presence probably reflects a special service rather than traditional plays and festivities.[85] The disappearance of the plays and processions that had formerly marked St Margaret's Day does not mean that parishioners forgot their patron saint, despite the restrictions placed upon them. Popular devotion to St Margaret had traditionally expressed itself in the custom of brides renting the 'circlet' of St Margaret from the parish to wear upon their wedding day. In 1540–41, St Margaret's parish displayed a continued

83 *London VCH*, p. 253.

84 W.H. Frere and W.M. Kennedy (eds.), *Visitation Articles and Injunctions* (3 vols., 1910), II, 5; *London VCH*, p. 253.

85 WAC, E3 (1537–47). The 1536 injunctions were published in September, so the first St Margaret's Day after this date would have been 20 July 1537: *London VCH*, pp. 265–6. There is no record of St Margaret's parish celebrating Dedication Day with a special service before this time.

enthusiasm for this custom by paying £3 'to Alice Lewis goldsmithes Wiff of London for a Serclett to mary maydens in' – this despite the many blows already dealt to the cult of saints in previous years. The continued use of the circlet (which may have been considered a fertility symbol) even during the reign of the Protestant Edward VI echoes local use of Our Lady's girdle, a relic housed at Westminster Abbey as late as 1535, 'which women with chield were wont to girde with'.[86] The continuing devotion to the local saint is also made strikingly clear in the churchwardens' accounts for 1544–46, which are elaborately decorated with the dragon of St Margaret's legend. As a symbol of the parish, the focus of a popular festival and the object of devotion, the memory of St Margaret endured for another twenty years, when St Margaret's Day and the festivities associated it with were revived once again when Queen Mary came to the throne.[87]

As if to compensate for the suppression of St Margaret's Day, payments to celebrate Ascension Day became correspondingly more numerous in the parish. Lacking one of the traditional means of expressing corporate identity, St Margaret's parishioners seem to have invested their Ascension Day celebrations with greater meaning. Ascension Day, which fell upon the sixth Thursday after Easter, was itself preceeded by Rogationtide, when parishioners traditionally beat the bounds of their parish on the Monday, Tuesday and Wednesday of that week. This activity culminated in Ascension Day, when the fasting that had accompanied Rogation ended with an Ascension Day feast. Although there is little evidence that Rogation at St Margaret's was marked by the elaborate activities visible at the neighbouring St Martin's, the parish nevertheless clearly put greater efforts into the celebration of Ascension Day. In 1539, the churchwardens paid for two great crosses to be borne 'before the procession on Ascencyon day'. By 1546, it seems that the parish was now collaborating with the newly constituted cathedral (formerly Westminster Abbey) in celebration of Ascension Day, paying for bread, ale, beer and wine on 'Ascension evyn', and for 'the prebendaries & quyer for the mynster after masse was done'. In addition, St Margaret's churchwardens supplied bread and ale for the choir on Ascension Day itself. The following year, 1547, similar payments are recorded, but then disappear for the rest of Edward's reign.[88]

Other signs of the initial reforms that would culminate in the Protestant Reformation appeared in the later 1530s. Cromwell's injunctions of 1538 directed parish churches to buy 'one boke of the whole Bible of the largest volume in Englyshe'. This bible, known as the Great Bible, was published in 1539.[89] In 1539–40, St Margaret's churchwardens dutifully noted 9s 9d paid for 'the halfe parte' of a Bible 'accordingly after the Kinges Injuncyons' and a desk upon which to place it. Another injunction of

---

86 WAC, E3 (1540–41, 1550–52); Duffy, *Stripping*, p. 384. St Margaret's circlet was originally donated to the parish by the wife of one Anthony Goldsmith c.1510–11. It is not clear why the purchase in 1540–41 was necessary.

87 WAC, E3 (1544–46). See below, ch. 2, for the Marian revival.

88 WAC, E3 (1539–40, 1545–46, 1546–47); Hutton, *Merry England*, pp. 34–6.

89 Walters, *London Churches*, p. 33.

1538 held potentially serious consequences for the ritual displays of parish churches. This ordered that 'no candles, tapers or images of wax [were] to be set before any image or picture'.[90] Surveys of churchwardens' accounts in London and elsewhere in England demonstrate how effectively this order was enforced. The order's implications seem to have been wide-reaching, possibly (in some historians' eyes) undermining an already waning belief in the intercessory powers of saints. Indeed such was the effectiveness of the 1538 injunctions that even in remote provincial areas, such as the west country, not a single new image was purchased for any parish for which Henrician churchwardens' accounts survive.[91] The evidence at St Margaret's, however, would not suggest that belief in the intercessory powers of saints had substantially declined. Unlike the records of most parishes, St Margaret's accounts make no reference to the removal of any image from the church in the wake of the 1538 injunctions. Indeed the marked attachment to images found within the parish in the Henrician period not only is striking but points to the depth of attachment to aspects of traditional religion that the parish would later display throughout successive Tudor 'reformations'. As late as 1545 the parish paid the large sum of £16 10s for a picture of the 'Concepcion' to set before the high altar. St Margaret's also responded to the Crown's dissolution of the chapel of the Rounceval guild at Charing Cross in the early 1540s by removing the images housed within the chapel – partly run by the parish fraternity of St Mary Rounceval – and setting them up in St Margaret's church.[92]

Although St Margaret's appears to have been unafraid to display an attachment to images, with all that such veneration might imply, this certainly did not mean that the parish courted trouble with the Crown or the ecclesiastical authorities: the Crown's intervention in the area had already revealed its awesome destructive potential, and the vital importance of retaining good relations with the government. It was a prudent move, therefore, when the parish supplemented its supply of images in 1539–40 with windows acknowledging the authority of the Crown and Cromwell. A glazier in this year received 10s for 'settyng up of the Kinges Armes & of my lord princes Armes, & of my lord privy seeles [Cromwell's] Armes in the Est Wyndowe of the Trynities Chapell'. This was the specific combination of arms that greeted the reader on the title page of the Great Bible, which the parish had recently purchased.[93]

90 WAC, E3 (1539–40); the injunctions specified that the cost of the bible was to be divided between the rector and the churchwardens, Frere and Kennedy, *Visitation Articles*, II, 36, 38; Hutton, 'Local impact', p. 116.

91 Whiting, 'Abominable idols', p. 45. Hutton's sample parishes confirm this finding. Only one of his parishes, St Nicholas, Bristol, recorded the purchase of a new image after 1538 until Mary's accession: Hutton, 'Local impact', p. 117. Hutton's study should also have revealed the purchase of an image at St Margaret's (since this parish was included in his sample), for which see below.

92 WAC, E3 (1545–46).

93 WAC, E3 (1539–40). The exact significance of this act is difficult to determine, especially since a further payment for setting up the arms stated that this was 'By the advise & comandementt of mr Lancaster herrot at Armes', although this may simply mean that the herald ensured that the arms were correctly depicted.

A similar degree of prudence may lie behind the choice of preacher invited by the wardens of the Rounceval guild on Lady Day of the same year that the new window was installed. The wardens chose Dr Anthony Kitchin, a former monk of Westminster who was also a royal chaplain and vigorous supporter of the royal supremacy. The hospital and chapel of St Mary Rounceval, supported by the Rounceval guild by the early sixteenth century, were both already effectively in the process of being dissolved by the Crown. The selection of Kitchin as preacher may well represent a typical attempt by St Margaret's to make the best of a bad situation by soliciting the support and favour of a religious conservative who was none the less first and foremost a King's man.[94]

Finally, the increasing powers which the sovereign had assumed were acknowledged in the very preambles to St Margaret's churchwardens' accounts. The regnal years cited for the account of 1542–44 used Henry's full titles for the first time – 'defendor of the Fayth and in Erth of the Church of England Also of Ireland Supreme hedd'.[95] For a church located so close to the Court, it was perhaps understandable that it was the royal supremacy that was the one aspect of the Henrician reforms which St Margaret's seems to have been most ready to acknowledge. As such forms of acknowledgement occurred largely in the period after the passing of the Act of Six Articles, when the King seemed to be leading the church in a more conservative direction, they may also not have strained the consciences of St Margaret's more conservative parishioners.

It is probably significant that, even in the early stages of the Reformation, St Martin's responded more promptly to the demands of religious change than St Margaret's. This is readily apparent in the parish's response to the injunctions of 1538. Despite the proliferation of images at St Margaret's, the injunctions appear to have been more rigorously enforced at St Martin's. As early as 1538–39, the parish sold off 'the cote and showes [shoes] of the picture of oure lady', an expense clearly linked to the injunctions. Entries in the churchwardens' accounts for 1530–40 are surprisingly unambiguous and show that St Martin's had already complied with the injunctions in other ways. At that time, the wardens received 9s 'for old Iron and lat[t]en candilstykes that stode before Images in the churche'. In an equally unequivocal gesture the wardens also paid for 'Amendying the Church walls where lyghts stode' – presumably to avoid the ghostly reminder of candles snuffed out and images removed. These efforts to sever any links with 'superstitious' practices seem to have been partly

---

94 WAM, Rounceval guild accounts, 1538–40; *DNB*, s.n. Anthony Kitchin; J. Strype, *Memorials of Thomas Cranmer* (2 vols., 1840), I, 187–9; Rosser, pp. 316, 319–20; *KW*, III, 22–4. Kitchin had subscribed to the Act of Supremacy and to the articles of 1536. His strong support for royal authority in religious affairs was later confirmed when, upon his election as bishop of Llandaff in 1545, he recited an oath that contained a striking denunciation of papal authority. As king's chaplain, any sermon given by Kitchin in 1540 would not merely have reflected government religious policy but quite likely have vindicated the claims of the royal supremacy.

95 WAC, E3 (1542–44). At St Martin's, the churchwardens had adopted these titles two years previously, in the accounts for 1540–42: see Kitto, p. 66.

connected with the appointment in December 1539 of a new vicar, Robert Beste, whose later sympathy with Protestant reform will be discussed in the following chapter.[96]

St Martin's, unlike its mother parish, never appears to have celebrated its patronal feast day in any special way. After 1536, of course, such activities would have been prohibited in any case. Instead the late 1530s and early 1540s saw parishioners put most effort and expenditure into the celebration of Corpus Christi and Rogation. References to these holy days are fairly sparse at St Martin's until the late 1530s, although a lone payment in 1526–27 records 12d spent on 'garnysshying' four torches for Corpus Christi. The feast traditionally involved carrying the sacrament in procession, accompanied by banners, torches and flags. The procession would proceed to different parts of the parish, where portions of a special service would be performed.[97] At this time the parish may not have celebrated the festival very elaborately. There are no further references to Corpus Christi until 1538, from which time its celebration is regularly recorded in St Martin's churchwardens' accounts. The previous year, however, the parish had made the substantial investment of £4 to purchase a 'Cannype Clothe', which would have been supported by staves and held over the priest who held the pyx in procession. It seems unlikely that such a purchase would have been made if the festival lacked popularity, at least among parish notables.[98] The 1530s also saw the first expenses listed for Palm Sunday. In 1532–33, 16d was paid for 'the Pagantes played on palme sonday', while in 1534–35, the accounts first record payments for palms, yew and box 'agaynste palme sonday'. In 1539–40 pageants are again referred to when 2s was 'resceyved of the pleyers that played in the Churche'.[99]

Celebrations connected with Rogation week first put in an appearance in parish accounts in 1539, when the parish paid four poor men 'to bere baners in Crosse weke'. Rogation or 'crosse weke', like Corpus Christi, brought parishioners together to form a procession. By the following year, 1540, the procession had evidently grown, for the accounts now include payments for nine men 'for bearying of the crose and baners in crosweke'.[100] As with Corpus Christi festivities, the accounts list increasingly regular payments for Rogation week from the late 1530s, suggesting the need to express a growing corporate awareness.

Surprisingly, St Martin's parishioners appear to have arranged more elaborate celebrations of these festivals during the 1540s. In 1543, a new and regular payment was introduced with garlands for the vicar to wear during the Corpus Christi procession, while the next year the parish paid for the necessaries for Palm Sunday, food on Holy

---

96 Kitto, pp. 59n, 60, 62. For Beste see below, ch. 2.

97 Kitto, pp. 14, 14n.

98 *Ibid.*, p. 55; Walters, *London Churches*, p. 47. It could also have been placed over the high altar in addition to its use in procession.

99 Kitto, pp. 28, 40, 60. Although payments for palm, yew and box became regular features of the St Martin's accounts, no further references to pageants occur.

100 *Ibid.*, pp. 63, 63 n.4, 72.

Thursday, garlands and torches for Corpus Christi, garlands and banners for Rogation week and a candle for the feast of All Saints.[101] It is, of course, quite possible that, in the past, support for some of these customs had been supplied on a voluntary basis by well-disposed parishioners and so had not been recorded in earlier churchwardens' accounts. What is striking, however, is that the 1540s saw the parish either introduce new customs or assume the cost and organization of those previously funded on an ad hoc basis.

The focus on Corpus Christi and Rogation at St Martin's may also relate to the particular concerns of the parish. In theory, greater concentration on the feast of Corpus Christi could carry significant religious overtones during a period when the nature of the sacrament was hotly debated. Reformers would have considered the festival idolatrous since its procession with the sacrament worshipped the corporal presence of Christ in the Eucharist. Rogation too could be considered to be tainted with idolatry, since the processional crosses were presumably objects of veneration. The increasing prominence of these holy days, especially Corpus Christi, might appear to be puzzlingly at variance with St Martin's prompt and scrupulous response to the 1538 injunctions. If the explanation is purely a religious one, then it might relate to the fear and uncertainty generated by the more conservative Act of Six Articles in 1539 and the subsequent episcopal repression of 1542, as Bishop Bonner of London attempted to stifle controversy in the capital over the nature of the mass and to re-establish conservative doctrine.[102]

The more formal and regular celebration of these ceremonies must also have related to other changes which overtook St Martin's parish in the 1530s and 1540s. A burgeoning population and the acquisition of some very well-to-do parishioners may have affected the manner in which holy days were celebrated. As we have seen, a number of these new parishioners had been guildsmen and churchwardens at St Margaret's and so accustomed to organizing more elaborate rituals. But sheer numbers and access to additional wealth are not sufficient explanation for the emphasis placed on particular holy days. Moreover, it is notable that St Martin's parish did not merely adopt those festivals most popular at St Margaret's. Rogation processions, for example, did not figure largely at St Margaret's, while the celebration of Corpus Christi may well have declined at St Margaret's during the 1530s.

Instead St Martin's parishioners chose to focus their attention on festivals that helped to define the parish in both symbolic and geographical terms. Corpus Christi, with its analogies to the human body and the corporate body of townspeople, has often been viewed as an occasion upon which local communities tried to reassert social harmony in the face of existing tensions.[103] Both Rogation and Corpus Christi

101 *Ibid.*, pp. 91, 105–6.

102 Brigden, pp. 276–7, 296–7, 299–300, 334, 339, 351.

103 Phythian-Adams, 'Ceremony and the citizen', pp. 58, 63, 74–5. See also Hutton's discussion in *Merry England*, pp. 40–4.

also required parishioners to form a procession. The beating of the parish bounds involved in Rogation, in particular, physically marked out the limits of the parish – an extremely important task given St Martin's new circumstances. Not only had the Crown recently annexed a throughly urbanized area to the parish, it had also bought up and enclosed large tracts of arable ground. It is clear that increased population on the one hand, coupled with the loss of large green spaces on the other, created a new awareness of the pressure on parochial space. It may not be a coincidence that a survey of parish commons took place only a few years later in 1549, the document forming the first entry in the minute book of the vestry – a body that was itself taking shape only during this period.[104]

Such an explanation assumes that disruptive forces, such as the change in parish boundaries, population increase and the dissolution of St Mary Rounceval may actually have served as a catalyst to the growth of a distinct parochial identity. The rising importance of collective projects and activities also finds its parallel in the development of formal parish government at St Martin's during the 1540s and 1550s – a topic discussed in subsequent chapters. St Martin's parishioners still seem to have attached considerable importance to Rogationtide and Corpus Christi in the 1550s. After the accession of Queen Mary in 1553 and the restoration of Catholic practice, most of the gifts that the church initially received from its parishioners were the paraphernalia associated with Corpus Christi and Rogation. Indeed the popularity of Rogation appears to be connected to issues of urban development and the use of open space well into the seventeenth century.[105]

Patterns of gift-giving to the parish church also hint at this more invigorated parochial life. It is true that, after the royal injunctions of 1536, both parishes experienced a sharp drop in the number of gifts presented to the local church. St Margaret's parish seems not to have received a single gift from any one individual after 1536. The absence of any communal projects or gifts arranged by parishioners acting in consort indicates a similar restraint. At St Martin's, however, while one-off gifts of money or candlesticks declined after 1536, communal projects flourished. Parishioners great and small contributed to the rebuilding of the church in 1542, while significant numbers were prepared to contribute to the purchase of an organ in 1544.[106]

The consequences of the Henrician upheavals in Westminster were numerous and complex, and many held long-term implications for the urban and social development

---

104 The 1549 survey is printed in Kitto, pp. 579–80. St Martin's parishioners may have been further inspired to draw up such a formal survey by the Edwardian proclamations regarding enclosure and the enclosure riots that took place elsewhere in England in 1549. The St Martin's survey does not appear to be a response to the questions of the royal commissioners investigating enclosure. See Larkin and Hughes, *Tudor Royal Proclamations,* I, 427–9, 451–3, 471–2. See below, ch. 6, for a fuller discussion of enclosure and common lands in the sixteenth and seventeenth centuries.

105 Kitto, pp. 146, 158. See below, ch. 6.

106 Kitto, p. 137.

of the area. Local government too, would be profoundly affected. But already the locality had been transformed, and parochial life in Westminster's principal parishes was starting to undergo important structural alterations. On the eve of the Edwardian reformation, St Margaret's was still a flourishing and wealthy parish. Its church, only recently enlarged and beautified, provided a richly decorated environment for worship, and was lavishly stocked with ornaments and vestments of the highest quality. The parish was also characterized by its numerous fraternities and wealth of parochial customs and traditions. But it was also a parish that was extremely vulnerable. Its ceremonial life had already been attenuated by the restrictions on saints' days and images. It had enjoyed intimate links with the Abbey, which had now been dissolved, and the heart of the parish had been dramatically reconfigured by the new Whitehall Palace. Its many fraternities, whose role was so central to the locality, had cause to fear the chantries act, already in preparation by 1545, while the spectacle of the dissolved Rounceval hospital already offered a bleak picture of what was to come. St Martin's parish, however, had in a sense gained from the Henrician changes. A substantially increased population, and its comparatively undeveloped parochial organizations, had enabled it to respond creatively to the forced changes in parish life, developing new corporate feasts and energetically rebuilding its church. These different tendencies – of quietly obstructive conservatism and enthusiastic adaptation – would be greatly accentuated in the following decade.

Chapter 2

The Impact of the Reformation
in Westminster 1547–62

ON Easter day 1555, a priest of Westminster Abbey, John Cheltham, was preparing to administer communion to parishioners at St Margaret's church. Suddenly, at the elevation of the host, a man with a knife rushed forward and stabbed the priest. Blood fell on the consecrated host. Chaos ensued among the packed congregation: women shrieked, and commented one contemporary, 'ther was sych a cry and choutt as has not byn'. Richard Dod, a former churchwarden, managed to wrest the knife away from the assailant, and with the help of others was able to restrain him. The sacrilege was such that parishioners were forced to leave St Margaret's and go to another, uncontaminated church to continue the service. The assailant was one William Flower, formerly a monk of Ely, now a married man living with his wife in Lambeth, who had committed the deed while being (as he claimed) 'compelled by the spirit', and 'greatly offended in his conscience with the priest'. When subsequently examined by Bishop Bonner, Flower maintained that for the past twenty-six years he had not believed that the sacrament was transformed into the body of Christ after the words of the consecration were spoken. It is certainly possible that Flower went to St Margaret's church precisely because it was known to offer services on a lavish scale and for its associations with the soon-to-be-revived Westminster Abbey: he explained to Bishop Bonner that, while he had first gone to St Paul's Cathedral, he had not acted there because the 'spirit' had not spoken to him there as it was subsequently to do in St Margaret's. While Flower eventually voiced regret for the attack, he refused to recant his views concerning transubstantiation. Accordingly, Flower was burnt at the stake in St Margaret's churchyard, but only after the hand which had delivered the offending blows had already been severed from his body.[1]

---

1 John Strype, *Ecclesiastical Memorials* (6 vols., 1822), III, pt 1, 336–7, 341–2; *The Diary of Henry Machyn, Citizen and Merchant-Taylor of London, 1550–1563*, ed. J.G. Nichols (Camden Society o.s. 42, 1848), pp. 84–5; *CSPVen 1555–56*, pp. 50–1; *APC 1554–56*, p. 118; John Foxe, *Acts and Monuments*, ed. S.R. Catley (8 vols., 1838), VII, 68–76; Foxe concedes that in stabbing the

The collective trauma experienced by the parishioners of St Margaret's in the wake of these events can only be surmised. A subsequent formal service of reconciliation, necessary to purify the church and presided over by the bishop of London, followed by a substantial reconciliation 'feast', doubtless did something to restore the spirits of the parishioners.[2] But the events of 1555 encapsulate the potential violence and bitterness of religious divisions in the years that followed the death of Henry VIII. The reigns of Edward VI and Queen Mary saw an end to the uneasy adjustments made under Henry, with more direct and far-reaching religious change imposed by the Crown. The close proximity of the Westminster parishes to the Abbey and Whitehall Palace meant that the radical changes of these years would inevitably have a profound impact upon them. Nevertheless, as we shall see, the experiences of parishioners in St Margaret's and St Martin's could differ significantly as prominent inhabitants and office-holders sought various ways of coming to terms with the pressures of reformation and counter-reformation.

THE EDWARDIAN REFORMATION

The death of Henry VIII heralded important changes in Westminster. The Lord Protector Somerset sought to make his mark in the area, building an enormous new palace on the Strand and exerting a significant unofficial influence in the town.[3] Other prominent courtiers acquired important houses in the area during Edward's reign. Parliament itself also laid down more lasting roots in Westminster from November 1548, with the House of Commons taking up a permanent new home in the chapel of St Stephen's (located within the precinct of the old Westminster Palace), newly acquired by the Crown.[4]

Most strikingly, however, this was a period of major religious change, in stark contrast to the piecemeal changes of Henry's reign. In a few short years, the Edwardian Reformation imposed dramatic changes upon parishes throughout England.[5] Chantries

---

priest Flower 'did not well nor evangelically', but includes Flower among his martyrs for his refusal to recant his beliefs concerning transubstantiation. These events have been erroneously described as taking place at Westminster Abbey: Brigden, p. 593. See Stow, I, 347, for the ceremonies to purify All Hallows Bread Street in 1532, after a quarrel between two priests led to bloodshed in the church.

2 WAC, E4 (1555–56).

3 *Acts*, pp. xxxv, xxxvii, nos. 72, 76, 78–80; WAM 38892. On the sacrilege involved in the construction of Somerset House see Brigden, pp. 473–4.

4 William Cecil bought a house in Canon Row, where his neighbour was John Thynne. William Paget and John Russell, earl of Bedford, obtained the Strand townhouses surrendered by the bishops of Carlisle and Exeter respectively: Bindoff, *House of Commons*, s.n. John Thynne; *CSPD Ed VI*, nos. 471, 479. *London P&P*, I, 324; A. Hawkyard, 'From Painted Chamber to St Stephen's Chapel: the meeting place of the House of Commons at Westminster until 1603' in C. Jones and S. Kelsey (eds.), *Housing Parliament* (Edinburgh, 2002), pp. 76–9.

5 For the most recent accounts of the Edwardian Reformation see D. MacCulloch, *The Tudor Church Militant* (1999); C. Davies, *A Religion of the Word* (Manchester, 2002); S. Alford, *Edward VI* (Cambridge, 2002).

and fraternities were dissolved, and lights and images were banished from churches along with most of the traditional forms of Catholic worship. In parish churches, Protestantism was to be propagated through the purchase of bibles and Erasmus's *Paraphrases upon the New Testament.* From June 1548, parishioners were to receive communion in both kinds and to hear divine service in English.[6] These sweeping changes were enforced by an unparalleled level of official 'policing' activity. Local authorities were frequently required to report to ecclesiastical and government officials on the implementation of these reforms, preparing chantry certificates and surveys of church goods.

In this more thoroughgoing reformation, Westminster would receive its fair share of attention. Royal injunctions for Westminster diocese issued as early as September 1547 required that divine service in all the parish churches of Westminster would finish before 9 a.m. every Sunday, so that both clergy and laity would be able to attend the sermon made in the Abbey (unless, it was specified, they had a sermon preached in their own church).[7] Dean Benson was himself a strong promoter of the reforms: his will made generous bequests to the foreign reformers Bucer and Fagius, as well as to Hugh Latimer.[8] Benson's early death did nothing to stem the flow of reform, as he was replaced by the strong Protestant Richard Cox (who was almoner and tutor to Edward VI), while the increasingly conservative bishop of Westminster, Thomas Thirlby, was removed to the diocese of Norwich. The dissolution of the bishopric of Westminster in 1550, and its absorption within the diocese of London (with the Abbey officially designated the second 'cathedral' of the bishop of London), also placed all of Westminster's parishes under the firm control of the redoubtable Bishop Nicholas Ridley, whose visitation of the metropolis in 1550 launched a major campaign to ensure conformity to new Protestant reforms.[9]

---

6 Hutton, 'The local impact of the Tudor Reformations' in C. Haigh (ed.), *The English Reformation Revised* (Cambridge, 1987), pp. 119–20, 124.

7 GL, 9531/12, pt 1, ff. 266v–267v (partly transcribed in W.H. Frere and W.P. Kennedy (eds.), *Visitation Articles and Injunctions of the Period of the Reformation* (3 vols., 1910), II, 133–4). This need not represent a deliberate government focus on Westminster: a similar order was apparently made for the clergy of London diocese to attend sermons at Paul's Cross: J.G. Nichols (ed.), *Narratives of the Days of the Reformation* (Camden Society o.s. 77, 1859), p. 23. The injunctions also required Westminster's parsons, vicars and chantry priests to attend every divinity lecture made in St Stephen's College, but the dissolution of chantries and the royal acquisition of the college soon afterwards means that it is unclear how far this article (or, indeed, the rest of the injunctions) were implemented thereafter. See GL *ibid.* for various other Edwardian injunctions with notes from Thirlby implementing them.

8 D. MacCulloch, *Thomas Cranmer* (New Haven, 1996), p. 422; MacCulloch, *Tudor Church Militant*, p. 84.

9 GL, 9531/12, pt 1, ff. 363v–365v; Frere and Kennedy, *Visitation Articles*, II, 131; *London VCH*, p. 295; WAC, E3 (1549–50). For Ridley's visitation articles see GL, 9531/12, pt 1, ff. 304v–306 and Brigden, pp. 463–4, 468–9. The diocesan union of London and Westminster was effected by letters patent, and was confirmed only in 1552 by act of parliament (which also granted the bishop of London peculiar jurisdiction in Westminster, which the dean and chapter had not enjoyed): C.S. Knighton, 'Collegiate foundations, 1540 to 1570, with special reference to St Peter Westminster' (Cambridge Ph.D., 1975), p. 72n.

With no lord mayor or aldermen to react to religious change by helping or hindering government directives, it was the parishes of Westminster which played a central role. The impact of these reforms on the beliefs of Westminster's parishioners is difficult to trace. We can, however, analyse how far and how rapidly the different parishes responded to the new directives, and the implications this may have had for the religious lives of their inhabitants.[10]

The history of the Reformation in Westminster is, not surprisingly, one of overall religious conformity rather than active resistance. Indeed, the most recent account of the Reformation in the parish of St Margaret's Westminster, noting the apparently orderly nature of the implementation of Reformation legislation there, has suggested that the parish may well have been both socially and intellectually predisposed to welcome the Reformation.[11] An entry in the parish accounts for 1549–50, noting pews broken in the crush when 'doctor lattymer dyd preache' in the church might bolster further this impression of a parish enthusiastic in its reception of Edwardian Protestantism.[12] A closer examination of the sources, however, reveals a far more complex pattern, and St Margaret's seems on the contrary to show all the hallmarks of a parish of profoundly conservative religious sentiments.

In England as a whole, considerable diversity of religious practice existed during the first few months of Edward's reign. St Margaret's parish moved cautiously towards reform rather than following the more avant-garde example of some London parishes. Those London parishes which anticipated Protestant reform attracted the unfavourable attention of a government that feared the disorder which might accompany unauthorized changes. In February 1547, the parish of St Martin Ironmonger Lane rashly removed all images in the church and mounted the king's arms on the rood loft in place of the crucifix. The Privy Council reined in such zeal, however, by immediately ordering the parish to restore the crucifix.[13]

Images elicited strong feelings both pro and con in London. But an order of November 1547 ordered the removal of images from City churches, months before a similar order to bishops throughout England, which was not issued until February

---

10 While I have sought to use testamentary material, alongside other sources, for evidence of the religious attitudes of parishioners, the number of surviving Westminster wills for this period is insufficient to produce a statistically significant sample. For broader problems in the use of will preambles as sources for interpreting religious belief see E. Duffy, *The Stripping of the Altars* (1992), pp. 504–23; M. Spufford, 'The scribes of villagers' wills in the sixteenth and seventeenth centuries, and their influence', *Local Population Studies* 7 (1971), pp. 28–43; J.D. Alsop, 'Religious preambles in early modern English wills as formulae', *JEH* 40 (1989), pp. 19–27; C. Marsh, 'In the name of God? Will-making and faith in early modern England' in G.H. Martin and P. Spufford (eds.) *The Records of the Nation* (Woodbridge, 1990); A. Ryrie, 'Counting sheep, counting shepherds: the problem of allegiance in the English Reformation' in P. Marshall and A. Ryrie (eds.), *The Beginnings of English Protestantism* (Cambridge, 2002), pp. 85–7.

11 Rosser, pp. 275–9.

12 WAC, E3 (1549–50).

13 Brigden, p. 424; *London VCH*, p. 288.

1548. St Margaret's parish paid for the 'takyng downe of the Roode the Tabernacles and the Images' between Christmas 1547 and May 1548. It is quite possible, then, that St Margaret's acted only after the bishops were ordered to oversee the removal of images from parish churches outside London. The lights of the church seem to have been extinguished back in September 1547 and the parish paid £8 10d for 'the Whytying of the Churche' by Christmas 1547. It was probably not until May 1548 that workmen were engaged to take down 'the hie Aulter table'.[14]

As such hallmarks of 'superstition' were removed, the accoutrements of Protestantism were introduced. The image gave place to the word. At the same time that St Margaret's wardens removed the high altar table, they also paid 'for the Wryghtyng of the Scriptures apon the same bordes' (i.e. wainscott boards for the high altar). In addition, they purchased thirty-five ells of cloth for 'the Frunte of the Rode lofte Where as the 10 Comaundementes be Wrytten' and paid 46s 8d to a painter for writing the Commandments.[15] Much earlier (some time before Christmas 1547) the wardens had paid for what was evidently a type of lectern.[16] The parish also acquired a bible and a copy of the 'papaphraces of Erasmus', a required text for parish churches according to the injunctions of 1547. Of the ninety-one parishes surveyed by Professor Hutton, forty-one had bought Erasmus's *Paraphrases* by the end of 1548.[17]

Certain of these purchases made at St Margaret's were ultimately funded out of a sale of church goods which took place around May 1548, a particularly bad time for the parish financially. Historians have generally noted that it was more expensive to refurnish Catholic churches than to dismantle them, yet by the end of May 1548, St Margaret's parish was £9 17s 2d in debt. This debt is all the more remarkable given the previous affluence of the church and parish, and the evident value of just a single one of its wealth of devotional objects. It appears likely, then, that the parish was parting only with the bare minimum of church goods necessary to stay afloat financially. It may be significant here that the greatest profit that accrued to the parish came from pawning (rather than selling) 'A Crose of Sylver and Gylte', which brought in £20.[18]

Although most entries in the churchwardens' accounts for 1548 and 1549 appear to chart the progress of Protestantism, others are ambiguous. The Easter celebrations of 1548 do indeed seem curtailed and make no mention of the traditional customs associated with Easter. On the other hand, a payment later in the year refers to hanging up the 'dome cloth' (the Doom cloth with its picture of either the Last Judgement or of Christ seated in majesty with uplifted hand). The accounts covering

---

14   *Ibid.*, p. 289; WAC, E3 (1547–48); M. Aston, *England's Iconoclasts* (Oxford, 1988), pp. 247–8, 251, 258–61.

15   WAC, E3 (1547–48).

16   *Ibid.*: 'the stone in the body of the Churche for the priest to declare the pistelles & Gospelles'.

17   *Ibid.*; Hutton, 'Local impact', p. 124.

18   Frere and Kennedy, *Visitation Articles*, II, 117–18, 123; Hutton, 'Local impact', p. 124; WAC, E3 (1547–49).

the first part of 1548 also record the purchase of altar hangings and a 'lyteel Coffer upon the hie Aulter for to sett in the Sacrament'.[19] Given the controversial nature of the debate over the Eucharist, it is particularly surprising to see the parish making these purchases when the Edwardian Reformation was already well under way. As we have already seen, St Margaret's was almost unique in the country as a whole in acquiring images well into the 1540s. Other signs of religious conservatism during Edward's reign can be detected in payments for funerals. Obits, torches, tapers and bells were still listed at St Margaret's in 1548, but by March of that year only weekly totals of money received were recorded, without any details. As late as May 1549 the parish still recorded payments for tapers at burials, even though nearly two years earlier the *Book of Homilies* had condemned the superstitions of 'purgatory, of masses satisfactory . . . of hallowed beads, bells, bread, water, palms, candles, fire [and] such other'.[20]

A related issue was that of chantries. In the autumn of 1547 chantries through-out England had been dissolved by statute on the grounds that the doctrine of purgatory was false. At the same time, fraternities, which by implication acted as communal chantries, were dissolved.[21] The dissolution of fraternities and chantries at St Margaret's, with its strong corporate traditions, obviously had a devastating impact.[22] After all, it was these fraternities which had been central to so much of local life: acting as important units of social organization, maintaining almshouses and church fabric, providing loans, and also giving the principal support for the feasts and rituals that punctuated the liturgical year. Since there were no fewer than eight fraternities at St Margaret's, a substantial number of parishioners would have been affected, especially among the parochial elite, who often belonged to more than one fraternity.

Evidence suggests, however, that the parish did not in fact sever its ties with the fraternities immediately. On the contrary, continued support for their chantry priests provides some of the most striking evidence for the religious conservatism of St Margaret's parishioners. From May 1548 to 1551, regular quarterly payments labelled 'rewards' were paid to the chantry priests and clerks of the Assumption guild, based at St Margaret's. The term 'reward' is certainly ambiguous – obviously the church-wardens were not eager to be too specific. The quarterly nature of the payments might represent a top-up pension or even the provision of certain services. Whatever the

19 WAC, E3 (1548–49).

20 WAC, E3 (1547–49); E. Cardwell (ed.), *Documentary Annals of the Reformation* (2 vols., Oxford, 1844), I, 45, n. 1. Prayers for the dead were also forbidden by I Ed. VI, cap. 14.

21 All fraternities were dissolved by I Ed. VI cap. 14 in November 1547 and their property made over to the Crown: see Frere and Kennedy, *Visitation Articles*, II, 128n. More generally, see A. Kreider, *English Chantries: The Road to Dissolution* (Cambridge, Mass., 1979).

22 Details of the sale of St Margaret's chantry lands are contained in *CPR*, Ed. VI, vol. 1, pp. 324, 411, 413; vol. 2, pp. 36, 59, 62, 233; vol. 3, pp. 10, 128–29; vol. 4, pp. 313–14; vol. 5, p. 297. For the sale of lands belonging to the previously dissolved Rounceval guild see *CPR*, Ed. VI, vol. 3, pp. 111, 242; vol. 4, p. 205.

46

nature of these rewards, the fact that the priests were paid out of parochial funds is significant. At the least, these 'rewards' demonstrate the influence that a large fraternity, such as that of the Assumption, could continue to wield even after its dissolution.[23] It is also notable the none of the purchasers of St Margaret's chantry lands came from the parish itself.[24]

The evidence for the performance of services in English at St Margaret's is mixed. The churchwardens' accounts reveal that the parish purchased 'vii salters in Englishe' sometime before May 1549. In London parishes, however, most accounts show the purchase of the Psalter in English during 1548.[25] The Prayer Book of 1549 seems generally to have been in use in the early summer of that year.[26] St Margaret's parish, though, seems to have dragged its feet over several aspects of the new service. The purchase of four 'bookes of the Servis in the Churche' (i.e. the Prayer Book) took place only after Christmas 1549 and possibly as late as May 1550, the date of Ridley's visitation. The late date of this purchase is highly unusual. Hutton points to the Prayer Book as one of the success stories of the Edwardian Reformation. Out of ninety-one parishes surveyed by Hutton, every one had obtained the Book of Common Prayer by the required date of Whitsunday 1549.[27]

A similarly reluctant attitude can be discerned towards the provision of communion in both kinds at St Margaret's. Back in March 1548, the *Order of the Communion* had been printed along with a proclamation enjoining its use. It specified that churches were to offer communicants both bread and wine at communion.[28] There is no evidence, however, that St Margaret's offered its parishioners communion in both kinds until the latter part of Edward's reign and then, it seems, only after official prodding. Some time after May 1551, the parish recorded receiving the surplus of melted-down plate, which had been used to make communion cups. The actual payment to the smith for producing four of the cups, however, was not made until 1552. Precisely when the cups were delivered and put into use is not clear. Payments for making a book of articles and '[our] byll to put in at the Bysshoppes vycitacyon' stand next to an

---

23 WAC, E3 (1548–50), E4 (1550–52); Kitching, p. 65. Some time in 1548, the Crown granted pensions of £5 a year for life to Richard Hall, John Hickley (Highley), Edward Story and Robert Wattes. Similar pensions were also granted to the two priests from the Rounceval hospital, William Langborne and Richard Kylgo: TNA, E101/75/22. The 'rewards' paid by St Margaret's parish may thus have been intended to supplement these amounts, which would have been below what the chantry priests had previously earned.

24 One of the purchasers, Christopher Nedeham, was an Edwardian churchwarden at St Martin in the Fields: *CPR* Ed. VI, vol. 2, p. 59.

25 WAC, E3 (1548–49); *London VCH* p. 291.

26 H.A. Wilson (ed.), *The Order of the Communion, 1548* (1908), pp. xix–xx.

27 P. Le Huray, *Music and the Reformation in England 1549–1660* (1967), pp. 13, 18, 23; N. Temperley, *The Music of the English Parish Church* (2 vols., 1979), I, 14; *London VCH*, pp. 292–3; WAC, E3 (1549–50), E4 (1550–51); Hutton, 'Local impact', p. 125.

28 Cardwell, *Documentary Annals*, I, 72.

entry for boat-hire 'when we wente for to speake for the Communion Cuppes'. It is possible, then, that St Margaret's parish was presented for not administering communion in both kinds. This impression is confirmed by the fact that the first payment recorded for 'bread & wyne for the Communion' at St Margaret's covers the period November 1552 to May 1553.[29]

There are other indications that transforming St Margaret's into a Protestant church required at least the threat of official action. The account ending in May 1550, the month of Bishop Ridley's visitation, contains many references to the sale of church goods. It is telling that these 'superstitious' items were sold to members of the parochial establishment. The sexton, John Ivery, the parish clerk John Ellis and the churchwarden Richard Dod all purchased 'superstitious' church goods such as torch coffins. Another former warden, the barber Thomas Stockdale, paid 10s for 'old brasse & Ierne [iron]'. Stockdale may well have been sympathetic to the old religion: in 1556 he witnessed the will of St Margaret's curate, Henry Mote, who had served the parish since Henrician times. In another case, the alebrewer and parliamentary representative for Westminster, Robert Smallwood, paid 10s for 'the Stones of the Crosse in the Churche yeard and the Alter in Saynt Cornelys Chapell'.[30] Further evidence suggests that these examples may fit into a pattern whereby church goods were purchased to preserve them, rather than their being acquired for secular use.

The case of Robert Smallwood is a particularly significant one in this context. Smallwood, a prosperous brewer, had served as St Margaret's churchwarden in 1540–42. He represented Westminster in parliament in 1545 and again in October 1553.[31] In 1550 Smallwood bought the 'superstitious' items noted above. In 1554, however, when the parish was enthusiastically restoring the church to its pre-Reformation state, the wardens recorded 4d given to labourers 'for the berying of the holy water stock from Mr Smallwoodes house to the churche', where it was then erected.[32] A grant from Westminster Abbey also suggests that Smallwood was considered sympathetic to pre-Reformation Catholicism. In April 1538, Smallwood was granted the right of presentation to the living of Launton, Oxfordshire. That living was later filled by the former prior of Westminster Abbey, Denis Dalyons, and seems part of the strategy adopted by many monasteries of granting livings in their gift to sympathetic laymen shortly before their dissolution.[33]

---

29 WAC, E4 (1551–53). A communion cup dated 1552 and belonging to St Margaret's parish is on display at Westminster Abbey.

30 Stockdale witnessed the will of St Margaret's long-time curate, Henry Mote, who retained his position throughout the Reformation period until his death in 1556: WAC, PCW, 187 Bracy.

31 WAC, E3 (1540–42), E4 (1554–55); Bindoff, *House of Commons*, s.n. Robert Smallwood.

32 WAC, E4 (1554–55). There is no reference to its sale in the churchwardens' accounts.

33 Knighton, 'Collegiate foundations', pp. 28–30. Dalyons was also one of the first prebendaries of the newly established Westminster chapter: *Acts*, pp. xl–xli. Smallwood's relationship with the monk Hugh Smallwood (annointed 1523) is unclear: B. Harvey, *Living and Dying in England 1100–1540* (Oxford, 1993), p. 116, n. 12.

Other prominent purchasers of church goods at St Margaret's parish also appear to have had sympathies with the old religion. Notable among these were William Jennyngs and Nicholas Ludford. Both men had been deeply involved in parish affairs, acting as churchwardens and guild officers. Ludford, however, actually served as church-warden during Edward's reign. He was a strange choice to help oversee the enforce-ment of Protestant practice, for Nicholas Ludford was England's most famous composer of Lady masses during the 1510s and 1520s. A member of the Chapel Royal, he had also supplied the parish with musical compositions during the 1530s, and his florid compositions were noted for the intricacy of their polyphony of the type most detested by the reformers.[34] That his attachment to the old religion endured is suggested by his behaviour during Mary's reign. Ludford was almost the first member of the parish to pay for prayers for the dead when Mary was restored, paying for bells and four tapers at the year's mind of his wife Anne on 23 December 1553, one of only two obits recorded in the parish before May 1554.[35] Ludford remarried shortly thereafter and it is notable that his new bride paid for the hire of St Margaret's circlet at her wedding.[36]

The religious sympathies of William Jennyngs, a groom of the chamber under Henry VIII, are even clearer. In 1553–54 Jennyngs donated 7s 'towards the lampe' in St Margaret's church. Jennyngs's devotion to the old forms of religion is most vividly revealed in his will of 27 August 1558. Jennyngs appointed John Feckenham, abbot of the restored Marian abbey, as one of the overseers of his will, leaving twenty loads of brick 'towards his buylding'. The building mentioned was the extensive resto-ration work Feckenham had undertaken at the Abbey, replacing jewels and relics and rebuilding the shrine of Edward the Confessor. Jennyngs also requested burial in the Abbey church, providing instructions for his funeral. He left 40s 'to my lord Abbot to syne [sing] and come with my bodie to the church' and 12d 'to every moncke that will waite and singe my bodye to the churche'. One monk was to be selected by Feckenham personally and paid 10s to sing thirty masses for Jennyngs's soul and all Christian souls.[37]

The bequests of men such as Jennyngs, and the pattern observed in the purchase of church goods, illustrate the existence of strongly conservative religious sentiments among prominent laymen at St Margaret's (and in Jennyngs's case, strong support for

---

34 D. Wulstan, *Tudor Music* (1985), pp. 256, 258–60; *The New Grove Dictionary of Music and Musicians*, ed. S. Sadie (20 vols., 1980), s.n. Nicholas Ludford; D. Skinner, ' "At the mynde of Nycholas Ludford" ', *Early Music* (August 1994), pp. 395, 399, 409. Smallwood was an executor of Ludford's will.

35 WAC, E4 (1553–54; 1554–55).

36 Skinner, 'Ludford', p. 399. Note also that Robert Wattes was listed in the chantry certificate of St Margaret's as beadle of the fraternity of the Virgin's Assumption, and yet subsequently served as 'conduct' in the Edwardian period: WAC, E4 (1550–51).

37 WAC, E4 (1553–54); Rosser, p. 383; TNA, PCC, Prob. 11/42A/11. Jennyngs left 20s to the poor of St Margaret's and 26s 8d to be distributed to the poor on the day of his burial; *DNB*, s.n. John de Feckenham. The diarist Machyn recorded the elaborate character of Jennyngs's funeral, 'with ii whyt branchys and a ii dosen skochyons of armes, and xvi torchys and iiii gret tapurs, and mony morners in blake, and pore men had gownes', Machyn, *Diary*, p. 177.

monasticism). Nevertheless, the isolated acts of individuals did not prevent a basic conformity to the Protestant practices set down by law. Even if St Margaret's church-wardens were sometimes slower to act than were their counterparts at other churches, the period after Ridley's 1550 visitation witnessed further changes to St Margaret's church. The remaining altars were removed and a communion table was purchased in line with Bishop Ridley's injunctions. Eventually the wardens also purchased two 'Communion Bookes' (the 1552 Prayer Book).[38]

Other events in St Margaret's at this time, however, once again suggest a reluctance on the part of the parish to cut itself off from its religious past. The year 1551–52 saw the first sale of vestments from the church. Vestments had been allowed by the 1549 Prayer Book, but after much controversy the rubric was revised in 1551. The sale at St Margaret's, then, was probably a response to this change in policy. A cope, a set of vestments and 'ii tynakyltes [tunicles] of Red Clothe Tissue' fetched £10 while three corporas cases of 'clothe of golde and tissue' sold for 4s. It is striking, however, how very few such items were actually sold by the richly furnished St Margaret's, especially as a 1547 inventory of parish goods had listed no fewer than twenty-one copes and thirteen corporas cases, as well as numerous other suits of vestments. Elsewhere in London and the home counties these sales were extremely common. Parishes in these areas, it has been argued, were highly conscious of the need to profit from these goods before the government did.[39] St Margaret's decision to retain most of its church goods rather than selling them probably derived from several motives. One was undoubtedly real devotion to Catholic ritual and the hope that such practices would one day be revived. A second motive may have been an essential conservatism on the part of parishioners and a desire to preserve what might be considered the community's heritage.[40]

Turning to St Martin's parish, it is clear that, despite the hints of religious controversy, the proponents of Protestant reform gained the upper hand relatively quickly under Edward VI. One reason for this must have been the leadership provided by the vicar, Robert Beste. Before he came to St Martin's, Beste had been a Franciscan friar in the Oxford convent, where in September 1530 he had been charged with incontinence and breach of the peace (charges possibly linked to unorthodox religious beliefs). At some point Beste joined the London convent of the Franciscans, where he remained until its dissolution in 1538. On 16 September 1539, Beste received a

38 WAC, E4 (1550–53); *VCH London*, p. 295; Hutton, 'Local impact', p. 125.

39 WAC, E4 (1551–53); H.B. Walters, *London Churches at the Reformation* (1939), p. 10; Hutton, 'Local impact', p. 125; M.E.C. Walcott, *The History of St Margaret Westminster* (1847), pp. 68–72.

40 Peter Heylin's seventeenth-century account of armed St Margaret's parishioners saving their church from demolition by Protector Somerset's workmen, who were said to be planning to use its stone on the building at Somerset House (quoted in Rosser, pp. 275–6) may actually have been a garbled account of the dismantling of St Mary le Strand in the same year (which undoubtedly did furnish stone for Somerset House, and whose dismantling any local hostility was insufficient to prevent).

dispensation to hold a benefice and change his habit. He officially became vicar of St Martin's on 22 December 1539 and it is seems likely that he was a royal appointment, perhaps even owing his appointment to Cromwell, who was acting as steward of the Abbey at the time.[41] Beste remains a shadowy figure for most of his time at St Martin's, but on 24 June 1554 it was recorded that 'a priest was put into Newgate for synging the Englyshe letany in his parishe Churche at Charing Crosse'. Beste was consequently deprived of his living in the same year, but on Elizabeth's accession he was apparently rewarded for his suffering in the Protestant cause by reinstatement as vicar. If Beste was sufficiently devoted to the new religion to risk imprisonment, then it is likely that evidence of Protestant change in parish practice reflected the positive support of the vicar, rather than a simple willingness to conform to government directives.[42]

As the process of clearing images from churches and introducing Protestant services began, St Martin's followed the example of swift compliance found generally in London. In certain ways, however, St Martin's anticipated official policy. Payments to the morrow-mass priest, for example, ceased in August 1547. In keeping with this, lights and prayers for the dead are recorded only twice after June 1547.[43] In other respects St Martin's acted promptly to implement Reformation policy. In January of 1548, the parish sold 100 pounds of 'olde metal' – all the plate that had been necessary to Catholic ritual. At the same time another 100 pounds of now useless wax was sold. A similar sale at St Margaret's did not take place until May. The wardens also began removing superstitious images from the church. It seems likely that St Martin's had cleared the church of images before the end of 1547, once again acting before the sister parish of St Margaret's. By January 1548, the parish was occupied in the later stages of this process. The wardens, for example, purchased 6s worth of glass 'for Repayringe of the wyndowes where the Trynytes were taken awaye'. Such a step suggests strong reformed views, since imagery in glass was condemned only by the more hard-line reformers as tending towards idolatry. By June 1548 the first major sale of superstitious church goods had also taken place.[44]

The remainder of 1548 and 1549 saw St Martin's complying promptly with official injunctions, enforcing orders suppressing Catholic forms of worship, but also showing itself swift in introducing its parishioners to Protestant tenets and practices.

---

41 A.B. Emden, *A Biographical Register of the University of Oxford A.D. 1501 to 1540* (Oxford, 1974), p. 47. In April 1539, Beste was prosecuted for eating flesh during Lent, along with a number of others, including some ex-monks: *L&P*, xvi, pt 1, no. 684. It is not clear precisely who held the right of appointment to St Martin's in these years (the last known appointment by the Abbey was William Skinner in 1522, while Hennessey does not list a patron for the living again until the Bishop of London appointed Thomas Welles in 1554: Hennessey, p. 294). In a consistory court case in 1546 Beste was curiously referred to as having been vicar of St Martin's for sixteen years, which must be a clerical error: WAC, Acc. 736, 15 September 1546.

42 Kitto, pp. 59, 64; *Narratives*, p. 288.

43 Kitto, pp. 124, 116–17.

44 *Ibid.*, pp. 121, 124; Aston, *England's Iconoclasts*, p. 316.

The churchwardens purchased the required text of the *Paraphrases* of Erasmus, white-washed the church and purchased a communion cup all during the summer of 1548.[45] In keeping with such changes, the parish soon after paid £8 16s 8d to have the ten commandments and various biblical texts written on the walls of the church.[46] There are no specific references at St Martin's to the purchase of the 1549 Prayer Book, but its acquisition can be inferred from a payment for 'the Carryage of the olde s'uyce bokes of the Churche to westmy'ster to the summer'. This entry refers to an order issued in December 1549 directing that old service books be defaced so that only the Prayer Book could be used. Only seventeen of the ninety-one parishes studied by Hutton, however, recorded their compliance with this order, once again placing St Martin's parish officials potentially among the most zealous in the country.[47]

It seems that Protestant doctrine was also expounded from the pulpit by visiting preachers. Some time after March 1550, the accounts refer to cleaning the church 'after mr Hoppers s[er]monds'. This entry probably refers to John Hooper, later Bishop of Gloucester and Worcester. Hooper had become chaplain to Protector Somerset in May 1549 and his severe brand of Protestantism attracted even greater attention during his famous Lenten sermons of 1550, which were preached at Court. Hooper is also known to have preached at various places in the capital during this period.[48]

The same year, 1550–51, St Martin's churchwardens organized a sale of church goods which must have completely stripped the church of vestments, altar cloths, banners and streamers. The items sold included thirteen complete 'suits' of vestments, a canopy cloth and a cloth of gold hearse cloth, trimmed with red velvet and 'enbrothered whyth angells'. The date of the sale again points to the zealousness of the parish officials. The use of vestments was a controversial issue among English Protestants, and only definitely banned by the 1552 Prayer Book.[49] The majority, if not all, of St Martin's vestments were sold by March 1551 – well ahead of the official ban. It

---

45 Kitto, p. 130. Communion in both kinds could have been offered to parishioners at an earlier date, even before the purchase of a communion cup. *The Order of Communion*, specifying communion in both kinds had been issued in March 1548: *London VCH*, p. 291. The Grey Friars' Chronicle states that this service began at St Paul's after Easter 1548, *Chronicle of the Grey Friars of London*, ed. J.G. Nichols (Camden Society 53, 1852), p. 55. Wriothesley's *Chronicle* notes that 'all the service' was in English at St Paul's and other London churches by May 1548: C. Wriothesley, *A Chronicle of England during the Reigns of the Tudors, A.D. 1485 to 1559* (2 vols., Camden Society n.s. 11 and 20, 1875–77), II, 2. A church administering communion in both kinds would undoubtedly have had an English service. There is no specific reference to the introduction of English services at St Martin's. In several instances the accounts do not record the purchase of items we know the parish to have possessed from indirect evidence. This is true for the communion table and the 1549 Prayer Book.

46 Kitto, p. 131.

47 Kitto, pp. 133; P. Hughes and J. Larkin (eds.), *Tudor Royal Proclamations* (3 vols., New Haven, 1964–69), I, 485–60; Cardwell, *Documentary Annals*, I, 85–6; Hutton, 'Local impact', p. 125.

48 Kitto, p. 136; *DNB*, s.n. John Hooper.

49 Kitto, pp. 136–8; E. Cardwell, *The Two Liturgies of Edward VI Compared* (1861), p. xxii.

seems likely that the sale made a clean sweep of the parish vestments, an unusual occurrence. The 1552 London surveys of church goods reveal that many churches still possessed vestments in the summer of that year. Only the City parishes of St Antholin and St Michael Bassishaw had been swept bare. Although a financial motive for the sale must be recognized, the early date and sweeping nature of the sale is indicative of strong reformed views among those involved.[50]

Evidence from the last year of Edward's reign confirms that St Martin's parish consistently exceeded the bare minimum to ensure Protestant conformity. Indeed some of the steps taken during this final year suggest that those of radical Protestant views had come to wield considerable influence in the parish. These steps may reflect the election of two new wardens in March 1552.[51] The expenses related to the communion service are of particular significance. St Martin's parishioners had, of course, been offered communion in both kinds from 1548. From 1552 this was funded out of a gathering from among parishioners, rather than out of the parish's ordinary revenues. Such was the enthusiasm for communion in both kinds that it appears to have been administered until December 1553, four months after Mary's accession.[52] On 26 March 1551, the churchwardens recorded with unusual precision that the parish had paid 4s for 'the knellynge stoylls in the Qwere and the foote passes [paces]'. These stools would have been used by parishioners kneeling as they received communion.[53]

Surprisingly, only a little over a year later the parish undertook the more expensive measure of building special pews for communion. The precise significance of this is not entirely clear, but it may suggest the presence of committed Protestants in the parish. Seats for communicants were also found at such London centres of Protestantism as St Bride Fleet Street, St Antholin's and St Benet Gracechurch Street. The matter of contention here was kneeling at communion. By implication, those parishioners at churches with communion pews or forms may have taken communion seated. More radical Protestants interpreted kneeling at communion as an affirmation of the real presence in the Eucharist, and so as a sign of idolatry. The 1552 Prayer Book, however, instructed parishioners to kneel, although the famous 'Black Rubric' was hastily appended to explain that kneeling was not to be interpreted superstitiously.[54]

It is particularly telling at St Martin's that six prominent parishioners donated money specifically to help meet the cost of the communion pews. It is possible that

---

50 Walters, *London Churches*, pp. 10, 18, 37. No returns from 1552 survive for either St Martin's or St Margaret's.

51 Kitto, p. 141. The new wardens were William Browne and Christopher Nedeham. For Nedeham in particular see below.

52 Kitto, p. 143, 148. The account ending December 1553 records 27s ½d 'payde and layde owt for bread and wyne for them that came to Co'munyon in the sayde two yeres space'.

53 Kitto, p. 138.

54 Walter, *London Churches*, p. 44; Cardwell, *Two Liturgies*, p. 291; Aston, *England's Iconoclasts*, p. 8; J. Strype, *Memorials of Thomas Cranmer* (2 vols., 1840), I, 415–16.

these men represent the core of a group of the hotter sort of Protestant, impatient for reforms along continental lines. But even if parishioners continued to kneel at communion, the erection of these pews remains important, for it demonstrates the extent to which parishioners were prepared to alter their medieval church to accommodate the Protestant practice of administering communion in both kinds to the laity.[55] It is significant that at the same time that the parish introduced communion pews, it also paid for the destruction of its rood loft.[56] Rood lofts were never officially banned during Edward's reign, but some felt that they retained superstitious connotations since they had formerly been covered with lights. Nevertheless, of the ninety-one parishes studied by Hutton only seventeen seem to have demolished their rood-lofts.[57]

By the end of Edward's reign, St Martin in the Fields could claim to be a truly Protestant church, both in its services and appearance. But the religious demands of the government were about to change dramatically.

THE MARIAN REFORMATION AND ITS AFTERMATH

The death of Edward VI on 6 July 1553 and the accession of his Catholic sister Mary meant the reversal of many changes introduced during the Protestant king's reign. Westminster in particular was at the centre of the restoration of Catholicism under the new Marian regime. While it has recently been suggested that the Edwardian government intended Westminster to act as a showcase for official Protestant policies, there in fact seems much more evidence for its being chosen by the Marian authorities to act as a showcase for restored Catholicism.[58] Certainly the Queen herself participated in Rogation processions in those parishes close to Whitehall in 1554. Machyn described the festivities when

> the quen['s] grace whent a prossessyon within sant James with harolds and serjants of armes, and iiii bysshopes mytred, and all iii days they whent her chapell a-bowt the feldes, first day to sant Gylles . . . the nest day tuwyse-day to sant Martens in the

---

55 Kitto, p. 144. The 'certen men' who banded together to pay for the communion pews were 'Master Pyrrye', John Evans, John Goldhurst, Richard Hamdon, Swafforde and one 'Burnop'. Of these men, Goldhurst had been a churchwarden for 1548–50, Evans was among those signing the 1558–59 accounts with the restored Protestant vicar Beste, and Hamdon supplied a service book to the parish in 1558–59 (although the parish had to pay him for it): *ibid.*, pp. 177, 178. Pyrrye may well be the Robert Perry who also donated goods to the Marian church. None of the other men who paid for the communion pews made any donations to the Marian church. Addleshaw and Etchells caution that in the seventeenth century seats or forms for communicants did not necessarily indicate that parishioners refused to kneel, but they are silent on the earlier period: G.W.O. Addleshaw and F. Etchells, *The Architectural Setting of Anglican Worship* (n.d.), pp. 119–23.

56 Kitto, p. 143, 147.

57 *London VCH*, p. 294; Hutton, 'Local impact', pp. 121–2.

58 MacCulloch, *Tudor Church Militant*, pp. 82–4, 111.

feldes, [and there] a sermon and song masse, and so thay dronke ther; and the iii day to Westmynster, and ther a sermon and then masse, and mad good chere, and after a-bowt the Parke.[59]

The Queen also made gifts to assist in the refurnishing of at least one of Westminster's parish churches.[60]

Most important of all for Westminster, the return of Roman Catholicism brought with it the refounding of the Abbey. Few monasteries were refounded under Mary, and of these Westminster was by far the most prominent.[61] Mary does not seem at first to have intended the restoration of the Abbey, being content initially to purge the cathedral chapter of Protestants and to replace them with her own chaplains.[62] Nevertheless, well before the revival of the monastic foundation, the Abbey was providing a lead for Westminster as a whole. Even before Mary's coronation itself, the obsequies and burial of Sir John Dudley were carried out at Westminster in a service that was sung entirely in Latin, with a procession beginning at 'the bake-syd of St Margatts'. Mass was performed there at Mary's coronation and at the start of parliament in the following October, and the new queen and her husband also regularly processed to the Abbey in great state to hear mass.[63] It was also at the Abbey that the political nation gathered amid splendid ceremony each year on St Andrew's Day to celebrate the restoration of Catholicism.[64] In 1555 the new dean Hugh Weston (a great favourite of the Queen and prominent hard-line opponent of Protestantism) was to be found carrying the blessed sacrament in an elaborate procession through the town of Westminster. The restoration of the monastic foundation in 1556, with the installation of the celebrated scholar and preacher John Feckenham as the new abbot, kept the Abbey still more in the public eye as a focus for revived Catholicism. At Feckenham's installation, he and fourteen monks 'whentt a prossessyon after the old fassyon in ther monkes wede', and many such processions followed. Feckenham spearheaded a determined revival of the Abbey, reclaiming the abbot's house from the strongly Protestant Lord Wentworth, vigorously defending the Abbey's right of sanctuary, and also in 1557 restoring the shrine of Edward the Confessor.[65] The restored Abbey also played a renewed role in the ritual life of Westminster's parishes, as we shall see.

---

59 Machyn, *Diary*, p. 61.

60 Kitto, p. 158.

61 D. Loades, *The Reign of Mary Tudor* (1992 ed.), pp. 299–302.

62 Knighton, 'Collegiate foundations', p. 154.

63 Machyn, *Diary*, pp. 44, 46, 74, 77, 122, 137, 163–4; Strype, *Ecclesiastical Memorials*, III, pt 1, pp. 55–6; *CSPVen 1556–57*, p. 878.

64 *CSPVen 1555–56*, p. 305; *CSPVen 1556–57*, p. 836; For King Philip riding in procession to the Abbey on St Andrew's Day see Strype, *Ecclesiastical Memorials*, III, pt 1, 324.

65 *DNB*, s.n. John de Feckenham; P. Tudor, 'John Feckenham and Tudor religious controversies' in J. Blair and B. Golding (eds.), *The Cloister and the World* (Oxford, 1996); Machyn, *Diary*, pp. 81, 119, 130. See also *ibid.*, pp. 121, 131, 132, 145–6. For the restoration of the Abbey see *CSPVen*

If Westminster stood at the epicentre of the revival of Catholicism, it also experienced some of the most vivid manifestations of opposition to this revival. William Flower's spectacular assault on a priest has already been mentioned at the beginning of this chapter. But Westminster also had first-hand experience of Wyatt's rebellion. Wyatt's troops clashed locally with those of the Queen at Hyde Park Corner before proceeding through the streets of Westminster to Charing Cross, while at the unprotected Whitehall Palace Dean Weston 'wore harness under his vestment' while celebrating mass before the Queen. After the defeat of the rebellion, several of Wyatt's supporters were hanged at Charing Cross and Hyde Park Corner, while Wyatt's head was set upon the gallows at Hay-hill, beside Hyde Park.[66]

Another source of dissatisfaction with the Marian regime that made itself felt strongly in Westminster was the presence of the Spanish entourage of King Philip. Elaborate funerals for dead Spaniards, celebrated 'after the fashion of Spain', were held in the Abbey, and also in all the Westminster parish churches.[67] But there were also, inevitably, a series of clashes between Englishmen and Spaniards in the streets of Westminster. Indeed, a clear indication of the local tensions is provided by the fact that the screams and drawn swords provoked by Flower's attack on the priest at St Margaret's led local Spaniards to fear that an attack on themselves was imminent.[68] A Spaniard was hanged at Charing Cross on 26 October 1554 for having killed a servant of Sir George Gifford in the Strand by Temple Bar. Just over a week later there was another large affray between Spaniards and Englishmen at Charing Cross, and within two months on New Year's Day 1555 a further uproar in the Abbey itself, as a group of 'debauched' Spaniards fired their pistols when the dean's men found them in the cloister, and the subsequent ringing of the alarm by a Spanish friar 'called all the street together'.[69] The rich clothing of the Spaniards made them a tempting target for theft, but the thieves received exemplary punishment – it was noted that they were often hanged not at the common places of execution but 'before the court, or the doors of the Spaniards that were robbed'. The prosecution of such assaults could also act as a focus for religious opposition. Among three Englishmen hanged at Charing Cross for robbing certain Spaniards in Westminster Abbey was a London poulterer, John Tooley, who declared his hatred of popery even from the cart which was taking him to execution.

1555–56, pp. 651, 809; and Machyn's account of the ceremonies surrounding the installation of the abbot: *Diary*, pp. 118–20; R. Rex, *Henry VIII and the English Reformation* (Basingstoke, 1993), pp. 125, 139. The restoration of the Abbey also entailed the dissolution of Westminster cathedral and the secular chapter: GL, MS 9531/12, pt 1, f. 407; Knighton, 'Collegiate foundations', pp. 156–7.

66 Strype, *Ecclesiastical Memorials*, III, pt 1, 136–44, 187; Machyn, *Diary*, pp. 52–4, 59–60.

67 Strype, *Ecclesiastical Memorials*, III, pt 1, 319, 322, 329; Machyn, *Diary*, pp. 75, 79. For other elaborate ceremonies involving Spaniards at the Abbey see Strype, *Ecclesiastical Memorials*, III, pt 1, 214, 324. Such examples rapidly decline after October 1555 – most of the Spaniards had departed by December: *CSPVen 1555–56*, pp. 213, 218; Loades, *Reign*, p. 207, n. 48.

68 *CSPVen 1555–56*, p. 51.

69 Strype, *Ecclesiastical Memorials*, III, pt 1, 320, 329.

This incident took place only three days after the burning of William Flower, and therefore seemed to call for another exemplary punishment. The dead Tooley was subsequently dug up from his burial underneath the gallows and his corpse burnt as a heretic after undergoing a ghoulish citation, trial, excommunication and sentence. The citation of the deceased Tooley was even set upon the church door of St Martin's.[70]

Westminster could hardly be unaware, then, of the tumultuous changes that the Marian succession brought in its wake, especially with the Abbey providing a striking focus for restored Catholic enthusiasm in the area, and a model for parishioners of conservative religious sentiments. Nevertheless, the formal re-imposition of Catholicism did not make itself felt immediately at the parish level. At least initially, the new Queen's fear of disorder and the need to consolidate her position meant that both Catholic and Protestant rites were tolerated. It was not until December 1553 that Parliament repealed the reforming statutes of Edward's reign, restoring the rites celebrated in 1546. In that same December, Machyn noted, a proclamation was issued 'that noman shuld syng no Englys serves nor communion after the xx day of Desember . . . and that evere parryche to make a auter and to have a crosse and staff, and all othus thinges in all parryches all in Laten, as hale [holy]-bread, hale-water, as palme and assesse [ashes]'. The tenor of this proclamation was confirmed by injunctions issued in March 1554, instructing parish churches to return to 'the laudable and honest ceremonies which were wont to be used' in the last year of Henry's reign. The reception given to the new Catholic regime, especially during the first few months, therefore casts an interesting light on just how fully (or not) the religious reforms of Edward's reign had been accepted.[71]

It is not entirely clear how quickly St Margaret's church resumed these old prac-tices. Latin services were certainly celebrated in the church before Christmas 1553. Some time between August and December 1553, the wardens purchased 'a Manuell an ymnall & a processional' and three 'Great Antiphoners 2 Grayels [graduals] and a Masse Booke'. On 23 December 1553, a glazier was paid for making a pane of 'paynted work' for St Margaret's chancel as well as setting up four 'paynted peces' into the east window of the chancel – work paid for by the Abbey church. As early as August the parish received gifts towards what would be the costly restoration of the church. By the end of 1554, not only had St Margaret's purchased most of the necessaries for Catholic worship, it had also resolutely sold off its Edwardian communion table, washed out 'the scripture of the high Alter table', and whitewashed 'the high allter endes & the 2 Chappelles' – these last two acts at least a month before Bishop Bonner ordered the razing of scriptures and writings painted upon church walls.[72]

70 *Ibid.*, pp. 342, 362; Foxe, *Acts*, VII, 90–7.

71 Machyn, *Diary*, p. 50; Cardwell, *Documentary Annals*, I, 124.

72 WAC, E4 (1553–55); WAM 37643A, 37643B; Cardwell, *Documentary Annals*, I, 168–70. In August 1553, the parish received 50s from Sir John Arundel, 'towardes byeng of the necessaryes to the Churche', while Edmund Wilgrece, a parishioner, donated 46s 8d 'towardes the Reparacions of the Churche' in 1556–57. Bishop Bonner's mandate on writings was dated 25 October 1554

Conservative sentiments in the parish were apparently stirred up still further by the tumultuous events surrounding Wyatt's Rebellion, and the march through Westminster of Wyatt's forces. Relieved by Wyatt's defeat, and perhaps rather shaken by the event, the parish paid for bread and drink 'on ashewenday to the Ryngers at the victory & overthrowe of wiat [Wyatt] and his Adherentes'. It is significant that the entry specifies that the bells were rung on Ash Wednesday 1554, the very day that Thomas Wyatt was sent to the Tower and the day before the Bishop of London ordered London churches to ring their bells and sing Te Deum Laudamus in celebration of Wyatt's defeat.[73]

Before May 1554 St Margaret's parish had acquired many of the essentials for Catholic worship. The wardens paid £4 13s for 'a Challis all gylte' and 10s for 'a blew Chesable of Satten of bridges [Bruges] with flowres with stole & fannell & for a holly water stock'. They also purchased a pyx, a censer, candlesticks, a lamp 'a ship for Frankenses', altar cloths, and corporas cloths, and paid for the rood cloth to be hung. At least some of the altars were in place by Easter 1554, including the high altar and the altar dedicated to Our Lady. Striking among the parish accounts are payments for the repair of church goods that had escaped destruction in the previous reign – 3s 8d 'for new Repeyringe of the sepulchre and the standerd for the tennable lightes'. In this process of Catholic restoration, St Margaret's appears comparable to other parish churches studied by Ronald Hutton, although acting sooner rather than later. Hutton finds 'considerable homogeneity' among churches in providing the externals of Catholic worship. By the end of 1554, most had acquired vestments, some or all of the ornaments and liturgical vessels of the Mass, some or all of the necessary service books and finally, they had all rebuilt the high altar.[74]

The Marian revival also brought back the pre-Reformation celebration of church holy days. At St Margaret's, the first Ascension Day of Mary's reign saw the traditional joint celebration with the former Westminster Abbey, with payments for bread, wine, ale and beer for the worshipful of the parish and 'for Mr Deane and his cumpany when they cam to Churche in procession on thascension evyn'.[75] The pre-Reformation popularity of St Margaret also reasserted itself, hesitantly at first, but then more confidently. The holiday was celebrated in 1554, and by 1555 many of the pre-Reformation customs associated with St Margaret's Day had been resumed. The church was decorated with garlands, Mr Rede was paid as in former times for 'the hyre of the

---

(Foxe, *Acts*, VI, 565–6), but Wriothesley recorded that many London parishes had removed royal arms and scriptural quotations from the walls of their churches by Easter 1554: Wriothesley, *Chronicle*, II, 113–14. For the restoration of Catholic practice in London more generally see Brigden, esp. pp. 574–93.

73 WAC, E4 (1553–55); Cardwell, *Documentary Annals*, I, 168–70; Machyn, *Diary*, p. 54; Brigden, pp. 543–5. Wriothesley, *Chronicle*, II, 109–11.

74 WAC, E4 (1553–56); Hutton, 'Local impact', p. 129.

75 WAC, E4 (1553–54).

cloths to hang the Quyre and Chapilles' and the 'waytes of London' played at the festivities.[76] The following year the parish paid for a new image of the saint, and the accounts for 1556–57 specifically refer to 'the gathering of the Vyrgynes' on St Margaret's Day.[77]

The enhanced importance of the Abbey under Mary also helped to revive the ritual and corporate life of the parish. The St Peter's day fair was held in the Abbey itself in 1554, followed by a procession and mass. In 1557, the revived Abbey and local parishioners united again when the fair was held in St Margaret's churchyard, followed later in the day by a 'godly prossessyon, the wyche my lord abbott whent with ys myter and ye crosse and a grett number of copes of cloth of gold, and the wergers, and mony worshephull gentyll-men and women at Westmynster, went a prossessyon'.[78]

The process of embellishing the church continued until Mary's death. The single most costly expenditure was for 'the Roode Mary and John'. This was restored in 1556–57 and its expense met partly through a 'gatheryng for the Roode'.[79] In addition to works of restoration, the parish also attempted to obliterate its Protestant past. During the last year of Mary's reign it sold off 'the Kinges armes that hung before the Roode loft' and dealt what might be seen as the final blow to the reformers' educative efforts when it paid for the making of three surplices from 'the Clothe that hung before the Rode loft wrytten with the Comaundements': an ironic reversal of the process whereby vestments had been cut up by Protestants to be used for secular purposes.[80]

It is easy to underestimate the extent of the embellishment of services at Marian St Margaret's. Items brought out of store or donated to the church do not always find their way into the records. This is borne out at St Margaret's by the evidence of inventories dating from the early years of Elizabeth, which include many 'superstitious' items not purchased or donated under Mary, suggesting that they were much older and had managed to survive the years of Edward's rule. The parish possessed more copes, for example, than can be accounted for by the acquisitions of Mary's reign.[81]

76 WAC, E4 (1555–56).

77 WAC, E4 (1556–57).

78 Machyn, *Diary*, pp. 66, 140–1.

79 WAC, E4 (1556–57).

80 WAC, E4 (1556–58).

81 Hutton, 'Local impact', pp. 129–30; WAC, E4, inventories of 1562–64 and 1564–66. By 1566 some of these copes appear to have been turned into hearse cloths, the rental of which provided the parish with substantial income. A particularly intriguing item in the 1566 inventory was a hearse cloth described as 'of old red tissue called St Cornelius Clothe' – possibly a survival from the old suppressed fraternity of St Cornelius or else a cloth from St Cornelius's altar. That the customs practised by the fraternities did not entirely fade away is suggested by the popularity of St George's cloth, for use at burials, which continued undiminished during Edward's reign. It is unclear if this cloth actually depicted the saint.

So far the discussion has focused upon the process by which Catholicism was revived at St Margaret's under Mary. There were however some significant omissions in this revival, although these omissions largely conform to the pattern found for the rest of England. Obits, and to a lesser extent lights at burials, never regained their pre-Reformation popularity at St Margaret's. More strikingly, the once vibrant fraternities of St Margaret's were not re-established during Mary's reign. In fact few fraternities reappeared in other parts of England. Some historians have attributed these gaps in the revival of Catholicism to the gradual decline in the cult of saints and waning belief in the efficacy of prayers for the dead, a decline which they date from Henry's reign. St Margaret's parishioners did not display quite the same rejection of images and the cult of saints as found in some of the parishes studied by Robert Whiting, as the revival of ceremonies relating to St Margaret makes clear.[82] It may be, however, that devotion to the patronal saint in a parish with such a history of strong corporate feeling should partly be interpreted as an assertion of communal identity as much as belief in the particular intercessory powers of an individual saint. But this makes the failure to revive the fraternities even more puzzling. After all, St Margaret's fraternities had not functioned simply as corporate chantries. They had served a whole range of local corporate needs that had nothing to do with beliefs in purgatory and saints.

Why, then, were fraternities not revived? Financial reasons must have played a significant role. One of the chief difficulties in resurrecting the fraternities was that the confiscation and sale of their lands meant that they no longer had any financial basis upon which to operate. In addition, those fraternities which had adopted quasi-governmental functions were precisely those wealthy ones, such as that of the Virgin's Assumption, which had possessed a landed income. Such responsibilities now devolved, logically enough, upon the parish. The parish simply assimilated the strengths and organizing tradition of the guild structure, drawing on the very men who had been most active in the fraternities.[83] At least some of the social advantages of the fraternities, then, were retained without the actual revival of fraternities and their religious activities. During the few years of Mary's rule, parishioners may also have been reluctant to make the long-term investment necessary in refounding the fraternities, especially given the absence of a secure Catholic succession to the throne.[84]

Such feelings of insecurity are easily imagined and would have been heightened by the dramatic events that took place within St Margaret's parish itself, such as William

---

82 Hutton, 'Local impact', pp. 131–2; R. Whiting, ' "For the health of my soul": prayers for the dead in the Tudor south-west', *Southern History* 5 (1983), pp. 75–7, 83–4; C. Burgess, ' "By quick and by dead": wills and pious provision in late medieval Bristol', *EHR* 405 (1987), pp. 856–7. In London, the only fraternity to be refounded was that of the Name of Jesus, which met in the Shrouds of St Paul's; see Brigden, pp. 581–3.

83 See below, ch. 4 on parish elites.

84 Cf. P. Marshall, *Reformation England 1480–1642* (2003), pp. 99–100; Marshall, *Beliefs and the Dead in Reformation England* (Oxford, 2002), pp. 115–18.

Flower's sacrilegious attack and the public spectacle of his death in the flames of a bonfire lit in St Margaret's churchyard. The presence of Wyatt's troops on the streets of Westminster and the subsequent hanging of three of Wyatt's supporters at Charing Cross, within sight of the parish, must have generated a corresponding fear of the disorder potentially unleashed by a kingdom divided by religion. It may also have instilled a lasting parochial distrust of individual Protestant enthusiasm: the parish accounts for 1554–55 contain the order that 'Joan Wylson the heretyck' should be buried 'withowte the Churchyarde wall'.[85] A return to the stability of the pre-Reformation years must have appeared very desirable. It is perhaps this kind of conservatism that one can detect at work in St Margaret's.

All in all, the bulk of surviving evidence at St Margaret's paints a convincing picture of religious conservatism, at least among those in decision-making positions. Of course, religious attitudes that must be pieced together in this fragmentary way can never provide a complete picture of parochial religion. Nevertheless, during Edward's reign the parish supported its former chantry priests, resisted communion in both kinds for as long as possible, was tardy in its purchase of the 1549 Prayer Book, resisted selling its church goods and, when it did sell such items, seems to have sold them to those who might be expected to conserve them. The explanation for such conservatism rests largely with the lead provided by parish notables. Many can be identified as religious conservatives. A number of the most influential were actually employed as lay officials of Westminster Abbey.[86] The role of the clergy also needs to be considered. St Margaret's curate, Henry Mote, was unlikely to have encouraged any moves towards reform. Mote, who was not a university graduate, was appointed by the Abbey during Henry's reign. He seems to have been a fairly anonymous figure and served the cure continuously as Westminster's own 'vicar of Bray' until his death in 1556.[87]

If St Margaret's presents a picture of religious conservatism, it is also notable that the parish does not seem to have been widely divided in its response to the Reformation. No doubt there must have been some parishioners of Protestant convictions, but the parish elites in this long-established parish, with its strong communal organizations and cohesive social structures, seem to have held firm in ensuring that the parish made only the most minimal concessions to the Reformation.

By contrast, St Martin in the Fields, as we have seen, had manifested a certain degree of enthusiasm for the Edwardian reforms. Nevertheless, the return to Catholicism

---

85 WAC, E4 (1554–55). This was presumably on the instruction of the curate, Henry Mote. On the hanging of Wyatt's troops see Machyn, *Diary*, p. 55.

86 Harvey, *Living and Dying*, p. 166; Rosser, pp. 158–60.

87 The list of St Margaret's curates provided in Hennessey, p. 439, is not to be trusted and, unlike entries for other parishes, sources are not provided for many of the names. Henry Mote served the cure from 1532 until his death in 1556 (see WAC, E3 and E4, where he signs himself as such on St Margaret's churchwardens' accounts and Rosser, p. 339). I have not been able to verify who served as curate 1556–58.

under Mary was accomplished relatively swiftly, even if the enormity of the task of restoration testifies to the effectiveness of the Edwardian churchwardens.[88] St Martin's churchwardens obediently set about purchasing some of the basic items of Catholic worship. By the end of October 1553, the parish had acquired an 'old portace [breviary]', a 'Messe booke and a Crosse', a manual, a pair of candlesticks and a holy water sprinkler. The accounts also show the wardens acting in response to official directives, such as the return to Henrician services, made mandatory after 20 December 1553, and the publication of royal injunctions on 4 March 1554.[89] The heavy expenses borne by the parish were only a little alleviated by the sale of Edwardian church goods.

Edwardian parish churches, of course, contained relatively few items which might be sold. It is notable that very few parishes made any effort to sell such goods. In this respect St Martin's parish was highly unusual. Between March and May 1554, the parish sold a copy of the bible and a copy of Erasmus's *Paraphrases*. The latter was purchased by one of the parish's Edwardian churchwardens, Christopher Nedeham, who had purchased land formerly belonging to one of the fraternities of St Margaret's and as warden of St Martin's had supervised the destruction of the rood loft and the erection of communion pews.[90] It is possible, therefore, that this purchase is the Protestant equivalent of the process already observed at St Margaret's, whereby religious enthusiasts bought the church goods which they valued, for safe keeping.

Efforts to restore the church to its pre-Reformation state proceeded gradually and as money allowed. In 1555 parishioners were assessed to meet the cost of rebuilding the rood loft. In 1556, St Martin's paid £3 for 'the Carvinge off the Roode with the Mary and John', while it later obtained a statue of St Martin, complying with the order requiring parish churches to display images of their patron saint. Hutton's study found that few Marian parishes bought saints' images other than those required by law. But unusually, St Martin's parish owned a picture of St Gregory (donated by a parishioner) as well as purchasing one of Christ. Sometimes, however, the efforts to restore the church appear to have been rather makeshift. During Elizabeth's reign the wardens mention 'a grave stone wch wee founde standinge and Combringe the Rome of the Church wch had served for the hie Alter beinge Krackte'.[91]

The revival of the traditional celebration of church holy days began with Easter 1554. The elaborateness with which such holidays were celebrated at St Martin's increased markedly in 1557. In part this reflects the financial situation of the parish.

---

88 Doubtless the pressure to conform was felt intensely at a church so close to Whitehall. But the same basic findings hold true for the sample parishes located in various parts of England studied by Hutton: Hutton, 'Local impact', pp. 129–30.

89 Kitto, pp. 146–9; Machyn, *Diary*, p. 50; Cardwell, *Documentary Annals*, I, 120.

90 *London VCH*, p. 299; Kitto, p. 151; *CPR* Ed. VI, vol. 2, p. 59.

91 Kitto, pp. 158, 162–3, 164, 173, 181.

It may be significant that the holidays upon which the parish spent the most money, apart from Easter, were Rogation (rather than Corpus Christi) and those days associated with the patronal saint. All of these holidays in some way focused attention upon the corporate identity of the parish, and were those least likely to carry divisive confessional overtones. We have already seen how important the Rogation ceremony was for St Martin's parishioners in particular, also fulfilling the secular purpose of beating the bounds of the parish. It may have appeared preferable to certain parishioners to emphasize this holiday rather than one, such as Corpus Christi, which involved carrying the 'popish' sacrament in procession.[92] At St Martin's the former popularity of Rogation was probably boosted when (as we have seen) Queen Mary herself participated in Rogation processions in those parishes close to Whitehall in 1554.

Other purely secular festivities, such as May games, seem to have enjoyed a popular revival in the Marian parish of St Martin's. In May 1555, Machyn noted that there was 'a goodly May-gam at sant Martens in the feld, with gyant and hobehorsses, with drumes and gonnes and mores [morris] danse and with othur mynsterelles'. A few days later a still more elaborate set of May games – in Machyn's view 'a goodly May-gam . . . as has ben syns' – was held in St Margaret's parish with giants, guns, drums, devils, three morris-dances, bagpipes and viols, minstrels, many people in disguise, 'and the lord and the lade of the May rod gorgeously'.[93]

These accounts of large communal rituals involving massed ranks of parishioners present a picture of outward unity. Beneath this surface, however, degrees of enthusiasm for the more directly religious aspects of the Marian revival clearly varied. There is some evidence to suggest a degree of opposition. It is notable that the last pair of Edwardian churchwardens – Christopher Nedeham and William More – were replaced three months before their term of office would customarily have ended. Significantly, their replacements took up their office from 25 December 1553, just days after the issuing of a proclamation that stipulated the return to late Henrician forms of worship. It was only at this point that the parish abandoned communion in both kinds. The Edwardian vicar, Robert Beste, may well have provided an initial focus for resistance, as his provocative stance in continuing with English services suggests.[94] This focus was removed, however, with Beste's ejection in 1554. He was replaced by Thomas Welles, whose firm Catholic sympathies are indicated by the fact

---

92 *Ibid.*, pp. 154, 156, 165. In 1557 the accounts record payments to 'the players vppon Ester Daye in the morenenge [*sic*]', echoes of the pre-Reformation plays held on Palm Sunday at St Martin's.

93 Machyn, *Diary*, p. 89. Machyn describes on the same day an elaborate procession of St Clement Danes' parishioners. On the revival of May games, and the somewhat equivocal government attitude towards them see R. Hutton, *The Rise and Fall of Merry England*, (Oxford, 1994), pp. 101–2.

94 Kitto, pp. 141, 151; Hughes and Larkin, *Tudor Royal Proclamations*, II, 5–8, 35–80. Churchwardens had in the past served for two-year terms beginning on Lady Day. After the early removal of the Edwardian wardens, the new churchwardens were elected on 25 December every second year (Kitto, p. 167), although the account of the previous wardens was generally rendered in the following March, when the surplus was given to the 'new' churchwardens.

that he was deprived on Elizabeth's accession – a fate suffered by only five London clergymen between 1558 and 1564.[95]

Welles was clearly not without his own supporters. A study of the gifts presented to the Marian parish of St Martin's suggests not mere reluctant compliance with the new regime on the part of parishioners but the existence of genuine enthusiasts for the reforms. Indeed, many more gifts were presented to St Martin's church than to St Margaret's during Mary's reign, although this may simply reflect the greater needs of the parish. A 'fayre streamer' for processions, for example, was a gift from 'the Bachelers of the parryshe'. Queen Mary herself presented silk altar hangings and a small organ to St Martin's, perhaps recognizing the needs of this church so close to Whitehall (or perhaps recognizing its recalcitrant character). Most notable among those presenting gifts to the parish were men who sat in parliament for Westminster in the 1540s and 1550s – John Reade (1547), John Russell (1545) and John Beste (1558). Reade gave the parish 'A coorse Alter clothe, and a bannar off tawney taffata', Russell donated a corporas and corporas cloth, while Beste presented the parish with 'ii graylls [graduals], one Antiphone, a precessyone' & a manuell in p'tchment'.[96]

Doubtless such gifts were in keeping with the social standing of members of parliament and their position within parish government, but no such gifts are recorded during Edward's reign. In the case of John Beste, possible Catholic views are also suggested by his family's later connection with St Martin's Marian vicar, Thomas Welles. When he made his will in 1565, Welles was living in the house of Beste's widow, 'my welbeloved in Christ', to whom he left one half of his goods. It is worth noting that another Westminster member of parliament, Robert Smallwood of St Margaret's, also held clear Catholic sympathies.[97]

There were other parishioners at St Martin's whose religious opinions were even more clearly Catholic. Among these was Arthur Stourton, the Marian Keeper of Whitehall Palace, whom the parish accounts describe as one of the 'masters of the parish'. When he was buried at St Martin's in 1556, Henry Machyn, describing his funeral, noted that he was

> a reyseyver of all copes of clothe of golde that was takyn out of all chyrches, and he dyd delevered [*sic*] them unto serten parryches agayne to them that cowld know them, the whych wher taken away by Kyng Edward the VIth . . . and now when that good qwyne Mare cam to the crown, she lett evere parryche for to have them agayne . . . if they were note gyffen to odur places in the reyme of England.[98]

95 Kitto, p. 219, n.2; *London VCH*, p. 308.

96 Kitto, p. 158. Bindoff, *House of Commons*, I, 143–4. Others donating church goods to St Martin's include Nicholas Lizard, the King's Serjeant Painter; the widow of the baker Thurston Mayre; William Hale, gentleman and churchwarden 1525–30; and Robert Perry, 'Clarke off the checke of the garde'.

97 TNA, PCC, Prob. 11/48/6. Smallwood was MP in 1545 and 1553 (October).

98 Kitto, p. 157; Machyn, *Diary*, p. 165. Bindoff (*House of Commons*, s.n. Arthur Stourton) passes over these comments in Machyn, although citing the diary entry. For further discussions of religious practice in the Westminster parishes during the early years of Elizabeth see below, ch. 9.

Men such as Stourton, and possibly the parliamentary representatives for Westminster, may have provided a focus for such Catholic feeling as existed within
St Martin's. At the very least, their presence explains the conformity found in a parish
that also contained strong Protestants. Ultimately, the Reformation records for
St Martin's depict a parish highly conscious of the twists and turns of religious policy,
but also one which attempted to retain at least the façade of parochial unity, even if
different factions might gain control of local institutions. In the Edwardian period,
churchwardens sought to protect themselves by insisting on recording in the formal
accounts that controversial acts were carried out 'withe the assente and consent of the
hole parrysh or the moost of the same parryshnors'.[99] In other cases, such as receipts
for lights and obits, the record falls silent altogether. The ambiguity of the records and
the emphasis on consensus suggest an attempt to make sure that this period of religious upheaval did not produce groups of 'winners' and 'losers' among the parish
governors.[100] It is particularly noteworthy in this regard that when a potentially divisive audit of all St Martin's churchwardens' accounts for the previous fifty years was
conducted in May 1554 by the violently anti-Protestant Dean of Westminster, Hugh
Weston, it did not turn into a witch-hunt of parishioners with Protestant credentials. Parish officials insisted that even this audit had been carried out 'by a comen
and agreable assent of the parishe of thys churche'.[101] For all that those of Protestant
sympathies retired from their prominent role in parochial administration, the
parish conspicuously did not divide along religious lines, which certainly attests to
the social cohesion of parish elites, as well as (perhaps) to feelings of uncertainty
about the future.[102]

Nevertheless, it seems clear that both St Margaret's and St Martin's conformed to
Catholic practice during Mary's reign, albeit with different degrees of enthusiasm.
Both parishes also contained Catholic enthusiasts who actively and voluntarily
promoted their religion. Such enthusiasm was cut short by the death of Mary in
November 1558.

The accession of Elizabeth heralded yet another change in the religious fortunes of Westminster. Elizabeth's coronation took place in an Abbey that was still officially a monastic

---

99 Kitto, p. 137.

100 E.g. *ibid.*, p. 134.

101 *Ibid.*, p. 150. Those giving signed consent to the audit included two of the 'certen men' who had
provided the money for the Edwardian communion pews, Robert Perye and John Evans (Kitto,
p. 144). As a result of the audit, four previous Edwardian churchwardens were fined by the
Commissioners for 'imperfections' in their accounts, but not the last two, whose term of office had
been foreshortened (Browne and Nedeham), while two Henrician churchwardens (Hale and Worley)
were also fined similar amounts, although their gifts to the Marian church imply more conservative
sympathies (pp. 153, 157).

102 For recent work which has also emphasized the degree of social cohesion among local communities
in the face of the threat of confessional polarization see, for example, N. Jones, *The English Reformation: Religion and Cultural Adaptation* (Oxford, 2002).

foundation.[103] Nevertheless, the impending revolution was made clear at the state opening of Elizabeth's first parliament, when the former Edwardian dean of Westminster, Richard Cox, newly returned from exile, made an extraordinary attack on the institution of monasticism at a service in the Abbey itself and in the presence of the abbot and monks.[104] The dissolution of the recently revived Abbey followed soon afterwards around July 1559 – a dramatic and unequivocal destruction of the central focus of the Marian reformation in Westminster.[105] The reversion of the Abbey to the status of a collegiate church in May 1560 did, however, free it from the jurisdiction of the bishop of London, and the parish of St Margaret's was also placed under the sole jurisdiction of the ex-Abbey, exercised by one of the prebendaries acting as archdeacon of Westminster (although the other parishes of St Martin's and St Clement's remained under the control of the bishop of London).[106]

The new regime meant a new reformation of parish religion, and the outward response of each of the Westminster parishes to this new Elizabethan 'reformation' was very much in character with their previous conduct. A survey of 127 Elizabethan parishes has concluded that the implementation of the Elizabethan Reformation was slower and less effective than its Edwardian counterpart, although the process was more speedy in London, with some London parishes dismaying officials with their swift conversion to Protestant practice and unauthorized iconoclasm.[107] Not surprisingly, perhaps, St Martin's – with its Edwardian vicar restored – followed the pattern of rapid compliance found in the capital. As early as August 1560, the parish bought two psalm books 'in meter by note', while it also acquired the appropriate service books and displayed the Ten Commandments in the church.[108] The parish also reintroduced seats for communicants, although this practice was never especially widespread in Elizabethan London.[109] Moreover, the parish did anticipate official policy on at least one occasion. In March 1561, the parish paid a scrivener for writing a 'testimoniall for pulling downe of the Rood lofte'. Although no Elizabethan regulation

---

103 On the coronation see C.G. Bayne, 'The coronation of Queen Elizabeth', *English Historical Review* 22 (1907); *CSPVen 1558–60*, pp. 16–17.

104 *CSPVen 1558–60*, p. 23. Bishop Bonner took sanctuary in the Abbey after Elizabeth's accession (Feckenham having formerly served as his chaplain). Feckenham was reportedly offered the Abbey and the retention of the monks if they would administer sacraments in the new fashion and take the oath of supremacy. He and the monks declined: *ibid.*, p. 95. On Feckenham's later career see Tudor, 'John Feckenham', pp. 312–22.

105 Knighton ('Collegiate foundations', p. 166) notes that it is hard to pinpoint the exact date of the dissolution.

106 This ecclesiastical jurisdiction exercised by the collegiate church over St Margaret's presumably harkens back to its status as vill under the abbots of Westminster. For the dissolution of the Abbey and the establishment of the new collegiate church see 1 Eliz. I c. 24; *CPR 1558–60*, pp. 397–403.

107 Hutton, 'Local impact', pp. 134–7; P. Collinson, *Archbishop Grindal, 1519–1583* (1979), pp. 101–2. Cf. R.M. Fisher, 'The Reformation of church and chapel at the Inns of Court, 1530–1580', *Guildhall Studies* 3, 4 (April 1979), pp. 223–47.

108 Kitto, pp. 185, 190–1.

109 *Ibid.*, p. 186; *London VCH*, p. 319.

initially mentioned rood lofts, they had been dismantled in some London parishes as a result of both popular and officially inspired iconoclasm. The government, however, was fearful of unregulated iconoclasm and the diversity of practice among parishes. In response to these concerns, the Ecclesiastical Commission issued orders in October 1561 limiting the size of all rood lofts. While St Martin's may not have acted as early as some London parishes, it did act well before this government order.[110] There were undoubtedly those who quietly dissented from such action: as we have seen, the parish's deprived Marian vicar seems to have remained in the parish, taking refuge with the family of former parishioners who seem to have shared his religious views.

St Margaret's parish also appears to have followed London's pattern of swift compliance, as noted by Hutton. Looking beyond this checklist, however, it is clear that the parish required considerable official pressure to banish all vestiges of Catholicism and that officials recognized that in some areas the parish was dragging its feet. There seems to have been a significant and direct intervention in parish affairs by the Protestant authorities in May 1562. At that time, the accounts for 1561–62 were uniquely 'allowed' and signed by the archdeacon of Westminster, William Latimer, a royal chaplain, biographer of Anne Boleyn, and noted Protestant. The accounts signed by Latimer were followed by an inventory of church goods. In contrast to a similar inventory produced in 1560, this one is purged of the superstitious church goods which had previously been listed.[111] But this was not all. Three months after the accounts were signed by Latimer, the new churchwardens elected by the parish were forced to renounce their offices, and were replaced instead by two wardens chosen by the new dean of Westminster. The fact that the churchwardens' accounts make no reference to this extraordinary occurrence underlines the dangers of underestimating the degree of opposition in St Margaret's and other parishes by looking only at the terse records of apparent acquiescence that parochial sources provide.[112]

---

110 Hutton, 'Local impact', pp. 135–6; Kitto, pp. 191, 193. Hutton notes that most rood lofts in southern and midland English parishes were cut down by the end of 1561. The process was slower elsewhere in the country.

111 WAC, E4 (1561–62); *Alumni Cantabrig.*, s.n. William Latymer; *Acts*, no. 190; 'William Latymer's Cronickille of Anne Bulleyne', ed. M. Dowling, *Camden Miscellany* 30 (Camden Society 4th ser., 1990), pp. 27–30. From June 1560 the jurisdictions of Westminster (St Margaret's parish) and St Martin le Grand were united under an archdeacon of Westminster, who was one of the prebendaries. Wills were proved under this new jurisdiction from 25 June 1560, *Acts*, pp. xxxvi–xxxvii.

112 The churchwardens' accounts seem to record an orderly transition from one pair of churchwardens (John Skynner and John Hunter, who served from 25 May 1560 to 9 May 1562) to the next (William Stanton and William Worley, who served from 10 May 1562 to 18 May 1564). But a notarial document among Westminster Abbey muniments records that two different wardens had in fact been elected – John Savage and William More – and that Stanton (Staunton) and Worley were appointed by the dean after the others had been required to renounce their new offices: WAM 38126. Staunton was an Exchequer official who served as MP for Westminster in 1572 (Hasler, *House of Commons*, William Staunton) and was one of those appointed to the Court of Burgesses when it was established in 1585: see below, ch. 7.

CONCLUSION

The mid-Tudor years had brought dramatic change to Westminster, involving substantial jurisdictional upheavals and the removal and subsequent revival of many central institutions and rituals of parish life. The presence of Whitehall Palace within its boundaries sometimes meant that Westminster was in the eye of the storm of successive Tudor reformations. But the Westminster parishes were not merely the passive recipients of government coercion. The experience of parishioners varied substantially, according to a number of factors.

First of all, the importance of parish notables and local clergy in implementing religious policy should be emphasized. The presence of an evangelical vicar such as Beste seems to have been a major influence in St Martin's, while the churchwardens elected by the parishes might occasionally play a significant role in promoting or hindering religious reforms. The interference in the terms of office of the last Edwardian churchwardens in St Martin in the Fields, and of the churchwardens elected in St Margaret's in 1562, are clear indications that some churchwardens, at least, were recognized as holding religious convictions that might interfere with their implementation of government religious policy (or at least of being susceptible to influence from those opposed to religious changes). This is not to suggest that all churchwardens necessarily held strong views over the reforms that they were required to implement. The status of the wardenship as an important local office (held on several occasions by future MPs) is enough to explain the presence of some more conservative figures among the Edwardian churchwardens, although in the case of St Margaret's it seems most likely that figures such as Ludford were chosen for their conservative sympathies.[113] Local notables and clergy undoubtedly played an important role, then, in providing a focus for those of differing religious views.

Another potentially crucial influence may lie in the social and institutional differences between the two parishes that are explored in other chapters of this study. The different social and administrative make-up of different parishes, the continuity and traditions of local parochial institutions, the cohesiveness of local elites, the room for local initiative, could all have an important role to play in explaining some of the contrasts in their responses to the Reformation. Perhaps St Margaret's, with its long-established parochial structures and administration, its lavishly furnished church, its prominent families that had been resident there for generations, and its long tradition of self-regulating fraternities, would always have been more hostile to large-scale changes in parochial religious practice, and more unified in its opposition to the dispersal of its parochial possessions. The less established parish of St Martin's, however, with its

---

113 If, as seems possible, John Beste shared the conservative religious views of his wife (see above), then his election as one of the Edwardian churchwardens at St Martin's (for 1550–52) might conceivably represent an attempt to create a balance between reforming and conservative religious forces in the parish, or even an attempt by Beste himself to limit the damage being done by the Edwardian Reformation.

weaker institutional structures and traditions, its ad hoc administration, its sparsely furnished church, its many new residents and its relative lack of traditional communal institutions, may have been better equipped to respond flexibly to religious changes. The same forces would account for St Martin's less unified response to religious change, with much more evidence of religious controversy and possibly of two factions, Protestant and Catholic, each of which implemented its policies enthusiastically when it was in a position to do so.

By Elizabeth's reign, the parishioners of Westminster had endured a bewildering series of changes in the structures of religious life. They emerged from this experience in different and distinctive ways. St Margaret's conservative instincts still appeared prominent, perhaps inspired by the revival of the Abbey and intensified by the communal trauma of the Easter-day stabbing of a priest and the subsequent burning of the miscreant in the churchyard. At St Martin's, an apparently consistent enthusiasm for each change in governmental policy seems to represent the swings in parochial power from Protestant to Catholic lay enthusiasts, and back again. In their different responses to the Reformation, we can already perceive the seeds of the distinctive paths of religious development on which the two parishes were to embark in subsequent years.[114]

114 See below, ch. 9, for later religious developments.

Chapter 3

———◆———

Town, cloister and Crown

THE upheavals of the 1530s and successive Tudor reformations brought disruption to most aspects of local society in Westminster. Lines of authority within the area, and indeed its whole collective identity, were thrown into disarray. The dissolution of Westminster's abbey gave rise to special problems, given the earlier prominence of the abbot in the medieval government of the town. Would the new dean and chapter retain the authority that the Abbey had previously exercised here? Or rather, would the Crown's heavy-handed intervention in the locality mark the end of medieval patterns of government and the creation of its own jurisdiction in the area surrounding the royal Court? Alternatively, would a new city emerge and take strength from the very suppression of the monastery, with an invigorated corporate, civic identity?

As this chapter will reveal, the answer to these questions is not a simple one. Relations between Abbey, Crown and townspeople were certainly redefined during the century following the Reformation. The relationship was not a static one, however, but one of interdependence and periodic tension – a situation that continued even with the relative stability introduced by Elizabeth's succession to the throne. Deans of Westminster remained surprisingly important in the locality, but overall the balance of power in Westminster shifted in favour of the Crown. As we shall see, new avenues of influence became available to the monarch in Westminster, even if the Crown did not always seek to wield it. In particular, a 'courtly' element was added to town government with the creation of the new post of high steward, a position that was generally held by the monarch's chief minister or favourite. At the same time, the expansion of the metropolis brought social and economic problems which in themselves drew attention to unresolved issues of local authority. The Reformation and its aftermath had also left Westminster's townsmen with little formal role in government. For this reason, as we shall see in the final section of this chapter, certain groups of townsmen pursued the goal of independent corporate status for the town, a goal that was never abandoned during our period, with concerted attempts at incorporation in 1585, 1607 and again in the 1630s.

POWER RELATIONS IN WESTMINSTER 1540–1612

The substantial changes in Westminster's town government after the Reformation need to be seen in the context of its earlier history. If there is one continuity between medieval and early modern Westminster, it is the structural anomaly of its urban government – an anomaly that was ultimately linked to the presence of a powerful religious institution in its midst. Medieval Westminster undoubtedly owed its original existence as an urban centre to the presence of the Abbey, but, as the royal Court became increasingly focused on the town, Westminster's local government began to seem increasingly anachronistic. Although effectively a city in an economic and social sense, the medieval town was not incorporated by charter. Instead the Abbey presided over a manorial system of government more usually associated with agrarian communities. This should not imply, however, that all was simply under the thumb of the abbot. As we have seen, Westminster – and especially St Margaret's – did have its own traditions of informal self-government, which operated at the parish level. In addition, by the early sixteenth century – and possibly earlier – the lay officers of the abbot's court had become a self-electing body, whose members usually held office in the town's religious fraternities.[1] It was through the more informal activities of these fraternities that townsmen responded to the social and economic problems of the later Middle Ages.

Changes ushered in by the Reformation, however, struck at the roots of urban government in the town. This was particularly so since, at the level of both town and parish, local authority in Westminster was tied to religious institutions – the monastery of St Peter's and the powerful lay fraternities of St Margaret's. Successive Tudor 'reformations' saw Westminster Abbey dissolved under Henry VIII and reconstituted as a collegiate church only to be refounded as an abbey under Mary and re-established yet again as a collegiate church by Elizabeth.[2] Such large-scale changes also found their parallel on the parish level. St Margaret's parish fraternities had provided an ad hoc form of local government but now these too were abolished with the nationwide dissolution of fraternities and chantries in 1547.

The 1540s and 1550s, then, were a crucial period in the history of Westminster's government. Unfortunately, surviving materials seldom provide us with a clear picture of what was happening. Indeed there is considerable evidence to suggest that this confusion may have been shared by contemporaries. In particular, many of the changes affecting Westminster Abbey led to uncertainty over matters of jurisdiction, especially when secular and ecclesiastical authority overlapped. For example, it is unclear what happened to the abbot's June court at the dissolution, but it seems to have continued

1 Rosser, pp. 234–5. See also above, ch. 1.

2 The daily running of the collegiate church and its internal administrative history are discussed in C.S. Knighton, 'Collegiate foundations, 1540 to 1570, with special reference to St Peter in Westminster' (Cambridge Ph.D., 1975).

under the auspices of the new dean and chapter.[3] The erection of the short-lived see of Westminster, created by Henry VIII in 1540 but dissolved by Edward VI in 1550, added further jurisdictional, as well as terminological, confusion.[4] For example, the use of the term 'city' to denote St Margaret Westminster (the ancient vill) apparently dates from this foundation,[5] but continued in use long after the bishopric was abolished and even though Westminster was never incorporated.[6] The very rapidity of change, with authority shifting between Crown and Abbey (or collegiate church), sometimes led to minor clashes over jurisdiction. In 1555, for example, Queen Mary appointed her trusted comptroller of the household, Sir Robert Rochester, as (under) steward, bailiff, escheator and coroner of Westminster and its liberties. She did so by authority of the 1540 Act (32 Hen. VIII c.20) which bestowed former monastic franchises on the Crown. The following year, however, the monastery was refounded and Abbot Feckenham reasserted the Abbey's right of appointment by granting the reversion of the office of steward to one John Throckmorton. On Rochester's death in 1557, the stewardship accordingly passed to Throckmorton, who held it until his death in 1580.[7] Changes in the body authorized to grant the office of bailiff of Westminster generated even greater confusion.[8]

Although the 1540s and 1550s witnessed the overturning of so many elements of ecclesiastical and local government, the period also saw two more long-lasting innovations: the creation of the office of high steward, and the granting to Westminster of the right to return members to parliament.

---

3   See below, ch. 7, for further discussion of the process by which the abbot's court was transformed into the Court of Burgesses.

4   See above, ch. 1.

5   *L&P*, xvi g. 379 (30); W. Maitland, *The History and Survey of London from its Foundations to the Present Time* (2nd ed., 2 vols., 1756), II, 1329; WAM 6559, f. 1.

6   E.g. W. Bidwell and M. Jansson (eds.), *Proceedings in Parliament 1626* (4 vols., New Haven, 1991–96) I, 488. See also below, ch. 4. Contemporaries seem to have distinguished between the 'city' of Westminster (St Margaret's) and its 'liberties' (the other parts of Westminster, which included St Martin in the Fields, the combined St Clement Danes and St Mary le Strand): e.g. Surrey History Centre, LM/1989; *The Petition of the Citie of Westminster* (1643).

7   Bindoff, *House of Commons*, I, 144; III, 455–6. Rochester's brother was a martyred Carthusian: D. Knowles, *The Religious Orders in England* (Cambridge, 1974), III, 424. Throckmorton was succeeded by Sir Thomas Cecil, who was appointed for life: *Acts*, no. 335.

8   The office of bailiff of Westminster took on a new character during the mid-Tudor period. Originally, the offices of bailiff and seneschal (or 'steward') were the two main representatives of the abbot's authority and appointed by him: Rosser, p. 231. Although bailiffs were less distinguished men than high stewards, it was a responsible position within the locality. In particular, it was the bailiff who served as returning officer at parliamentary elections. Appointments to this office were made either by the Crown or by the abbot and subsequently the dean and chapter. In practice, however, the bailiff seems to have acted as an agent of the high steward, keeping him informed of affairs within the city and its liberties (WAM, 'The Offices of High Bailiff and Searcher of the Sanctuary' (typescript by L.E. [Tanner] in Deanery files); *HMC Hatfield*, XV, 189–90). During the early years of Elizabeth, controversy broke out over who held the legal right to this office.

The creation of the office of high steward was a significant innovation in the post-Reformation town. Its real importance lay in the extension of royal authority that the office introduced into this important area surrounding the Court – an area where the abbot had formerly stood as the chief local notable. The first high steward for Westminster seems to have been Sir Anthony Denny, a trusted member of Henry VIII's Privy Chamber and strong Protestant, who was probably appointed by either the bishop of Westminster or the Crown in 1545.[9] Denny retained this position until his death in September 1549, but no successor seems to have held this office until 1561, despite the fact that the Seymours exerted an important unofficial influence in the area in the Edwardian period.[10] From 1561 onwards, however, Westminster's high stewards were consistently men who were either chief ministers of the Crown or royal favourites. Particularly notable is the fifty-year period when William Cecil, Lord Burghley, and then his son Robert Cecil, earl of Salisbury, held the high stewardship in succession.

Officially, the high steward was appointed by the Westminster dean and chapter, which formally issued letters patent.[11] In practice, however, it is difficult to determine how much choice deans actually possessed in the selection of high stewards. It is true that the dean and chapter liked to emphasize in formal records that the high steward was merely their appointee, referring in lofty tones to 'the Deane and Chapter and their Steward' or 'the dean or his Steward'.[12] Nevertheless, the dean and chapter may well have felt obliged simply to accept the Crown's recommendation when making appointments (after all, the position of dean was itself a Crown appointment).[13] On at least one occasion, matters became rather more complex. In 1628, when Dean John Williams attempted to appoint the earl of Holland to the vacant high steward-ship without reference to the King, he encountered the full weight of royal displeasure. Williams was briskly instructed that King Charles 'expected his pleasure' in the appointment, and a few days later the dean and chapter laconically noted receipt of a

9 There is some ambiguity about the appointing authority. The chapter minute reads: 'It is agreed by the dean and chapter that Mr Denye shall have the stuardshippe of all the liberties of Westminster within [replaces 'with/within the citie and nere about there adjoyning unto'] the countie of Middelsex' (*Acts*, no. 32). Bindoff, *House of Commons*, I, 144 notes that Denny received a fee from the bishopric in 1548–49.

10 For the Seymours see *Acts*, nos. 63, 64, 72, 76, 78, 79; for Denny see Brigden, pp. 384–5; D. Starkey, *The Reign of Henry VIII* (1985), pp. 133–6.

11 J.F. Merritt, ' "Under the Shadowe of the Church"? The Abbey and the town of Westminster 1530–1640' in C.S. Knighton and R. Mortimer (eds.), *Westminster Abbey Reformed 1540–1640* (Aldershot, 2003), p. 155 n. 7.

12 E.g. WAM 9886; WAM 6561, p. 7.

13 Manchée, p. 6. Influence potentially worked in more than one direction, whatever the formal tech-nicalities of an appointment, and certainly contemporaries thought that high stewards might influ-ence the choice of deans (e.g. Bodl., MS Ashmole 1729, ff. 173–174v; John Hacket, *Scrinia Reserata* (1693), pt 1, 44). Even if the power of nomination was not intrinsic to the office of high steward, the high steward was often a sufficiently influential political figure in his own right to play a role in the appointment. See generally Merritt, 'Under the Shadowe', p. 155 n. 9.

royal letter, informing them of the king's desire to confer the office of high steward upon his own preferred candidate. Not surprisingly, the dean and chapter now concurred with this choice.[14] Equally, deans and chapters were also susceptible to pressure from high stewards. When Robert Cecil received his patent for the office of high steward in 1598, he had no qualms in returning it to the Abbey with the instruction that the dean and chapter should remove a clause requiring their approbation of his choice of deputies, a matter in which they promptly acquiesced.[15]

The experience of Westminster differs from other towns where the post of high steward was created in this period. In most towns, the initiative for choosing high stewards – and for including the office in corporate charters – seems to have come from the town itself. This was not the case in Westminster, where there was no town council or central executive. The origins of the office remain unclear, whatever the role of the dean and chapter in later appointments. In practice, however, the high stewardship tended to act as a conduit for royal patronage, even if this new official might also act as a mediator between townspeople and the Crown.[16]

High stewards in Westminster seem to have exersized most influence from c.1561 to 1612, when William Cecil and Robert Cecil held the position in succession. As leading royal ministers the influence they wielded in Elizabethan and early Jacobean Westminster was, as we shall see, pervasive and often decisive. Indeed, William Cecil even referred to 'we to whom the governance of the sayde Citie [of Westminster] under her Maiestie doth belong' by virtue of his office as high steward.[17] The Cecils' influence was also partly linked to the way in which it operated on a number of different social and political levels. On the parish level, for example, many prominent members of St Martin's parish and vestry had reason to consider the Cecil family as their patrons.[18] Unlike so many high stewards elsewhere in England, both father and son were also normally resident in the locality and maintained impressive residences there. Burghley House fronted the Strand in the parish of St Clement Danes, while Robert Cecil, who was actually born in Westminster, developed a substantial urban estate in

14 TNA, SP16/116/10, fol. 15 (cf. SP16/117/2, f. 2; 16/117/22, f. 24); WAM Chapter Act Bk II, f. 44 (19 September 1628). Williams's acerbic correspondence with the King via Viscount Conway focused on the relative powers of the dean and of the chapter, but it was Williams's deteriorating relationship with the King which was the real issue. The King's choice for high steward was the lord chamberlain, Philip Herbert, later earl of Pembroke and Montgomery.

15 *Acts*, nos. 498, 500. In 1612, Chamberlain reported that the 'baliwick' of Westminster was reputed to be worth £500 a year: *The Letters of John Chamberlain*, ed. N.E. McClure (2 vols., Philadelphia, 1939), I, 352.

16 On the office of the high stewardship and its history see V. Hodges, 'The electoral influence of the aristocracy 1604–1641' (Columbia University Ph.D., 1977), pp. 202–13; C.F. Patterson, *Urban Patronage in Early Modern England* (Stanford, 1999), pp. 30–40, 243–54. In Westminster, as elsewhere, the terms 'steward' and 'high steward' do not seem to have been used consistently in contemporary documents, and the two offices may not always have been filled simultaneously.

17 *Wyllyam Cecill knight, high steward of the citie of Westminster ... To the Baylyffe* (1564).

18 See below, ch. 4.

the parish of St Martin's, where he erected Salisbury House. Robert Cecil's claim of his special attachment to the area 'having been bred and born within these poor liberties of Westminster', is likely to have been as much a recognition of its usefulness as a power base as an avowal of a sentimental allegiance.[19]

The dominance of Cecil influence was also reflected in the second long-term change to Westminster government to emerge from the mid-Tudor period: the acquisition of two new parliamentary seats. From at least 1545 (and possibly from 1542) Westminster returned members to parliament. Although the instrument granting Westminster the right to return members has not survived, it seems to be connected to the creation of a see of Westminster in 1540.[20] Thereafter these parliamentary seats became an important avenue of patronage from both within and outside the locality. Under Elizabeth the Crown was less actively involved in the government of the town, and the choice of parliamentary representatives became just one more area in which Cecil influence could make itself felt. Elsewhere in the country, other high stewards nominated at least one of a town's MPs, especially in those cases where the high steward had helped the town to gain a parliamentary seat in the first place.[21] This had not been the case in Westminster, although it was asserted by Dean Williams in 1628 that the high steward of Westminster customarily chose one of the two MPs.[22]

It is certainly true that the Cecils were able to wield substantial electoral patronage. To begin with, members of the Cecil family themselves sat for the area. The young Robert Cecil gained his first parliamentary experience representing Westminster in 1584 and 1586. Lord Burghley's grandson, Richard Cecil, sat for Westminster in 1593, while William Cooke (later Sir William) was a cousin of Robert Cecil's and was returned for Westminster in 1601.[23] Other Westminster MPs in the Elizabethan period were officials in the Exchequer and the Court of Wards, the government departments most closely linked to Lord Burghley.[24] Even if such men were promoted by the Cecil interest, however, they were also prominent local residents who continued

---

19 J. Disprose, *Some Account of the Parish of St Clement Danes* (2 vols., 1868), 1, 146 (on Burghley House); *HMC Salisbury*, XX, 213.

20 Bindoff, *House of Commons*, I, 144. The bishop of Westminster first took his seat in the House of Lords in 1542.

21 J.E. Neale, *The Elizabethan House of Commons* (1949), pp. 210, 234–7.

22 BL, MS Cotton Julius C, III, f. 402r–v.

23 Hasler, *House of Commons*, s.n. Robert Cecil, William Cooke II; *Acts*, no. 498. It should be stressed that Cooke's immediate family could claim strong ties with the Westminster area. Sir William Cooke was the son of William Cooke I, an Elizabethan St Martin's vestryman: Merritt thesis, pp. 330–1.

24 Richard Hodges (1559), William Staunton (1571), John Dodington and John Osborne (1572) and Peter Osborne (1588–89) were all Exchequer officials, although only Peter Osborne, the lord treasurer's remembrancer, held a position of any great importance. Similarly, both Robert Nowell (1563) and Thomas Wilbraham (1572) were both attorneys in the Court of Wards when elected for Westminster.

to live in the area even after serving in parliament.[25] The Elizabethan period also saw a shift in the types of men who served as MPs, which appears partly linked to Cecil electoral patronage. Until the 1560s, when the family gained a dominant position in the area, more than half of Westminster's members of parliament had been local men involved in day-to-day parochial affairs as churchwardens or masters of parish fraternities, even if they also possessed other administrative experience that made them suitable to stand for parliament. After 1559, only two members, William Staunton (1571) and John Dodington (1572), served in the comparatively humble office of churchwarden.[26]

In the Elizabethan period, then, power in Westminster was largely concentrated in the hands of the Crown and the Cecil family. It can be difficult to disentangle Crown influence from Cecil family influence, given the key position of the family at the heart of government, and it may well be that contemporaries did not always make this distinction. What is clear is that the Crown generally did not intervene actively in the government either of the town or of the former Abbey, and that royal involvement in the locality had the effect of paving the way for the Cecil ascendancy.

But where did the dean of Westminster fit into this equation? While Cecil patronage was influential in Westminster from at least 1561 onwards, it is important to recognize that the dean of Westminster remained a key figure in the locality, retaining many of the powers which the abbots had formerly enjoyed. The dean and the Cecils were certainly not involved in any sort of power struggle. On the contrary, Gabriel Goodman, who served as dean of Westminster for forty years (1561–1601), was a friend and former chaplain of Lord Burghley.[27] Goodman seems very much to have been Burghley's man, and in the locality the particular interests of each figure appear to have harmonized quite naturally.[28] Moreover, their spheres of influence tended to be complementary rather than conflicting. The influence of the Cecils was most evident in the parishes of St Martin's and St Clement's, whereas the dean and chapter's sway remained particularly strong in the parish of St Margaret's, the old 'vill' of Westminster.[29]

---

25 This discussion is based on Bindoff and Hasler and the identification of these men in parish records, especially parish rate books. Both Peter Osborne and his son John were related to the Cecils through their Cooke relations. The only man who does not fit easily into this pattern is the courtier Sir Thomas Knyvett of Escrick, Yorkshire, and in his case the Cecil influence must still account for his first election in 1584. On Knyvett see Merritt, 'Under the Shadowe', p. 157 n.16.

26 For Westminster's MPs during the 1540s and 1550s see above, ch. 2.

27 For more on Goodman's religious views and the significance of his lengthy tenure as dean see below, ch. 9, and J.F. Merritt, 'The cradle of Laudianism? Westminster Abbey, 1558–1630', *JEH* 52 (2001), pp. 627–9.

28 Burghley did, however, seem to have expected to play a role in appointments to prebendal stalls in the Abbey: see Merritt, 'Under the Shadowe', pp. 158–9.

29 For the distinction between the manor and the 'vill' of Westminster see Rosser, pp. 14–15, 226–30. For more on the Cecil network at St Martin's see below, ch. 4, and Merritt, 'The Cecils and Westminster 1558–1612; the development of an urban power base' in P. Croft (ed.), *Patronage, Culture and Power. The Early Cecils* (New Haven, 2002), pp. 231–46.

Equally important was the fact that the dean retained major secular powers through-out Westminster by reconstituting the abbot's old manorial court. These were powers that might appear to have been eroded by a 1585 act of parliament, which created a new 'Court of Burgesses', an institution partly erected to oversee law and order in the area. It has been customary for commentators to maintain that the 1585 Act marks the point at which 'arbitrary' clerical rule in Westminster was replaced by the more representative government of the laity.[30] But it seems more appropriate, it will be argued, to portray the Act as establishing what was largely a revamped version of the old abbot's court, even if it did seek to provide a more effective structure for its activities.[31]

In fact, the 1585 Act went out of its way to preserve most of the secular powers and liberties of the 'Abbey'. For example, the traditional right of sanctuary was specifically maintained. The newly formed Court of Burgesses was also presided over by the dean of Westminster and the high steward, or his deputy.[32] But this was not all: the dean and chapter did not exaggerate when they argued some fifty years later that by this Act the Queen and parliament 'were so exceeding Tender of the priviledges of the Church of Westminster, that . . . this Act did rather *adde* some power unto it, then take any thing from it'.[33] For, if anything, the Act actually enabled the dean to regain some of the secular powers that pre-Reformation abbots had lost to the laity. By the early sixteenth century Westminster's chief pledges, who manned the abbot's court, had become a self-electing body, much to the annoyance of the abbots, who had formerly appointed these local men.[34] But the Act now restored the power of the dean (or high steward) to appoint what were now called burgesses. It was even stipulated that the burgesses were not 'to hear examine and determine any Thinge, by vertewe of this Acte' without the consent of the dean or high steward. As a final reassurance to the power of the collegiate church, a final proviso stipulated that nothing contained in the Act should be prejudicial to the dean and chapter or their successors, and that they should enjoy all the privileges, authority and benefits which they and their officers had ever enjoyed before. The dean and chapter must have taken satisfaction from the ultimate shape of the 1585 Act. Indeed, the retrenchment of clerical power in Westminster government was so firm that it was later singled out for specific attention during the parliamentary debate on church reform in 1641. The dean, John Williams, argued against proposed restrictions on clerical involvement in secular government, noting the devastating impact that such a measure would have on Westminster: 'if some Salve or Plaister shall not be applied to Westminster in this point, all that Government and Corporation is at an end'.[35]

---

30 Maitland, *History*, II, 1348.

31 See below, ch. 7.

32 27 Eliz. I c. 31; Manchée, p. 220.

33 WAM 6559, p. 2 (italics mine).

34 Rosser, pp. 234, 363.

35 Hacket, *Scrinia Reserata*, pt ii, 175.

Continuing clerical involvement in Westminster's government would have also been evident in other areas. Deans of Westminster from at least the Elizabethan period normally sat as Middlesex JPs, thereby commanding significant powers of summary justice, which they continued to exercise when a new Westminster sessions authority was established in 1618.[36] Goodman and many of his successors were certainly active Middlesex JPs, and several of the Westminster prebendaries also later served as JPs in the town.[37] It was also presumably by virtue of his position as JP that Goodman occasionally acted as a commissioner for lay subsidies and approved parish expenditure derived from the poor rate.[38] Deans of Westminster even swore in a host of minor local officials, from hogdrivers to appraisers.[39] Less surprisingly, the Abbey also possessed ecclesiastical jurisdiction over the parish of St Margaret's, which meant that it proved wills within a peculiar court of Westminster and operated its own church court.[40]

These powers gradually helped to consolidate the position of the dean and chapter after the radical changes of the 1540s and 1550s. Yet this consolidation was more of a rearguard action by Goodman's Abbey, in the face of potential threats to its authority, rather than a display of extraordinary initiative. The apparent institutional stability that marked Westminster's government in Elizabeth's reign was essentially predicated on administrative inertia and an unwillingness to confront increasing anomalies. Many aspects of local government in the town remained unresolved, and even the collegiate church, as it struggled to retain its clerical privileges and restore its finances, suffered as a result. Indeed, the dean and chapter were unable to gain royal approval for their own statutes, drafted around 1560–61, forcing the collegiate church to drift partly into government by custom.[41]

Nevertheless, Elizabethan Westminster did experience substantial stability in its government, largely owing to the personal links and co-operation between the Queen, Lord Burghley and Dean Goodman. All three were exceptionally long-lived, and a fundamental harmony of interests between Crown, high steward and dean was maintained in Westminster throughout the second half of the sixteenth century. As we

---

36 For membership of the 1618 commission see TNA, C181/2, ff. 331–2. See also below, ch. 7, for the Westminster Sessions authority.

37 WAC, F304; LMA, WJ/SR (NS), 1/1–106; *Middlesex Sessions Records*, n.s. I (1612–14), ed. W. LeHardy. For prebendaries as JPs see Merritt, 'Under the Shadowe', p. 162.

38 E.g. TNA, E179/142/202, E179/253/1a, cited in R.C. Barnett, *Place, Profit and Power* (Chapel Hill, N.C., 1969), p. 70; WAC, E149, f. 26v.

39 WAC, WCB2, pp. 77, 79.

40 WAC, Peculiar Court of Westminster, will registers; WAM A1/1 and A2/2. See also the discussion in ch. 9.

41 The legality of these draft statutes was contested for several hundred years until 1911, when it was officially established that the statutes had no legal authority and that the collegiate church was governed by custom and royal letters, and that, where the custom was not clear or continuous, the statutes were to act as evidence as to what custom had been: E. Carpenter (ed.), *A House of Kings* (1966), pp. 452–3.

shall see, it was not necessarily in the interests of any one of these to see the creation of a stronger and more formal system of government for the town. Goodman always worked to preserve the status, fortunes and clerical privileges of the Abbey, and he was undoubtedly aware that large-scale change would potentially involve a diminution of the Abbey's traditional authority in the area. This is not to say that Goodman or Burghley were indifferent to problems of public order that became such a focus of attention in the 1580s. Quite the contrary was true, but they seem to have been largely content to allow the work of local government to fall disproportionately on to Westminster's parishes, with more direct intervention by the high steward only in times of crisis. What they did not do is conceive of a *political* solution to the increasing social problems associated with the town's spiralling population.

THE GROWTH OF INSTABILITY IN EARLY STUART WESTMINSTER

Town politics and patronage became more volatile in the early Stuart period, although this was far more apparent after the death of Robert Cecil, earl of Salisbury, in 1612. For most of this period, the Crown continued to show as little interest as before in intervening directly in the daily government of the town. The Crown did show some interest in strengthening the power of the Marshalsea Court, most notably in 1611 when a new Court of the Verge was established with a broader remit than the old Marshalsea Court, but the new court still dealt only with matters of debt, covenant and trespass, and was never intended to address the more general problems of law and order that bedevilled the town itself.[42] Only the Abbey displayed any concerns over the court's jurisdiction, mostly notably in 1621 when those royal household figures involved in the Court of the Verge seem to have challenged the Abbey's privileged jurisdiction and immunities in the area.[43] As we will see, in the early 1630s there was royal concern about disorder in the suburbs, and in Westminster in particular, but while this did generate schemes for reorganization of local government there does not seem to have been any intention to secure direct royal control over the area.[44]

The growing volatility of town politics and patronage in the early Stuart period partly reflected the collapse of the Cecil patronage that had earlier dominated the town.

---

42 D.G. Greene, 'The Court of the Marshalsea in late Tudor and Stuart England', *American Journal of Legal History* 20 (1976), pp. 276–9; TNA, SP16/168/49; 16/531/47, 125. Bodl., MS Rawlinson A 169, ff. 2–4, is a contemporary and mostly accurate account of the development of the court. See also W.R. Jones, 'The Court of the Verge: the jurisdiction of the Steward and Marshal of the Household in later medieval England', *Journal of British Studies* 10 (1970); D.J. Johnson, *Southwark and the City* (1969), pp. 286–8; G.E. Aylmer, *The King's Servants: The Civil Service of Charles I* (revised ed., 1974), p. 45.

43 *Cabala* (1654), pp. 68–9; Merritt, 'Cradle', pp. 636–7 and n. 58.

44 See below. One royal concern was addressed when the Court of the Verge was reconstituted as the Palace Court in 1630: Greene, 'Court', p. 279.

Initially, Jacobean Westminster was marked by a degree of continuity and stability, as Cecil patronage continued to operate on many levels within Westminster.[45] Robert Cecil, who had succeeded his father as high steward in 1598, clearly kept a close eye on the locality, albeit mostly through the use of intermediaries, and his surviving papers reflect concerns over plague, public order, residential development and religious patronage. Cecil links with the Abbey also continued: although Dean Goodman had died in 1601, the dean appointed in 1605, Richard Neile, was another former Cecil chaplain.[46] Cecil patronage also continued to determine Westminster's parliamentary representation. Two members of the Cecil inner circle were returned during Salisbury's remaining years – Sir Walter Cope in 1604 and Sir Julius Caesar in 1610. Nevertheless, elections in Westminster often paired up such MPs, who increasingly might be seen as 'courtier' candidates, with local men who were generally associated with St Margaret's parish. Edmund Doubleday (1614), for example, served as an overseer of the poor for St Margaret's, sat on the Court of Burgesses and was a local justice of the peace. As warden of the Mint, he was also the type of government bureaucrat who so often represented Westminster in parliament.[47]

The death of Salisbury in 1612 led to substantial changes in the network of influence that had developed in Westminster over the space of some fifty years. Both deans and high stewards were henceforth more deeply immersed in the labyrinthine politics of the Stuart Court, while their shorter tenure in office may have limited their influence on the parish level. It is particularly striking that after Goodman's death every subsequent dean of Westminster before the Civil War went on to become a bishop, while deans Richard Neile, George Montaigne and John Williams all ultimately rose to become archbishops of York.[48] In each case, we are dealing with what might be termed courtier clerics – men who moved easily at Court, keen to please the monarch and with one eye on further preferment, even if conscientious in their role as dean. John Hacket later noted that the deanery was seen at this time as 'a fortunate Seat . . . near the Court' and he likened it to 'the Office of the King of Persia's Garden at Babylon, which was stored with his most delicious Fruits . . . He that was trusted with that Garden, was the Lord of the Palace.'[49]

45 See below, ch. 4, for the parochial networks of Robert Cecil.

46 A more politically prominent figure than Goodman, Neile held the influential position of clerk of the closet, but he could also boast that he was Westminster born and bred, the son of a tallow chandler who had even attended Westminster school. Neile's early career and Westminster background are discussed in A. Foster, 'A biography of Archbishop Richard Neile (1562–1640)' (Oxford D.Phil., 1978). For the significance of Neile's presence in Westminster in religious terms see below, ch. 9; Merritt, 'Cradle', pp. 645–6.

47 See also ch. 4.

48 Deans of Westminster served as follows: Lancelot Andrewes (1601–5), Richard Neile (1605–10), George Montaigne (1610–17), Robert Tounson (1617–20), John Williams (1620–43, suspended 1637–40).

49 Hacket, *Scrinia*, pt i, 44.

The new high steward after Salisbury's death was the royal favourite Robert Carr, then Lord Rochester and later earl of Somerset. If Carr's appointment reflected his growing influence with the king, it also illustrated the way in which the extensive Cecil patronage was carved up among the many who aspired to Salisbury's old positions.[50] As dean of Westminster, George Montaigne was already in place when Carr received his patent as high steward, but thereafter Montaigne continued to ally himself closely with both Carr and the powerful Howard family which supported the young favourite. Montaigne even preached a sermon at the controversial wedding of Carr (now earl of Somerset) to the notorious divorcée Frances Howard.[51]

But how did such Court manoeuvring affect Westminster? On the level of town government, this generally meant that town officers appointed by successive deans were increasingly men associated with the mercurial fortunes of Court favourites rather than those with more long-standing local ties. Carr's appointment, for example, was accompanied by two other new appointments. Walter James became bailiff and escheator of Westminster, while Samuel Baker received a patent for the offices of coroner and clerk of the market. Neither man was a significant local figure, and both seem to have been nominated by the high steward. It is significant that when the dean and chapter ratified the nominations they specifically limited the term of office to 'the naturall life' of Carr.[52] At least in theory, such offices had previously been considered life appointments. Carr had little time to establish himself in Westminster, however, and the town's MPs during his ascendancy – Edmund Doubleday and Sir Humphrey May (at this time known only as a groom of the Privy Chamber) – were not specifically associated with him.[53] Carr's lack of a townhouse in Westminster – he lodged at Court in the Cockpit – further emphasizes his relatively shallow links with the locality and certainly contrasts with the impressive houses maintained by Burghley and Salisbury.[54]

With the scandal of the Overbury murder and Carr's subsequent fall from power, a new favourite emerged at Court, and rapidly assumed Carr's Westminster offices. George Villiers, later duke of Buckingham, received his patent as high steward of Westminster on 8 December 1618. As in the case of Carr, new officers were appointed at the same time, but only for the duration of Buckingham's life, and Buckingham subsequently reshuffled his own men around the posts of bailiff and

---

50 Appointed on 5 December 1612: WAM, Chapter Act Bk II, f. 10. Salisbury's stewardship of York, for example, passed to the earl of Northampton.

51 *DNB*, s.n. George Montaigne.

52 WAM, Chapter Act Bk II, f. 10. Nothing more is known of James and Baker – certainly James was not a local man.

53 T. Moir, *The Addled Parliament of 1614* (Oxford, 1958), p. 189.

54 *SL*, XIV, 46. Carr had also become Keeper of Whitehall Palace in 1611. Although an earlier Keeper had lived at the Cockpit, Sir Thomas Knyvett, Carr's predecessor, normally seems to have stayed in his King Street house in St Margaret's: *ibid.*, 46; WAC, e.g. E149 (1599–1608).

coroner on several occasions.[55] In making these appointments it would appear that neither Carr nor Buckingham sought to cultivate local patronage networks. Of course, the long years of Cecil influence meant that local links and Cecil links had gradually come to seem much the same thing, but none of Salisbury's immediate successors served long enough for this process to occur, even if they had been canny enough to encourage such a development. After Buckingham's assassination in 1628 the office of high steward was bestowed upon Philip Herbert, earl of Pembroke and Montgomery, a prominent courtier who, like Carr, resided at Court. Pembroke did not play a major role in formulating national policy and his post of Lord Chamberlain would have given him a natural interest in the environs of the Court. He may therefore have played more of a role in the locality than either Carr or Buckingham, but it remains unclear how extensive a patronage network he possessed in the area before the Civil War.[56]

If town officials changed more rapidly in the post-Cecil period, this was also matched by greater contention over parliamentary elections. With his virtual monopoly of local appointments, the duke of Buckingham was able to secure the return of his brother, Sir Edward Villiers, as a Westminster MP in 1621, 1624 and 1625. Nevertheless, Buckingham could not count upon the smooth running of elections. In fact, three out of five parliamentary elections in Westminster during the 1620s appear to have been contested, as was the Short Parliament election of 1640, while in 1628 it is clear that Buckingham's preferred candidate was decisively (indeed derisorily) rejected. There could be no more vivid manifestation of the newly volatile nature of Westminster politics. By contrast, in the period leading up to the Civil War there were only two contested elections in the City of London after 1604 and there had certainly never been a case of a disputed election during the many years when Westminster's parliamentary seats had been an exclusively Cecilian preserve.[57]

The declining influence of the high steward in the area may partly explain such increasingly disputed elections. The 1628 election, however, reflected a sharper discontent with royal policies. Westminster had been selected as the first locality for the collection of the controversial Forced Loan in 1626, as well as an an earlier, initial royal benevolence. This had presumably reflected a confidence on the government's part that Westminster's inhabitants, with their Court links, might prove more supportive of royal policy. It was also relatively easy to call the relevant subsidymen individually before the Privy Council in order to demand their compliance. While

---

55 See Merritt thesis, pp. 148–9.

56 Like other high stewards in the past, Pembroke was able to secure the appointment of his own preferred candidates as bailiff and escheator: his steward Anthony Hinton was made bailiff in December 1628 (WAM, Reg. 13, f. 267), and was replaced by George Perry in 1639 on Pembroke's specific recommendation (WAM, Chapter Act Bk II, f. 71v). A relative, Edward Herbert, was appointed recorder soon after Pembroke took up his post (Chapter Act Bk II, f. 44v). In the 1640s, Pembroke became involved in managing the affairs of the former collegiate church.

57 D. Hirst, *The Representative of the People?* (Cambridge, 1975), p. 219.

St Margaret's and St Martin's had capitulated, there had been vociferous opposition in the rest of Westminster, most notably in St Clement's.[58] The election of 1628 witnessed the decisive rejection of the high steward's candidate and also of previous Westminster MPs, in favour of local vestrymen (in the shape of Thomas Morrice and Joseph Bradshawe). The other candidates were rejected, a contemporary reported, 'because, as is said, they had discontented their neighbours in urging the payment of the loan'.[59] The election for the Short Parliament in 1640 also witnessed a contested election in which Court candidates were decisively rejected in favour of two candidates with strong local connections. One was the prominent St Margaret's apothecary William Bell. Westminster's other member, the noted lawyer and future parliamentarian John Glynn, also possessed specifically Westminster ties. Not only did he serve as both JP and recorder of Westminster but he had also provided legal advice to St Margaret's parish on its response to ship money.[60]

The elections of 1628 and 1640 make it clear that Westminster's electorate could no longer be expected simply to endorse 'Court' candidates. But there were other issues at stake in the disputed parliamentary elections of the 1620s. Perhaps the most interesting election of the early Stuart period took place in 1621, when it was the involvement of the dean that sparked resentment among some of Westminster's inhabitants. This disputed election sheds light on the role that deans might play in elections, but it is particularly revealing of the Abbey's wider relations with the Westminster parishes.

Initially, Westminster's election for the 1621 parliament had proceeded normally, with the election of Sir Edward Villiers (presumably the high steward's candidate) and Edmund Doubleday as MPs for Westminster. This took place after the bailiff's receipt of a precept from the sheriffs and notice having been given of the election. The problems began when Doubleday died only days after being elected. Complaints then arose over the manner in which Dean Williams arranged for a successor to be elected. This resulted in the parishioners of St Martin in the Fields, St Clement Danes and St Mary le Strand contesting the election of the new MP, William Mann.

---

58 R.F. Williams (ed.), *The Court and Times of Charles I* (2 vols., 1848), I, 130–1, 133, 151, 154, 157, 159, 166.

59 *Ibid.*, I, 327.

60 *HMC De l'Isle*, VI, 235–6. Glynn was appointed recorder of Westminster in May 1636 (WAM, Chapter Act Bk II, f. 62v). He was also steward of Westminster by 1639, and a member of the sewers commission for Middlesex for some years: Keeler, p. 187. For his consultation with St Margaret's see WAC, E20 (unfol.). Given that the recordership and stewardship were in the gift of the high steward, Pembroke, it seems likely that Glynn was Pembroke's choice, and indeed Conrad Russell has seen Glynn as Pembroke's client: C. Russell, *The Fall of the British Monarchies 1637–1642* (Oxford, 1991), p. 215. If so, it is interesting that Glynn's connection to Pembroke does not seem to have labelled him a 'Court' candidate. This may provide evidence that Pembroke was understood to be hostile to some of the policies of the Personal Rule. It should be noted that Westminster's electors rejected another candidate, the lawyer Holborne, who had been a more obvious member of the 'opposition' to Personal Rule government: he had served as John Hampden's counsel in the Ship Money case: *ibid.*, p. 120.

A petition to the parliamentary committee of privileges, signed by sixty Westminster inhabitants, furnishes most of the evidence for what occurred.[61]

A central figure in the events was that wily politician, Dean John Williams. Williams had become dean of Westminster in 1620 and already seemed intent on stamping his personal authority on the area. It is notable that when Williams was created lord keeper and also bishop of Lincoln (soon after the election for the 1621 parliament) he made sure that his appointment to both posts was celebrated with great splendour in Westminster itself.[62] Doubleday's death seems to have provided the newly arrived Williams with an opportunity to flex his muscles in the locality, with controversial results.

According to the later petitioners, Williams chose a day for the election of a new MP, whom he 'appointed and nominated' to be William Mann. This was done 'upon the former precept but noe publique notice thereof gyven'. Instead, petitioners claimed that 'only *private* notice was given the night before about vii or 8 of the clock to every particular house in the parishe of St Margaret', this after private 'conference' at the Abbey. Nevertheless, rumour of the election spread from parishioners of St Margaret's 'to some of their frends' dwelling in the other Westminster parishes.[63] The men of the 'liberties' (i.e. the Westminster parishes aside from St Margaret's) managed to organize themselves quickly. They went to Westminster Hall at the appointed time and 'made choice of Mr Edward Forsett a sufficent and worthie gent for theire Burgesse although he never made suyte or stoode for the same'. Significantly, Forsett was a vestryman of St Martin's, as well as a Middlesex JP. But the petitioners found that the dean was intent on returning William Mann, a St Margaret's vestryman and 'collector of his rentes and one that receyveth fee and wages from the Colledge [collegiate church]'. The petitioners described how, on the day of the election, Mann entered Westminster Hall in the company of the bailiff of Westminster, an attorney who had assumed 'the managinge' of the business and 'a grete multitude of others (whereof some were gentlemen of worth) but the greatest part were serving men, Apprentices, women, children, watermen [and] Porters'. With this support, Mann was returned 'notwithstandinge that they were admonished that a verie great number of them who cried for Mr Manne were children and other people . . . who had no voice'.[64]

---

61 Surrey History Centre, LM/1989.

62 *Letters of John Chamberlain*, II, 387, 406.

63 Surrey History Centre, LM/1989. Italics mine.

64 *Ibid.* For Edward Forsett see also below, ch. 4. Although Sir Arthur Ingram and Robert (later Sir Robert) Pye supported Mann's election, Sir Edward Wardour, who appears to have been present, objected to it, particularly on the grounds that many people voted who were not eligible to do so. Wardour also noted that Dean Williams 'refused to number them by the Poll', *CJ*, I, 528–9. Pye was a client of Buckingham's (Aylmer, *King's Servants*, pp. 311–13), while Ingram's connection with Westminster remains unclear, although surprisingly his name appears on the indenture for the 1620 election (see WAM 9629). Wardour was a Westminster resident, while his father, Chidiock Wardour, had been a prominent St Martin's vestryman under Elizabeth, see below, ch. 4. The bailiff of Westminster was William Jeve, a Buckingham appointee.

The petitioners were clearly anxious to portray the dean as the villain of the piece. But who were these sixty petitioners? It is notable that they were not drawn from among the foremost gentry and aristocracy in the area. Rather, they were parishioners of lesser social rank: eight of them merely signed with a mark, although they were mostly prosperous craftsmen and middling sort, with not a single gentleman among them. These were not, however, inconsequential men. Four signatories were prominent members of St Martin's vestry, and at least twenty-one others were currently serving or would go on to serve in significant offices in the same parish (including seven future vestrymen).[65]

Most striking about the petitioners is the absence of parishioners from St Margaret's, while at least thirty-three signatories have been identified as St Martin's men. An additional petition to parliament concerning the same matter specifically described itself as being from the inhabitants of the parishes of St Martin's, St Clement Danes and St Mary Savoy (i.e. Mary le Strand). This petition maintained that 'of ancient times' members of these particular parishes 'have allwayes accustomed to give their voices' in Westminster parliamentary elections but that this custom had been ignored in the recent election.[66] Most of all, petitioners criticized the unwarranted priority which St Margaret's parish had received, with members of the other parishes receiving no formal notification of the intended new election. Williams apparently remained unrepentant about the pre-eminence that he allotted to St Margaret's. Writing later to Sir Robert Cotton, when the latter aspired to a Westminster parliamentary seat in 1628, Williams asserted that, while one of the candidates was selected by him on recommendation from the high steward, the other candidate was chosen by 'the Towne, that is by the Vestry'. This vestry, it is clear, was that of St Margaret's.[67]

Williams insisted that this vestry was an independent force whose decision he merely rubberstamped. They submitted the 'town' nominee for his approval, but only as a matter of courtesy, 'and if they pitch upon any Neighbour of ther owne, especially upon any one of the 12 burgesses, they are like that little god Terminus, that will not be removed from theyre opinions'. Williams's insistence on the vestry's independence is not convincing, however. The chief members (if not all) of St Margaret's vestry, whom Williams mentioned by name, were actually officials of the collegiate church or men who had obtained favourable leases from it.[68] One was William Mann, and another was Peter Heywood, who had himself served as an MP for Westminster in 1626. Indeed, Heywood's parliamentary activities were limited to serving on a

---

65 Surrey History Centre, LM/1989. From St Martin's vestry: Simon Greene, John Thorpe, John Johnson and Gabriel Brewer. Future St Martin's vestrymen: Charles Kynaston, William Goodacres, Henry Wickes, Henry Lidgold, Anthony Hill, William Stacey and Samuel Clarke.

66 The signatures to this petition do not survive. Surrey History Centre, LM/1331/27.

67 BL, Cotton Julius C, III, f. 402r–v.

68 Ibid. Those mentioned as leading vestrymen at St Margaret's were William Mann, William Ireland, Thomas Morrice and Peter Heywood.

committee concerned with a bill to prohibit clergymen from acting as JPs, which was specifically amended in committee to allow exemptions for deans, among others.[69] Williams let slip where the real power lay when he suggested that Cotton might win this 'town' seat by donating history books to the vestry, which would then form part of the library of Westminster Abbey, even if officially they were to be presented to St Margaret's vestry.[70]

Williams's comments are revealing, and support the impression gained from the 1621 petition that the old 'vill' of Westminster (i.e. St Margaret's parish) still played a central role in the politics of the locality. This may have been appropriate during the medieval period, when the more populous vill constituted the economic heart of Westminster and its properties formed a significant proportion of the Abbey's revenues.[71] By the seventeenth century, however, the vill no longer towered over the other Westminster parishes as it had done previously. The 1621 petitioners specifically emphasized that these other Westminster parishes now formed the 'greatest part' of Westminster as a whole, which was why the failure to inform them of the intended election was so deeply resented.[72]

When due process was observed in parliamentary elections, however, it does seem that the candidate preferred by the dean and St Margaret's could still expect to be elected. It is striking that Williams managed to have Mann returned again as a Westminster MP in 1624 and 1625, although there appear to have been further protests in the latter year.[73] Even in 1628, when Court candidates were rejected, the 'patriot' MPs who were elected were both members of St Margaret's vestry. St Margaret's hegemony was a fact of life in the town as a whole and also evident in the numerical superiority of St Margaret's men on the Court of Burgesses, the only body in Westminster (apart from the Westminster sessions) which brought together members of different parishes.

What seems to have ignited particular resentment in 1621, however, was the manipulation of this situation by the dean. The intensity of the hostility, however, can be understood only when it is recognized that some of Westminster's townspeople had been involved in a more long-running attempt to gain incorporation for the town, moves that had put them at odds with the Abbey. As we shall see, this push for reform partly stemmed from a desire for more effective local government to deal with major

---

69 I am grateful to Dr Andrew Thrush for allowing me to read the History of Parliament's provisional biography of Heywood, which notes Heywood's involvement in this committee.

70 BL, Cotton Julius C, III, f. 402r–v.

71 Rosser, pp. 43–5, 52–4.

72 Surrey History Centre, LM/1989.

73 *CJ*, I, 569a, 800. Mann's 1621 election was not overturned. The Commons' Journals reveal nothing of the content of a petition tendered by Sir John Danvers regarding the conduct of the Westminster election in 1625, but it may be significant that in the following year's election Mann seems to have been replaced as the Abbey's favoured candidate by Peter Heywood.

social problems and urban expansion.[74] Yet for those pressing for reform, the deficiencies of Westminster's existing government were the consequence of its anachronistic and unrepresentative character.

THE STRUGGLE FOR INCORPORATION 1585–1636

In 1607, King James approved a bill for the incorporation of Westminster.[75] Westminster, so it seemed, would stand at last side by side with the City of London, with its urban government mirroring that of its more powerful neighbour. But the royal assent turned out to be little more than a mirage and ultimately Westminster's government never underwent such a radical reordering. What, however, were the forces behind this (and other) bids for incorporation?

So far we have said little about the place of townspeople within the nexus of relations involving the Abbey, high steward and Crown. During the medieval period, the relations between townspeople and Abbey had been far more harmonious than was often the case elsewhere. This relative lack of friction appears to have been related to the economy of late medieval Westminster. This was sufficiently diverse to avoid the more polarized Abbey/town split found in towns with great monasteries, such as Bury St Edmunds.[76] The upheaval of the Reformation, though, left the jurisdictional boundaries between the town and the dean and chapter ill-defined. This in itself did not bring about an inevitable clash of interests. There is also little evidence that the inhabitants of post-Reformation Westminster specifically attacked the secular powers of the dean and chapter as part of a principled objection to clerical authority within towns.[77]

Nevertheless, by the 1580s, the escalating problems of poverty and disorder associated with the urban expansion of Westminster brought into sharp relief certain anomalies in its government, anomalies that were ultimately linked to the continuing secular powers of what was now the collegiate church. A fundamental problem was that the men who struggled to govern Westminster's expanding parishes did not have access to a whole panoply of powers that were provided elsewhere in the country by the structures of an established town government. Although the Crown had granted Westminster the right to call itself a 'city', this was a city that had no right to make

---

74 These issues are discussed more fully below, ch. 7.

75 LPL, Shrewsbury Papers, MS 709, f. 149.

76 Rosser, pp. 245–7. Note also the more harmonious situation in Chichester: S. Thomas, 'Chichester and its cathedral on the eve of the Reformation', *Urban History* 29 (2002).

77 There are difficulties in comparing Westminster with other English towns. Cathedral towns necessarily had bishops, as well as a dean and chapter, and served as administrative centres in a way that the collegiate church of Westminster did not. For attitudes towards cathedrals see Merritt, 'Cradle', p. 625, n. 7.

laws, and no power to tax or to run its own courts. It was also a 'city' without its own income, and therefore with no money to pay an independent bureaucracy.[78] These facts help to explain what was a long and drawn-out campaign to replace weak manorial government with a more powerful corporate structure, a project that would necessarily wrest power away from the Abbey.

1585: AN ACT 'TO MAKE TRYALL WITH'

As we have seen, the 1585 Act for the government of Westminster essentially ensured the continuation of clerical authority in the town. But this was not the original purpose of the bill. In fact, the triumph of the dean and chapter was achieved only through a highly effective rearguard action to defend itself against what was a significant threat to its authority. The most recent published account of the Act notes that the bill went through a great many amendments in both Lords and Commons, but entirely misses the point that much of the controversial nature of the bill arose from its origins in local conflicts between the townspeople and the dean and chapter.[79] Indeed, the early Stuart dean and chapter complained specifically that at the time of the 1585 Act 'the Townsmen of Westminster endeavoured . . . to have a Corporacion and to exempt themselves out of the Jurisdicion of the Deane and Chapter'.[80]

There is a great deal of evidence to support this later assertion. The 1585 Act for the 'good government' of the city and borough of Westminster was originally a private bill and was referred to as being 'for the alteration of the government of the said cittie'.[81] It seems to have been initiated by those substantial townsmen of Westminster who also served on the vestry of St Margaret's parish – the most administratively sophisticated of the Westminster parishes. There is little doubt, however, that they consulted with the vestrymen of the other Westminster parishes. The co-operation of these fellow vestrymen was central to the legislation. The dominant role played by St Margaret's parishioners, however, is borne out by a list appended to its parish vestry minutes of the 'Charges layde owt concerninge the Acte of parliamente for the Cittie of Westminster and the Lyberties of the same'. These charges were met by St Margaret's parish. The parish also undertook the refurbishment of the building, located in St Margaret's, where the newly created Court of Burgesses would sit.[82]

---

78 See further discussion of this point in ch. 7 below.

79 D. Dean, *Law-making and Society in Late Elizabethan England* (Cambridge, 1996), pp. 254–5.

80 WAM 6561.

81 Webbs, *Manor and Borough*, I, 214, n. 1; *Acts*, no. 376.

82 WAC, E2413, ff. 6–8. An ornamental plaque listing the names of those who contributed to the expenses of the bill was subsequently hung in St Margaret's church: WAC, E5 (1587–88), f. 26v. The controversy surrounding the Act and the involvement of Westminster's leading townsmen is mentioned in BL, Lansdowne MS 43, f. 178.

Expenses incurred by St Margaret's parish in promoting the bill reveal the prominent but ambiguous role played by members of the Cecil family. This is hardly surprising given that, as we have seen, most of Westminster's parliamentary representatives
during Elizabeth's reign were associated with the Cecils. In 1584–85, the young Robert
Cecil and Sir Thomas Knyvett (a St Margaret's man) represented Westminster in
parliament, and St Margaret's parishioners paid them and other officials a series of
gratuities to smooth the passage of the bill.[83]

Despite the importance of the bill to the future of Westminster, the local dean
and chapter remained surprisingly ignorant of the course of the legislation. On 25
March 1585 they recorded in their Chapter Act book that

> whereas some of the inhabytantes of the cittie of Westminster did exhibite a bill into
> the parliament for the alteration of the government of the said cittie, which bill beinge
> passed the lower howse *unwyttinge unto us*, it pleased the lordes of the higher howse,
> upon oure humble petition, to graunte unto us a certen proviso in the said bill for the
> preservinge of oure lyberties and pryvledges, which proviso they delyvered unto us to
> be considered of by oure learned counsell.[84]

Given Goodman's close links with Burghley, this lack of advance knowledge is striking.
It is possible that Burghley was unaware of the bill's implications for the Abbey. If this
was the case, it would imply that the bill was initially presented more as a straightforward 'law and order' bill, with the fact that it introduced incorporation either not
stated explicity by the townsmen or introduced at a later stage.

What is clear is that the original bill represented a far more substantial assault on
the secular powers of the dean and chapter than that which emerged in the final Act.
The legal advice that the chapter sought on the impact of the proposed legislation
makes it clear that the Abbey's rights ran the risk of being seriously infringed.[85] For

---

83 WAC, E2413, ff. 6–7. At Christmas St Margaret's presented Sir Robert Cecil, Sir Thomas Knyvett
and the Recorder of London with a marzipan each 'in the name of the Inhabitance'. On one occasion, a dinner was held at the Court of Wards for those on the committee for the bill, while another
time 'muskedyne and Cakes' were deemed appropriate for Westminster's MPs. These gratuities and
frequent payments for 'boatehier' suggest the consultation needed to shepherd the bill through
parliament. Among payments for the Lower House, one to 'my Lord Treasurers man for dra[w]inge
the Booke at my Lordes Commaundment' suggests Burghley's involvement at some stage., *ibid*.
This reference to the 'Booke' otherwise known as the 'king's bill', was the stage of the process of
granting borough charters when the exact wording of the grant was composed: S. Bond and N. Evans,
'The process of granting charters in English boroughs 1547–1649', *EHR* 91 (1976), p. 107.

84 *Acts*, no. 376.

85 These survive as 'Mr Vales notes and Rem[em]braunces for some amendment of the bill for the
good government for westminster': TNA, SP 12/177/27. Dean (*Law-making*, p. 254, n. 162)
notes that Vale's opinions on the bill were 'mostly unfavourable', but misses the rather obvious
explanation that Vale was presumably the attorney employed by the dean and chapter, at the prompting of the Lords. Later, in 1587, Vale received a patent for 'court keping [*sic*]' (*Acts*, no. 403), and
at the same time was also made the dean and chapter's receiver general jointly with George Burden.
Among charges for the new Westminster courthouse were those for cushions 'one for Mr Vaelle and
one for Mr Bayllyffe' (WAC, E2314, f. 8).

example, the bill effectively abolished Westminster's right of sanctuary, so that the close and the sanctuary would have been subject to all aspects of the legislation.[86] It was also noted that the bill further eroded the secular authority of the dean and chapter by permitting the Middlesex justices to appoint officers 'in defaulte of' the dean and high steward 'which allwaies have bene named & appointed by the high Stewarde onelie'. This was considered to be the thin end of the wedge, and 'against reason & the liberties'.[87] The Abbey's attorney also seemed to object to what he considered to be the novel claims to ecclesiastical jurisdiction being made for the proposed new court, which would become the Court of Burgesses.[88]

As we have seen, the 1585 Act in its final form actually preserved many of the privileges of the dean and chapter. But this was only after a series of fraught meetings between Lords and Commons, and the final stipulation that restricted the powers of the newly created Court of Burgesses to determine anything without the consent of the dean or high steward was actually a scrawled, last-minute amendment to the bill.[89] In addition, it is more than likely that these concessions to the Abbey were agreed only because the act was explicitly presented as a temporary measure (and in fact required renewal at every subsequent parliament). Indeed, an account of the debate in parliament over the bill actually states that it was intended to be a temporary measure 'to make tryall with'.[90]

Plainly there was a strong desire among many townspeople in 1585 for a more centralized and lay-dominated government for Westminster, with more independence for the burgesses than emerged, and at least the shadow of a proper incorporated governmental structure. Even if the 1585 Act still left the dean in a prominent position, it is important to recognize that hopes of substantial change still remained, and in this context even the limited degree to which the Court of Burgesses imitated the terminology and practices of London government is significant. As we shall see in a later chapter, the reality of administration followed medieval, manorial structures, and differed substantially from the centralized and judicial functions of London's government.[91] Nevertheless, to those people eager for a stronger government on London's model, the imitation of London's structures and terminology was not a matter of mere pretentiousness, but rather gave symbolic expression to their aspirations. This new Court of Burgesses may have been under the dean's control, but it still nursed a potential civic identity.

---

86 Sanctuary had nearly been abolished during Mary's reign, when only a dramatic speech in Parliament by Abbot Feckenham had saved the Abbey's rights. Dean Goodman had also defended sanctuary during the 1560s: H.F. Westlake, *Westminster Abbey* (2 vols., 1923), II, 426–7, 429. The right of sanctuary was also a recurrent issue in the City of London: Archer, pp. 299–302.

87 TNA, SP 12/177/27. Further comments related to the problem of governing Duchy of Lancaster properties, located within the liberties of Westminster but not subject to its jurisdiction.

88 *Ibid.*

89 HLRO, 27 Eliz. I c. 47 (*sic*).

90 BL, Lansdowne MS 43, f. 178; *Proceedings in the Parliaments of Elizabeth I*, ed. T.E. Hartley (3 vols., Leicester, 1981–95), II, 60, 72, 98, 102.

91 See below, ch. 7.

1607: 'FOR AVOIDING OF OPPRESSION'

The ambiguity of Westminster's position and the extent of local ambitions resurfaced again in 1601, when a coat of arms was granted to the 'city' of Westminster. The text of the grant is notable partly for the very lack of reference to the dean and chapter, despite the fact that the arms partly incorporated elements of the coat of arms used by the dean and chapter itself. Instead, the formal grant is addressed to members of the Court of Burgesses and their assistants and, after noting the importance of the city as the principal seat of the monarch, of parliament and of the ancient Wool Staple, it stipulates that the arms have been granted 'uppon due consideration that the said Cittie maye have the honnor of Armes as other Cities and Burroughes'. The grant of arms also shows that, even if Westminster lacked a proper civic government, its burgesses were clearly determined to acquire as many of the symbolic trappings of incorporation as possible.[92]

Such symbols of civic prestige were clearly treasured by at least some of Westminster's officials. A striking example of a nascent civic spirit is detectable in the extraordinary will penned by Morris Pickering, an original member of the 1585 Court of Burgesses, and one of those to whom the grant of arms was addressed. Pickering's 1603 will reads like a one-man attempt to create for Westminster a set of traditions, a civic esprit de corps and a sense of identity similar to that experienced by the elite of London citizenry. Yet it is also possible to read the will as a sign that such an identity had not developed as much as early members of the Court of Burgesses had hoped. To the parishioners of St Margaret's, Pickering left a black velvet burial cloth, to be 'as large and fayer as . . . may be hadd or done with the armes of the said citty of Westminster'. This cloth was to be used only at the funerals of burgesses, their wives and 'especiall good frendes' who lived in the parish. Pickering also strived to promote a sense of fellowship among the burgesses. For example, he bequeathed 40s yearly to Westminster's burgesses 'for them to make merry withall, for the better contynewance of brotherly love and Amytie (the which god graunte to multyply among them)'. Cautiously, Pickering stipulated that this sum was to be paid out only 'if the Acte nowe Enacted for the good government of the said cittie of Westminster or any other hereafter to be made to like effect, shall contynewe in force'. Additionally, Pickering left to the burgesses of the city 'by what name, or title forever they shalbe called' a standing cup of silver worth £40. This was to be as large and fair as possible, with the arms of the city and the names of Pickering and his wife engraved upon it. Pickering intended that the cup be kept 'as a monyment for ever, and used at all such feastes and tymes, as the sayd Burgesses and governors . . . shall meete together to be merrye in'. Many other gifts were made by Pickering to individual burgesses, and £5 for the burgesses and assistants to make a banquet on the day of his funeral.[93]

92 Manchée, pp. 209–10.

93 WAC, PCW, 482 Elsam; Manchée, pp. 209–10. The Pickering cup is illustrated in Manchée, pp. 250–2. For Pickering's other bequests see Merritt thesis, pp. 121–2.

Pickering's careful reservations over the duration of the Act and even the title of 'burgess' bear testimony to the degree to which a stronger and more permanent form of city government was still anticipated by certain townspeople. It should be noted, however, that Pickering's will did not seek to promote civic identity by setting it in opposition to Abbey interests. Pickering himself had been a verger of the Abbey from 1572, and his will also made many bequests to Westminster prebendaries and servants of the dean and chapter, thereby underlining the intimate connection that still linked the government of Westminster to the former monastery.[94] Nevertheless, the unfulfilled desire for corporate status was soon to manifest itself in more direct opposition to the dean and chapter.

Only a few years later, the campaign for incorporation came tantalizingly close to achieving its goal, when a bill drafted for the incorporation of the town gained royal approval in 1607. Of course a good deal had happened since the 1585 Act. Early Jacobean Westminster was a dynamic place, with the refurbishment of aristocratic townhouses along the Strand, plans for Britain's Burse under way, and the growing importance of St Martin's and St Clement Danes, two Westminster parishes which had been far less significant in the medieval period. Indeed, St Martin's was increasingly identified as the parish of choice for the discerning gentleman.[95] But the social and environmental problems singled out in the preamble to the 1585 Act had not abated. Population increase, poverty and relatively unchecked building continued to dog the Westminster parishes. Of course such problems were not limited to Westminster, and similar difficulties aroused concern in the City of London, especially in relation to its many 'disorderly' outlying suburbs. Part of the City's response was to review the jurisdictional status of these problematic areas. A new charter of 1608 sought to define more clearly the City's authority and the status of various suburbs and liberties. The overall pattern, however, was one in which the City gained more supervisory powers over some liberties while seeking at the same time to avoid any extra administrative burden.[96]

In this context, the early years of James also witnessed a well co-ordinated campaign by Westminster townsmen to achieve their own longed-for incorporation, an important initiative which has escaped the notice of historians. This time, the promoters of incorporation got as far as producing a complete draft royal charter of incorporation, again apparently without the involvement of the dean and chapter.[97] This proposed incorporation was justified by its supporters as enabling the better government of

---

94 *Acts*, no. 273.

95 See below, ch. 5.

96 Pearl, *London*, pp. 30, 32; W. de G. Birch, *The Historical Charters and Constitutional Documents of the City of London* (1887), pp. 142–5. Concern over the renewal of a commission to deal with disorders in and around London had been raised in 1606: *HMC Hatfield*, XVIII, 229.

97 The 65-folio draft charter survives as WAM 6586, which is given the date of 1607 in WAM 6561, p. 5, which itself dates from the 1630s.

the town, the better relief of poor inhabitants, but also 'for avoyding of oppression'. Again, the dean and chapter seem to have been crucial in their opposition to the scheme, and the margins of the surviving draft charter are punctuated with their objections.[98]

The proposed charter seems to embody a systematic attempt to remove the powers successfully preserved by the dean and chapter in the 1585 Act and to create instead an institution run by and for the townspeople. The powers of the new corporation were to extend over exactly the same area previously described as the town and its 'liberties', taking in the parishes of St Margaret's, St Martin's, St Clement Danes (encompassing St Mary le Strand) and including the dean himself 'within the yeard before his dore'.[99] The chief burgesses were to be elected by the townsmen, and not (as the 1585 Act had required) chosen by the dean or high steward. On the making and establishing of laws and ordinances (which the 1585 Act had specified that the dean or steward should be 'parties' to), the new charter excluded both the dean and chapter and the high steward. A further section urged the creation of a 'Court of Record & Cognizance of all pleas in Westminster', thereby taking away the court baron of the dean and chapter. It was also specified that the corporation should have the view of frankpledge (formerly granted to the abbots of Westminster and subsequently the dean and chapter) and should also receive fines and amercements from all those arrested by their sergeants at the mace within Westminster. The new corporation also wanted its own market for the sale of horses and cattle to be held in Tothill every Monday, and their own fair in Westminster, again threatening the fair and market from which the dean and chapter profited.[100]

Another related document specifies that the intention behind the bill was explicitly to imitate the structures of government in the City of London. Even the selection of Westminster's MPs was to be taken in hand by the new corporation, with the stipulation that members be chosen from among the principal burgesses. This document twice punctiliously insists that the high steward should be chosen or appointed 'by the Deane of Westminster & his sucessors as Tyme out of mynde he hath Bene . . . And as they by Auncient Charters have Acthoritie so to Appoint', but this represents a rather token sop to the concerns of the dean and chapter, as the proposed incorporation left the high steward with little real function in the locality.[101]

---

98 These objections are collected together in WAM 6587, but this is now badly torn and incomplete. An apparently accurate copy of them was made in the 1630s in WAM 6561, pp. 5–7, and this is the text that I have used.

99 WAM 6561, p. 6.

100 *Ibid.*, pp. 5–7. These various provisions are typical of borough incorporations: see Bond and Evans, 'Process', pp. 104–5; R. Tittler, *The Reformation and the Towns in England* (Oxford, 1998), pp. 87–96, 161–76, 188–95, 345–6; M. Weinbaum, *British Borough Charters* (1943).

101 WAM 6557. This document appears to be a précis in English of the contents of the proposed incorporation. It is dated as 'temp. Eliz.' in the the Muniments' slip index, but references throughout the document to the king make it clear that it must date from the early Stuart period.

In their arguments against the scheme, the dean and chapter protested that the petition for incorporation came from 'a popular faccion of the meanest sort of the Inhabitants of Westminster' who wished to enjoy 'diverse liberties and privileges' which the dean and chapter had always exercised. The proposal and its presented rationale were 'verie scandelous to the Deane and Prebends, and their Officers, and verie preiudiciall to the said Collegiate Church'. Basing their stand on the fact that they had continually exercised authority in the town since the Reformation, the dean and chapter protested that any complaints about the nature of that government constituted a personal attack and must be justified. It was 'a great imputacion to them and their Officers' that the government should be altered 'by reason of their misgovernment, want of charitie, and oppression, before they be convicted of such Crimes, and the Cause be heard'. If there were indeed 'anie defect' in the dean and chapter or their officers they desired that it be made known, stressing that 'they are willing to be reformed and to submitt themselves unto anie censure'. For the proposed charter itself, the dean and chapter pointed out every single provision that represented a diminution of the authority that the 1585 Act had preserved, and particularly urged the 1585 proviso that nothing contained in the Act should be prejudicial to the dean and chapter or their successors. The jurisdiction and privileges that would be given to the townsmen, it was warned, 'must of necessitie be occasion of continual broyles' between the townsmen and officers of the dean and chapter for their several jurisdictions 'as is daylie apparant, betweene the Universities and the Towns wherein they are seated'.[102]

In the end, however, the Westminster dean and chapter succeeded in blocking this 1607 draft charter for incorporation, in the same way that they had managed to neuter the 1585 Act. Although the bill for incorporation progressed as far as receiving the royal assent and a charter was drafted, it was ultimately foiled.[103] The promoters of the incorporation had certainly been fearful that they might be outflanked: after royal approval had been gained they had anxiously petitioned that the 1585 Act should continue only until the new corporation had been passed under the Great Seal, and 'that then the said [1585] Acte shalbe utterly voyde, repealed and of none effecte for ever after to all ententes and purposes whatsoever'. This foreboding that the incorporation would be blocked at the last minute, and the 1585 Act retained, proved to be all too accurate.[104]

---

102 WAM 6561, pp. 5–6.

103 While the 'humble Requeste of the Inhabitants of the Cyttie of Westminster' (LPL, Shrewsbury MS 709, f. 149) to the King comments that 'it hath pleased his moste excellent Matie of his glorious favor to incorporate the said Cyttie', this must have represented only the very early stages in the progress of the passage of the charter (possibly just the securing of a sign manual from the King). I have been unable to find references to the charter passing the signet (TNA, SO3), which makes it unlikely that it reached the Privy Seal, let alone the Great Seal. I am grateful to Simon Healey for his advice on this.

104 LPL, Shrewsbury Papers, MS 709, f. 149.

There are a number of possible reasons for their lack of success. Even if the chapter exaggerated in claiming that the bill was merely the work of 'a popular faccion' of the meanest sort, it is still quite possible that the townsmen were themselves split, and that some prominent burgesses from St Margaret's were more supportive of the Abbey's interests. These were presumably 'the chiffest persons of the Towne' who, the dean and chapter reported, both disclaimed the work of the 'faction' and signed a certificate to the Attorney General dissociating themselves from the proposed incorporation.[105] It is also possible that the then dean, Richard Neile – a Cecil protégé – ultimately enjoyed the support of Robert Cecil, whose own authority as High Steward might potentially have been threatened by the new corporation.[106] There is certainly evidence that the dean and chapter seem to have petitioned Salisbury directly, presenting the proposed incorporation in the worst possible light.[107] Clearly the proposed incorporation must have had powerful backers to intercede for it if it gained the king's assent and it is possible that Sir Thomas Knyvett – an influential courtier and MP at the time of the first attempted incorporation in 1585 – was involved. But it seems most likely that the opposition of Robert Cecil and the dean proved overwhelming.

THE 1630S: WESTMINSTER AND THE REORGANIZATION OF
METROPOLITAN GOVERNMENT

The anomalies of Westminster's existing government, and the consequent pressure for incorporation, would not disappear, however. For example, a Jacobean petition for a separate Westminster sessions complained that the authority of the Court of Burgesses was overthrown every time the Middlesex sessions summoned Westminster officers to it, and that Westminster's government could not be 'perfect and plenary' without its own commission of the peace (which was indeed finally established in 1618).[108] Westminster's spiralling population and attendant social problems continued to cause concern, and by the early 1630s the call for incorporation was being made once more.

The 1630s were remarkable as the first time since the reign of Henry VIII that the Crown seems to have contemplated a significant reform to structures of government in

---

105 WAM 6586, ff. 3, 16 (marginal notes). The fact that the paper described below (*HMC Hatfield*, XXII, 289–90) describes a petition drawn up 'without the consent of the Dean *and burgesses*' further implies that at least the majority of the burgesses were among those 'chiffest persons' who wrote to the Attorney General.

106 It is also likely that the City of London would have been opposed to the creation of such a rival jurisdiction.

107 Among the Hatfield papers (MS 109/86) is an undated paper entitled 'A brief of such privileges and grants as is desired to be granted from the King unto the meanest sort of people in Westminster without the consent of the Dean and burgesses'. This is essentially a summary of the points in WAM 6561, pp. 5–7. The editor of *HMC Hatfield* (XXII, 289–90) dates this document tentatively to 1636, but it seems more logical to assume that it is a debating paper presented to the first earl in 1607, rather than to the second earl, who did not succeed to his father's position of high steward.

108 WAM 6562, f. 1r–v.

the area. One important impulse behind this shift seems to have been specific royal concerns over the inability of Westminster's existing government to control disorder and disease effectively.[109] In 1631–32 Westminster's authorities were soundly chided for their lack of energy in implementing the new Book of Orders. Separate Privy Council letters addressed to Westminster's JPs and to the dean and chapter complained that

> hereabouts, where his Ma[jes]tie is most resident and the number is greater of those that are in authority and ought to see reformacion, there is more abundance of such kinde of people [vagrants] and less care taken for the execution of the Lawes and good orders provided in that behalfe then in other places more remote, which is a great scandal to Justice, whereof even strangers doe take notice to the disgrace of our nacion.[110]

The Privy Council registered constant complaints in this period about the personal inconvenience caused to the King as a Westminster householder by vagrancy, new building and air pollution in the area around Whitehall Palace.[111] In a meeting of November 1633 the Privy Council expressed particular concern over new buildings and the growth of 'disorderly people' when recommending the 'establishing . . . an uniforme government in the cittie and suburbs, both for the markets & for the wel ordering of trades; and for al things belonging to the policie of a wel disposed bodie to be under one command'. The specific proposal was that all of the metropolis be absorbed within 'the two incorporations of London & Westminster'.[112]

What emerged was the much-watered-down phenomenon known to historians as the 'New Incorporation of the Suburbs'. This reflected overridingly economic concerns and made little attempt to erect a new form of political government for the area.[113] Clearly, if the Crown had briefly contemplated a rationalization of Westminster's governmental anomalies, it had soon retreated. Nevertheless, previous accounts of the 'New Incorporation' have downplayed long-running concerns over social disorder, and have also passed over the Westminster context of these negotiations. In fact, this limited form of economic incorporation was implemented only after the failure of a very different campaign for a separate political incorporation of the city of Westminster, and after prolonged pressure from the Abbey to protect its interests against the proposed 'New Incorporation'.

The proposed corporation of Westminster, apparently submitted in 1633, is an intriguing project.[114] It is striking that (unlike the incorporation attempts of 1585

---

109 For the impact of disease in this period see below, ch. 8.

110 TNA, PC2/41, pp. 374, 467.

111 TNA, PC2/42, pp. 78, 220, 255, 259; P.C. 2/43, p. 239. See also below, ch. 6.

112 TNA, SP16/250/51.

113 V.L. Pearl, *London and the Outbreak of the Puritan Revolution* (Oxford, 1961), pp. 33–7; Johnson, *Southwark*, pp. 314–16.

114 The proposal, with comments by Dean Williams, survives in a contemporary copy as WAM 6561, pp. 1–4, on which see below. The surviving evidence for this campaign is difficult to interpret – many of the crucial documents are undated, and they have often been confused by historians with

and 1607) the 1633 proposal seems to have been drawn up with the active, even enthusiastic, co-operation of the dean and chapter.[115] According to Dean Williams's later testimony, this incorporation plan was proposed to him by some of the inhabitants of Westminster 'for the better reiglinge of their Inmates & imployinge of their poore'.[116] The proposal seems to represent what would ultimately be a cautious extension of the 1585 Act. Rather than a new corporation, this would take the form of 'a Charter Supplemental' to the previous act. A new, perpetual town government would be created; it would be 'a full and perfect Corporacon', licensed to purchase and receive lands to the value of at least £200 a year for the public use of the corporation. It would have the power to admit freemen or members of the liberty or corporation and 'to exclude all others that intrude upon them to overcharge and impoverish their whole liberties, and to overthrow the good orders there established'. It would have its own commission of the peace[117] with two chief burgesses, for whom a certain amount of civic pageantry would be provided: 'for the better and more ornament for their persons and respect for their places' they would have two serjeants or mace-bearers 'carrying little Maces before them when they walke abroad'. A common seal would also be provided.

While some of the trappings of civic identity would therefore be provided, this was nevertheless a rather limited, clerical form of incorporation which would still preserve the powers of the dean and chapter. The new Corporation would be comprised of the dean and chapter, the high steward, bailiff, twelve burgesses and twelve assistants – in other words, precisely the personnel of the Court of Burgesses. The dean would appoint all the officers of the corporation, including the recorder, coroner and clerk of the market. No mention was made of elections to the Court of Burgesses, but, since the proposal was merely for letters patent supplemental to the 1585 act, its members were presumably still to be selected by the dean. Many of the principal features of the 1607 incorporation proposal were therefore absent: no chamberlain, no high bailiffs, no change in the selection of town officials, no court of record, no power to make apprentices, no new markets or gaol and no selection of MPs by the corporation. The reality of this proposed corporation was made starkly evident in the final sentence of the proposal, which claimed that the inhabitants did not want the extra expense of a new corporation but instead 'with more advantage doe desire to shelter themselves under the shadowe of the Church and their highe Steward for the time'. Such wording was clearly calculated to procure the dean's assent, and heightens

the 'New Incorporation of the Suburbs' which was implemented in 1636. It is, however, possible to reconstruct the essence of what seems to have been proposed.

115 This is especially ironic as its promoters seem to have included at least one person – George Hulbert – who had been involved in the petition against Dean Williams over the disputed parliamentary election of 1621: Surrey History Centre, LM/1989; WAC, F3 (1635–36).

116 WAM 25095.

117 Westminster came under the jurisdiction of the Middlesex justices of the peace, although a separate subdivision for Westminster had been established in 1618: see below, ch. 7.

the suspicion that this proposed incorporation was the work of those Westminster notables who had always enjoyed a close working relationship with the Abbey. The lack of significant changes to existing authorities in the area may also have been crucial to securing the support of the high steward.

It is easy to see why Dean Williams was happy to endorse this proposed corporation 'under the shadowe of the Church'. He recommended that a petition be drawn up with the advice of the famous lawyer John Selden, the Westminster recorder, Edward Herbert, and one 'Mr Mason'.[118] It might then be submitted to the King via the earl of Pembroke and Montgomery, who was not only Westminster's current high steward but also the lord chamberlain. The earl's petition to the King, on behalf of the collegiate church and inhabitants of Westminster, still survives. It requests a 'perpetuall succession of Magistracie with like power of punishing offenders, with like priviledges, as other your Majesties Townes Corporate within this yor Kingdome', but stresses the qualification 'the right of the said Church being allwaies preserved'.[119]

The sudden conversion of the dean of Westminster to the benefits of a corporation – even in this highly moderated form – is not difficult to explain. The previous year had seen a series of exchanges between the Privy Council and the City of London over the need to deal with disorders in the suburbs. The Privy Council had specifically proposed that 'part of the suburbs' should be incorporated within the City of London, or that a new incorporation of tradesmen and artificers covering all the liberties and outparishes should be created.[120] In the face of this threat, the dean was understandably anxious to pre-empt the absorption of Westminster within a larger incorporation. One solution would be to obtain a separate incorporation for Westminster, but under the strict control of the Abbey. Soon after, Williams's political enemies among the Westminster prebendaries would accuse him of plotting a 'treaty' with the townspeople. According to this highly slanted account, Williams had acted without consulting the chapter, partly in order to form a corporation which would then undermine the authority and reputation of the Abbey. On this charge at least there is no reason to doubt Williams's innocence, and the justice of his claim that by the proposed scheme the 'royalties and liberties' of the church were left 'full and compleat, in the hands of the Church'.[121]

Nothing seems to have resulted from this proposed corporation 'under the shadowe of the Church' and the 1633–34 accounts for St Margaret's sadly recorded the parish

---

118 TNA, SP16/342/44.

119 As Williams was urging the presentation of the petition in 1633, it seems reasonable to date this otherwise undated petition to 1633, rather than the 1636 suggested in *CSPD 1636–37*, p. 315.

120 Pearl, *London*, p. 33; Johnson, *Southwark*, pp. 314–15.

121 WAM 25095. The contemporary copy of the proposal and of Williams's comments on it (WAM 6561, pp. 1–4) would seem to have been made in pursuit of this charge against Williams in 1635. The copy of the dean and chapter's objections to the 1607 incorporation, which are appended to this document and described as the reasons 'against a like Corporation formerly projected anno 1607', represents a mischievous and unwarranted attempt to equate two entirely different proposed corporations, presumably the better to support the charge against Williams.

outlay 'for our part of the Charges towards th'obteyning of a Corporacion for the Citie and liberties, wherein, nevertheless, wee lost our endeavor'.[122] Instead in 1636 the better-known 'New Incorporation of the Suburbs' was finally established. But this did not occur without the outraged protests of the dean and chapter, who did all that they could to oppose the scheme. Their protests drawn up against 'the New Intended Corporation of the City of Westminster . . . in such forme & manner as is *nowe desired* also make it clear that, at least as it was first proposed, the 'New Incorporation of the Suburbs' probably aimed at far more wide-ranging powers than those that ultimately emerged.[123] Amid doleful warnings of the dangers of corporations erecting 'popular Governments' whose 'Insolencyes' would later need to be suppressed, the dean and chapter protested that all their privileges and powers of nomination would be 'suppressed and trod underfoot'. It seems clear that the proposed new incorporation made no explicit allowance for the preservation of other powers and jurisdictions, except for a clause which specified only that it would not violate any of the liberties and privileges of the City of London.[124] The dean and chapter undoubtedly feared that as a consequence the form of government established in Westminster by the 1585 Act would be completely overthrown. Accordingly, they therefore rehearsed many of their objections to the 1607 incorporation, and they sounded a truly apocalyptic note:

> the priviledges granted to the Church by so many Kings and Queenes of England must all bee subverted, the profits of the Church diminished and their Rents delapidated, their officers dishonoured and displaced, and many of them Quite undone, and the Authority of the Dean and Chapter must bee shut up within the wall of the Church yard, or the Gates of their Cloysters.[125]

The complaints of the dean and chapter may partly account for the rather weak and half-hearted nature of the eventual Incorporation of the suburbs, which finally stipulated that the jurisdictions and 'formes of government already established' in Westminster as well as the other suburbs were to remain intact, as were also the 'libertyes, priviledges imunities' and other rights granted to the dean and chapter 'or lawfully used by them and their high Steward'.[126] The dean and chapter still sought to exclude Westminster altogether from the new incorporation, protesting now at the problem of overlapping jurisdictions. Moreover, as the government of Westminster had

---

122 WAC, E18, payments 1633–34, n.f. Cf. F3 (1635–36); F2002, ff. 101, 103v.

123 Italics mine. The dean and chapter's protests are recorded in WAM 6559.

124 The dean and chapter noted this by shrewdly drawing attention to the fact that, unlike the 1585 Act, the bill included no 'salvo' for preserving the 'ancient power and Jurisdicon of the Steward Marshall and Coroner of his Majestyes Houshold': WAM 6559, p. 3. This was an astute point to have raised at the time when Charles was concerned with the authority of the new Palace Court: see Greene, 'Court', p. 279.

125 WAM 6559, p. 3.

126 WAM 6558. The desire to underline its separate status may also explain why, in 1636–37, St Margaret's paid 18s to a goldsmith for cutting a silver seal 'with the Armes of this Towne', WAC, E20 (1636–37), n.f.

already been established by an Act of Parliament, they insisted, its case was therefore 'quite different from any other parte of the Suburbes'.[127]

In the event, Westminster *was* included within the New Incorporation of the Suburbs, although the fact that the governor of the New Incorporation was Peter Heywood, a friend of the Abbey, may have provided some reassurance. While the new Corporation stirred up major opposition from the City of London it does not appear to have had a significant impact on the suburbs themselves, with many reluctant to enrol with the new corporations, and the new Corporation soon fell into abeyance with the calling of the Long Parliament.[128]

The New Incorporation did little, then, to change how Westminster was governed. The Caroline government had ultimately rejected both a wide-ranging political incorporation of Westminster along with the other suburbs, and also the low-key incorporation of the City of Westminster 'under the shadowe of the Church'. As in the past, the Crown had been unwilling to see the development of an independent government in Westminster. The 1630s had instead witnessed an increasing level of Crown involvement in the area, and the breakdown of the dean's relations with the king over a range of issues. This resulted in Williams's effective banishment from the area and his public suspension in 1637, with the administrative affairs of the Abbey passing into the hands of the Crown.[129] Nevertheless, for all this interference, the Crown had still made little attempt to address the fundamental structural weakness of town government in Westminster. By 1640, Charles I seems to have grasped the dangers of this state of affairs. As royal authority crumbled more generally and protests became more threatening in 1640, the Privy Council anxiously ordered the burgesses to secure public order in the area. It was rather late in the day, however, to will the Court of Burgesses to act as an effective civic government.[130]

The century that followed the Henrician 'revolution' in Westminster witnessed a remarkable degree of administrative conservatism. Unresolved issues and anomalies thrown up by the ad hoc reforms of the 1530s became gradually entrenched. While some of the Abbey's powers were diminished, the dean and chapter hung on with remarkable resilience to much of the control of daily government in the locality. The

---

127 WAM 6560.

128 For the details and fortunes of the New Incorporation see TNA, SP16/318/44; Pearl, *London*, pp. 34–5; Johnson, *Southwark*, pp. 314–16; Bodl., Bankes MSS 12/46 (a draft of the terms of incorporation from which a bill was to be prepared for the King's signature); J.F. Larkin (ed.), *Stuart Royal Proclamations* (2 vols., Oxford, 1983), II, 234.

129 Hacket, *Scrinia*, pt ii, 89, 90, 132. Charles showed little hesitation, after Williams's suspension, in subduing the Abbey as he saw fit, peremptorily claiming the right to appoint all Abbey officers and to dispose of all the Abbey's fines and leases 'according to our royal will and pleasure': WAM, Chapter Act Bk II, f. 64v. WAM 25109 is a memorandum of the appointment of the royal commission to hold a visitation of Westminster college (25 January 1636/7). See also TNA, PC2/50, p. 232 (3 April 1639), which documents the allocation of a prebendal house by the Privy Council commission for the visitation of the Abbey.

130 TNA, PC2/52, p. 568 (21 June 1640).

social problems created by the rapid pace of urbanization presented a strong case for full-scale reform of Westminster's government. But the Crown, with its close links to Westminster's deans and high stewards, was usually prepared to listen to the Abbey's complaints that such reforms would threaten its status. By 1640 Westminster was one of the greatest administrative anomalies in the kingdom. It was a town whose population was many times greater than that of most provincial urban communities, but which had not been granted the corporate status that these lesser provincial centres enjoyed, despite at least three official attempts to procure it.

There was clearly the kernel of a corporate, civic identity in Westminster, with its title of 'city', its Court of Burgesses, its parliamentary representatives and coat of arms. But this was a city that was largely stillborn, with the aspirations of those townspeople who had pushed for incorporation in 1607 ultimately frustrated. Authority, status and administration therefore became concentrated within its separate parishes. As the greater authorities of Crown and dean and chapter stymied further action, it fell to parochial elites to assume the burdensome administration of the would-be City of Westminster. It is these elites who will be the focus of the next chapter.

Chapter 4

—◆—

Parish elites

THUS far we have examined the degree to which political power in Westminster was wielded by the Crown, the Abbey and powerful courtier families such as the Cecils. As we have seen, the exact balance of power might vary, but the net effect was to leave Westminster without larger civic institutions to govern its increasingly diverse and expanding population. The 'townspeople' have so far appeared as a frustrated, amorphous voice – villified as a group seeking the incorporation of the town. But the locality hardly provided a forum in which 'townspeople' might be said to be constituted – all the less so with the failure of attempts at incorporation.[1] Instead, Westminster residents came together principally within their respective parishes, and it was parochial structures which shaped their daily lives. It is at the parish level, then, that we must seek the urban notables who governed the area.

Westminster's local governors played a substantial role in the area, yet they have remained largely anonymous, despite the fact that they undertook many of the same tasks as London's more celebrated civic elite. If day-to-day government in Westminster was essentially parish government, it was nevertheless the case that the parishes concerned were increasingly large and important, with their officials commanding substantial wealth and influence. Indeed, the power wielded by Westminster's vestries was so enormous that by the eighteenth century they came under a national spotlight in parliament, as a series of legal cases challenged the power and legitimacy of what were seen as oligarchical and sometimes corrupt organizations.[2]

---

1 The manor of Westminster is poorly documented after 1514. Even in the late medieval period, Rosser has demonstrated how the institutions of the guild and the parish were becoming more prominent in local government, a trend that intensified during the sixteenth century for a number of reasons. The creation of the Court of Burgesses would have further weakened the prominence and significance of manorial institutions.

2 Webbs, *Parish and County*, pp. 236–8, 244–5, 253–5, 257–61, 266. Cf. J. Innes, 'Managing the metropolis: London's social problems and their control, c.1660–1830' in P. Clark and R. Gillespie (eds.), *Two Capitals; London and Dublin 1500–1800* (Oxford, 2002), p. 67, n.48 and I. Archer, 'Government in early modern London: the challenge of the suburbs', in *ibid.*, p. 145.

This chapter will examine those individuals who wielded the most influence at this decisive level of local government. Initially, it will chart the rise of the vestries which would later acquire so notorious a reputation for oligarchical control. Secondly, it will analyse the social identity of these parish elites, charting their interactions with each other, and also with the larger institutions of Abbey and Crown. Finally, it will tackle the broader issues of authority and responsibility among these local governors. How were they able to legitimize their role and maintain their authority, particularly in their dealings with the more socially elevated individuals and high-profile institutions located in their midst?

THE PARAMETERS OF PARISH OFFICE

Historians have long seen the sixteenth century as a key period in the development of the English parish. Both the growth of the state and the policing of Reformation religious policy required parishes to assume new powers and responsibilities.[3] In Westminster, for example, the need to respond to changing religious policy seems to have prompted the growth of more formal self-government in St Martin's parish. But the parishes of Westminster developed an importance far beyond that which is usually attributed to parochial organizations. Indeed, they exercised powers that were usually the preserve of civic government in London, or of county government in other areas of the country. Each Westminster parish, for example, assessed and collected the subsidy, a task undertaken by the ward in London, while the government negotiated separately with each Westminster parish over purveyance, which was otherwise organized on a county basis.[4]

If Westminster parishes performed far more tasks than was customary, so the workload was correspondingly heavy for the key officials responsible for them: the churchwardens. By the sixteenth century, this ancient office encompassed overlapping ecclesiastical and secular spheres. Churchwardens' tasks included managing parish finances, maintaining religious and moral order and, as secular officers of the parish, implementing certain government legislation. As elsewhere, Westminster's churchwardens were required to undertake an array of tasks related to the increasing use of the parish as a unit of civil administration. These ranged from organizing special levies for maimed soldiers, prisoners and houses of correction and support of the militia, to the maintenance of highways and bridges, the presenting of recusants and the collection of rates.[5] Churchwardens in the Westminster parishes would have been additionally

---

3 Webbs, *Parish and County*, pp. 9–41; D. Palliser, 'Introduction: the parish in perspective' in
   S. Wright (ed.), *Parish, Church and People* (1988); B. Kumin, *The Shaping of a Community* (Aldershot, 1996); J. Youings, *Sixteenth-century England* (Harmondsworth, 1984), pp. 338–9; N.G. Pounds, *A History of the English Parish* (Cambridge, 2000).

4 Kitto, pp. 437, 581–2; WAC, F2, vol. 1, f. 73; F2, vol. 2, f. 378; F3 (1628–29), n.f. Cf. WAC, E2413, f. 8.

5 Webbs, *Parish and County*, pp. 20–5. The Webbs suggest (p. 22) that London churchwardens were always elected by the vestry, but churchwardens predate vestries. For the office elsewhere see

burdened by the sheer size and populousness of their parishes, especially from the late sixteenth century. Parish litigation also occupied an increasing amount of the church-wardens' time as lawsuits arose over illegal building, unpaid taxes and the management of bequests.[6]

The different jurisdictions operating in Westminster also complicated parochial administration. For secular tasks, all parishes tended to be responsible to the Middle-sex justices. For ecclesiastical matters, as we have seen, this was not the case. Instead, from Elizabeth's reign onwards, St Margaret's churchwardens dealt directly with the Abbey via the archdeacon of Westminster. By contrast, St Clement's and St Martin's wardens came under the authority of the bishop of London, and were sworn in yearly before the archdeacon of Middlesex at St Clement's church. As a consequence, matters of religious conformity and moral regulation might be tackled in very different ways in neighbouring parishes.[7]

The churchwardens were thus situated near the sharp end of parish administration, but they formed part of a larger network of parish office-holders that included overseers of the poor, constables, scavengers and surveyors of the highways. Churchwardens in Westminster had usually risen through the ranks to their current positions. At St Martin's, for example, higher office was almost always preceded by office-holding at a lower level. The vast majority of churchwardens there served first as overseers of the poor – a position of financial and moral responsibility that demanded a thorough knowledge of the local community.[8] Similarly, virtually every churchwarden at St Margaret's in the Elizabethan and Jacobean periods had first held office as overseer or collector for the poor, including even those men of somewhat higher social status who became MPs for Westminster – a pattern still observable as late as 1640.[9] In practice, such a system held the advantage of ensuring that churchwardens possessed considerable administrative experience, as well as being known to more senior parish officials.

E. Carlson, 'The origins, function and status of churchwardens, with special reference to the diocese of Ely' in M. Spufford (ed.), *The World of Rural Dissenters, 1520–1725* (Cambridge, 1995), pp. 164–207.

6 Often the wardens held these responsibilities jointly with the parish constables. In St Martin's, however, it is notable that many tasks assigned elsewhere to the constables were here undertaken or supervised by the churchwardens, such as the collection of moneys to support houses of correction, maintain bridges and pay for compensation related to the practice of hue and cry, J. Kent, *The English Village Constable 1580–1642* (Oxford, 1986), pp. 45–7; WAC, F2 vol. 2, ff. 239, 284; 22 Hen. VIII c. 5; F2, vol. 2, ff. 196, 208, 217; Kitto, p. 254. For the escalating workload see WAC, F2002, f. 36v.

7 E.g. Kitto, pp. 191, 239. On procedure at visitations see also K. Fincham, *Visitation Articles and Injunctions of the Early Stuart Church* (2 vols., Church of England Record Society 1 & 5 (1994, 1998), 1, xiv, xxii; M. Ingram, *Church Courts, Sex and Marriage in England, 1570–1640* (Cambridge, 1987), pp. 44–6, 324–9, 345–9.

8 Between 1600 and 1625, 75 per cent of all churchwardens served as overseers of the poor, i.e. seventeen out of twenty-three. Overseers' accounts are missing for seven years from 1574 to 1625, which might have increased this percentage: WAC, F301–350.

9 Based on analysis of WAC, E4, E5, E6, E8, E13, E14; E144–152. William Bell, an MP in 1640, had earlier served as overseer of the poor.

The range of lesser parochial offices available to male residents may also have helped to promote social stability by integrating a broader cross-section of the community into local government.[10] Certainly, Westminster's parishes in the late Elizabethan period seem to have provided healthy office-holding ratios. In 1600, 40 per cent of all St Martin's subsidy-payers either had held or would go on to hold office as overseer of the poor, churchwarden or vestryman.[11] The ratio of offices to householders was also a favourable one at the beginning of the seventeenth century. In 1605, approximately fifty-two local offices existed in St Martin's, creating a ratio of one office for every 6.5 householders.[12] But the size of the parochial bureaucracy did not keep pace with the parish's rapid population increase, which reduced these ratios to 1 in 12 by 1619.[13] Evidence for the more populous St Margaret's parish suggests that it was better served by parish officers during the Elizabethan period, but that it too failed to create significant numbers of new offices to deal with its burgeoning population.[14] Yet calculation of ratios can be seriously misleading: not all householders would be eligible for these positions at any one point in time, and many were held by single individuals in progression.

Finally, another reason why office-holding at these levels gives a misleading impression of participation in parochial government lies in the fact that, as parish government was increasingly formalized, so these minor officials were overshadowed by the increasing importance of the parish vestry.

THE EMERGENCE OF THE WESTMINSTER VESTRIES

The emergence of vestries is one of the most important developments in early modern urban communities. Throughout the country, the post-Reformation period witnessed the development of parish vestries, which concentrated power in the hands of a small elite. In London, as well as in other larger towns, these were often 'closed' vestries,

10 V. Pearl, 'Stability and change in seventeenth century London', *London Journal* 5 (1979), pp. 15–17; Boulton, pp. 263–8; S. Rappaport, *Worlds Within Worlds* (Cambridge, 1989), pp. 182–3.

11 TNA, E179/142/235. I have excluded constables and scavengers – offices for which complete lists of office-holders do not survive.

12 WAC, F332. The number of offices may have varied slightly, but I have counted the following as officers: vestrymen, churchwardens, sidesmen, vestry clerk, parish clerk, schoolmaster, beadles, sextons, parish herdsman, assessors for hay, overseers for the poor, constables, scavengers, surveyors for the highways, bearers, rakers, Westminster burgesses and assistants, and the bailiff and under-bailiff of Westminster. Jurors were also selected from the parish to serve at the Middlesex (and later, Westminster) Sessions and the Westminster Court of Burgesses (e.g. WAC, WCBI, f. 265).

13 WAC, F346. During the period 1603–25 the parish experienced a threefold increase in population, but acquired only one additional constable, beadle and sexton, and for the year 1625, a third churchwarden: WAC, F2001, ff. 114v, 135v; F2002, f. 36v.

14 In 1588 St Margaret's had twenty-seven sidesmen alone: WAC, E2413, pt 1 f. 10. During the Elizabethan period St Margaret's enjoyed twice St Martin's ratio of constables to householders: Archer, p. 225.

which were self-electing, as opposed to the more open parish meetings that had theoretically regulated medieval parish business.[15] In the capital, faculties for vestries were
increasingly granted by the bishops of London during the Jacobean period. By the
1630s, however, the ecclesiastical authorities were so concerned by vestries as an
intrusion of lay power into religious affairs that an official investigation into the origins and structure of the capital's vestries took place.[16] Nevertheless, Westminster's
vestries continued to grow in importance, and the origins of these unelected bodies
became an increasingly contentious matter in the eighteenth century. Indeed, in the
1790s the volume documenting the existence of St Martin's Elizabethan vestry was
apparently hidden away in the roof of the parish church to prevent its appearance in a
court case challenging the powers of the current select vestry.[17]

As Westminster's vestries were to become a byword, either for oligarchic corruption or lay intrusion,[18] it is particularly important to trace their disputed origins, and
to uncover the manner of their development. As we shall see, while it is indisputable
that they represented the emergence of more oligarchic forms of parish government, a
number of different forces lay behind the vestries' appearance and consolidation. It is
unhelpful simply to view their emergence as evidence of a deliberate strategy whereby
a small elite overthrew traditions of medieval communality. In the case of the Westminster parishes, vestries seem to represent the formalization of the powers of pre-
existing parish elites in the face of increasing administrative burdens and the social
pressures associated with the town's expansion. It is this relatively silent transition
which may help to explain why later arguments over the origins of Westminster's
vestries were so difficult to resolve.

We shall begin with St Martin's parish. Here, the crucial transition would
appear to have taken place in the 1550s and partly reveals itself through the changing
process by which churchwardens were elected. The churchwardens' accounts, which
survive from 1525, show that normally two new churchwardens took office every
two years. Until 1546, the wardens of the parish were said to be 'electe and chosen
by consent of the hole bodie of the same parishe'.[19] From 1546 to 1583, however,
the wardens are described simply as 'chosen and appointed'. The body responsible
for this choice is not recorded until 1583, when the wardens are said to be elected

15 Archer, pp. 69–74; Webbs, *Parish and County*, pp. 37–40; Kumin, *Shaping*, pp. 250–55.

16 For St Martin's return see LPL, Carte Misc. 7/79/5. No returns survive for St Clement Danes or St
    Margaret's.

17 Webbs, *Parish and County*, p. 261 n.1 (see also pp. 184, 196, 236–7, 243–5, 248–9, 250,
    253–5, 257–61, 266). Cf. P. Seaward, 'Gilbert Sheldon, the London vestries and the defence of
    the Church' in T. Harris, P. Seaward and M. Goldie (eds.), *The Politics of Religion in Restoration
    England* (Oxford, 1990), pp. 49–73.

18 The Webbs exempt the parish of St George Hanover Square from this general picture of vestry
    corruption in Westminster: Webbs, *Parish and County*, pp. 240–1, 245.

19 Kitto, pp. 21, 58. Two-year terms of office for churchwardens became the norm in the City during
    the fifteenth century: *London VCH*, p. 224.

by the 'masters of the parish'. The use of the term 'vestry' for the appointing body first occurs in 1588, after which time the vestry, usually in consultation with the vicar, selected new churchwardens.[20]

Similarly, the very process of producing formal churchwardens' accounts is related to the development of a small governing body within St Martin's parish. The creation of a more formal body seems to have resulted from concern over financial procedure combined with the need to respond to the religious changes of the Reformation period. Changes to church furniture and fabric, to the conduct of divine service, the need to draft responses to government enquiries about church property and the sale of church goods – all put a tremendous burden on parish administration and decision-making.[21] The question of responsibility undoubtedly loomed large in those times of shifting political and religious allegiances. Not surprisingly, then, the emergence of a group formally recognized as acting on behalf of the St Martin's parishioners took place gradually during the 1550s.

The turning point came in 1553 when, as we have seen, Dean Weston of Westminster supervised an audit of St Martin's parish accounts covering the previous fifty years. The audit was conducted by a committee of twenty-five men. The parishioners who signed the audited accounts were mainly former churchwardens, but those auditors who had not served became part of a pool from which future wardens were selected. Thereafter, parish accounts were always signed and 'allowed' by a group of named parishioners. The introduction of collective responsibility in the parish also coincided with increasing references to the 'masters of the parish'. It was this group, rather than individual churchwardens, who now shouldered the collective burden of controversial decisions and monitored the expenditure of funds.[22]

Vestries are generally seen as a post-Reformation phenomenon, although there is little doubt that medieval parishes depended on their 'chief parishioners' to carry out many duties. The term 'vestry' was used as early as 1507 in the London parish of St Christopher le Stocks, but in general post-Reformation vestries gained a higher profile as they undertook the wider range of tasks increasingly allocated to the Tudor parish by parliamentary statute. Certainly Bishop Grindal used the term in 1567 in a circular letter to the London clergy when its meaning must already have been clear.[23] At St Martin's, the term 'vestry' seems to have been used interchangeably with 'masters of the parish' until the 1580s, and the latter phrase lingered on in use for at least another twenty years. It is only possible to trace the existence of St Martin's vestry as a formal body, with regular meetings and clearly defined membership, from the late Elizabethan

20 Kitto, pp. 352, 399.

21 Cf. M. Carlin, *Medieval Southwark* (1996), p. 98.

22 Kitto, pp. 137, 150. See above, ch.2.

23 Webbs, *Parish and County*, pp. 38–9n.

period, since a continuous sequence of vestry minutes survives only from the 1590s. Although lists of Elizabethan vestrymen do not survive, it appears that these 'masters of the parish' were mostly former churchwardens.[24]

While it is thus possible to observe the working of a *cursus honorum* from church-warden to vestryman in St Martin's, it is notable that during this period St Martin's vestry also included a sprinkling of gentlemen as members, who did not work their way through the ranks. The prosperous landowner Thomas Poultney is an interesting case in point. By the time of his death in 1594 he was a vestryman, yet he had earlier refused to serve as churchwarden when elected.[25] The inclusion of prosperous gentle-men such as Poultney is remarkable in itself: parochial government was normally considered the preserve of the middling sort, and the bureaucratic character of paro-chial administration might have made it seem more appropriate for those of non-gentle status. While gentlemen might be expected to exert an unofficial role in the locality, it is striking that throughout this period several gentlemen played a signifi-cant role on the vestry.[26] A figure like Poultney was presumably admitted to the vestry as a courtesy to a large local landowner: there is little evidence to show that he took an active part in parish affairs.[27] But other gentlemen parishioners, as we shall see, played a more prominent role in St Martin's vestry.

More broadly, the Jacobean period saw what one might call the 'professionalization' of St Martin's vestry. The functioning of the body was put on a more formal footing and its meetings became more frequent as the sheer weight of parochial business increased exponentially. It is notable, then, that the first list of St Martin's vestrymen (a body of twenty-four men) dates from 1606, while from 1607 the names of those attending vestry meetings were now regularly recorded.[28] A vestry minute of 1609 specifically stated that the vestry was the body responsible for allowing the church-wardens' accounts – presumably narrowing what appears to have been a wider choice of auditors from among parishioners during the Elizabethan period.[29] It also became

24 The evidence is derived from those signing parish accounts and documents. Nevertheless, it is clear that vestrymen did not always sign the accounts. William Portington, for example, was one of four men elected to the vestry in October 1598, but his signature does not appear on accounts until 1608: WAC, F2001, ff. 95v, 34v; F2, vol. 1, f. 95.

25 *Register of St Martin in the Fields 1550–1619* (Harleian Society 25, 1898), p. 139.

26 This development in St Martin's, however, foreshadows the later structure of the vestry of St George Hanover Square (a parish carved out of St Martin's) during the eighteenth century, when the involvement of gentlemen or even peers marked out the area from the rest of the metropolis: Webbs, *Parish and County*, pp. 240–1.

27 The Webbs provide examples elsewhere in England of vestry office related to the occupation of certain lands. The vestry could also be treated as a representative body of ratepayers: Webbs, *Parish and County*, p. 215.

28 WAC, F2001, ff. 45, 46. The Webbs state that vestries were frequently composed of twenty-four men, perhaps a hold-over from manorial courts with their juries of twelve and twenty-four: Webbs, *Parish and County*, pp. 178–9, 215.

29 WAC, F2001, f. 57v.

the normal practice in the Jacobean period for only a few vestrymen to examine these accounts and the accompanying inventory of church goods, which were then officially 'allowed' by the vestry as a whole.[30]

It was during the Jacobean period, too, that the vestry became an increasingly narrow elite. Although twenty-four men were listed as vestrymen in 1606, by 1612 half of these men had died and they were not replaced. Power thus became concentrated in the hands of a few individuals, with a consistent group of twelve men signing parish documents by the 1610s. Any further deaths were replaced by recruitment from among recent churchwardens, but this was certainly not automatic, and not all churchwardens were elected to vestry membership.[31] While this development represented a narrowing of the vestry, there is no doubt that these men took upon themselves an extraordinary weight of business. At most meetings the vestry assigned particular tasks to small working groups of about four men, who would later report back to the vestry as whole – a substantial amount of year-round work for men who were also successful businessmen.

The vestry's dominance over all aspects of parochial business is increasingly clear.[32] This becomes most apparent in their relationship to St Martin's churchwardens, the officials so often designated by statute as responsible for implementing new laws at the parochial level. At St Martin's, however, churchwardens increasingly appear in a more subordinate role during the early decades of the seventeenth century, sometimes merely acting as assistants to individual vestrymen during special investigations. More generally, they merely implemented policies which had actually been decided upon in the vestry.[33] Indeed, the vestry ultimately insisted on the right to approve the allocation of every pew in the church, considering the matter too controversial to be determined by the churchwardens alone.[34] In the same way, the vestry drastically reduced the financial independence of churchwardens. In 1619 the vestry imposed a spending limit of 40s on the wardens, with larger expenditure forbidden unless specifically authorized by the vestry.[35] Such rigorous procedures stemmed partly from a series of financial disputes, but they also reflected an apparent belief that parochial affairs had now

---

30 E.g. 1607 and 1613: WAC, F2001, ff. 47v, 84.

31 *Ibid.*, ff. 45, 101, 132v, 155v.

32 This is not to imply that significant religious influence could not be wielded by parishioners who were not members of the vestry: see below, pp. 309–15.

33 Parallel changes had taken place at St Margaret's during the 1590s, a time-lag which presumably resulted from different patterns of population growth.

34 See below, ch. 6.

35 WAC, F2001, f. 128. The 40s limit appears to have been in force elsewhere in the capital, but even if the vestry was here formalizing existing practice, it forms part of a broader pattern of the increasing formalization of vestry control over churchwardens in St Martin's. It was ordered at the same meeting that new churchwardens must be bound to 'six of the most auntient of the vestry' to make a proper account of their expenditure (cf. f. 103). At a meeting in October 1634, however, it was decided that this regulation was insufficient. There was still an acute problem that some churchwardens were

become so financially complex and full of pitfalls that only management by an experienced committee could ultimately be trusted.[36]

At much the same time, the vestry increased its supervision of the overseers of the poor – parish officials who administered a yearly income in excess of £500. The vestry now regulated admission to parish almshouses, and controlled the allocation of pensions to poverty-stricken widows, invalids and orphans. As the competence and honesty of other lesser officials came under scrutiny in 1617, the new and heavier workload of the vestry was partly recognized when the wages of the vestry clerk were doubled 'in respect that the meetings held in the Vestry will hereafter be muche more frequent then heretofore'.[37] Vestry meetings were scheduled for the first Thursday of every month, but there could be as many as three meetings in a single month, and some of these could occupy an entire day.[38] Laconic entries in the vestry minutes such as 'Answere given to many peticions' also indicate that surviving records may greatly underestimate the breadth and intensity of vestry activity in the local community.[39]

There are few sources to tell us whether this consolidation of vestry power encountered much resistance from within the parish.[40] We can only speculate on how far other parishioners may have resented such oligarchical control. It is easier to trace the concerns of external authorities at this monopolizing of local power. Certainly the religious power of vestries in the metropolis as a whole came under scrutiny from Bishop Juxon in 1635–36. The chief concern was clearly the extent of religious authority exercised by laymen – but questions about the origins of vestries potentially queried the basis of their authority. St Martin's bland response to Juxon's enquiry simply avoided discussing the religious dimension of the vestry's activities, although this was considerable.[41] The parish's formal return also vastly downplayed the scope of vestry power overall. Instead, it maintained that the parish was ordered by the vicar and churchwardens, with twenty of 'our Auncienter Parishioners' merely

---

too poor to advance moneys on behalf of the parish, leading them to raid the parish stock. New types of bonds were therefore proposed for churchwardens – whatever their degree or quality – with the 'Ancientest Vestrymen', F2002, f. 102v.

36 Accusations of financial impropriety were levelled against the sexton, one of the beadles and the parish clerk in 1617, while a larger financial dispute connected with the rebuilding of St Martin's church a decade earlier finally came before Star Chamber in 1619, WAC, F2001, ff. 107v, 109v, 111r–v.

37 *Ibid.*, f. 109v.

38 WAC, F3 (1629–30). There were three meetings in the months of October 1619, April 1620, and March 1621, for example: F2001, ff. 116, 136v–138, 141–3, 149v–150. Vestry meetings may also be under-recorded, as the dispute with Coppin shows (see below).

39 WAC, F2002, f. 33; cf. f. 27v.

40 Archer (pp. 73–4) notes the difficulty of unearthing such material.

41 This aspect of the return and St Martin's tussles with the ecclesiastical authorities are discussed below, ch. 9. In May 1626, an earlier government inquiry into church fees had also sought information about 'how they held their vestry', WAC, F3, f. 7.

'assisting' them.[42] Parish documents, however, show quite clearly that in the 1620s and 1630s most parish business was conducted by a core of twelve vestrymen, with the churchwardens playing a very subordinate role. The episode highlights the degree to which the practicalities of parish government had led to the speedy evolution of new procedures, whereas the theoretical basis of parochial authority still lagged behind such realities. Vestrymen had to downplay their authority when responding to Juxon's inquisition, but in other contexts they were anxious to assert it, as we shall see.

In St Martin's, we have seen how the vestry emerged in a relatively undeveloped parish as it became more populous and also a more fashionable area. By contrast, early modern St Margaret's had inherited a long medieval tradition of parish government. In the absence of sophisticated structures of local government, townsmen had come to control much local administration through their membership in the many parish fraternities or as members of the abbot's manorial court. Indeed, parish, guild and manorial court all provided overlapping arenas in which local people might participate in neighbourhood affairs. Nevertheless, a clearly defined elite had emerged by at least the fifteenth century, and parish accounts of the early sixteenth century commonly refer to the 'worshypfull' of the parish.[43] This group would seem to be the same as that which regularly sat on the abbot's court in the early sixteenth century, a body which a contemporary petition described as being self-electing and including 'the grettest vitaylers . . . in the seid towne'.[44]

Although a parish elite clearly existed in pre-Reformation St Margaret's, it appears to have been fairly broadly based, and did not rigorously exclude others from participation in parish government. Parish accounts, for example, were approved by between fifteen and twenty-five named men 'with diverse others', who probably listened while the accounts were read aloud.[45] The experience of the Reformation period does not seem to have resulted in a dramatic narrowing of the ruling group at St Margaret's. Yet the dissolution of the fraternities inevitably reduced the opportunities for office-holding and for lay participation in this parallel arena. The energies that had previously been divided between parish and fraternity became more exclusively centred on the parish. The initiative which had been displayed by St Margaret's fraternities in dealing with local poverty, for example, now translated itself into parish-based schemes of social welfare.[46] Nevertheless, the parish continued to draw from a relatively large pool of applicants for various parochial offices.[47]

---

42 LPL, Carte Misc. 7/79/5. These vestry returns for London require careful and sceptical reading. For an example of another deeply misleading vestry return see P. Lake, *The Boxmaker's Revenge* (Manchester, 2001), pp. 316–22.

43 Rosser, pp. 234–6, 287, 290–1; WAC, E3, 1530–31.

44 Rosser, pp. 362–5. Dr Rosser suggests a date of 1511 for this petition.

45 E.g. WAC, E3 (1530–32, 1540–42).

46 See below, ch. 8; Merritt thesis, pp. 270–2.

47 Merritt thesis, pp. 175–6.

The Reformation did not serve to forge a governing elite at St Margaret's as it did at St Martin's, largely because such a group already existed. But changes in the distribution of power within the parish are evident from the mid-1570s. The period between 1576 and 1600, in particular, seems to have witnessed the consolidation of an elite group and the formation of a parish vestry. These changes were not dramatic, but they probably limited access to higher office, and gave more exclusive control over parochial finances to the vestry – decades before parallel moves at St Martin's. The first evidence of such a change dates from June 1576, when the curate and five parishioners formulated an order for the selection of future churchwardens. This order specified that only men who had formerly served as churchwardens were entitled to vote.[48] Thereafter, a group of about twelve men – almost all former churchwardens – regularly signed parish accounts. The 1580s, of course, saw the creation of the Court of Burgesses, and this may have heightened the sense of exclusivity that vestrymen possessed, since St Margaret's burgesses seem to have been chosen from among their number. By the 1590s, a series of orders were made, most of which restricted the powers of serving churchwardens while increasing those of the vestrymen.[49]

In 1593 a more detailed set of orders was promulgated by St Margaret's vestry 'for better government and benefyte for the Churche'. These orders included provisions which limited the financial freedom of the wardens and forbade them from altering church furniture and fabric without the consent of the vestry. The regulations also narrowed even further the pool of potential candidates for the office of churchwarden. This order may not have significantly altered the composition of the vestry, but it certainly indicates a tightening of the governing elite balanced by a desire to maintain at least the appearance of consensus.[50]

Other procedures were also modified in 1593 to increase the power of St Margaret's vestry. Sextons and clerks were now to be chosen by the vestry, with no involvement from the churchwardens. The 1593 orders also displayed a growing preoccupation with status, which emerged in relation to burial and pewing. For example, high constables, burgesses and vestrymen were specifically exempted from certain restrictions over pews. By contrast, similar privileges at St Martin's were extended to churchwardens, but made no mention of the extra-parochial offices of high constable or burgess.[51] It is difficult to cite any one reason why these changes should have occurred when they did at

---

48 WAC, E5 (1574–76). They were to choose two men from a list of six candidates. After these two were chosen, the vacancies of the candidates were filled by new men selected by the outgoing churchwardens.

49 WAC, E5 (1588–90), f. 27v. The term 'vestry' was in use by the 1580s (E5 (1586–87), f. 24), but no general term for the parish governors is to be found in parish documents in the early Elizabethan period.

50 WAC, E2413, pt 2, ff. 1–2; E5 (1574–76); Merritt thesis, pp. 177–8. Westlake states that a select vestry was formed at St Margaret's in 1590, but provides no evidence: H.F. Westlake, *St Margaret's Westminster* (1914), p. 80.

51 WAC, E5 (1588–90), f. 27v; E2413, pt 2 ff. 1–3v. For orders regulating church seating see below, ch. 7.

St Margaret's, but they seem to be related to that preoccupation with status and with the growing threat of poverty and disorder which marked the parish during the late Elizabethan period and led to the creation of the Court of Burgesses.[52]

The centralization of power in the hands of the vestry in Elizabethan St Margaret's in many ways foreshadowed developments in Jacobean St Martin's. Nevertheless, remnants of earlier, more inclusive procedures are still visible in the later ritual surrounding the selection of churchwardens. A detailed account from 1669 claimed that traditionally St Margaret's parishioners were warned of the impending election by a tolling bell on the Thursday before Whitsunday, whereupon they repaired to the church, where the minister and vestry were seated at a table in the chancel. Here the churchwardens' accounts were formally received by 'the ancient vestrymen', who then appointed some previous wardens to make a formal audit of the same accounts. The vestrymen would then adjourn to the vestryroom to elect the new churchwarden out of a list of former overseers of the poor. The name of whichever individual had gained the most votes was then announced by the Reader in the open church before the parishioners 'to the end they may have notice of the same'.[53] An even more abridged form of parochial elections survived in St Martin's. By the 1620s, the election at St Martin's actually took place more than a week before the public meeting. New parish officers were nominated at a vestry meeting and 'confirmed and allowed' at a further vestry meeting the following week, before being then 'published in the Churche at Morning prayer' on Easter Sunday.[54] Ultimately, what had once been a more open selection of office-holders by parishioners had become a mere formality, as the choice of candidates was removed both spatially (in St Margaret's) and temporally (in St Martin's) from the public gathering of the community.

PATRONAGE AND SOCIAL NETWORKS

ST MARTIN'S: THE CECIL NEXUS, THE KING'S WORKS
AND GENTRIFICATION

Thus far a pattern of emerging oligarchy within Westminster's parishes has been traced. But who were these men who participated in parish government? If parish government became more oligarchical, then was this an 'oligarchy' that operated in the pursuit of particular special interests? To answer this question we need to examine

---

52 See below, ch. 7.

53 Webbs, *Parish and County*, pp. 248–9. This account was composed as a result of a challenge in 1667 to the right of the vestrymen to select the churchwardens. Churchwardens' accounts for the early seventeenth century seem to record the votes taken by the vestry, with names of candidates listed followed by dots, which appear to represent votes: e.g. WAC, E6 (1603–04), (1605–06), f. 27v.

54 WAC, F2002, f. 28r–v.

who these parish officials were and to reconstitute their social networks. Occupational groupings, for example, could form the basis of significant social networks: occupational clusters were to be found in at least some parts of Westminster,[55] and the evidence from recognizances taken at the Middlesex sessions in the early seventeenth century suggests that occupation may ultimately have provided the most functionally important social bond, particularly among St Martin's parishioners.[56] Other forces could be significant – ties of patronage to the Court, or to the Abbey or to prominent aristocrats – while the very experience of office-holding might itself create significant social bonds between office-holders. As we shall see, the social world of parish officials reflected the larger developments at work within Westminster society. Once again, it is clear that the parishes displayed quite distinctive characteristics. In St Martin's, parish elites increasingly embodied newer trends in relation to the prominence of the royal Court and urban development. By contrast, parish officials at St Margaret's were associated with older economic and social interests, and parish identity there owed much to the character of the medieval vill of Westminster.

As an increasingly fashionable residential area, we might expect courtly figures and members of the gentry to play a major role in the running of the parish of St Martin's. As we will see, a handful did indeed play an important role. Nevertheless, in doing so they still operated within the multiple links of patronage, profession and economic interest which characterized the office-holders of the parish. To understand these complex ties it is most useful to begin with St Martin's churchwardens.[57] Churchwardens not only conducted the day-to-day parish business of parishes; they also formed a pool from which members of the vestry were selected. Between 1525 and 1625 the occupations of about 75 percent of the ninety-nine St Martin's churchwardens have been identified. These findings confirm many of the generalizations often made about the occupations mostly widely practised in Westminster.[58] Residents, for example, provided services to Crown servants, the Court and the gentry living in St Martin's.

55 A poll tax for part of St Margaret's parish from 1641, for example, suggests that, even among poorer groups, men such as porters often lived side by side: TNA, E179/253/10. This pattern also seems to have obtained in the parish of St Clement Danes.

56 See the analysis of LMA, WJ/SR (NS) 2/1–123 and LMA 1/29–81 in Merritt thesis, pp. 207–11. For use of similar evidence see Boulton, pp. 242–7; K. Wrightson and D. Levine, *Poverty and Piety in an English Village: Terling 1525–1700* (1979), pp. 101–3. For examples of professional solidarity among particular occupations see the activities of Westminster's shoemakers, cutlers and chandlers: BL, Lansdowne MS 21/30, 26/66 (shoemakers of Westminster to Lord Burghley, 1575 and 1578); C.W. Welch, *History of the Cutlers' Company of London* (2 vols., 1923), II, 193; LMA, WJ/SR (NS), 5/9.

57 While statistical analysis of churchwardens has been attempted, it has not been possible to make a similar meaningful analysis of vestrymen as (1) the full official membership is rarely stated; (2) patterns of attendance and workload could vary enormously between members; and (3) not all vestry meetings were recorded, making even a calculation of vestry attendance potentially misleading.

58 Rosser, pp. 119–66; M.J. Power, 'The east and the west in early modern London' in E.W. Ives, R.J. Knecht and J.J. Scarisbrick (eds.), *Wealth and Power in Tudor England* (1978), p. 183. I have used the occupational categories devised by A.L. Beier in his 'Engine of manufacture: the trades of

The clothing and victualling professions are well represented among churchwardens (eighteen), while five plied trades involving transport. Thirteen churchwardens were employed in the building trades, the largest single occupational grouping found among wardens. This prominence of men involved in the building trades seems to reflect a concentration of these occupations in St Martin's more generally. Certainly by the late Elizabethan period, the opportunities for legal and illegal building in the western part of the metropolis were considerable, while by the later seventeenth century craftsmen such as carpenters were important among the speculative developers who fuelled the expansion of the West End. Other St Martin's churchwardens in our period were employees of the Crown (twelve), but nine were so employed in connection with the Office of Works and five of these as officers of the King's Works, perhaps reinforcing the link between the Crown and the building trades.[59]

The Office of Works, which was such a force in St Martin's parish, was the organization responsible for building and maintaining royal palaces and fortifications throughout the country. The elite craftsmen and administrators employed by the King's Works figured prominently not only among churchwardens and other important officers (such as overseers of the poor) but also on St Martin's vestry itself. Indeed no other single group enjoyed such a high profile within parish government as a whole, and this Works connection was one of the most striking aspects of parochial government, especially in the Jacobean period. Among its leading parishioners, St Martin in the Fields numbered men holding the leading administrative posts in the King's Works throughout the period between the Reformation and the Civil War. These included offices such as the surveyor, comptroller, paymaster, master mason, chief joiner in the Tower of London, chief glazier, chief locksmith and the purveyors of the Works at Westminster and London. In addition, every master carpenter who served the Crown between 1519 and 1629 was also a prominent St Martin's parishioner.[60]

One reason why Works employees played such a dominant role among St Martin's officials was doubtless the financial experience that men such as the surveyor, comptroller and paymaster could bring to parish affairs. In addition, master craftsmen within the Works office would also have possessed sound financial experience partly derived from acting as their own purveyors.[61] In fact, developments in the conduct of financial affairs in the Works office closely mirrored the chronology of such changes in the administration of St Martin's parish. During the same decade – the 1550s – the Office of the King's Works, like St Martin's parish, also witnessed the development

---

London' in A.L. Beier and R. Finlay (eds.), *London 1500–1700: The Making of the Metropolis* (1986), p. 148. There is insufficient evidence to determine the occupational structure of the parish statistically.

59 Merritt thesis, pp. 188–9. E. McKellar, *The Birth of Modern London* (Manchester, 1999), pp. 97–104.

60 Occupational information derives primarily from parish records, wills and TNA, E351. *KW* III, pt I, pp. 406–12.

61 *KW* III, pt I, pp. 3, 18.

of collective financial responsibility. This was no coincidence. Many of the Works officers involved in the introduction of this system lived in St Martin's, and it was as parish notables that two successive master carpenters (John Russell and John Colbrand), along with the comptroller of the Works (Thomas Fowler), the sergeant painter (Nicholas Lizard) and the chief glazier (Peter Nicholson) developed a system which required 'masters of the parish' such as themselves to allow future expenditure and to sign parish accounts. Of course, other men besides officers of the Works signed these parish accounts, but the collective presence of these Works employees would doubtless have been significant. To Works officials serving as parish officers, it must have seemed natural to emulate good business procedure when transacting parish business.[62]

Officials of the King's Works were also in a position to offer regular, if short-term, employment to large numbers of local craftsmen and labourers. Indeed the Works office itself was located within the parish, at Scotland Yard. Not surprisingly, men connected with the King's Works played a major role whenever St Martin's parish church required repair or enlargement, most notably in 1542, the 1590s and 1606–9.[63] When St Martin's church was effectively rebuilt in 1606–9 the former Works' clerk, John Thorpe, surveyed the land for the new churchyard, and supervised the work on the church along with William Portington, the King's master carpenter. It was also decided that these two, 'men well experienced in Surveyinge and architecture shold make bargines for that work'.[64] Similarly, the decoration of the church interior was undertaken by the noted joiner Samuel Jeniver, who was a Works craftsman as well as a St Martin's parishioner.[65]

London historians are accustomed to tracing livery company involvement in parish government, but, as we have said, livery companies did not exist in Westminster. It is therefore tempting to see a parallel type of influence exerted in St Martin's by employees of the King's Works. The administrative duties required by parish and Works office also brought many of the same men together, merely wearing different hats. The ways in which such identities were blurred is suggested by parish documents which sometimes use official Works titles rather than an individual's surname. Thus a vestry minute of 1618 refers to 'Mr Carpenter', rather than Mr Portington, who was the King's master carpenter.[66] Similarly, in 1609, the monthly executive meetings of

---

62 *KW* III, pt I, pp. 3, 57–8, 407, 411–12; Kitto, pp. 158, 166, 178, 195. For the Russell family in Westminster see D.R. Ransome, 'Artisan dynasties in London and Westminster in the sixteenth century', *Guildhall Miscellany* II, 6 (1964).

63 Merritt thesis, pp. 226–8, 230–2, 238–9.

64 WAC, F2001, f. 45; TNA, STAC8/101/19. On this and subsequent occasions St Martin's benefited from its Works connections in many small, practical ways: F2002, f. 69. Building materials seem to have passed through the Works' waterside storeyard at Scotland: WAC, F2 vol. 1, ff. 163, 176.

65 He later served as a St Martin's overseer of the poor. Jeniver also worked on the Banqueting Hall at Whitehall Palace and Hatfield House: Merritt thesis, pp. 238–9.

66 WAC, F2001, f. 123.

King's Works' officers consisted of six men, five of whom were St Martin's parishioners. Of these five, two were vestrymen, one was a future vestryman, while two others were prominent parishioners.[67] The role played by members of the King's Works in parish government was also perpetuated by their readiness to put forward the names of colleagues for future office: thus Henry Wickes, paymaster of the Works, and Thomas Bagley, chief glazier, figured among four men nominated to become overseers of the poor in 1623.[68]

It would be misleading, however, to suggest that the King's Works men in St Martin's necessarily formed a closed grouping or a faction antagonistic to others in local government. The 1601 will of the bricklayer Thomas Bendge (warden 1599–1601), for example, nominates the master carpenter Portington as an executor, as one might expect to find in the will of a man who was regularly employed by the Works office. But the will also highlights Bendge's specifically parochial links through the use of three witnesses from outside his area of employment, two of whom were former wardens and one of whom was a former overseer of the poor.[69] Moreover, the prominence of the Works element in St Martin's local government should not obscure other ties linking St Martin's office-holders.

Many office-holders were allied by ties of marriage or blood. For example, John Beste, an MP for Westminster in 1558 and 1559 and St Martin's churchwarden for 1550–52, was later followed in office by his brother and heir Robert Beste, who served as churchwarden 1565–67.[70] Other office-holders were linked by ties of marriage,[71] or occupation, or by residence in the same part of the parish. Only forty wills survive for

---

67 *KW* III, pt I, pp. 111–18. Those attending would have been the lord treasurer's representative, Edward Forsett (also a Middlesex JP), the Master Carpenter Portington, the Comptroller Thomas Baldwin, the Surveyor Simon Basil, the Master Mason William Cure, and the Paymaster Andrew Kyrwyn. Forsett and Portington were vestrymen, Baldwin had been elected warden and later became a vestryman, Basil was a leading parishioner, while Kyrwyn lived in St Martin's and was to be succeeded in office as Paymaster by Henry Wickes, who later became a St Martin's vestryman. Kyrwyn's financial conduct within the Works office had been seriously questioned earlier and it is interesting to note that he never held office in St Martin's.

68 WAC, F2001, f. 164v.

69 WAC, F2001, f. 95; TNA, PCC, Prob. 11/98/53. Other examples of alliances forged among vestrymen outside the Works' network include the close links between John Thorpe (one of the period's earliest land-surveyors and one-time clerk of the Works) and Simon Greene (woodmonger and later 'Purveyor of his Majesties Stable'). They enjoyed close ties of marriage and friendship, and often seem to have acted together on parochial business: see below and Merritt thesis, pp. 191–2.

70 Bindoff, *House of Commons*, s.n. John Best. Similarly, another Westminster MP, John Reade, keeper of the wardrobe at York Place and later at Westminster Palace, acted as churchwarden from 1542 to 1544, and was followed by his nephew Robert Reade, who held office as churchwarden at St Martin's 1565–67 (*ibid.*, s.n. John Rede). Other examples of churchwardens who were also kinsmen include John Golightly, keeper of the mews at Charing Cross (warden 1550–52) and William Golightly (warden 1563–65, whose precise relationship to John is unknown); and the father and son churchwardens Robert Pennythorne senior and junior, who served in 1540–42 and 1568–69 respectively: Merritt thesis, pp. 189–92.

71 The chandler John Matthew (warden 1616–18) married Eleanor Derricke, daughter of the saddler Patrick Derricke (warden 1591–93): *Register of St Martin-in-the-Fields*, p. 82.

the ninety-nine churchwardens who served between 1525 and 1625, but they display similar parochial commitments and links to other office-holders. Office-holders invariably left a bequest to the poor, while many requested burial in the body of the church.[72]

Fellow office-holders were often the recipients of bequests. The brewer Derrick Heldon, for example, left the vestryman and woodmonger Simon Greene 20s to buy a ring 'for a Remembraunce'.[73] In particular, men who served in office together often found an important place in each other's wills.[74] This suggests that the shared experience of office-holding produced a lasting impression on those involved, and engendered a group feeling among the parish governors. For the vestryman and joiner Henry Waller, for example, St Martin's vestry could actually fill the role normally played by family members. Leaving no immediate heir, Waller directed that his possessions were to be divided among his twelve nephews and nieces. Fore-seeing some difficulty with this arrangement, however, he specified that if any dis-pute should arise 'they [should] cause fower or sixe of the better sorte of the vestrie of . . . St Martin in the feildes . . . to hear and determine the same without sute of lawe'. Waller also left £4 for a dinner to the vestrymen of St Martin's, as well as arranging bequests for his 'good freindes & neighbors', almost all of whom were highly placed officials in the parish.[75]

A more unusual feature of St Martin's vestry was the active involvement of mem-bers of the gentry in parish government.[76] Initially, a few gentlemen on St Martin's vestry in the Elizabethan period may have been granted their position as vestrymen largely as a courtesy, and their membership is revealed only by a chance passing refer-ence. In this category one might include men of local importance such as George Bredyman, the keeper of Whitehall Palace, and Thomas Poultney, the owner of much land in the western part of the parish.[77] By contrast, Chidiock Wardour, clerk of the pells and a Middlesex JP, was exceptional as a gentleman parishioner who played an active role in parish government during Elizabeth's reign.[78] The Jacobean period,

---

72 In 1589 the merchant tailor William Downes requested burial 'in a vaulte to be made under my pew whear I now sitt', TNA, PCC, Prob. 11/74/81.

73 TNA, PCC, Prob. 11/88/86.

74 In 1558, the baker Roger Lee left a bow and arrows to his fellow warden Henry Haughton, while in his 1626 will William Stacy left 30s to William Clarke 'Apothecarie in the Strand' to make a ring 'to weare in rembraunce of me'. Stacy and Clarke had served jointly as churchwardens in 1620–21. Similarly, in 1609 Raphe Allanson singled out for a bequest 'my partner Henry Waller', who seems to have been his business partner as well as his fellow churchwarden in 1601–3: TNA, PCC, Prob. 11/88/86, 11/150/143, 11/113/41, 11/41/60; WAC, F2001, f. 164v.

75 TNA, PCC, Prob. 11/139/2.

76 This phenomenon seems to have been rare in early modern England, although some gentlemen served as churchwardens in Jacobean Romford: M. McIntosh, *A Community Transformed* (Cam-bridge, 1991), p. 233.

77 Kitto, pp. 272, 398; *SL*, XIV, 46, 46n, 47.

78 WAC, F2001, ff. 18, 28, 40, 44, 44v; Hasler, *House of Commons*, s.n. Chidiock Wardour.

however, witnessed the increasing participation of gentlemen in St Martin's parish. By 1606, Wardour had been joined on the vestry by Sir George Coppin, a clerk of the Crown, Arnold Oldisworth, clerk of the Hanaper, Edward Forsett, a divine right theorist and Middlesex JP with close links to the Cecils, and even Sir Thomas Windebank, a clerk of the signet, although the latter played little role in day-to-day-affairs. All of these men shared a similar legal or administrative background which also rendered them particularly useful in dealing with the growing complexities of St Martin's parish government.[79] The vestry minutes also begin to give pointed recognition to the activities of such gentlemen on behalf of the parish in this period. This is particularly true of Coppin, whose roles in securing the gift of a communion cup, and in presenting to the parish letters patent for a new churchyard, are celebrated in lengthy formal entries in the vestry minutes.[80] Other gentlemen vestrymen seem to have limited their active involvement to occasions when some form of patronage was to be exercised, such as the selection of a parish clerk. Their intervention could be decisive: in 1604 Oldisworth and Sir William Cooke were able to overturn a 'former agreement' made by the vicar, vestry and 'other Ryght Wor' [shipful] persons' to appoint another candidate as parish clerk.[81] The need to defend gentry status could also draw in gentlemen who were otherwise less active in parish government. Such concerns presumably motivated a man such as Sir Robert Brett, a gentleman usher, to attend a vestry meeting in April 1608. His signature is attached to an order relating to the building of pews in the church – an issue of obvious interest to status-conscious gentlemen, but also one which would act partly as a focus for social rivalry, as we shall see.[82]

One important connection which drew these different members of the St Martin's vestry together (and the gentry and members of the King's Works in particular) was a link to the Cecil family. As we have already seen, the Cecil family had based itself in Westminster during the sixteenth century, with both Lord Burghley and his son Robert occupying major townhouses and serving as high steward of Westminster in unbroken succession from c.1561 to 1612. The Cecil link with many of Westminster's MPs has already been noted, but their influence also extended into the various levels of

---

79   See below. Sir William Ashton was an active vestryman in the 1620s and 1630s: e.g. F2002, ff. 50, 51v, 72v, 81, 103, 106.

80   WAC, F2001, f. 44r–v.

81   WAC, F2001, f. 170v. Sir William Cooke was the son of William Cooke (a kinsman of Lord Burghley's and clerk of the liveries of the Court of Wards), while Oldisworth was a Middlesex JP, MP, clerk of the Hanaper and vestryman by 1606. These two were distantly related and both also held offices in their native Gloucestershire. Hasler, *House of Commons*, s.n. William Cooke II, Arnold Oldisworth. For another example of gentry involvement in the selection of parish clerk see WAC, F2001, ff. 18, 45; F316, f. 3v.

82   His signature appears with that of fellow knight, Sir John Spilman, the King's jeweller, whose origins are less clear. WAC, F2001, f. 53. Among those names on a grant for a new churchyard for St Martin's are Brett and Spilman. Other gentlemen listed are Sir Thomas Windebank, Sir George More, Sir Jerome Bowes and Francis Barty (Bertie): TNA, C66/1711, m. 20.

parochial government, especially in St Martin's parish. Many members of St Martin's vestry had reason to regard the Cecil family as patrons.[83]

In particular, many of the St Martin's officials who enjoyed Crown employment in the royal Office of Works were also employed periodically by the Cecils. Building work at Theobalds, Salisbury House, Britain's Burse and Hatfield House involved many of the master craftsmen who sat on St Martin's vestry. The active vestryman Thomas Fowler, comptroller and paymaster of the Works, enjoyed particularly close links with the Cecils, supervising building work at Theobalds, and in his will of 1595 he not only bequeathed a prayer book to Lord Burghley but also provided the opportunity for either Burghley or Robert Cecil to rent his substantial Strand townhouse for a modest sum. Fowler's appointment as one of the two original chief burgesses appointed to the Court of Burgesses in 1585 presumably reflects Burghley's approval.[84] His colleague in the Office of Works, the Master Carpenter William Portington, may not have enjoyed the more personal links of Fowler, but he was sufficiently trusted by Salisbury to help supervise the earl's building work in the Strand, approving accounts and advancing money.[85] Other parish officers who also worked on Cecil properties included craftsmen such as Thomas Slowman (bricklayer), Samuel Jeniver (joiner) and Samuel Clarke (ironmonger), and the celebrated surveyor John Thorpe.[86] It was not just members of the King's Works who enjoyed links with the Cecils. The fashionable tailor Christopher Collard – another influential St Martin's vestryman and member of the Court of Burgesses – was on first-name terms with Burghley's household steward Thomas Bellot, and even appears to have acted informally as a member of the earl's household in some capacity beyond his sartorial duties.[87]

Other, more gentlemanly members of St Martin's vestry were not mere employees of the Cecils, but were deeply trusted allies of the family, most notably Sir George Coppin, Raphe Dobbinson and Edward Forsett. Sir George Coppin, a clerk of the Crown in Chancery, started his career in Burghley's household and attended the old man during his last illness. Coppin moved among a network of other Cecil intimates including Sir Walter Cope, while his sister Bridget was married to John Bowle, Salisbury's household chaplain.[88] While Coppin was a Cecil client with Court connections, for day-to-day affairs in Westminster Burghley (and later Salisbury) relied on

83 See above, ch. 3. For a fuller discussion see J. Merritt, 'The Cecils and Westminster 1558–1612: the development of an urban power base' in P. Croft (ed.), *Patronage, Culture and Power* (New Haven, 2002), pp. 231–48; Merritt thesis, pp. 194–200.

84 TNA, PCC. Prob. 11/87/8; Merritt thesis, pp. 194–5; Manchée, p. 212.

85 Merritt thesis, pp. 232, 238; Hatfield House, Salisbury MSS, Bills 32.

86 Merritt thesis, ch. 5; Hatfield House, Salisbury MSS, Bills 16, 32, 33; WAC, F2001, ff. 56A, 110A, 142; WAC, F329, F333; *HMC Hatfield*, XXI, p. 177; John Summerson (ed.), *The Book of Architecture of John Thorpe* (Walpole Society 40, 1966), pp. 2–3, 5.

87 Merritt thesis, pp. 197–8; Hatfield House, Salisbury MSS, Bills 14, 22, 33.

88 Merritt thesis, pp. 198–200; CUL, MS Ee.III.56, no. 80: Burghley to Sir Robert Cecil, 5 February 1595/6; Hasler, *House of Commons*, s.n. George Coppyn; BL, Salisbury MSS, Bills 18; Summerson,

another St Martin's vestryman, Raphe Dobbinson. Dobbinson was so trusted by Salisbury that in December 1607, when the earl resigned from a number of civic posts
(namely bailiff, coroner and clerk of the market), Salisbury formally made them all
over to Dobbinson. Moreover, Dobbinson seems in practice to have been serving in
the office of high bailiff (perhaps as Salisbury's deputy) from as early as 1600, and
held the post until 1612.[89] Equally, the vestryman Edward Forsett was a trusted client
of the Cecils, being charged with the crossexamination of the Gunpowder plotters and
thereafter continuing to act in an investigative capacity for Salisbury as lord treasurer,
as well as assuming the role of local JP.[90]

Common links to the Cecils and the King's Works office might help to unify
parish government in St Martin's. Nevertheless, it is important to recognize that there
were also serious divisions, sometimes even between groups who shared the same
patron. The parish petition for the rebuilding of St Martin's church in 1606 had
urged the need to make it a place fit for gentlemen and Crown officials, and it is the
complications surrounding the presence of such figures in the locality which helped to
spark a major dispute that erupted among the Jacobean vestry.[91]

It was the parish's struggle to cover the costs of the rebuilding of St Martin's church
in 1606–9 which provided the occasion for the dramatic emergence of these social
tensions into the open. Ironically, this enterprise also represented a shining example of
how the parish might harness communal energies and benefit from its links with the
building trades and Office of Works.[92] Financing the project and supervising the expenditure of over £1,000 was an enormous task, and occupied many leading parishioners,
among whom were the vestrymen Sir George Coppin and Raphe Dobbinson. Despite
the successful completion of this massive refurbishment, co-operation between Coppin
and the other vestrymen broke down during the later stages of the building. Coppin and
certain vestrymen, but principally Dobbinson, traded accusations of fraud and mis-
management which finally led to a case heard in Star Chamber in 1616.[93]

The dispute centred on allegations that Coppin had failed to account for all the
money that he had helped to procure for the work, despite acting as 'treasurer' for the

---

The Book of Architecture of John Thorpe, p. 73; N.E. McClure (ed.), *The Letters of John Chamberlain*
(2 vols., Philadelphia, 1939), I, 554; *DNB*, s.n. John Bowle.

89 Merritt thesis, pp. 198–200. Dobbinson styled himself variously gentleman or yeoman, but his
    origins are obscure. For his regular communications with Salisbury see *HMC Salisbury*, 8, p. 344;
    14, p. 284; 15, pp. 186–90; 17, p. 307; *Acts*, no. 541. For Dobbinson's activities as bailiff see also
    LJ II, 513, 515 (where his name is given incorrectly as Robinson). He ceased to serve as high bailiff
    in the year of Salisbury's death.

90 Merritt thesis, pp. 324, 347; *DNB*, s.n. Edward Forsett; *KW*, III, pt i, 110–11, 116, 119, 134.

91 TNA, STAC8/101/19.

92 Merritt thesis, pp. 237–41; see also J.F. Merritt, 'The social context of the parish church in early
    modern Westminster', *Urban History Yearbook* 18 (1991).

93 TNA, STAC8/101/19; WAC, F3, ff. 13, 23.

project. His uncooperativeness then led the vestry to question his handling of parish funds more generally. One recurring theme of this dispute was the discomfort which Coppin felt when required to work in theoretical equality with fellow vestrymen who were, nevertheless, his social inferiors. Indeed Coppin agreed to produce a general account of expenditure only after one of the 'principall gents in the . . . vestrie' explained that exception was taken on this matter 'by men of good reckoninge' – and this several years after the building was completed.[94] It is significant that Coppin bowed to pressure only from men who were evidently either his social equals or superiors: throughout the long years of the quarrel, he always insisted that the vestry had no authority over him.

But Coppin was not merely uncooperative. Although Cecil patronage could not ensure harmonious relations among St Martin's parish elites, it is probably significant that the participants in the dispute determined to resolve it outside the parish only after the death in May 1612 of the first earl of Salisbury, doubtless the most influential man in the parish and the natural arbitrator. Even so, shared Cecil links probably explain why George Montaigne, a former Cecil chaplain, tried to mediate in the conflict by attending vestry meetings in 1612–13. At the time Montaigne was dean of Westminster, and the parish was technically outside his ecclesiastical jurisdiction – therefore his involvement seems to have occurred because he was known personally to many members of the vestry.[95]

In 1614 Coppin accused Dobbinson of inciting other parishioners against him, and apparently brought his case before the bishop of London. Coppin also appears to have made counter-accusations of fraud against Dobbinson and Thorpe. The bishop then attempted to arbitrate between the two parties, though with little success.[96] Far from marking the end of hostilities, the bishop's intervention further intensified the dispute. A particularly stormy vestry meeting in February 1615 found St Martin's vicar reproving Coppin that 'he troubled the whole Companie' and that 'he was so full of Contumelious wordes as neither befitted the place nor his person'.[97] The case finally found its way into Star Chamber in 1616. Unfortunately, the judgement handed down by Star Chamber has not survived. Whatever its decision, however, the matter was kept alive until well into the 1620s, after both Coppin and Dobbinson had died.[98]

Coppin's own explanation of the quarrel played up social distinctions within both the parish and the vestry itself – perhaps the better to enlist Privy Council support in Star Chamber. Social climbing had created faction within the parish and so, he implied, had led parish officers to abuse their positions. The result, Coppin alleged,

94 TNA, STAC8/101/19.

95 WAC, F2001, ff. 76–77, 80–1.

96 TNA, STAC8/101/19.

97 *Ibid.*

98 Dobbinson died in 1622 and Coppin in 1620: *Register of St-Martin-in-the-Fields*, pp. 173, 157.

was that certain vestrymen had allocated new pews in the 'highest' places in the church to themselves, whereas 'Earles lordes Knightes and other bountifull benefactors to the same Church were destitute of any convenient Pewes or places'. And yet, as Coppin explained, he had obtained funds via the Privy Council on the understanding that they were to be employed on St Martin's church, 'being a parishe Church where some of the principall lordes of his Majesties privie Councell were for the most part residinge'.

The fellow vestrymen whom Coppin specifically identified as the architects of this 'conspiracy' were Raphe Dobbinson, John Thorpe and Christopher Collard. But these were unlikely leaders of a populist conspiracy against the nobility. Dobbinson, explained the status-conscious Coppin, was the bailiff of Westminster 'and the rather for his place . . . of an arrogant proud [and] malicious disposicion'. And yet, like Coppin himself, Dobbinson clearly regarded the earl of Salisbury as his chief patron. To a lesser extent this was also true of Collard. As we have seen, Collard not only acted as tailor to both Salisbury and his servants but was also clearly an intimate of the household. If Coppin's enemies were not populist conspirators against the social hierarchy, however, it is clear that they may have represented a social threat to Coppin in another way. Thorpe and Collard were evidently men who were energetically scaling the social ladder in a manner that lesser gentry like Coppin might have found uncomfortable. Thorpe, the son and brother of stonemasons, was one of England's earliest land-surveyors, with a highly educated interest in architecture, whose activities would have led him to rub shoulders with members of the gentry. The tailor Collard sent his son to Westminster school and subsequently to university, where the latter studied for the ministry. Both men were also singled out as particular friends and patrons of learning by the writer Henry Peacham (quondam tutor in the earl of Arundel's household and later schoolmaster at St Martin's).[99]

Coppin's accusations clearly present an exaggeratedly polarized view of social relations among St Martin's governors. Coppin sought to identify broader social divisions as a means of legitimating his position in the eyes of the higher authorities. In the process he sought to portray a socially levelling conspiracy among vestrymen who in fact mostly enjoyed mutually beneficial relations with the court and nobility. Nevertheless, while Coppin may have overstated such divisions, it seems clear that underlying social tensions and potentially abrasive clashes among those of differing social rank were one of the many forces at work among Westminster's governing elites.[100] For all that Cecil patronage was crucial to many of St Martin's governors, this quarrel should remind us that sharing the same patron did not necessarily override these other interests and divisions.

By the 1620s and 1630s, St Martin's vestrymen shared less in terms of occupation and patronage, even if they operated as a tightly knit group. Their sources of

---

99 TNA, STAC8/101/19; Salisbury MSS, Bills, 14, 20, 33; Summerson, *Book of Architecture of John Thorpe*, pp. 2–6; H. Peacham, *The Gentlemens Exercise* (1612), p. 172. For Peacham's 1620 appointment see WAC, F2001, f. 148.

100 For church seating see below, ch. 6, pp. 214–23.

patronage also became less uniform. This partly reflected a broader power vacuum in the area, especially by the 1630s. The fragmentation of the Cecil patronage removed one unifying factor and it is not clear that any of Westminster's later High Stewards achieved the same concentration of local influence. The King's Works also played a less decisive role in parish government by the 1620s and 1630s. This was partly because population growth and the increasing social complexity of the area had diluted their importance in the community. By the 1630s, St Martin's vestry largely consisted of wealthy members from the service sector, but the tight networks of patronage ties that typified the Jacobean period were no longer evident, and a prominent parish activist such as the vintner George Hulbert – who was a JP and also president of the Military Company – seems to have had no wider patronage ties whatsoever.[101]

The role of gentlemen on St Martin's vestry also became less prominent in the 1620s and 1630s: those gentlemen who died or left the vestry were not replaced by men of similar social status, and the vestry itself became increasingly small and oligarchical in its organization.[102] The decline in direct gentry involvement may stem from the creation of a Westminster sessions, which provided a new and more prestigious channel for their involvement in local affairs, as JPs. What is clear even in the 1630s, however, is that Westminster's gentry were not simply uninterested in local affairs, nor did their desire to sustain their social position in the area diminish. Social relations could still be problematic, as we will see. If early Jacobean divisions were exposed by the church-building dispute, the same concerns over maintaining social hierarchy in church now revealed themselves in the 'need' to build a separate 'Lords' gallery' in St Martin's by the 1630s.[103]

ST MARGARET'S: BUREAUCRATS, VICTUALLERS AND ABBEY PATRONAGE

A quite distinctive set of social networks characterized the parish governors of St Margaret's Westminster. Here was a parish that contained the royal palace of Whitehall in its midst, and yet we find that gentlemen impinged far less directly upon its government. This partly reflected the fact that the gentry were less prominent in the parish as a whole. From the later sixteenth century onwards, St Margaret's contained

---

101 *CSPD 1638–39*, p. 521; WAC, F2002, ff. 101, 103v, 106. Hulbert played a significant role in the attempts towards incorporation, and also seems to have played a principal part in a series of clashes between St Martin's parishioners and the earl of Bedford in the later 1630s over the earl's creation of Covent Garden: *CSPD 1638–39*, p. 134. I plan to deal with these disputes in more detail elsewhere.

102 The involvement of members of the peerage in the vestry's activities in the 1640s (charted in J.S.A. Adamson, 'The peerage in politics: 1645–1649' (Cambridge Ph.D., 1986), pp. 89–97) reflects the unique political situation of that decade, and should not be seen as representing a continuation of earlier trends.

103 See below, ch. 6.

fewer aristocratic townhouses or fashionable new developments than was the case in
St Martin's. In addition, the role of gentlemen as a force for change within the parish
was less pronounced than in St Martin's, even when the numbers of gentry resident in
St Margaret's increased in the 1620s. When a new gallery was added to the church in
the 1630s, it is notable that this was no 'Lords' gallery': 120 out of 143 pewholders
were simply listed as 'Mr'.[104] Nevertheless, a constant trickle of minor government
bureaucrats – especially exchequer officials – were always active among parish office-
holders, a pattern that had been set in the medieval period, when the Exchequer had
been the first royal department to set up an establishment independent of the Court.[105]
During Elizabeth's reign, Exchequer officials such as William Staunton and Thomas
Cole figured prominently among St Margaret's parochial elite and as Westminster
MPs. This traditional association took on new significance during the Elizabethan
period, however, since the Exchequer was one of the departments with which Lord
Burghley, Westminster's high steward, was associated, and the link with Burghley
may explain the favoured status that Exchequer officials received from the Abbey.[106]
In the Caroline period Sir Robert Pye and Arthur Squibb continued the Exchequer
link with St Margaret's parish government, but the association never exercised a decisive influence over the running of the parish.[107]

In fact, the dominant groups in St Margaret's parish government were principally drawn from those elements which had played a major role in the area in the
medieval period – namely, the food and drink trade. A thriving service sector had
developed in the medieval period and the provision of food and drink had become
a mainstay of the local economy. The large and prosperous inns and taverns of
thoroughfares such as King Street supplied a constant stream of visitors and residents
all packed into this busy part of the metropolis. Wealthy bakers, brewers, butchers,
and fishmongers had also played a leading role in St Margaret's parish and the victuallers
of the town had been identified as a self-perpetuating elite in the early sixteenth
century.[108] By the beginning of the seventeenth century, these same occupations still
predominated among St Margaret's office-holders: nearly half of the churchwardens

---

104 However, a number of office-holders in the 1620s and 1630s subsequently took to styling themselves as 'gentlemen' in Abbey leases, including the linen-draper James Parcall, the brewer
Bartholomew Parker and the apothecary William Bell: see n. 126 below.

105 Rosser, pp. 19–21. Others include minor royal servants and bureaucrats such as William Towe
(warden 1590–92), described as yeoman of His Majesty's litter, and Marmaduke Servant, an usher
of the Court of Wards and Liveries.

106 See above, ch. 3; Merritt thesis, p. 145. The dean and chapter in 1590 granted a lifelong lease of a
prebendal house to John Fortescue, chancellor of the Exchequer, despite the lack of sufficient housing for the prebends themselves at the time, simply 'in regard of his office in the Exchequer': *Acts*,
nos. 416, 431.

107 WAC, E2413, f. 16; G. Aylmer, *The King's Servants* (1961), pp. 311–13. Pye's links went back to
the 1620s and his association with Buckingham: E15 (1626–27), f. 16r–v.

108 Rosser, pp. 362–5.

serving between 1590 and 1610 were in the food and drink trade, for example – by far the largest occupational grouping among St Margaret's office-holders.[109]

The new Palace of Whitehall and the flourishing law courts had undoubtedly helped to sustain and expand St Margaret's service sector. But office-holders at St Margaret's did not necessarily limit their economic activities to Westminster. A minority of them clearly found it to their advantage to belong to London livery companies such as the Vintners, Grocers and Butchers – a comparative rarity among St Martin's officials.[110] Whether or not membership of livery companies gave these men a distinctively 'London' orientation is unclear. It would, however, have meant that they could function commercially in the City and this may have been important for those operating on a larger scale.[111] Three St Margaret's office-holders even reached the uppermost levels of livery company membership. Cuthbert Lynde (churchwarden 1601 and 1607) served as warden of the Grocers' Company and remembered them in his will, Thomas Morrice (churchwarden 1616–18 and later vestryman) was an upper warden of the same company, and Edmund Doubleday (who served in a number of parish offices) became master of the Vintners' Company.[112] It is also clear that livery company membership could hold some larger social meaning for some of these St Margaret's men, as the 1614 will of William Carter (churchwarden 1604–6) demonstrates.[113] Nevertheless, despite the fact that some St Margaret's office-holders belonged to London livery companies, the wills of office-holders more generally do not suggest a London orientation. Most men seem to have owned property in St Margaret's parish itself, occasionally supplemented by holdings elsewhere in Middlesex or perhaps Surrey. Few recorded properties in the City of London.[114]

109 Between 1530 and 1625, it has been possible to identify the occupations of only 50 per cent of St Margaret's churchwardens. Twice as many victuallers (especially brewers and bakers) served as church-warden as did the members of any other occupational grouping. Occupations have been derived primarily from wills, vestry minutes and churchwardens' accounts.

110 E.g. TNA, PCC, Prob. 11/124/93. Other St Margaret's churchwardens with livery company membership include Joseph Bradshawe (Brewers' Co., Prob. 11/163/37), John Brigham (Grocers' Co., WAM 35932, 36514, 28714), John Butcher (Butcher's Co., WAC, PCW, 4 Camden), William Stanlake (Grocers' Co., PCW, 218 Camden) and Christopher Bennell (Haberdashers' Co., PCW, 130 Camden). The St Martin's vestryman Derrick Heldon was, however, a wealthy member of the Brewers' Company c.1600. I owe this latter information to Dr Ian Archer.

111 The Masons' Company was pressurized by the Crown into offering membership to Nicholas Ellis, the King's Master Mason (and St Margaret's churchwarden 1546–48) so that he could serve as official viewer to the City, J.S. Loengard (ed.), *London Viewers and Their Certificates 1508–1558* (London Record Society 26, 1989), pp. xvi–xvii, xix.

112 *List of the Wardens of the Grocers Company from 1345 to 1907*, ed. W.W. Grantham (1907), pp. 23, 25. Lynde served as churchwarden in 1601 and 1607. TNA, Prob. 11/112/66; GL, MS 15201/2, pp. 196–215; WAC, E13, f. 44v.

113 Carter bequeathed £22 15s to the Vintners' Hall, apologizing for the smallness of the sum and referring to 'all my good Freindes the worshipfull Company of the Vintners wheare I was graste [graced] with all and soe brought upp': WAC, PCW, 4 Camden; see also TNA, PCC, Prob. 11/124/93.

114 Officials with Westminster property who also held land elsewhere include the grocer William Stanlake, with lands and tenements in Surrey and Middlesex (WAC, PCW, 218 Camden), the haberdasher

We have noted the predominance of the food and drink trade among St Margaret's office-holders, but some men are less easily pigeon-holed. Edmund Doubleday, for example, pursued parallel careers as a bureaucrat and vintner. He was ubiquitous in late Elizabethan St Margaret's, signing parish accounts from 1590, and serving as overseer of the poor that same year and as high constable of Westminster in 1592–95. By the 1590s he had also acquired numerous leases from the Abbey.[115] If we turn to Doubleday's professional career, we find him acting as a scrivener and public notary as early as 1587. There then followed a much later legal education at the Middle Temple, which may have propelled him into a position in the Mint office in 1601. In the meantime, advantageous marriages to wealthy Westminster widows brought him property in Westminster, including the Saracen's Head in King Street. Marriage to the widow of a vintner seems to have prompted him to seek admission to the Vintners' Company. Thereafter, his rise within the trade was such that in 1610 he was accounted one of its wealthiest members and by 1616–17 Doubleday was master of the Company. Doubleday's membership was evidently more than nominal (he even took on an apprentice), yet this did not stop him from obtaining other minor government positions.[116] But one wonders whether it was particularly his status within Westminster's victualling world that accounts for his election as MP in 1614. Doubleday's links to the locality remained central to him and when he died in 1620, only days after having been elected MP for Westminster for the second time, he requested burial 'near the vestry' in St Margaret's church.[117]

Occupational ties are one of the most obvious bonds between St Margaret's office-holders. Yet vestrymen and churchwardens also shared links of kinship and friendship of much the same sort as has been demonstrated for office-holders at St Martin's. They witnessed each other's wills, acted as overseers and bequeathed one another mourning rings. Similarly, many members of this elite were related by marriage. Morris Pickering (warden 1586–88) had two sons-in-law who became parish officials – Edmund Doubleday and Thomas Tickeridge (warden 1606–8), who was probably a grocer. The alebrewer Samuel Haselwood (warden 1596–98), was succeeded as churchwarden only four years later by his brother-in-law, the baker Christopher Ricroft.[118]

Christopher Bennell, with property in Croydon, Surrey (WAC, PCW, 130 Camden) and the alebrewer Samuel Haselwood, with 'Beaste and Cattell' and 'Meadowe errable and pasture groundes' in Chelsea (TNA, PCC, Prob. 11/104/69).

115 WAC, E147, f. 1v; E6 (1592–93), n.f.; *Acts*, nos. 415, 419.

116 *Acts*, no. 396, n.636; *Minutes of Parliament of the Middle Temple*, ed. C.T. Martin (3 vols., 1904), I, 428; GL, MS 15201/2, pp. 196–215; TNA, C66/1559, m. 14; C66/1822. I would like to thank Dr Andrew Thrush for the last two references, and for allowing me to consult a draft History of Parliament biography of Doubleday.

117 Among his many other Westminster-related offices, Doubleday sat on the Court of Burgesses and became successively JP for Middlesex and then Westminster, when that subdivision was created; TNA, PCC, Prob. 11/137/70v–72; Merritt thesis, pp. 148, 202–3.

118 WAC, PCW, 482 Elsam; TNA, PCC, Prob. 11/104/69.

Other forms of influence worked alongside personal and occupational links, however, and perhaps the most important single patronage network operating within St Margaret's parish was that controlled by the dean and chapter of Westminster. Just as the walls of the collegiate church towered over the adjacent church of St Margaret's, so it tended to loom large in the affairs of the parish. Even after the Reformation, the 'Abbey' continued to be a major landowner in the parish, while the dean was able to retain many of the secular jurisdictional powers of the old abbot.

Several members of St Margaret's vestry, such as William Ireland and William Mann, not only played a major role in parish affairs but also served the Abbey quite directly. Mann, for example, appears to have started life in the timber business but soon assumed a prominent place in public life. From 1590 he served successively as an overseer of the poor, a churchwarden and a vestryman, and by 1610 he had gained a seat on the Court of Burgesses, a body dominated by St Margaret's men. At the same time, Mann also seems to have acquired positions of increasing trust within the collegiate church, beginning in 1598 with that of joint surveyor of the works and joint receiver for the rents of Westminster and Knightsbridge. He also built up an impressive property portfolio. By 1608 no fewer than thirty-one tenements located within St Margaret's had been leased to him by the Abbey – a feat presumably made possible through his privileged links to the dean and chapter. Mann's already dominant position on St Margaret's vestry must have been further boosted in 1618, when he obtained a lease of the house normally occupied by St Margaret's curate, and a lease of the profits on burials within St Margaret's chancel.[119] His career seems to have culminated in his 1621 election as Westminster MP – with the dean's explicit backing. We have seen elsewhere the controversy that this event aroused. Nevertheless, it seems fair to say that Mann truly personified the intimate ties between Abbey and parish. When he died in 1635, his house was found to be a repository for some of the most important documents and records pertaining to the collegiate church – a fact partly explained by his appointment as registrar of the Chapter House.[120] Yet throughout this time of Abbey preferment, Mann continued as an active vestryman of St Margaret's and in 1618, when he became a justice of the peace for Westminster, he seems to have done so in his capacity as a St Margaret's man, dealing especially with business in his own parish.[121]

Few of those who held office in St Margaret's were as intimately linked to the Abbey as Mann and few built their careers in quite this manner. Nevertheless, many of the parish elite held leases from the Abbey, or were familiar with its personnel – from schoolmasters to deans and prebendaries[122] – and some enjoyed Abbey 'perks',

---

119 *Acts*, nos. 491, 544; WAM, Chapter Act Bk II, ff. 20r–v, 35. This last lease was made jointly with William Ireland. Mann eventually became a receiver of fines in King's Bench: see *CSPD 1603–10*, pp. 397, 422, 425; *CSPD 1580–25*, p. 515.

120 See above, ch. 3. WAM, lease book xiii, f. 226 (I am grateful to Dr Andrew Thrush for this reference); WAM 9589.

121 TNA, C181/2, f. 331; LMA, WJ/SR (NS) 16/29.

122 E.g. WAC, PCW, 217, 227, 407, 482 Elsam; TNA, PCC, Prob. 11/104/69.

including appointment to minor local offices.[123] Other St Margaret's officials benefited from the ecclesiastical holdings of the chapter. For example, George Bright (warden 1570–72) farmed the parsonage of St Bride, Fleet Street, while St Martin's parsonage was leased first to Thomas Cole (overseer of the poor in 1576 and Westminster MP), and then later to the St Margaret's grocer John Fabian (warden 1606–8).[124] Other churchwardens also received favourable long-term leases, such as those granted for ninety years to the butcher John Savage in 1554, and to the hosier Richard Ferris in 1569.[125] Right up to the Civil War, a significant proportion of St Margaret's churchwardens leased land and property from the Abbey.[126] It is difficult to judge precisely how much profit accrued to the St Margaret's men who obtained leases from the collegiate church. It may have been significant: the massive immigration into the capital resulted in a generally buoyant land market, and this would presumably have been especially true of many properties located close to Whitehall Palace.

It is, of course, possible to paint a picture in which St Margaret's parish governors appear to be mere appendages of the dean and chapter and its interests. But such a picture would be highly misleading. As we have seen, parliamentary elections and efforts towards incorporation can highlight tensions over the role of the Abbey that are not otherwise visible. It seems likely that relations between Abbey and parish ran more smoothly under Dean Goodman's lengthy tenure, and certainly by the seventeenth century Dean Williams considered St Margaret's vestrymen to be awkwardly independent. Appointments of the parish clerk in 1601, and of both parish clerk and organist in 1616, also found the parish resisting direction from the dean and chapter.[127]

Perhaps the most notable feature of St Margaret's office-holding elites was their aspiration to play a broader role in the government of Westminster. The parish tended to identify strongly with the civic identity of Westminster and sought to enhance its own status by emphasizing the town's aspirations. Their particular interest seems to have derived from the fact that the old 'vill' of Westminster was contiguous with St Margaret's parish.[128] As we have seen, the parish had played the principal role in

123 For further details see Merritt thesis, pp. 202–5.

124 WAM 38045; *Acts*, nos. 241, 531.

125 *Acts*, nos. 164, 247, 405.

126 E.g. William Bell (warden 1628–30, WAM 284476, 35883); James Parcall (warden 1630–32, WAM 35881–2, 36464–5, 36480–1, 35911); Thomas Moore (warden 1638–40, WAM 35607); James Chapman (warden 1632–35, WAM 51019); John Brigham (warden 1632–34, WAM 35932, 36514, 28714, 35942, 36530).

127 *HMC Hatfield*, XI, 587–8; WAC, E2413, ff. 26v–27v.

128 The creation of a diocese of Westminster in 1540 resulted in the bestowal of the courtesy title of 'city', which continued in use after the dissolution of the bishopric and cathedral. Nevertheless, the term 'city' seems to have been applied to the area of St Margaret's only, with the rest of Westminster often referred to as the 'liberties' of the city of Westminster: e.g. W. Bidwell and M. Jansson (eds.), *Proceedings in Parliament, 1626* (4 vols., New Haven, 1991–96), I, 488.

lobbying for incorporation in 1585: payments for the campaign were included in the vestry minute book as part of parochial expenditure, and the parish absorbed the costs of furnishing the courthouse. Parishioners of St Margaret's also figured more prominently among Westminster's parliamentary representatives than did candidates from other parishes. It was therefore presumably seen as natural that St Margaret's parish elite dominated the Court of Burgesses, holding eight out of twelve seats. Indeed, seats on the Court of Burgesses were (according to the 1585 statute) specifically intended for 'artificers' and merchants – the parish's 'natural' leadership. This was not an arena in which gentlemen would compete for power and social position. It is also notable that special pews reserved for burgesses were located in St Margaret's church, but not in St Martin's or St Clement's.

Having noted the different characteristics of St Margaret's governors, it would, however, be misleading to draw an absolute distinction between St Margaret's and other Westminster parishes. Some St Martin's officials had links to the Abbey as well as the Cecils, some were engaged in the food and drink trade, and others served on the Court of Burgesses alongside St Margaret's men.[129] There are also dangers in suggesting too narrow and exclusive a view of local occupational groups: one historian, for example, has written that the parish of St Clement Danes consisted almost solely of gentlemen and their servants 'to the virtual exclusion of other social and occupational groups'. Yet wider use of evidence reveals large numbers of tailors, butchers, cutlers and shoemakers in the locality.[130] Nevertheless, as we have seen, the distinctive medieval profile of St Margaret's is still very much visible among its early modern officeholders. Many prominent personnel in the parish still continued to reflect the presence of the Abbey, the law courts, the government bureaucracy associated with the Palace of Westminster and the victualling trades that serviced them. In comparing this parish with St Martin's, what is most significant is the persistence of traditional parochial governing elites, even during a period of major social change – by the early Stuart period the parish still possessed relatively few significant new links with prominent courtiers and fashionable society, despite its immediate proximity to a nascent West End.

STATUS AND OBLIGATION IN LOCAL SOCIETY

The conflicts between Coppin and others in St Martin's have already demonstrated that the authority and status commanded by parochial office-holders in Westminster

---

129 Merritt thesis, pp. 194–5, 199–200.

130 Beier, 'Engines of manufacture', p. 155; Merritt thesis, pp. 207–8; WAC, WCB1, WCB2, passim; LMA, MJ/SBR/3, ff. 18, 28, 30. There are fundamental problems of evidence which make meaningful statistical analysis of occupational structures in this period impossible. For post-1660 developments, when other forms of evidence become available, see J. Boulton, 'The poor among the rich: paupers and the parish in the West End, 1600–1724' in P. Griffiths and M. Jenner (eds.), *Londinopolis* (Manchester, 2000), pp. 203–6.

were not straightforward matters. In Coppin's eyes, at least, the superior social rank of Westminster's courtly residents should have outweighed any authority that socially inferior residents might derive from their status as local office-holders. But was this merely the skewed perspective of a hot-headed gentleman, or does this conflict highlight larger structural problems in how authority operated in Westminster and how it was constructed by residents there? How far were parish officials in practice able to enforce parochial obligations on parishioners in such a socially and politically complex area?[131]

We may begin with questions of social obligation and parish identity. What did it actually mean to be a parishioner and what obligations did this entail? In Westminster, the answers to these questions were more problematic than in rural or even City parishes and reflected what were distinctive features of the area. In particular, the presence of the royal court increasingly problematized the question of parochial membership and responsibility. By the seventeenth century this had created some very practical problems for local officials, especially in St Martin's. One major source of confusion and conflict was the fact that some parishioners claimed exemption from local duties and offices on the grounds that they were royal servants. Should these individuals be exempted from the fines normally levied on those who simply chose to evade office? The Privy Council constantly asserted the right of 'meniall servants in ordinary' such as 'his Majestie's footemen, littermen, coachmen, and groomes of the stable' to be exempted from local rates and parochial responsibilities such as watching and warding. Given their relatively humble status, the Council maintained that these individuals should not be liable for any charge or assessment 'but what they themselves are willing in *neighbourhood* to contribute thereunto'.[132] The Council's allusion to a sense of neighbourly obligation suggests the continuing strength and ubiquity of this assumption, yet their attempt to reduce it to a purely voluntary donation actually undermined it. The seventeenth century witnessed increasingly urgent attempts by parish officials to fight the growing tendency of individual parishioners to exploit a supposed 'Court' affiliation to avoid burdensome local rates and the duty to watch and ward.[133]

By the end of 1627, the problem had become so acute that the high constable of Westminster presented a petition to the Privy Council in the name of himself and the other constables and inhabitants. In particular they argued that

> the major part of the inhabitants doe consist of his Majestie's servants, men of the best and most sufficient estates and abilities, whereof divers beeing shopkeepers, victuallers

---

131 See also discussions below, chs. 6 and 8.

132 *APC 1616–17*, p. 420; TNA, PC2/42, p. 379. Italics mine.

133 This is not to say that a desire to avoid local rates and duties to watch and ward was in itself an early modern phenomenon. In the supposedly more community-conscious medieval period, absence from London wardmotes incurred a fine, while it also seems to have been necessary to impose fines on those refusing the offices of constable, scavenger and beadle: C.M. Barron, 'Lay solidarities: the wards of medieval London' in P. Stafford, J. Nelson and J. Martindale (eds.), *Law, Laity and Solidarities* (Manchester, 2001), pp. 223–4.

and the like, some haveing two severall shopps, who by reason of his Majestie's said service doe not only claime a priviledge and personall freedome from all personall service and all other taxations and charges whatsoever, but do also thereby take themselves to be exempted from the ordinarie and lawfull government of the said cittie.

The result of this situation was twofold. Firstly it led to an increase in 'others . . . [who] daily . . . straine themselves to be sworne his Majestie's servants'. The second effect was to burden yet more the shrinking pool of residents eligible to bear local office and pay local taxes. Such men, 'beeing poore shopkeepers and tradesmen', not only struggled to pay a larger tax bill. They also lost out when forced to close their shops to undertake parish business – and all this, it was reported, when 'his Majestie's servants remaine in their shopps and will not stirr'.[134] It is difficult to determine how far the Court's desire to protect poorer parishioners was being exploited by wealthier ones, but nevertheless it is clear that the presence of the Court served to problematize and divide local allegiances and obligations. This was not, however, a matter that could easily be resolved. Two years later, St Martin's paid for a copy of a Privy Council warrant 'whereby it was ordered that his Maties Servantes should serve offices', and in 1633 the vestry complained to the Privy Council once more about the King's servants refusing to pay local rates. While the Council listened sympathetically, they repeated their earlier stipulation that 'their Ma[jes]t[ie]s meniall servants in ordinary shall be exempted from all personall service, unless they will voluntarily undergo the same'.[135]

Theoretically, the Crown was prepared to adopt a sterner line when dealing with more socially elevated courtier-residents. When seeking to impose more stringent watching and warding in 1617, the Privy Council stipulated that the privileges granted to more menial royal servants should not extend to 'diverse persons of quallity', including those employed by 'his Majestie's Exchequer and Receipt, [nor] . . . other officers of attendance who have their dwellings within Westminster'. While these more elevated residents could claim privilege from *personal* service, they were required to pay for the hire of a replacement to fulfil their parish obligations (as indeed were those humbler Westminster parishioners who were themselves the servants of government bureaucrats or courtiers).[136]

Such gentry residents presented continual problems to local office-holders who sought to instruct them in their duties as members of the parish community. Problems surfaced in a number of areas, from charitable contributions and the payment of local

---

134 *APC 1627–28*, pp. 194–5 (21 December 1627).

135 WAC, F3 (n.f.) (1629–30); TNA, PC2/42, p. 379 (10 January 1633).

136 *APC 1616–17*, pp. 419–20. For an example of a Westminster parishioner attending prominent courtiers see the case of the barber Robert Shaw, who paid £4 8s to be excused from the office of constable of St Martin's in 1623 on the grounds that he was tied to 'daylie attendance' on the marquess of Hamilton and the earl of Montgomery, and had gone into Spain to attend the prince of Wales: WAC, F2001, f. 166.

rates to the allocation of pews in church. Not the least of the difficulties faced by parishes in dealing with such residents was that of determining precisely what constituted residency.[137] Many members of the upper gentry and aristocracy living in Westminster resided in the parish only for part of the year, and this rendered problematic the question of where their loyalties should be located (and most importantly, where they were liable to pay rates). Of course the very nature of Westminster society – with its law terms, royal Court, intermittent parliaments and the beginnings of a fashionable gentry 'season' – generated a host of temporary residents. Not surprisingly, regular tussles ensued, not just over royal servants but also over who was truly 'resident'. Thus one John Baker claimed that his position of postmaster of Colchester meant that he was exempt from local service, although the vestry complained that he was 'a constant dweller' in his Westminster parish, and that his Colchester duties were actually performed by a deputy.[138] Baker was not alone. Many well-to-do Westminster residents owed at least a partial allegiance to other parts of the country. Indeed, at least four St Martin's vestrymen can be found serving as MPs for constituencies in other parts of the country in the late Elizabethan and early Jacobean periods.[139] As we shall see, the issue of residency had enormous financial implications for parishes, especially in relation to moneys available for desperately needed poor relief.[140]

The social complexity of life in the Westminster parishes meant that by the seventeenth century local officials were almost constantly engaged in careful negotiations with local gentlemen. This was particularly true in the matter of rating individuals for the purposes of taxation, a task usually undertaken by parish vestries.[141] Often gentlemen wanted to be involved in the process of rating, or at least to be consulted. In St Clement Danes, the sense of social distance between parishioners was carefully maintained even in the parish rate books themselves, which first listed men according to social status – 'Noblemen and knightes', then 'Esquires and gentlemen' – with the remainder of the parishioners grouped under topographical headings.[142] Other Westminster parishes did not indicate social divisions quite so starkly in their records, but the potentially tense relations between Westminster's social and office-holding elites are regularly apparent.

137 On the problem of residency and rating see Webbs, *Parish and County*, pp. 14–15, 39; A.H. Smith, 'Militia rates and militia statutes 1558–1663' in P. Clark, A.G.R. Smith and N. Tyacke (eds.), *The English Commonwealth 1547–1640* (1979); E. Cannan, *History of Local Rates in England* (1912), pp. 70–1.

138 TNA, PC2/42, p. 379. Baker had refused to serve as overseer of the poor, and subsequently reneged on an agreement to pay a fine. For problems over defining residency see also below, chs. 6 and 8.

139 Chidiock Wardour, Arnold Oldisworth, Edward Forsett and Sir George Coppin.

140 See below, ch. 8.

141 A. Fletcher, 'Honour, reputation and local office-holding in Elizabethan and Stuart England' in A. Fletcher and J. Stevenson (eds.), *Order and Disorder in Early Modern England* (Cambridge, 1985), pp. 92–115. See also below, ch. 8.

142 WAC, B19, ff. 1–28.

The delicate nature of social relations in Westminster is nicely illustrated by an example from 1630. When building works took place at the Westminster house of the privy councillor Sir Thomas Wentworth, his brother-in-law, Lord Haughton, reported that a local notable 'Mr Ireland' (presumably the St Margaret's vestryman William Ireland) was 'so careful of your service as while I was your Lordships tennant he came or sent dayly to inquire of the health of my sisters catts, and what rest they had taken the night before'. William Mann, 'another senator of Westminster' (as Lord Haughton revealingly described him) also offered his services: 'in Mr Irelands absence [he] did stand sentinell all the whole day by the doore while the house was open with the building'.[143] We have, of course, encountered Mann before as an Abbey official, Westminster JP and wealthy linchpin of local government. Presumably as a representative of the locality, the social deference implicit in Mann's behaviour was intended to tap into ideas of status and reciprocity. Certainly it was important for officials to be on good terms with rising privy councillors in their midst, and the desire here seems to have been to bind Wentworth with ties of mutual assistance and good neighbourhood (and perhaps the focus on domestic pets is all the more telling for the appearance of uncalculating social intimacy which it implies). As we will see, Westminster's officials had constant problems in ensuring that new noble residents paid their rates and helped to alleviate the severe and costly social problems that dominated the area. Clearly by 1630 there was a recognition that the social education of new elite residents had to begin as early as possible. The fact that Wentworth's first donation to the poor the following year was one of the most generous in the parish suggests that this policy was not entirely unsuccessful.[144]

Of course it was useful if parishes could call upon local intermediaries to smooth the way with elite residents, if the need arose. As we have seen, the vestryman Christopher Collard acted as an intermediary between St Martin's parish and the Cecil family partly on the basis of his having acted as tailor to the first earl of Salisbury. In 1622, Collard was requested by the vestry to attend William Ashton, a member of Salisbury's household, to facilitate a direct interview with the second earl over the thorny issue of an unpaid annuity.[145] The same Sir William Ashton later himself acted as an intermediary when the vestry (of which he was now a member) needed to prevent the earl of Bedford from selling his pew.[146]

Clearly, office-holders were forced to play an awkward role between aristocratic residents and the parish community. At the same time, it was also vital that Westminster's officials have their own status recognized by the gentry and nobility – a status that was presumably acknowledged more easily by the mass of middling and

---

143 Sheffield City Archives, Strafford Papers 12/143.
144 WAC, E153 (n.f.) (1631–32). Wentworth paid a 'benevolence' of 40s.
145 BL, Salisbury MSS, Bills 14; WAC, F2001, f. 157v.
146 WAC, F2001, f. 157a.

lower-ranking parishioners. Lord Haughton's wry reference to a 'senator of Westminster' echoes the condescending remarks of Dean John Williams on the stubborn clannishness of St Margaret's vestrymen and the Westminster burgesses.[147] Resentment at the airs and graces adopted by local officials could spill over into more acrimonious exchanges. Even officials of the rank of justice of the peace could encounter problems. Lady Theodosia Tresham was accused of telling the Westminster JP George Long that 'your authoritie set aside you are a scurvy companion', and that she would be revenged upon him.[148] Tensions over authority could work the other way, however. In 1639, the grocer Bryan Barneby, an overseer of the poor and later a Westminster burgess, was complained of for 'scornfully behaving himself' before the Duchess of Richmond's executors when conducting parish business.[149]

The balance between the burdens of local office-holding and the rewards of authority and status brings us to the problem of office evasion. Other urban areas experienced this problem, but in Westminster parochial office was likely to have been more demanding than elsewhere. Disincentives may be traced to the escalating pressures of office, and the fact that officers were increasingly answerable to the Privy Council for their actions (or inaction). The political importance of the area meant that even constables and scavengers could find their behaviour rigorously scrutinized. A failure to clean the Strand at the time of parliament in 1621 led to a Privy Council order that constables, scavengers and rakers should be assembled, and that whoever was responsible for the failure should be imprisoned.[150] We have already noted how householders used replacements to watch and ward. This was not in itself a major problem for Westminster's officials – indeed, this seems to have become common practice over the course of the seventeenth century.[151] But men's reluctance to serve in more significant local offices was an increasing headache for Westminster's governors. The humble offices of scavenger and surveyor, not surprisingly, proved unpopular, and there are occasional examples of men paying fines to avoid the office of constable.[152] But examples of men refusing to serve in higher local office gather pace in the seventeenth century.

---

147 BL, Cotton Julius C, III, f. 402.

148 *Middlesex County Records*, ed. J.C. Jeaffreson, III (1888), 34.

149 *Ibid.*, p. 72.

150 *APC 1619–21*, pp. 369–70. Cf. *CSPD 1633–34*, p. 387.

151 See for example the case in the 1630s of John Markett, who hired four different people to watch for him at different times, although he did watch on two nights himself. This was noted in the course of a Sessions case without any suggestion that Markett had done anything wrong: LMA, WJ/SR (NS) 51/28. The problem of those refusing to watch and ward seems to have been particularly acute in St Margaret's: e.g. LMA, WJ/SR (NS) 7/17.

152 E.g. WAC, F2 vol. 2, ff. 228, 414; F2001, f. 166. Few men actively avoided the constableship, perhaps attracted by its serving as a stage on the *cursus honorum* to the prestigious office of churchwarden: Kent, *English Village Constable*, pp. 78–9. There is, however, a danger that parish records under-record such cases, see below.

There is very little recorded evidence of men refusing to serve as churchwardens or vestrymen before the seventeenth century (the first recorded case dates from 1587).[153] In April 1607, however, Thomas Baldwin, Comptroller of the King's Works, refused to serve as churchwarden and was fined £5 'according to the Auntient Custome in that case used.'[154] St Martin's also experienced a flurry of cases in the early 1630s when a number of men paid fines (in the shape of 'voluntary' sums given to the poor or towards the repair of the church) to be spared appointment to the onerous position of overseer of the poor. While these men presented formulaic excuses of their regular employment outside the parish, none of them seems to have been averse to holding parochial office as such. Several had held other parish offices, and two can be found serving as vestrymen in 1641 – a fact which suggests that their real concern was to skip some of the more demanding posts along the traditional *cursus honorum*.[155] In fact, there is no real evidence that fining out became a mere money-raising device in this period, as seems to have happened in London for the more prestigious but financially draining office of alderman.[156]

One way of compensating for the demands placed upon office-holders was to boost the status and prestige that accrued to such positions. From the later Elizabethan period onwards Westminster parish officers sought to enhance the symbols of their status. They secured preferential treatment in the arrangement of church seating, and in St Martin's vestrymen also received preferential burial arrangements in the old churchyard.[157] St Martin's vestry also steadily enhanced the surroundings in which they met, with the provision of more luxurious chairs and furnishings in the vestry room and the erection of a separate vestry house in 1614. Men clearly still valued this specifically parochial recognition of status – perhaps the more so given the absence of livery companies or civic office, which offered a social ladder to Londoners.[158]

---

153 Kitto, p. 400.

154 WAC, F2001, f. 46. For another example of fining out from the office of churchwarden see F2002, f. 37.

155 WAC, F2002, ff. 78v, 83r–v. John Waterer and Edmund Edlyn were excused office in the early 1630s but were acting as vestrymen in November 1641 (ff. 84r, 94, 120). There is a danger of underestimating the problem, however, as some office evasion was not mentioned in parish records, but recorded elsewhere: e.g. LMA, WJ/SR (NS) 11/22.

156 R. Wunderli, 'Evasion of the office of alderman in London, 1523–1672', *London Journal* 15 (1990). For rather more widespread office evasion in early Stuart London see A.M. Dingle, 'The role of householder in early Stuart London, c.1603–1630' (London Ph.D., 1975), pp. 113–19.

157 On burial privileges and office-holding in 1609 see WAC, F2001, f. 56. All Westminster parishes had differential burial fees that were ranked according to the social group, residency or office-holding of the deceased: e.g. TNA, E178/5842 (St Clement Danes), E215/1307 (St Martin's). See also the 1630s burial fees in LPL, Carte Misc. 7/79/5. For church seating see below, ch. 6.

158 WAC, F2, vol. 2, f. 234.

The desire of vestrymen to affirm their collective power and legitimacy is evident also in the shifting terminology used by the vestry to describe itself, which seems to reflect the ways in which this oligarchy sought to legitimate itself to different groups within (and possibly outside) the parish. At St Martin's, the growing use in parochial documents of the term 'ancients' may be crucial here. It seems clear that, while the 'ancients of the parish' might imply a wider body than the membership of the vestry,[159] in practice it became the term that vestrymen preferred to use when describing themselves.[160] Thus a number of orders from the later 1630s are described in the vestry minutes as having been passed with the 'Consent of the Auntients of the parish at the vestry', followed by the signatures of as few as six of the normally active vestrymen. By 1640, one St Martin's vestryman even asked to be accompanied to the grave by 'the auncients of the parish'.[161] The emergence of this phrase as an alternative to terms such as 'masters' or 'better sort' may reflect a desire to reaffirm a communal identity that transcended divisions of wealth, as well as a concern to appropriate the right to define local 'custom' in the face of rich and poor alike.[162] It is intriguing to note that this term was particularly used at times of plague, when social relations came under particularly severe strain, and the legitimacy of those imposing the hated plague orders and associated taxation was most in doubt. By later in the seventeenth century, however, the use of this term was clearly seen as a device designed to blur the lines of authority, and a 1696 petition against select vestries (apparently including those in Westminster) specifically objected to how vestrymen 'assume to themselves the name of Ancients'. There could be no clearer example of how the vestries had taken upon themselves the authority to speak and act for the parish community as a whole.[163]

159 It was sometimes used in London specifically to denote a body other than 'a vestry of selected persons': Archer, p. 69.

160 In St Martin's own submission to Juxon they implied this distinction, claiming that the vicar and churchwardens governed with the assistance of twenty of our 'Auncienter Parishioners', whose number was 'supplied successively out of the ancients' by the vicar and wardens: LPL, Carte Misc. 7/79/5.

161 WAC, F2002, f. 113. Cf. ff. 106, 114v, 118; TNA, Prob. 11/184/119. Note also the use of the term 'the Ancyentes of the vestrie' as a body approving expenditure in St Clement Danes: WAC, B19 (1623–24). The term 'ancients' is not among those mentioned in Professor Wrightson's discussion of terms used by parish elites more generally: K. Wrightson, 'The politics of the parish' in P. Griffiths, A. Fox and S. Hindle (eds.), *The Experience of Authority in Early Modern England* (Basingstoke, 1996), p. 34; H.R. French, 'Social status, localism and the "middle sort of people" in England 1620–1750', *P&P* 166 (2000), pp. 75–6, 98.

162 Cf. below, ch. 6. The occasional use of another phrase – 'the gentlemen of the vestry' – in parish documents of the early 1630s may reflect the usage by a new parish clerk (WAC, F3, entry for 5 July 1632). Nevertheless, the usage was clearly intended to lend dignity to *all* vestrymen, regardless of rank, rather than distinguishing between groups of vestrymen. The term was also used of those mostly lower-status vestrymen who stayed during the 1636 plague: WAC, F3 (1636–37), F363 (July 1636).

163 Webbs, *Parish and County*, p. 250; *CJ* XI, 550. This topic raises more issues than can be discussed here. I hope to pursue a wider study of vestries in the metropolis elsewhere.

CONCLUSION

The post-Reformation period in Westminster was marked by the narrowing of local oligarchies, as administrators felt themselves to be squeezed between increasing numbers of poor on the one hand and an influx of more socially elevated residents on the other. The parochial elites that emerged did not, however, represent a single dominant political or economic interest. Many of them enjoyed links of some kind with the royal court, the Abbey or with prominent aristocrats, but this reflected the inevitable ties of mutual convenience that the area fostered. Westminster's office-holders were not simply the clients of higher authorities, who moved them around the chess-board of local politics, but neither were they a fiercely independent local middling sort squaring up to such authorities, however much it might suit the agenda of some elements to portray them as such. In addition, while the experience of office-holding could help to forge a sense of unity and cohesion among these narrowing elites, the broader social tensions in the area could invade the vestry too.

The 'masters of the parish' identified in St Martin's and St Margaret's represented a range of different interest groups, then, and it was through the interplay of these many different elements that the supposed voice of the community was developed and proclaimed. But this was always a particular, self-appointed voice. Increasing their social status while also trading on their claim to speak for the parish community (with all the legitimacy which that entailed) helped the more senior parish officers to find sufficient reward and a role for themselves in the tangled politics of the area. We should be wary, however, of taking their claim to speak and act for the parish at face value. The narrowing of the governing elite made it all the more important for the vestry to insist that it acted as the voice of the local community. It was very much in the vestry's own interests to blur the dividing line between the interests of 'parish', 'community' and 'vestry'. But while the social transformation of early modern Westminster placed increasing pressure on notions of parish community and social obligation amid a large, fluid and socially diverse population, the vestries' determination to keep alive such notions was an important feature of the locality in this transitional period. In the process, the local elites were still able to wield significant power – both symbolic and actual – in a Westminster where so much authority and responsibility was still exercised on the parish level.

2 Whitehall Palace and its environs, mid-sixteenth century. Detail from the contemporary 'Agas' map.

Chapter 5

◆

The rise of a fashionable society

I live i' th'Strand . . . I'll have
My house the academy of wits, who shall . . .
Write panegyrics of my feasts . . .
The horses shall be taught, with frequent waiting
Upon my gates to stop in their career
Toward Charing Cross . . . my balcony
Shall be the courtier's idol, and more gazed at
Than all the pageantry at Temple Bar
By country clients.[1]

So declares Celestina in James Shirley's play *The Lady of Pleasure*, staged in 1635.
Her words evoke the way in which Westminster had become the most fashionable
quarter of the capital by the early seventeenth century. Here was the site of a lifestyle of
conspicuous consumption, a heady world of luxury and leisure, which could by the 1630s
be most easily conjured up by a series of allusions to Westminster's topography. Shirley's
depiction of the refined and luxurious existence played out among the gentry introduces us
to a new theme in the history of early modern Westminster. For many literary, cultural and
economic historians, the Westminster of the late sixteenth and early seventeenth centuries
is most familiar as the location of what later became known as the 'West End'.[2]

From the late sixteenth century onwards, changing patterns of behaviour among
the gentry and aristocracy profoundly influenced the character of development in the

---

1 James Shirley, *The Lady of Pleasure*, ed. R. Huebert (Manchester, 1986), act I, scene ii, ll. 79–95.

2 L. Stone, 'The residential development of the West End of London in the seventeenth century' in
B.C. Malament (ed.), *After the Reformation* (Philadelphia, 1980); R.M. Smuts, *Court Culture and
the Origins of a Royalist Tradition in Early Stuart England* (1987), ch. 3; L. Stone, *The Crisis of the
Aristocracy* (Oxford, 1965), pp. 385–97; F.J. Fisher, 'The development of London as a centre of
conspicuous consumption in the sixteenth and seventeenth centuries', reprinted in F.J. Fisher,
London and the English Economy, 1500–1700, ed. P. Corfield and N.B. Harte (1990); A.J. Cook,
The Privileged Playgoers of Shakespeare's England (Princeton, N.J., 1981).

capital, and particularly in Westminster. The Jacobean period witnessed the consolidation of a pattern whereby significant numbers of the gentry and aristocracy expected to travel from the provinces to the metropolis on a regular basis. A number of factors gave momentum to this phenomenon. Among the most important of these was the fact that the royal Court had become less peripatetic by the sixteenth century, and with the building of Whitehall Palace the Court was more firmly based in Westminster. The Court acted as a magnet to all those who sought royal patronage, and its increasing size and lavishness would provide an important economic and cultural stimulus to the locality.[3] Aristocrats and gentlemen alike were also drawn to the area by the increasing frequency with which parliament met, while individual parliaments met for longer as well. In the Jacobean period, for example, parliament was regularly in session between 1603 to 1610 and again in the 1620s, necessarily resulting in longer and more expensive stays on the part of lords and MPs.[4] Another significant force behind visits to the capital was the need to attend to business at the Westminster law courts. Of course men and women in the medieval period also came to the capital for the same reason, but the rise in litigation which took place in the early modern period meant that such trips to the capital seem to have increased in frequency. The impact of litigation is suggested by one esimate made in 1570s, when it was said that consumption of grain in the capital during the law terms jumped by thirteen per cent.[5]

During the later sixteenth century, travel by coach also meant that visits to the capital could more easily involve the entire family, encouraging visitors to stay longer and spend more money. It was a phenomenon that was increasingly noted by contemporaries. Speeches in parliament – including those by James I himself – denounced the expenditure on foreign luxuries that visits to the capital entailed, while the decline of hospitality in the countryside was also presented as the dark accompaniment to pleasure-seeking in town.[6] But this was also a period in which a more positive valuation of gentry life in the capital was emerging. As early as 1579 the anonymous dialogue *Cyvile and Uncyvile Life* reveals a discourse promoting the values of civility and urbanity,

---

3   S. Adams, *Leicester and the Court* (Manchester, 2002), pp. 114–16; D. Starkey (ed.), *The English Court* (1987), pp. 18–19; A. Bryson, *From Courtesy to Civility: Changing Codes of Conduct in Early Modern England* (Oxford, 1998), pp. 126, 129.

4   D. Smith, *The Stuart Parliaments, 1603–1689* (1999), p. 236; cf. TNA, SP14/164/10. Even when parliament did not actually meet – for example during the 1630s – there were constant rumours of parliament being called (Smith, *Parliaments*, p. 119) and this expectation in itself may have affected confidence in the market for luxury goods and housing.

5   Rosser, pp. 122, 131–3; Fisher, 'Conspicuous consumption', pp. 105–18; I. Archer, 'Material Londoners?' in L. Orlin (ed.), *Material London ca. 1600* (Philadelphia, 2000), p. 176.

6   F. Heal, 'The Crown, the gentry and London: the enforcement of proclamation, 1596–1640' in C. Cross, D. Loades and J.J. Scarisbrick (eds.), *Law and Government under the Tudors* (Cambridge, 1988), pp. 212–15. As Dr Heal shows (p. 212), the proclamations originally derived from orders as early as 1545, which required members of the gentry to return to the country and provide for the military defence of their shires. The Jacobean proclamations were distinctive in their new emphasis on shifting patterns of gentry behaviour, which were seen to threaten the social fabric of the country. See also Fisher, 'Conspicuous consumption', pp. 112, 118.

which found their most natural outlet in forms of gentry sociability that were most easily realized in the city.[7] The confluence of these various phenomena created the critical mass of gentry and aristocratic residents that would help to generate the cultural phenomenon of the London 'season'.

That Westminster played host to increasing numbers of visiting gentry and aristocracy is clear. It is also evident that this period was marked by the development of the notion of a distinctive gentry urban lifestyle, based on a shared, self-contained and exclusive culture of gentry sociability.[8] But the precise impact on Westminster of this emerging lifestyle of the urban gentry – on land and property usage, on local employment, and on the local economy and society – has not been traced before. This chapter is intended to focus on the practicalities of this emergent fashionable society, tracing the manner in which both visiting and resident gentry and aristocracy lived in Westminster, how they acquired accommodation, what sort of households they maintained, what sort of amenities they required and how far the locality was able to provide them.

Yet Westminster was not a mere tabula rasa on to which the values and lifestyles of aristocratic and gentry society could be effortlessly imprinted. Accordingly, it is the interaction of old and new, of the medieval suburb and the new gentry lifestyle, which is the focus of this and the next chapter.

TOWNHOUSES

In the early seventeenth century, Westminster's aristocratic credentials were most impressively conveyed by the great townhouses which lined the Strand. Palatial mansions such as Arundel House, Salisbury House, Northampton House and York House stood as symbols of privilege, power and luxury. As landmarks in the capital, their place along the curve of the Thames was clearly marked out on maps of the period. These great townhouses provide an obvious starting point for any exploration of the development of the area as a fashionable quarter, and have received considerable attention from historians of the period. Nevertheless, they did not represent a single, co-ordinated development. Rather they emerged in a piecemeal way as a complicated and gradual adaptation of older properties to new ownership and new uses, and can be properly understood only in this context.

Great townhouses had been a feature of the Strand thoroughfare since the medieval period. Before the Reformation, medieval bishops had built large mansions fronting the Thames on both Fleet Street and the Strand. Here they could live in aristocratic

---

7 *Cyvile and Uncyvile Life: a discourse where is disputed, what order of Lyfe best beseemeth a Gentleman* (1579) – another issue reprinted in W.C. Hazlitt (ed.), *Inedited Tracts* (1868), pp. 1–93. See the discussions in Bryson, *Courtesy*, pp. 114–18; F. Heal, *Hospitality in Early Modern England* (Oxford, 1990), pp. 104–6.

8 Bryson, *Courtesy*, pp. 113–14, 134–5.

style as befitted members of the House of Lords, whenever they were in the capital. In addition, they used their properties as bases from which to replenish their provincial households. At the time of the Reformation, however, many of these ecclesiastical properties passed into the hands of wealthy laymen, often as a result of disadvantageous property 'exchanges' made under pressure from the Crown. The most striking example was Wolsey's York Place, which became the new Whitehall Palace. But many of the 'new men' favoured by the Tudors, such as the Seymours, Russells, Pagets, Thynnes, Dudleys and Sidneys, also acquired former ecclesiastical properties along the Strand and Fleet Street. When the great duke of Somerset decided to build himself a showpiece house in the Strand he demolished no fewer than four bishops' mansions in the process.[9] Similarly, the Strand townhouses of Tudor lords such as the earls of Arundel and the earls of Bedford ultimately had their origins in the inns and palaces of England's bishops.[10] In St Margaret's parish, another enclave of aristocratic housing developed in Canon Row, as laymen took possession of houses formerly occupied by the canons of St Stephen's Chapel.[11]

As lay ownership of property along the Strand began to dominate, the Crown did retain certain properties itself. These were normally tenanted by royal favourites or members of the royal family. Durham House, for example, came into Crown hands in 1536, and was occupied for over twenty years by Sir Walter Raleigh during the later sixteenth century, having earlier housed the royal favourite Robert Dudley before he obtained his own house in St Clement Danes in 1570.[12] After the fall of Somerset, the Crown employed Somerset House as grace and favour lodgings: it was used as a

9   S.J. Madge, 'Worcester House in the Strand', *Archaeologia* 91 (1945), p. 160; C.L. Kingsford, 'Bath Inn or Arundel House', *Archaeologia* 72 (1922), pp. 247–8; C.M. Barron, 'Centres of conspicuous consumption: the aristocratic town house in London 1200–1500', *London Journal* 20 (1995), pp. 1–16; Phyllis Hembry, 'Episcopal palaces 1535–1660' in E. Ives, R. Knecht and J. Scarisbrick (eds.), *Wealth and Power in Tudor England* (1978), pp. 146–66.

10 These two houses were both located in the parish of St Clement Danes. Arundel House was formerly the inn of the bishops of Bath and Wells, while the first Bedford House (later Worcester House) had served as townhouse for the bishops of Carlisle and was obtained by Lord Russell in 1539. Russell House was located on the south side of the Strand and was occupied prior to the Elizabethan erection of the better known Bedford House (located north of the Strand and south of Covent Garden): Kingsford, 'Bath Inn', p. 247; Madge, 'Worcester house', p. 160; *London P&P*, III, 191.

11 Houses in Canon Row included those of the earl of Hertford, who had inherited it from his mother, the widow of Protector Somerset, and those of John Thynne (Somerset's steward), Richard Cecil (father of Lord Burghley) and Sir Edward Hoby. Sir John Gates and Sir Anthony Denny also acquired former church property in St Margaret's. *London P&P*, III, 324; Bindoff, *House of Commons*, s.n. John Thynne, Richard Cecil, Anthony Denny, John Gates. In the last years of Elizabeth, Stow also wrote of the houses there 'now in building' of the earl of Derby and the earl of Lincoln: Stow, II, 102.

12 The rights of the see were reasserted in 1603, but see *SL*, XVIII, 84–93; S. Adams (ed.), *Household Accounts and Disbursement Books of Robert Dudley, Earl of Leicester* (Camden Society 5th ser. 6, 1995), pp. 25–6; L. Stone, *Family and Fortune*, (Oxford, 1973), p. 93. In 1570 Leicester bought Paget House, a former episcopal property, see C.L. Kingsford, 'Essex House, formerly Leicester House and Exeter Inn', *Archaeologia* 73 (1922–23), pp. 1–54.

residence for the Princess Elizabeth during Mary's reign and periodically occupied by ambassadors thereafter. York House, too, was leased by the Crown for almost all of Elizabeth's reign.[13]

The desirability of houses along the Strand and Fleet Street was boosted in the Elizabethan period by the erection of large houses by two of the greatest courtiers of the period, Lord Burghley and the earl of Leicester. By the latter stages of Elizabeth's reign this area had become intensively developed, with the result that rising stars at Court faced difficulties in finding an appropriate house or even a site upon which to build. Thus, in his search for a Thames-side site for what was to become Salisbury House, Robert Cecil was reduced to purchasing and tearing down an old house belonging to the son of the earl of Worcester, and then acquiring adjoining properties piecemeal in order to augment a very cramped site – a complex series of transactions that necessitated an Act of Parliament.[14]

The Jacobean period witnessed an exceptional spurt in building activity connected with the large townhouses of the Strand. Some noblemen were able to demolish older houses and build from scratch, as in the case of earl of Northampton, who built a luxurious new residence on the site of old buildings near Charing Cross between 1605 and 1609.[15] Older houses could be notoriously damp and uncomfortable. The old York House, for example, was described by Archbishop Hutton in 1596 as 'somewhat rheumatic', while a few years later its then occupant, Lord Keeper Egerton, referred to the the 'small comfort in this unsavoury house'. Not surprisingly, when the duke of Buckingham acquired the house in 1620 he promptly had it pulled down, and by 1626 the new York House was admired by the French ambassador as 'the most richly fitted up' of any house he had visited in the capital.[16] Other building of the Jacobean period, however, did not involve demolition, but rather the redevelopment and refurbishment of older houses. For example, the ageing Somerset House was enlarged, 'beautified' and modernized (bringing in piped water from Hyde Park) for the benefit of Queen Anne. It was now rechristened 'Denmark House', and the playwright Middleton celebrated this transformation in 1616: 'a stately palace and majestical, / Ever of courtly breeding, but of late, / Built up unto a royal height of state'.[17] In the case of Arundel House – probably the most famous of the aristocratic

---

13 *London P&P*, III, 269–71.

14 Stone, *Family and Fortune*, pp. 92–4. The main part of the building appears to have been completed by 1602, with additional work continuing until 1610 and resulting in Great Salisbury House to the east and Little Salisbury House to the west: *SL*, XVIII, 120–1.

15 The house was luxuriously appointed, with only the most choice furniture and tapestries and designed to accommodate the Earl's vast collection of paintings: L.L. Peck, *Northampton: Patronage and Policy at the Court of James I* (1982), pp. 64, 73–5; E.P. Shirley, 'An inventory of the effects of Henry Howard, K.G., earl of Northampton', *Archaeologia* 42, 2 (1869), pp. 353–69.

16 *SL*, XVIII, 53–5; *Egerton Papers*, ed. J. Payne Collier (Camden Society 12, 1840), p. 221.

17 E. Howes, *Annales* (1631), p. 1026; *London P&P*, I, 495. Charles I granted the house to Henrietta Maria and a Catholic chapel was built here: *KW*, IV, pt ii, 261.

Strand townhouses in the early Stuart period – Inigo Jones was employed to remodel extensively this old Tudor house in Italianate style between 1614 and the early 1630s. There its picture gallery and gardens provided a carefully designed setting for the earl's famous collection of sculpture and paintings.[18]

The great townhouses of the Strand thus represented a combination of medieval survivals and adaptions, along with a smaller number of new major aristocratic residences. The significance of these great houses stems partly from their role as exemplars of aristocratic living and taste. They were noted for their contents – fine paintings, rich furnishings, exquisite tapestries and the curious and precious objects collected by their owners. They also had a major cultural and artistic impact, playing an important role in the history of collecting and connoisseurship. Higher expectations of comfort and luxury among the nation's elite also fuelled a change in the ways in which other buildings came to be designed and furnished. Indeed, this largely Jacobean building and remodelling of the Strand's great houses and gardens coincided with other large-scale rebuilding work at Court, as well as in the capital more generally. London's livery company halls were widely refurbished, while many churches throughout the metropolis were also enlarged and beautified during the Jacobean period.[19] In Westminster itself, the two main churches attended by the gentry, St Martin in the Fields and St Clement Danes, were substantially rebuilt and redecorated in the first decade of the seventeenth century, partly to accommodate influential gentry parishioners who expected to worship in a socially appropriate setting.[20]

These great mansions on the Strand undoubtedly made a profound impact on contemporaries: not only was their location a prestigious one on the highway linking the City and Court, but their ostentatious display of wealth and power in their turn lent prestige to the area, and played no small role in establishing Westminster as a centre of fashionable living. Nevertheless, it must be emphasized that this impact derived precisely from their exceptional character. The great townhouses were never representative of the mode of life adopted by most members of the aristocracy in the capital, let alone the members of the gentry. By the early seventeenth century the size of noble households had declined, and the demand was now for luxury and comfort rather than space to accommodate the enormous retinues of medieval aristocrats. Intensive development in the more desirable parts of Westminster, coupled with restrictions

---

18 D. Howarth, *Lord Arundel and His Circle* (New Haven, 1985), pp. 57–8, 102–4, 106, 113; Richard James, *Marmora Arundeliana* (1628). By the 1630s, the galleries and garden of Arundel House contained 32 statues, 128 busts, 250 sarcophagi and other fragments: R. Strong, *The Renaissance Garden in England* (1979), pp. 170–4; Kingsford, 'Bath Inn', p. 252.

19 J. Archer, 'The Industrial History of London 1603–1640' (London M.A. thesis, 1934), p. 46; F.J. Furnivall (ed.), *Harrison's Description of England* (4 parts, 1877–1908), IV, 237–40; J.F. Merritt, 'Puritans, Laudians and the phenomenon of church-building in Jacobean London', *HJ* 41 (1998), pp. 935–60; C. Platt, *The Great Rebuilding of Tudor and Stuart England* (1994).

20 J.F. Merritt, 'The social context of the parish church in early modern Westminster', *Urban History Yearbook* 18 (1991), pp. 20–31; cf. below, ch. 6.

on building on open fields further to the west, meant that few major new houses were erected by the aristocracy. In less developed areas, such as the western and northern portions of St Martin's and St Margaret's parishes, aristocratic building was limited, while major new houses such as Leicester House, Goring House and Tart Hall were built only in the 1630s. A number of influential courtiers preferred to lodge at Court, including two of Westminster's high stewards, the earl of Somerset and the earl of Pembroke.[21] Even a major urban developer such as the first earl of Clare, who put together a substantial portfolio of urban property in St Clement Danes and adjacent parishes, never possessed his own townhouse.[22]

Significant as the great aristocratic houses of Westminster were to its identity, in many ways it was the more modest residential housing suited to gentlemen and professional men that was to emerge as a defining feature of urban development in the area in the period before the Civil War.[23] As we will see in a later chapter, the building of houses tailored to new forms of urban living emerged significantly only in the later 1620s and 1630s, and their appeal also extended to members of the peerage.[24] For most of the period we have considered, however, such specialized housing was unavailable. Denizens of the fashionable London season instead had recourse to the local market in temporary accommodation. It was the fact that gentlemen and even peers often required short-term accommodation which partly accounts for their distinctive impact on the local economy and society. It is to this lively market in temporary accommodation that we now turn.

LODGINGS

In the period before the Civil War, lodgings suitable for gentry visitors seem almost always to have been in short supply. For this reason, the pursuit of good-quality accommodation was a major undertaking, best accomplished through an extensive network of friends and kinsmen. Letters written by gentry in Westminster to friends

---

21 *SL*, XIV, 46; R.T. Spence, *Lady Anne Clifford* (Stroud, 1997), pp. 99, 101, 111.

22 *Letters of John Holles 1587–1637*, ed. P.R. Seddon (Thoroton Society 31, 35–6, 1975–86), I, Introduction, p. xxvi. For the use and regulation of open space in the Westminster parishes see below, ch. 6.

23 In a speech in Star Chamber in 1616, James I deplored the increase in the number of buildings in the capital and specifically linked this to the tendency of gentlemen to flock to the metropolis instead of maintaining good housekeeping in the country: C. McIlwain (ed.), *The Political Works of James I* (Cambridge, Mass., 1918), p. 343. For the suggestion that some impoverished gentlemen had given up their country properties for a chamber in the capital see E. Lamond (ed.), *A Discourse of the Common Weal* (Cambridge, 1893), p. 19.

24 It was only in the later 1620s, for example, that leasees of the earl of Salisbury built the fine houses on the west side of St Martin's Lane. The characteristics of these houses seem to have been borne in mind by builders in the earl of Bedford's development in Covent Garden which took place in the 1630s: Stone, *Family and Fortune*, p. 110. See also below, ch. 6.

in the country constantly recount the varying price of lodgings, the difficulty of finding them and rumours of soon-to-be-vacant houses. Not surprisingly, gentlemen and their families sought lodgings in neighbourhoods convenient for the activities they were likely to pursue.[25] Attending parliament, seeking preferment at Court, pursuing a legal case or even shopping might all benefit from a base in the western suburbs of the metropolis – especially in the Westminster parishes.[26] It is true that visitors were unlikely consciously to have sought lodgings within the precise jurisdiction of Westminster. Nevertheless, as we have seen, the social cachet of certain areas within Westminster is clear from topographical allusions in contemporary plays.

If accommodation was difficult to find, this was partly because gentry visitors were preoccupied with location and also because competition was fierce for those houses which matched gentry expectations of comfort and convenience, especially when parliament was in session. In 1597, Rowland Whyte reported to Sir Robert Sidney that 'all the Houses near Charing Cross, and Holborn, were taken up, er[e] I came from you, and Mr Lesieur, with my self, have lefte few Houses unsought for, and yet can heare of none fit you to lye in'.[27] Sir William Trumbull found similar problems in 1616, when John More went house-hunting for him. Viewing the house of one Mr Gates, More found little to praise, it being 'lowe roofte, yll contrived, narrow stayres, foggy aire, [and] no cellerage'. The house was also too far from Court, which, as More shrewdly commented, 'is as bad as to have a shop out of trade'. More's remarks on other houses in Westminster also suggest the limitations of the housing stock, as well as the priorities of the more discerning gentry house-hunter. More complained that houses he had seen near Charing Cross, for example, were 'both without gardens and private courtes and therefore wholly unfitt; neither will it be easy to finde a house fitted with a garden near the Court unlesse . . . it be in St Martins Lane, where houses are very dear, or in Drurie Lane, where they are cheaper but some what farre remote'.[28] This scarcity of housing pointed to a good commercial opportunity, which More himself was later to exploit.[29] The dearth of good houses for rent was a complaint that was still made in the later 1630s, and this despite the earl of Bedford's new development in Covent Garden. As late as 1639, the Master of Ceremonies,

---

25 Those members of the gentry and aristocracy who did not rent properties in Westminster tended to end up in in one of the adjacent parishes, such as St Giles in the Fields, St Andrew Holborn or St Dunstan in the West, the last two of which also held the advantage of proximity to the Inns of Court. Thus Lord Haughton, son of the earl of Clare, stayed in the vicinity of Fleet Street at 'one Clarks a taylor neere Dorsett hows' in 1626, *Holles Letters*, II, 333.

26 As early as 1601 it was recognized that proclamations ordering gentry to return to their country estates could be implemented effectively only if City officials co-ordinated their efforts with Middlesex JPs, so that gentry 'delinquents' could not escape merely by residing in Westminster, Heal, 'The Crown, the gentry and London', p. 215.

27 A. Collins (ed.), *Letters and Memorials of State* (2 vols., 1746), II, 63.

28 *HMC Downshire*, VI, 534.

29 See below.

Sir John Finet, could write to Viscount Scudamore about difficulties that he and Scudamore's wife had encountered in house-hunting: 'all that . . . wee can do by our indeavours, cannot in this great Citty (so little in conveniencyes of lodgings) finde one as yet sufficiently capable and commodious for your Lordship but eyther the distance from Court, the want of good ayre, the streightnes of roomes, or illnes of neyghbourhood makes it liable to exceptions'.[30]

At the upper end of the social scale, members of the aristocracy regularly borrowed or rented each other's houses. Changes in the finances or political fortunes of the families who owned great townhouses might mean that these properties were available to let, if not necessarily for sale. The house of the disgraced earl of Arundel, for example, was occupied by Lord Hunsdon in the early 1590s, while that portion of Salisbury House known as 'Little Salisbury House' was regularly let to members of the aristocracy after the death of Lord Treasurer Salisbury in 1612.[31] The latter appears to have been much in demand. When the newly sworn lord treasurer Sir Henry Montagu wanted to rent part of Salisbury House in 1621, he found that the second earl had no room to spare. Montagu then decided that Bedford House would suit his desire for a house near the Court, but he was frustrated yet again when the lord chancellor begged him to wait another year, since Bedford House had been promised to the Archbishop of York.[32] Similarly, when Exeter House (on the north side of the Strand) was sought as a temporary residence for the Spanish Infanta and her entourage in 1623, it was inhabited not by the earl of Exeter but by the earl's tenants, whom the peer was reluctant to disturb.[33] Indeed, members of the peerage played an elaborate form of musical chairs in their search for suitable and spacious accommodation. It is not surprising to find that such information regularly found its way into the reports of newsletter writers. In December 1631, for example, it was related that the earl of Essex and his family would borrow Warwick House for a stay in the capital just 'as my lord of Bristol did last somer' while Lady Warwick 'meanes to remoave [sic] to Sir Edioard [Edward] Hungerfords by Charing Crosse'.[34]

Peers might also be forced to compete with the Crown for the more desirable townhouses in Westminster and adjacent parishes. Durham House, although in possession of the see of Durham, was regularly used by the Crown for a range of purposes, including the housing of ambassadors and the ceremonies associated with creating Knights of the Bath.[35] Cecil House, on the north side of the Strand, also served as an ambassadorial residence and was occupied by the Dutch ambassador when it burnt

30 TNA, C115/N8/8827.

31 Kingsford, 'Bath Inn', pp. 251–2; Stone, *Family and Fortune*, pp. 93–4.

32 *The Letters of John Chamberlain*, ed. N.E. McClure (2 vols., Philadelphia, 1939), II, 331.

33 *London P&P*, II, 27; *CSPD 1619–23*, pp. 561, 611.

34 TNA, C115/M35/8386.

35 *SL*, XVIII, 91–2.

down in 1627.[36] By the 1630s Sir John Finet blamed the unwillingness of London aldermen to house ambassadors as a major reason why the Crown had been increasingly forced to requisition the houses of aristocrats for this purpose. The truth of this is unclear, but it is the case that between 1623 and 1636 the officers of the King's Works fitted up no fewer than eleven such houses for ambassadors, most of them in the western suburbs of the metropolis.[37] One solution to the problem of ambassadorial housing in Westminster was to formalize a system of 'contracting out'. Thus in the early 1630s the Crown agreed to pay £300 a year for the house of Sir Abraham Williams in New Palace Yard to be kept for the king's 'use', to receive ambassadors. The house was to be elegantly equipped with hangings, furniture and linen, while the amount also included payment to Westminster residents in adjacent houses to lodge any whom the main house could not accommodate.[38]

For those not fortunate enough to borrow or share a house with friends, the available options varied considerably. Gentry families might find themselves in spacious apartments located within aristocratic houses or even victualling houses. The choice was ultimately determined by a combination of luck, good social connections and the size of one's purse. It is extremely difficult to compare prices for lodgings as surviving sources seldom specify what amenities the overall figure included. Where information does survive, however, it suggests (as one might expect) that short-term and furnished accommodation was a good deal more expensive than leasing a house for a period of years.[39] At the upper end of the social scale, the earl of Cumberland paid £16 per month to hire a house in St Martin in the Fields when he attended parliament in 1621. Cumberland expected to be able to entertain guests in a manner commensurate with the status of a peer who was greeted by the King's and Prince's trumpeters when he arrived in Westminster. The rented house was large enough to accommodate a family party comprising the earl himself, his daughter Frances and her husband Sir Gervase Clifton and Lord and Lady Clifford, and the rent included all necessary bedding, linen, brass and pewter. The house itself possessed a great chamber, five lodging chambers, two garrets, a hall, a kitchen and two cellars. This was clearly a

---

36 *Ibid.*, 125.

37 *Ceremonies of Charles I: The Note Books of John Finet, 1628–1641*, ed. A.J. Loomie (New York, 1987), p. 73, cf. pp. 86–7; *KW*, III, pt i, 153–4. French ambassadors lodged at Arundel House in 1617 and in Suffolk House (formerly Northampton House) in 1624: Kingsford, 'Bath Inn', p. 252; LMA, WJ/SR/ (NS) 12/158.

38 TNA, SO3/10, March 1633.

39 In Covent Garden in the 1630s, townhouses tenanted by gentlemen cost a minimum of £25 a year, whereas nearly half the houses costing £40 a year or more were occupied by peers or gentlemen: Smuts, 'The Court and its neighbourhood', p. 137. As early as 1614, Chamberlain reported that the widow of the great courtier Sir Walter Cope had taken a house on Drury Lane, at a rent of £30 a year, which was a great come-down from her mansion on the Strand, but probably good-quality gentry accommodation, *Chamberlain Letters*, I, 594. In 1634, the fashionable Lady Carlisle rented a house in the Strand for £150 a year from Thomas Carey, soon to be English ambassador in Venice: Knowler, I, 176.

substantial house by the standards of the metropolis. Nevertheless, the limits of aristocratic living in the capital are underlined by the fact that the house rented by Cumberland, although working out to an annual charge of nearly £200 a year, still required him to board out his servants at a cost of 10s per week.[40]

Lesser members of the gentry also needed to track down accommodation and negotiate terms whenever they came to the capital. The agreement entered into by Sir John Wynn in 1606 suggests the situation that some members of the gentry may have encountered. At the cost of £100 for nine months (from Michaelmas to Midsummer), accommodation was to be provided for Sir John, his wife and daughter, a chambermaid and three men, with stabling for three geldings. The cost was to include hay, straw and three bushels of provender weekly as well as fire and candlelight for their chamber. The Wynns were required to bring sheets and linen for their chamber, and their own maid was to undertake all washing using soap and starch, although the maid of the house would do washing 'by buck' (bleaching). Because the house was actually shared, the agreement seems to have been especially detailed. It specified, for example, that Sir John's wife might entertain her friends 'with meat', but not with lodgings, while Sir John's men were to be civil, and not quarrelsome or drunken.[41]

The market in lodgings was generally a competitive one, and the Wynns, like other families, lived in a range of houses over the years. The correspondence of the Smyths of Ashton Court, a wealthy West country family, reveals that between 1628 and 1641 the family always stayed within Westminster, but not always in the same parish. In 1628, Thomas Smyth stayed at Lord Paulet's house in Petty France, 'at the lower end of Tuthill Street', while subsequent visits saw him staying in St Clement Danes, first at the sign of the Reindeer and then at the sign of the Prince's Arms 'at one Mr South's house, a cutler at Denmark House'. In 1631, Mary Smyth reported that her husband had just taken a house in Drury Lane. The location in this instance was determined partly by price, since the houses in Covent Garden were found to be too small, except for the largest, which were available only at £4 to £5 per week. By 1640, however, Thomas Smyth was to be found staying in St Margaret's parish, where he found lodgings at the Saracen's Head, near Palace Gate, moving the next year to St Martin's, where he occupied a house in the Strand, near Bedford House. The mobility of the Smyths appears to have been quite common, and was probably related to the type of accommodation sought in the year in question. A family party demanded a larger, more commodious house, while Thomas Smyth obviously accepted more modest lodgings during solitary visits to the capital.[42]

40 Chatsworth House, Bolton MS 99, f. 224: sum paid to Mrs Ogle, 'dwelling in the Strand over against the New Burse'.

41 *Calendar of Wynn of Gwydir Papers 1515–1690* (1926), no. 403. The house was located near the Rolls Chapel, in Chancery Lane and so technically outside Westminster.

42 J.H. Bettey (ed.), *Calendar of the Correspondence of the Smyth Family of Ashton Court 1548–1642* (Bristol Record Society 35, 1982), pp. 88, 95, 106, 111, 149, 164, 176.

Although house-hunters used informal networks to track down accommodation, it is clear that a more market-oriented system was already in full swing by the 1620s, with houses intended for wealthy tenants advertised by the posting of bills in public places.[43] But who provided rented accommodation in Westminster? Landlords seem to have varied as much as the type of housing available. Some gentlemen stayed in accommodation provided by innkeepers and victuallers. In 1622, Sir Sampson Darrell and Sir Ambrose Turville were said to live in the house of an 'ordinary keeper' near Charing Cross.[44] Lesser gentry may have found themselves in the relatively humble position of the impoverished Lady Cave, who lodged in a victualler's house among 'a number of gentlemen that victual in the house, every man in his chamber apart'.[45] It seems clear, however, that letting property to provincial gentlemen provided a valuable second income to men who pursued a variety of other professions. In the early 1620s, for example, George Barnes, a haberdasher in the Strand, provided lodgings for Sir Francis Nethersole, while Elias le Talliard, a goldsmith 'near Charing Cross' rented rooms in his house to Sir William Somerset; and Edmund King, a prosperous scrivener who prepared documents for the parish of St Martin in the Fields, housed one Ambrose Wheeler, 'gent'.[46] Although it is difficult to say much about the quality of rooms or houses provided, it is striking that the craftsmen and retailers active in the lodgings market occupied the higher spheres of their own professions. Lord Haughton may have lodged with a skinner in 1620, but Francis Peirson, the man in question, actually supplied robes of state to members of the House of Lords, while Thomas Smyth did not lodge with just any glazier in 1641, but with Thomas Bagley, the King's master glazier.[47]

Surviving correspondence suggests that most rented houses required the occupant to furnish the property to a required standard. Nevertheless, more specialized furnished 'luxury' accommodation was available and men such as John Cleeves of St Clement Danes evidently responded to a perceived demand. For over thirty years Cleeves kept a large and 'fair' house by 'the sign of the Black Boy', specifically to lodge gentlemen during term time, having set up in business around 1605.[48] There were many reasons why this more specialized housing was popular for those not wanting to rent a property. The cost and inconvenience involved in transporting one's furnishings

43   TNA, SP14/164/10.

44   TNA, SP14/134/88.

45   *Wynn Papers*, no. 597. Lady Cave had been forced to close her house in Holborn. The victualling house in question was located in the Old Bailey, actually outside Westminster, but the type of accommodation was also to be found in Westminster, see below.

46   TNA, SP14/134/86 (return of sojourners and lodgers remaining in Westminster and the Strand, 22 December 1622).

47   *Holles Letters*, II, 242; *Correspondence of the Smyth Family*, p. 176.

48   LMA, WJ/SR (NS) 41/16, 41/28, 41/38. Richard Denham, a member of the Court of Burgesses, described the house as 'an ordinary for gentlemen of quality' and certified that Cleeves's establishment was a respectable one.

from the country could be considerable, especially if the stay was not lengthy or did not involve all the family. When the earl of Clare contemplated a relatively short stay in the capital in 1627, he noted that it would be 'infinite trubblesome' to move all necessaries for keeping house. Instead he proposed 'to take sum lodgings furnished, where one might have linnens, things for the kitchen vyz. suche [as] My Lord Say hath in Holborne at this time, and suche had or hath Sir Arthur Ingram at Doctor Hethers'. The Dr Heather who had obliged Sir Arthur Ingram was the famous William Heather, former chorister of Westminster Abbey and friend of William Camden, who established a professorship of music at Oxford. Heather, and later his widow, regularly provided high-quality accommodation for members of the gentry in the house he leased from the Abbey. Located within the close of the collegiate church, the house would have been particularly desirable given its proximity to the Court, and it seems that Heather was not the only member of the Abbey establishment to rent out furnished lodgings. In 1626, Lewis Bayley, bishop of Bangor, was to be found writing from his lodging 'in Westminster cloister at Mr Frost his house', while as early as 1605 prebendal houses were sometimes made available to certain favoured members of the gentry.[49]

Furnished and unfurnished lodgings all formed part of a lucrative rental market and may have affected property prices more generally. The earl of Clare, a canny urban landlord who acquired a sizeable number of properties in St Clement Danes in the early seventeenth century, commented on what seemed to be the escalating prices that even mediocre houses could command. Hearing in 1627 that the earl of Bedford wanted to sell his 'little hows at Westminster', he noted its limitations: 'roomes he hath ennough, but little, a little hall, and little parlor, the rest answerable' and yet, to his astonishment, the house was said by locals to be worth £500.[50] The inevitable result of such conditions was a rapid rise in urban building on leasehold, with the development of St Martin's Lane, and later Covent Garden, Queen Street and Drury Lane, seeking to capture the new market of gentry and aristocratic residents.

Nevertheless, it would be wrong to paint the character of the demand and development of the gentry housing market in entirely rosy colours. Factors affecting the market often pushed in opposite directions. Demand for housing could be uneven and clearly was highest during periods when parliament was in session. Restrictions on new building in the capital from the late Elizabethan period up to the Civil War, although frequently flouted, still seem to have kept a restraining hand on unfettered speculative building.[51] That being said, the famous case of John More, clerk of the

---

49 *Holles Letters*, II, 348, 456–66, 68–9; National Library of Wales, Carreglwyd III/10. I would like to thank Simon Healey of the History of Parliament for a transcript of this letter. *Wynn Papers*, no. 348. For Heather see *DNB*. Frost held the position of 'chaunter' at the Abbey: WAM 34165, 35681.

50 *Holles Letters*, II, 354. Clare's rentals from urban properties accounted for approximately half his income by the later 1620s: *ibid.*, I, 'Introduction', pp. xvii–xxxi.

51 T.G. Barnes, 'The prerogative and environmental control of London building in the early seventeenth century: the lost opportunity', *California Law Review* 58 (1970), pp. 1332–63 and discussion below, ch. 6.

signet, who was singled out in Star Chamber in the 1630s, and heavily fined after building a large number of houses in St Martin's Lane, suggests that the temptation to build was almost irresistible. More claimed that he had watched his neighbours in St Martin's Lane building illegally for the past seventeen years before finally succumbing himself. More's case, however, was extreme and it is clear that his punishment was intended to be exemplary.[52]

The housing market was also periodically dampened by royal proclamations requiring the gentry to return to the country and resume their traditional provincial responsibilities. Proclamations against gentry residence were issued on no fewer than seventeen occasions between 1596 and 1640, although the extent of enforcement varied considerably. The three main periods of enforcement clustered around 1595–1601, 1622–24 and 1632–36. The proclamations did, however, permit individuals to transact essential business during the law terms, while members of the royal household and Privy Council were exempted. In early 1623, during what appears to have been one of the strictest periods of enforcement, Sir John Coke was told that if he had not already decided upon 'your house in St Martin's Lane', that he could take his pick of rented accommodation there or elsewhere 'at indifferent prices' given that the two proclamations against gentry residence had so emptied the City and suburbs.[53] Another contemporary noted in 1624 that prices had fallen because of the proclamations, but 'if Parliaments bee heereafter so frequent as the King promiseth, houses in Westminster will hold upp well enough'.[54] Over the early Stuart period as a whole enforcement was intermittent and, while the level of prosecution intensified in the 1630s, petitions and warrants surviving from the same decade demonstrate that it was increasingly possible to obtain a written dispensation from the proclamation.[55] Overall, the proclamations did not prevent gentry residence in Westminster or its attendant property market, but it may have affected the latter's buoyancy. Finally, it is important to remember that some members of the gentry and aristocracy still chose to reside outside Westminster – and this not just in nearby parishes such as St Bride's and St Dunstan in the West but even within the City of London itself.[56]

52 *HMC Cowper*, II, 47.

53 *Ibid.*, I, 127; Heal, 'The Crown, the gentry and London', pp. 211–15, 219–20. Even in 1623, however, Lady Bedford expressed mild surprise that the proclamation had deterred Lady Cornwallis from coming to town that winter, since 'I wolde have gotton you a dispensation': *Private Correspondence of Lady Jane Cornwallis*, ed. Lord Braybrooke (1842), p. 85.

54 TNA, SP14/164/10.

55 The Bankes manuscripts in the Bodleian Library (38/29) contain many petitions and warrants relating to the proclamations. Between 1632 and 1640, 238 dispensation warrants were issued: Heal, 'The Crown, the gentry and London', p. 223.

56 Stone, *Crisis*, p. 397; J. Robertson, 'Stuart London and the idea of a royal capital city', *Renaissance Studies* 15 (2001), p. 39. On gentry and aristocratic residence in London in 1595, see BL, Lansdowne MS 78/67, ff. 165–167. Some peers inherited medieval houses in the City, such as the earls of Pembroke, who possessed a house at Baynard's Castle: Spence, *Lady Anne Clifford*, p. 99.

To sum up, the period from the late sixteenth century to the Civil War saw an increasing gentry and aristocratic presence in Westminster, although numbers could fluctuate significantly year by year within this broad upward trajectory.[57] The significance of this presence, however, can easily be misinterpreted since the exact constituents of this elite population were constantly shifting. The overall picture of gentry residence is of one characterized by high mobility.[58] From year to year, gentlemen often flitted between the Westminster parishes, occasionally straying into adjacent London or Middlesex parishes, such as St Giles in the Fields. For most it was also a year-by-year decision whether to come to the capital at all. The strong market for lodgings suggests that, while the desire to be in the capital was high, only a minority were actually prepared to maintain a permanent town establishment, and historians such as Stone have probably overestimated the latter phenomenon.[59] As we shall see in later chapters, this distinctive pattern of gentrification had long-term consequences for Westminster's social and economic development.

SHOPPING

In the early modern period new imported luxuries, easier access to the capital for entire families and new patterns of consumption made shopping one of the more important activities taking place within the Westminster parishes. This was not an entirely new phenomenon, since Westminster shops had traditionally sold a range of luxury goods aimed at those attending the royal law courts, Westminster Palace and, later, Whitehall Palace. In the fifteenth century the occupations of St Margaret's residents, for example, included goldsmiths, tailors, embroiderers and even spectacle-makers.[60] Nevertheless,

57 One very rough guide to gentry residence in Westminster is provided by the poor-rate records of St Martin's for the early Stuart period. These show that numbers of titled ratepayers fluctuated over the period, ranging from as few as eighteen recorded in 1607–8 (after thirty in 1606–7) to fifty-six recorded in 1618–19. The 1620s regularly saw around fifty titled men and women assessed in the parish (WAC, F333–356). The changing use of assessment and 'benevolences' makes it difficult to provide entirely reliable figures.

58 See also below, ch. 8.

59 Figures cited by Stone of peers who 'had a townhouse' or 'a fairly permanent residence' (*Crisis*, pp. 395, 397) are problematic, since they do not distinguish between short-term accommodation and longer leases, a confusion partly exacerbated by surviving source materials: poor rate records do not specify forms of occupation. Stone *does* note that in the 1620s and 1630s, even among the peerage only forty-one had houses of their own as opposed to fifty-nine living in rented houses or lodgings (*ibid.*, p. 396). F.J. Fisher ('The development of London', pp. 180–1) also observes that 'it was still the custom for them [the gentry] to stay in hotels and lodgings rather than to possess town houses of their own' in the early Stuart period. Barron ('Centres of conspicuous consumption', pp. 1, 12–13) notes the medieval pattern whereby peers increasingly preferred to rent accommodation in London rather than purchasing it.

60 Rosser, pp. 146, 148–9, 161–5. On medieval shopping in the capital see D. Keene, 'Shops and shopping in medieval London' in L. Grant (ed.), *Medieval Art, Architecture and Archaeology in London* (1990), pp. 29–46.

from the late Elizabethan period onwards there was a growing recognition of the commercial potential represented by new gentry residents and seasonal visitors. This was to lead to the creation of Britain's Burse, the first major attempt to develop the area commercially as a centre for the sale of luxury goods.

For gentry visitors to the capital, shopping formed an important part of their stay. This was not simply a leisure activity. Fashionable purchases made in the capital undoubtedly played a role in maintaining status, as well as indulging one's personal taste. Beyond this, however, most visitors came armed with the shopping lists of provincial friends and relatives. Executing these commissions efficiently displayed one's superior knowledge and taste as well as advertising the fact that one belonged to a family able to travel to the capital in the first place. In this way, shopping in the capital must have had the indirect effect of oiling the wheels of patronage and sociability within provincial society.[61] Shopping thus provided the opportunities for reciprocal gifts and favours that formed an important part of the 'social commerce' of the period.[62] Relying on others to make important purchases was, of course, fraught with difficulty and so letters tried a variety of expedients to make sure the item was what was required. Writing to Lady Cornwallis in 1624, Nicholas Bacon enclosed a length of thread that was the exact length of his pair of pistols, so that a case could be made for them.[63]

Fashionable clothing and accessories probably topped the shopping list of many visitors, especially those items requiring luxurious fabrics or specialist handling and finishing. Such demands explain the numbers of tailors, shoemakers, embroiderers, glovers and milliners – to say nothing of the jewellers and goldsmiths – who crowded into the parishes of St Martin's and St Clement's. These individuals provided a steady stream of merchandise to short-term visitors, to the great magnates in their mansions along the Strand and to those who lodged at Court. There were many such as Mrs Dodson, a needlewoman who lived in Hartshorn Lane, just off the Strand, who not only produced work herself but taught others and supplied patterns to them.[64]

Appropriate dress was essential to social and political success, and was not just the preoccupation of the frivolous-minded. Writing to his brother in the country, Henry Oxinden reminded him that 'most men, especially such as have power, doe thinke themselves disparaged to keep company with men of mean attire'. Oxinden's advice on the type of dress necessary for those coming to town – what to buy and how to make do – must have been echoed by many of the more knowledgable country gentry advising less-travelled friends and relatives. He advised that 'Brother Barrow' should

---

61 E.g. D. Gardiner (ed.), *The Oxinden Letters 1607 to 1642* (1933), p. 176. For the later seventeenth century see S.E. Whyman, *Sociability and Power in Late-Stuart England* (Oxford, 1999).

62 *Ibid.*, pp. 88–9, 185; Bryson, *Courtesy*, pp. 123–4.

63 Cornwallis, *Correspondence*, p. 96.

64 LMA, WJ/SR (NS) 40/12. St Margaret's appears to have had fewer residents involved in the production and sale of clothing, although one Jane Ryhova, wife of John Daniel of Tothill Street, produced 'tyres' and head-dresses and included the Countess of Essex among her clients: *Les Reportes del Cases in Camera Stellata 1593–1609*, ed. W. Baildon (1894), pp. 408–9.

be consulted when dealing with any tailors, to ensure that James Oxinden would not be 'cousened' or fobbed-off with yesterday's fashions. Finally, since an 'indifferent' cloak would not do in the novel circumstances of a visit to the capital, Henry Oxinden generously offered to 'lend you my best for 2 or three especiall weeks (if needs requiere)'.[65]

The quality and stylishness of goods obtained in the capital – not just Westminster – was one of its attractions to those in the provinces. Sir John Wynn particularly asked for 'a pair of good London boots to keep out the water', while the earl of Clare felt he could only rely on the skill of one Mrs Ward of Milford Lane, near St Clement's church, when he needed to acquire a cap with a discreet fringe of red hair, to be realistically sprinkled with grey.[66] Provincial gentry were even able to make provision for their remembrance by posterity when visiting Westminster. Craftsmen in the area were able to sell partially assembled tombs, which could be shipped down to their country where the final erection of the monument would take place. Although some of this work took place in Southwark workshops, by the 1630s the fame of 'the Tombmakers at Charing Crosse' had become proverbial.[67]

The examples provided above should make it clear that shopping, and hankering after new and luxurious fashions, was common to men as well as women in this period. Nevertheless, contemporaries regularly presented such concerns as a distinctively feminine 'vice'. Plays and royal speeches alike associated women with an obsessive and destructive desire for consumer goods. In a speech in Star Chamber, James I lashed out at 'the pride of women' which forced their fathers and husbands to take them to London 'because the new fashion is to be had nowhere but in London'.[68] There were other aspects of the urban lifestyle which generated these particular anxieties about the gender order (as we shall see), as well as a venerable tradition of seeing the meretricious attractions of the city as emasculating for men, as well as particularly enticing for women. Nevertheless, the dean of Westminster's refusal to allow women wearing yellow ruffs into Abbey services in 1620, and the Abbey preacher who condemned idle women 'seeking after the fashions', reflected the fact that lavish expenditure on fashions, and the social and moral anxieties which went with it, were firm features of the locality.[69]

Emblematic of this development in Westminster was the construction of Britain's Burse (or the New Exchange as it came to be called). This marked the single most

---

65   *Oxinden Letters*, pp. 169–70.

66   *Wynn Papers*, no. 284; *Holles Letters*, III, 495.

67   Sheffield City Archives, Strafford Papers 6, p. 38. For a 1601 agreement concerning the construction of a tomb between the Lucy family and the masons and tombmakers, Isaac James (a St Martin's parishioner and office-holder) and Bartholomew Atye: TNA, SP46/23, ff. 145r–v.

68   *Political Works of James I*, p. 343.

69   Merritt, 'The cradle of Laudianism? Westminster Abbey 1558–1630', *JEH* 52 (2001), p. 640. On views of London see L. Manley, *Literature and Culture in Early Modern London*, (Cambridge, 1995), ch. 2; P. Lake, 'From Troynouvant to Heliogabulus's Rome and back again', and J.F. Merritt, 'Introduction: perceptions and portrayals of London 1598–1720' in J.F. Merritt (ed.), *Imagining Early Modern London* (Cambridge, 2001).

systematic and high-profile attempt to locate luxury retail shopping in the western part of the metropolis in the pre-Civil-War period. Westminster's hold on the vast trade in luxury goods was hardly exclusive, and its shopping district did not outshine that of the City of London's Royal Exchange. Nevertheless, by the seventeenth century the expansion of the Court and the increase in the sheer numbers of the wealthy and fashionable residing in Westminster seem to have boosted the retail economy. The creation of Britain's Burse was a deliberate attempt to exploit – and perhaps encourage – the capital's prosperous westward development.

The building of Britain's Burse in 1609 was also part of a more general strategy of property development undertaken by Westminster's high steward, Robert Cecil, earl of Salisbury. Costing over £10,000, it was constructed along the Strand, next to Durham House, its façade entirely faced in expensive stone and adorned with sculptures. The purpose of the building was to provide arcades of specially designed shops, located in a pleasant and luxuriously decorated environment.[70] Shop leases were limited to haberdashers, stocking-sellers, linen-drapers, seamsters, goldsmiths, jewellers, milliners, perfumers, silk mercers, tiremakers, hoodmakers, stationers, confectioners, girdlers and those dealing in china, pictures, maps or prints. Booksellers were also permitted, and the first edition of *Othello* was published in 1622 by Thomas Walkley at the Eagle and Child in Britain's Burse. The idea seems to have been to provide unusual and costly items to catch the eye of those who came to browse. There were a hundred shops in all, although they were described as 'being as it were small chests rather than shops'. The earl of Salisbury promoted the venture heavily, speeding the building along its way and arranging a formal opening of this 'New Exchange' in April 1609.[71] The entire royal family attended the occasion, which was marked by an entertainment written by Ben Jonson, with scenery designed by Inigo Jones.[72] Despite this auspicious beginning, the fortunes of Britain's Burse were somewhat mixed and initially the shops were difficult to let. By and large, however, they were successful in the 1610s, suffered during the trade depression of 1621, only to recover again during the 1630s.[73]

---

70 Stone, *Family and Fortune*, pp. 101, 105, 112, 113; L. Stone, 'Inigo Jones and the New Exchange', *Archaelogical Journal* 114 (1957), 106–21.

71 Stone, *Family and Fortune*, pp. 103–4; *SL*, XVIII, 94–6. It is interesting to note that Cecil defended the venture to the City at much the same time (1606–7) that Westminster's inhabitants were preparing another bid for incorporation – a bid he was likely to have opposed. Cecil claimed that he was determined to leave future inhabitants of Westminster with 'some such Monument as may adorn the place, and happily derive some effect of present benefit and future charity to the whole Liberty'. He also suggested that Londoners should be willing to share some of their prosperity – 'some little quill of profit to pass by their main pipe': *HMC Salisbury*, XX, 213.

72 J. Knowles, 'Jonson's *Entertainment at Britain's Burse*' in M. Butler (ed.), *Re-presenting Ben Jonson* (Basingstoke, 1999), pp. 114–51; Archer, 'Material Londoners?', p. 186. The suggestion that the verses spoken on this occasion emphasized the 'distinctive aristocratic ethos' of the New Exchange seems unwarranted.

73 Stone, *Family and Fortune*, pp. 104–9.

Yet Britain's Burse offered not just a concentration of luxury goods, but also an environment in which shopping became more of a sociable activity. Habits did not change overnight: in the decade after the opening of Britain's Burse the earl of Cumberland still sent servants to buy him a ruff and cuffs in the Burse, as well as choosing hats and bands from a selection brought to him privately in his lodgings.[74] But for others, shopping afforded opportunities for social exchange and discourse. The surveyor Francis Carter warned against the Cecils' attempts to build on remaining areas of space in the Burse by observing that 'it begins to be an appointed place of meeting, for men to walk and stay on for another'. This offered commercial opportunities, he continued, as 'in that staying, a man sees one thing or other that he will buy, [as] I know by my own experience and proof'.[75]

It would also be easy to exaggerate the degree to which Britain's Burse constituted a socially exclusive setting in which the gentry shopped only among their equals in decorous surroundings. It would certainly not have made commercial sense for the shopkeepers of Britain's Burse to have narrowly restricted themselves to what was still only an intermittent gentry presence. In fact, Britain's Burse was not the hermetically sealed haven of gentry exclusivity that some modern accounts suggest. Shortly after the shops had opened, it was noted that the 'playing of foils and cudgels', the barking of dogs, and ball games 'which breaketh the windows' all disrupted the serene ambience in which customers might most easily be persuaded to part with their money. A pair of stocks had to be erected to deal not only with those caught pilfering and stealing but also with rowdy shopkeepers.[76] The Privy Council noted in the late 1630s that Britain's Burse was also pestered by the erection of sheds up against the shops, which were used to house inmates and 'other uses not fit to be continued', creating both 'present annoyance' and the risk of plague.[77] Yet however much it might struggle to suggest a world of social exclusivity and decorous living, Britain's Burse undoubtedly managed to manufacture an impression of exclusivity in an urban environment that could attract both the gentry and the well-to-do middling sort anxious to distance themselves from those of lower social status. It was in this sense appealing to the increasing taste for social distance and exclusive forms of sociability that were central to the new ideals of gentry urban culture.[78]

Ultimately, Britain's Burse was not just significant as a shopping development that flaunted its aristocratic associations. At the time it was also seen as a project that would dramatically intensify the drift of certain luxury trades away from the City and towards the western part of the metropolis. Even before it was built, the Lord Mayor

---

74 Chatsworth House, Bolton MS 97, f. 102; MS 95, f. 46.

75 Cited in L. Peck, 'Luxury and war: reconsidering luxury consumption in seventeenth-century England', *Albion* 34 (2002), p. 8.

76 TNA, SP14/49/5; C. Pendrill, *The Adelphi* (1934), pp. 50–1, 56, 61.

77 TNA, PC2/49, pp. 164–5.

78 Bryson, *Courtesy*, ch. 4.

of London had objected to the unfair advantage that it would enjoy over the Royal Exchange, 'being near unto the Court of Whitehall in the midst of the Nobility and where much of the Gentry lodge and reside, as also in the high way by which all Termers pass to Westminster'. He particularly warned that it would ultimately draw 'Mercers, Goldsmiths and all other chief traders to settle themselves out of the City in those parts'.[79] Although Britain's Burse may not have undermined City retailers severely, the very fact that it was erected suggests a recognition of an economic shift starting to take place within the capital. In 1635, for example, the Goldsmiths Company petitioned the Privy Council about the increasing drift of goldsmiths away from Cheapside and Lombard Street in the City and towards the western suburbs. The petition noted no fewer than twenty-five goldsmiths located in the Strand and Fleet Street in addition to others resident in 'Westminster' (i.e. St Margaret's parish). The company protested that this concentration outside the City walls (and the company's jurisdiction) would be to their detriment, but clearly the lure of being situated closer to many of their customers proved too much for many goldsmiths.[80] By 1639, silver smiths, silver-drawers, jewellers, engravers and gilders appear in significant numbers among the occupations practised in Westminster. The foreign luxury goods of all kinds so coveted by fashionable Englishmen could be bought with increasing ease, in many cases from a range of French craftsmen and retailers who settled in the western suburbs of the metropolis after Henrietta Maria became queen.[81] The conditions that encouraged luxury trades to site themselves further westwards are clearly apparent in our period, and ventures such as Britain's Burse first exploited these opportunities systematically. It was only the post-Restoration period, however, that saw the real consolidation of this area as the leading shopping district in the capital, boosted by City retailers who quickly sought to re-establish trade after the devastation inflicted by the 1666 Fire of London.[82]

SIGHTSEEING

As the seat of national government and the site of the royal Court, the law courts and parliament, Westminster played host every day to large numbers of people who poured

79 Cited in Stone, *Family and Fortune*, pp. 96–7.

80 *CSPD 1635*, pp. 237–8. See also P. Griffiths, 'Politics made visible: order, residence and uniformity in Cheapside, 1600–45' in P. Griffiths and M. Jenner (eds.), *Londinopolis* (Manchester, 2000), pp. 178, 181, 186–7, 189.

81 TNA, SP 16/414/96, 97, 139. It is likely, however, that the Strand had traditionally contained a certain number of goldsmiths: Archer, 'Industrial history', p. 73. See also *Harrison's Description of England*, I, 237–40 for the rising standard of living among the gentry and aristocracy. Howes's 1631 edition of Stow's *Annales*, pp. 869, 1039–41, also discusses the development of the market for luxury goods in the capital.

82 S. Porter, *The Great Fire of London* (Stroud, 1996), pp. 177–8; T. Reddaway, *The Rebuilding of London after the Great Fire* (1951), pp. 42, 47, 300–2, 306 n.2.

into the town to pursue legal and administrative business or to present petitions. But alongside those whose business took them to Westminster, the locality was also visited by large numbers of men and women who came to view the singular sights and activities associated with the area.

As we have seen, Westminster lodged many visitors to the capital and was also a tourist destination in itself. Of course, visitors did not limit their sightseeing to Westminster alone. The Tower of London, St Paul's Cathedral, the Royal Exchange in London, the Bear Garden and theatres in Southwark all attracted their share of visitors and are noted in diaries and letters home. Perhaps the chief attraction of Westminster, however, was its association with the monarch.

For many well-to-do foreign and English visitors, the opportunity to observe some aspect of the life of the royal Court was clearly the highlight of a journey to the capital. Catching a glimpse of the monarch, hearing a sermon in the Chapel Royal, touring the various royal gardens and apartments or perhaps attending royal tournaments and entertainments – all were possible features of a visit to Westminster. What emerges from many accounts is the relative ease of access to at least parts of the Court and to official occasions (however much access may have been strictly regulated in the innermost parts of Whitehall Palace). James I, for example, seems to have revived the ancient custom of dining publicly in the Presence Chamber. In the more decorous and private Court of Charles I, a great dinner celebrating peace with Spain appears to have been a public occasion, a toast proposed by the King being interrupted by 'the disturbance of the disorderly multitude scrambling for the boxes of sweet meates, thrown . . . among them by the king and the great lordes'.[83] Others commented on seeing the monarch, in a manner that suggests that seeing (not meeting) the sovereign was often all that was really desired or expected.[84] Of course, part of this access was linked to the custom whereby the monarch received petitions from subjects, a process that was subjected to some regulation. Monarchs were regularly approached by petitioners on the way to the Chapel Royal, at table and at Whitehall, while passing through the Privy Gallery – a thoroughfare that was also a place to lounge, stroll or catch the eye of the influential.[85] Indeed, access to the Chapel Royal itself appears to have been surprisingly open, at least in the Jacobean period. When guards were asked why they did not stop a man later apprehended as a pickpocket there, they replied that the fellow had been dressed 'in a very good and seemely apparell, like unto a Gentleman or Citizen' and so they did not query his entry – a policy that suggests that

---

83   *KW*, IV, pt ii, 29; N. Cuddy, 'The revival of the entourage: the bedchamber of James I, 1603–1625' in D. Starkey (ed.), *The English Court: From the Wars of the Roses to the Civil War* (1987), pp. 182, 184; Loomie, *Ceremonies of Charles I*, p. 96.

84   *KW*, IV, pt ii, 29; *The Diary of William Whiteway*, ed. D. Underdown (Dorset Record Society 12, 1991), p. 151.

85   *KW*, IV, pt ii, 17. Access to the king was far more limited under Charles I: K. Sharpe, 'The image of virtue: the court and household of Charles I, 1625–1642' in Starkey, *English Court*, pp. 226–60.

visitors and possible suitors to the monarch were expected.[86] This suggestion is confirmed by the experience of Sir Richard Paulet, who attended the Chapel Royal when he came up to the capital for the parliament of 1610. After receiving communion, Sir Richard's maidservant was discreetly approached by an attendant, who asked for the name of her master, since the King required a record to be kept of all who received there.[87] For those of gentlemanly status, at least, this relative ease of access extended to other activities connected with the Court. Simonds D'Ewes, while a student at the Inns of Court, thought it only natural to turn up for an ambassadorial reception at York House. Although D'Ewes had some difficulty gaining admission at first, he was ultimately able to see both Prince Charles and the duke of Buckingham.[88]

The Tiltyard at Whitehall Palace was also a major attraction for visitors to the capital. Tournaments and festivities held at Whitehall Palace attracted crowds from throughout the capital and this was one way in which at least a part of the Court would have been on view to the public more generally.[89] Members of the public could attend these occasions on payment of a fee. During the reign of Queen Elizabeth, annual exercises were held in the Tiltyard to celebrate the monarch's birthday. In addition, Elizabeth moved the Grand Feast previously held at Windsor to Whitehall, as part of the development of annual St George's Day ceremonies into a great public spectacle. Viewing stands ultimately became a permanent fixture. Indeed this structure held its attractions even during times when public festivities were not on the agenda. In one scandalous incident, the local watch discovered the royal jester Archie Armstrong in the judge's seat in the Tiltyard, in the company of a woman and with 'his points undone'.[90] Viewing galleries of a more specialized kind were built for ambassadors as the occasion required, although important guests could also be accommodated at the windows of houses overlooking the Tiltyard itself. During the reign of James I, Lady Walsingham's lodgings were frequently put to use in this way. The Tiltyard was also occasionally used for bear-baiting, as least during the reigns of Elizabeth and

---

86 *The Arraignment of John Selman* (1612), p. 6. The deacon, Francis Walsingham, had to join a throng of fellow-petitioners along the King's route to the Chapel Royal when he tried to present a paper to the King: Francis Walsingham, *A Search Made into Matters of Religion* (St Omer, 1609), pp. 31–3. I would like to thank Dr Anthony Milton for the latter reference.

87 Hampshire Record Office (HRO), MS 44M69/F6 (Diary of Sir Richard Paulet, 1610), entry for 1 April.

88 *The Diary of Simonds D'Ewes 1622–1624*, ed. E. Bourcier (Paris, 1974), p. 170. Tickets were required for access to events in the Cockpit: *A Deep Sigh Breath'd through the lodgings at Whitehall* (1642), sig. A3v.

89 A tradition dating back to the reign of Richard II involved Coronation feasts taking place at Westminster Hall, accompanied by the ritual entry of a royal champion on horseback, who threw down a gauntlet against any challengers, a tournament then following the next day or shortly thereafter: A. Young, *Tudor and Jacobean Tournaments* (c.1987), p. 103.

90 *Ibid.*, pp. 84–6, 103; WAC, WCB2, pp. 26–7. See also LMA, WJ/SR (NS) cal. vol. 37–40, p. 182, for a case of a man found 'suspiciously' with two 'wenches' in the Tiltyard one night.

James, making it a major source of outdoor entertainment and ceremony, not just in Westminster but in the capital as a whole.[91]

Royalty could also be glimpsed in one of the most popular 'sights' of Westminster – Westminster Abbey – where the royal tombs were a magnet for visitors. Such was the popularity of visits to view the 'monuments at Westminster' that the chapter appointed an official keeper of the monuments from at least the 1580s, and a patent for this lucrative post, which included the profits from 'showing' the monuments, sold for £250 in 1615. In the 1590s a satire by the poet John Donne had even featured 'The man that keepes the Abbey tombes, / And for his price doth with who ever comes / Of all our Harries, and our Edwards talke'.[92] Foreign and English visitors alike visited the Abbey, both before and after the Reformation, and scholarly works on the Abbey, as well as a little guidebook to the tombs written by William Camden, began to be available from the later sixteenth century. Presumably this guide might have purchased by a visitor such as the earl of Huntington, who paid 2s to be shown the 'toomes' in 1606 – but the burial place of kings also attracted humbler visitors, such as a Jacobean mariner who arranged an outing to see the monuments with a friend.[93]

Westminster Hall was another popular venue for visitors to Westminster. The business of the law courts attracted a huge variety of visitors who included sightseers such as Lady Margaret Hoby in 1600, and law students who came to take notes on cases in progress.[94] Part of the hall also contained stalls, which sold not only items such as law books and legal stationery but also ribbons, trinkets, toys, gloves, combs and looking glasses. In this way stallholders profited not only from the Hall's serious legal business but also from those waiting in attendance on the law courts or tourists curious to the see the venue of so many famous state trials, from that of Sir Thomas More to the infamous Overbury murder case.[95]

Finally, it is also clear that many of the great aristocratic houses of Westminster routinely opened their doors to visitors.[96] Many visitors commented on the picture

91 Young, *Tournaments*, pp. 86–9.

92 *Acts*, no. 541; Durham Cathedral Archives, Hunter MS 44 ('Memorials taken out of my brother William Neile's Almenack Bookes' by Richard Neile, 1624), p. 217v; 'Satyre IV', *The Complete English Poems of John Donne*, ed. C.A. Patrides (1985, rpt, 1990), p. 233.

93 *HMC Hastings*, I, 368; LMA, WJ/SR (NS) 41/9; *The Diary of Baron Waldenstein*, ed. G.W. Groos (1981), pp. 37, 41. A surviving copy of Camden's *Reges Westmonasterii Sepulti* (1600) is inscribed as being purchased in Westminster for 10d on 28 July 1600: CUL (shelfmark: SSS.44.10).

94 D.M. Meads (ed.), *Diary of Lady Margaret Hoby* (1930), p. 152; *Diary of Simonds D'Ewes*, pp. 61, 77, 191. For cutpurses and pickpockets apprehended in Westminster Hall see LMA, WJ/SR (NS), 21/142, 28/132.

95 *CSPD 1634–35*, p. 591. Archbishop Laud recorded a small fire there in 1631, 'by burning of the little shops or stalls kept therein': *London P&P*, III, 484.

96 Strong, *Renaissance Garden*, p. 51, notes that Leicester's garden at Kenilworth Castle 'was basically the formal garden of Whitehall and Hampton Court transferred to the nobleman's great house'. As in the medieval period, it seems that most noblemen reserved their prestige-building for their country houses, although peers such as Arundel represent an important exception: Barron, 'Centres of conspicuous consumption', pp. 10, 11, 14.

galleries and public rooms of these houses, and they must have been well known in the locality. Some houses could be visited and viewed without the need to meet the owners. This was true of Sir Walter Cope's house, with its notable collections of coins, pictures and curiosities. Similarly, the famous collection of statues and pictures displayed at Arundel House was also open to members of the public, or at least to those of gentlemanly status.[97] The formal gardens of the great aristocratic houses also attracted visitors and a tour of them was part of the hospitality that the owners of such houses could provide. In the early Stuart period, the gardens of Arundel House elicited admiration, while in the Elizabethan period the substantial gardens of Burghley House in the Strand – including a walled mount garden and orchard – reflected the personal interest of the great Elizabethan statesman and it is known that they were presided over by the famous herbalist John Gerard.[98]

OUTDOOR RECREATIONS

More than any other part of the capital, early modern Westminster witnessed the creation of designated green spaces, specifically set aside for leisure. Although London saw the setting out of Moorfields in the Jacobean period, this afforded one of the few public places for Londoners to walk amid trees and flowers.[99] But in Westminster such ventures were encouraged by the presence of the gentry and aristocracy and, as a result, parks and gardens were equipped for a variety of outdoor recreations that were particularly tailored to their needs. Green spaces partly provided a venue where members of fashionable society could socialize and be 'seen'. Equally, Westminster's gardens were prized as places of refuge and quiet conversation, which offered sweet, health-restoring air.[100] Both the preservation and the formalization of green spaces, however, was initially due to the elite sporting tastes of those linked to the Court.

The first major initiatives took place under Henry VIII, who took the opportunity to equip Whitehall Palace with tennis courts, a cockpit for cock fighting, bowling alleys and of course the Tiltyard. These sporting facilities suited the tastes of a young and active king, who keenly participated in all types of sport and hunting and encouraged his

---

97 *HMC Hastings*, I, 362; C. Williams (ed.), *Thomas Platter's Travels in England in 1599* (1937), pp. 171–2. In 1623, after attending a Gowrie Day sermon, D'Ewes went with a friend to to see 'the elephant that was come out of Spaine', and then on to view the pictures and statues 'at My Lorde of Arundels howse without Temple barr', *Diary of Sir Simonds D'Ewes*, pp. 150–1. J. Newman 'A draft will of the earl of Arundel' *Burlington Magazine* 122 (1989), pp. 692–6.

98 P. Henderson, 'A shared passion: the Cecils and their gardens' in P. Croft (ed.), *Patronage, Culture and Power: The Early Cecils 1558–1612* (New Haven, 2002), pp. 100–1 and plate X. Gerard dedicated his *Herball* to Burghley in 1597.

99 M. Galinou (ed.), *London's Pride: The Glorious History of the Capital's Gardens* (1990), pp. 49–51.

100 *SL*, XX, 58–9; For later see L. Williams, ' "To recreate and refresh their dulled spirites in the sweet and wholesome ayre": green space and the growth of the city' in Merritt, *Imagining*.

courtiers to do likewise.[101] The attractions of promenading and the enjoyment of green spaces amid the dirt and noise of the capital were also to be found in the more formal setting of private gardens and those open spaces maintained and developed by the Crown. Banquets had been held in St James's Park since the sixteenth century. The earl of Leicester, for example, had prepared one for Queen Elizabeth in 1562 to celebrate May Day, and banqueting houses were still located there in the seventeenth century. Similarly, Hyde Park was acquired by the Crown from Westminster Abbey in 1536, when it became part of the extensive royal hunting grounds, which stretched almost all the way to Hampstead Heath. Timber stands were erected in the park, where the King or other observers could watch the progress of the hunt. Banqueting houses were also set up in Hyde Park, the first as early as 1546, when one was said to have been built for the French ambassador.[102]

As the century wore on, however, other sports also gained popularity in fashionable society. In 1598 Sir Robert Dallington praised the French game of pall-mall as a 'gentlemen-like sport', which 'yields good occasion and opportunity of discourse, as they walke from the one marke to the other'.[103] By 1635, one Archibald Lumsden received a crown grant to set up all the necessaries 'for the game of Pall Mall within . . . [the] grounds in St James' Field', and to charge his customers accordingly.[104] It was the more traditional sport of bowls, however, that gave rise to Spring Gardens, one of the better-known pleasure gardens of the early Stuart period.[105]

Here outdoor pursuits combined sport with a chance to eat, drink and stroll in a landscaped setting. Spring Gardens was adjacent to the royal Court and so came under the formal control of the lord chamberlain, via a keeper appointed by him. Although the chief attraction was the bowling green, it effectively operated as a fashionable and expensive ordinary, where the gallants of the day paid 6s each for a meal. Its courtly setting attracted numerous gentlemen and lords, but the 'continual bibbing and drinking Wine all Day long under the Trees' led to two or three quarrels a week, according to the newsletter writer Garrard. Ultimately Spring Gardens may have been the victim of its own success. In 1634 a notorious quarrel between Lord Digby and Sir William Crofts prompted Charles I to close the bowling green for a day and then indefinitely, chiefly because of concerns over violence committed in what was held to be 'the King's garden'.[106]

---

101 Stow, II, 102.

102 D.J.H. Clifford (ed.), *The Diaries of Lady Anne Clifford* (Stroud, 1990), pp. 72, 74; *KW*, IV, pt ii, 157–60.

103 *London P&P*, III, 8–9.

104 *CSPD 1635*, p. 404.

105 The first reference to bowling alleys in Westminster dates from 1460: Rosser, *Medieval Westminster*, p. 216. Strong (*Renaissance Garden*, p. 178) notes that even in the early Stuart period Sir John Danvers's famous Italianate garden at nearby Chelsea contained an oval bowling green, 'an essentially English feature'.

106 Knowler, I, 261–2.

The demand for places of outdoor recreation in Westminster certainly did not abate with the closure of Spring Gardens in 1634. Its success may well have prompted the creation of a public bowling green on the east side of Leicester Fields, which itself was laid out for formal walks in 1631. The subsequent suppression of Spring Gardens, however, paved the way for the creation of one of the most elaborate public venues designed specifically for the gentry and aristocracy in the pre-Civil War period. The 1635 building of Shaver's Hall in fields behind the Royal Mews – near the Court, but not too near – provided a range of activities which allowed gentlemen to divert themselves as well as to forge useful social and political contacts. The earl of Clarendon later described it as a 'fair house for entertainment and gaming, with handsome gravel walks with shade'. Here 'very many of the nobility and gentry of the best quality resorted both for exercise and conversation', and it was here that Clarendon recalled having encountered men such as the earl of Bedford.[107] The house, which contained dining rooms, gaming rooms and kitchens, was designed in the most luxurious fashion possible, the roof also having been leaded and enclosed with an ornamental railing to permit visitors to enjoy a roof-top stroll. The house and gardens were built at an estimated cost of over £4,000 and included lavish facilities. The grounds were divided into two distinct sections, with the upper part containing a tennis court and a bowling alley. Access to the lower part of the grounds was via a tunnel, which went under a footpath and led to a second bowling green and an area with gravelled walks and gardens.[108]

Despite the aristocratic overtones of Shaver's Hall – peers such as Lord Dunbar were said to have lost £3,000 here at one sitting – its origins were less elevated. The entire complex was, in fact, built by Simon Osbaldeston, the earl of Pembroke's 'gentleman barber', who had acquired a good deal of experience in running such an establishment as Pembroke's deputy at Spring Gardens. Clearly Osbaldeston had built his establishment with the market carefully in mind and conscious of the pitfalls of the earlier complex. The name of 'Shaver's Hall', was ironically bestowed upon it after its opening, although at first there was said to be 'no conceit . . . of the builder's being a barber'. The losses of gamblers 'shaved' there coupled with Osbaldeston's former occupation, however, quickly led to the nickname, one writer mischievously remarking that 'my Lord Chamberlain Pembroke' would 'chafe abominably' when he came to hear of it.[109]

The gambling at Shaver's Hall was arguably less important than the opportunities that this and other such venues provided for a range of forms of gentry sociability and public assembly – conversation, promenading, eating and drinking, and so on – in a

---

107 C.L. Kingsford, *The Early History of Piccadilly, Leicester Square, Soho and their Neighbourhood* (Cambridge, 1925), pp. 54–5, 79–84.

108 Kingsford (*ibid.*, pp. 82–3) cites a 1651 parliamentary survey, which describes the building in great detail. The cost was estimated by Garrard in 1635: Knowler, I, 336. Osbaldeston paid a fine to St Martin's parish to compensate it for building on lammas land: e.g. WAC, F362, n.f.

109 *CSPD 1635–36*, p. 462. Pembroke does not seem to have financed the venture. He was, however, said to frequent the place 'where they bowl great matches': Knowler, I, 435.

socially exclusive setting. These venues helped to create a social arena that was outside the Court itself although within its social ambit. But even under the aegis of the Court the creation of new amenities for exclusive forms of social display and interaction flourished in this period. In the seventeenth century, Hyde Park also seems to have become increasingly popular as a fashionable outdoor venue, where friends met and members of the Court displayed themselves in their coaches. Ben Jonson alluded to the parade of coaches as early as 1620, while the duchess of Newcastle recalled girlhood memories of the 'Ring' in Hyde Park. To celebrate an official 'opening' of the park in 1638, the dramatist James Shirley even wrote a play entitled *Hyde Park*, a work that involved its characters in the foot-races which were so popular a feature of the park.[110] St James's Park also increasingly developed as a setting for formal walks and diversions during the reign of James I. The famous Hollar engraving of 'Summer', depicting a fashionably dressed lady, is set against a vista of promenading figures in St James's Park – obviously her appropriate social setting. Utilization of green spaces also had a gender component. Hunting, walking in royal gardens or carriage rides, all were deemed suitable for respectable upper-class women, while sporting facilities, with their associations with gambling, drinking and prostitution, appear to have been more male-dominated locations.[111]

How exclusive were these venues? There were degrees of privileged access to certain areas around Westminster, and private walks only available to the peers and courtiers with the necessary keys.[112] Pleasure gardens, however, were not necessarily socially exclusive. Admission to Spring Gardens appears to have been open to all who could afford it, although some might have preferred a more exclusive atmosphere. In 1620, Sir Thomas Littleton came across one of his creditors, the merchant tailor Robert Holloway, in Spring Gardens, where the latter had been advised by his physician to walk 'into some fresh and sweet ayer'. Disconcerted, Sir Thomas sneered that he did not expect to see men of Holloway's 'vocation admitted to come thither'. When Lord Digby was later reproached for brawling there, he airily explained that 'he took it for a common bowling place, where all paid money for their coming in'.[113] Places like Shaver's Hall, Hyde Park and St James's may have enjoyed a greater social cachet, but there is little suggestion that they pursued formal policies of social exclusion. We may perhaps assume that similar considerations governed admission as noted earlier for the Chapel Royal – with relatively open access to well-dressed men and women who conducted themselves in an appropriate manner. If so, it seems likely that

---

110 *London P&P*, II, 250. Shirley's dedication to the Lord Chamberlain Pembroke records that he wrote the play at the earl's request. Presumably this 'opening' related to the building of the New Lodge in 1634–35 at a cost of about £800: *KW*, IV, pt ii, 159.

111 *London P&P*, I, 187; *KW*, IV, pt ii, 241–52; A. Griffiths and G. Kesnerova, *Wenceslaus Hollar: Prints and Drawings* (1983), p. 81.

112 See below, ch. 6. The earl of Cumberland paid 2s on a visit to Westminster in 1614 for 'a double key for the Covent Garden gate to goe the nearest waie to the markett': Chatsworth House, Bolton MS 95, f. 156.

113 TNA, STAC8/176/9; Knowler, I, 261–2.

aristocratic fashions and pleasures were increasingly enjoyed by those of prosperous middling status. It was wealth, not birth, that was the crucial criterion. Nevertheless, these social amenities ultimately derived their rationale and appeal from their sense of social exclusivity. Here were places where members of the gentry and aristocracy could mix publicly with those of similar manners and fashions, and these were social interactions which served crucially to validate and reinforce those status-conscious values that were shared in such settings.[114]

EATING AND DRINKING

The heavy concentration of eating and drinking establishments within Westminster formed a venerable part of its medieval history. The presence of the law courts, government bureaucracy and the Court all within the confines of the town had fuelled the demand for inns, taverns and victualling houses. Indeed, the monks of Westminster had owed much of their prosperity to the rents paid by local brewers and innkeepers. In medieval Westminster, most of this activity was concentrated within St Margaret's parish, along the two main arteries of Tothill Street and King Street, with another cluster of inns and taverns along the Strand, running eastwards towards the City.[115]

By the early modern period, population increase and rising numbers of gentry and aristocratic visitors to the capital led to an explosion in the numbers of alehouses, inns and taverns. Westminster's hostelries served a diverse clientele and there was an establishment to cater for every pocket.[116] The range of people passing in and out of the town every day makes it unlikely, however, that such places were entirely dependent on the upper echelons of society. At the cheaper end of the market were alehouses, whose clientele included not only the poorer sort more generally but also the many servants employed by an increasing gentry population. Local authorities found it difficult to keep up with the proliferation of alehouses, particularly those at the cheaper end of the market. In June 1634, the Middlesex justices licensed 285 alehouses in the parishes of St Margaret's and St Martin's alone, but also suppressed a further 162 in the same area.[117] Such establishments were necessary, but contemporaries often associated them with crime and vice and the large numbers of poor who also made up the population of Westminster.[118]

114 Bryson, *Courtesy*, pp. 115, 133.

115 Rosser, pp. 122–33.

116 See M. Carlin, 'Provisions for the poor: fast food in medieval London', *Franco-British Studies* 20 (1995), pp. 35–48; S. Pennell, ' "Great quantities of gooseberry pye and baked clod of beef": victualling and eating out in early modern London' in Griffiths and Jenner, *Londinopolis*, pp. 228–49.

117 *CSPD 1634–35*, p. 107. The exact figures are: St Margaret's, 159 licensed and 77 suppressed, St Martin's, 126 licensed and 85 suppressed.

118 P. Clark, *The English Alehouse: A Social History 1200–1830* (1983), pp. 145–51, 166–76.

A different sort of hostelry was usually frequented by gentry customers. Edward, viscount Conway, regularly dined in local taverns, and it was not uncommon for Conway to spend as much as 13s on a supper in a tavern.[119] In 1620, it was recorded that nearly a hundred taverns were to be found between Charing Cross and Temple Bar.[120] Taverns could be substantial and highly respectable venues. The members of St Martin's vestry, for example, frequently met at the Salutation Tavern, in Brewer's Alley, to discuss parish business. Thomas Larkin, the King's master locksmith, owned the Sun Tavern in King Street, opposite the turning into New Palace Yard. This prime location must have made the business a profitable one, and a plan of the property reveals the large kitchen and huge oven that served the establishment.[121] Some hostelries must have aimed to cater for the more socially elevated market that the gentry migration to Westminster afforded. This is borne out by a proclamation of 1634, which, to encourage gentlemen to live more willingly in the country, forbade the dressing or eating in inns of all game and fowl, such as 'Pheasant, Partridges, Ducks as also Hares'.[122]

The tables of the rich, and the many eating houses located in the town, also fostered a demand for a variety of fruits and vegetables. This demand in turn was answered by commercial gardeners, a large number of whom were based in Westminster. Commercial gardeners had been based in Westminster since the medieval period when along with York, the town had supplied the needs of gardeners throughout the country. One of these, Henry Russell, provided plants for Henry VIII's garden at Chelsea, while the Banbury family, located in St Margaret's parish, operated a business near Tothill Street for over fifty years. In 1597, Gerard praised another 'painful planter', Henry Banbury, who was especially known for the many excellent varieties of apples and pears he stocked. That these commercial gardens were still flourishing well into the Stuart period is attested by the newsletter writer James Howell, who in 1629 sent Sir Arthur Ingram 'a hamper of Melons, the best I could find in any of Tothilfield gardens'.[123] Other commercial gardeners less known to history obviously operated in the locality, and on a substantial scale. In 1633, one St Margaret's gardener broke into the garden of another and stole four thousand liquorice plants, said to be worth £10 – the same amount that the future Secretary of State Edward Nicholas paid per quarter to rent a house in King Street.[124]

---

119 *CSPD 1634–35*, pp. 590–1. On the definition of inns and taverns see Clark, *Alehouse*, pp. 5–15.

120 BL, Harleian MS 6850, ff. 31–2.

121 E.g. WAC, F2, vol. 2, f. 357; J. Schofield, *The London Surveys of Ralph Treswell* (1987), pp. 143–4.

122 Knowler, I, 176.

123 J. Harvey, *Early Nurserymen* (1974), pp. 39–44; J. Howell, *Epistolae Ho-Elianae* (5th ed., 1678), p. 199.

124 LMA, WJ/SR (NS), 36/197; *CSPD 1631–33*, p. 376; see also ch. 6.

Urban travel and social relations

The spread of new forms of land transport was a marked feature of seventeenth-century England. The impact of these new developments on local society was perhaps most immediate and striking in Westminster, where aristocratic residents and members of the Court were more quickly able to adopt modish and convenient forms of transport. It was here that the increasing use of coaches began not only to generate new demands and practical problems but also to stimulate changes in the ways in which the more affluent members of society conducted themselves, and experienced the metropolis.

Travel by water was the traditional (and most convenient) means of transport in medieval London. The great medieval houses along the Strand had been designed to face on to the Thames, which served as the capital's main highway, and some lords kept their own barges. During the fifteenth century, an increase in the traffic passing between the City and Westminster encouraged the development of the Strand's street frontage, which was leased out to innkeepers and small traders.[125] Nevertheless, travel by water continued to play a dominant role, with the aristocratic houses of the seventeenth-century Strand still served by stairs down to the Thames. Further down river, the Privy Bridge – a substantial two-storeyed structure – served Whitehall Palace, while the main approach by river to Westminster Palace and New Palace Yard was at the King's Bridge.[126] The Crown itself retained the services of about forty watermen who were called upon to act on public occasions, including John Taylor the Water Poet. More generally, foreigners such as the Swiss traveller Thomas Platter commented on the richly furnished wherries that plied their trade along the river, taking well-to-do customers even relatively short distances.[127]

By the early seventeenth century, however, the watermen of the Thames were having to compete with coaches for passengers and they soon lodged formal complaints with the Crown. The wealthiest residents of the capital maintained their own private coaches, but hackney coaches were increasingly popular and were widely used by members of the gentry. By 1634, one Captain Bailey kept a coach stand at the Maypole in the Strand, attended by drivers in livery. In that year it was also said that four men could travel in a hackney coach from Temple Bar to Westminster for 12d, while Sir Edward Conway was able to hire a hackney coach for an entire day for 6s.[128] During the reign of Charles I, the use of hackney coaches, in particular, seems to have exploded.[129] By the mid-1630s it was being estimated that there were some six thousand hackney coaches operating

---

125 Barron, 'Conspicuous consumption', p. 5; *SL*, XVIII, preface, p. xxi.

126 *KW*, IV, pt ii, 295, 302–3.

127 Bernard Capp, *The World of John Taylor the Water-Poet 1578–1653* (Oxford, 1994), p. 15; P. Razzell (ed.) *The Journals of Two Travellers in Elizabethan and Early Stuart England* (1995), p. 12; TNA, E163/13/18, ff. 17–18, 43; LMA, WJ/SR (NS) 14/8.

128 Capp, *John Taylor*, pp. 15, 31–3; Knowler, I, 227; *CSPD 1634–35*, p. 591.

129 Rushworth claimed that at the accession of Charles I in 1625 there were no hackney coaches standing in the street and that only twenty coaches were available for hire in and about London – a

within a four-mile radius of London. Nevertheless, the congestion and damage that coaches left in their wake did concern the authorities. Accordingly the Caroline Privy Council tried various means of restricting coach use – setting a minimum distance for coach journeys, limiting their use to peers and trying to reduce congestion at Blackfriars playhouse by prohibiting coaches from waiting for playgoers. These schemes raised a good deal of dissatisfaction, yet, despite some strictness in enforcement, it is clear that the Crown was waging a losing battle. In one case a ban broke down as soon as the man responsible for the regulation and licensing of hackney coaches (the Marquis of Hamilton) left town.[130]

Already by the Jacobean period coaches had become a necessary adjunct to a fashionable lifestyle: by 1636 it was possible to associate old-fashioned Elizabethan virtue with noblemen who still habitually walked on foot in the capital.[131] Travel by foot and on horseback was also partly displaced by newly fashionable sedan chairs and litters, which became sufficiently numerous to display an identifying number.[132] Splendid coaches became a sign of wealth and status, often adorned with coats of arms and furnished with richly embroidered cushions. Accordingly, an elaborate etiquette revolving around the use of coaches began to develop. The correct way to accompany a visitor to his coach or to acknowledge the salute of someone passing by in a coach was a necessary part of a gentleman's social education.[133] Henry Peacham, however, gently mocked these social nuances in *Coach and Sedan*, where it was debated 'whether an empty coach, that had a Lords dead painted Coate and Crest . . . upon it without, might take the wall of a Sedan that had a Knight alive within it'.[134] The lending and borrowing of private coaches also locked social elites into complex forms of obligation and patronage. During various visits to Westminster, the earl of Cumberland borrowed coaches belonging to other men with links to his own part of the country,

---

claim that seems a severe underestimate, although the increase in the number of hackney coaches seems to date from this period: J.F. Larkin and P. Hughes (eds.), *Stuart Royal Proclamations* (2 vols., 1979–83), II, 495, n.1.

130 H. Peacham, *Coach and Sedan* (1636), sig. F; *Stuart Royal Proclamations*, II, 494–6; Knowler, I, 175, 181, 266; J. Scally, 'The political career of James, Third Marquis and First Duke of Hamilton to 1643' (Cambridge Ph.D., 1993), pp. 103, 150. Sharpe, *Personal Rule*, pp. 405–6. Note Thomas Wentworth's request for a dispensation in Bodl., Bankes MS 64/27.

131 Peacham, *Coach and Sedan*, sigs. C3v–C4. The increasing use of coaches during the Elizabethan period was noted by Stow (I, 84).

132 E. Jones ('The first West End comedy', *Proceedings of the British Academy* 68 (1983), p. 223n) cites Brome's 1633 play *The Sparagus Garden*, in which one character pursuing another is told she has gone 'Downe towards the Strand I tell you, in a new Litter, with the number one and twenty in the breech on't'. Restrictions on the use of sedan chairs during time of plague were introduced in 1636: TNA, PC2/48, p. 283.

133 Bishop Lewis Bayley, for example, carefully gauged every mark of respect he received on visiting the capital in 1627: 'Sir Thomas Savage I saw passing in a coach, I being in another, and so very lovingly saluted me & so passed away': National Library of Wales, Carreglwyd MS III/10.

134 Peacham, *Coach and Sedan*, sig. B2v.

including the Archbishop of York, Sir Thomas Wharton and Sir George Calvert.[135] The early Stuart period also saw the parade of coaches in Hyde Park emerge as both a leisure activity and a socially accepted form of self-display.[136] Indeed, the importance of the coach as a social symbol quite literally accompanied the fashionable to the grave. As early as 1618, the corpse of Lady Haddington, daughter of the earl of Sussex, had 'a solemne convoy of almost an hundred coaches (and torches in aboundance) that accompanied her from Westminster to Whitechappel' on her way to burial in Essex, while a similar procession conveyed the body of Lord Banbury out of Salisbury House in 1632.[137]

The use of coaches also stimulated the emergence of distinctive forms of urban sociability among members of the gentry and aristocracy, especially as expressed through formal 'visiting'. The ritualized etiquette of urban 'visiting' may have been elaborated more fully in the later seventeenth century, but the practice itself was clearly established much earlier. Early in the Jacobean period Thomas Gataker had reprimanded members of St Martin's gentry for unnecessary visiting on the Sabbath, while in 1642 the urbane Henry Peacham warned of 'perpetual visits of vain and useless acquaintance'. The hectic round of visits to friends, acquaintances, relations and patrons was not gender-specific. Peacham's strictures were aimed at male visitors, but it is also clear that the pastime was particularly popular among women: in the 1630s Daniel Featley denounced from the pulpit of Westminster Abbey those women who filled their afternoons with 'idle visits'.[138] Access to sedan chairs and the family coach potentially gave elite women greater levels of freedom, and they seem to have exploited this opportunity to undertake expeditions shopping, mixing with friends and attending sermons, without male relations.[139] Lady Halkett saw herself as something of a pioneer in the 1630s, attending places such as Spring Gardens only in the company of other women, yet even after the Restoration she still felt the need to justify this conduct as perfectly proper.[140] The undercurrent of concern over the freedoms made possible by these modes of transport is suggested in contemporary satire. Most of this satire, however, concentrates on travel by women of lower status, including 'Citizens-wives' going by coach to leafy districts outside the capital 'under a colour of seeing

---

135 Chatsworth House, Bolton MS 99, f. 110; MS 97, f. 103; MS 95, f. 116.

136 See above. Cf. Whyman, *Sociability and Power*, pp. 87, 92, 94–5, 100–5; P. Waddy, *Seventeenth-century Roman Palaces* (New York, 1990), pp. 60–2.

137 *Chamberlain Letters*, II, 195; TNA, C115/M35/8406.

138 Peacham, *Art of Living*, p. 245; Merritt thesis, pp. 339–40; D. Featley, *Clavis Mystica* (1636), p. 277.

139 Clifford, *Diaries*, pp. 64, 71–2, 74–5; V. Larminie, 'The undergraduate account book of John and Richard Newdigate, 1618–21', *Camden Miscellany* 30 (Camden Society 4th ser. 39, 1990), pp. 187, 206–7. For the late seventeenth century it has also been suggested that control over use of the family coach was a form of power particularly exercised by elite women: Whyman, *Sociability*, p. 105.

140 *The Autobiography of Anne Lady Halkett*, ed. J.G. Nichols (Camden Society n.s. 13, 1875), p. 3.

their children at nurse to banquet with their sweet-hearts and companions'. Similarly, the spread of coach travel among women of all social classes in the 1630s was mocked as social pretension, which might also accompany sexual misconduct: 'tradesmens wives, waiting-maids and young wenches', who after experiencing travel by coach, 'ever after . . . account themselves companions for the best Ladies'.[141]

The social consequences of coach travel for urban life were far-reaching in other ways.[142] Some of the practical requirements of coach travel generated commercial opportunities for the area: the use of coaches fuelled a demand for stabling and ultimately for houses that could accommodate private carriages. Great houses such as Arundel House had separate coach houses, and the provision made for stables and coaches was one of the selling points of houses built in Covent Garden in the 1630s. The shortage in Westminster of places to park or store coaches is suggested by the prosecution in 1632 of a man who was said to keep coaches in St Martin in the Fields while actually residing elsewhere.[143]

Other aspects of coach travel were more onerous for the locality. To be experienced at its best, travel by coach required broad, straight and well-paved streets of the sort not generally found even in well-to-do parts of Westminster. In 1601, the portion of the Strand that led from the earl of Bedford's house to Charing Cross had a 'noisome' channel running near the doors of the houses, while the ground itself was said to be so high and sloping that coaches and horses frequently overturned. The need to improve roads used by the monarch in his coach became an increasingly problematic issue, especially as the financial responsibility for the upkeep of roads was a controversial matter, and could prove costly for the local parishes. Similarly, parishes baulked at the cost of maintaining roads for new aristocratic houses located some distance from built-up areas, as in the case of Goring House.[144]

It can also be argued that the very use of coaches reinforced a sense of social distance between their privileged occupants and others on the road. Coaches increasingly injured pedestrians, while their capacity for speed led to frequent quarrels with pedestrians and those driving other vehicles. A typical dispute erupted in St Martin's Lane when a coach found its way blocked by a man paving the road. When the coachman found that he could not easily turn the vehicle around, he came to blows with the paviour who had inadvertently blocked his path.[145] Occupants of coaches remained

---

141 Peacham, *Coach and Sedan*, sigs. C1v, F4v; cf. L. Gowing, ' "The freedom of the streets": women and social space, 1560–1640' in Griffiths and Jenner, *Londinopolis*, pp. 130–51.

142 Some scholars find a parallel between the privacy that coaches afforded their occupants and trends in architecture, which allowed an increasing sense of the individual to develop through the arrangement of private rooms: see Jones, 'First West End comedy', pp. 238–9, 243; L. Manley, *Literature and Culture in Early Modern London* (Cambridge, 1995), pp. 505, 507.

143 LMA, WJ/SR (NS) 34/55.

144 *HMC Salisbury*, XIV, 101–2, 183; XXIV, 198; WAC, E18, f. V. Presentments against all the Westminster parishes for not maintaining the highways properly came before the Middlesex and Westminster JPs on a regular basis: e.g. LMA, WJ/SR (NS) 34/150.

remote and largely unknown by passers-by, although the livery of coachmen or the arms on highly decorated private coaches were probably familiar to the nobility and may have become known to local residents. None the less, the complexities of social interaction introduced by coaches is suggested by a case in which a St Margaret's constable actually apologized for his behaviour when he was struck by Lord Fielding after stopping the peer in a hackney coach. As the constable explained, he could not necessarily tell from the outside of a coach whether or not there was a lord inside.[146]

SERVANTS

The lifestyle of Westminster's elite required the employment of large numbers of servants. Coachmen, stableboys, porters, gardeners, messengers and a whole range of domestic servants kept the fashionable houses of Westminster running. Their numbers were augmented by a veritable army of household servants employed at Court. While numbers employed at Court fluctuated significantly over time, a book compiled in March 1638 lists 245 servants working everywhere from the counting house and gardens to the kitchens, cellar and buttery, with a further 133 acting as servants to these higher servants. In addition to these named servants, it is clear that the royal household also employed others more fleetingly, according to demand.[147]

Although the Crown would have been the single largest employer of servants in Westminster, many men and women would have found work in gentry and aristocratic households. The households of great aristocrats were undoubtedly hubs of activity, especially those along the Strand. In 1584–85, for example, Robert Dudley, earl of Leicester, is thought to have operated a household of between a hundred and a hundred and fifty people while at much the same time Lord Burghley's household numbered at least a hundred. It is sometimes difficult to distinguish between official servants 'in ordinary' and the larger penumbra of servants who were employed on an 'extraordinary' or casual basis, but clearly every great house had its hangers-on, hoping for occasional work.[148] A great institution like Westminster Abbey also attracted those seeking odd jobs or for crusts from the great table.[149] By the end of the sixteenth century, the large noble retinues characteristic of the medieval period were becoming far less common.[150] Nevertheless, the

---

145 LMA, WJ/SR (NS) 34/64, 142; 41/5.

146 HLRO, MP 29 June 1641. During this tense time politically, it is possible that Fielding deliberately travelled in an unmarked coach: cf. LMA, WJ/SR (NS), 41/6.

147 TNA, SP16/386/97. On the numbers at the royal court in the sixteenth century see Adams, *Leicester and the Court*, pp. 25–8, 116.

148 Adams, *Household Accounts*, pp. 28–30.

149 In 1617 the Dean specifically complained about the number of 'hangbies' that the Abbey seemed to foster, ordering servants and strangers to keep away from the buttery and cellars 'nor to bring his freendes to the buttery hatch', WAM Chapter Act Bk II, ff. 23r–v.

150 Stone, *Crisis*, p. 395.

number of servants employed in Westminster is unlikely to have declined. Increasing gentry and aristocratic numbers in the town would have maintained a large servant population, as well as boosting the opportunities for servants in Westminster's many inns and taverns.

Among servants to be found in Westminster were those who accompanied their masters from the provinces, and therefore experienced their own distinctive version of the West End 'season'. Many gentry families visiting the capital were accompanied by servants – particularly personal servants. Indeed, the number of Catholic servants brought into the capital by their masters during parliament time was raised as a matter of concern in the House of Commons in 1624.[151] More typically, families such as the Oxindens paid a maidservant's coach-fare to bring her from Kent, while other servants travelled with the family when first coming to the capital.[152] The trustworthiness of provincial servants seems to have been the main advantage, although Henry Peacham, in his *Art of Living in London*, warned gentlemen, 'if you bring one with you out of the country, except you have a great eye over him he will quickly be corrupted . . . with much acquaintance'.[153] Yet many nobles and members of the gentry hired lesser servants from the locality on a short-term basis after they had arrived in the capital. Indeed the increasing scale of the practice is suggested by a patent granted under James I to establish a formal employment agency for domestic servants, as well as Peacham's advice to rely upon recommendations when employing a new servant rather than to 'adventure every straggler'.[154]

Short-term employment, with demand picking up when parliament was in session, would not have been uncommon. Indeed, it seems likely that some relatively unskilled servants would have passed from household to household, and possibly even into and out of Crown employment. Little information survives about the scale of casual employment, but destitute servants often appeared in cases heard before local JPs.[155] In 1633, one John Thomas described how he used to 'carry links [torches] to gentlemen about the Court' but was now 'a poor fellow out of service' who lived in humble lodgings in Longditch.[156] The casual nature of employment is also suggested by the testimony of William Ammon, who told how he was in the habit of going to the stables of the duke of Lennox, where finally 'one of the grooms, an Italian, put him on work there this fortnight or so'.[157]

151 C. Russell, *Parliament and English Politics 1621–1629* (Oxford, 1982), p. 160.

152 *Oxinden Letters*, p. 129 (1637). See also *Holles Letters*, II, 279.

153 H. Peacham, *The Art of Living in London* (1642), ed. V. Heltzel (Ithaca, N.Y., 1962), p. 247.

154 *Ibid.*, p. 247; TNA, E163/18/11 (licence granted to Clement Budden and William Barley, to keep a registry of servants and to act as house and land agents in London and Middlesex).

155 E.g. LMA, WJ/SR (NS) 51/18.

156 LMA, WJ/SR (NS) 38/3.

157 Ammon also confessed how he had ultimately used this access to where the footmen usually slept to climb into the house and steal various items of clothing: LMA, WJ/SR (NS) 40/17.

The terms of casual employment may have prompted the emergence of what was clearly an informal network of servants that transcended the households of particular employers, with men and women gathering in alehouses or at each others' places of employment. Joan Dessall, for example, recalled how she and another maidservant went out for an errand, stopping at the 'the sign of the Cock, in Tuthill [Tothill] Street' where they socialized with two of the servants working there. Similarly, when Dinah Ackersley lived in Soho near the stables of Sir Robert Naunton, she grew to know Sir Robert's servants, including his porter, Richard Rose. Thereafter they periodically visited her where she later worked in St Clement Danes, where she would provide them with drink. On the occasion of St James's Fair, Dinah introduced Rose to her sister and her brother-in-law, a 'comfet-maker', and the foursome gathered for a drink in Covent Garden, before passing through Piccadilly to attend the fair itself.[158]

The common practice whereby servants were lodged separately from their masters also helped to generate such contacts between different employers' servants. A 1570 deposition relating to a burglary in the Exchequer paints a vivid picture of the life of one Thomas Brown, 'horsekeper' to John (later Sir John) Stanhope. Brown was paid 40s per year by Stanhope, who lived in St Stephen's Alley in St Margaret's parish. Brown did not live with his master, but lodged separately at the nearby Boar's Head, where he shared a room with another 'horsekeper' employed by Sir John Salisbury. Brown often accompanied Stanhope on visits: one day he went with Stanhope to the lodgings of Henry Knollys in the Old Bailey, and then on to visit Lady Hoby in Blackfriars. When not accompanying his master, though, Brown seems to have been left relatively free, and he describes dining with a servant of the earl of Oxford and 'one Cragge of the pastry' at an inn in Westminster, where they paid 6d each for cold shoulder of mutton, bread and drink. On another occasion, Brown dined at the Boar's Head, where he lodged, and then 'walked up and downe in the palace' (i.e. New Palace Yard) with one James, a servant and 'horsekeper' to the earl of Hertford, after which the two returned to drink at a favourite inn.[159] Depositions from servants in the household of the Exchequer official William Staunton confirm this sense that servants periodically had time on their hands. Staunton's young servants frequently asked permission to go out to play games in Westminster Hall or to play stoolball in New Palace Yard, sometimes in the company of their employers' fourteen-year-old daughter.[160]

Servants employed in a lesser capacity, such as messengers and those who looked after horses and carriages, would often have operated outside the household and may

---

158 LMA, WJ/SR (NS) 40/1–5, cf. *ibid.*, 5/92. Peter Clark has noted how alehouses enabled immigrants to the capital to become integrated within the locality: see his 'Migrants in the city: the process of social adaptation in English towns, 1500–1800' in P. Clark and D. Souden (eds) *Migration and Society in Early Modern England* (1987), pp. 267–91. For a group of linkmen who served various gentlemen but lodged together in Spur Alley, off the Strand, see LMA, WJ/SR (NS) 51/18.

159 TNA, E163/13/18, pp. 17–18. Brown mentions taking the sacrament at St Margaret's parish at Easter, but he does not seem to have done so in the company of his master.

160 *Ibid.*

have been far more loosely attached to it. Records of the period make it clear that large numbers of servants were employed in this fashion. Gentleman who came to Court, visited friends or went to the theatre would always be accompanied by servants, who spent a good deal of time 'in attendance', simply waiting. The accounts of Robert Dudley, earl of Leicester, are regularly punctuated with payments to the servants who attended him wherever he went. In 1559, for example, 12s went towards 'your lordship's servants' dyner when your lordship dyned at my Lord of Pembrokes'.[161] Servants who were 'in attendance' on peers or members of parliament were formally granted immunity from prosecution during parliament time, but this also ensured that there were substantial numbers of unoccupied servants left waiting for long periods around the Parliament House, and it is not surprising that disorderly scuffles occasionally occurred.

Violent quarrels involving groups of liveried servants were also a periodic feature of life in Westminster.[162] The very wearing of livery may have intensified rivalries among servants, especially when alcohol was added to the equation. In 1638, for example, one Carr, a servant of the marquis of Hamilton, found himself the centre of a 'tumult' when he was arrested in front of Wallingford House. When the constable took Carr to a nearby house at Charing Cross, many of the marquis's other servants followed and a crowd seems to have gathered. In their attempt to 'rescue' Carr, the other servants broke into the house, setting ladders up against it and beating up the arresting official, who later died.[163] More generally, masters clearly attached importance to the wearing of livery, possibly because it accorded the wearer access to the houses of the wealthy. Sir Robert Naunton brought a complaint before the Westminster JPs in 1627 when one of his servants abandoned his service without leave, carrying his livery with him.[164]

Concerns over large numbers of liveried servants congregating within a small area seem to have peaked during meetings of parliament. These young men evidently developed their own forms of sociability which might, however, wear a threatening aspect. In 1624, in response to recent 'outrages', the House of Lords issued orders disbanding 'named companies' formed by the servants of peers, which met in a nearby tavern – an order which had to be repeated in 1628. At the heart of the problem was a mock 'company' of coachmen, headed by the coachmen of leading peers, who imitated the conventions of a livery company and seem to have used the tavern as their equivalent of a livery hall.[165] Tensions could also emerge between liveried servants and private

---

161 Knowler, I, 217–19; Adams, *Household Accounts*, pp. 60, 62, 63.

162 E.g. LMA, WJ/SR (NS) 44/38.

163 Knowler, II, 165. It is possible that anti-Scottish and anti-English sentiments may have been at work here.

164 LMA, WJ/SR (NS), 19/133; Chatsworth House, Bolton MS 99, f. 86v (payments for footmen's badges).

165 *LJ* III, 264, 446; *LJ* IV, 13. HLRO, MP, 28 June 1625 (with text of an earlier example from 16 March 1623/4). Problems of disorder were probably made worse by the immunity from arrest which the servants of peers enjoyed during parliament time, leading to many debates about who counted as a 'servant', e.g. *LJ* II, 513, 515, cf. above, ch. 4.

citizens – the former insisting on the dignity of their master. A London merchant named Fox found this to his cost during a dispute with the earl of Dover's waterman over the price of a fare. The waterman dubbed the thrifty Fox 'a three penny companion', whereupon Fox asked jeeringly if the badge upon the waterman's sleeve was a goose. The waterman replied no, that it was a swan, and the earl of Dover's arms, a remark which supposedly prompted Fox to continue that it was 'a fooles coate and a knaves coate'. When brought before the Court of Honour, Fox denied that his quip referred to the earl of Dover, but he was still fined heavily – £200 to the earl of Dover and £200 to the King.[166] In a similar case in 1606, it was claimed that a St Martin's parishioner had defamed Viscount Cranbourne (Robert Cecil) – a dangerous thing to do in the Cecil stronghold of Westminster – leading to a violent quarrel with the servants of another nobleman.[167]

Another crime that constantly lurked on the edge of fashionable society was theft. Access to the houses of noblemen and to the Court itself would appear to have been remarkably open, partly because of the way in which they employed large numbers of people on a casual basis. William Frigg, a tailor who had worked occasionally in the house of Sir Thomas Fernefold, returned there even when there was no work, chatting to maidservants in the kitchen and helping himself to bread and butter – although not to the silver salt, as he assured magistrates in 1635.[168] In 1628, when William Wastwater, formerly a servant to a gentleman usher, was out of service he continued to visit his friends still employed at Court, casually dropping into the chamber of the Maids of Honour.[169] Similarly, in 1637 George Garrard described how the king's servants waited 'Pell-Mell without any Order, lodge still in Court and feed there, though they be out of their Month or Quarter'.[170]

Ostentatious displays of wealth combined with easy access must have encouraged theft in Westminster, and not just on the part of servants, although this group did appear frequently before the justices of the peace. Not surprisingly, opportunistic theft was rife, as the earl of Holland found in 1631 when two velvet cushions were stolen from his coach when it was left standing outside a house he was visiting.[171] The mixture of planning and impulse behind thefts, however, was not always clear. Nathaniel Day, formerly a solider serving with the earl of Lindsay, and lately in Ireland, was found wandering about in a house he conceived to be that of my 'Lord of Lindseys',

---

166 TNA, C115/N9/8854.

167 *HMC Hatfield*, XXIV (Addenda), p. 69.

168 LMA, WJ/SR (NS) 44/13.

169 *Ibid.*, 20/11.

170 Knowler, II, 140. Garrard claimed that disorder at Court was affecting both 'above and below stairs' although he was primarily discussing the liberties taken by 'every mean courtier'. See also the discussion in Scally, 'Political career', pp. 120–1, and the measures to dismiss sixty-one servants in 1638 in TNA, SP16/386/97.

171 LMA, WJ/SR (NS) 31/5, 31/14.

but he denied stealing a cabinet.[172] The ease with which Day was able to enter the house should not surprise us, however, since the openness of the houses of the well-to-do would appear to have been one of the features of town life. This is illustrated by the steps taken in 1637 to protect the house of the future secretary of state Edward Nicholas, then absent from town. Measures included leaving candles at the window and spreading reports that Nicholas's servants were resident, while, intriguingly, particular care was taken to leave the front door open during the day as a sign of occupation.[173] Such precautions exemplify the complex dialectic of exclusivity and accessibility which typified gentry society in Westminster.

CONCLUSION

In October 1642, a pamphlet lamented the decline of Whitehall Palace during the King's prolonged absence. There was now 'no racket nor balling in the Tenis Court, no throng nor mumbling of Coaches before the Court Gates', no 'continuall throng of Gallants' at the entrance to the Court. This spelt doom not only to the many perfumers, jewellers, tire-women, confectioners, glovers, silkmen and dancing masters who had flocked about the palace, but also, it noted mischievously, to the pages and gentlemen ushers who had pocketed bribes to prefer tradesmen to 'Court custome'. Similarly, it was joked, 'Chambermaides and Damsels of the Napery' would now be forced to return home to the country where their herdsmen fathers lived or to marry coachmen who themselves would be reduced to running country inns.[174]

This partly satirical pamphlet illustrates the wider point that the fashionable society of the pre-Civil War period – however exclusive and self-contained it might consider itself to be – existed in tandem with a large penumbra of men and women who depended on and profited from it. The relative openness of townhouses, the Court and pleasure gardens to everyone with wealth and suitable attire, the extraordinary fluidity of the 'fashionable' population, whose dwelling place, length of residence, furniture and servants could change every season – all these helped to make Westminster a dynamic centre of elite consumerism, populated by a partly deracinated gentry who created their own temporary 'societies' every season.

But even if the constituents of fashionable society changed from year to year, its economic impact on the locality was more sustained, and the commercial opportunities more long-lasting. In fact, a substantial proportion of the non-gentry inhabitants of Westminster must have been engaged in various ways – directly or indirectly – with

---

172 *Ibid.*, 41/1.

173 *CSPD 1637*, pp. 372–3. Many accused of theft from gentry houses and caught wandering around them claimed to have entered the house in search of employment, e.g. LMA, WJ/SR (NS) 12/161, 12/165.

174 *A Deep Sigh . . . at Whitehall*, sigs. A2r, A2v, A3v–A4r.

this emerging elite society. Tradesmen could profit by letting houses, running amenities or selling wares, while the poor and unskilled might work in stables and coach-
houses, aristocratic households, or one of the area's prosperous inns. The well-to-do of
the capital were also exposed to aspects of this fashionable courtly society. They might
copy new tastes and fashions – they could purchase goods in Britain's Burse, browse
round the stalls in Westminster Hall, walk in the Spring Gardens, ride in the newly
fashionable coaches and dine in one of the many taverns.

The rise of fashionable urban living could sometimes clash abrasively with the
lives of less privileged local inhabitants. Aristocrats might spurn local office-holders,
the newly fashionable coaches could (literally) ride rough-shod over local residents,
and local industries could struggle to reconcile their needs with the demands of
decorous urban living.[175] Local resentment at the pretensions and luxurious excesses
of fashionable society would have been understandable – after all, its all-too-apparent
evils were regularly attacked from press and pulpit and sometimes we can glimpse the
result. In April 1616 Westminster witnessed one of the increasingly fashionable night
burials, as Sir John Grimes was solemnly buried in a procession of more than two
hundred torches, attended by several members of the nobility. Shortly afterwards,
however, an elaborate parody was enacted one night by 'rude knaves' who buried a
dog with great solemnity in their own torch-lit ceremony in Tothill Fields.[176]

Such sardonic attacks were rare, however, and it may be that Westminster's non-
gentry residents saw little reason to mock a society from whose tastes and foibles they
often stood to gain. This is not to suggest that the denizens of the emerging fashionable
society were integrated into Westminster society. In most cases, one assumes, they
gave little thought to it. Among Westminster's many gentry and aristocratic residents,
relatively few involved themselves in local affairs to any great extent, and therefore few
acquired the local status and authority that went with such involvement.[177] The fluidity
of much of the gentry population and the instability of their living arrangements
may have generated among them a sense of freedom, but it also limited the sort of
sustained role or status that they could command in the locality. Nevertheless, as a
group, their cultural and economic impact on the locality was profound.

---

175 See below, ch. 6.

176 *Chamberlain Letters*, I, 623.

177 The distinction between birds of passage and more or less full-time residents is an important one
here, for which see above, ch. 4.

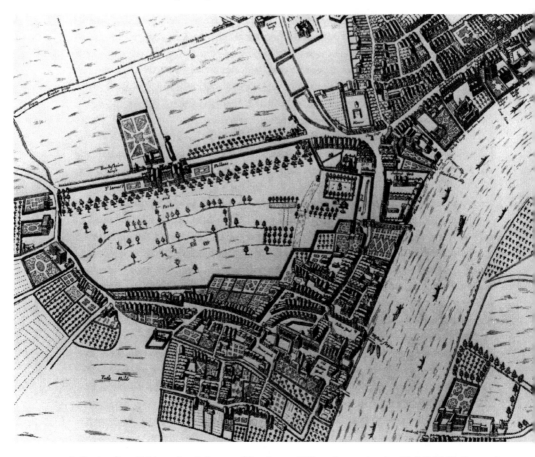

3 Section from Faithorne's 1658 map of London and Westminster, showing Tothill Fields (bottom) and the relatively undeveloped area north of St James's Palace. Note the newer buildings of Tart Hall, Berkshire House and the Gaming House.

Chapter 6

Space and urban identities

WRITING in 1613, St Martin's lecturer Robert Hill completed the dedicatory epistle of one of his works with the wry address 'from your Parish of Saint Martin in (or rather now by reason of many new buildings *neere*) the Fields'.[1] Hill's joke encapsulates what contemporaries would have regarded as the most striking development in early modern Westminster – the steady encroachment of new buildings on formerly semi-rural land. Even in the early seventeenth century, Westminster's inhabitants could thus appreciate the ironic contrast between pastoral placenames and increasing urbanization.

Arguments over the nature and use of land and space provide an important means of investigating social relations in the developing town. Space, after all, was not a neutral commodity, and on a whole range of levels – from the construction of new planned housing to the disposition of a church pew – Westminster's inhabitants appropriated space in ways which promoted their own values, economic interests, and social status. As this chapter will show, the use of land and space in Westminster involved a constant series of negotiations between shifting interest groups and individuals. What was at stake was not merely the deployment of land and space, but also the social and cultural character of Westminster.

THE SUBURBAN INHERITANCE

The pervasive economic influence within Westminster of the royal Court, government bureaucracy and the Abbey is a relatively familiar theme to historians of the capital. Perhaps less widely known to early modern historians is the extent to which Westminster remained 'suburban' in character. Not surprisingly, political and Court historians have been less interested in this aspect of the town's development and yet it

---

1 Robert Hill, *The Pathway to Prayer and Pietie* (1613), epistle dedicatorie, italics mine.

is crucial to understanding the constraints on its emergence as a fashionable, courtly enclave.

To define Westminster as a suburb is to place it within a metropolitan London context. The very fact of the town's location outside the walls of London and outside London jurisdiction gave impetus to certain forms of economic activity from the medieval period onwards.[2] In particular, the area attracted those who engaged in trades that were relegated to the outskirts of London either because they were unpleasant and polluting or because they required more space than the crowded confines of London could easily provide. This, combined with the presence of the vast London food market on its doorstep, meant that butchering, brewing and market gardening all flourished within the town.[3] By the sixteenth century, open fields within Westminster also began to be used for brickmaking, a smoky process which also disfigured the landscape.[4] Although these suburban activities all continued to flourish into the seventeenth century, their coexistence with aristocratic urban development became increasingly problematic.

In the case of the meat trade, for example, early modern butchers continued to operate in surprisingly close quarters to pen-pushing bureaucrats, elegant courtiers and superior shopkeepers. This was a pattern that had its roots in the medieval development of the capital, with attempts to ban slaughtering within the City in 1361. In Westminster, butchers primarily located themselves in St Clement Danes – just beyond Temple Bar and the boundary with the City – and in St Margaret's parish, already an urban centre in the medieval period, with a potentially large contingent of meat-eaters.[5] The open fields that bordered St Margaret's also made this parish an attractive one for butchers, who could graze cattle there before slaughter.[6] Surveys of open fields from the 1630s reveal that certain fields in St Margaret's and St Martin's belonged to butchers, while in 1641, large numbers of 'slaughtermen', including Basil

---

2 G. Rosser, 'London and Westminster: the suburb in the urban economy in the later Middle Ages' in J.A.F. Thomson (ed.), *Towns and Townspeople in the Fifteenth Century* (1988), pp. 55–6; Archer, pp. 12–13, 134–8, 184–5, 186–9, 225–30; D.R. Ransome, 'The struggle of the Glaziers Company with the foreign glaziers, 1500–1550', *Guildhall Miscellany* 2 (1960), pp. 12–20.

3 Rosser, pp. 119–22, 133–43; Rosser, 'London and Westminster', p. 53. Rosser notes (*ibid.*, pp. 51–2) that the 'most critical function performed by the suburban economy was the provision of food'. He also comments that for food producers and sellers in the surrounding countryside, the entire area of metropolis – city and suburbs together – 'represented a single pitch for the retail of their wares' (*ibid.*, p. 53).

4 See below.

5 E. Sabine, 'Butchering in mediaeval London', *Speculum* 8 (1933), pp. 344–5, 348, 350; BL, Harleian MS 6363, f. 22; Rosser, p. 138; cf. M. Carlin, *Medieval Southwark* (1996), pp. 185–7, 237–9.

6 In 1624, one Westminster butcher described how he had bought sixty-two sheep at Leighton Buzzard, Bedfordshire, which he then arranged to be driven down to the capital and placed in Tothill Fields for the night: LMA, WJ/SR (NS) 12/160. This was obviously plausible, even if he was actually accused of stealing the sheep from an innkeeper who was grazing them in St James's Field (*ibid.*, 14/33).

Hedgeman, 'his Ma[jes]ties herdsman', were to be found living in Mill Way, just west of Whitehall.[7] Pasture areas were also located in the northern portions of St Martin's parish, and it should be remembered that the famous Piazza at Covent Garden was built upon what had been known until the 1630s as the 'great pasture'.[8]

It is clear that many of the butchers in Westminster were prosperous individuals who operated on a substantial scale. Like their medieval predecessors they served in prominent local offices. But other contemporary records reveal how common it was for individual men and women to keep a few animals. Westminster burgesses and justices of the peace alike faced a constant barrage of complaints over the problems created by the keeping of livestock in crowded urban conditions. One newcomer to St Margaret's parish, for example, was found to have converted his kitchen into a cow-house, while others kept hogs and swine in their houses, too often allowing the animals to rootle under their neighbours' windows. Of course the burgess court was partly established to deal with cases of nuisance, but the nature and frequency of complaints suggest that these conditions were beginning to arouse greater opposition.[9]

It was the professional part of the trade, however, that increasingly became the object of complaint in certain parts of Westminster. Indeed, the 1585 Westminster Ordinances contained detailed provisions concerning butchering and arranged for the appointment of town hog-drivers and poundkeepers.[10] By the seventeenth century, demands on space and fears over the spread of disease all brought pressure to bear upon local butchers. This was particularly true in St Clement's parish, where butchers were accused of polluting St Clement's well, spreading waste in the fields adjoining Lincoln's Inn and contributing to the spread of plague. The latter concern may have particularly reflected elite sensibilities, especially those of St Clement's lawyers and gentry residents.[11] But such concerns were more widely felt: in 1612 the Court of Burgesses banned butchers from carrying 'Beast offels' through the streets at unreasonable hours, because (it was claimed) it not only annoyed the inhabitants but also infected the poor.[12]

---

7 LMA, WJ/SR (NS) 32/200, 32/201; TNA, E179/253/10, ff. 6–7v.

8 See below. For the driving of hogs along Long Acre in 1630, on their way to the pound, see LMA, WJ/SR (NS), 29/7.

9 Cf. Carlin, *Medieval Southwark*, pp. 186–7, 239; WAC, WCB1, pp. 12, 177. One St Martin's victualler was presented for 'feeding his hogges with carrion and anoying his neighbores', LMA, WJ/SR (NS) 34/68. The illegal sale of meat during Lent meant that butchers frequently came into contact with the law: see also BL, Landsdowne MS 43/25, the answers of the Westminster butchers concerning the sale of fish in Lent (1584).

10 Manchée, pp. 217–19; WAC, WCB2, p. 79; BL, Harleian MS 1831, f. 181; cf. LMA, WJ/SR (NS) 21/17, 21/30.

11 WAC, WCB1, p. 253; TNA, SP16/331/1; LMA, WJ/SR (NS) 45/113, 45/114; cf. Sabine, 'Butchering', pp. 342–3.

12 WAC, WCB1, p. 177 (cf. p. 253).

The Westminster that was the centre of a substantial meat trade also began to jostle with the Westminster that was emerging as a centre of fashionable living and courtier residences. As early as 1600, leases granted in Drury Lane forbade lessees from setting up slaughterhouses, although these had previously operated in this part of St Clement Danes.[13] In the 1610s, the frequency with which butchers drove sheep from Tothill Fields through the streets of the town led the Court of Burgesses to impose substantial fines.[14] By 1639, however, the Privy Council itself intervened more dramatically in a case of annoyance involving Matthew Gunson, a butcher whose shop was located in the Strand 'betweene Yorke howse & the new Exchange' (Britain's Burse). Gunson was given six months to move his shop, but, more importantly, the Council took the opportunity to order that 'no Butchers shopp att all shall be from hence forth kept in the Strand'.[15] Here was one of the first unequivocal examples of a government-led attempt to alter permanently the character of built-up parts of Westminster, removing from a main street one of the more distinctive features of the medieval town.

Brewers were another traditional group within Westminster that found themselves under pressure by the seventeenth century. Brewers in medieval Westminster had been among the wealthiest individuals in the town, and their seventeenth-century counterparts were still an important group locally, some operating on an enormous scale.[16] In 1625, two Tothill Street brewers were among only fifteen in the metropolis chosen to brew 1,660 tons of beer for the Navy in the space of two weeks.[17] A number of brewhouses were situated by the riverside, but they seem to have operated freely in residential areas throughout Westminster. Nevertheless, by the seventeenth century the location of large brewhouses began to arouse some hostility. Most of these complaints focused on brewhouses in St Margaret's parish, where the biggest brewers had established themselves.[18]

13 P. Croot, 'Before and after Drury House: development of a suburban town house 1250–1800', *London Topographical Record* 18 (2001), pp. 33–5.

14 WAC, WCB1, p. 12. The 1585 Ordinances had already imposed a fine of 12d for hogs found wandering off the common at Tothill into streets or churchyards: Manchée, p. 217.

15 TNA, PC2/50, p. 441. Gunson was also immediately required 'not to kill any Butchers meate whatsoever there'.

16 Much brewing, however, was undertaken on a smaller scale, with households brewing their own ale as necessary. Frequent prosecutions for illegal 'tippling' demonstrate how often townspeople supplemented their income by selling some of the ale they produced: Rosser, pp. 126–8; Carlin, *Medieval Southwark*, pp. 204–8. The extent to which Westminster brewers supplied London or the surrounding countryside is not entirely clear, although some Westminster brewers belonged to the London Brewers' Company, including the Elizabethan St Martin's vestryman Derrick Heldon.

17 *HMC Cowper*, I, 200.

18 Because brewhouses were expensive to build and equip, it seems as if brewers generally took over established sites, if possible. One survey notes the names of brewers previously operating on the same site, e.g. 'Bennet who hath lately taken Aliffes house' and Bonde 'who hath taken the Braddflints house': TNA, SP16/346/4.

The cause of the problem was the unpleasant smoke associated with brewing on such a scale, particularly the use of cheap sea-coal. In 1633 the King himself registered complaints that may well have reflected those of other Westminster residents. The choking smoke, it was said, not only caused annoyance but also endangered the health of the entire royal family. In particular, brewers in Tothill Street – whose gardens backed on to the wall of St James's Park – were ordered to stop brewing temporarily during the pregnancy of Henrietta Maria, it being noted that the fumes might also endanger the health of 'both their Ma[jes]ties, and the Princes their Children, as their Maties have found by their own experience.' What is clear, however, is that this heightened royal sensitivity merely marked the beginning of more systematic attempts by the Privy Council to regulate the worst aspects of commercial brewing in Westminster.[19] Four years later, the Council conducted a survey of brewhouses in Westminster, with particular attention to the type of fuel used, although most brewers claimed to use wood and 'charked cinders', each insisting that any sea-coals in their possession were merely 'to burne in his dwellinge house as hee saieth'.[20] These conflicts underline that fact that processes such as brewing existed side-by-side with residential development throughout our period and also that levels of toleration seem to have been declining, perhaps as other sources of air pollution increased.

Intensive urban development also created tensions through the demand for building materials, some of which were produced locally. Parish officials in Westminster were particularly concerned about the increasing use of fields for brickmaking.[21] Clay for brickmaking appears to have been dug in Westminster from the first half of the sixteenth century, probably linked to the convenience of fields and an increasing demand for brick.[22] Brick-kilns and brickmaking were tolerated, but the process of making bricks scarred the landscape, as well as taking land out of pasture. By the early 1630s, St Martin's vestry attempted to deal with the increasing damage caused by digging for 'brikearth, lome, sand and gravell', by fining those whose work was carried out on land that formed part of the parish commons. Brickmaking also caused air

---

19 TNA, PC2/43, p. 239. Among the brewers affected were wealthy men such as George Prynne, Bartholomew Parker and Abraham Bradshawe. Prynne and Parker were also substantial landholders in the locality. In 1631 both men acted as assessors for 'his Majesty's composition hay' and were recorded as holding twelve acres and nineteen acres of land respectively in St Margaret's parish, LMA, WJ/SR (NS) 32/200.

20 TNA, SP16/346/4.

21 Although brick buildings were still relatively few in the early seventeenth century, the Crown increasingly stipulated building in brick and bricks were also used for chimneys, ovens, wells, garden walls and sometimes for the sides of buildings: J. Schofield (ed.), *The London Surveys of Ralph Treswell* (London Topographical Society 135, 1987), p. 28; S. Thurley, *The Royal Palaces of Tudor England* (New Haven, 1993), p. 15.

22 In the mid-sixteenth century one Edward Kingston subdivided Geldings Close (part of modern-day Soho), using over three acres for digging clay and brickmaking and a smaller area for 'grasinge for his horse and other cattle', C. Kingsford, *The Early History of Piccadilly, Leicester Square and Soho* (Cambridge, 1925), pp. 18, 157 (depositions from Wilson *v.* Bristowe). Cf. Kitto, pp. 581–2.

pollution and, like brewing, this began to provoke complaints from Westminster's royal residents. One kiln 'which is . . . verie noysome, and offensive to the King and Queenes ma[jes]tie in their passage to Hyde Parke' was suppressed by the Privy Council in the 1630s.[23] But brickmaking itself seems to have continued unabated, leaving officials to collect rates from an area designated in 1636 as 'the Brick Kilins'.[24] More generally, the concern to regulate brickmaking suggests that the formerly remote areas where men had dug for clay, made bricks and shovelled gravel now found themselves much closer to inhabited areas, while the shrinking amount of common land brought this work under greater scrutiny.[25]

But traditional 'suburban' features of Westminster did not all centre on noxious practices. Gardens, orchards and even specialist nurseries had been commonplace in medieval Westminster, perhaps encouraged by the skills of gardeners serving the royal household, Abbey and nearby episcopal palaces.[26] By the early modern period the increasing demands of the metropolitan food market saw the expansion of market gardening in parts of Westminster.[27] The marshy character of lands stretching out westward to Pimlico made it largely unsuitable for building, but different types of produce grew easily here. As a result, large swathes of land were given over to gardens, without the pressure for substantial building development found elsewhere.[28] The profits of large-scale gardening allowed more than one gardener to end his days as prominent member of the local community. A fine monument in St Margaret's, for example, celebrated the life of the gardener John Varnham (d. 1586), whose charitable activities, we are told, included finding plentiful employment for the local poor in weeding his plots.[29] In addition, local people frequently grew produce and sold the surplus, either in gardens attached to their houses or in one of the many small garden plots located on the fringes of built-up areas. Much of the land which

---

23 WAC, F2002, ff. 91–92; TNA, PC2/42, p. 78. See also *Stuart Royal Proclamations*, ed. J. Larkin and P. Hughes (2 vols., 1973–83), II, 283.

24 LMA, WJ/SR (NS) 32/201; WAC, F363, n.f.

25 The 'Gravell Pittes' are recorded in a 1549 survey, while in 1638 St Martin's officials gave a shilling to a poor girl 'that lay in a Gravell Pitt' near Ebury Farm, WAC, F365, f. 48. Gravel pits are also shown on the 1585 map in Kingsford, *Piccadilly*. In 1623, one John Collins paid £12 a year for gravel pits near 'Pikadilly': WAC, F2, vol. 2, f. 404.

26 See above, ch. 5.

27 F.J. Fisher, 'The development of the London food market, 1540–1640', *Econ. Hist. Review* 5 (1935), pp. 46–64.

28 Rosser, pp. 9–11, 133–7; J. Harvey, *Early Nurserymen* (1974), pp. 39–41. In 1623, St Martin's officials describe travelling to the western boundary of the parish, to the 'herbe gardens right against the Neathouse', WAC, F2, vol. 2, f. 402. A 1631 survey of 'landholders' specifically mentions gardens in 'Streaton ground', the 'horsferry ground and all that levell to Pimlicoe' and an area called the 'Vinegarden', LMA, WJ/SR (NS) 32/200, 32/201.

29 Strype, II.vi.41. In 1633, St Martin's apprenticed one of the parish orphans to William Taylor of Westminster, gardener, WAC, F360, n.f. Houses in Tothill Street and the Woolstaple, surveyed by Ralph Treswell, show gardens and orchards to the back, see Schofield, *Surveys*, figs. 2, 53.

appears to be 'vacant' on maps of the Tudor–Stuart period actually consisted of orchards and gardens, such as the enormous area to the north of Charing Cross known as St Martin's Field.[30] Nevertheless, in many portions of Westminster – especially those areas north of the Strand – gardens came under pressure as garden plots were either swept away in piecemeal development or retained to form a garden for new, good-quality houses.[31]

Westminster's role as a centre of food production and distribution created competition for space in other ways. The situation of its market place brought particular problems. In any town, keeping a market within its physical bounds and preventing nuisance were all necessary parts of market regulation. But in Westminster the close proximity of market, royal Court and the Palace of Westminster gave rise to special tensions. A butcher in the marketplace whose meat was hung out in the highway 'where the Judges comonly pass by' presumably received sterner treatment from the burgesses than the simple offence of blocking pedestrians might otherwise have warranted.[32] In 1628 residents of King Street complained to the Privy Council that the street was narrowed by people renting market space and 'setting Tressells, Boords, Tubbs and other trash in the Streete'. The resulting crush caused 'quarrells and broyles' among traders and pedestrians, in addition to the annoyance caused to 'their Lordships themselves, the members of both houses of the Parlament, the Judges, Lawyers, and others passing to and fro in Parlament and Terme tymes'.[33] The petitioners claimed that the Elizabethan market house had been built in the 'round wolstaple' specifically to free King Street of its former market, but clearly any market in this part of Westminster was likely to incommode judges and MPs.[34] It is notable, however, that the petitioners were Westminster residents who had themselves been inconvenienced.

30 *SL*, XXXIII, 288.

31 E.g. Croot, 'Drury House', pp. 35, 39, 48–9. Covent Garden, of course, had originally supplied the monks of Westminster Abbey with apples, cherries, pears, plums and nuts, although by the seventeenth century buildings increasingly supplanted gardens: Rosser, p. 136; *SL*, XXXVI, 1, 23–4.

32 WAC, WCB2, p. 119. The butcher's shop was said to be 'in the Woolstable or Markett place'. Cf. WCB1, p. 139, where fishmongers at the market were ordered to keep to their standings 'to th'end that all Coaches and Carts may passe that way without lett or impediment'. In 1636, complaints in Star Chamber about the 'nuisance' of fishmongers' shops near Somerset House was primarily linked to their possible contribution to the plague, which was rampant that year: LMA, WJ/SR (NS) 46/11.

33 *APC 1628–29*, pp. 129, 199.

34 The bare outlines of the market house are depicted by Treswell in his survey of the houses surrounding the Woolstaple: see Schofield, *Surveys*, fig. 53. It was built on land owned by the dean and chapter. A list of contributions for the building of a market house in 1568 are to be found in BL, Lansdowne MS 10/26. A new market house was built there in 1606, with the assistance of Lord Burgley's former steward, Thomas Bellot, who also neogiated its charitable status with the dean and chapter: *Acts*, nos. 538 and n.273, 541 and n.346; WAM 37027. This was one of only two suburban markets in the capital, I. Archer, C. Barron and V. Harding (eds.), *Hugh Alley's Caveat: The Markets of London in 1598* (London Topographical Society, 137, 1988), pp. 11–12; Carlin, *Medieval Southwark*, pp. 201–4.

Attempts to highlight the inconvenience or loss of dignity suffered by notables or the monarch could often represent a polemical ploy in disputes between different groups of Westminster inhabitants, as we will see.[35]

Westminster's suburban inheritance was still then very much in evidence in the early seventeenth century. The suburban character of parishes such as St Margaret's and St Martin's still encouraged men and women to pursue by-employments undertaken by their medieval predecessors, such as gardening or the keeping of poultry or pigs.[36] Men described in local records as 'the landholders' of St Margaret's were still called upon to provide a yearly supply of hay for the royal mews,[37] while the town's butchers were men who represented an important local economic interest. But this period also witnessed signs of conflicting pressures on the use of space, particularly as the social composition of the area began to alter.

The way in which this conflict would be resolved is suggested by the case of Henry Holford of St Martin's. Holford had enclosed an area near Covent Garden to be used for pasture. Increasingly, however, he found himself struggling with members of the nobility as well as local butchers. Noblemen's coaches began to cut through the area, spoiling the pasture and failing to close the gate, which in turn led to butchers dumping their waste there. Ultimately Holford proposed his own solution to this problem, which was not to close the pathway, or even to appoint a gatekeeper. Instead he asked permission to build houses 'fit for subsidy men' – a use that would preclude all others.[38] Increasingly in the seventeenth century, it was Holford's solution that was to be embraced, as new housing in Westminster progressively squeezed out much of the pasture and undeveloped land that sustained the suburban economy.

THE CROWN AND THE SPATIAL ECONOMY OF WESTMINSTER

Thus far we have considered how Westminster's traditional suburban activities co-existed with newer demands for space. Many of these newer demands were linked to elite development in the area, but we have yet to examine the Crown's direct impact on the use of space. A decisive event here was Henry VIII's decision in the 1530s to build a great palace at Whitehall, on the site of Cardinal Wolsey's York Place. This

---

35 By the Restoration period, there was a series of proposals to ban the traffic from carts from the Strand and King Street during the time Parliament met: *HMC Seventh Report*, pp. 135a, 136a, 166a. Traffic problems were also emerging in St Martin's from as early as 1614, when the parish wrote a petition 'touching the turning the Westerne waynes into London throughe holborne and not to annoy this street and parishe' – presumably these wains (waggons) were vehicles transporting agricultural products from the countryside, WAC, F2, vol. 1, f. 199.

36 Cf. Carlin, *Medieval Southwark*, pp. 186–8; Rosser, 'London and Westminster', p. 54.

37 LMA, WJ/SR (NS) 32/200.

38 *HMC Hatfield*, XIV, 101–2. Holford's letter dates from the first decade of the seventeenth century.

move was to have a decisive influence over the character of the area for the next century or more, carrying profound implications for the usage of large tracts of land and bringing long-term changes to the local land market and economy.

With the building of Whitehall Palace between 1531 and 1536, Henry VIII undertook a major programme of works which vastly enlarged the palace and sought to rationalize the appearance of a range of inherited buildings. Eventually Whitehall Palace came to occupy no less than twenty-three acres, more than three times larger than any other royal palace.[39] To allow for this expansion, however, it was necessary for the Crown to acquire adjacent properties, since the site was in a heavily urbanized area, hemmed in by neighbouring buildings on King Street and the river Thames.[40] This constituted a major intervention in the locality, as we have seen.[41]

Just as significant as the seizure of parts of central Westminster for the Palace of Whitehall was the Crown's simultaneous move to gain control over large tracts of open fields to the north and west of the palace, within the parishes of St Margaret's and St Martin in the Fields. An extensive range of royal hunting grounds was thereby acquired within easy riding distance of the palace, stretching from Hyde Park to the newly emparked St James's Park. The acquisition and preservation of open land near the palace was also a practical measure to secure a pure and constant water supply to the sprawling palace.[42]

The Crown was able to acquire such extensive tracts of land with relative ease because much of it lay in the hands of the church. Henry VIII did not obtain this property as a result of the monastic dissolutions: the land deals that the Crown negotiated with various ecclesiastical landlords actually preceded the dissolution of the monasteries.[43] Nevertheless, it is clear that the series of very favourable land exchanges between the Crown and these landlords was possible only in a climate in which religious bodies felt themselves to be in a weak position.[44]

In this way a good deal of property in St Martin's and St Margaret's fell into Crown hands during the Henrician period. Nevertheless, pressure on royal finances

39 G. Rosser and S. Thurley, 'Whitehall Palace and King street, Westminster: the urban cost of princely magnificence', *London Topographical Record* XXVI (1990), pp. 57–9; Thurley, *Royal Palaces*, pp. 54–5; 28 Hen. VIII c. 12.

40 28 Hen. VIII c. 12 also redefined the precinct of the palace of Westminster to include Whitehall, including the entire length of King Street (Rosser and Thurley, 'Whitehall', pp. 74–5).

41 See above, ch. 1.

42 Thurley, *Royal Palaces*, pp. 72–3, 166, 169; Kingsford, *Piccadilly*, pp. 15–17.

43 One exception here is five acres in St Martin's Field belonging to the Monastery of the Vale Royal in Cheshire: *SL*, XX, 3.

44 Not surprisingly, the major landowner with whom the Crown dealt was Westminster Abbey. But ecclesiastical owners of the open areas to the north of Whitehall, St James's Palace and the Mews at Charing Cross also included Eton College, Abingdon Abbey and the Master and Hospital of Burton Lazars. These institutions surrendered their land in the area between 1531 and 1536: *SL*, XXIX, 1–2, 21; *SL*, XXXIII, 27, 288; *SL*, XXXIV, 416.

in the reigns of Elizabeth and James forced both monarchs to lease out most of this property, following a more general policy of leasing or selling off church property that had been acquired during Henry's reign.[45] The history of properties in these relatively undeveloped portions of Westminster (i.e. to the west of St Martin's Lane and north of St James's Palace) becomes more complicated at this point. The subletting of properties and the granting of leases in reversion also led to confusion among contemporaries.[46] While many locals did obtain Crown leases, it is also clear that speculative property deals flourished under Elizabeth and James.[47] For example, former church property located in St Martin's Field (north of Charing Cross and the royal Mews) was ultimately leased by the Crown to a group of London financiers who lent money to James I.[48] Similarly, St James's Farm, part of lands previously belonging to St James's Hospital, was leased by the Crown to Thomas Poultney some time before 1575, but his son could secure the future of the property in 1590 only by gaining an assignment of the reversionary lease that had already been granted to one of the Queen's musicians.[49]

It should be emphasized that this open land owned by the Crown remained largely free from buildings until well into the seventeenth century, despite the buoyancy of the land market in Westminster. It was not until the 1620s, for example, that a handful of significant buildings began to appear on land opposite St James's Palace, while aristocratic houses built on open fields during the 1630s, such as Leicester House, were still isolated developments, and were considered desirable precisely because of their spacious and airy situation.[50] Nevertheless, there is some evidence that makeshift dwellings associated with poor immigrants and agricultural workers had begun to spread in these areas by the Jacobean period. Many of these structures were probably of the sort described in a 1650 Parliamentary survey of lands in Soho. These included 'Cottages, Cutts, Shedds' and 'meane habitacions', most with mud walls and thatched roofs. Such structures were interspersed with gardens, orchards, stables and cowhouses.[51] The early

45 *SL*, XXIX, 1, 21.

46 The most famous instance of this was the case surrounding the possession of Geldings Close, to the north of the Mews at Charing Cross, for which see Kingsford, *Piccadilly*, pp. 17–27. See also *SL*, XXXI, 132–8.

47 The manor of Ebury, near Knightsbridge, for example, was granted by Elizabeth in 1567 to one of her gentlemen pensioners, William Gibbes, who sold it within a week to William Whasshe, while reversions to the property were also sold by the Crown: *CPR 1566–69*, no. 353; C.T. Gatty, *Mary Davies and the Manor of Ebury* (2 vols., 1921), I, 42–5.

48 *SL*, XXXIV, 380. The property originally belonged to the Master and Hospital of Burton Lazars. London financiers used this property and others to secure a loan of £67,000 to the Crown in 1610.

49 *SL*, XXIX, 26–7.

50 Edmund Howes, *Annales* (1631), p. 868; *SL*, XXIX, 2; *SL*, XXXIV, 433, 441. Leicester House was built on former church property in St Martin's Field, which passed to the Crown and then on to several others, before ending up in Leicester's hands in the 1630s: *ibid.*, 416. The fields directly in front of the house remained open for the next forty years, although there was some scattered building not far away: *ibid.*, 424, 433.

51 *SL*, XXXIII, 288. The land involved was to the east side of Colman Hedge Lane.

seventeenth century also saw other, more miserable dwellings erected in fields, even more temporary in nature, and of the sort routinely demolished by local authorities.[52]

Of course urban development in Westminster also concerned the Crown directly. Nothing could alter the fact that Whitehall Palace lay in the heart of a busy town, and further development of this already built-up area could not help but affect the lives of courtiers and crown servants. As we have seen, the fear of disease had prompted Henry VIII to move parish boundaries to avoid the carriage of bodies along King Street, as this would have involved passing through the precinct of the Court on their way to burial.[53] The enormous increase of poor, unhygienic housing in Westminster in the century following Henry's death meant that the town also suffered increasingly during plague time, to the understandable consternation of those at Court. Such concerns explain the Privy Council's frequent dismay over poor tenements in the vicinity of Whitehall, such as the substantial sheds in Old Palace Yard near the 'Parliament Stayres', which, it was complained in 1637, had recently been turned into dwellings.[54] 'Boothes and sheds' erected against the wall of the tennis court at Whitehall were removed according to King Charles's specific direction, partly because they were 'very unseemely by reason of their neerenesse to his Ma[jes]t[ie]s Courte and no lesse offensive to his Ma[jes]t[ie]s sighte'.[55] Similar urban crowding resulted in another order to demolish new coach houses and stables in Canon Row, which caused annoyance not only by their location near the common sewer but also by their proximity to the Lord Privy Seal and 'ye houses of other noble persons adioyning'.[56] More substantial new building might also create problems, as in the case of houses in St Martin's Lane, whose sewage flowed naturally into Scotland Yard.[57] So feverish was the demand for housing in the area around the Court that the Crown even struggled to protect stone from its own buildings, including the ruins of the old Westminster Palace, which were used by unscrupulous developers.[58]

It also seems likely that the royal desire to preserve certain areas of privacy and decorum within the environs of Whitehall was partly prompted by the nature of its constricted town site. From early on, galleries running across King Street had been designed to permit access from one side of the palace to the other while avoiding what was a major throughfare. Correspondingly, successive monarchs always felt the need

52 WAC, F2001, f. 147; *APC 1619–20*, pp. 266, 574.

53 *L&P*, vii, 1423; viii, 28.

54 TNA, PC2/48, pp. 456–7 (1637). For plague and the Crown see below, ch. 8.

55 TNA, PC2/42, p. 259.

56 TNA, PC2/48, p. 89 (1637).

57 In 1625, officials from King's Works investigated the source of filth that regularly accumulated in Scotland Yard: WAC, F2002, f. 111.

58 *CSPD 1635–36*, pp. 25, 301; TNA, E178/5493; BL, Charters, Cotton XXIV; *APC 1628–29*, p. 269.

to maintain more private areas within the palace as well.[59] It is also clear that monarchs such as Charles I sought to maintain the more secluded situation already enjoyed by St James's Palace. In 1630, for example, he went to far as to order all passages and foot-bridges through St James's Field to be closed, except for a door out of the tennis court 'which is to be for the kings private use & ye addmittance of whom his Matye shall please'.[60]

So far we have mostly considered the Crown's desire to regulate the environs of the royal palaces. The Crown also intervened in Westminster as part of its broader policy towards new building and the expansion of the capital. Even here, however, the particular problems of Westminster seem to have loomed increasingly large in the minds of policy-makers.

The progress and enforcement of royal building policy in the capital in Tudor and Stuart times is a complex subject. Certainly, the Crown was never entirely con-sistent in its policy of enforcement, even in an area on its doorstep, like Westminster. A series of proclamations, the first published in 1580, attempted to prevent further building within three miles of the City gates as a means of restricting growth, which was associated with the inevitable rise of poverty, disorder and disease. But proclama-tions were a blunt instrument with which to tackle such a difficult and pervasive phenomenon. The 1580 proclamation, which pertained to both London and West-minster, was repeated many times, apparently to little effect.[61]

The Jacobean period saw the issuing of similar orders, but gradually a subtle shift began to make itself felt in Crown policy. A proclamation of 1615 placed a new emphasis on building quality, and even specified the size of bricks to be used.[62] These orders received further support with the creation of a new and enlarged commission in 1615, which seems to have become the Commission for Buildings, a body that was periodically renewed up to the Civil War. Nevertheless, early Stuart attempts to regu-late building still faced many obstacles, including lack of manpower.[63] In part, the

---

59 This is a complex issue and bound up with the politics of each reign. For the disposition of space within the royal apartments and complex of buildings that made up Whitehall Palace, the best account is Thurley, *Royal Palaces*, 128–33, 137–9. See also the essays in D. Starkey, *The English Court* (1987), especially Neil Cuddy on the Jacobean court.

60 *SL*, XXIX, 25.

61 The clearest single account of building-related proclamations in the capital is to be found in *KW*, III, 140–3.

62 *KW*, III, 140–1. One effect of the 1615 proclamation, with its strictures on good materials and building practice, was to ensure that new housing targeted financially secure individuals. This had also been the theme of earlier orders for the metropolis, and in 1607 a royal proclamation actually speci-fied that the King wished to encourage houses that 'in regard of the charge of building, cannot but be inhabited but by persons of some ability': M. Smuts, 'The court and its neighbourhood: royal policy and urban growth in the early Stuart West End', *Journal of British Studies* 20 (1991), p. 134; C.M. Barron, *The Parish of St Andrew Holborn* (1979), pp. 48–9; *Stuart Royal Proclamations*, I, 172.

63 A Privy Council order of 1635 instructed the aldermen of London and Westminster's JPs to order constables to be more vigilant, but, considering the size of the task and the many other responsibili-ties of constables, such demands may well have been unrealistic: TNA, PC2/43, p. 81. In Westmin-ster reporting on illegal building was theoretically one of the tasks performed by burgesses.

royal policy of issuing licenses, granting exemptions, and allowing new builders to compound, undermined government credibility by giving the impression that its motives were largely financial.[64] The Commissioners for Buildings also appear to have been less active during the first year of Charles I's reign. A 1630 proclamation against new building noted that a similar proclamation of 1625 had not produced 'so full effect hitherto as wee expected', while the commissioners themselves had been a source of 'contemptuous disregard'.[65]

It was in the 1630s, however, that royal regulations on new building began to be more strictly enforced, and Westminster was the scene of some of the most vigorous royal intervention. Part of the reason for this may lie in the identity of the only individual on the Commission for Buildings who had architectural expertise, Inigo Jones. Jones was not actually appointed to the Commission until 1620, although it is likely that his was the guiding hand behind the architectural provisions of the 1615 proclamation.[66] Jones was undoubtedly a major force behind the intensified regulations of the 1630s. It is more rarely noted, however, that Jones was also a member of the Westminster commission of the peace, the body directly responsible for the practical enforcement of government building regulations in the area. In his capacity as JP he would have observed the pressures to build in Westminster coming from both gentlemen and poor immigrants, and he would also have routinely confronted the poverty and crime that contemporaries connected with poor housing. Moreover, as Surveyor of the King's Works, Inigo Jones also held special responsibility for maintaining the environs of the palace, and was required at different times to have enclosures torn down in St James's Field, and to act to protect the water supply of Whitehall and even of the Court of Star Chamber itself. Dealing with the impact of local development in Westminster, especially that associated with the poor, was thus an important aspect of Jones's work.[67]

The increasing importance attached to Westminster in the Crown's building regulations is revealed also in the text of the proclamations themselves. Caroline building proclamations, unlike their predecessors, specified that the area subject to building restrictions should be measured not just from the City gates but also 'from His Majesty's Palace at Westminster'. This not only served to extend the proclamation's remit further westwards throughout Westminster but also manifested again a particular concern with the environs of the palace.[68] The New Commission on Buildings also

---

64 A commission with the power to compound with illegal builders was first established in 1608, while a proclamation of 1607, although draconian in its language, did permit new building by special licence: *KW*, III, 140.

65 *SL*, XXXVI, 26; *CSPD 1629–31*, p. 9. For the second earl of Clare's building see Croot, 'Drury House', p. 40.

66 *KW*, III, 141.

67 *Ibid.*, 142–3; e.g. TNA, PC2/48, pp. 107–8; 2/49, pp. 173, 293, 493–4, 503–4; 2/50, p. 65; LMA, WJ/SR (NS) 38/193, 39/172, 41/39. Jones was active as a Westminster JP, taking recognizances, by November 1630: *ibid.*, 30/1 (cf. *CSPD 1629–31*, p. 371).

68 Compare *Stuart Royal Proclamations*, I, 485–8, 597–8 with II, 20–6, 280–7.

singled out Westminster parishes for especially close supervision in the 1630s. Granted, many entries in the Privy Council registers relate to the development of Covent Garden and the tussles between the earl of Bedford and his neighbours. Nevertheless, Inigo Jones and the Westminster JPs found themselves called upon to act far more often than had their predecessors. The Caroline period was also marked by dramatic enforcement drives, although it is clear that licences were granted with some frequency, generally with the petitioner promising to ensure that the houses were fit for subsidy men, or some other similar phrase.[69]

It is clear that King Charles brought special considerations to bear in relation to building in the western suburbs, which included Westminster. In particular, the King's main rationale for permitting certain building 'in those places wch are neere to the Court' was 'to accommodate noble men, & publique officers or men of qualitie attending his M[ajes]ties service'.[70] The idea that one might reduce disease and poverty near the Court by preventing the erection of poor tenements was not a new one (although the proclamations of 1625 and 1630 stand out from their Jacobean predecessors in their return to an Elizabethan concern with increasing numbers of poor immigrants and inmates and the danger created by their lack of government). What does seem more novel is the Crown's conscious encouragement of the notion of a separate residential quarter for aristocrats and royal servants, even if Westminster had always held such associations to some extent.[71]

This new sensitivity to the advantages of a separate and distinctive courtly estate bordering on the royal palace was itself partly a response to and recognition of the emerging fashionable society in the area, which made the presence of suburban economic activity and poor housing seem increasingly inappropriate to royal eyes.

A COURTLY NEIGHBOURHOOD IN TRANSITION

The building of new houses suitable for the gentry and aristocracy was undoubtedly one of the most significant developments to take place in early modern Westminster.

---

69 The most intense period for the prosecution of offenders was 1632–36. The attorney general prosecuted 175 cases of illegal building in the metropolis from 1631 to 1642; with forty of these coming to trial: T.G. Barnes, 'The prerogative and environmental control of London building in the early seventeenth century: the lost opportunity', *California Law Review* 58 (1970), p. 81. More severe penalties were also introduced for local office-holders failing to bring transgressors before the Commissioners: *Stuart Royal Proclamations*, II, 282–3.

70 *CSPD 1636–37*, p. 398; TNA, SP16/250/51. In this same document, the King voiced his concern over what he held to be increasing disorder as a result of new building in the neighbourhood of Whitehall, a circumstance which grew from the fact of 'the inhabitants being for the most part of base qualities or condition'.

71 It has been suggested that by the 1630s the King and the Privy Council differed over building policy in the capital. While the Council was eager to prosecute all offenders, King Charles wanted to allow some leeway to permit good-quality building by the rich that would ornament the capital, while stamping out poor tenements: *SL*, XXXVI, 32.

As we have seen, parishes in the western part of the metropolis, including those in Westminster, had always held an attraction for peers, gentlemen and government bureaucrats. In St Margaret's parish, titled residents particularly favoured areas such as Canon Row and Dean's Yard. Traditionally popular areas, such as the Strand, retained their popularity, as old episcopal houses passed into the hands of the Crown and aristocracy. Many of these houses were significantly redeveloped in the early seventeenth century. Meanwhile, piecemeal development by small entrepreneurs took place in partially built-up areas. In St Clement Danes, for example, large houses with gardens, specifically intended for 'the use of some great person', were built in Drury Lane in the 1620s, amalgamating several smaller sites.[72] Garden plots and modest dwellings also began to give way to more up-market housing and much-needed stabling, although development north of the Strand still remained limited in the pre-Civil War period. Elsewhere, pressure to expand on to nearby vacant land increased. Much of this vacant land was situated either in areas where the Crown was particularly sensitive to development or else in open fields which were officially part of parochial common land. As we shall see, attempts to create more substantial properties with large, spacious gardens ran into particular problems with parish authorities since this inevitably restricted the varied communal uses to which the land had previously been subject.

Nevertheless, members of the peerage had certain expectations about their privileged entitlement to space. Even in the cramped conditions of the metropolis the prospect from a courtier's house was due extra consideration. When a tailor complained in 1605 that his view of the Thames would be impeded by new building, Sir Walter Cope remarked bluntly that the view that would remain after the building 'wee thincke to be of sufficient prospecte for a man of his qualitie'. By contrast, there was far more concern that proposed new building might blight the gardens of Arundel House and Somerset House.[73]

Of course gentry residents did not necessarily require the same spacious gardens to their properties that great aristocrats might seek, or even the commanding views. Indeed gentlemen and lesser peers alike readily adopted the new kind of modest, upper-class housing being developed in places such as Lincoln's Inn Fields, the west side of St Martin's Lane and, later, Covent Garden. These houses possessed a light and airy quality, with open gardens at the back, rather than the tenement-filled backyards that had been typical of the area. Their most striking innovation, however, was the replacement of the traditional large gatehouse and courtyard – which had characterized aristocratic townhouses – with a shallow courtyard that could be entered directly from the street, shielded only by railings.[74] Despite this apparently greater accessibility, however, the gentry still sought to preserve socially differentiated space in certain contexts, be it in

72 See above, ch. 5. Croot, 'Drury House', p. 42.
73 *HMC Hatfield*, XXIV (Addenda), pp. 36–7.
74 J. Schofield, *The Building of London* (1984), pp. 168–70.

church, at home or in the coaches and sedan chairs in which they travelled. Indeed, the taste for more modest housing developed in tandem with new codes of gentlemanly sociability that emphasized intimacy and exclusivity rather than the large-scale displays of wealth and patronage that traditional, large-scale households afforded.[75] The impact of the gentry on the use of space in the locality may also partly be traced through fashionable society's increasing fascination with more exclusive pleasure gardens, such as Spring Gardens, Shaver's Hall and even Hyde Park itself.[76]

It is also important to remember that the overall pattern of housing in Westminster remained quite traditional, with fine houses on thoroughfares situated quite close to shops, taverns and poorer housing in back alleys. In the Westminster parishes, alehouses favoured by poor labourers might adjoin the townhouse of a privy councillor.[77] Although drunken and disruptive behaviour among poorer neighbours might bring censure, there is little evidence that the widespread pattern of socially mixed housing was in itself seriously questioned. Tailors, shoemakers, bakers and carpenters still expected to live in close proximity to the gentlemen and aristocrats who made up an important part of their clientele.[78]

The earl of Bedford's development of inner Covent Garden, the most regulated and large-scale building project undertaken in early modern Westminster, was designed to be radically different from this older housing pattern.[79] The earl's petition for a licence specifically sought permission to build in Covent Garden and Long Acre 'howses and buildings fitt for the habitacons of Gentlemen and men of ability'.[80] Such promises were, of course, the traditional means of obtaining a licence to build in this period. What was truly novel about the Covent Garden development was how it planned to configure urban space. There were to be no narrow alleys or yard tenements. Instead, clear spaces between and behind the houses would permit fresh air and light to enter from both the front and back, while the provision of piped water and proper sewers also contrasted with the dark and dank houses that many gentlemen would have found elsewhere in Westminster.[81] Strict regulations on the use of

---

75 A. Bryson, *From Courtesy to Civility: Changing Codes of Conduct in Early Modern England* (Oxford, 1998), pp. 116–17, 132.

76 Of course it was always a struggle for these areas to maintain their social exclusivity: see above, ch. 5.

77 *HMC Salisbury* XV, 227 (a letter of complaint addressed to Robert Cecil). In the same letter, it was complained that many carpenters and other labourers were lodging in Worcester House, and that 'their people there do annoy the neighbours very dangerously and in fashion too unreverent to be reported to you'.

78 See above, ch. 5; *SL*, XX, 116; Smuts, 'Court and its neighbourhood', pp. 127–8, 140. For a similar medieval pattern see Rosser, pp. 120, 129–33, 161–5, 201–7.

79 For a recent account see D. Duggan, ' "London the ring, Covent Garden the jewell of that ring": new light on Covent Garden', *Architectural History* 43 (2001), pp. 140–61. I plan to publish elsewhere a study of the disputes surrounding the creation of the parish of St Paul Covent Garden.

80 *SL*, XXXVI, 26.

81 Smuts, 'Court and its neighbourhood', pp. 143–4.

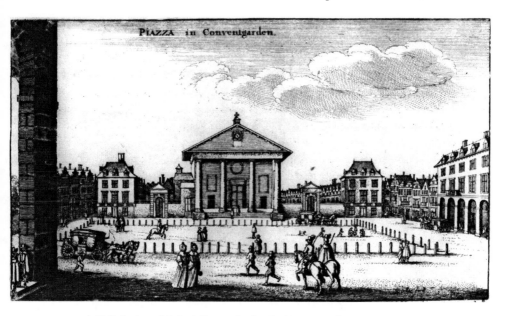

PIAZZA in Conventgarden.

4 Hollar's view of St Paul Covent Garden, looking across the Piazza, c.1658.

building materials and other attempts to maintain the architectural uniformity of the area also characterized the new Covent Garden houses.[82] The pattern of streets within inner Covent Garden was another of its novelties. Streets took the distinctive form of concentric squares around the open Piazza, instead of a more traditional pattern of linked thoroughfares. The result was a self-contained enclave that was relatively cut off from surrounding areas.

The design of the houses, coupled with the unusual street plan, not only provided better living standards for occupants. It effectively excluded the poor by eliminating the types of areas in which the poor traditionally congregated – or at least this was the theory. In reality, the situation was considerably more complex. In part, this was because Covent Garden actually consisted of two distinct areas. The newer, more innovative housing occupied only about twenty acres of an open central area known as 'the great pasture'. But outer Covent Garden included many older, timber-built structures, including poor tenements and alleys of the sort

---

82 For building specifications in leases, see *SL*, XXXVI, 29–31. Some houses were required to be uniform with those on another street (*ibid.*, 4), but specifications in the Bedford leases do not give direct stylistic direction (*ibid.*, 5). The quality of workmanship on the houses also varied. In the late 1660s, the diarist Evelyn noted that houses in the subsidiary streets 'in Covent Garden and other places' needed rebuilding after twenty or thirty years. Indeed there were some structural faults even in the houses most closely supervised by Inigo Jones himself: *ibid.*, 6–7.

that the new development planned to banish.[83] There may have been expectations that this poorer housing would be replaced, since Bedford's licence allowed him to demolish houses as well as build new ones, but this never occurred.[84] As a result, the elegant houses of inner Covent Garden were still fringed with streets such as Long Acre – the northernmost boundary of Bedford's estate – where old tenements jostled alongside newer, good-quality residences, as well as poorer areas close to the Strand, such as Falcon Alley, Vinegar Yard and Whitehart Yard.[85]

The fact that inner Covent Garden was located not far from older and less salubrious housing is not surprising in itself. But other forces worked against the social exclusivity that was a feature of the new development in its planning phase. In 1638 the Privy Council specifically rejected a plan to build alleys between Covent Garden and Long Acre. Even so, the dreaded alleys that 'pestered' other portions of the metropolis began to develop, although the Westminster JPs (including Inigo Jones) worked very hard to track down and suppress these obscurely located cul-de-sacs.[86] Other attempts to maintain the 'tone' of the area might be opposed by the residents themselves. Thus the Privy Council's attempt to limit the number of taverns in Covent Garden to two was actively opposed by petitioners who included Sir Edmund Verney and the Duc de Soubise.[87]

Although it was possible to impose a whole series of regulations about the building of houses – their width, the use of building materials and so on – it was not necessarily possible to dictate who actually occupied them. There was, of course, an undoubted cachet attached to the fine three-storey buildings in the Piazza, which housed peers and upper gentry from the start, but these were not the only residents to be found in Covent Garden. Nearly four-fifths of the housing in Covent Garden belonged to tradesmen and others, rather than to gentry. In common with most urban landlords, Bedford did not built the houses himself, instead issuing leases to build, which were snapped up by well-to-do builders, tradespeople and a few royal servants.[88] Indeed, the leasing of houses was a highly speculative business – only fifteen of the first 182

---

83 *SL*, XXXVI, 26–7; Smuts, 'Court and its neighbourhood', p. 136, n.64.

84 Instead, financial pressures led the earl to sell off parts of his estate in outer Covent Garden, precisely these areas of pre-1631 building, *SL*, XXXVI, 27, 33. Smuts suggests that the 1634 Star Chamber case brought against Bedford 'may have been intended to force him to redevelop outer Covent Garden – or simply as retaliation for his failure to have done so on his own' ('Court and its neighbourhood', p. 145, n.87). Ultimately the earl was compelled to pay £2,000 in order to confirm his earlier licence and receive immunity from retrospective prosecution for pre-1631 building.

85 Smuts, 'Court and its neighbourhood', pp. 138, 142, 146. Inhabitants in Long Acre kept animals in their yards, including turkeys: LMA, WJ/SR (NS) 31/7.

86 Houses that did not conform to the building proclamations – even if they were not the shoddy tenements inhabited by the poorest sort – also continued to be built even in the fashionable areas near the Piazza. The earl marshal and other privy councillors blocked illegal building between Long Acre and Covent Garden, by noting that the real problem lay with houses fit only for persons of 'mean quality', TNA, PC2/49, p. 493; PC 2/50, p. 65; Smuts, 'Court and its neighbourhood', pp. 138, 146–7.

87 TNA, SP16/314/83.

houses were occupied by the original lessee. This need not have affected the social profile of residents, although it does appear that even in the highly select central Piazza one house was let to a bricklayer, and another to a tailor from St Giles's.[89] Richard Brome's play *The Weeding of the Covent-Garden* even mocked the low social status of the early inhabitants of the new development.[90] That being said, the houses did prove extremely popular with prosperous gentry and peers as the building progressed, even if it was personal taste and the ability to pay that ultimately determined the type of resident.[91]

Bedford's development at Covent Garden undoubtedly marked an important turning-point in the architectual history of the capital. Its distinctive pattern of development – regular streets and relatively uniform houses punctuated with areas of green space – was copied in areas such as Lincoln's Inn Fields and Great Queen Street as well as the planned estates of the post-Restoration period in Bloomsbury, Soho and St James's Square.[92] However, as Malcolm Smuts has convincingly argued, the initial impetus for this socially segregated housing appears to have come from the Crown, rather than from the demands of aristocrats or gentlemen. The swift adoption of such housing by the privileged classes in part demonstrates how well the houses addressed what were real problems of urban living in the expanding metropolis.[93]

Although the houses built in Covent Garden constitute the single largest development of new housing erected on previously open land in Westminster, a few substantial houses were built in locations more distant from existing built-up areas. In the pre-Civil War period, this was an option available only to a handful of courtiers. Building in an area of open fields, such as St Martin's Field or St James's Field, left the

88 *SL*, XXXVI, 27.

89 *Ibid.*, 4, 77.

90 The play's 1658 prologue explains that the work was written ten years before 'when it [Covent Garden] was grown with weeds, / Not set, as now it is, with Noble Seeds': *ibid.*, 322.

91 Sixteen out of seventeen residents living in the Piazza in 1641 were peers or of gentlemanly status (including two ladies and one gentlewoman), Smuts, 'Court and its neighbourhood', pp. 143, 149. On the other streets of inner Covent Garden, however, the households consisted of members of the professions as well as gentry. About twenty per cent of the houses in the new streets of Covent Garden (seventy out of approximately three hundred) are once again said to have been occupied by 'armigerous or professional households' (*ibid.*). A tendency of scholars to conflate gentry and professional groups has made it easy to underestimate the latter.

92 P. Hunting, 'The survey of Hatton Garden in 1694 by Abraham Arlidge', *London Topographical Record* XXV (1985), pp. 83–110. In 1659, John Evelyn reporting seeing the foundations laid in St Andrew Holborn 'for a streete and buildings in Hatton Garden, designed for a little towne' (*ibid.*, p. 87; Smuts, 'Court and its neighbourhood', p. 144, 148). Features of the earl of Salisbury's houses built on the west side of St Martin's Lane in the 1610s and 1620s anticipated those of Covent Garden, but it must be emphasized that the original leases laid very few restrictions on methods of building (see L. Stone, *Family and Fortune* (Oxford, 1973), p. 110). Although the houses were contiguous, they did not really constitute socially segregated enclaves, given that the houses on the east side of the street were occupied by artisans and traders, *SL*, XX, 116. The lane was becoming increasingly fashionable, however, from the 1620s.

93 Smuts, 'Court and its neighbourhood', p. 149. Smuts also suggests that the desire to bring architectural uniformity chimed in with 'more widespread cultural impulses'.

builder free to plan a larger house and to make the most of its spacious position by setting the house within formal gardens. Most of the noblemen who were able to build in this fashion obtained their land – generally from the Crown – in the late 1620s and early 1630s. Most of these aristocratic developers were closely linked to the households of Henrietta Maria and Charles. For example, Lord Goring (vice-chamberlain of the Queen's household and Master of her Horse) obtained land to build a house below the Mulberry Garden in St James's Park. In the years after 1633, Goring erected a fine house there, which he ornamented by creating the 'Fountain Gardens', partly on the site of former gravel pits.[94] Although most of the area opposite St James's Palace was reserved for royal recreation, some time around 1626–27 the earl of Berkshire was apparently allowed to build himself a mansion facing the palace itself. Once again, it is notable that Lord Berkshire was a former Master of the Horse to King Charles when the latter was still Prince of Wales.[95]

Royal favour also undoubtedly played a part in the creation of elegant houses with impressive gardens in St Martin's Field, a huge area north of the Mews at Charing Cross. Sir William Howard, a crypto-Catholic with links to Henrietta Maria, built his house on land leased from the earl of Salisbury around 1627, despite official regulations against such new building and its position on the lammas lands of St Martin's parish.[96] Perhaps the best-documented house to be built in this area was Leicester House, located near Newport House, although not so close as to impinge on it or to prevent either house from developing large formal gardens.[97] The earl of Leicester purchased several different adjoining properties around 1630, before obtaining a licence to build in 1631. The house itself was under construction between 1631 and 1635 and was luxuriously furnished by Leicester with purchases acquired in France while he was ambassador there from 1636 to 1641. The earl casually described it as a 'little House; which was not built for a Levie, but only for a privat Family', but, whatever its level of informality, the cost of this little jewel-box of a house, with its rich furnishings, came to no less than £8,000.[98] At the time when they were built, these houses were still dotted upon a landscape of fields and orchards. Some streets were laid out around Leicester House in 1630 and later in 1648, but the development of a grand square, as a socially exclusive enclave, was ultimately a post-Restoration phenomenon.[99]

---

94 Gatty, *Mary Davies*, I, 100–1.

95 *SL*, XXIX, 2. A few other houses must have been built here during the sixteenth century, since partly timbered houses belonging to Sir Henry Henne and Sir William Poultney survived the Restoration (*ibid.*).

96 *SL*, XXXIV, 361–2. WAC, F3551, f. 30; WAC, F2002, f. 100. The earl of Newport purchased the house in 1634 and extended its grounds; this was reflected in the larger sum he paid to St Martin's for lammas money – 52s a year: Knowler, I, 207.

97 Morden and Lea's map of 1682 shows the relative position of the houses, (see Kingsford, *Piccadilly*, p. 80). Architectural details shown on the map have been questioned: *SL*, XXXIV, 453.

98 *SL*, XXXIV, 416–18, 441.

99 *Ibid.*, 416, 424, 427–8.

As we have seen, Westminster in the period before the Civil War did begin to witness the beginnings of planned urban estates. That being said, the extent of this phenomenon is too often read back from the later seventeenth century, and it should be remembered that most grand squares took shape in the late 1660s under the influence of the earl of St Albans's St James's Square.[100] It should also be recognized that even by the 1670s and 1680s, when the four big West-End 'estates' of Salisbury, Newport, Leicester and Portland had come into being, these were laid out as independent units, with their own network of streets and with little thought for the relationship of one development to the other.[101]

Aristocratic estates were not, therefore, a dominant feature of pre-Civil-War Westminster. Gentry and aristocratic housing was still more typically integrated within existing socially mixed areas, although the ensuing problems invited the solution which Covent Garden had preferred.[102] But aristocrats could never hope to insulate themselves entirely from the local community. As we shall see, even those who built their new houses in far-flung parts of the Westminster parishes soon found themselves having to negotiate their way through a maze of local claims and interests.

COMMON LANDS: DEFINING COMMUNAL INTERESTS

Thus far our discussion has focused on the interplay between Crown policy and economic forces in shaping land use. But the attitudes of individual parishes towards land usage brings another factor into play. The role of parishes is a particularly important one because disputes over the deployment of space gave rise to claims about the nature of the community and local society. In these circumstances, parishes asserted their role as guardians of communal rights and interests. Such claims over communal lands normally tend to be associated with remote provincial areas, but these issues still carried resonance for suburban parishes in the capital.

This was particularly true in the case of St Martin in the Fields, the least developed of the Westminster parishes. As we shall see, at crucial times throughout our period St Martin's vestry attempted to reassert itself as the voice of important local and communal interests.

The infringement of common lands within St Martin's – the product of increasing enclosure and emparkment – aroused particular concern. All parishioners, including many of the poorest, traditionally enjoyed access to common lands at certain times of the year. Among the poor, a significant number pieced together a living partly by keeping a few animals – making access to lammas land vital to their survival – and the

---

100 See *ibid.*, 424; E. McKellar, *The Birth of Early Modern London* (Manchester, 1999), pp. 17–20.

101 *SL*, XXXIII, 2, 4, 21.

102 See also M. Power, 'The east and the west in early modern London' in E. Ives, R. Knecht and J. Scarisbrick (eds.), *Wealth and Power in Tudor England* (1978), pp. 172–5, 177–9, 181.

parish would sometimes compensate poor parishioners for the death of their animals.[103] St Martin's officials had an obvious financial motive in supporting the maintenance of common lands, since some of those denied access might well end up seeking relief from the parish. But by upholding common lands, parish officials also restricted various undesirable activities, as well as reaffirming the authority and integrity of the parish itself.[104]

The physical integrity of St Martin's as a parish was closely linked to its defence of common lands. As we have seen, the boundaries of St Martin's parish had been altered in the earlier sixteenth century, and the process had also involved the emparkment of large tracts of land. Not surprisingly, parish governors were therefore highly conscious of major changes to the landscape, particularly those which seemed to undermine communal rights. Nevertheless, the history of St Martin's attempt to defend common lands reveals that the range of local interests that needed to be accommodated was far more complex than parish rhetoric might suggest.

Much of what we know about St Martin's common lands derives from a series of surveys conducted by parish officials during the course of the sixteenth century.[105] A 1549 survey accused a number of individuals of enclosing the common lands of the parish, and argued that the enclosures constituted a threat, not only to tradition and custom but also to public order.[106] The ditches and hedges that enclosure introduced, for example, were now places where 'theves and harlotts do lye And resort unto Dystruction of the kyngs Subietts in wynter season And in the somer tyme all the harlots do Continew And lye ther'.[107] St Martin's parish carried out a further survey in 1575 which made similar complaints, but it was in 1592 that matters finally came to a head. In this year parishioners from both St Martin's and St Margaret's decided to act more dramatically in order to defend their dwindling common lands from enclosure. A formal petition was made to Lord Burghley as High Steward, but when Burghley directed that a formal inquest should look into the matter, the parishioners embarked upon their own form of 'enclosure riot'. Perhaps misled or misinformed by Burghley's apparent concern and favour – or perhaps concerned by the lack of official action as Lammas Day approached – parishioners took matters into their own hands, and on 1 August 1592 some forty people armed 'with Pickaxes and such-like Instruments, pulled down the Fences and broke the Gates' of fields that had been enclosed.[108]

103 WAC, F2001, f. 163.

104 The parish did not, however, derive an income from the land until the seventeenth century, when it received fines for improper usage: see below.

105 The surveys of 1549 and 1575 are printed in Kitto, pp. 579–81 and derive from the vestry minute book.

106 Enclosure was a very topical issue in 1549 and parishioners may have been inspired to draw up a formal survey by the Edwardian proclamations regarding enclosure, and by enclosure riots elsewhere in England that year. The St Martin's survey does not seem to be a response to the questions of the royal commissioners investigating enclosure. See *Tudor Royal Proclamations*, ed. P.L. Hughes and J.F. Larkin (3 vols., New Haven, 1964–69), I, pp. 427–9, 451–3, 471–2.

107 Kitto, p. 580. See the same claim made in the 1592 survey: WAM 17212.

108 BL, Lansdowne MS 71/18, f. 34.

This is a bare outline of the events of 1592, but the episode deserves a more detailed examination for what it reveals both about the complexity of interests connected with enclosure and also the way in which the claims of parish identity and communal interest might be manipulated. What is perhaps most striking initially about this 'riot' is its mannered and ritualized character. It has been suggested that the parishioners may have been emboldened by news of riots in the City of London and other suburbs during that summer, but equally such disturbances may explain why protestors conducted their demonstration in so orderly a fashion, constantly emphasizing the legitimacy of their actions.[109] A generally sympathetic report of the incident made to Burghley by the under-steward Richard Tenche also emphasized the controlled nature of the protest. Although protesters had made 'some small Breach in every Enclosure', Tenche also stressed that

> some of them, thus assembled, were of the best and ancientest of the Parishes; that they carried with them no Weapon . . . and had divers Constables with them, to keep her Majesty's Peace. And, having thus laid open such Grounds, as they challenged to be their Commons, they quietly returned to their Houses, without any farther Hurt doing.[110]

Other witnesses identified some of those involved, and confirmed the impression that this was a very formal protest led by senior parish officials. Among those said to be present were the bailiff of Westminster, Mr Henry Wells, 'the Officers of St Martin's', the bailiffs 'Mr Peach and Mr Rasie' and one Mr Coles,[111] a burgess who had served as high constable of Westminster the previous year. All the more striking given the Cecil influence within Westminster was the alleged claim by protestors that 'wee have my Lord Threasorers Bayly that keepeth Tyballes'. At various times during the course of their activities, protesters also apparently maintained that they acted with the authority of the Queen's council and the lord treasurer. Finally, to cap this impression of legal rectitude, it was said that Coles 'ledd them the way from field to field with a written roll in his hand'.[112]

Over two days, the number of participants grew and the lammas land protest worked its way from close to close, throwing open gates and pulling down rails, allegedly informing one witness 'that the next day they would be twoo hundred there, and that they must breake open up to Knightesbridge and Chelsey'. Herdsmen brought cattle into the 'liberated' closes and allowed them to graze there, warning that they

---

109 R. Manning, *Village Revolts* (Oxford, 1988), p. 205.

110 BL, Lansdowne MS 71/18; Strype, II.vi.79.

111 This was probably Thomas Cole, who also leased the tithes of St Martin's from Westminster Abbey, which may also have given him his own personal agenda in the dispute. For his lease see *Acts*, nos. 261, 456 and n.883.

112 BL, Lansdowne MS 71/19, 20. For the value attached to written documents in this period see A. Fox, 'Custom, memory and the authority of writing' in P. Griffiths, A. Fox and S. Hindle (eds.), *The Experience of Authority in Early Modern England* (1996), p. 103.

would impound any cattle found there not belonging to parishioners of St Martin's or St Margaret's.[113]

Of course, the 'enclosers' saw matters in a very different light. Significantly, they urged Burghley to bring a case before Star Chamber, being especially fearful that 'they [the protestors] are about by a jurie to be chosen emunge them selves to procure a verdicte to warrant theire former douinge'. In the event, the inquest that had been originally planned seems to have taken place in December of the same year. A very lengthy presentment was produced for the occasion, and it detailed all lands intended to be accessible to commoners not just from St Martin's but also from the 'mother' parish of St Margaret's. This document stated that St Martin's parish had regularly reasserted its rights via enclosure surveys in 1549 and 1575, as well as at 'divers times since by laying open the said enclosures at the accustomed times'. This 1592 survey also shrewdly portrayed the Crown as another party wronged by the enclosers, thus extending the scope of the quarrel beyond the parish. The conversion of ground from arable and common to meadow and pasture had, they claimed, 'spoyled and defaced' the Queen's 'spacious and pleasant walkes' and had disastrously reduced the quantity of royal game 'which in the memorie of manie persons yet liveing and before the Converting . . . did usually there breede and frequent in greate nombre and plentie'.[114] Such arguments seem to have been successful, and the December inquest found decisively in favour of the parishioners.[115] The passage of a law the following year prohibiting enclosures within three miles of London gave the parishioners further reassurance.[116]

But was this outcome the straightforward victory for local, communal interests that it might appear? Historians since the time of John Strype have been aware of the episode, but they have tended to follow Strype in presenting a fairly black-and-white picture of enclosers and their opponents. The presence of parish notables in the protest certainly suggests a united front among locals, but this appearance may be deceptive. Despite the rhetoric of community interest often employed, it is important to recognize that the struggles of the 'parish' with the enclosers did not represent a simple division between community-minded parishioners and grasping outsiders. In fact, most of the enclosers were established residents of St Martin's parish, and some

113 BL, Lansdowne MS 71/18–20, 22. See also Strype, II.vi.79–80; P. Williams, *The Tudor Regime* (Oxford, 1979), pp. 335–6.

114 BL, Lansdowne MS 71/24; WAM 17212. The objection seems to have been to land being enclosed and permanently used for pasture, whereas arable land was in theory still open to all for grazing after harvesting.

115 *Ibid.* A note on the back of this document signed by Burghley's deputy Richard Tenche reports that the parties charged were summoned on 12 December to answer the parishioners' charges, and that he, with the consent of the jury, required them to lay open their grounds at or before the next feast day of St Thomas the Apostle (21 December) on pain of a fine of 12d for every acre not laid open by then. None of the historians who have previously commented on the enclosure riot – who have relied on material in the Lansdowne manuscripts – has noted how the struggle ended.

116 35 Eliz. I c. 6. Even in the 1630s, prosecutions were being made against enclosers in Chelsea under the terms of the Elizabethan act: *CSPD 1631–32*, p. 73; Manning, *Village Revolts*, p. 205.

of the biggest enclosers were actually parish officials. Thomas Poultney, who held St James's Farm of the Queen, was regularly censured and it was alleged in 1592 that he 'threateneth Death to any that shall presume to open' the fields. Yet Poultney appears among the vestrymen auditing the parish accounts as early as 1586.[117] Also among the chief enclosers listed in 1592 was the tailor John Childe, who was accused of impounding poor men's cattle when they came on to his land. Yet Childe not only served as a St Martin's churchwarden, he was also closely involved in the communal rituals of the parish, each year offering refreshment to St Martin's Rogationtide procession when it passed through his property at Ebury Farm.[118] Another St Martin's churchwarden, John Erpe, was listed as an offender in 1592, and yet he had earlier been one of those who prepared the 1575 survey of St Martin's lammas lands.[119] It should also be emphasized that these enclosers denied the antisocial role that the protesters attributed to them. They noted that the interests of the Queen and public order were necessarily bound up with those of her tenants (i.e. themselves) and they emphasized how the dispute was leading to 'the undoinge of a number of pore men whose whole wealth dependeth here upon havinge dearly bought severall leases (In some yeres scarce hable to pay theire rent)'.[120]

On further inspection, then, what historians have presented as a clash between parish society and rapacious outsiders was in fact much more of a conflict among different elements within Westminster's elite. The victory of those who defended access to common lands in part represents their success in convincing both contemporaries and later historians that it was they alone who spoke for a single, unified parish society, with a uniform set of needs.

While St Martin's officials appear to have won the battle with enclosers in 1592, they had not, however, won the war. Over the next half century the parish struggled to maintain lammas rights, but as we shall see, the nature of the conflict began to shift.[121] In the first decades of the seventeenth century the vestry continued to pursue transgressors in courts such as King's Bench and the Exchequer as well as before the Privy Council. The 1610s saw a further crisis over enclosure and in 1620, after much anxious discussion, the vestry drew up a petition for a new commission to prosecute new

---

117 Kitto, p. 398 (Acct of 1586–87), 582; Strype, II.vi.79, 80. Poultney's descendants continued to be prominent landowners in the locality for another century: Kingsford, *Piccadilly*, p. 24.

118 Merritt thesis, p. 371.

119 Kitto, p. 582.

120 BL, Lansdowne MS 71/24. While Strype's account quotes from part of this document (pp. 79–80), he omits the passage quoted above, apparently the better to support his preferred rendering of events as a simple clash between parish society and grasping outside developers.

121 There is surprisingly little information available concerning St Margaret's lammas lands in this period. The 1592 survey makes it clear that the parishes shared rights of commoning, with St Margaret's parishioners referred to as 'intercommoners' (WAM 17212). Nevertheless, St Margaret's vestry expressed little concern over lammas access and St Martin's continuing struggles, perhaps because they had access to their own common at Tothill. For one useful listing of major landowners in St Margaret's parish in 1631 see LMA, WJ/SR (NS) 32/201.

enclosures of lammas land.[122] This followed some tense encounters between parish officials and enclosers on Lammas Day, although the seventeenth century never witnessed
comparable levels of 'direct action' to that of 1592. One long-running dispute involved
the newly formed Military Company, which enclosed part of St Martin's Field for its
drilling yard.[123] By May 1618 St Martin's vestry resolved on direct confrontation with
the Company, ordering that the lammas common was 'to be claymed and prosecuted in
a due course at Lammas next by the churchwardens, with assistance of other parishioners'.
This massed attempt to gain access on Lammas Day was clearly effective: the captain
and various members of the Military Company personally attended the vestry five days
later to acknowledge parochial rights of commoning.[124]

Some of the threats to common land that provoked protests at this time echo
those of the previous century – but in a more intensive form. Complaints about the
damage to pasture caused by brickmaking, for example, seem to escalate in this
period. Vestry minutes particularly emphasized the hardship that the poor endured as
a result of people digging clay during the period between Lammas and Candlemas
(i.e. between August and February) when the lands were meant to be open to parishioners. Although fines were introduced by St Martin's parish in 1632, it is notable
that the parish did not try to impose a blanket ban on these activities. Instead the fines
seem to represent a half-way house between a punishment and a levy imposed by the
parish, which could be used to help poor residents who were now perhaps less likely to
engage in animal husbandry than their sixteenth-century counterparts.[125]

The infringement of lammas land through building became far more of an issue
in the seventeenth century, especially with a series of building developments in
St Martin's Field in the later 1620s and 1630s. In social terms, this marked a significant
change in that it increasingly pitted parish rights against the demands of its most socially
elevated residents – an element that had not figured in earlier disputes. Withstanding

---

122 WAC, F2001, ff. 23, 32a, 34, 112, 116a, 145a, 146a. In 1594 the vestry approved a parish-wide
collection to support the cost of a suit begun in King's Bench and the Exchequer in defence of the
commons of St Martin's against 'Mrs Jones of Sct Giles': Kitto, p. 583 (for the money collected see
ibid., p. 584). For later appeals to the Privy Council see below.

123 On the Military Company see below, ch. 9. The building of the wall around the Military Yard also
created other disputes with local landowners: see e.g. TNA, E124/27, ff. 197, 227r–v. The discussion of the Company in SL, XXXIV (St Anne Soho), 431, seems to be unaware of these quarrels and
underestimates the Company's conflict with the parish.

124 WAC, F2001, ff. 112, 117a, 121, 121a. Evidence of similar clashes may be teased out of the
vestry minutes: for example, Robert Baker's enclosure of lammas lands seems to have been revealed
only on Lammas Day 1621, as the vestry minute rebuking him is dated the next day (2 August):
F2001, f. 152a.

125 WAC, F2002, f. 92. See also f. 91r–v. The vestry similarly complained of the way that people took
away grass and 'herbage' from the land which properly belonged to the use and benefit of the parish
and 'especially to the poore of this parishe from Lammas day till Candlemas day'. The extent to
which large numbers of poorer inhabitants grazed animals on lammas lands is unclear. Ironically,
the payments to the parish may actually have funded individuals who had little or nothing to do
with agriculture.

the ambitions of such builders was never easy, but St Martin's vestry became increasingly adept at ensuring that the parish at least received compensation for the permanent loss of lammas land. Once again, this money was used to augment the far from adequate amounts collected via the parish poor rate. By the 1630s St Martin's parish was receiving annual payments from developers ranging from the earl of Salisbury (for 'manie faire dwellinge houses' with accompanying gardens erected and enclosed at Swan's Close), to descendants of the rags-to-riches Robert Baker (for enclosing part of Windmill Field) and Simon Osbaldeston (for his pleasure palace of Shaver's Hall).[126] The parish also did its best to claim compensation on behalf of the vicar of the parish for the titheable property that was lost by this new building.[127]

St Martin's vestry was thus able to ensure at least partial reparation for the land lost.[128] It could be argued that the parish officials were essentially presiding over a process whereby lammas land was converted from a general resource for all the parish, especially the poor, into a form of income used to supplement the parochial poor rate.[129] But the vestry did not simply acquiesce in this process, even if change may appear to have been inevitable. In 1634, when the earl of Newport enclosed lammas land in Scavenger's Close with a brick wall, he was required to leave and maintain 'a faire sufficient foot way' through it, and to pay 50s yearly for the use of St Martin's poor.[130] Similarly, when land was enclosed for the new Leicester House, the parish obtained a ruling from the Privy Council that not only required the payment of a yearly fine but also specified that there were to be 'fitt spaces left for the Inhabitants to drye their clothes there as they were wont, and to have free use of the place . . . and all the foot wayes through that close to bee used as now they are.'[131]

126 E.g. WAC, F3 (1626–27), f. 3v; F354, 359, F362. For Baker see F. Sheppard, *Robert Baker of Piccadilly Hall and His Heirs* (London Topographical Society 127, 1982); for Shaver's Hall see above, ch. 5, and Kingsford, *Piccadilly*, pp. 81–2. For Salisbury's payments see e.g. Hatfield House accounts, Box G/13, f. 13v. Robert Baker was charged by St Martin's vestry in 1612 to pay 30s annually on lammas day 'in Recompence of the Lammas common' for building houses on enclosed land 'neare the Windmill': WAC, F2001, f. 74v. Note also the example of lammas common being enclosed for a bowling alley: *ibid.*, f. 84a.

127 For example, Sir William Howard paid 10s a year to compensate for lammas land lost, but also 1s a year to the vicar in respect of tithes: WAC, F2002, f. 69v. Henry VIII's grant of land in 1542 was specifically to compensate the parish for the loss of '*titheable* places': Merritt thesis, p. 60, n.74 (my italics).

128 It should be noted, however, that unpaid fines for encroachment on lammas land progressively accumulated, amounting to £10 10s. by 1641 (WAC, F367, f. 35) – an amount which included moneys owing from the earls of Salisbury and Leicester, and Lord Mountjoy.

129 This was certainly what the landowners would have preferred. Raphe Wood, one of the witnesses of the 1592 'enclosure riot' whose fields were entered, claimed that he had said 'yt he would rather yeld some tribute to the poore of parishe then be troubled in this sort' (BL, Lansdowne MS 71/19).

130 WAC, F2002, f. 99v (cf. f. 69v). The entry was signed at a later date by the earl of Newport in the presence of witnesses, to ensure his compliance. Cf. F2002, ff. 69v, 100; F3, 1628–29, n.f.

131 *SL*, XXXIV, 432–3 (quoting TNA, SP16/181/27); TNA, PC2/41, p. 50. The fine was to compensate for land formerly used to graze cattle. Enforcing the ruling was problematic. St Martin's vestry minutes for 1635 record Sir William Ashton and various others going to treat with Leicester about lammas ground 'which he hath built uppon and inclosed' (WAC, F2002, f. 104).

Although these small victories may appear to be merely symbolic, they neverthe-less represented significant re-assertions of parochial rights vis-à-vis its new aristo-cratic residents. By the early Stuart period, the need to ensure that aristocrats and gentlemen acknowledged that they had social and financial duties towards the parish in which they resided had become increasingly important in Westminster, especially in the parish of St Martin's.[132] This was a matter rendered all the more urgent by increasing difficulties with noble residents over local taxation. Ironically, the parish sometimes found such individuals reluctant to contribute towards the cost of main-taining good-quality roads to the west, in areas of new aristocratic settlement.[133] More generally, however, the seventeenth century saw the protection of common pasture begin to mutate into the right of the parish vestry to define 'common' rights and to decide on the necessary compromises (such as the payment of fines) which would ensure that parochial claims were recognized, even as those very lands began to be swallowed up.

PERAMBULATION: DEFINING PAROCHIAL SPACE

As we have seen, Westminster's parishes could intervene when access to common land was threatened by the changing use of open space. The parishes also affirmed their geographical limits through the yearly ritual of the parish perambulation.

The Rogationtide procession had an obvious practical value in confirming dis-puted boundaries. This was especially true in Westminster, where Henry VIII's adjustment of parish boundaries contributed to disputes which were not resolved until the mid-eighteenth century.[134] Usually the contested areas were located in fields,[135] but even in more urban areas it was felt necessary to establish boundaries with care. In 1608, for example, an engraved stone was placed in the wall of Salisbury House to mark the boundary between the parishes of St Martin's and St Clement Danes.[136] St Martin's northern boundary with St Giles in the Fields also prompted disagree-ment, although a boundary marker had been placed at the top of Drury Lane in 1612. In 1620, however, the 'ancient inhabitants' of the two parishes met together to

132 See above, ch. 4.

133 WAC, F2002, f. 78r–v. Failure to pay may have been related to quibbles over taxation and resi-dency. As early as 1618 the Middlesex justices sought clarification over residency and the obliga-tion to pay for repairs to highways, at which time it was noted that payment was required if an individual 'doth doe inhabite [the parish] by the space of six dayes yearly': LMA, MJ/SBR/3, f. 57.

134 For example, a grant of 18 Eliz. erroneously stated that Gelding Field was in the parish of St Margaret's rather than St Martin's, and required the passage of a further act in the same year to correct the mistake: *London P&P*, II, 121 (citing *The Times*, 13 February 1849); H.F. Westlake, *Westminster: A Historical Sketch* (1919), pp. 110–11.

135 WAC, F2, vol. 1, ff. 176, 194.

136 WAC, F2, vol. 1, f. 94.

reconcile their memories of where the parish boundary traditionally stood.[137] It may have been such disputes that led St Martin's in 1624 to commission a map of the 'whole parishe' from one of its vestrymen, the noted surveyor John Thorpe, which may have lessened disagreements thereafter.[138]

Clear boundaries were also important in ensuring that parishes received all tax income due to them, and this undoubtedly spurred officials to mark them, especially in more urban areas, where the sums involved might be significant. It may also explain why even in a parish with more puritan clergy and vestrymen, such as the Jacobean St Martin's, the ancient ceremony of perambulation continued to be observed with great diligence. The link between parochial boundaries and rates emerged most seriously as a bone of contention at the end of our period, when the new parish of St Paul Covent Garden was created in 1646. During the 1630s and 1640s, the process of carving out this new parish from the larger St Martin in the Fields threw up many problems, but some of the fiercest disagreements centred on the question of rates. Not only was the independent status of St Paul's unclear since it was initially deemed a 'chapelry' of St Martin's, but no agreement on the exact boundaries between the mother and daughter parish took place until the day before the consecration of St Paul's church itself.[139]

Parish perambulations could have a broader ritual and social significance beyond these purely practical considerations. We have already noted the communal and religious importance of parish perambulation in Westminster in the first half of the sixteenth century.[140] But how prominent was this ritual thereafter and what roles did it fulfil? In St Margaret's parish the custom appears to have continued uninterrupted from Mary's reign into Elizabeth's, but there is no reference to its celebration at St Martin's before 1584. This would confirm what we already know of the more conservative temper of St Margaret's, but it would be rash to assume that St Martin's parishioners did not go on perambulation earlier in Elizabeth's reign: indeed, the parish had bought the homilies for perambulation as early as 1561.[141] Nevertheless, it is clear that the custom enjoyed increasing popularity during the latter half of Elizabeth's reign, especially from the 1590s. Celebrations at St Martin's grew more elaborate,

---

137 WAC, F2001, f. 147. See also the reference to St Giles 'comeing on over our ground' in WAC, F3 (1637–38).

138 WAC, F2, vol. 1, f. 176; F3, f. 14. Unfortunately, this 'plott' does not seem to have survived.

139 *SL*, XXXVI, 53–5. The Privy Council ultimately became involved in these disputes: see TNA, PC2/49, pp. 71, 145–8, 598; PC2/50, p. 367; PC2/52, pp. 637–8.

140 See above, chs. 1 and 2.

141 Kitto, p. 363; e.g. WAC, E4 (1559–61), n.f. Hutton argues convincingly against the view that the practice of perambulation suffered a prolonged decline after the Reformation (*The Rise and Fall of Merry England* (Oxford, 1994), pp. 175–6). Cf. K. Thomas, *Religion and the Decline of Magic* (1971), pp. 62–5; D. Underdown, *Revel, Riot and Rebellion* (Oxford, 1985), pp. 77–81, 90–1, 96–7. Rogation processions figure in the surviving records of every City of London parish except St Mary Aldermanbury by 1639 (Hutton, *Rise*, p. 176), but it is incorrect to state that St Martin's began to make Rogation processions only in the 1590s (and to imply that there were none in St Margaret's).

with the ringing of bells and the parish supplying drink and sometimes food for those parishioners who had helped to beat the bounds.[142] From 1608, the St Martin's church-wardens recorded paying money directly to poor parishioners to allow them to 'drinck withall', while in 1613, over 14s was distributed to forty-four 'poor people that went the perambulacion in mony to drincke withall'.[143] Such liberal provision for festive drinking among poorer parishioners is particularly striking in a parish where the vestry was of such a sternly puritan character. Leading men of the parish also might provide hospitality, as in the case of John Childe, a wealthy tailor who lived at Ebury Farm, in the westernmost part of the parish, where the procession seems regularly to have stopped for refreshment.[144]

Payments for food and drink also seem to have constituted a form of charity and are partly related to periods of dearth. If we examine the amounts spent on perambulation in St Margaret's, these rose dramatically during the difficult decade of the 1590s. The churchwardens there specifically made the link between perambulation and relief of the poor when presenting their account. In 1594, for example, they noted that the parish spent £7 10s. on bread, cheese, fish and 'other victualles' when 'the worshipfull of the parish & very many others of the porest sort went the peramulation to Kensington, in this harde & deere tyme in all thinges'.[145] Thereafter, the amounts contributed by the parish could vary tremendously from year to year, possibly in response to need within the parish and in the wake of disease.[146] Similarly, at St Martin's the cost of perambulation rose dramatically during difficult times for the poor in the late 1610s and early 1620s (£7 10d in 1622), while payments to poor people at Knightsbridge hospital (the westernmost destination of the procession) became a feature of perambulation.[147]

It seems likely that Rogationtide processions held more significance for the West-minster parishes than for those elsewhere in London. The town lacked the civic pro-cessions which flourished within the City of London, while the pre-Reformation processions that had been such a feature of parishes such as St Margaret's had also been prohibited. Nor do the Westminster burgesses seem to have organized any public ritual associated with the town or to have offered any public hospitality. The Rogation holiday therefore represented one of the very few occasions in Westminster

---

142 Kitto, pp. 484, 496.

143 WAC, F2, vol. 1, ff. 88, 212.

144 E.g. WAC, F2, vol. 1, ff. 176, 194. Cf. F. Heal, *Hospitality in Early Modern England* (Oxford, 1990), pp. 379–80.

145 WAC, E6 (1594–95), f. 9v.

146 In 1622–23, St Margaret's spent £12 17s 6d on food and drink whereas in the following year the parish only parted with £2 7s 6d: WAC, E13 (1622–23), f. 18v; (1623–24), f. 38.

147 In several of these years it was noted that the inhabitants going on perambulation were 'many in number', WAC, F2, vol. 1, ff. 155, 280, 377, 400, 420. Even before this time, the parish occa-sionally gave alms to 'the poore that went the perambulacion', see *ibid.*, ff. 176, 233.

when members of the local community were able to reaffirm neighbourly bonds in a public manner.[148] In large and increasingly populous parishes, such as St Martin's and St Margaret's, this was particularly important. In theory, all the parish participated,[149] and did so as inhabitants and parishioners rather than as ratepayers, though this is not to say that the procession ignored social distinctions. Nor was this entirely a solemn procession of a few parochial elites. Children had a special role in the perambulation of parish boundaries and in 1619 St Martin's purchased nearly 150 'Silke pointes' for boys to sport during the procession. Inevitably the involvement of children could lead to some boisterous behaviour. In 1629, St Martin's vestry were obliged to pay 3s to a woman 'from whom certaine boyes which went the Perambulacon snatched divers Oringes and Leamons', and in 1633 12d to a poor boy 'who had his head broke in the perambulacon by other boyes'.[150] It is important here to note the sense of parochial responsibility for acts committed during perambulation. It would also appear that increasing importance was attached to Rogationtide activities during times of escalating tension. In this regard, it is notable that in 1640–41 St Margaret's spent a record amount of nearly £20 at Kensington, when the 'worshipfull of the Vestrie and others of this Parish went the Perambulacon'.[151]

Despite this evidence of widespread involvement in parish perambulations, further examination reveals that the procession was not, in the end, quite the uniting of a whole community that might have been ideally intended.[152] To begin with, none of St Martin's gentry residents seem to have participated in the celebrations. Apart from the minister, the highest-ranking participants were parish officials of the middling sort. They were the ones who administered the parish on a day-to-day basis. For them, it would appear that Rogation processions would have acknowledged their status and responsibility, undiluted by the need for deference to gentry residents.[153] Parish officials organized the procession and, it might be argued, reinforced a sense of their own position through the 'parish' hospitality that they helped to oversee.

148 Although Elizabethan proclamation had emphasized the secular and practical grounds for Rogation, prayers were included in the ceremony. In the early Stuart period, visitation articles asked whether perambulations took place regularly and with appropriate prayers: Hutton, *Rise*, p. 105; K. Fincham (ed.), *Visitation Articles and Injunctions of the Early Stuart Church* (2 vols., Church of England Record Society I and V, 1994, 1998), I, xvi, 29.

149 It is, however, unclear whether women participated. Boys are specifically mentioned as part of the procession, but not girls.

150 WAC, F2, vol. 2, f. 328; F3 (1629–30); (1633–34), n.f.

151 WAC, E23 (1640–41), n.f., but cf. E16, f. 31v, when less than £13 was spent at an earlier perambulation in 1628.

152 Professor Hutton charts what he sees as the return of the Rogationtide rite in the early Stuart period, but we should not assume that it was necessarily the inclusive ritual that it may have been in the pre-Reformation period.

153 E.g. Kitto, p. 484; WAC, F2, vol. 2, f. 233. St Martin's parish records normally make great play of any involvement by members of the gentry and aristocracy, but they are never mentioned in connection with Rogation, unlike members of the vestry.

The more expansive character of the ritual also began to be curtailed at St Martin's from 1622, largely on the grounds of cost.[154] What emerged was a more exclusive ritual altogether. In a striking compromise, it was decided to alternate a 'closed' annual perambulation (perhaps only by the vestry) with a 'full' perambulation involving all the parishioners to be held once every three years. This larger perambulation would seem to have lasted three days, but still had its more exclusive element. The beginning and end of the three-day perambulation was marked by a perambulation dinner for the 'ancients of the parish'. Revealingly, the 1631–32 account makes plain the member-ship of this group by referring to the dinner as being provided for 'divers of the Auntient *Vestrymen*' of the parish.[155] Such dinners illustrate the increasing tendency of the parish officials, normally drawn from the prosperous middling sort, to consider them-selves as the symbolic manifestation of the local community. The inclusive, communal celebration of Rogationtide was now framed by the more exclusive festivities of the 'community' of parish officials.

THE PARISH CHURCH AND SOCIAL IDENTITY

The desire to demarcate parochial space was not limited to perambulations and com-missions into lammas lands: it could also become an issue inside the very parish church itself. We have already noted that a distinctive feature of Westminster was the strong autonomy of its parishes. Westminster's parish churches thus commanded consider-able local significance, perhaps all the more so given the lack of civic buildings or livery company halls in the area.

Of course the primary function of the church was as a venue for religious services. The Reformation had altered the character of churches as ceremonial spaces, yet parishioners still continued to worship together, even if it was as much the sermon as the sacrament that brought them there. Rites of passage marked the entry and the passing of inhabitants, memorials celebrated the deeds of the living and the dead, and at the Easter communion the whole community was – at least in theory – united together in a 'feast of charity' in which prior reconciliation was mandatory.[156] It was here, too, that transgressors of social norms could be publicly shamed. Those convicted of drunkenness or sabbath-breaking could be required to admit their fault

---

154 Certainly rising costs was a major concern in the 1620s, when the parish was suffering a crippling debt from the 1625 plague rate: in 1629 the vestry ordered that the perambulation costs should not exceed £5: WAC, F2002, f. 68v. Other factors may have been concerns about keeping such a large procession in order and perhaps a desire of parish elites to distance themselves from the poor.

155 WAC, F2001, f. 168a, italics mine. See also F3, ff. 6v–7; (1627–28), f. 97; (1629–30), n.f.

156 Note the insistence on this by St Martin's puritan lecturer Robert Hill: *The Pathway to Prayer and Pietie* (1613), 'A Communicant instructed', pp. 27–8 (but note his complaint (*ibid.*, 'Christs Prayer Expounded', p. 137) that 'at the publique confession of sinnes, in great Congregations scarce fortie are present upon the Sabbath day').

publicly in church after morning prayer on the Sunday, while those convicted of sexual misdemeanours performed public penance in church in a white sheet.[157]

The interior of the church could also, of course, serve as a arena for public celebration as much as for public shaming. Burials in prominent parts of the church continued after the Reformation, and funeral monuments vied for space, size and prominence.[158] Even in the post-Reformation period, burial in the chancel was particularly sought after, and the families of Lady Anne Cecil and Lady Porter must have been gratified to have secured fashionable night burials of the deceased in the chancel of St Martin's.[159] Generally, however, aristocrats resident in Westminster seem to have preferred to be buried either in Westminster Abbey or in the country.[160] Below the peerage, however, competition for burial space and prominence was still intense. Where gentry monuments might celebrate family descent, the monuments belonging to those of lesser social status commemorated qualities and values other than those of lineage. Monuments belonging to local notables emphasized their role as office-holders, good neighbours and local benefactors. Thus the monument of Richard Bedoe in St Clement Danes specified that he was 'one of the ancientiest of this parish and a Feoffee of the Poor', while that of the vintner Richard Jacob noted that he passed through all offices 'both in the parish as also in his Company'. In St Margaret's, the gardener John Varnham was celebrated in verse 'Who in his Life lived well, / by Labour, Travaile, and Paine: / In helping of the Fatherless, / And widowes very Poore; / And setting ever them to worke / which went from Doore to Doore'.[161]

But Westminster's churches did not limit themselves to the commemoration of the dead; certain important events in the communal life of the parish also allowed the living to receive public recognition. Those who paid towards the rebuilding of St Martin's in 1606–9 received recognition in the 'Armes and Streamers' that were hung in the church, while a description of the rebuilding was engraved in brass and set into the wall of the east end of the church. In St Margaret's church, an ornamental plaque listed those who contributed to the expenses of the 1585 Act for the government of the town.[162] In the 1630s, St Margaret's vestry paid for a new table of the names of 'all the best'

---

157 E.g. LMA, DL/C/617, n.f. (March 1604/5, May 1605); DL/C/306, ff. 55b, 383; WAC, E19, f. 46v.

158 Great care was taken in 1630–31 to ensure that the ten monuments that were moved to make room for the new gallery were erected properly elsewhere: WAC, F3, 1630–31, n.f. See also V. Harding, ' "And one more may be laid there": the location of burials in early modern London', *London Journal* 14 (1989); Harding, *The Dead and the Living in Paris and London, 1500–1670* (Cambridge, 2002).

159 WAC, F3 (1632–33). Night burials in the chancel could be expensive: see *CSPD 1637*, p. 435, for a reference to a night burial in St Martin's chancel costing over £11.

160 Accounts for 1632–33 list payments from several people for burying out of the parish, including the earl of Somerset and the countess of Shrewsbury, although one vestryman buried his wife out of town (WAC, F3, 1632–33, n.f.).

161 Strype, II.iv.114, II.vi.41.

162 WAC, E5 (1587–88), f. 26v.

benefactors to the parish poor, with their names 'drawne in letters of Gold'. Such monuments served to celebrate the deeds of benevolent parishioners, but such public commemoration was also clearly intended to act as a spur to further donations.[163]

The interior of the church could thus embody a number of different messages, some personal, some corporate.[164] Other messages concerning the nature of local society were conveyed through the disposition of seats which provided Westminster's different social groups with an important means of protecting, declaring and enhancing their status within the locality.

We must begin a discussion of church seating with a caveat. Church services provided one of the few occasions when, at least in theory, the whole community gathered together under one roof. In practice, however, this was not strictly possible in the teeming parishes of St Margaret's and St Martin's. By the seventeenth century neither parish church was capable of holding all its parishioners, and when on occasions such as Easter the whole parish was required to attend, both parishes followed the practice used in some other parts of the metropolis of 'staggered' communions, which actually took place over a period of six weeks.[165] Such steps indicate that attendance levels at normal Sunday services and sermons regularly fell short of one hundred per cent, although it would be misleading to assume that parishes were strictly divided between 'attenders' and 'non-attenders'.

Despite this, the idea that the church service represented the community at prayer still remained a potent one.[166] But if the church service supposedly represented the community at prayer, then it was here that the divisions over who constituted the 'community', and how the community's hierarchy should be represented, became most urgent and pointed. As we shall see, the arrangement of church seating was in itself an artificial representation of the community, a performance whose choreography different groups struggled to control. In this way the arrangement of church seating, with all its symbolic implications, focused attention upon the underlying tensions in Westminster society.[167]

Modes of allocating church seating varied significantly in the parishes of early modern England. Historians have sometimes been content simply to repeat the

---

163 WAC, F2 vol. 1, ff. 92, 115; E20 (n.f.). St Margaret's also paid 30s for a frame to a table of the names of parish benefactors: E16, f. 35. Cf. I. Archer, 'The arts and acts of memorialization in early modern London' in J.F. Merritt (ed.), *Imagining Early Modern London* (Cambridge, 2001), pp. 89–113.

164 J.F. Merritt, 'Puritans, Laudians and the phenomenon of church-building in Jacobean London', *HJ* 41 (1998), pp. 950–4.

165 See below, ch. 9.

166 This inclusive notion of the parochial community was also bolstered by the more practical desire to ensure payment of tithes and monitor religious conformity: see J. Boulton, 'The limits of formal religion: the administration of holy communion in late Elizabethan and early Stuart London', *London Journal* 10 (1984).

167 In Westminster Abbey itself, the escalating conflict between the dean John Williams and some of his prebendaries spilled over into the question of the dean's seating arrangements: *CSPD 1635–36*, pp. 218, 347.

truism that the ranking of seats in church reflected the social hierarchy of the parish, with the most important parishioners occupying the front pews, while groups of lesser status occupied seats of descending importance, with further social segregation (if space permitted) between sexes and ages, in the form of separate pews for women and youngsters. More recently, however, there has been a growing appreciation of the fact that seating within the church seldom corresponded exactly with the local social hierarchy. On occasion, the criteria of wealth, age, ancestry and office might be conflicting rather than mutually reinforcing. In localities where new socially elevated residents arrived, or where pews were attached to landed property that changed hands, the spatial disposition of the local inhabitants might easily lag behind changes in local society.[168] The history of church seating in the rapidly developing town of Westminster provides an excellent opportunity to investigate such disjunctions further.

Both St Martin's and St Margaret's struggled with the problem of rapid population growth, and the inevitable competition for seating that this created. Both parishes crammed in additional seats wherever possible, built new pews and galleries, and ultimately created chapels of ease.[169] Both parishes, moreover, witnessed systematic attempts to regulate seating according to criteria that gave a high priority to elements such as office-holding. Nevertheless, as we shall see, the distinctive social complexion of the parishes promoted different anxieties and led to correspondingly different patterns of spatial distinction within the church.

THE STRUGGLE FOR STATUS: SEATING AT ST MARTIN'S

Problems of space dogged the church of St Martin's throughout the sixteenth and seventeenth centuries. The sheer pressure of numbers would seem to lie behind the partial rebuilding of the tiny medieval church in 1542, otherwise an unpropitious time for church-building. Thereafter, the Elizabethan church underwent a number of smaller programmes designed to increase the building's capacity. In 1570 a large number of pews were introduced into the church, with eighty-one parishioners donating money for new pews, possibly their own.[170] By 1597, a new gallery was built on the

---

168 N. Alldridge, 'Loyalty and identity in Chester parishes, 1540–1640' in S. Wright (ed.), *Parish, Church and People: Local Studies in Lay Religion* (1988), pp. 94–7; S. Amussen, *An Ordered Society* (Oxford, 1988), pp. 137–44; M. Aston, 'Segregation in church' in W.J. Sheils and D. Wood (eds.), *Women in the Church* (Studies in Church History 27, Oxford, 1990); J.F. Merritt, 'The social context of the parish church in early modern Westminster', *Urban History Yearbook* 18 (1991); M. McIntosh, *A Community Transformed* (Cambridge, 1991), pp. 199–201; P. Griffiths, *Youth and Authority* (Oxford, 1996), pp. 104–9; Boulton, pp. 146–7, 286–7; J. Maltby, *Prayer Book and People in Elizabethan and Early Stuart England* (Cambridge, 1998), pp. 197–9, 207, 210, 259, 260, 261; A. Heales, *The History and Law of Church Seats or Pews* (1872), pp. 127–55; C.W. Marsh, 'Sacred space in England, 1560–1640: the view from the pew', *JEH* 53 (2002).

169 See below, ch. 9.

170 Kitto, pp. 253, 255.

south side of the church and an older gallery or 'loft' was modified to allow for more pews. A major rebuilding of the church in 1606–9 was partly prompted by the need for new and better pews, but even this work could not satisfy the demand for seats, and yet another gallery appeared within the church in the 1630s. Over-crowding was still a common occurrence in the 1630s, and on important occasions such as communion-taking and burials the parish regularly needed to repair pews that had been damaged in the crush.[171]

Of course insufficient seating was not merely an inconvenience; it also held financial implications. Pew rents had been collected in St Martin's since at least the 1520s and by the seventeenth century generated a significant income for the parish.[172] Insufficient seating might fuel competition between parishioners, but it also created the danger that the 'unplaced' would refuse to pay parish rates more generally. This issue sufficiently concerned parish officials that they sought legal advice over the matter in 1613.[173] St Martin's officials spent a remarkable amount of time regulating church seating, from attending day-long vestry meetings on seat allocation to producing a yearly 'plot' of the pews and painting letters on the seats, to brokering settlements among parishioners whenever expanded church seating created another set of 'winners' and 'losers'. Changing the seating plan could also prove difficult, since a few parishioners had actually constructed their own pews.[174] In October 1619, for example, St Martin's vestry agreed that 'the foremost pew of the middle gallery' was to be occupied only by Charles Kynnaston, Isaac James, Samuel Clarke and William Mitchell, since they had erected it themselves.[175]

But what sort of principles governed the allocation of seating? Few details relating to pewing survive for most of the sixteenth century, although it is clear that men and women sat separately, a custom still observed in the seventeenth century. As early as 1567, St Martin's constructed 'a pewe for the church wardens and sidemen [*sic*] to sytt in', but no other pews specifically for office-holders are recorded in the sixteenth century.[176] Growing competition for seats, however, meant that the vestry needed to establish more formal criteria for placing parishioners. Possible criteria included social status, office-holding and length of residence in the parish. Differences of opinion

---

171 *Ibid.*, pp. 498–501; WAC, F3, 1635–36, 1636–37, n.f.

172 Kitto, p. 37 (1534–35). It is likely that earlier quarterly collections included pew rentals (e.g. pp. 9, 10, 11).

173 To the relief of parish officials, legal advice informed them that 'for coverings of our Church and for paying of the debts which the parish owes, we may taxe them whether they be placed or no': WAC, F2, vol. 1, f. 179.

174 E.g. WAC, F2, vol. 1, f. 177; F2, vol. 2, f. 329. In 1604 the churchwardens noted that 'Mr Greenes pewe and the Pewe where Captaine Wood, Mr Fowle and Mr Dobinson doe sitt [was] made of their owne charges': WAC, F2, vol. 1, ff. 40–41.

175 WAC, F2001, f. 136v.

176 Kitto, pp. 143, 223, 233. In 1627, wardens paid to enlarge 'the Maides gallery' at St Martin's, WAC, F3, 1627–28, f. 105. Cf. M. Aston, 'Segregation in church'.

occurred primarily over the weight to be given to each of these factors. A 1606 reference to keys of pews 'for those householders who sitt in the gallery' suggests that householder or rate-paying status would have been a minimum requirement for pew-holders.[177] But beyond this minimal criterion, the competition for seats in St Martin's took on a sharper edge as the social complexion of the parish began to alter. As we have seen, increasing numbers of gentlemen chose to reside in St Martin's in the later Elizabethan and early Stuart period. The first reference to seats needed specifically for these residents dates from 1604, when the churchwardens received money 'towards the Inlargement and makeing of new pewes for lordes knightes Ladies and gentlemen of the better sorte'.[178] Shortly thereafter, it was decided to enlarge St Martin's in a programme which virtually rebuilt the church. Ironically, this building programme actually led to a highly acrimonious quarrel among the members of St Martin's vestry in which the disposition of seats played a major role.

The great rebuilding of St Martin's in 1606–9 was partly intended to furnish the church with 'decent and sufficient Pewes and seates according to the severall dignities and degrees of the said Inhabitantes'.[179] The problem, of course, was to decide precisely how those different dignities and degrees should be recognized, and even the vestrymen seem to have been divided on this point. As we have seen, Sir George Coppin (one of the few gentlemen active on the vestry) countered accusations of financial impropriety with claims that certain middling-rank vestrymen had kept the 'principall Pewes' in the church for themselves, leaving earls, lords and knights 'destitute of any convenient Pewes or places . . . which . . . hath ever since contynued discontentement and faction in the said parishe'.[180]

Although the 'plot' outlined by Coppin appears unconvincing, what he did identify was a tension inherent in the newer social structure of St Martin's. This potentially pitted members of the gentry and aristocracy against those whose 'right' to desirable seats was linked to their place within the local hierarchy of the parish. In the decade during which the Coppin dispute simmered away – the 1610s – the parish continued to experience disagreements over pewing. St Martin's vestry seems to have been particularly concerned to secure privileged positions for parochial officials, even those of humble background. New pews were built for both the churchwardens and the overseers of the poor in 1610.[181] The erection of a separate vestry-house in 1614,

---

177 WAC, F2, vol. 1, f. 61.

178 WAC, F2, vol. 1, f. 28. At St Botolph Aldersgate, one of the few City parishes with significant numbers of gentlemen, pews for knights, ladies and burgesses are first mentioned in 1601: *London VCH*, p. 320.

179 TNA, STAC8/101/19.

180 *Ibid.* For this episode see above, ch. 4, and Merritt, 'Social context', pp. 21–30.

181 WAC, F2 vol. 1, f. 131; F2001, f. 126. In 1619 a special pew near the font was ordered to be 'made fitt for the Midwives': F2001, f. 133. Seats for 'the poore in the Church' are also first mentioned in 1609 and were probably limited to those receiving parish pensions: F2 vol. 1, f. 130.

complete with twenty-four stools luxuriously covered in 'Russia leather', also under-lines a desire to formalize and dignify the status of these vestrymen.[182]

The criteria for seating allocation also took account of length of residence in the parish. While it was common for parishes to attach importance to length of residence, at St Martin's even this relatively simple criterion might carry socially specific over-tones. Throughout pewing disputes in the 1610s and 1620s, the vestry tried to main-tain the rights of long-established residents against the claims of newer, more socially prestigious parishioners. In December 1616, the vestry and the vicar, Dr Montford, considered the case between Lady Waller and one Mrs Greene (probably the wife of the woodmonger and vestryman Simon Greene). Mrs Greene, they noted, had been assigned a seat by the churchwardens before 'my lady Wallers habitacion in the parishe'. For this reason they upheld Mrs Greene's right to her pew 'according to the auncient usuage and custome of this parishe'. Another pew would be found for Lady Waller, 'if she mislike to contynue in the pew with Mris Greene' but only 'as neare as the church-wardens can finde any fitting'.[183]

Clearly the demands of at least some gentry residents made for a tense situation, which led the vestry to police all aspects of seating with extraordinary care. A 1619 vestry order warned the sexton to restrict access to pews except to those specifically allocated a seat by churchwardens. Nevertheless, the order was not to apply to 'persons of great ranke and quality', who might occupy a seat if its designated occu-pant was absent.[184] Under such pressure, less socially powerful groups increasingly found themselves excluded from seating. Indeed, in the same year it was explicitly ordered that children and waiting-women should be banned from pews on the grounds that they troubled 'parishioners of all condicione which have been placed by order and have right to sitt therein'. In deference to rank, however, the vestry drew back from the brink, and exempted the children of noblemen from this order.[185] The possibility of a serious social blunder must have seemed quite daunting to senior parish officials, and, however difficult the behaviour of St Martin's gentry, they were influential people whose charity was crucial to parish finances. In 1630 St Martin's vestry restricted the power of churchwardens to make these delicate decisions, perhaps fearing that mistakes might be made, especially if lower officials felt intimidated by their social betters. Instead, a new order prohibited churchwardens from placing anyone of the rank of esquire and above, until vestry consent had been obtained.[186]

Despite their fears of offending gentlemenly parishioners, the vestry consistently resisted pressures from them. In 1617 there was a direct clash with the young earl of

---

182 WAC, F2 vol. 2, f. 234. For the preferential treatment received by parish office-holders and their families in relation to burial see above, ch. 4.
183 WAC, F2001, f. 107.
184 *Ibid.*, f. 131a.
185 *Ibid.*, ff. 133, 126.
186 WAC, F2002, f. 73v.

Salisbury over the failure to appoint special pews for his servants. This dispute continued over a number of years (during which time the earl withheld payment of parish rates) and seems only to have been resolved in the earl's favour in 1622, at the 'speciall instance' of the bishop of London, the former Cecil chaplain George Montaigne.[187] More than a decade later, the vestry was also prepared to act promptly to prevent the private sale of a pew by the earl of Bedford to the courtier Sir Richard Wynn.[188] It seems likely that Lady Roe adopted a more successful strategy in obtaining a desirable pew. When she was assigned a seat, vestry minutes noted approvingly that she had already shown her 'love & liberality' to the parish by gifts 'adorning the Pulpitt & the Communion table'. There is no reason to think that her gifts were given solely with this specific end in mind, but it was behaviour that suggested a proper regard for the parish community.[189]

The most substantial attempt to remedy the problem of seating members of the gentry and nobility was the erection of a new gallery on the south side of St Martin's church in the early 1630s. This seems specifically to have been intended for members of the gentry and aristocracy, and it is often referred to in later accounts as 'the Lords' gallery'.[190] The gallery had the advantage of preventing nobles from usurping traditionally high-status pews occupied by the more middling sort of parochial officials, while at the same time offering them a space that was socially differentiated. 'Benevolences' of between £20 and £30 were received from the earls of Bedford, Suffolk, Salisbury and Berkshire, as well as from influential courtiers such as Lord Goring, Sir Thomas Edmondes, Sir Thomas Roe and Sir Francis Cottington. Such sums did not, however, 'buy' a place, and parish officials carefully monitored the use of pews, patrolling and amending them as necessary for practical and aesthetic reasons.[191] But squabbles over seating in the new gallery would seem to have been just as common as before. An all-day meeting of St Martin's vestry in December 1630 included a discussion of 'certain Complaynts and Excepions taken by some of the Nobilitie touching places in the new Gallery'. The bishop of London was increasingly brought in to adjudicate, and in March 1631 'divers' of the vestry attended the then bishop of London, William Laud, over pew disputes concering the wives of Sir Henry Vane and Sir Francis Cottington.[192]

---

187 WAC, F2001, ff. 117v, 151, 155v.

188 WAC, F2002, f. 106 (1636).

189 WAC, F2002, f. 71. Her gifts were an embroidered carpet for the communion table, a cushion for the pulpit and a pulpit cloth, all of them of red velvet: F3, 1628–29, n.f. She is identified in the churchwardens' accounts as the wife of Sir Thomas Roe.

190 An addition to the south gallery had first been suggested by Montford to the vestry in 1623, although he simply referred to 'suche parishioners as are not yet placed in the churche', and did not refer directly to any intention that it should seat more socially elevated residents: WAC, F2001, f. 172a.

191 WAC, F3, 1630–31; F2002, ff. 87v, 88.

192 WAC, F3, 1630–31. The duchess of Buckingham is also recorded as complaining over seating at this time. The vestry also attended Laud's chancellor, Dr Duck, in January and June/July 1630 concerning aspects of pewing and the placement of monuments, all organized in consultation with Laud himself (F3, 1629–30, 1630–31).

The prominence of women in these contested cases is of particular interest, especially since men and women normally sat separately at St Martin's.[193] Historians have noted the disproportionate number of women who brought cases before the London church courts in this period and earlier.[194] The similar prominence of aristocratic women in arguments over church seating in Westminster may derive partly from similar limitations in women's public role. But in the case of more socially elevated women, the need to manifest their social importance may have paralleled the quest for status which they (and their husbands) pursued among their social equals in arenas well outside the world of the parish. It is also possible that prominent courtiers would have attended services at Court, sometimes leaving their wives alone to attend the parish church and to defend their status in the process.[195] Further down the social scale, there was no special seating for the wives of office-holders, even when their husbands may have sat in a special pew, but these women were seldom involved in seating disputes, except perhaps when aristocratic women scorned to sit with them.[196]

Another striking aspect of the quarrels over seating in the new gallery is the increasing intervention of Laud, the current bishop of London. It is likely that Laud was already primed to deal sternly with the vestry, whose puritan inclinations he had recently encountered.[197] During one period in the early 1630s, St Martin's churchwardens were summoned before the bishop with monotonous regularity to answer seating-related complaints from various members of the gentry and aristocracy. Indeed, in 1631, when Laud became aware that St Martin's churchwardens were now required to obtain vestry approval for any seating decision, he cancelled the order 'as beinge against my Episcopall Jurisdiction', and formally entered and signed this counter-order in St Martin's vestry minute book.[198] These regular appeals to the bishop of London are significant for the light that they shed on relations in the community. Technically, the bishop (as ordinary) had the authority to allocate seats in parish churches, but in practice it was generally assumed that pewing would be organized by churchwardens and vestrymen. The regular appeals to the bishop are not just a barometer of social discontent but also evidence of an increasing readiness among the

193 For another example of pew disputes involving aristocratic women see WAC, F2002, f. 36 (Lady Finet (wife of Sir John Finet, Charles I's master of ceremonies) and her gentlewoman).

194 L. Gowing, *Domestic Dangers* (Oxford, 1996), pp. 30–4.

195 J.C. Cox, *Churchwardens' Accounts* (1913), p. 187.

196 There were special pews for the wives of prebendaries in Westminster Abbey by the 1630s, if not earlier, WAM, Chapter Act Bk II, f. 73v. The Abbey apparently provided a pew for members of the Court of Burgesses (Manchée, p. 220), but their wives do not seem to have been similarly favoured. Boulton notes (p. 147) that women's involvement in seating disputes may also be explained by changes to their status after remarriage. For widows and seating see below.

197 See below, ch. 9.

198 WAC, F2002, f. 73v. Laud presumably became aware of the order during his hearing of the Cottington and Vane cases two months earlier. See also F2002, f. 72v. Cf. McIntosh, *Community Transformed*, pp. 199–200, where the new gentry, in the shape of Sir William Ayloffe, appealed to the archdeacon over seating when he could not persuade the churchwardens to allocate him a better pew.

aristocracy, in particular, to bypass the authority of parish officials. This is all the more significant if the arrangement of church seating was perceived as a symbolic representation of power in the locality. If the vestry controlled the assignment of pews, they had, as one historian has put it, a power over 'the process of defining and reifying the social order'.[199] To challenge this power was to challenge the ability of local office-holders to impose their own reading of social status within the locality.

PATROLLING THE POOR: SEATING AT ST MARGARET'S

Spatial arrangements within St Margaret's church were as complex as those of its sister parish, but reflected somewhat different preoccupations. Although the church had been enlarged in the late fifteenth century to accommodate an already substantial urban congregation, it experienced overcrowding again by the second half of the sixteenth century – several decades before similar problems emerged at St Martin's. As early as 1571–72 individuals were prepared to pay extra to have neighbouring seats kept empty, and the frequency with which the accounts list sums received for a 'remove' also suggests the constant jockeying for position that took place.[200] The first recorded pew regulations at St Margaret's date from 1593 and echo some of the concerns found later at St Martin's. The orders especially noted part-time residents in the parish, presumably those with houses in the country, who came to the capital only for the law terms or to visit the Court. Any individual, the order stated, who had a pew 'and dothe not frequent the same once in three monethes' was to lose their seat.[201] Churchwardens may have been reluctant to enforce such an order, particularly if the offender were of high social status – the specification that any warden failing to execute the order was to be fined over 6s for his negligence certainly hints at this.[202]

By and large, however, Elizabethan regulations at St Margaret's focused attention on patrolling the division that separated those of the middling sort and above from those who barely managed to cling to householder status. For this reason, the vestry drafted orders that tried to ensure the social status of pew-holders. For example, the 1593 regulations declared that any existing pew-holder who 'shall happen to be decayed, and after to take releife of the Paryshe' was to surrender their pew.[203] It may be significant that such an order dates from the economically troubled decade of the 1590s, with its heightened sensitivity to social disruption. On at least one occasion the accounts reveal the churchwardens actively pursuing this policy: in 1595–96, 2s

199 Amussen, *Ordered Society*, p. 143.

200 WAC, E5, 1571–72; 1584–85, ff. 17–18; Merritt thesis, p. 255.

201 WAC, E2413, pt 2, f. 2. Residence specifications were also prominent in pewing regulations in the new church of St Paul's, Covent Garden in the 1630s and specifically addressed the problems created by short-term leases: *CSPD 1639*, p. 218; TNA, SP16/421/154.

202 WAC, E2413, pt 2, f. 2.

203 *Ibid.*

6d was paid to 'Jane Jones widow in recompence of her pew, to leve & forsake the same beinge a very poore woman'.[204] Widows would have been especially vulnerable to this regulation and certainly widows figured largely among parish pensioners (at St Margaret's and elsewhere).[205]

This emphasis on excluding the poor should perhaps be kept in mind when noting that immoral behaviour, which contemporaries often associated with poverty, was also grounds for losing a pew at St Margaret's. The orders of 1593 stated that any person convicted of 'whoredome, bauderye or any other notable cryme' would be deprived of his or her pew.[206] This order echoes the preoccupations of the Court of Burgesses, a body dominated by St Margaret's men, which regulated personal conduct as well as disciplining masterless persons.[207]

Rate-paying was also linked to seating in church and could, of course, be taken as a measure of status. In Southwark, the amount paid in rates at least partly determined seating in the church, and was associated with civic responsibility.[208] At St Margaret's, by 1609 the vestry actually directed that any pew-holder, male or female, who failed to pay parish rates (the poor rate and plague rate are specifically mentioned) or any 'service to be done or performed to the Kinge' would lose their pew.[209] Such an order underlines the difficulties created by delinquent ratepayers, and both St Margaret's and St Martin's formulated similar orders. At St Martin's, however, complaints were directed against those who were able to pay but did not (parishioners who maintained residences in more than one parish were a particular problem for St Martin's). By contrast, St Margaret's pewing regulations seem to focus on those who had actually lost householder status. Once again, the preoccupation was with threats to status posed by those from below rather than from above.

Office-holding was as important a criterion in St Margaret's as in St Martin's, but St Margaret's parish designated special seats for office-holders at an earlier date and introduced many restrictive seating practices some twenty years earlier than St Martin's. The special seats allocated to office-holders during the sixteenth century would also seem to reflect St Margaret's more sophisticated parish government in the Tudor period, with designated pews for overseers of the poor as early as 1560, and a new pew for churchwardens in the 1580s (although there is evidence of a special seat for them from at least the 1550s) and for the burgesses of Westminster by the 1590s.[210]

204 WAC, E6 (1595–96), f. 18. Another order dealt with problems of status relating to remarriage: WAC, E2413, pt 2, f. 2v.

205 Archer, pp. 9–14.

206 WAC, E2413, pt 2, f. 1v.

207 There is no record, however, of any person losing their pew for such a reason.

208 Boulton, pp. 146, 287.

209 WAC, E2413, pt 2, f. 10v.

210 WAC, E4, 1559–60, 1565–66, 1581–82, 1596–97, f. 10. By contrast, the only special pew recorded at St Martin's during the sixteenth century was that built for the sidesmen and churchwardens in 1567: Kitto, p. 233. Pews for office-holders do not seem to have become widespread in the City of London until the early seventeenth century: *London VCH*, p. 320.

Despite these innovations, however, St Margaret's never suffered from acrimonious seating disputes. In particular, long-term residents of the parish were not pitted against newer residents of higher social status. It is true that more titled residents began to acquire pews at St Margaret's from the 1620s, and a substantial number of new pews were erected in the 1620s and 1630s.[211] Indeed by the late 1630s a new gallery was constructed, to which some 143 parishioners contributed 'benevolences', but while 120 of those renting pews in this new gallery are styled 'Mr', no peers are listed, and virtually no record of any conflict over seating arrangements survives.[212] More disruption was probably caused by the occasional invasion of the church by the House of Commons for the purpose of communions and fast sermons, although again no record of any conflict over seating survives.[213]

It seems highly unlikely that seating disputes were entirely absent from St Margaret's, but these would appear to have been resolved within the parish. The easy proximity of the ordinary – the dean of Westminster – may also have ensured that any potential disagreements were quickly nipped in the bud. This is confirmed by a solitary reference to a pewing dispute dating from the late 1630s, at a time when the dean was imprisoned, and the controversy was therefore referred to Archbishop Laud, then acting in Dean Williams's place. We know of the pewing dispute only because associated legal costs were recorded by the churchwardens. This example suggests that it was more normal for complaints to be settled by the informal mediation of Westminster's dean or archdeacon.[214]

The relative calm that governed the process of church seating may, of course, reflect the fact that St Margaret's governing elite formed a more united and socially cohesive grouping than that of St Martin's. As we have seen, many office-holders were members of the victualling professions – brewers, bakers and butchers – groups that had played a leading role in parish affairs since medieval times.[215] They also seem to have been united by their fear of the poor immigrants who flooded into Westminster in the later sixteenth century. It had been this fear of the poor and the scale of population increase that had led to the creation of the Court of Burgesses, a process that had been largely promoted by St Margaret's men.

CONCLUSION

As we have seen, the exploration of contested space – from the church pew upwards – sheds important light on the different social forces at work within Westminster

---

211   It is possible that peers known to have houses in the parish attended services at the Abbey or at the Chapel Royal. WAC, E15 (1626–28), ff. 15v, 16v, 37v; E17 (1630–31), ff. 31v, 37, 38.

212   WAC, E23 (1640–41).

213   For the use of St Margaret's by the House of Commons see below, ch. 9.

214   WAC, E21 ff. 66, 69. There are no other such payments recorded in the accounts.

215   Rosser, pp. 133–43, 234–5, 363.

society. Victuallers and craftsmen, 'men of qualitie', parish officials and the Crown all struggled to appropriate space in Westminster and to dictate its usage. In the process, many different principles might be invoked: the need for social distance and distinction, the prevention of disease, the right of those of a certain social rank to better views and cleaner air, the immemorial rights of the parish community to enjoy access to common lands, the need to control disorder, and the rights of those performing local offices to commensurate spatial status within the parish. These were not, however, the watertight principles of implacably opposed social groups. A certain fluidity of interests characterized many individuals, so that a spokesman for parochial rights in one context might easily appear as an 'antisocial' encloser or illegal builder in another. Similarly, the impact of the Crown itself worked in different directions, preserving large swathes of green space yet ultimately stimulating development in the area.

This chapter has emphasized the Tudor–Stuart period as a crucial time of transition, with the coexistence of very different uses of space within the Westminster parishes. Each of these reflected a different 'Westminster': the home of the royal court and its hunting grounds; the chief venue of fashionable gentry society; the bureaucratic and administrative quarter; the prominent centre of the meat and brewing trades; the semi-rural outskirts; and the suburb 'pestered' by poor immigrants. None of these identities, however, entirely dominated the shape of the locality and so the result was a townscape of striking contrasts. Forces were at work which would encourage the development of a more select, self-consciously fashionable enclave,[216] yet high-living aristocrats still lived cheek by jowl with the tradesmen who serviced their needs, peers were forced to defer to local craftsmen in the disposition of church seating, and owners of elegant new mansions still partly shared their grounds with local laundry-women, while the procession of royal judges squeezed past the carcasses of the local meat market, and members of the royal household choked on the fumes from local breweries and starch houses.

---

216 This would take place largely in building further west and north than our period witnessed.

Chapter 7

The Westminster Court of Burgesses: neighbourhood, disorder and urban expansion

A CONTEMPORARY account of life in Westminster in 1585 portrayed its busy thoroughfares and back alleys in the blackest fashion. The Elizabethan town stood on the brink of moral chaos and social breakdown. Its rapid expansion and the 'general concourse' of so many people living and passing through its crowded streets had led to 'soondry great murders, Ryottes, Routes, fraies, roberies . . . Adulteries and oder incontynente lief [sic] . . . and many oder the lieke shamefool synnes'. That, at least, was how it was described in a draft of a parliamentary act designed to reorganize its government – a text doubtless couched in the bleakest terms possible in order to justify its proposed legislation.[1] This characterization of the area undoubtedly employs the standard rhetoric of the period, whereby a large and shifting population was associated with a combination of moral turpitude and crime. Yet Elizabethan Westminster *did* face very real social problems connected with urban growth and high levels of immigration. Ultimately the architects of the bill sought to pave the way for major structural alterations in Westminster's local government and as we have seen, they were unsuccessful in their bid for full-scale incorporation. Nevertheless concerns over disorder, particularly in an area surrounding the royal Court, were sufficiently serious to result in a parliamentary act specifically said to be for the 'good government' of Westminster.

This 1585 Act formally established a Court of Burgesses, with the stated intention that this new body would tackle problems of disorder and provide the town with a means to ensure 'good government' more generally in the locality. The powers given to the court meant that it never dealt directly with the violent crime so vividly evoked in parliament in 1585. The types of 'disorder' which the Court of Burgesses regulated most often were those forms of behaviour particularly associated with urban expansion – keeping 'inmates', illegal building, vagrancy, sexual immorality and working as

---

1 TNA, SP12/117/29, f. 1. See above, ch. 3, for the history of the 1585 Act.

a 'masterless' person. Even if these were not the murders and 'Ryottes' mentioned in the draft Act, however, they were nevertheless seen as undesirable manifestations of an urban expansion which, in contemporary eyes, generated violence, theft and immoral behaviour.

The Court of Burgesses and its workings have never received proper analysis, and yet the court occupies a particularly intriguing position in the history of early modern Westminster. To begin with, it was a unique Westminster phenomenon. Nowhere else was there an organization that combined the aspects of an ecclesiastical court, a London ward jurisdiction and a leet court in quite this way during the early modern period. Moreover, it confined its attention solely to Westminster residents and was made up of local inhabitants. In this way it differed from an authority such as the Middlesex sessions, which continued to punish serious crimes such as murder and theft, not just from Westminster but from across the county.[2] The prominent role played by a cleric – the dean of Westminster – who presided over the burgesses also made this court distinctive within the early modern metropolis.[3]

The chance survival of two minute-books of the court covering the years 1610–16 enable us to gain some fascinating glimpses of how this institution operated.[4] There are obvious limitations to these sources: details are relatively sparse, with no surviving depositions, while the six-year time-span provides only a snapshot of the range and volume of business that came before the court in our period. Nevertheless, they offer rich and important insights into the working of early modern Westminster, and the ways in which the local community responded to the pressures of urban expansion. As we will see, notions of neighbourhood, sexual morality and personal reputation emerge as the significant preoccupations of a town seeking to regulate itself in the face of the first great waves of suburban expansion.

DISORDERED BEGINNINGS

Before we can discuss the impact of the court on Westminster residents, it is important to understand the historical framework within which the Court of Burgesses operated. The formal creation of the Court of Burgesses can be dated to 1585, but in fact this

---

2 The purpose of this chapter is to explore the distinctive Westminster institution of the Court of Burgesses, rather than the more general topic of crime in Westminster. The records of the Middlesex Sessions before the Civil War are problematic, and cases from Westminster formed only a portion of its business, although a separate division for Westminster was created in 1618 (see above, ch. 3). There has been no systematic analysis of crime in London or rural Middlesex for the early seventeenth century, which might contextualize the Westminster material. Records for the post-Restoration period are more amenable to statistical analysis: see R.B. Shoemaker, *Prosecution and Punishment: Petty Crime and the Law in London and Rural Middlesex* (Cambridge, 1991).

3 The dean together with the high steward's deputy normally presided over the court, see below.

4 The minute books appear to be mid- to late seventeenth-century copies of the originals.

act gave a new lease of life to a far older institution – the manorial court traditionally presided over by the abbots of Westminster. In the pre-Reformation period, the abbot's manorial court had wielded secular powers in the manor of Westminster and it had been the only body to exercise authority throughout the town's four pre-Reformation parishes. Indeed, the abbot's June court was the principal local court serving the town by the late medieval period.[5]

The June court operated in a very urban environment, but its brief was largely that of a traditional manor court of the kind more usually associated with agrarian communities. The court met once a year, presided over by the abbot's bailiff or seneschal. Twelve prominent tenants of the vill, known as chief pledges, sat on the court and presented offenders according to the nature of the court's jurisdiction. As a leet court, the abbot's court regulated matters such as the baking of bread, alebrewing, butchering and various types of nuisance. Suspicious or antisocial behaviour, such as 'night-walking', prostitution and scolding, also came before the court.[6] The abbot also exercised a number of royal prerogatives within the Westminster manor, including the view of frankpledge, the assize of bread and ale and the trial of certain offences against the king's law.[7]

By the early sixteenth century, the figure of the Westminster chief pledge had become an increasingly prominent one. As Dr Rosser has shown, the members of the abbot's court had actually become a self-electing body, whose members usually held high office in St Margaret's religious fraternities.[8] In this way they occasionally grouped together and assumed certain duties more usually associated with a formal town executive.[9] It was from this tradition of informal self-government – and perhaps assertiveness – that the later role of the Westminster burgess was to emerge.

Of course, the dissolution of Westminster Abbey problematized the existence of the abbot's court. The jurisdictional status of the former Abbey also became increasingly complicated during these years and it remains unclear whether the abbot's court continued to function under another name during the latter years of Henry VIII's reign.[10] In May 1547, however, the Edwardian dean and chapter authorized Sir Wymond Carew, brother-in-law to Sir Anthony Denny (the new high steward of

---

5 Rosser, pp. 228–32. The four pre-Reformation parishes were St Margaret's, St Martin in the Fields, St Mary le Strand and St Clement Danes. WAM 5299A (temp. Jas. I), describing the 'bounds' of the 'Cittie of Westminster and the liberties thereof', states that it had been usual to summon persons from within this entire area before both the Court of Burgesses and 'the Court leet of the manor of Westminster'.

6 Rosser, pp. 230, 233, 238–44. During the sixteenth century, leet courts expanded the range of offences they punished to include social misbehaviour, M. McIntosh, *Controlling Misbehavior in England, 1370–1600* (Cambridge, 1998), p. 37.

7 Rosser, p. 230.

8 *Ibid.*, p. 234.

9 *Ibid.*, pp. 285–93.

10 See C.S. Knighton, 'Collegiate foundations, 1540 to 1570, with special reference to St Peter Westminster' (Cambridge Ph.D., 1975), pp. 26–7, 72, n.1, 121.

Westminster), to preside over a leet court.[11] Although it is clear that the dean and chapter were partly able to exercise the secular authority formerly wielded by Westminster's abbots, it is not known whether the chief pledges were able to retain the autonomy they had earlier enjoyed.

Little is known about the leet court during the Marian period and the early years of Elizabeth, but it is mentioned as a functioning body in 1584–85.[12] Despite its apparent resilience, it seems likely that the population increase in the locality drew attention to the court's shortcomings. There were widespread fears about the unfettered expansion of the metropolis during Elizabeth's reign. In suburban Southwark, for example, the parish of St Olave's appointed a surveyor of inmates in 1585, the very year that the Court of Burgesses was established in Westminster. In Westminster itself, the early 1580s found St Margaret's parish officials expelling vagrants as part of a concerted campaign.[13] It is also possible that the focus of Westminster's leet court failed to adjust to newer expansion in the parishes of St Martin's and St Clement's, which had seldom figured in the records of the abbot's court.[14] The creation of the Court of Burgesses may therefore have been intended to bring these parishes more firmly within the jurisdiction of a single court and to redirect its attention towards issues linked with immigration.

By the 1580s, it would appear that population increase and poverty in Westminster had eroded the already limited ability of its various local bodies to maintain order and had compounded existing structural deficiencies. Local officials, it was complained, held 'no lawful warraunte' to punish offenders except at the leet court, which met only twice a year. The meeting times of the court were so well known, it was said, that 'Sooch malefactors doo avoide and flee from the said City and Liberty untill the said Courte and Sitting be past, And then in moquerye retoorne and contynue without any punishmente'.[15] There was clearly a need, then, for a court that would meet much more frequently and for officials who would co-ordinate activities throughout all of the parishes. The problem of lax law enforcement in Westminster was also said to be

---

11 Carew was to levy fines 'to the use and commodite of the said Dean and chapter', keeping one half of the fines for himself and it seems logical to assume that the yearly court still met in the usual manner. The dean and chapter, for their part, agreed to pay the costs of dinners for the steward and other officers when the court was in session. Instruments of punishment were also specifically placed in Carew's care and his duties included maintaining the stocks, pillory and cucking stools: *Acts*, no. 58. For the use of such instruments see McIntosh, *Controlling*, p. 64, Archer, pp. 242–3, 251. For Denny's appointment see above, ch. 3.

12 27 Eliz. I c. 31.

13 WAC, E146, 1581 (*sic*). By 1593, the Southwark parish of St Saviour's was ordering its churchwardens to report fortnightly on inmates: Archer, pp. 184–5.

14 For the period before 1540, the June court seems to have dealt mostly with St Margaret's parishioners. I owe this information to Dr Rosser.

15 TNA, SP12/117/29, f. 2. This draft claims that the leet court met twice a year, which, if correct, differs from the once-yearly meetings of the abbot's court: Rosser, p. 230. The problem of pursuing recalcitrant offenders when leet courts meet so infrequently was also a difficulty for the Guildable Manor in Southwark: see M. Carlin, *Medieval Southwark* (1996), p. 114.

compounded by the paucity of JPs living in the town. This lack of resident justices of the peace in Westminster was specifically raised in debates over the 1585 bill, while the preamble to the bill also emphasized the need for an efficient law enforcement body to tackle the area's most pressing problems.[16] Behind this discussion of structural problems, however, was also the conviction that a larger moral problem needed to be addressed – an assumption with important consequences for the ultimate scope of the new Court of Burgesses.[17]

It is clear that the supporters of the 1585 legislation had initially hoped to address these problems by achieving full corporate status for the area. Instead, the Court of Burgesses that emerged from the Act, while a body with a range of law enforcement powers, did not constitute a central governing body for Westminster and it should not viewed as a counterpart of London's Court of Aldermen.[18]

Many of the idiosyncratic features of the Court of Burgesses stem from its origins in this failed incorporation bid.[19] Just as the failure of this attempt was due to opposition from competing authorities in the area, so the Court of Burgesses was encumbered by numerous restrictions to its powers. A clause in the Act specified that it should continue only until the end of the next ensuing Parliament and thereafter the act was renewed on seven successive occasions, in each case for only a short period of time, until 1640.[20] Given these circumstances it is not surprising to find that an act as temporary as the 1585 Act was intended to be, preserved a whole array of existing jurisdictions: indeed the ordinances of the new court specified a range of authorities whose power must not be encroached upon. The list is a mighty one and included the jurisdictions of 'the Steward, Marshal or Coroner of the [royal] Household, the Middlesex justices, the dean and chapter of Westminster, the Mayor, Society and Clerk of the Staple, the High Constable, the Bailliff of the Liberties, the Town Clerk, [and] the Clerk of the Markets . . . in the City and Liberties'. The relationship between parish government and the burgesses was also left unclear. There never seems to have been a shared political will to resolve these conflicting jurisdictions, and this lack of clarity would dog the operation of the Court of Burgesses for the next hundred years

---

16 BL, Lansdowne MS 43, f. 172. The lack of resident JPs and the inability of the Middlesex Sessions to cope with offences taking place in Westminster were still sources of complaint in the 1610s; see below.

17 See below.

18 Manchée, pp. 5–6, notes the oddities of the 1585 legislation and its temporary character but still holds that 'the main purpose of the Act was to create in Westminster a civic government somewhat similar to that of the City of London, with certain reservations to secure the ancient rights of the Abbey'. Cf. a similar explanation in *Cambridge Urban History vol. II* (Cambridge, 2000), p. 334.

19 See above, ch. 3.

20 The 1585 Act was renewed in 31 Eliz. I c. 10 (1589); 35 Eliz. I c. 7 (1593); 39 Eliz. I c. 19 (1597); 43 Eliz. I c. 9 (1601); 1 Jas I c. 25 (1603); 21 Jas I c. 28 (1624); 3 Chas I c. 4 (1627); 16 Chas I c. 4 (1640). The act was made permanent in 1640, an event the Webbs suggest may have come about by 'legislative inadvertence': Webbs, *Manor and Borough*, pp. 214–15.

and more.[21] The unsettled basis of this new Court of Burgesses is also firmly underlined by the very absence of administrative details from the text of the 1585 Act – including the thorny issue of how the court was to be funded. Indeed it was left to a separately issued list of 'Orders and Ordinances', dated 27 May 1585, even to specify the nature of the court's activities.[22]

THE BURGESSES AND LOCAL SOCIETY

Whatever the confused origins of the 1585 Act, its impact for good or ill was still considerable. The administrative significance of the act was to create a Court of Burgesses presiding over a system of twelve wards. The court consisted of twelve burgesses, each of whom was aided by an assistant burgess. Every Tuesday, all burgesses and their assistants (twenty-four men in all) were to come together to form a Court of Burgesses, presided over by the dean of Westminster, and the high steward or his deputy.[23] In practice, deans of Westminster attended regularly, while high stewards were normally represented by a deputy. Once together, they heard cases primarily relating to the harbouring of 'inmates', illicit sexual activity, illegal building, market regulation and nuisance.[24] Those burgesses absent without good cause were to be fined 4d on each occasion. On Saturdays, burgesses (probably in turn) were to be found at Westminster's local market, where their presence was meant to ensure that standards of wholesomeness and honesty were properly maintained.[25]

But who were the burgesses and what sort of social and administrative authority did they exercise? The 1585 Act did not allow for the election of burgesses; instead, they were merely to be appointed by the dean or high steward, while assistant burgesses were chosen by the court as a whole. Even so, when the office of burgess was first created, it was clearly intended to be one of considerable dignity and power. Ironically, although no Westminster corporation was created in 1585, the terms and social cachet assigned to what was presumably meant to have been a Court of Aldermen were not correspondingly downgraded. A burgess held his office for life, if he desired, and once a member of the Court of Burgesses he had reached the pinnacle of local status. The burgess-ship was the highest office a man could hope to obtain in the

21 Webbs, *Manor and Borough*, pp. 215–19, 224–31. A more recent discussion of law enforcement in eighteenth-century Westminster is contained in E.A. Reynolds, *Before the Bobbies: The Night Watch and Police Reform in Metropolitan London, 1720–1830* (1998). It is, however, dangerous to extrapolate backwards from this period into the pre-Civil-War period.

22 It is not clear exactly who drafted these ordinances, but it seems likely that they were agreed upon by the burgesses and ultimately by Lord Burghley, the current high steward of Westminster: Webbs, *Manor and Borough*, p. 214. The 1585 Ordinances are printed in Manchée, pp. 212–21.

23 *Ibid.*, p. 220.

24 See below.

25 Manchée, p. 214.

locality, except for that of bailiff or possibly member of parliament. It only remained for him to serve as one of Westminster's two chief burgesses, a position that rotated yearly among court members and therefore seems not to have carried additional status.[26] There was no office of lord mayor to progress to, or the hope of a knighthood (as became customary for lord mayors of London in the sixteenth century). It is, however, unlikely that Westminster burgesses were considered comparable in social status to an aldermen of London or to the lord mayor. Nevertheless, the very names 'burgess' and 'Court of Burgesses' sought to convey a sense of prestige and distinction.

Other attempts were made to boost the social prestige of burgesses. The will of one of the first burgesses, Maurice Pickering, had sought to establish the ritual paraphernalia that would represent the burgesses as a town government in waiting, including special feasts, plate and a burial cloth for the exclusive use of burgesses.[27] Charges of arrogance made against the burgesses in the Jacobean period certainly survive: Lord Haughton, as we have seen, mockingly termed the burgesses 'senators', and one malefactor vowed to his mistress that he would take her far beyond the reach of 'the proudest Burgess of them all'.[28] But this sense of self-importance may have been bolstered by higher aspirations. Additional bids for incorporation in the Jacobean and Caroline periods reveal that townspeople expected the burgesses to play a central role in any formally incorporated city government that might emerge, and to form a pool from which the town's MPs would be chosen. Yet the consciousness that burgesses might not have been receiving the respect owing to them is suggested by proposals put forward to incorporate Westminster in 1633. The two chief burgesses, it was suggested, for the 'better and more ornament for their persons and respect for their places' should in future be accompanied by two serjeants 'carrying a little Mace before them when they walke abroad'.[29]

But what type of man served on the Westminster Court of Burgesses, and how did these individuals relate to the local community? The 1585 Act designated that burgesses were to be 'merchauntes, Artificers, or Persons usinge anye Trade of buyeng or selling within the said Cittie or Boroughe', conditions which would seem to reflect the interests of the townsmen behind the attempted incorporation. Nevertheless, the act conceded that burgesses could also ultimately be chosen from among others 'willing' and living within the 'Cittie or Boroughe and the liberties of the same'. This concession explains how two minor Exchequer officials with close links to Lord Treasurer Burghley – John Dodington and William Staunton – came to be among the original twelve burgesses appointed in 1585. None the less, later appointments to the Court

26 27 Eliz. I c. 31. Burgesses did occasionally ask to be discharged from their position: e.g. WAC, WCB1, p. 55.

27 See above, ch. 3.

28 Sheffield City Archives, Strafford Papers, 12/143; WAC, WCB1, p. 7.

29 WAM 6561, pp. 1–2.

of Burgesses suggest that burgesses were generally intended to be prosperous trades-men and artificers with business interests in the locality.[30]

In practice, burgesses were usually parochial officials and therefore already familiar figures of authority in the local community. That being said, the office of burgess sat at one remove from the parish *cursus honorum*. The very fact that the 1585 Ordinances required burgesses and their assistants to attend the Sunday morning sermon at the Abbey meant that burgesses were not attending their parish church. This suggests an attempt to reinforce the sense that the burgess was a civic official serving all of West-minster, and not just his individual parish.[31]

How, then, was the role of the individual burgess understood? The 1585 Act specified that every burgess with his assistant was to 'doe and deale in everie thinge and things as Aldermens deputies in the Cittie of London'.[32] Like London's deputy alderman, the Westminster burgess dealt directly with the ward he served and, as we shall see, helped to settle local disputes. Burgess and deputy alderman alike performed a wide range of tasks and each was supported by inquestmen and a form of wardmote inquest. Nevertheless, the position of Westminster burgess was clearly more presti-gious than that of deputy alderman.[33] Unlike the deputy alderman, however, the bur-gess did not exercise powers of summary conviction. These were reserved to the burgesses collectively, sitting as a court.[34] In fact, the burgess was not truly analogous to any one City official and, as we have seen, his earlier antecedent was really the medieval West-minster chief pledge.

At the heart of the working of the Court of Burgesses lay the relationship between the individual burgess and his ward. This unique Westminster ward system was singled out for praise during the passage of the 1585 Act through parliament.[35] It must be emphasized that the Westminster 'ward' was a very different unit from the

---

30   27 Eliz. I c. 31. Both Dodington and Staunton had also filled the comparatively humble office of churchwarden (at St Margaret's), while both men had served as Westminster MPs in the early 1570s: see Merritt thesis, p. 145. For a later list of burgesses, which seems to confirm this preponderance of tradesmen and artificers, see CUL, MS Gg.I.9, pp. 45, 62ff., although in 1610 the court included one of the King's porters and an official of the Court of Common Pleas: WAC, WCB1, p. 47.

31   *Ibid.*, p. 220. It may also have been intended to act as a pointed reminder of the extent to which the power of burgesses ultimately derived from that of the dean and chapter.

32   27 Eliz. I c. 31.

33   The deputy alderman, although a man of substance, a common councilman and probably a vestryman in his parish, did not belong to that group of elite merchants who became city aldermen. In Westminster, however, the burgess was more likely to have progressed steadily through lower parochial offices, such as constable and churchwarden, before eventually attaining the burgess-ship. I am indebted to Dr Ian Archer for discussing the social position of the deputy aldermen with me.

34   For the court exercising summary jurisdiction see WAC, WCB1, pp. 36, 38, 81; WCB2, ppf. 7, 94. Burgesses also appear to have lived in the ward they were responsible for: WAC, F2001, f. 133.

35   BL, Lansdowne MS 43, f. 179, also printed in T.E. Hartley (ed.), *Proceedings in the Parliaments of Elizabeth I* (3 vols., Leicester, 1981–95), II, 58–60.

wards of the City of London. In London a 'ward' referred to a larger administrative unit that typically included several parishes.[36] In Westminster, by contrast, the 'ward' was a subdivision of the parish. Therefore each parish contained several wards: no fewer than eight wards were situated in St Margaret Westminster, three in St Martin in the Fields and one in St Clement Danes and the Strand.[37] Each ward was to be served by a burgess and an assistant burgess, men who lived locally. The historian Strype, writing in the early eighteenth century, noted that a Westminster ward was originally known not by a name related to a geographical location but according to the name of the burgess who represented it, for example 'Mr Fowler's ward' or 'Mr Colbrand's ward'. This practice self-consciously imitated that of twelfth- and thirteenth-century London, where the names of each ward changed when a new alderman entered office, but it may have also reflected an attempt to underline the personal relationship between the individual burgess and the locality that he patrolled.[38]

The smaller size of Westminster's wards provided the potential for close interaction between the burgess and his immediate neighbours, and it is clear that the Westminster burgess (assisted by his deputy) personally involved himself in the daily running of his ward. Inhabitants regularly visited the houses of individual burgesses for business ranging from arbitration to the issuing of certificates of good behaviour. The importance of the wards meant that the workload of individual burgesses was far heavier than that of the burgesses sitting collectively as a court. They were expected to possess a good knowledge of the wards in which they lived, and from time to time they were asked to report on their wards for a variety of reasons – most often to survey the number of poor or those likely to need parish relief in the future.[39] Their inquiries might extend even further. In April 1611, for example, the court ordered the burgess Matthew Head to 'enquire of the behaviour of all Inhabitants of Knights bridge and to certify att the next Court'.[40] The inquestmen and wardmote inquests would also have been important here. Although virtually no record survives of their activities in Westminster, the inquestmen presumably acted as presenting jurors, and they formed part of a system which kept the burgess informed about affairs in his ward. In this

---

36 C.N.L. Brooke, *London 800–1216: The Shaping of a City* (1975), pp. 162–3. The closest parallel in London was the precinct: F.F. Foster, *The Politics of Stability* (1977), p. 29; Archer, p. 83; V. Pearl, 'Change and stability in seventeenth-century London', *London Journal* V (1979), pp. 15–25; A.E. MacCampbell, 'The London parish and the London precinct, 1640–1660', *Guildhall Studies in Local History* 2 (1976), pp. 107–24.

37 See 27 Eliz. I c. 31; Strype, II.vi.57. For the ward boundaries in 1585 see also BL, Lansdowne MS 44/48, which the catalogue erroneously describes as pertaining to London. The relationship of the twelve Westminster wards to the twelve chief pledges of the old manor court remains unclear: Rosser, p. 233.

38 Strype, II.vi.57; Brooke, *London*, p. 163. Some examples of the use of named wards in Westminster may also be noted in the 1642 collection for distressed Irish Protestants: TNA, SP28/193, ff. 266v, 276v.

39 See WAM 9353.

40 WAC, WCB2, p. 56.

respect, the smaller size of the Westminster ward may have been to its advantage – certainly the minutes of the Court of Burgesses give the impression that burgesses were well-informed.[41] But how did burgesses exercise their authority, and what preoccupations do their activities reveal? To answer these questions, we need to turn to the surviving minutes of the court.

THE COURT OF BURGESSES AT WORK

As noted above, the only pre-eighteenth-century minutes to survive for the court cover the period 1610–16. Although dating from nearly thirty years after the passage of the 1585 Act, the minutes hold special interest because they allow some comparison between the court's duties in theory and how it chose to implement them in practice. The minutes show the court dutifully enforcing the provisions set down in the separately issued list of 'Orders and Ordinances', dated 27 May 1585, which specified the nature of the business to be conducted by the Court of Burgesses.[42] The ordinances themselves seem to have been based largely upon the types of cases dealt with by the abbot's old manorial court, and so may well simply represent an attempt to formalize time-honoured practice.[43] Indeed, many of the cases handled by the burgesses would have seemed familiar to their earlier counterparts who served on the old manorial court. Cases involving sanitation, the protection of the common at Tothill, the curbing of the encroachment of new building, the regulation of the local market and of antisocial behaviour, such as scolding, fill the minute books of the Court of Burgesses.[44]

Market regulation was an important part of the court's function and one that derived from the powers formerly exercised by the abbot of Westminster. The regulation of weights and measures used by bakers, brewers and colliers was one of the obligations imposed on the burgesses by the 1585 Ordinances.[45] Complaints about the wholesomeness of victuals sold at the market could also be brought before the burgesses, while the court also settled disputes between those selling their goods in the

---

41 In the eighteenth century, a leet jury and an annoyance jury were sworn in October and then again in April, a practice which is hinted at in the Jacobean court minutes: WAC, WCB1, pp. 32, 53, 115, 216, 232; Manchée, pp. 217, 219. On the circumstances in which a jury was called see below, p. 236. It is possible that inquestmen were selected by parish vestries. In Elizabethan London, the wardmote 'was given no choice at all over the members of the inquest', which was controlled by parish vestries: Archer, p. 68. For a brief set of instructions for a wardmote inquest see CUL, MS Gg.I.9, p. 52. This document dates from c.1660 and also contains an oath for constables, indicating that they were expected to present inmates, *ibid.*, p. 50; for earlier cf. WAC, F2001, f. 162.

42 Manchée, pp. 212–21.

43 WAC, WCB1 covers the years 1610–13, while WCB2 covers 1613–16. For offences brought before the old manorial court see Rosser, pp. 232–44.

44 Some of these issues are discussed above, ch. 6.

45 Cf. Rosser, pp. 139, 232–44; Manchée, p. 213.

market. The porters of Westminster, for example, complained to the court about London 'foreigners' who carried coals into Westminster and so robbed them of their business.[46] As in the medieval period, it was the absence of London guild regulations that prompted the Westminster authorities to undertake these responsibilities. The standards that burgesses sought to maintain were actually based on those employed in the City of London, as were other details of market regulation and the powers allotted to searchers. This desire to conform with London standards is suggested all the more clearly by a directive of the court in 1615 that required one of the burgesses to obtain a copy of the market orders for Cheapside and Newgate Markets.[47] Only the orders concerning butchers seem distinctive to Westminster and this was due to the fact that butchering had been banned inside the City since the fourteenth century, while remaining an important trade practised within Westminster.[48]

But how did the Court of Burgesses proceed against offenders? The minutes of the court show that a presentment against an individual was usually not challenged, so that it served as both indictment and conviction in one, as was normally the case with leet courts.[49] Presentments came from a variety of sources, including constables, wardmote inquests and the burgesses themselves.[50] These presentments tended to be firmly linked to the offences set out in the 1585 Ordinances, yet it is possible to discern small shifts in presentments which may have reflected either public concerns or the preoccupations of the burgesses themselves. So for example, we find clusters of presentments related to fire hazards, tobacco-sellers and unfinished apprenticeships.[51] A certificate of inhabitants complaining about starch-making in a part of St Margaret's parish also suggests that groups of neighbours might approach the burgess court directly over a particular grievance.[52]

Most people appearing before the Court of Burgesses were there to receive some form of punishment or correction, since the guilt of accused men and women was

46 WAC, WCB1, p. 209.

47 WAC, WCB2, p. 121. For market regulation more generally see I. Archer, C. Barron and V. Harding (eds.), *Hugh Alley's Caveat: The Markets of London in 1598* (London Topographical Society 137, 1988).

48 Manchée, p. 218 (Ordinances); Rosser, p. 138; e.g. WAC, WCB1, p. 253. See WCB1, p. 177 for regulations concerning the times for carrying 'Beast offels' through the streets.

49 McIntosh, *Controlling*, p. 36.

50 E.g. WCB2, p. 158. The court operated closely in conjunction with constables, officials who acted as administrative agents for various higher authorities, but especially the justices of the peace. Authority over the constables seems to have been blurred in practice, and in the Jacobean period constables were sworn before *both* the Court of Burgesses and the Middlesex justices: e.g. WAC, WCB1, pp. 15, 17; WCB2, pp. 19, 21; W. Le Hardy (ed.), *Calendar of Middlesex Sessions Records*, n.s. II (1936), 95–6, 286. Twenty-three constables served in St Margaret's parish, four in St Martin's and three in St Clement's: Strype, II.vi.57. The areas constables patrolled, however, do not seem to have coincided with burgesses' wards, at least in St Martin's and St Clement Danes.

51 WAC, WCB2, pp. 129, 131 (fire); WCB2, pp. 88, 96, 103, 120, 142–3 (tobacco); WCB2, pp. 39, 51 (apprenticeships).

52 WAC, WCB2, p. 36.

treated as a foregone conclusion. It was theoretically possible to challenge presentments, however, as a handful of jury trials recorded in the minutes indicate. These
trials evidently took place in front of a jury convened outside the weekly meetings of
the court, and the cases themselves pertain almost exclusively to sexual offences
(adultery and incontinency), although one trial involved three women accused as
scolds.[53] The penalties commonly handed down by the court included fining as well
as the taking of sureties to ensure compliance with a court order. Nevertheless, the
court also had sharper means at its disposal, including imprisonment in the Gatehouse prison, and physical penalties, such as whipping, carting and the use of the
stocks and cucking stool. Such punishments were clearly in use by the earlier leet
court as early as the mid-sixteenth century, a period which also saw the creation of
Bridewell in London and the increasing use of physical punishments in the capital
more generally. Nevertheless, by the Jacobean period, there was no suburban jurisdiction that punished offenders so harshly and on so regular a basis as the Court of
Burgesses did. On one occasion William Littlebury, a servant who had 'reviled' a
constable, was even whipped 'at the open bar at court'.[54] Another punishment favoured by the court was 'banishment' from the city and liberties of Westminster.
This involved whipping the offender through the streets at the cart's tail, all the way
from the Westminster Gatehouse, near the Abbey, to Temple Bar in the Strand.[55] This
sounds suspiciously as if 'undesirables' were simply deposited over Westminster's border with the City, a policy that would have done little for metropolitan social problems more generally. Nevertheless, the desire to 'purge' the area of the 'basest and
baddest sort of parsons', who were thought to congregate in Westminster, was clearly
one of the original aims of the act.[56] These harsher physical punishments were almost
exclusively reserved for those found guilty of moral offences. That being said, the
Westminster Court of Burgesses was unusual among London courts in the combination of offences that it regularly punished.[57]

The desire to expel sexual offenders – sometimes whipping them at the cart's tail
as they walked from the Westminster Gatehouse to Temple Bar – suggests that the
symbolic impact of expulsion may have been considerable. This was not unparalleled:

---

53 WAC, WCB1, pp. 6, 8, 23, 57, 150, 213 (for regrating victuals at Westminster market), 245;
    WCB2, pp. 21, 30.

54 WAC, WCB2, p. 7.

55 E.g. WAC, WCB1, p. 35; WCB2, p. 117. Other offenders were simply told to leave Westminster,
    but without formal expulsion. The Ordinances suggest that the penalty of whipping at the cart's tail
    was for offenders who had already been expelled from the town but had subsequently returned
    without leave (Manchée, p. 216), but cases in the court minutes do not spell this out as the reason
    for such treatment.

56 BL, Lansdowne MS 43, f. 179.

57 London's Bridewell, however, did make use of similar physical punishments, Archer, pp. 201, 204,
    207. Manorial courts potentially dealt with a similar range of offences, but seldom punished them
    this systematically and not in the London metropolitan area; see below.

as early as 1508, the manorial court had imposed what was apparently the unprecedented penalty of banishment from the town upon thirty-one individuals who were
said to be 'ill-governed of their bodies'.[58] By the early seventeenth century, however,
the banishment of offenders had become a relatively frequent event – even if it did not
always involve whipping along a punishment 'trail'.[59] Given Westminster's border
with the City of London, banishment might seem a strange punishment. Nevertheless,
the ceremonial character of formal expulsion from Westminster may have reinforced
a sense of communal authority and social cohesion.[60]

For all this stress on punishment, the Court of Burgesses was especially concerned with establishing the personal reputations of those who came before it. As we
shall see in the next section, it was this strong concern with personal reputation when
dealing with a range of offences which was meant to act as a counterweight to the evils
associated with the sense of anonymity that unregulated urban expansion created.

IMMIGRATION, REPUTATION AND URBAN EXPANSION

So far the discussion has emphasized points of continuity between the Court of Burgesses and its medieval predecessor. Yet it is possible to over emphasize these elements.
Although the burgesses prosecuted many traditional manorial court offences, the largest
number of cases involved a more novel preoccupation with immigrants into Westminster and those who housed them.[61] In this the court's activities remained faithful
to the 1585 Act, which in its very first sentence provided a catalogue of the ill effects
springing from new building and subdivision of tenements. Such activities, the Act
stressed, bolstered a greatly increased population, 'many of them gyven whollie to
Vyce and Ydlenes'.[62] Nevertheless, it would be wrong to portray the court as simply
launching a coercive assault on *all* immigrants. In fact, a far more subtle process was in
operation, which revolved around the flexibility of the term 'inmates'. The court ordinances placed a ban on settled inhabitants keeping 'inmates', as sub-tenants were
known.[63] However, references to 'inmates' in the court minutes reveal that this

---

58 Rosser, p. 244.

59 See below. Carlin notes that expulsion could be a penalty for anti-social behaviour in late fifteenth-
and early sixteenth-century Southwark, with carting as an additional punishment in the sixteenth
century: *Medieval Southwark*, p. 113. Nationwide, McIntosh finds expulsion emerging as a punishment in the lesser courts in the later fifteenth century, but decreasing by the later sixteenth century:
Controlling, p. 39. Archer (p. 251) suggests that, for the Elizabethan period, expulsion was more
common in Middlesex and Westminster than in London.

60 L. Gowing, *Domestic Dangers* (Oxford, 1996), p. 24; McIntosh, *Controlling*, p. 75, n.57.

61 McIntosh notes that lesser courts used bylaws or ordinances in relation to subtenants for more than
any other offence. The use of bylaws declined, however, perhaps in response to national legislation
in 1589: McIntosh, *Controlling*, p. 195.

62 27 Eliz. I c. 31.

63 Manchée, p. 212.

category was not always a hard and fast one.[64] It generally seems to have been used to refer to poor, possibly unskilled individuals, crammed into shared accommodation – perhaps a single room or cellar. But in practice the court often seems to have blurred the distinction between tenants (who were treated more leniently) and inmates – a distinction that had been drawn far more firmly in the 1585 Ordinances. In effect, an 'inmate' could become a 'tenant' if he or she were able to produce a testimonial of good behaviour.[65] In all cases, the court relied heavily on evidence of good behaviour and personal reputation in the way it chose to enforce the by-laws affecting newcomers.

Westminster was unusual in the early modern metropolis in its thoroughgoing operation of a testimonial system. Although there are parallels to Westminster's treatment of inmates and newcomers in other parts of the capital, its implementation elsewhere seems to have been extremely piecemeal.[66] In Westminster, by contrast, the system was rigidly policed. The 1585 Ordinances had forbidden any person from accepting tenants without first receiving a written testimonial of their 'good behaviour and conversation' from their last place of residence. The testimonial was then to be registered with the burgess of the appropriate ward. The surviving minutes clearly demonstrate that the Court of Burgesses devoted a remarkable amount of its time and energy to enforcing the testimonial system.

Given the difficulties of controlling immigration, it may be that the court thought it best to subject newcomers and the working poor to stringent regulation, rather than simply seeking to expel them. In particular, it was the anonymity of newcomers that was felt to leave the community open to crime and evil example. It was this anonymity that the testimonial system – and its rigorous enforcement – were designed to combat. In this sense the system operated as an insurance policy against a range of social and moral ills. In addition, the very act of presenting a certificate of good behaviour to the burgess meant that newcomers became known to local officials. Although this undoubtedly had its coercive aspects, it may also have provided a means whereby the 'respectable' poor could establish a good reputation in a new locality.

Even though enforcement may have been selective, the court acted with impressive thoroughness and decisiveness in stripping away the anonymity of newcomers.

---

64 Cf. the discussion in N. Goose, 'Household size and structure in early Stuart Cambridge' in J. Barry (ed.), *The Tudor and Stuart Town, 1530–1688* (1990), pp. 78, 93.

65 Manchée, pp. 212, 216. Cf. WAC, WCB1, pp. 15, 26, 50, 58, 59, cases in which 'inmates' are said to be without testimonials, even though the Ordinances required testimonials only from tenants, since inmates were simply to be removed. One John Shaw was described as both an 'inmate' and a 'tenant', within a single entry: *ibid.*, p. 49.

66 The closest parallel is to be found in Southwark, but here the impetus came from individual parishes, which employed a surveyor of inmates from the late sixteenth century. The task of such men, however, was merely to expel individuals unless they could provide a surety against becoming chargeable on the parish: Archer, pp. 184–5; H. Raine, 'Christopher Fawcett against the inmates', *Surrey Archaeological Collections* 66 (1966), pp. 79–85. The responsiveness and activity of Southwark's manorial courts is less clear, although within the Guildable Manor newcomers and landlords were meant to enter into bonds to prevent tenants from claiming poor relief: Boulton, pp. 273, 291.

It sent to Windsor, for example, to discover why authorities there had arranged for Elizabeth Brookes to be tied to a cart's tail and whipped. Similarly, it sought out information on the behaviour of two women previously living in St Dunstan in the West, where the deputy alderman, Mr Tinkinson, could report 'no good of them'.[67] Clearly, it was possible for the infamous reputation of men and women to follow them around the capital and surrounding area.

A great deal of the work undertaken by burgesses individually, and by the court collectively, related to the testimonial system. The administration of this system formed part of a much broader preoccupation of the burgesses with assessing and documenting the reputations of individual men and women. Thus, burgesses were required to judge the fitness of victuallers, or of officials such as beadles, and also provided character references to the justices of the peace.[68]

Turning to the enforcement of the testimonial system, several striking points emerge. One is that the Court of Burgesses targeted those who accepted illegal tenants – perhaps more so than the poor who occupied this often makeshift accommodation. This was partly a result of the manner in which the 1585 Ordinances were framed, but also seems to have been a matter of policy.[69] Clearly the onus was laid upon the landlord to ensure that tenants had presented testimonials to the local burgess *before* he accepted them. The treatment meted out to landlords as well as to keepers of inmates varied considerably. This allowed the burgesses to temper their penalties to reflect the varying motivation and social status of offenders. Some were bound over for sums of between £10 and £20 to ensure the removal of inmates within a specified time.[70] Many Westminster residents (possibly those who were well-off or first-time offenders) merely received a warning, while others were fined 40s.[71] Those who took in poor immigrants, however, were often the poor themselves, attempting to supplement a meagre income. When Edward Pudley of St Margaret's appeared before the burgesses charged with keeping inmates, the normal fine of 40s was waived because he was said to be 'a very poore man and not well able to pay 40s'. Nevertheless, he could not be left unpunished and so was ordered to sit in the stocks for six hours 'with a paper on his head testifying his offence'.[72] Others found keeping inmates included a

67 WAC, WCB1, p. 42, WCB2, p. 18. Cf. WCB1, p. 282.

68 WAC, F2001, ff. 101, 119; LMA, WJ/SR (NS) 41/20, 41/38; In London, the beadle of the ward might theoretically do similar work, but, since he served several parishes, his efficiency may be open to question: Archer, p. 220.

69 Notable in this respect are Westminster's 1564 plague orders, which associate inmates with disorder, but place the blame entirely on the 'gredinesse' of landlords who charge such high rents that the inmates 'can not maynteyne them selves without sekyng the same by sundry kyndes of disorder': *Wyllyam Cecill knight, high steward of the citie of Westminster . . . To the Baylyffe* (1564).

70 E.g. WAC, WCB1, pp. 1, 2, 4, 9, 16, 19, 90; WCB2, p. 5.

71 WAC, WCB1, pp. 110, 113, 114; WCB2, p. 21.

72 WAC, WCB2, p. 83.

waterman and a labourer living in Thieving Lane.[73] Particular opprobrium attached to individuals who seemed deliberately to offer accommodation to 'lewd, vagrant and pilfering people' or men such as Symon Ellis, 'a common receiver of lewd, idle and begging People'.[74] Theoretically, landlords were required to ensure that tenants practised some 'lawfull science or manuall occupation'.[75]

The court itself obviously considered the keeping of inmates to be a serious issue, despite what may have been limits on its resources and on the penalties that it could impose. It is noteworthy that when one of the burgesses, the saddler Patrick Derrick, was accused by his own assistant burgess of neglecting his duties, the first action of the court was to order three other burgesses to survey Derrick's ward for the presence of inmates.[76] How seriously those who kept inmates regarded the court is difficult to judge. The fact that the prosecution of inmates or those who kept inmates formed the bulk of the court's business in itself suggests the widespread flouting of regulations. One St Margaret's man was sufficiently bold to ignore ten separate warnings to rid his premises of inmates. The burgesses sentenced him to the stocks but others may have been willing to run the risk of punishment, knowing the court to be overburdened with business.[77]

The fate of inmates and illegal tenants – as opposed to those who housed them – is generally unclear. Normally the landlord or 'harbourer' was responsible for ensuring that they vacated the property. Similarly, these poor men and women were generally just instructed to leave the city and liberties of Westminster, and it seems likely that constables had some responsibility for enforcing the order.[78] Yet the concern about them was part of a larger fear of those who did not fit into existing household structures and hierarchies. It is true that the court did sometimes expel from Westminster inmates who were skilled workers, currently in employment.[79] Generally, however, it was preoccupied with masterless men and women. Here poor young immigrants to the capital were the object of particular attention. Such newcomers tended to settle in suburban areas, such as Westminster, even if they later moved into the City of London proper. In the suburbs they could take up various forms of employment, free from the restrictions of the London livery companies. Suburban areas were also a magnet for the significant numbers of young people who failed to complete London apprenticeships.[80] Similarly,

73 WAC, WCB1, p. 284, WCB1, p. 13.

74 WAC, WCB1, p. 274. WAC, WCB2, p. 173.

75 Manchée, p. 216.

76 WAC, WCB2, p. 157. In spite of the accusation, Derrick was actually sworn as chief burgess the following year: *ibid.*, p. 174.

77 WAC, WCB2, p. 81.

78 E.g. WAC, WCB1, pp. 7, 16, 19, 49. In some cases, inmates were bound for sums of money to leave Westminster.

79 WAC, WCB2, p. 39, WCB1, p. 283.

80 Archer, pp. 218, 242, and S. Rappaport, *Worlds Within Worlds* (Cambridge, 1989), pp. 311–15 – these two suggest than more than half of apprentices recruited in the mid-sixteenth century failed to complete their terms.

when Henry Powell, 'lately from the country', set up a cobbler's stall 'to the great prejudice and hindrance of diverse poor people . . . who have ever been bred and dwell apprentices within this Citty', he was ordered to find himself 'Journeywork' with some 'honest master'.[81] Many immigrants, however, would have been unskilled. Indeed, the 1585 Act specifically drew attention to the threat posed by recent migrants 'for the most parte withowte Trade or Mysterie'. Of course, the many hostelries located in Westminster provided large numbers of unskilled jobs in the service sector, but this employment would have been far less stable than that provided for apprentices by London livery companies, nor did it teach a craft.[82] In the main, however, the court seems to have been most concerned to ensure that the young men found themselves a master and so were incorporated into some household structure which would theoretically provide employment as well as moral guidance.

The Court of Burgesses also intervened when women were discovered to be living by 'their own hand'. Although financially such women might live very precariously, it was their independent status that rendered them suspect. One single woman who sold apples in a stall under a house in Petty France, for example, was ordered to find herself some 'honest service' within a month or face further punishment.[83] In these circumstances, it was assumed that the absence of a master would lead to immoral conduct. These fears were partly generalized ones, but, because poverty might limit a woman's marriage prospects or drive her into prostitution, officials feared that single women would give birth to illegitimate children who, as officials were keenly aware, might then require support from the parish.[84]

Other men and women were specifically identified as vagrants in the court minutes. Unlike masterless men and women, it seems that these people could claim no fixed abode. From the court's point of view, the real difficulty lay in catching the homeless who made up the floating population of Westminster. Richard Whetstone, when taken as a vagrant by the authorities, 'did openly confess, that he had lived soe by the space of four yeares last past within this Citty and Libertyes'. Authorities could do little to control these very poorest of the poor, who flooded into the capital as one wave of immigration followed another from the 1560s.[85] It seems likely that vagrants were

81 WAC, WCB1, p. 36; WCB2, pp. 36, 39, 105. The court was also sometimes required proof of completed apprenticeships from young men: WAC, WCB1, pp. 282, 283; WCB2, pp. 39, 51.

82 R. Finlay and B. Shearer, 'Population growth and suburban expansion' in A.L. Beier and R. Finlay (eds.), *London 1500–1700: The Making of the Metropolis* (Harlow, 1986), pp. 52–3. The 1585 Ordinances limited the number of alehouses in Westminster to one hundred, but a survey of 1631 found no fewer than 551 in operation: Manchée, p. 220; *CSPD 1629–31*, p. 557.

83 WAC, WCB2, pp. 139v (sic)–140.

84 Archer, p. 194; Boulton, p. 129; Raine, 'Christopher Fawcett', pp. 79–85. On people living 'at their own hand' see also P. Griffiths, 'Masterless young people in Norwich, 1560–1645' in P. Griffiths, A. Fox and S. Hindle (eds.), *The Experience of Authority in Early Modern England* (Basingstoke, 1996), pp. 146–86.

85 WAC, WCB2, p. 73.

either sent directly to the Middlesex sessions or dealt with summarily either by constables or JPs living within the locality – the ordinances of the Court of Burgesses merely authorized burgesses to fine constables who were dilatory in their pursuit of vagrants. A flurry of Privy Council orders in the 1610s complaining that beggars and vagrants were more common in Westminster than in the City of London or other shires reflect both the scale of the phenomenon and the inability of the existing authorities to control it (as well as the extra sensitivity that the government always felt towards the situation in Westminster).[86]

The zealousness of the Court of Burgesses in prosecuting those who flouted these orders meant that the burgesses spent much of their time disciplining recent immigrants to the capital. But they were also occupied with a related problem. If the weekly prosecution of inmates and masterless men and women marked a change from Westminster's medieval manorial court, so too did the court's attempt to regulate the subdivision of existing buildings and to monitor the quality of new building. The medieval court had certainly dealt with building encroachments, but in Westminster, as in other urban centres, the second half of the sixteenth century witnessed an explosion in the number of buildings subdivided to provide lodgings for poor immigrants from the countryside.[87] Many flimsy, makeshift tenements were thrown up to accommodate the new urban poor, while existing buildings were intensively developed. Large houses were subdivided and then extended, with new additions sometimes stretching out into the street. Even previously uninhabited portions of buildings, such as cellars and garrets, were now converted into cheap housing. Poor immigrants to the capital crowded into densely packed tenements which officials associated, not without cause, with poor sanitation and the spread of plague. There was even the suspicion that such housing was a breeding ground for conspiracies and possible riot.[88] Royal proclamations had attempted to restrict building in London and Westminster since 1580, but the frequency with which these proclamations were renewed attests to the problems officials faced in enforcing them.[89] The enforcement of these royal proclamations, however, did not come within the scope of the Court of Burgesses. Neither did the

---

86 WAC, WCB1, p. 195; *APC 1615–16*, pp. 210–11, 695–6. Large numbers of vagrants were still being expelled by the Westminster sessions in the 1630s: TNA, SP16/189/48, 16/420/17. For further discussion of poverty and immigration see below, ch. 8.

87 Rosser, p. 241; D. Keene, 'Growth, modernisation and control: the transformation of London's landscape' in P. Clark and R. Gillespie (eds.), *Two Capitals: London and Dublin 1500–1840* (2001), pp. 7–38.

88 P. Hughes and J. Larkin (eds.), *Tudor Royal Proclamations* (New Haven, 3 vols. 1964–69), I, 486. For Westminster see BL, Lansdowne MS 35, ff. 101–106; WAC, F6039. C.M. Barron, *The Parish of St Andrew Holborn* (1979), pp. 46–7.

89 For a discussion of royal building policy in the capital see T. Barnes, 'The preogative and environmental control of London building in the early seventeenth century: the lost opportunity', *California Law Review* 58 (1970). The royal proclamation was reinforced by statute in 1593, at the insistence of London citizens: Barron, *St Andrew Holborn*, p. 48.

1585 Ordinances specifically attempt to regulate new building or the subdivision of existing properties.[90]

The court did hear some cases related to illegal building, although such cases always formed only a small proportion of the court's business, at least in the Jacobean period. But it focused its attention on housing likely to be inhabited by poorer tenants, rather than speculative development intended for a more prosperous clientele (which did indeed take place in Westminster, and was generally prosecuted elsewhere). As an issue, illegal building was frequently dealt with in tandem with inmates. It is clear that burgesses were meant to inform themselves about building within their wards. In October 1611, for example, three St Martin's burgesses were appointed 'to informe the Court of all new Buildings and Inmates within there several wards on Tuesday next'.[91] When cottages were erected in Petty France the court briskly ordered those responsible to pull them down immediately or pay a fine of £20, while the carpenter working on the project was told not to 'proceed to work or build there upon pain of Imprisonment'.[92] Shoddy tenements and cottages on the fringes of built-up areas seem to have been a particular target. Burgesses were also frequently required to assess the suitability of buildings for subdivision and conversion.[93] When two shoemakers of St Martin's parish built new stables near Covent Garden, the court ordered them to attend the steward's chamber and to give their bond not to convert the stables into tenements, a ploy commonly used to evade building regulations.[94] Generally, however, cases involving the subdivision of existing properties came before the court more frequently than those concerning new building itself. All such work on the part of the court reflected Westminster's increasing population, as did its regular efforts to prosecute nuisance.[95] The Court of Burgesses alone must have had only a limited impact on the spread of illegal building, which we know took place on a scale that was far larger than its appearance before the court would indicate. Nevertheless, the Court formed part of a large, if very loosely co-ordinated network of enforcement bodies stretching from the Star Chamber to the Middlesex (and later Westminster) sessions to individual parishes.

90 This despite the fact that sworn viewers for building existed in Westminster before 1585 although no record survives of their activities: see WAM 16320.

91 WAC, WCB1, p. 106.

92 WAC, WCB1, p. 76. Occasionally the court minutes provide evidence of the more widespread problem in controlling new building due to dispensations granted by influential courtiers, such as Sir Walter Cope: WAC, WCB1, p. 125, see also pp. 103–4. By 1619 the emphasis of government policy changed, with quality control rather than the prohibition of new building being enforced: see above, ch. 6.

93 For example, WAC, WCB1, p. 44; WCB2, p. 139. Conversions were sometimes permitted.

94 WAC, WCB1, p. 212. The reference to the 'Steward' probably refers to the the high steward's deputy, Sir Humphrey Chambers. For further discussion of building and population increase see ch. 8.

95 WAC, WCB1, pp. 196, 285.

REGULATION OF PERSONAL CONDUCT: PUNISHMENT
AND ARBITRATION

The discussion thus far has concentrated on the offences most directly related to population growth. But another important side to the Court of Burgesses' activities was its
regulation of personal conduct. The 1585 Act had singled out the 'repressinge and routinge
owte of Vice' as one of the chief aims of the new legislation. Regulative and moral offences
punished by the court included fornication, bridal pregnancy, slander, scolding, bastard-
bearing, disrupting the sabbath and drunkenness. Traditionally, many of these offences
could be punished by leet courts, including verbal violence, such as scolding. It is also true
that most of the moral offences listed above could be presented before church courts.
Nevertheless, it is significant that the 1585 Act envisaged that the Court of Burgesses itself
would discipline such conduct. Ultimately, the Act served strongly to bolster an aspect of
manorial court jurisdiction.[96] This may have run counter to trends in the capital more
generally, where the yearly wardmotes only regulated such offences spasmodically, and
cases of social misbehaviour either came before the deputy alderman, who could deal with
them summarily, or the church courts, as was still partly the case in the Westminster
parishes.[97] Still more unusual was the presence of the dean of Westminster as a presiding
figure, which may have given the Court of Burgesses a distinctive ecclesiastical tone.

The court meted out its fiercest physical punishments for immoral conduct. These
punishments are all the more striking because most individuals who came before the
Court of Burgesses were merely fined or simply given a warning. Women who had given
birth to illegitimate children were a particular target. Here the authorities were prompted
by a combination of moral outrage and concern for parochial finances, since illegitimate
children were seen as a potential burden on parish rates. Sometimes the woman alone
was punished, presumably because her partner remained unknown. Occasionally the
court punished groups of women together, in a ruthless manner suggestive of brutal
enforcement drives. On 13 February 1611, for example, the court noted that

> whereas Elizabeth Wittingham and Margaret Geary and Elizabeth Young have all
> confessed themselves guilty of Incontinency and to have each of them a Child and
> were never married and because they could not shew no reson why they should not

---

96 This seems to follow national rather than metropolitan trends: where manorial courts flourished in
the early Stuart period, they increasingly presented regulative offences beyond the traditional range
of agrarian concerns, including cases of sexual misconduct: J.A. Sharpe, *Crime in Early Modern
England* (1984), pp. 26–7, 83–5. For the ecclesiastical jurisdiction of the archdeacon of Westminster see below, ch. 9.

97 While the London wardmote of the fifteenth century had dealt with such offences, by the sixteenth
century the wardmote began to focus more narrowly on cases of nuisance: Archer, pp. 68, 78.
Occasional presentments against 'suspicious' persons do still occur in wardmote inquests of the
early Stuart period, but they are very much the exception: GL, MS 3018/1, ff. 69, 77v, 91v–92;
MS 4069/1, ff. 118v, 145v, 157. The churchwardens of St Martin's and St Clement's still continued
to present cases of immorality to the London consistory court: e.g. LMA, DL/C/306, ff. 556, 613;
DL/C/308, f. 267; DL/C/318, ff. 10, 28, 142, 160, 213, 235, 409. It is not clear why some
cases went before the burgesses and others to the church courts.

be punished according to the Law . . . [they] shall be carried to the round house and there to be stript from the wast upward – and all of them to be whipped and then presently to be banished this Citty and Liberties.[98]

The court was not scandalized merely by illegitimate births. Fornicators were punished even when a child had not resulted from the liaison.[99] Francis Metcalf, a clerk of St Margaret's, was even presented by his local burgess for committing incontinency with Elizabeth Pool 'late deceased'. He denied the charge, a jury was sworn and he was found guilty 'upon the oathes of three sufficient witnesses'. The punishment of bridal pregnancy also suggests that the court hoped to curb immoral behaviour even if its direct financial impact on the community was negligible.[100] It is not clear, however, that the court always pursued a consistent policy, or even that burgesses necessarily agreed over the punishment of regulative offences. In a case of September 1612, certain burgesses seem to have felt that the punishment ordered for two young people convicted of incontinency was too harsh. A rare marginal note records that 'this order was amended from Whipping to Carting because 2 burgesses did affirm that when a young man and a maid did commit Incontinency together they ought but to be Carted & not whipped'.[101] This would certainly suggest that, while fornication would be punished as an offence in its own right, it was bastard-bearing which provoked the most severe punishment, even if some burgesses were happy to contemplate harsher punishments across the board.

At its most invasive, the burgess court disciplined individuals whose activities only held the potential to violate community standards. For example, David Lodwyn, a nobleman's servant, was required to enter into a bond 'not to frequent or be seen in the Company of Grace Paddon'. In another case, the court forbade Henry Peacher to receive Agnes Hill, the wife of William Hill, into his house, to keep her company 'or in any thing to take her part or in any wise to meddle with her in any thing whatsoever'.[102] Similarly, those merely found living 'suspitiously' could find themselves before the burgesses. Unica Baynes, the wife of William Baynes, formerly of 'Pickle Hearing' and lately settled in Westminster, was banished from the town when it was noted that 'her husband [was] now living from her, at the East Indies, and none in the house but herself and one Thomas Palmer who lived in the nature of a soldier, and very suspitiously together'.[103] Presumably it was thought best to act before her unconventional behaviour progressed to the immoral or criminal.

---

98 WAC, WCB1, p. 35.

99 For example, WAC, WCB1, p. 21.

100 WAC, WCB1, p. 45.

101 WAC, WCB1, pp. 201–2.

102 WAC, WCB2, p. 153; WCB1, p. 19.

103 WAC, WCB2, p. 169. Gowing notes that accusations of illegitimate pregnancy and immoral conduct were more frequently made against women in Wapping, where sailor husbands were often absent: *Domestic Dangers*, pp. 89, 134, 264.

The Court of Burgesses also provided mechanisms for controlling other aspects of personal behaviour through the prosecution of slander and scolding – offences that were closely related. Cases heard before the court may represent only the tip of the iceberg, since many would undoubtedly have been settled by individual burgesses at the ward level.[104] Women were most often accused of scolding by local officials – sometimes by burgesses and in once case by churchwardens.[105] More rarely, a woman's neighbours would present her as a scold, but, even in cases promoted by officials, neighbours may have been the ones to instigate proceedings. Recent research has reminded us of the complex series of motives and assumptions contained within accusations of scolding, especially in the context of the metropolis. In the absence of depositions for the Court of Burgesses, however, these are difficult to reconstruct. Cases before the burgesses characterize scolding in terms of a pattern of abusive speeches, sometimes involving threats of violence. Scolding may also have been more commonly presented when the woman was of low social status and was already accused or suspected of some other form of criminal behaviour. In the case of Margaret Betts, her accusers maintained that on a Sunday morning, during the time of divine service, she was seen sweeping the 'kennel' by her door, swearing that if any did 'sweep down the dirt to her Doore she would strike him over the face with her broom'. Even worse, she threatened to cut the throat of a woman passer-by and 'Nicholas Sharpe sayeth that there is not a worse Scold in all Westminster'. Accordingly, she was sent to the Gatehouse prison until able to provide sureties for her good behaviour.[106]

Generally the circumstances surrounding cases of scolding are obscure, and admonishment by the court was the most frequent result. This warning, however, may have carried considerable force since it was usually accompanied by the threat of ducking if the offender persisted. Between the years 1610 and 1616, only four out of twenty-five recorded cases involving scolds resulted in punishment.[107] These figures suggest that the burgesses may have felt that admonition rather than punishment was more likely to promote social harmony and more properly 'feminine' behaviour.

Nevertheless, this evidence should not lead us to neglect the indirect influence the court may have exercised over the behaviour of women. Most women may not have received punishment but the example of those who were punished – and punished severely – should not be underestimated. As Laura Gowing reminds us, whatever the exact scale of punishment 'the nature of crime and the symbols of its punishment loomed large in the popular imagination'. In Westminster, the public

---

104 See below.

105 WAC, WCB1, pp. 76–7.

106 WAC, WCB1, p. 173. Gowing, *Domestic Dangers*, pp. 122–3, 129. Cf. McIntosh, *Controlling*, pp. 58–65; M. Ingram, ' "Scolding women cucked or washed": a crisis in gender relations in early modern England?' in J. Kermode and G. Walker (eds.), *Women, Crime and the Court* (1994).

107 For women found innocent of scolding see WAC, WCB1, p. 245; WCB2, p. 21. Married couples were sometimes threatened with ducking in cases of verbal abuse, e.g. WAC, WCB1, p. 236.

spectacle provided by the punishment of Maudlin Tichon of St Martin's parish must have been extraordinary, all the more because it was exceptional. In 1611, Tichon was presented by one of St Martin's churchwardens and convicted after a jury trial in which many witnesses came forward, reporting that she 'misbehaved herself in Scoulding and abusing of her Neighbours with most reproachful Speeches'. Accordingly, the burgesses decided that the 'Antient Custome of the Citty' should be used and that she 'should be fastened to a Boate tayle and so to be drawn through the water to the otherside of the Thames and this order to be executed this afternoon'. This is the only recorded instance of this horrific punishment during the six years covered by the surviving court minutes and how far it was an 'Antient Custome' is unclear.[108] Yet this is not the only example of harsh physical punishment imposed by the burgess court in cases of scolding. When Alice Webb, said to be a common disturber of her neighbours 'with her tongue', also 'abused' the constables and 'misbehaved' herself towards one of the burgesses, she was ordered to 'wear the mortars about her neck home to her house and the Constables to see them fast stapled with Iron'. The court further ordered that this gruesome device, designed to fit into the mouth and stop the wearer from speaking, was to be left in place 'until the Court shall order the contrary'.[109]

Another form of verbal violence that came before the court was slander. The 1585 Act specifically authorized the Court of Burgesses to prosecute slander, an offence which was sometimes brought before manorial courts on the grounds that it disturbed the peace.[110] This differed from most other offences in that presentments were made not by local officials but directly by the individuals concerned. The cases coming before the Westminster burgess court follow the pattern noted at the church courts at York and London. Most contained a sexual component and most involved married rather than single women. The wife of Henry Hodgskins, for example, was called 'a blink'd ey'd whore and bastard bearing whore'. Servants who made carelessly provocative speeches could also find themselves before the burgesses. Mary Davye, a maidservant to Andrew Burrow, a spurrier of St Margaret's, was reported to have said that 'the most parte of English women were whores', whereupon the court ordered her mistress to punish her directly.[111]

Slander cases could become very complicated when neighbours traded accusations. The neighbours of Elizabeth Reynolds heard her say that 'Mary Raphe had murthered the Child in her belly'. Mary Raphe, in turn, was reported to have called her accuser's husband a 'Rogue Rascall Knave and Newgate bird'.[112] In this case, possibly because of the seriousness of the initial accusation, the dean of Westminster

108 Gowing, *Domestic Dangers*, p. 122; WAC, WCB1, pp. 76–8.

109 WAC, WCB2, p. 18.

110 Sharpe, *Crime*, pp. 25–6.

111 J. Sharpe, *Defamation and Sexual Slander in Early Modern England: The Church Courts at York* (Borthwick Papers 58, 1980), pp. 10, 21–2, 27; Gowing, *Domestic Dangers*, pp. 125–38; WAC, WCB1, pp. 38, 171.

112 WAC, WCB1, p. 174.

intervened. The husbands of the two women were ordered to accept arbitration from 'their neighbours', whereupon 'Mr Raphe chose Mr Brownrick and Thomas Reynolds chose Mr Fisher and Mr Dean nominated Mr Kirkham indifferently to heare and determine the said matters'.[113] Despite this impartial arrangement, the parties had little success in dampening the animosity between the two women. About six weeks later, the women were again in court. On this occasion, Elizabeth Reynolds was accused of having said that Mary Raphe had sent a maidservant 'to robb the said Elizabeth Reynolds house'. The court called witnesses but decided this speech was actionable elsewhere and so the matter was referred to the common law courts.[114]

To members of the Court of Burgesses, such a case must have represented a failure. It indicated that the ward system had not functioned as intended, for one of the most significant features of government by the Westminster burgesses lay in the extensive use of arbitration, especially at the ward level. Undoubtedly arbitration played an important role in many places, but it often leaves little evidence behind in historical records. Nevertheless, it is clear that many courts – civil, ecclesiastical and common law – accepted or even promoted arbitration that led to parties settling out of court. Similarly, studies of the role played by constables in this period present him less as an official gaining prestige through large numbers of arrests, but rather as an intermediary who defused tensions within the community before they reached breaking point.[115]

In particular, the 1585 Ordinances forbade men and women from commencing lawsuits without first obtaining the consent of their local burgess. Instead, when neighbours fell into controversy over 'uncharitable speeches or other annoyances' they were expected to seek the arbitration of the local burgess. Similarly, the court also acted to reinforce the local powers of burgesses by refusing to hear all but the most serious cases.[116] Those who attempted to bypass their ward and bring a complaint directly before the Court of Burgesses (or any other court) were almost invariably referred back to their local burgess and ordered to accept his arbitration.[117] In the context of rapidly expanding parishes, the role designated for the Court of Burgesses was to re-establish social harmony among neighbours, on a face-to-face basis. Of course arbitration, particularly mediated by men of high social status, might have its coercive side and ultimately involved the imposition of community norms. It may also have been

---

113 WAC, WCB1, pp. 169–70, 174.

114 WAC, WCB1, p. 191.

115 Sharpe, *Crime*, pp. 45, 77; Archer, p. 78; J. Kent, *The English Village Constable 1580–1642: A Social and Administrative History* (1986), pp. 295–6.

116 Manchée, p. 215.

117 For example, WAC, WCB1, pp. 31, 65, 170, 229. For a currier who tried to take a suit for uncharitable speeches to King's Bench before 'he had complained to the Burgess and Assistant of that Ward' see WCB2, p. 131. For a similar case involving the Marshalsea court see WCB2, pp. 168–9. Other courts mentioned include 'the Prerogative Court att Paules' (WCB2, p. 44), the 'Spirituall Court' (WCB2, p. 79; WCB1, p. 239) and the Court of Arches (WCB1, p. 224). See also WCB2, p. 67.

less satisfying for the parties involved. The very act of bringing a case to court and hearing the evidence aired may have been what some men and women actively sought. This is partly confirmed by the very creation of ordinances which strongly discouraged lawsuits. Indeed, the range of courts which Westminster residents were admonished from using by the burgesses suggests a fairly sophisticated knowledge of law courts among local inhabitants and an ability to use them.[118]

Nevertheless, the symbolic and practical importance of neighbours resolving disputes – and indeed remaining in charity – was upheld by the court on a daily basis. Burgesses arbitrated in a wide range of disagreements between Westminster residents, and not merely those involving 'uncharitable speeches'. When a difference arose between the St Margaret's fishmonger James Morley and Ann Aldorfe, for example, the court ordered them to consult with the burgesses William Mann and Henry Weatherfield and 'in consideracion of 6s mutually given each other to stand to and abide such award'. In another case, a dispute over the pawning of a doublet was settled by the burgess William Stanlake, upon the agreement of the parties to abide by his decision. Similarly, a controversy between the gentleman Sir John Bentley and one Mr Home was referred to the local burgesses to 'examine and end'.[119]

The solutions adopted by the Court of Burgesses in such disputes often resembled those in use in church courts. In particular, the court attempted to restore charity among neighbours by requiring the parties to apologize to one another.[120] When the wife of Henry Hodgskins, shoemaker, and that of Richard Ward traded insults, for example, the court ordered the parties to meet 'at Mr Derricks House or Mr Colbecks House his Assistant and . . . then & there ask each other party forgiveness for their offence . . . for their scandalous words'.[121] The court sought a similar solution in December 1610, when Anne Baynham appeared before the court for calling her mistress 'whore'. Because she could not prove the accusation, the court ordered that 'the said Anne Baynham is in sober and comely sort kneeling on her knees [to] ask her forgivenesse for wrongfully accusing and slandering her at the place where she accused her and before such persons as then heard the same accusacion'. The servant was also warned that if in future she were to slander or upbraid her mistress, she would be brought to court and whipped.[122] Such a re-enactment served to reaffirm community values and was doubtless thought to set a good example.

---

118 Cf. Gowing, *Domestic Dangers*, pp. 164ff; J. Sharpe, ' "Such disagreement betwyx neighbours": litigation and human relations in early modern England' in J. Bossy (ed.), *Disputes and Settlements* (Cambridge, 1983), pp. 174–8, 183.

119 WAC, WCB1, p. 33; WCB2, pp. 65, 69. Cf. S. Hindle, 'The keeping of the public peace' in Griffiths, Fox and Hindle, *Experience*, pp. 229–31.

120 For a formal reconciliation conducted by the local minister at St Martin's in the 1580s see WAC, F2001, ff. 6, 12.

121 WAC, WCB1, p. 39.

122 WAC, WCB1, p. 23. See also WCB1, pp. 32, 232; WCB2, p. 164. Cf. Sharpe, 'Such disagreement', pp. 180–1.

Recent work on church courts and leet courts has emphasized the way in which men and women actively used these courts against unruly neighbours and to help them settle disputes.[123] This also holds true for the burgess court at Westminster, which shared some characteristics of both these courts. Certainly the Court of Burgesses depended on the willingness of neighbours to serve as witnesses and inquestmen and to inform themselves of one another's business. The court also became a means through which the respectable members of the community could discipline and possibly disassociate themselves from the unruly poor. Neighbours, for example, complained that Richard Butler, a bricklayer of St Margaret's, was a common drunkard, while on another occasion the court noted that complaint had been made of the labourer John Chamberlein for 'maintaining of unlawful Games in his House and else where as for raffling for Pewter and such like'.[124] The empowerment of neighbours, however, necessarily had its coercive side. When Sibbele Barrow came before the court, she was told that if her 'Neighbours' ever again complained about her, she would be 'putt in the Cooking stool and Ducked'.[125]

It is difficult to assess whether the Court of Burgesses was distinctive, either in its treatment of women or in the way in which women related to it. Because the court did not normally hear party-against-party suits and instead presented 'offenders', it provides fewer opportunities to study women making active use of legal proceedings. In addition, the surviving court minutes are too limited to allow us to chart change over time. Nevertheless, women in Westminster had access to many other courts and we know that the London consistory court prosecuted cases of slander and scolding from women from St Martin's and St Clement Danes.[126] Certainly some of the features that provided an arena for the contesting of gender were particularly to be found in Westminster. The demographic patterns which historians have noted in London – where high mortality rates increased the proportion of households headed by women, and the number of widows remarrying and gaining greater leverage within households owing to their wealth and age – would have been true for Westminster as well.[127] Anxieties about the position of women may have been heightened further by the large population of female servants, the high numbers of women running alehouses and the substantial number of semi-autonomous women in the shape of hucksters and market traders, such as the herb women of Westminster market, to say nothing of the pretty

---

123 Sharpe, *Defamation*, p. 27. Ingram, *Church Courts*, pp. 165, 307–8, 324–5, 367. Gowing argues that the early seventeenth century saw women using the London consistory court in a new way, which represented one means by which gender relations were constantly contested and renegotiated; *Domestic Dangers*, pp. 263–76.

124 WAC, WCB1, pp. 79, 71. See also WCB2, p. 175.

125 WAC, WCB1, p. 22.

126 Cf. Gowing, *Domestic Dangers*, pp. 217–18; L. Gowing, ' "The freedom of the streets": women and social space, 1560–1640' in P. Griffiths and M. Jenner (eds.), *Londinopolis* (Manchester, 2000), p. 138.

127 I. Archer, 'Material Londoners?' in L. Orlin (ed.), *Material London ca. 1600* (Philadelphia, 2000), pp. 184–5; Boulton, pp. 127–9.

women used (it was said) to attract customers to shops in the New Exchange.[128] The severe physical punishments meted out to women by the court – particularly those reserved for scolds, most of whom were women – while not unique to Westminster, might conceivably have reflected such anxieties, although they may have loomed large simply because of the frequency of the court's meetings and hence the greater opportunities to administer punishment.

More generally, the court seems to have made itself available as a means of re-asserting social hierarchy. Even parents and masters turned to the court to help bolster their authority. Thomas Sparke, a cordwainer of St Margaret's, sought the court's aid in dealing with his apprentice, whom he accused of drunkenness, staying out late at night and failure to attend divine service.[129] The court was also prepared to act in support of parents against their own children, especially when neighbours may have been affected by the disruptive behaviour. Edmond Hill of St Clement Danes, for example, was privately whipped 'for his disobedience to his Father and Master', while the same punishment was meted out to the daughter of a St Margaret's waterman, whose misdemeanours included 'misbehaving herself toward her Father & Mother', scolding and calling her neighbours 'whore'. Such punishments illustrate how the dis-ordered private household might be reformed through the action of neighbours and local officials. There could be no more striking example of how the Court of Burgesses sought to uphold all traditional forms of authority, both social and familial.[130]

CONCLUSION: URBAN ANONYMITY AND THE ROLE OF THE COURT OF BURGESSES

Created in order to address the problems generated by a burgeoning population, and increasing levels of poverty, immigration, and immoral conduct, the Court of Burgesses sought above all to combat the anonymity that might be seen as the inevita-ble consequence of urban growth. Different forms of disorder and unregulated behav-iour were assumed to be inextricably linked: immigrants and 'inmates' threatened disorder by existing outside settled hierarchical structures, sexual incontinency created financial burdens on the parish in the shape of bastards but also contributed to a breakdown of social relations associated with criminal behaviour more generally. Despite (or perhaps because of) gentrification, the court mostly dealt with the middling and lower orders of society. It was here where the need to combat anonymity was perceived to be most significant. At all social levels below the gentry, therefore, the

128 For female servants see V. Elliot, 'Single women in the London marriage market: age, status and mobility' in R.B. Outhwaite (ed.), *Marriage and Society: Studies in the Social History of Marriage* (1981), pp. 88–9, 91–2; Archer, 'Material Londoners?', p. 188.

129 WAC, WCB1, p. 240. London livery companies sometimes intervened in a similar manner: Archer, p. 239.

130 WAC, WCB1, p. 97; WCB2, p. 112; cf. Gowing, *Domestic Dangers*, p. 269.

court strove to re-emphasize the bonds between neighbours, masters and servants, landlords and tenants, and parents and children. It tried to ensure that new immigrants were either properly integrated into these structures (after their moral probity had been assured by the necessary testimonials) or expelled from the town altogether. In this war against anonymity and disorder, the individual burgess served in the frontline. His ward divided parishes into smaller neighbourhood units. He was to ensure the moral probity and financial independence of newcomers. In conjunction with constables and the inquest, he was also to seek out forms of unregulated conduct, be it adultery or illegal building. Additionally, his knowledge of local affairs was bolstered by ordinances requiring his arbitration in neighbourhood disputes.

It is not clear whether the scrutiny that burgesses were expected to maintain was informed by a sense of 'godly magistracy'. The fact that more serious crimes – such as theft, assault and murder – were dealt with by the Middlesex sessions rather than the burgess court makes it difficult to use the court minutes as a comprehensive guide to the preoccupations and values of its members. Nevertheless, the burgess court undoubtedly saw itself as dealing with forms of criminality linked to the expansion of the metropolis. 'Godly' ideas of moral discipline would certainly have been entirely compatible with some of the extraordinarily harsh penalties inflicted by the court for moral offences. Yet it seems unlikely that the court acted as the self-conscious voice of 'godly magistracy', given the prominence of the deans or their deputies presiding over the court, and the substantial built-in majority of burgesses from the religiously conservative parish of St Margaret's. While the religious preferences of members of the court are not always clear, very few have been identified as having puritan sympathies, and the court in the 1610s did not involve any of the most obviously 'godly' members of Westminster society and parish government. The Court of Burgesses would seem to exemplify the pattern noted by some historians, whereby a rigorous social discipline and an anxiety to patrol it in all its forms from the family upwards, while quite compatible with 'godly' discipline, could also emerge from essentially conservative religious forces.[131] The fact that the court itself was in essence a revamped leet court, with its membership based on the structure of the old abbot's court, simply reinforces this sense that the harsh social discipline exerted through the court was not necessarily novel in its inspiration, even if it was being called upon to deal with a rapidly changing locality. How far the court's discipline was perceived by Westminster's inhabitants as repressive social control, imposed by an unrepresentative oligarchy, rather than as a traditional form of moral oversight which reinforced communal and neighbourly

---

131 M. Spufford, 'Puritanism and social control?' in A. Fletcher and J. Stevenson (eds.), *Order and Disorder in Early Modern England* (Cambridge, 1985); M. McIntosh, *A Community Transformed: The Manor and Liberty of Havering, 1500–1620* (Cambridge, 1991), pp. 250–1, 253–5, 257; M. Ingram, 'Reformation of manners in early modern England' in Griffiths, Fox and Hindle, *Experience*, pp. 74–7. The providentialist language employed in the debates and wording of the 1585 Act need not be seen as distinctively puritan: see A. Walsham, *Providence in Early Modern England* (Oxford, 1999), pp. 327–31.

values is difficult to say. It is perhaps plausible to suggest that both views were held, with equal reason.

Clearly, the Court of Burgesses represented a determined attempt to address the social problems of the developing locality: the minute books of the court present a picture of a very active institution. But the court in all probability would have seemed most efficient and meaningful in the parish of St Margaret's, where most of the burgesses and constables were located, and whose poor benefited from the fines collected by the court. Such an organization reflected the earlier importance of the old vill of Westminster, but this same structure made it difficult for the court to keep pace with the development of areas outside the vill, namely St Martin's and St Clement Danes.

Although the Court of Burgesses was the most high-profile local institution in Westminster, contemporaries were aware of the limitations that prevented its playing a broader role in the government of the locality. Fundamental here was the court's lack of executive authority, which contrasted sharply with London or indeed with most corporations. It is striking, for example, that the Court of Burgesses exercised little deliberative or law-making role. Instead it functioned almost exclusively as a means of enforcing the series of orders set down in the 1585 Ordinances.[132] The bid for a charter in 1607 specifically recognized this difficulty by proposing new powers to enable burgesses to frame 'statutes and orders'.[133] It is true that the burgesses could seek to respond to the severity of social problems by varying the level and intensity of their punishments. As we have seen, burgesses could refer back to 'ancient custom' when devising penalties proportionate in exemplary force (in their eyes) to the escalating social and moral problems of the age. But the court's inability to create its own statutes and orders undoubtedly limited its ability to respond creatively to the problems engulfing the area. In addition, since the court did not own or administer any corporate property, it lacked the separate income which would have enabled it to pay its own civil servants or bureaucracy.[134]

In the capital as a whole, however, the Court of Burgesses stood out among suburban authorities. Unlike other suburbs, Westminster enjoyed certain advantages which helped it to tackle problems specifically related to the large number of poor immigrants that the metropolis attracted. The Westminster Court of Burgesses met far more frequently than London's suburban leet courts, while its strict enforcement of a

---

132 The Ordinances first set down in 1585 do not appear to have been formally updated until 1719: Webbs, *Manor and Borough*, p. 215; Manchée, p. 221.

133 WAM 6557, p. 1. These were especially to pertain to the governance of 'inhabitants', 'craftsmen' and 'vittellers'. The 1607 charter would also have created a Common Council with the authority to make laws and orders for the good government of the city, as in London: *ibid.*, p. 2.

134 WAM 6561, p. 3. The court did, it is true, swear in a range of minor officials as various as musicians (to serve as official waits for the city), appraisers, porters, hog drivers, viewers of buildings and searchers for unwholesome flesh, unwholesome fish and unwholesome poultry (e.g. WAC, WCB2, pp. 77, 79, 121, 122; Webbs, *Manor and Borough*, pp. 216, 220). But there is no evidence that the court paid these officials.

testimonial system, including the punishment of inmates, made it unique among suburban governments of the period (by contrast, most leet courts operating within the
suburbs limited their activities to market regulation and cases of nuisance).[135] It is a
moot point, of course, whether this testimonial system was really enforced systematically, given the large numbers of people passing in and out of the town, and the
high levels of short-term employment available from the royal Court and seasonal
gentry residents. Nevertheless, the energy which the burgess court devoted to its
implementation is impressive. Even if Westminster's demographic problems were more
severe than those of other suburban areas, the town potentially had more means available to combat them. Whatever the deficiencies of the court, the direct involvement of
local burgesses, to which the court minutes bear witness, contrasts notably with the
notorious 'trading justices' active in late seventeenth- and early eighteenth-century
Westminster and Middlesex.[136]

Westminster was also notable in our period for the many levels of overlapping jurisdiction active in the area. The Court of Burgesses' overview of moral offences, for example,
was to some extent duplicated by the activities of the church courts, while the Middlesex
sessions, the Court of the Verge (later the Palace Court) and the array of commissioners
created by the Privy Council might all at times overlap with the burgesses' purview. These
layers of overlapping jurisdictions could ensure a remarkable intensity of investigation and
prosecution.[137] Constables in St Martin's, for example, were ordered by the parish vestry to
share information on inmates with burgesses on a weekly basis. The extent of cooperation
probably varied, yet the personal links between certain burgesses and JPs and the overlapping of personnel should have facilitated co-ordination.[138] There is also evidence that
burgesses and parish officials expected to co-operate.[139] Nevertheless, it is important to

---

135 They made no attempt to control the number of inmates within their jurisdiction. Even in the relatively well governed Southwark, the leet court concentrated on nuisance and market regulation: Archer,
pp. 226–7. For the limited scope of the Finsbury leet court see E. Levy, 'Moorfields, Finsbury and the
City of London in the sixteenth century', *London Topographical Record* 26 (1990), pp. 87–9.

136 Webbs, *Parish and County*, pp. 337–42.

137 Archer, pp. 235–6. For a relatively optimistic view of London's 'fragmentation' in a later period see
J. Innes, 'Managing the metropolis: London's social problems and their control, c.1660–1830' in
Clark and Gillespie, *Two Capitals*, pp. 65–9, 72–7.

138 WAC, F2001, f. 162. There was some overlapping of personnel between the Middlesex sessions
and the Court of Burgesses. Westminster justices such as William Mann and Edmund Doubleday
had sat on the Court of Burgesses, while Sir Humphrey Chambers had presided over the court as
the representative of Westminster's high steward. More generally, during the Jacobean period the
number of Middlesex justices living in Westminster had increased substantially and included such
active JPs as the Westminster prebendary Gabriel Grant, Edward Forsett of St Martin's and Michael
Moseley of St Clement Danes as well as the minister of St Clement Danes, Roger Bates: see LMA,
WJ/SR (NS) 1, *passim*.

139 The accusation that a young girl was being maltreated in a house of ill-repute quickly brought both
a St Martin's churchwarden and a burgess to the house in question: see LMA, WJ/SR (NS) 5/32.
See also the reference to scavengers' books 'rated and signed by such of the Burgesses and Assistants
as were present': WAC, F2002, f. 33.

recognize that overlapping jurisdictions could potentially inhibit effective action, and it is possible to document clashes. A petition from the Jacobean period, which appealed for the creation of a separate Westminster sessions, drew attention to such problems. It complained that 'common annoyances and disorders are much increased' because Westminster officers were required to attend the Middlesex sessions instead of the local burgess court and leet court. Moreover, 'meane people . . . of the worst conversation and meanest ability' habitually gained licences to act as victuallers from ignorant Middlesex justices who issued them without securing certificates from West-minster burgesses or local inhabitants.[140]

More generally, there is reason to think that the burgesses were unable to sustain a dominant status within this network of overlapping authorities. This is partly apparent in the court's dealings with parishes and the local justices. Loyalty to the parish seems to have remained stronger than loyalty to the city and liberties, even among the court's chief office-holders.[141] Indeed, when the court clashed over jurisdiction with the West-minster parishes, it was usually the loser. In May 1612, the 'chief parishioners' of St Martin's complained that certain constables had been sworn by the Court of Burgesses without first having secured their approval 'who doe best know who are fitt and serviceable men for that purpose'. The court therefore agreed that in the future none would be sworn without a certificate 'or sufficient assurance from the Burgess and Assistant and other the chief of that Parish . . . that he hath born such other offices as is used in that Place to be borne by him before he come to be constable'. Such disagreements foreshadow eighteenth-century disputes created by Westminster's over-lapping jurisdictions, when parish vestries and local justices tended to act in consort, often ignoring the burgess court altogether.[142]

The Privy Council also often chose to sideline the court, especially in connection with new policy initiatives. Despite the fact that the 1585 Ordinances required the Court of Burgesses to supervise the work of constables, the Jacobean Privy Council ignored the court. Instead they simply wrote to local JPs, urging them to direct the constables to conduct weekly searches for vagrants in victualling houses and inns so as to suppress the 'continewall robberies, burglaries and pilferries' that afflicted the locality.[143] In 1616 a new provost marshall was appointed for Middlesex, while from 1618 a newly constituted Westminster sessions now formed a separate division within the existing Middlesex sessions. By the 1630s, the enforcement of new government initiatives such as the Book of Orders was also delegated to local JPs and the dean and

---

140 WAM 6562, f. 1r–v.

141 This is borne out in the surviving wills of burgesses. While fellow vestrymen, kinsmen and those practising the same occupation are remembered as recipients of rings or as overseers, the shared experience of burgess-ship is seldom mentioned. See above, ch. 4, for the wills of office-holders.

142 WAC, WCB1, p. 167; Webbs, *Manor and Borough*, pp. 215, 224–5.

143 *APC 1615–16*, pp. 210–11.

chapter.[144] The 1630s also saw the Crown's concern over new building receive renewed attention via the appointment of new commissioners, essentially taking over the work of the burgesses, while King Charles also explored the possibilities of boosting the powers and authority of his own Court of the Palace of Westminster. Clearly, the Crown did not envisage any broader role for the Court of Burgesses in the government of the locality.

The Court of Burgesses was a unique creation of the fears, preoccupations and hopes of the 1580s. Its destiny, however, was to take its place among the host of lesser bodies policing Westminster. Nevertheless, it clearly met a local need: the court continued to function during the Civil War and Interregnum and was still a hive of activity in the eighteenth century.[145]

144 TNA, PC2/41, pp. 373, 467.
145 Manchée, pp. 8–9, 221–37 and *passim*.

Chapter 8

Poverty, plague and the politics of communal responsibility

WESTMINSTER played host to grand centres of conspicuous consumption and affluent leisure, from Whitehall Palace to Shaver's Hall. But beside the grand townhouses of the aristocracy and the pleasure gardens of the gentry lurked the darker side of life in the Westminster parishes. The area's development as a courtly suburb saw a parallel growth in poverty, largely fuelled by poor immigrants to the metropolis. There can have been few other places in the country where the extremes of wealth were placed in such close and vivid juxtaposition. Harrowing images of the homeless and destitute emerge from local records: a poor boy found in the street whose feet had nearly rotted away, poor infants left at the doors of great houses, women giving birth in the street and poor men and women huddling in ditches or under hedges, sometimes crying, sometimes too cold and weak to move. Such spectacles were a feature of Westminster life, as was the periodic discovery of corpses belonging to poor unidentified men and women, who had died in fields or near brick kilns on the outskirts of the town.[1]

These bleak images provide a glimpse of the effects of suburban expansion and the harsh conditions endured by poor migrants to the capital, which Westminster parishes shared with other suburban areas of London.[2] But poverty did not necessarily wear such an extreme aspect. More commonly, poor men and women in Westminster pieced together what was often a precarious living over the space of many years. Ironically, this was partly a function of the developing West End. An expanding service sector in Westminster created jobs, but many of these offered only casual, short-term employment. Seasonal gentry visits, the periodic absence of the royal Court, the irregular calling and dissolving of parliaments, and the occasional devastating outbreak of plague, all contributed to an economy that was often buoyant, but could be unpredictable.

---

1 WAC, F340, n.f.; F359 (1632–33); E144 (1567), n.f.; E149 (1606–7), f. 21; F301, f. 14; F388, n.f.

2 See above, ch. 7.

Even the normal ebb and flow of the law terms led Thomas Dekker to fashion a 'complaint' for the town in which 'Westminster' lamented the law vacations, which 'doe blow abroad the wealth that before I have gotten together'.[3] Smaller retailers and artisans, as well as servants and casual labourers, could suffer as a consequence. For every Robert Baker, who in a few short years rose from humble tailor to wealthy property-holder, who styled himself 'gentleman' and employed sixty men making 'pickadils' in his shop on the Strand, there were a great many others who failed to prosper, each year a struggle to survive on the edge of poverty.[4]

If some of the factors contributing to poverty were distinctive to Westminster, so too were some of the structures of society and government which framed the experience of poverty. In Westminster, unlike neighbouring London, the absence of livery companies removed one safety-net which potentially cushioned skilled workers and their families from the economic effects of illness, misfortune or death. Nor did Westminster possess the other civic institutions that made provision for the poor in the City. There were, of course, other institutions that were unique to Westminster, such as the royal Court and Abbey, which could have an impact on the resources available to the poor. Indeed, fears of poverty and especially the crises brought on by plague could lead to significant intervention by the Crown in its surrounding neighbourhood, as we will see. Westminster's increasingly gentrified population represented another possible source of wealth that could potentially mitigate the suffering of its poor residents, if it could be tapped effectively.

Nevertheless, if we are to be able to understand the scale of poverty in Westminster, the efforts made by the authorities to relieve it, and the experience of the poor themselves, then it is necessary to focus on the institutions which always stood in the front line of attempts to tackle Westminster's social problems – the parishes. It soon becomes evident that the different circumstances and social profiles of St Martin's and St Margaret's could result in very different responses to the problems of poverty and plague. The study of how Westminster society responded to poverty also enables us to examine issues that highlighted fundamental questions of communal identity in Westminster, at both ends of the social scale. For example, which poor people did parishes consider themselves responsible for, and how narrowly was this sense of community interpreted in practice? And given that the 'gentrification' of Westminster was one of the area's most notable developments in this period, how far were the parishes able to persuade the gentry that they were members of the local community with specific obligations towards the poor?

As we will see, the broader issue of poverty raised questions of belonging and responsibility in acute form, and nowhere more so than in Westminster's parishes.

---

3 Thomas Dekker, *The Deade Term. Or Westminsters Complaint for Long Vacations* (1608), sig. C1r; John Norden, *Speculum Britanniae, Description of Middlesex* (1593), pp. 47–8.

4 On Baker's career see F. Sheppard, *Robert Baker of Piccadilly Hall and His Heirs* (London Topographical Society 127, 1982) and on 'pickadils' specifically, p. 9.

POPULATION AND POVERTY

The growth of Westminster parishes such as St Martin in the Fields and St Clement Danes has traditionally been viewed as a continuation of London's western expansion. But in fact, the nature of Westminster's development seems to have related as much to the growth and rising importance of the old 'vill' of Westminster, an urban centre since the medieval period. While most of those living in London's eastern and northern suburbs were engaged in the production of goods, Westminster's growth, as has been emphasized, was fuelled by a service economy, a pattern established during the Middle Ages.[5] This had an impact on the nature and distribution of the poorer population of the town during the sixteenth and seventeenth centuries.

That the town of Westminster was home to an increasingly large population of poor people is obvious from contemporary comments. Yet the range and depth of poverty is difficult to chart with any precision. A handful of Elizabethan surveys sheds some light, but the evidence that they provide is incomplete and difficult to compare.[6] Nevertheless, it is possible to gain a general impression of the changing geographical distribution of population and poverty in Westminster during the late Tudor and early Stuart period.

Throughout this time, the most densely populated parish was St Margaret's, which also seems to have experienced higher levels of poverty. In the early 1570s, for example, St Margaret's spent on its poor four times as much as did St Martin's (£245 over eighteen months as against £67 spent by St Martin's, and £138 by St Clement's). By 1578 St Margaret's also supported four times more parish pensioners than the neighbouring St Martin's (seventy-two compared to eighteen).[7]

Density of population also suggests differing levels of poverty. Surveys dating from 1582 and 1595 reveal that subdivided property tenanted by inmates was both more widespread and more intensive in St Margaret's than elsewhere in Westminster. Thus while in 1582 St Martin's officials did not identity subdivision of properties as a problem, in the same survey St Margaret's parish reported that the Catherine Wheel, a single property in Tothill Street, had been divided into seventeen tenements, whose cramped quarters housed fifty-three lodgers.[8] The extent of urban crowding is even more vividly depicted in a 1595 survey which covered just one of St Margaret's eight wards. Within this single district (an area covering the Sanctuary, the Almonry, and

---

5 A.L. Beier, 'Engine of manufacture: the trades of London' in A.L. Beier and R.A.P. Finlay (eds.), *London 1500–1700: The Making of the Metropolis* (1986), pp. 154–6; R.A.P. Finlay and B. Shearer, 'Population growth and suburban expansion' in *ibid.*, pp. 44–6, 52–3.

6 See the discussion in Merritt thesis, pp. 273–4. Some of the surveys are contained in Burghley's papers, perhaps collected in the run-up to the 1572 parliament, which introduced a compulsory, nationwide poor rate (see below).

7 BL, Lansdowne MS 14, ff. 89–90; MS 16, ff. 167–68; WAM 25029 (cf. WAC, F305, n.f.).

8 BL, Lansdowne MS 35, ff. 101–6. St Clement's parish reported seventy-two inmates, but only forty-four lived in subdivided tenements.

some of the alleys off Tothill Street) there were said to be 246 poor inhabitants, including children and inmates. Many of the poor were concentrated in tiny cramped alleys situated directly off the prosperous and impressive houses of Tothill Street – Pickaxe Alley, Green's Alley, Skinner's Alley and St Anne's Alley.[9] This pattern of housing, with the rich occupying the main thoroughfares and the poor clustered in nearby alleyways, was typical of early modern cities more generally.[10]

This information points to high levels of poverty at St Margaret's. However, the only survey that provides sufficient information to gauge the extent of poverty in any of the Westminster parishes in our period relates to the parish of St Martin's.[11] This survey of 1603 reveals that 6.7 per cent of St Martin's householders received regular relief as parish pensioners, while an additional 15.8 per cent 'want relief & are likely to Come to have Relief', creating a combined total (with dependants) of 14.9 per cent, out of a total parish population of about 2,950.[12] These percentages are roughly consistent with those of other urban surveys in the period.[13] What is perhaps more striking, given St Martin's emergence at this time as a fashionable district, is that these statistics are not dramatically different from those estimated for the relatively poor Boroughside district of Southwark in 1622. In this more workaday suburban area 7.4 per cent of householders received pensions, while 18.6 per cent needed occasional relief.[14]

More generally, poverty in Westminster was associated with a rapidly rising population. This growth can be charted from a range of sources, which also reveal differing rates of increase in different areas of the town. Population growth was a feature of St Margaret's from the late fifteenth century onwards, and already by 1548 the parish contained approximately 3,500 inhabitants – a figured not reached at St Martin's until the early seventeenth century.[15] During Elizabeth's reign, St Margaret's population

---

9   WAM 9353.

10 Boulton, pp. 167–92.

11 A survey exists for a portion of St Clement Danes in the 1630s (TNA, SP16/359/22), but this lists only the poor 'within the Dutchy of Lancaster'.

12 WAC, F6039. Population estimates based on parish register.

13 Similar surveys suggest that poor relief was allocated to roughly 5 per cent of the population of a town, with a further 10–20 per cent potentially in need of relief in times of dearth and disease: P. Slack, *Poverty and Policy in Tudor and Stuart England* (Harlow, 1988), p. 74; cf. P. Slack, 'Poverty and social regulation in Elizabethan England' in C. Haigh (ed.), *The Reign of Queen Elizabeth* (Basingstoke, 1984), p. 232. In London, the fragmentary evidence suggests that between 5 per cent and 7 per cent of householders depended on regular relief, but there was great variation between poor suburban areas and the smaller, more prosperous parishes of the inner city. In 1595, 44 per cent of householders were in need of relief in the Portsoken portion of St Botolph Aldgate, a notoriously poor suburban parish: Archer, pp. 152–4, 188–9, 197.

14 Boulton, pp. 95–6, 115–16. I have worked on the assumption of a household size of 3.8, a figure used for other suburban areas of London, including by Boulton for Southwark. A larger household size of 4.5 would bring the figures for St Martin's and Boroughside even closer.

15 Rosser, pp. 177–9 (based on 2,500 communicants, as reported in St Margaret's 1548 charity certificate).

seems to have doubled, and it now became the object of deep concern.[16] As we have seen, the 1585 Act for the government of Westminster specifically identified immigrants as unskilled labourers, who were likely to swell existing numbers of poor. St Margaret's population continued to rise in the early Stuart period, reaching nearly 16,000 by the late 1630s.[17] As late as the 1650s, St Margaret's was still the more densely populated of the Westminster parishes, its many alleys 'pestered' with urban poor.[18] Seventeenth-century plague statistics also confirm that high population density at St Margaret's was a sign of poverty, for the parish suffered more severely during epidemics than the other less crowded Westminster parishes, despite relatively elaborate measures taken against the disease.[19] By the 1660s St Margaret's parish contained 4.2 hearths per household (the lowest figure for any of the Westminster parishes), with 47.6 per cent of its inhabitants unable to pay the hearth tax, compared with only 19.3 per cent in St Martin's.[20]

By contrast, the effect of Elizabethan population growth was rather different at St Martin's, where most of the parish had remained largely undeveloped before the sixteenth century. In 1548, it reported 700 communicants or approximately 980 parishioners.[21] Population estimates based on parish registers suggest a population of around 2,950 in the first years of the seventeenth century, still less than the 3,500 resident in St Margaret's in 1548. In addition, it seems likely that St Martin's more easily accommodated its Elizabethan population increase than did St Margaret's. By the early seventeenth century, however, contemporary complaints about St Martin's growth accompanied a threefold increase in its population between 1603 and 1625.[22] Although this same period witnessed the development of St Martin's as a fashionable enclave, it is clear from a range of sources that much of this Jacobean increase came from poor immigrants. During the next fifteen years St Martin's population now

---

16 In estimating parish populations I have followed Archer in averaging baptisms over five-year periods, and assuming 5 per cent under-registration and a birth rate of 37 per 1,000.

17 Parish registers imply an average population of roughly 15,790 for the period 1635–39.

18 M. Power, 'The east and the west in early modern London' in E.W. Ives, R.J. Knecht and J.J. Scarisbrick (eds.), *Wealth and Power in Tudor England: Essays Presented to S.T. Bindoff* (1978), pp. 170, 174–5; M. Power, 'Social topography of Restoration London' in Beier and Finlay, *London 1500–1700*, p. 203.

19 P. Slack, 'Metropolitan government in crisis: the response to plague' in Beier and Finlay, *London 1500–1700*, p. 63; R. Finlay, *Population and Metropolis 1580–1650* (Cambridge, 1981), p. 121. For more on the plague see below.

20 The mean number of hearths per household elsewhere in Westminster were 7.7 (the newly created St Paul Covent Garden), 5.0 (St Martin's) and 5.9 (St Clement Danes). St Giles Cripplegate, a poor parish in the northern suburbs, recorded 3 hearths per household: J. Champion, *London's Dreaded Visitation* (1994), appendix 1; Power, 'The east and the west', pp. 181–2.

21 Kitching, p. 64 (adding two-fifths to account for children under fourteen).

22 *CSPD 1625–26*, p. 525. Parish registers for St Martin's suggest a population of between 9,500 and 11,000 by 1625. A previous trebling of population at St Martin's had earlier taken place over about fifty years (c.1548–1603).

seems to have doubled – a significant factor in the overall growth of Westminster in the Caroline period.[23] Indeed it has been calculated that by the late 1630s the overall population of the Westminster parishes totalled between 35,000 and 42,000 inhabitants. Any one of Westminster's parishes, then, would have ranked alongside the most populous towns in England.[24]

The overall pattern is thus one of spiralling population growth and increasing poverty, with the impact of poverty felt most acutely at St Margaret's in the early 1580s, and at St Martin's by the late Jacobean period. It is this changing context, as we shall see, that provides the key to differing patterns of charity and official relief, the character of social relations and the response to disease.

CHARITY, THE ABBEY AND THE CROWN

So far our discussion of poverty has been couched in terms of individual parishes. Yet Westminster was unique within the metropolis in possessing two institutions that not only underpinned its economy but also offered charity to the poor of the area: the Abbey and royal Court.

The Abbey was a source of some charitable provision in medieval Westminster, and the charitable activities of the Westminster monks may have been more carefully targeted, and the alms more effectively distributed, than has sometimes been thought.[25] Whatever the extent of the monks' personal involvement in the town, the amount of alms which the Abbey distributed could still be significant. By the early sixteenth century the Abbey was spending roughly £400 a year on alms, including some £215 a year in doles, especially those commemorating the anniversaries of royal benefactors. Recipients of the larger doles undoubtedly consisted of many poor from London, although local residents of Westminster might sometimes be indicated by the testator. Even when the monastery was dissolved, it was ordered that the newly created cathedral and collegiate church should give £100 a year to 'poor householders'.[26] The collegiate church does not seem to have achieved anything like this sum, however.[27] The 'college alms' in the 1550s provided bread, meat and money for forty poor people every Sunday for a year. This may have been a reasonably generous amount in the

23 Smuts, 'Royal policy', p. 118 n.3.

24 *Ibid.*, p. 118.

25 N.S. Rushton, 'Monastic charitable provision in Tudor England: quanitifying and qualifying poor relief in the early sixteenth century', *Continuity and Change* 16 (2001), pp. 9–43, esp. pp. 25, 29–32.

26 B. Harvey, *Living and Dying in England 1100–1540* (Oxford, 1993), pp. 24–33.

27 C.S. Knighton, 'Economics and economies of a royal peculiar: Westminster Abbey 1540–1640' in R. O'Day and F. Heal (eds.), *Princes and Paupers in the English Church, 1500–1800* (Leicester, 1981), p. 59. Individual prebendaries or the dean himself did, it is true, occasionally give alms to the poor of St Margaret's.

early Elizabethan period, but the identical alms were still offered in the 1630s, when the numbers of poor people in the surrounding area had increased exponentially.[28] Even if the number relieved was small, it must be stressed that these alms were not distributed in a haphazard fashion – lists of recipients were drawn up carefully every week. In the case of other doles, the names of recipients were listed street by street.[29] In addition, the dean handed over control of these college alms to St Margaret's parish officials, perhaps in response to the 1572 statute which established a national poor rate to be administered at the parish level. The alms continued to be distributed within the former Abbey church, so reminding the needy of the ultimate source of this bounty.[30] But transferring control to parish officials underlined the fact that poor relief was now essentially the administrative task of the parish.

It seems clear that the Elizabethan Abbey normally offered little more than token relief to the poor of the town, despite continuing to provide occasional doles and to formally distribute the 'college alms'. Only a locally born dean, Richard Neile, over-saw new efforts designed to benefit poor local men and women. The Abbey (or the dean personally) did make charitable donations during plague epidemics, when extra provision was vital, but it could not be relied upon to make a substantial regular donations to the poor of the town.[31]

Much the same was true of the charity dispensed by the royal Court. Recent work on medieval Westminster has noted royal alms-giving, but has also emphasized its relatively undiscriminating character. By the early modern period the Crown still fig-ured as a source of some charity in the locality, for example the royal Maundy money continued to be distributed, although the sums distributed changed little and did not acknowledge the changing profile of poverty in the locality.[32] In addition, the Crown also continued to nominate individuals to places in the royal almshouses, built within the precincts of the Abbey by Henry VII. There is no suggestion, however, that such appointments were any different from the early Tudor use of such almsrooms 'as a

28 E.g. WAM 37494–37547; WAC, E145, f. 9; E153 (1634–35), n.f.

29 Surviving lists of those receiving alms from the mid-Tudor period make it clear that the recipients were not a single recurring cohort, but that they were drawn from a larger pool of names: WAM 37494–37547. See also WAM 37548.

30 WAC, E144, 1566, n.f.; E145, 1572–73, n.f.; 1578–79, n.f. For a 1599 traveller's description of the distribution of these alms see P. Razzell (ed.), *The Journals of Two Travellers in Elizabethan and Early Stuart England* (1995), p. 41. In the early eighteenth century Ned Ward complained 'that the parish poor of St Margaret's should be suffered to beg within the Abbey, even in prayer-time', but it is not evident that this took place in the earlier period: N. Ward, *The London Spy* (1993 ed.), p. 142.

31 See the list of charitable activities compiled by dean Richard Neile in WAM, Dean's Book 7, f. 7r–v. See also WAM 33682, f. 42v (1625 plague).

32 St Margaret's usually received £3 6s 8d (e.g. WAC, E154, E155), although for the difficult year 1625–26 the amounts were larger (E152, 1625–26, f. 15v). By contrast, the yearly gift to St Martin's was of 20s (e.g. F301): while this sum was raised to 30s in 1580–81 (F307) it re-mained at this level for the rest of our period (e.g. F362).

means of pensioning off retired servants'.[33] More publicly, the poor of St Margaret's, St Martin's and other Middlesex and Westminster parishes did receive alms from the royal almoner or sub-almoner when the monarch removed from Whitehall. These alms normally seem to have been distributed at Whitehall itself, probably to poor men and women who had petitioned directly or been recommended by the parishes.[34] At times of exceptional hardship, the Crown might also make substantial one-off donations to the parishes on Whitehall's doorstep – especially at times of plague – but generally the Crown did little to assist in dealing with day-to-day poverty, or with the multitude of beggars whom the palace attracted to the area.[35] Indeed in 1626 local JPs pleaded for the right to appoint a provost marshal to deal with the mass of 'lewd people' who came to Westminster and begged before Whitehall Palace.[36]

Financial assistance from Crown and Abbey could not therefore be counted upon to do much to relieve the local poor. Resources regularly available to help the poor, then, needed to come from elsewhere.

POVERTY AND ADMINISTRATIVE STRUCTURES

In the early modern capital, it was the imposition of compulsory rates that formed the cornerstone of poor relief. This system relied on structures of local government to operate, and therefore Westminster and the City of London organized poor relief very differently. London's government presided over a centralized system in which parishes contributed to a municipal collection administed by Christ's Hospital. This allowed for the redistribution of rate income from richer to poorer parishes, but it also meant that parish officials controlled only a portion of the poor rate they collected.[37] Beyond the level of City government, poverty was also a concern of the Privy Council, which periodically involved itself in London's affairs, for example during the crisis

---

33 Rosser, p. 297. Appointments to royal almsrooms are noted in State Papers Domestic throughout this period.

34 In 1637 moneys were sent to the parishes for distribution because of the plague: *CSPD 1637*, pp. 160–1. £11 12d was received by St Margaret's overseers from 'Mr Walter James Sergeant of his Maties backhowse [bakehouse]' at the King's remove to Hampton Court in 1625/6 (WAC, E152, 1625–26). St Margaret's generally fared better than St Martin's: WAC, E145 (1575–76), f. 19; E152 (1625–26); F304, n.f.

35 Note the £100 payments by the Crown to St Margaret's in 1625 (WAC, E152 (1625–26 plague account), f. 11) and to each parish in the wake of the plague outbreak of 1636 (E153 (1636–37); F363 (1636–37)). Also note the substantial donation of bread to St Margaret's poor in 1625: WAC, E152 (1625–26), f. 27.

36 *APC 1626*, pp. 306, 323.

37 This system emerged out of the poor relief legislation of 1563 and 1572. Out of this sum each parish then funded pensions for its own residents, subject to the approval of Christ's governors. Not surprisingly, the system sometimes generated tension, setting parochial officials against the hospital authorities in the quest for funds: Archer, pp. 159–61.

years of the 1580s and 1590s.[38] This involvement may partly have reflected the somewhat exaggerated fears of councillors during those decades. Sometimes, however, it was the very complexity of City bureaucracy that led the Privy Council to step in when it seemed that decisive action was required. Nevertheless, the City itself did have the power to make and enforce regulations connected with issues of poverty and disease.

In Westminster, as we will see, the twin concerns of poverty and disease prompted far more frequent intervention by the Privy Council. This was partly due to the absence of any coordinating administrative body for the whole area. In addition, because the royal Court lay within Westminster, those problems that concerned the Council acquired an even greater urgency than did similar issues in London. The Council's worries, however, centred on the interconnected problems of immigration, illegal building, vagrancy and plague – problems common to most poor suburban areas.[39] Other bodies that concerned themselves with issues of poverty in Westminster included the Middlesex (and later Westminster) JPs. They punished vagrancy and other crimes associated with the poor as well as playing a role in the administration of the poor law. In particular, JPs chose collectors and overseers for the poor from names submitted by each parish, with the stipulation that overseers should be 'substantial householders'. Middlesex justices also signed and approved accounts showing how parishes had spent the poor rate. In practice both tasks seem to have been a formality, but lack of evidence may mean that their role has been underestimated.[40] The Court of Burgesses, another body that functioned in the area, intervened directly and disproportionately in the lives of the poor, given the offences covered by the court's ordinances, but it was not directly involved in the distribution of relief. Moreover, as we have seen, the Court of Burgesses did not have the power to respond to extraordinary conditions of poverty in times of crisis, or to authorize special collections or fasts, as took place in the City of London.[41]

As we have seen elsewhere, this absence of a larger presiding authority left Westminster's parishes as the most prominent administrative structures in the town. And it was in the administration of poor relief and collection of the poor rate that the parish undertook what was possibly its most significant and certainly its most financially complex task. This system of relief essentially conformed to the pattern of parish-based relief set

---

38 *Ibid.*, pp. 229–30. See also Slack, 'Metropolitan government', pp. 66–7.

39 For the council and illegal building, especially in Westminster, see T. Barnes, 'The prerogative and environmental control of London building in the early seventeenth century: the lost opportunity', *California Law Review* 58 (1970). For the Privy Council and plague see below.

40 E.g. WAC, F319 (1592–93), f. 10; E145 (1573–74), f. 51v. After the death of Goodman, vestrymen who were JPs signed accounts at St Martin's, while the various deans of Westminster signed St Margaret's accounts until John Williams entered office, when JPs assumed this task. WAC, F229, (1602–03), f. 8v; E149 (1601–02), f. 26; E150 (1610–11), f. 25v; E151 (1620–21), f. 64.

41 See above, ch. 7. Archer, pp. 198–9.

down in the parliamentary statutes of 1572 and later those of 1598 and 1601.[42] Each Westminster parish thus exercised complete autonomy over its own finances, keeping all revenue from the poor rate and deciding how it should be spent. There was no citywide system of relief in Westminster, nor do the parishes seem to have co-operated with one another significantly. As a consequence, individual parish vestries often wielded tremendous power and controlled very large sums of money – vastly greater than those at the disposal of most parishes in England. The parishes of St Margaret and St Martin even organized separate houses of correction, institutions which were normally maintained only at the town or county level, a testimony to the parishes' independence and ambitions, as well as perhaps to the perceived scale of the problem of poverty in Westminster.[43]

PAROCHIAL INITIATIVES: THE ANTECEDENTS OF
WESTMINSTER'S POOR RATE

There was nothing new in parishes playing a prominent role in poor relief in Westminster, at least in the parish of St Margaret's. In the late medieval period, however, it had been resident townsmen, as members of parish fraternities, that had responded to the problems of the local poor.[44] As Westminster could not call upon the trade guilds or urban taxes upon which relief was based in other medieval towns, the role of these fraternities was vital. Their charitable activities demonstrated a sense of shared interests and communal responsibility which allowed Westminster residents to overcome these structural anomalies.[45]

Given this tradition of charitable activity, the impact of the dissolution of the fraternities at the Reformation was potentially devastating. A number of elements seem to have mitigated this loss, however. First of all, the process of dissolution occurred only gradually in Westminster. The site of the Rounceval hospital had been absorbed by the expansion of Whitehall Palace in the 1530s, even though its fraternity struggled on until its early dissolution in 1544.[46] The almshouses in Our Lady's Alley, funded by the Assumption guild, seem to have escaped confiscation. It is not clear who subsequently maintained them, but they continued to function until at least the early seventeenth century.[47] Moreover, as has been argued in earlier chapters, the organizing tradition of St Margaret's guilds seems to have been redirected towards the

---

42 E.M. Leonard, *The Early History of English Poor Relief* (Cambridge, 1900), is still a valuable account for the early modern period.

43 St Margaret's overseers of the poor routinely supervised an income of over £500 a year by the 1630s (e.g. WAC, E153 (1631–32), n.f.) On houses of correction see below.

44 Rosser, pp. 298–300.

45 *Ibid.*, pp. 295–8, 313–15, 319–20.

46 *Ibid.*, pp. 319–20; *KW*, III, pt 2, 22–4.

47 TNA, E178/4205.

parish as a whole after the Reformation, and this would also seem to hold true for at least one of the guild activities – relieving the poor. Obviously, the Catholic doctrine of works had partly inspired the charity of the fraternities. Although scholarship on late medieval charity has challenged the view that Catholic alms-giving was necessarily 'indiscriminate, clerically controlled and oriented towards the salvation of the donor rather than the objective relief of the recipient', these characteristics were found to some degree in medieval Westminster.[48] Nevertheless, the charity of St Margaret's guilds had been communally controlled and seems to have targeted specific recipients. It is therefore not surprising that St Margaret's parish was the location of one of several mid-century experiments in poor relief that preceded the parliamentary statute of 1572 which formally required poor rates to be levied throughout England.

The mid sixteenth century witnessed a number of experiments in English social policy whereby a handful of towns introduced compulsory poor rates (at least on a temporary basis) often following periods of crisis.[49] Many of these initiatives, however, were only fleeting experiments.[50] This makes the scheme developed in St Margaret's Westminster all the more remarkable. Surviving accounts of collectors for the poor show that St Margaret's parish had established what came close to being a compulsory levy to support the poor sometime *before* 1561. Precisely when the parish introduced this levy is not known, although the influenza epidemic of 1557 may have prompted local authorities to act, and the dissolution of the Abbey in 1559 may have accentuated the problem of provision for the poor. Approximately two hundred households were rated in the early 1560s, with collectors for the poor chosen by the curate, churchwardens and 'headboroughs' of the parish.[51] Most crucially, it is clear that this levy for the poor in Westminster progressed smoothly from at least 1561 until the introduction of the 1572 statute, a transition that required little alteration to the system already in place.

St Margaret's system seems to have built upon the success of earlier communal fund-raising and charitable activities – the pre-Reformation rebuilding of the parish church as well as the re-establishment of the Rounceval hospital spring to mind. It depended on the co-operation of leading parish officers, many of whom had held

---

48 Slack, *Poverty and Policy*, pp. 8–9; J.A.F. Thomson, 'Piety and charity in late medieval London', *JEH* 16 (1965), pp. 182–3.

49 Slack, *Poverty and Policy*, pp. 48–9, 122–3, 141.

50 *Ibid.*, pp. 114–22. The City of London, it is true, had ordered parishes to collect alms on a regular basis since 1533. Thereafter, officials were directed to encourage parishioners to contribute, but a wholly compulsory poor rate was not introduced until 1572 (*ibid.*, pp. 118, 121).

51 WAC, E144 (1561–62) (which shows the parish already collecting arrears), E144 (1566), n.f. It is not clear by what legal authority these collections were made. A 1552 statute had encouraged parishes to record amounts agreed by inhabitants for support of the poor, so that individuals became committed to a set of weekly payments in advance (Slack, *Poverty and Policy*, p. 123). While donations were still theoretically voluntary under the statute, the formal manner of the imposition and administration of this system in St Margaret's, including the listing of arrears, is striking.

office within St Margaret's fraternities.[52] The ease with which the parish was able to shift to compulsory rates suggests that it tapped a willingness to fund the systematic communal relief of the poor. The scheme was administered with characteristic efficiency and the level of default was low. Rates did not displace charity, as will be seen, but they provided St Margaret's with a regular income from which it could aid poor inhabitants.

Not only was St Margaret's clearly a precocious parish in its development of poor rate administration, but it is also the only area of Westminster that provides any detailed evidence of poor relief before the 1572 parliamentary statute. For the period after 1572, however, the funding of poor relief is well documented in both of the two Westminster parishes of St Martin in the Fields and St Margaret's. As we shall see, patterns of poor relief differed significantly in the two communities. Issues such as the relative importance of rates and charity reflected not only broader differences in the scale of poverty but also administrative traditions that emerged from differing social circumstances.[53]

NEGOTIATING THE POOR RATE: A PROBLEM IN SOCIAL RELATIONS

The introduction of compulsory poor rates throughout England in 1572 provided an opportunity for parishes in Westminster to introduce taxation which could help to combat escalating poverty in the area. Despite the obvious prosperity throughout Westminster, high levels of arrears in poor-rate payments became a distinctive feature of St Martin's parish in particular. The problem of tax arrears has not been discussed by historians of poverty, but it was to become central to the experience of this Westminster parish. These difficulties stemmed partly from the changing social complexion of the area as more well-to-do part-time residents came to live in St Martin's. But the issue of arrears was more than a financial inconvenience. Failure to pay the poor rate also highlighted issues of communal responsibility and certainly aroused resentment among parish governors. More generally, rating raised difficult questions. The matter of who should pay the poor rate and how far the system should expand to reflect increasing poverty created further tensions.[54]

When poor rates were first levied in St Martin's, the yield was relatively small and may initially have reflected relatively low levels of poverty in the early Elizabethan parish. Between 1577 and 1597 about 70 per cent of ratepayers were also assessed at

---

52 Rosser, pp. 287–90.

53 Poor-rate accounts for St Clement Danes in the Elizabethan and early Stuart periods are too patchy to allow sustained analysis.

54 For rural areas see S. Hindle, 'Exhortation and entitlement: negotiating inequality in English rural communities, 1550–1650' in M. Braddick and J. Walter (eds.), *Negotiating Power in Early Modern Society* (Cambridge, 2001), pp. 106–13.

the lowest assessment of ½d weekly. Indeed no one paid more than 2d weekly (about 8s a year) despite a top rate of 6d weekly, sanctioned by statute. During difficult years officials did not raise the assessments of existing ratepayers but instead chose to cause less offence to the more prosperous members of society by adding ratepayers at the lowest level. This meant, of course, that at times of shortage the burden of the rate fell more heavily on those who were actually less able to pay.[55] This pattern may point to the existence of a group who were normally able to survive without parish assistance, yet who lacked the surplus income to pay local rates. They could be called upon to help in times of crisis, but were likely to fall into poverty themselves.[56]

But administrative inertia seems to have bedevilled the rating system at St Martin's. Certainly, numbers paying the rate did not rise in line with population increase – indeed, they sometimes fell. In 1597–98, for example, only 193 households were assessed for the poor rate, the lowest number since 1580–81.[57] As a result, the income from the poor rate remained fairly static: between 1582 and 1597–98 the amount raised was a fairly constant £29 a year. This appears even less impressive if it is remembered that the later sixteenth century experienced price inflation of over 50 per cent.[58] The percentage of householders paying the rate continued to decline into the following century. While around 38 per cent of households were assessed for the poor rate in 1591,[59] by 1609 this rate had dropped to 35 per cent, shrinking by the 1620s to below 30 per cent, virtually the same level found in the relatively poor Boroughside area of Southwark in 1622. This 30 per cent level was considerably lower than the 67 per cent of householders who paid the rate in the 'socially mixed' parish of St Margaret Lothbury in 1624.[60] Not surprisingly, therefore, tax revenue at St Martin's failed to keep up with inflation or population increase. Although the parish's population trebled between 1603 and 1625, tax revenue only doubled – and this during a period when the percentage of poor in the population was probably rising.[61]

Despite these fundamental shortcomings, the parish's system underwent significant development after 1598. The poor law of 1598 abolished the previous maximum rate of assessment of 6d weekly, and the parish immediately took the opportunity (in tandem with a similar move in the City of London) to raise assessments significantly.

55 WAC, F304–324. In 1581, for example, when burials soared 48 per cent above the level of the previous year, officials responded by increasing the number of those assessed. All of these new ratepayers were brought in at the lowest assessment level. F308, n.f.

56 Cf. Boulton, pp. 115–16.

57 WAC, F324, ff. 1v–3v, 5v–7; F307, n.f.

58 WAC, F308–324; Archer, pp. 162–3.

59 WAC, F317, n.f. This is with a population estimate of approximately 2,260.

60 WAC, F335, n.f.; Boulton, pp. 115–16. Even so, St Martin's percentage was higher than that of St Margaret's: see below.

61 WAC, F329–352. This calculation does not take into account the further erosion of this income by inflation. WAC, F317, n.f.

Tax revenue soared, increasing threefold in a single year.[62] Of course, St Martin's had previously made little use of the upper assessment levels, but the new statute clearly encouraged local officials to think more systematically about its new, expanding gentry population as a source of income. Such a large-scale overhaul of the system was not repeated, but the parish did thenceforth attempt to tax members of the gentry at much higher levels. Indeed, it was the fact that the parish could now tax gentry residents at levels well in excess of the old maximum rate that may explain why the overall percentage of ratepayers was allowed to decline. In 1605, for example, the earl of Salisbury paid £4 a year and Sir Thomas Lake 52s a year.[63]

It is probably fair to say that St Martin's poor rate never realistically tapped the influx of wealthy gentry residents into the area in the early seventeenth century. Nevertheless, even if officials did not tax gentry residents sufficiently to keep tax revenue on a par with the rise in population, the assessments paid by gentry residents were still very important to the parish, and were exploited more efficiently after 1598. It is likely that many of the gentry thus targeted were part-time residents in the neighbourhood. Following the important legal precedent set by the 1589 Jeffrey case, the 1598 statute treated a non-resident occupier of lands as an inhabitant of the parish, and therefore liable to rating. Officials were now permitted to relieve the parish needy 'by taxation of every inhabitant or occupier of lands in the said parish in such competent sum & sums of mony as they shall think fitt'.[64] St Martin's, of course, attracted many courtiers, government officials and MPs with lands elsewhere. These were now subject to the poor rate. The impact of this can be seen by looking at a single year, 1605. In that year twenty-five knights and peers were assessed, only two of whom had paid under the old system, although many had contributed 'benevolences' previously. Their rates, totalling £35 7s, accounted for 34 per cent of all tax revenue. In other words, in 1605 7 per cent of St Martin's ratepayers accounted for a third of the overall income.[65]

But rating parishioners was only the first step. This potential income was not always easy to collect. In fact, there is evidence that officials faced increasing difficulties in collecting the rate from the late 1590s onwards. As early as 1605, the parish had obtained warrants to distrain the goods of debtors to the poor rate.[66] In 1613, officials referred to £43 19s 1d 'which wee could not collect', nearly 15 per cent of the total value of the amount assessed that year, while high levels of arrears marked the 1610s and 1620s, reaching a peak of nearly 24 per cent of the amount assessed in

62 WAC, F325, n.f.; Archer, p. 162. Rate income continued to rise, from £80 in 1598–99 to over £142 in 1605–6 (F332), £172 in 1615–16 (F342), and £312 in 1633–34 (F360), with the last amount raised from 1,079 ratepayers, although 12 per cent of ratepayers were in arrears to the tune of £48.

63 WAC, F335, n.f.

64 E. Cannan, *History of Local Rates in England* (1912), pp. 70–1.

65 WAC, F332, n.f.

66 WAC, F332, n.f.; F333, n.f.

1622.[67] From the late 1620s, the number of parishioners owing arrears was running at roughly 150 a year, but with the impact of plague in the mid-1630s the amount missing in arrears soared to over £300, owing from 638 individuals.[68]

Why were arrears so much of a problem for the parish? A disinclination to pay local rates was not, of course, uncommon in early modern society. But St Martin's officials saw the problem as lying with particular social groups, whose behaviour raised the question of just who was a parishioner and what responsibilities that entailed. One problematic group were clearly those individuals who owned fields and pastures in St Martin's parish but resided elsewhere. Officials had paid in 1605 for a special warrant to distrain 'for the poores money of the landholders'.[69] More problematic, however, were those members of the gentry and aristocracy who lived in St Martin's for only part of the year. The earl of Northampton, for example, figured more than once on lists of those paying arrears to the parish.[70] Mark Steward, a Hampshire MP, owned poor tenements in Covent Garden, many of which housed parish pensioners and those likely to seek relief from the parish. And yet, officials noted censoriously, 'he himself payeth not any thing at al[l] to the Relief of the poore'.[71] A 1595 book of presentment sent by St Martin's vestry to Lord Burghley suggests that the problem of dual residency had been recognized even earlier. The book was said to contain the names of 'gentlemen of account' residing in the parish, but having their livings elsewhere.[72]

Of course, difficulties in collecting the poor rate arose among ratepayers at both ends of the taxpaying spectrum. But the parish, not surprisingly, concentrated its efforts on those most able to pay. The significant percentage of poor-rate income that derived from local gentry and aristocracy made it all the more vital for St Martin's officials to chase up those who did not contribute. When the parish petitioned the Lord Keeper about 'divers great persons, who *refused* to pay to the relief of the poore' in the early 1630s,[73] this marked only the beginning of an endless series of petitions to the Privy Council for the recovery of arrears from aristocratic 'refusers to pay parish duetyes' throughout the decade.[74]

67 WAC, F340, n.f.; F349, n.f.; St Clement's officials paid for a warrant in June 1610 to pursue those who 'refuse to paye to the poore according to their cessments': WAC, B19, 1610–11, n.f.

68 WAC, F364.

69 WAC, F332, n.f.; F333, n.f.

70 E.g. WAC, F334, n.f.; F335, n.f.

71 WAC, F6039, f. 3. He seems to have resided at least occasionally in the parish. Ironically, Steward had sat on the committee that produced the 1598 poor law, although he appears not to have spoken on the subject: Hasler, *House of Commons*, s.n. Mark Steward.

72 Kitto, p. 573.

73 WAC, F358a (1631–32), f. 41.

74 Italics mine. F358a (1631–32), f. 40, F360 (1633–34), F363 (1636–37), n.f. Not long after, the parish of St Paul Covent Garden was carved out of St Martin's, thus depriving the mother parish of some of its wealthiest ratepayers: *CSPD 1640*, p. 344; *SL*, XXXVI, 53.

Non-payment of the poor rate at St Martin's was partly associated with a more general hostility towards new or unexpected taxes. The number of cases dating from the first decade of the seventeenth century suggests that the problem of dual residents was compounded by that of parishioners who may simply have found the unprecedented burden of taxation excessive. In 1604, the churchwardens found it necessary to send a list of names to the Lord Chancellor of those who refused to contribute voluntarily to the refurbishment of the church bells.[75] In 1607, the failure of 'obstinate & uncharitable persons' to contribute to the rebuilding of St Martin's church led to a rate being imposed upon the parish. In particular, St Martin's governors requested the 'authoritie to taxe and assesse all suche as are dwellers and *have howses in the said parish* that shall refuse to paye their proporcion with the rest'.[76] Here too, officials emphasized the problems posed by those who were not full-time residents. Any unusual form of taxation also seems to have encountered particular opposition. In 1612, collectors raising money to pave Drury Lane faced such hostility that the vestry agreed not only to defend them against any who tried to 'molest, trouble or impeead [*sic*]' them, but also to pay damages to the collectors, if necessary.[77]

St Martin's was not the only parish, of course, to run into problems over the poor rate. By 1608 St Margaret's churchwardens and overseers also complained of parishioners who refused to pay the poor rate, and they were authorized by JPs to distrain the goods of the defaulters if necessary.[78] But some inhabitants also complained to the JPs over what they saw as a rapid and unwarranted escalation of their rates.[79] For all the earlier precociousness and sophistication of St Margaret's rating system, however, revenue from compulsory rates there seldom represented even 50 per cent of income for the poor. The poor rate's relatively small yield at St Margaret's was partly linked to the small proportion of the population that was assessed for the rate – always a lower figure than that at St Martin's. This continued to be true even as the percentage of those assessed at St Martin's also dropped. In 1603–4, for example, almost the same number of parishioners were rated in St Margaret's as in St Martin's, despite the fact that at this time St Margaret's had twice St Martin's population. Indeed, St Martin's actually raised more money from their poor rate in this year than St Margaret's did.[80] Accordingly, at St Margaret's various forms of charity constituted the bulk of the parish's receipts for the poor.

75 WAC, F2001, f. 43.

76 Italics mine. WAM 57269.

77 WAC, F2001, f. 76. See also above, ch. 6.

78 WAM 9348.

79 See the example of John Thompson, who complained that he had lived in Westminster for two years and that, while he was first rated at 2s a year (the rate of his predecessor in the same house), the rate had subsequently risen to 4s and then 8s by early 1635: LMA, WJ/SR (NS) 41/22.

80 Parish registers suggest a population around this time of roughly 6,370 in St Margaret's and 2,950 in St Martin's. St Margaret's rated 317 householders (18.9 per cent) and St Martin's 304 (39.1 per cent).

PATTERNS OF CHARITY: THE LIVING AND THE DEAD

The introduction of compulsory rates was the most important single new development in early modern poor relief. Nevertheless, charity continued to play a major role in supporting the needy. This was true in early modern London, but especially true of early modern Westminster.[81] Both St Margaret's and St Martin's continued to rely on charity to assist their efforts to relieve the local poor. Nevertheless, this generalization hides important differences. The extent to which the two parishes relied on charity, and the forms of charity that predominated in each parish, differed significantly. In general terms, St Margaret's continued to be more reliant on charity than was St Martin's. In addition, by the seventeenth century St Martin's depended more on the charity of the living, while St Margaret's relied on the charity left behind by the dead. These trends partly reflected the social composition and cohesiveness of these parishes, but, as we will see, it seems that parish officials themselves were aware of these patterns and may have acted in ways that reinforced them.

The importance of charity to parochial finances was always highest at St Margaret's. The charity or 'benevolences' of men and women, living and dead, continually represented a significant percentage of the parish's poor receipts. In a plague year such as 1596–97 the percentage contribution was even more remarkable: all revenue for the poor totalled £257 7s, of which nearly £222 fell into the category of benevolences.[82] Not surprisingly, charity generally rose in line with the number of burials and, to a much lesser extent, with price increases.[83] But it is notable that even as the parish's population soared and poor-rate receipts rose through the first four decades of the seventeenth century, the parish's income from charity kept pace with the changes, so that the poor rate rarely, if ever, amounted to 50 per cent of the parish's overall receipts for poor relief. St Martin's also depended on charity to cover the costs of poor relief; it was not until 1605 that St Martin's poor rate alone even met the cost of the weekly pensions paid by the parish. Nevertheless, while officials relied on the charitable donations of St Martin's parishioners to make up the difference, they were never very considerable.[84] In the years from 1574 to 1590, benevolences in St Martin's averaged only about 27 per cent of receipts, while even during the more difficult decade of the 1590s they rose only to approximately 46 per cent. The 1590s totals were exceptional. During the Jacobean period, if the plague epidemics of 1603 and 1625 are excluded, the level of benevolences hovered at around 17 per cent of all receipts, and this pattern did not change to any great extent in the 1630s.[85]

81 Archer, p. 178; Archer, 'The charity of early modern Londoners', *Transactions of the Royal Historical Society* 6th ser. 12 (2002).

82 WAC, E147, ff. 6v, 8v–9v.

83 I owe the latter point to Dr Archer.

84 WAC, F335, n.f.

85 WAC, F301–352, F3345. Collections taken at the church door from 1609, which were administered separately by the vestry, would raise the overall levels of benevolences by nearly 20 per cent.

To explain this disparity in charity between the parishes we need to study the charitable donations in more detail, looking first at charitable 'benevolences' donated by living men and women, and then at bequests to the poor, made available after a testator's death.

At St Margaret's, large and regular gifts from just a few institutions and individuals accounted for the lion's share of the charity it received and these gifts contributed significantly to overall resources available to the poor. The Westminster dean and chapter, as we have seen, regularly provided weekly alms in the form of forty dishes of meat, forty loaves of bread and 40d in money – an annual benevolence that was valued at £34 13s 4d. Along with gifts from the royal almoner (which could amount to as much as £4 in 1574), other contributions to the local poor came from branches of government bureaucracy operating within St Margaret's parish (including the justices of the Common Pleas and King's Bench and the barons of the Exchequer), and from the Lord Mayor of London and the mayor of Oxford when they came to Westminster to be sworn in office.[86] In the seventeenth century, St Margaret's increasing role as the parish church of the House of Commons also meant that the parish was able to secure large donations towards the parish poor whenever the Commons met there for communion or on fast days.[87]

While institutional benefactions helped to boost revenue for relief of poverty, it was individual benefactors who were the crucial source of charity in St Margaret's. While there were many small donors, a number of the nobility made very substantial contributions. Among individual benefactors to St Margaret's poor, Lord Burghley and Lady Dacre towered above all others. Both gave one-off benevolences but also established more regular donations.[88] In the case of Lord Burghley, it was partly in his capacity as high steward of Westminster that he presented St Margaret's with a yearly benevolence. This consisted of sufficient bread and beef to feed seventy-four poor people, the alms being distributed jointly by the collectors for the poor and the bailiff

---

Collections are itemized in the churchwardens' accounts. The Caroline period shows a similar pattern. Although benevolences surged in the plague year of 1636–37, and with a resident parliament in 1640–41, they remained only a fraction of the amount received from rates, and until the 1630s the sum from benevolences was still less than that received at monthly communions (F353–367).

86 E.g. WAC, E147, 1590–91, f. 21v; E150, 1610, ff. 12–13. Several exchequer officials were St Margaret's vestrymen. Cf. also the benevolences of New Inn, Clement's Inn and Lyon's Inn to St Clement Danes: WAC, B19, B21.

87 See e.g. WAC, E152 (1625–26), f. 16; E16, f. 15v. The parish did not necessarily have direct control over these moneys, however: the 1628–29 churchwardens' accounts note that £28 10s proceeds of the Commons fast paid to Thomas Morice by the Committee of the Commons were to be distributed according to the Committee's direction (E16, f. 29). St Margaret's also presumably benefited from the poor box in the House of Lords that was filled with the forfeits paid by lords who arrived late (i.e. after prayers) in the chamber or were absent without excuse: *LJ* II, 401 (penalties for late attendance ran at 2s for an earl, and 12d for every other lord).

88 WAC, E145–147.

of Westminster.[89] As well as one-off benevolences of as much as £11 10s, Lady Dacre also left a substantial bequest to found almshouses for the local poor.[90] Lady Dacre's mother, the Marchioness of Winchester, also seems to have been generous on a similarly grand scale. In 1583 alone Lady Winchester gave £35 10s to be spent on the poor, while in 1585 she paid 30s weekly to a group of forty parish pensioners.[91] As general revenue rose – with the overseers regularly managing revenue of over £500 by the 1630s – an individual benefaction did not have the same proportionate impact, but collectively benevolences still made a decisive contribution, and one-off gifts were occasionally large. Lord Paget, who lived in Dean's Yard, made an anonymous gift of £200 to poor 'hospital' children (which was wisely invested and provided an annual sum in interest payments).[92]

At St Martin's, as we have seen, benevolences from its parishioners accounted for a much smaller percentage of receipts available to the poor. Bearing in mind St Martin's problems in collecting the poor rate among the aristocracy, it is striking that the most frequent and generous gifts to the poor tended to come not from the most wealthy or aristocratic residents but from parishioners who were regularly in residence, attended the parish church, and had links with local officials. Nevertheless, many such individuals belonged to gentry families. Members of the Cooke family, especially Anne Cooke (Lady Bacon) and her brother William (a St Martin's vestryman), were noted for their generosity. The death of William Cooke was sadly minuted in the collectors' book, where he was lauded as a gentleman who was 'very liberall unto ye poore as by ye recorde here remayning may appeare'.[93] Most of those residing in large townhouses along the Strand, such as the earls of Bedford, could also be relied upon for charity, although none matched the scale of a Lady Dacre. Those holding the office of lord keeper of the Privy Seal seem also to have contributed generously to the parish, presumably because most lord keepers occupied York House, which was located in St Martin's parish.[94]

The same contrasting patterns of donations between St Martin's and St Margaret's may also be observed if we study bequests. At St Margaret's, many of these donations took the form of funeral doles, which could amount to significant sums in a given

89 WAC, E146 (1588–89), f. 33. Larger numbers of poor might sometimes receive the doles, such as the 120 in January 1573 (E145 (1572–73), f. 8v).

90 E146 (1588–89), f. 32 and see below.

91 WAC, E146 (1583–84), f. 31; (1585–86), f. 38; (1588–89), f. 32. Lady Winchester's grandfather Sir John Brydges (a lord mayor of London) had operated an innovative scheme for poor relief in London in the early sixteenth century. For Brydges (Brugge) see Archer, p. 179.

92 WAC, E16, f. 30.

93 WAC, F316, f. 3v. Other regular parish benefactors included Henry McWilliam (a gentleman of the Privy Chamber), Lady Cheke, John Stanhope (later Lord Stanhope, a privy councillor), Sir Francis Knollys, Sir William Knollys and the earl of Rutland.

94 WAC, F323, f. 14; F324, f. 8v; F2001, f. 30.

year. In 1620–21, for example, sums distributed in bread or cash at funerals amounted to nearly £60 – almost a quarter of the income for the poor (excluding rates) that was received that year, and nearly twice the amount collected at parish communions.[95] But more important were larger formal bequests made by testators. Again, St Margaret's seems to have been much more effective than St Martin's in attracting such bequests. A steady stream of cash bequests flowed in to the parish, such as the £100 bequeathed to St Margaret's poor by the duchess of Richmond in the late 1630s. But other more elaborate bequests were increasingly in evidence. Sometimes this took the form of rental income. St Margaret's had possessed some landed income as a result of bequests to the poor before the Reformation, but, while virtually all of this was later confiscated since it was tied to chantry lands, the parish soon began to benefit from further lands left to the poor. In 1554, for example, the shoemaker Richard Castell left the poor of St Margaret's £6 yearly, issuing from various lands and tenements.[96] As early as the 1570s, St Margaret's testators were introducing sophisticated schemes for the poor such as almshouses, loan schemes and stocks for items such as firewood. In 1576, for example, Thomas Newnyns left money to establish a stock for the poor to work on, while around the same, Cornelius van Dun, a former yeoman of the guard, left money for almshouses.[97] More generally, the property portfolio of St Margaret's was enlarged throughout the period, and by the early 1640s parish officials were busy collecting revenues for the poor from properties as far afield as Barking to the manor of Albury, Surrey.[98] It is these bequests which helped to sustain the remarkably high levels of charitable donations evident in St Margaret's throughout the pre-Civil-War period. In a very real sense, then, St Margaret's was reliant on the charity of the dead.

By contrast, at St Martin's bequests began to play a significant role in poor relief only at the end of the sixteenth century. The parish received its first known rental income for the poor only in 1595, at the death of the vestryman John Colbrand, the Queen's Master Carpenter, who bequeathed 20s a year to St Martin's poor from his tenement 'The Owl', located in Westminster.[99] Similarly, it was only from about 1600 that testators began to establish more elaborate schemes to benefit the needy, such as interest-free loans.[100] The new century witnessed a gradual rise in the number, value and sophistication of bequests. Nevertheless, despite its increasing gentry population, St Martin's never attracted the number of large bequests that were common in

---

95 E.g. WAC, E151 (1620–21), ff. 33–6.

96 WAC, E145 (1576–77), f. 22v; *Parochial Charities of Westminster, First Report of the Trustees* (Westminster, 1890), pp. 27–8.

97 WAC, E145 (1576–77), f. 23v. In 1578, a certain Mr Patenson left £42 to the parish which was to be kept 'untill the same may be bestowed upon somme good bargaine as a lease . . . which may yeelde an yerely rente to the poore'. WAC, E145 (1578–79), ff. 26, 39v.

98 WAC, E23 (1641–42), n.f.; E24 (1642–44), f. 4.

99 WAC, F322, f. 8; F345, n.f.

100 E.g. WAC, F2, vol. 1, f. 117.

St Margaret's. It is also notable that funeral doles never seem to have been as prominent at St Martin's as they were at St Margaret's.

The role of parish officials in soliciting and administering charitable donations may partly explain these different patterns of charity. Some of the institutional charity directed towards St Margaret's, for example, may reflect astute manoeuvring by parish officials. The yearly benevolences given by branches of government bureaucracy, for example, seem to have originated as donations from individual office-holders, many of whom lived within the parish. Over time, however, they gradually became established as regular donations from the collective body of office-holders, which may represent prompting from St Margaret's officials.[101] St Margaret's seems also to have been adept at creating institutions that could attract substantial donations and channel private charity towards specific groups. Most notable here was the founding by parishioners in the 1620s of a hospital, which later became the King Charles School in Tothill Fields.[102] The hospital may have been established initially to cater for orphans left by the 1625 plague, but it was already receiving substantial bequests from noblemen and even the House of Lords by the late 1620s.[103] Its acquisition of royal letters patent in 1633 clinched the parish's ambition to make the school a favoured target for benevolences. Such 'benevolences' seem to have been actively encouraged by parish officials and they presided over a system that involved the attendance of the hospital children at the burials of benefactors. This soon took place so frequently as to suggest that it was virtually compulsory for the well-to-do.[104]

St Margaret's also excelled in the meticulous care devoted to the administration of charitable donations. Thus when the duchess of Richmond bequeathed £100 to the poor of the parish in the late 1630s, St Margaret's officials oversaw the distribution of this amount to no fewer than 1,137 poor people, every one of them named and listed in a book signed by the vestry and burgesses, a copy of which was presented to the duchess's executors.[105] Even a small donation of £10 from the future Secretary Edward Nicholas generated a careful list of 136 named recipients, specifying in each case their place of residence and occasionally their particular needs, which was presented to the donor.[106]

The precision with which St Margaret's officials recorded seemingly every funeral dole, from the Elizabethan period onwards, also of course reflects the concern of officials to ensure that these sums were distributed to the 'worthy' poor, and so reinforced the criteria behind parish-based relief. This would be in keeping with the practice of a number of St Margaret's parishioners, who donated money to the poor during their

---

101 Merritt thesis, pp. 288–9.

102 *Parochial Charities*, p. 46.

103 WAC, E16, f. 30; WAC, E16, f. 15v.

104 WAC, E19 (1634), ff. 19r–v, 24r–v.

105 WAC, E21 (1639–40), ff. 124, 126.

106 TNA, SP16/365/69.

lives, but sometimes insisted on specifically naming suitable recipients. Such a closely directed and discriminating form of charity suggests a certain familiarity with the poverty of their neighbours, possibly related to the more crowded conditions of the parish.[107] But it may also suggest a certain inflexibility, and even a hostility towards non-traditional or newer residents in the area.

St Martin's officials do not seem to have replicated the extraordinary charity machine that we can see at work at St Margaret's. By the Jacobean period, however, the parish does seem to have taken a more assertive role. The construction of parish-run almshouses at St Martin's c.1604, for example, was mainly facilitated by a series of carefully targeted bequests which must represent a degree of parochial orchestration. Thomas Evans, the Lord Chancellor's messenger for thirty years, left £100 towards the building of a parish almshouse, while Nicholas Fraunces, a French servant of the earl of Bedford, and Richard Woodlocke, a haberdasher and St Martin's vestryman, each bequeathed £10 towards the building of one room in the new almshouses.[108]

Nevertheless, as we have emphasized, St Martin's did not attract the same number or size of benevolences and bequests that funded St Margaret's poor relief effort. There are many possible reasons for this disparity. It is true that St Margaret's was a more religiously conservative parish than St Martin's, but charitable donations did not necessarily come from the most religiously conservative parishioners, as the case of Lady Dacre, a prominent benefactor of the puritan foundation of Emmanuel College, Cambridge, attests. If parish officials themselves influenced patterns of giving, this may simply have reflected the tendency to follow established parish practice, which had developed at an earlier date than at the more recently urbanized St Martin's.[109] Patterns of charity at St Martin's, by contrast, seem to highlight social differences between the two parishes. Despite the fashionable social profile of St Martin's, it seems clear that officials generally believed its gentlemen residents to possess relatively shallow links to the parish. Such individuals might not live long in the parish and were likely to buried in the country, where they had family links and potentially other charitable obligations. Thus, most bequests to the poor of St Martin's during the Jacobean period came from local, middling-rank residents. Whatever the precise reason, given the parish's lack of St Margaret's traditions of paternalistic relief or the sophistication of St Margaret's property portfolio, St Martin's instead made far more systematic and effective use of a rate-based system.

But not all charitable giving to the poor in Westminster passed through the hands of parish authorities. Private charity may have been vital in helping the poor to make ends meet, and could also reflect a sense of communal obligation that bypassed parochial

107 E.g. WAC, E145 (1578–79), f. 25v.

108 WAC, F2, vol. 1, ff. 35, 190; W.K. Jordan, *The Charities of London, 1480–1660* (1960), p. 147.

109 For a discussion of measures taken by parliament to encourage private charitable schemes see J. Kent, 'Social attitudes of Members of Parliament 1590–1624' (London Ph.D., 1971), pp. 80–5.

structures. Of course, charity distributed privately by individuals is nebulous and unquantifiable. It might be the aid that one neighbour gave to another, or it might be food or alms distributed at the doors of great noble households. Obviously, the Westminster parishes benefited more regularly from this latter kind of charity than did other parishes in the metropolis. Most nobles would have given alms on a more casual basis, as well as contributing to the more organized relief administered by the parish. The first earl of Salisbury, for example, presented St Martin's parish with a regular benevolence. But his charity also reached the poor through other channels. The earl's messengers, for example, regularly distributed alms as they rode through the parish on their way to their master's country residence at Hatfield. Indeed, the poor seem to have congregated at gateways leading through Covent Garden, waiting for the earl's liveried servants to ride by.[110]

Parochial charity in Westminster thus provides a study in contrasts. St Margaret's appears to have run a more traditional system based on personal charity, with large numbers of donors and bequests and the continuing popularity of funeral doles. More fundamentally, despite all of the benevolences received from individuals and institutions, St Margaret's was still crucially reliant on the contribution of the dead. St Martin's, by contrast, was dependent on the living, and her officials devoted their energies to ensuring the effective running of the poor-rate system. Charitable giving in St Martin's therefore appears to have been less personalized, and more directed towards the collection of funds to enable the parish authorities to deal flexibly with a larger and more diverse range of poor people. Nevertheless, the parishes were alike in witnessing parish officers playing an increasingly active role in administering and controlling charitable provision in the area.

RECIPIENTS OF RELIEF

But what of the poor themselves – who were they, and what was their experience of the town and its relief? Although popular conceptions of the poor often viewed them as a single constant category within society, the reality was considerably more complex, with individuals slipping in and out of poverty throughout their lives.[111] The experience of poor men, women and children in Westminster varied considerably, from poor unskilled immigrants who arrived destitute in the capital, to unemployed servants or agricultural workers scraping a living or suddenly labouring under some

---

110 For example, on 13 April 1607, one messenger gave 2s 6d to the poor as he rode between London and Theobalds: BL, Salisbury MSS, Bills 18. Lady Winchester ensured that her generosity was properly directed when she arranged for her household steward to distribute her alms jointly with St Margaret's collectors for the poor: WAC, E145 (1577), f. 7.

111 Cf. T. Wales, 'Poverty, poor relief and the life-cycle: some evidence from seventeenth-century Norfolk' in R.M. Smith (ed.), *Land, Kinship and Life-cycle* (Cambridge, 1985), pp. 351–404.

misfortune. The ups and downs of uncertain employment or a downturn in the economy did not merely affect living conditions. Less often noted is the psychological impact of poverty, which proved too much for some. Thomas Wood was a long-standing resident of St Martin's, where he had remained very poor, 'being a drayman to Croffts of Ebrew [Ebury] Farm', but, when he became too ill to work, he grew so depressed that he ultimately hanged himself.[112]

Those who received formal poor relief from parishes formed only a tiny proportion of those whom even parish officials would have considered poor. It is clear, however, that the authorities dispensing relief in Westminster were aware of how easily men and women might be catapulted into extreme poverty. For this reason, parishes made relatively frequent one-off payments to individuals who might otherwise become a long-term burden on the parish. Motives here were undoubtedly financial, but there is no reason to think that they were seen as cynical. When Roger Davis, 'a poor waterman', lost his boat, St Margaret's parish paid 20s towards the cost of a new boat, presumably because otherwise he would have been destitute.[113] Imprisonment, or even small fines, might be enough to drive people into debt, and it is notable that in these cases both St Martin's and St Margaret's officials were sufficiently attuned to the danger that they moved to pre-empt it, paying or returning fines or lending money to those in trouble.[114] Similarly, in 1637, Westminster JPs argued against the demolition of seven illegally constructed cottages in Long Acre, on the grounds that they were inhabited 'by persons of very poore and meane Condicion, who . . . have bene ancient inhabitants in the parish' and who 'would be likely to lye in the Streetes, or at the least to fall to the Charge of the parish' if they were to be ejected. Despite their 'poore and meane Condicion' and 'Charge of wives and children', the commissioners still noted that 'they are now able to live upon their Trades [they included a carpenter, a cobbler, a baker, a sawyer, and two gardeners] in some reasonable manner'.[115] As this example illustrates, however, the men and women who received this sort of consideration were normally more long-standing parishioners, possessed of a good reputation.

Life-cyclical events, such as births and deaths, often tipped men and women into poverty and of course were also likely to bring individuals into contact with the parish. At both St Martin's and St Margaret's, payments to 'childbed women' were not uncommon. Such payments seem to have paid the lying-in costs of poor women, and some may have compensated for the woman's temporary removal from paid work.[116] Women also suffered disproportionately from the death of a spouse, and in Westminster as

---

112 LMA, WJ/SR (NS) 29/9.

113 WAC, E23 (1640–41).

114 For example, poor victuallers who agreed to reform themselves after being fined for defective measures had their fines returned to them by the St Margaret's churchwardens because of their poverty: WAC, E16 (1629), f. 40v (cf. f. 31v).

115 TNA, SP16/370/35.

116 E.g. WAC, F343, n.f.; F345, n.f.; E151 (1619–20), f. 32v (1620–21), f. 49.

elsewhere in England, parishes tended to devote the majority of their resources towards their relief. Many of these women were elderly, but parishes in Westminster also paid younger widows to care for their own children.[117] The possibility of falling into poverty in old age haunted many in the early modern period.[118] In Westminster, even individuals with quite modest resources might seek to arrange some provision for themselves as they grew older. One Margaret Goulde, for example, made an arrangement with John Glassington, governor of Knightsbridge Hospital, whereby she would live her remaining days at the hospital and be supplied with meat, drink and laundry facilities, on the condition that she would leave her possessions to the hospital on her death, 'and accordinglie [she] forthwith brought one carre loden with beddinge brasse pewter and other utensills of reasonable good Value'.[119]

Although some men and women teetered on the brink of poverty and might hope to receive an occasional payment from their parish, there were others whose poverty required more systematic relief. In Westminster, as elsewhere, the distinction between the worthy and unworthy poor was the mainstay of the system of poor relief. Those who were thought deserving of charity fell into categories defined as much by parliamentary statute as local standards – widows, orphans, the elderly and lame, and blind or sick persons.[120] The able-bodied poor could generally expect little systematic relief. Expenditure in all the Westminster parishes was divided between weekly pensions for these 'impotent' persons and occasional payments for the 'extraordinary' poor – the latter granted cash sums according to the discretion of the vestry or overseers for the poor, as we have seen.[121]

The typical pensioner, in Westminster as elsewhere, was female, often an elderly widow. In 1606, for example, forty of St Martin's forty-three pensioners were women.[122] The payment of such pensions could swallow up 75 per cent or more of all parish poor receipts.[123] Although many pensions were effectively paid for life (mostly in the case of the elderly), it is important to recognize that some men and women

---

117 E.g. WAC, F350. n.f.; E150 (1615–16), f. 24v; E153 (1630–31, 1631–32. 1632–33, n.f.). Cf. Archer, p. 157.

118 Cf. C. Schen, 'Strategies of poor aged women and widows in sixteenth-century London' in L. Botelho and P. Thane (eds.), *Women and Ageing in British Society Since 1500* (Harlow, 2001).

119 TNA, REQ2/213/21. Cf. the bargain proposed by Mr and Mrs Noble: WAC, F2001, f. 183A.

120 39 Eliz. I. c. 3. section i permitted cash payments to the 'lame, impotent, old [and] blind'. These categories are reiterated in the overseers' accounts for St Martin's: see WAC, F308, n.f.

121 A comparison of the names of parish pensioners with those receiving a portion of private gifts donated to the parish poor shows little overlap between the two groups: see TNA, SP16/365/69 (list of St Margaret's poor receiving the gift of Edward Nicholas); WAC, F363 (list of twenty-eight individuals receiving portions of the 20s benevolence from the duchess of Buckingham in St Martin's in September 1636).

122 E.g. WAC, F310, f. 11; F332, n.f.

123 In 1606, for example, pensions cost the parish £132 16s 6d for fifty-nine individuals, out of total expenditure of £153 4d: WAC, F333. In 1616, out of a total expenditure of £254 nearly £200 was spent on pensions, with an additional £20 spent on 'necessaries' for the parish orphans: F342, n.f.

became 'pensioners' only for a period of weeks or months.[124] This might represent the time needed to recover from an illness, while widows could lose their pensions on remarrying.[125] In both the parishes of St Martin's and St Margaret's, pensions clearly underwent regular review. In practice, despite the substantial overall cost to parishes, the situation of those who received weekly pensions from the parish could still remain precarious. Indeed, amounts paid to pensioners tended to cover only a portion of their expenses. In 1603, St Martin's pensioners were said to have paid annual rents ranging from 20s to 40s, yet the average pension during this period only amounted to approximately 12d weekly or 52s a year. Yet the 'pauper budget' devised by Dr Archer for the mid-1590s estimates total expenses excluding rent, at between 65s 3d a year and 87s a year for a non-working widow. If rent is estimated at the lower end of the scale known to be paid by St Martin's pensioners (at 20s a year), then a solitary widow still needed to find between 33s and 55s a year from other sources to make ends meet, even after receiving her pension.[126] Those who were lucky enough to be allocated a place in the parish almshouses, however, may have fared rather better. The case of Joan Barton, one of St Martin's almswomen, is probably exceptional. Nevertheless, that fact that her apparel, food and lodgings were provided for her, in addition to her years receiving a share of gifts divided among the poor at funerals, ultimately enabled her to accumulate the sizeable sum of £50.[127]

But Barton's unusual example should not suggest that most who benefited from charity – whether pensioners or not – enjoyed easy circumstances. Most of those recognized by the parish as the 'worthy' poor supplemented their income by piecing together a living from various sources. They nursed parish foundlings, washed the church linen or served in relatively lowly offices, such as that of sexton. At St Margaret's, for example, one Father Maddockes received 8s a year for washing the dishes used when the dean and chapter distributed food to the poor in the Abbey church, while Robert Chapman earned the same amount by 'setting the people in order at the almes and the calling of them'.[128] Indeed, it is striking how many of the parochial tasks relating to the 'management' of the poor were undertaken by the poor themselves: in St Margaret's, poor women were paid 'for carrying the Almesbaskettes about the towne to gather the broken meat for ye town poore in ye Coreccion howse'.[129]

---

124 For some examples of how the value of pensions might vary over a single pauper's life see J. Boulton, ' "The most visible poor in England"? Constructing pauper biographies in early modern Westminster', *Westminster History Review* 1 (1997), p. 14.

125 WAC, F2001, f. 149; Boulton, 'Visible poor', p. 14.

126 WAC, F6039; Archer, pp. 194–5. The variation in figures derives from the two different budgets constructed by Dr Archer, one for a 'standard' budget and the other for a 'saver' budget. In 1612, an almswoman of St Margaret's, said to be 'one that lived by the Almes of the Parish', paid 30s a year for her chamber in the house of a cobbler: WAC, WCB2, f. 47. For poor relief as income supplement see Boulton, pp. 95–7.

127 TNA, C2/Jas I/S25/42. I hope to deal with this case in more detail elsewhere.

128 WAC, E145 (1572–73), f. 12v.

129 WAC, E19 (1634), f. 23; also in 1633–34, n.f.; and cf. E21 (1638–39), ff. 75, 77.

The only group whose full costs were routinely met by parishes were the parish orphans. In 1606 St Martin's parish supported fourteen orphans, each of whom received a pension of approximately 10d per week, while by 1622, the number had increased to twenty-nine.[130] Numbers of orphans supported by the parish do not appear to have increased in proportion to population – suggesting that the parish avoided assuming this burden whenever possible. Even plague epidemics resulted in only a small increase in numbers, except in 1636, when numbers soared from sixty-four to 122.[131] Some orphans received hornbooks and primers, while a few lucky children (apparently orphans of known parishioners rather than foundlings) attended school.[132] Others were paid to serve apprenticeships, some in the fashionable trades characteristic of the area (thus one instrument-maker in St Martin's was paid £4 for taking on a parish orphan as an apprentice for twelve years).[133] As we have seen, in the 1620s St Margaret's embarked upon an impressive long-term scheme for orphans when it established a hospital, which received royal letters patent in 1633.[134] Its royal status seems to have helped the foundation attract frequent generous benevolences. For the 'hospital children', as they were termed, the most unusual feature of their lives must have been the constant round of funerals they attended, a favour granted to those who promised a legacy to the institution which supported them.[135]

Other parochially based institutions impinged on the lives of certain poor people in Westminster. Those most favoured might obtain a place in parish almshouses, but poor men and women who breached social convention could be detained in houses for those deemed to be morally deficient, if not actually criminal. In the grim conditions of houses of correction it was clearly not unusual for inmates to wear leg manacles.[136] They could also be obliged to work in order to ease the costs of running the house.[137] A house of correction known as the 'Rounde howse' was functioning at St Margaret's by the early 1570s, and seems to have focused its energies on unmarried mothers. At St Martin's, a similar house of correction was built at the same time as the parish almshouses, around

---

130 WAC, F332, n.f.; F348, n.f.

131 See below.

132 In 1607, for example, the St Martin's overseers of the poor paid 16s to the unfortunately named Mr Thicknesse, for schooling a certain Mathias Getley for one year: WAC, F342, n.f.; F333, n.f.

133 WAC, E354 (1627–28).

134 *Parochial Charities*, p. 46; WAC, 1656/125. The governors of the school were all St Margaret's vestrymen: see WAC, 1656/1. The parish supplied everything, from their smocks, shoes and hornbooks to the special 'diett drinke' of herbs and spices that fortified the children in the spring: WAC, E15 (1626–27); E15 (1627), f. 39; E21 (1638–39), ff. 80–81.

135 E.g. WAC, E19 (1634), ff. 19r–v, 44. Surviving accounts of the school date from 1641: WAC, 1656/1.

136 See LMA, WJ/SR (NS) 51/19 (14 March 1638). For the diet of inmates see WAC, E20 (1636–38), n.f.; E21 (1638–39), f. 76.

137 Note the various proposals for this in 1618–23: LMA, MJ/SBR/3, f. 11.

1604.[138] By 1622, St Margaret's parish decided to build a new house of correction in Tothill Fields, which included a mill where the idle poor could be put to work. Its orders seem to have been modelled on those of London's Bridewell and other neighbouring houses of correction (and indeed by the 1640s parish accounts even referred to it as 'Bridewell').[139]

Even among the 'virtuous' poor, the distribution of relief partly served to emphasize their duties of deference and submission to those in authority. This was particularly true for those living in almshouses, where inmates were theoretically subject to draconian regulations. A single breach of the rules of the almshouses founded in St Margaret's parish on the bequest of Lady Dacre could cost the offender as much as one month's pension or lead to expulsion. Penalties fell upon all those who blasphemed, uttered uncharitable speeches or were found eating or drinking in an alehouse (unless working nearby). Each member of the community was also required to engage in some form of manual labour suited to his or her ability.[140] Duties of deference might not always be paid, of course, and even those pensioners fortunate enough to end up in the almshouses did not necessarily have a very positive view of the overseers of the poor. In St Martin's parish, one Thomas Morton was accused of 'using evill speeches, first in a generall manner vizt A greate deale of money is given to the poore of the parishe but whatsoever becomes of it the poore are sure to have little enoughe'. He also compounded his offence by upbraiding Nicholas Reade, one of the overseers of the poor, 'with very evill wordes to his face touching the allowances to the poore'.[141] Not surprisingly, Morton's pension was suspended.

Those who received relief may also have found that, in doing so, they did more than accept a role in which their deference and good behaviour was required. In some ways the very identity of the recipient might be absorbed by that of the benefactor: parish accounts in St Margaret's routinely refer to 'Mrs Goddard's women', 'Mrs Inglish's women' and 'Mrs Hughes' women', implying that the individuals concerned were not merely relieved but were in a sense appropriated by a benefactor.[142] Badging served further to label the poor. Each almsperson or child in Lady Dacre's foundation was required to wear the hospital badge in order (as the regulations explained) that he

---

138 WAC, E144 (1570–71), n.f.; F2, vol. 1 ff. 35, 44; WCB1, f. 35.

139 WAC, E24 (1642–44), f. 16v. This new house of correction was actually shared by the two parishes, with St Martin's making a regular donation to its expenses. Churchwardens paid for the transcription of 'presidente[s] and orders' from houses of correction in Middlesex, Surrey and from London's Bridewell, in preparation for its opening: WAC, E13 (1622–23), ff. 14, 18v–19; (1624–25), f. 21v. These houses of correction were distinct from the Middlesex houses of correction, for which each Middlesex parish was assessed c.1615, as a result of legislation in 1610 (7 Jas I c. 4): *Middlesex County Records*, ed. J.C. Jeafferson (4 vols., 1886–92), II, 103; WAC, F342, 1615–16, n.f.

140 Smith, *Parochial Charities*, p. 66.

141 WAC, F2001, f. 155.

142 E15 (1626–27), f. 42.

or she might be 'descerned thereby', and parish almspeople in St Martin's were also required to wear brooches and badges.[143]

Ultimately, the experience of the poor in Westminster was crucially dependent on the ways in which they were viewed by the parochial authorities. Often they had to petition formally for relief, and yet even one-off payments were far from automatic.[144] The poor were not destitute of 'agency': petitioners could do their best to emphasize the criteria that most appealed to vestrymen – such as length of residence and good character. Relief was a face-to-face matter, and the reputations of some individual paupers were clearly well known, as evidenced by references to 'madde Madge' and 'Tobacco Besse' in the St Margaret's poor-rate records, and the 'Countesse of Lambeth' in the house of correction.[145] Reputation could be vital to a pauper's welfare: it quite literally formed a sort of 'currency' when dealing with officialdom and soliciting relief.[146] As we have seen, Westminster's Court of Burgesses and its associated ward system also placed particular importance on personal reputation and differentiating the legitimate resident from the unknown poor. Clearly some individuals put their 'case' before parish officials, requesting relief, but there seems to have been some expectation that overseers of the poor – perhaps via neighbours, or other local officials, such as burgesses – would also inform themselves of those in need. In 1608, St Martin's overseers for the poor recorded 12s paid 'in private to sundry poore Inhabitants . . . whose want cannot be hidden, and yet they forbeare to crave Relief publiquely as the most sorte doe'.[147] Such an example suggests both pity and approval on the part of parish officials and it emphasizes the extent to which the experience of the poor was ultimately dependent on the attitudes, fears and financial pressures of middling-rank parish administrators.

DISTRIBUTION OF RELIEF

Fundamental to the experience of the poor, as we have seen, were the attitudes and values of those who were entrusted with the distribution of poor relief. But the

---

143 Smith, *Parochial Charities*, p. 66; WAC, F341. Cf. Boulton, p. 148, and Boulton, 'Going on the parish: the parish pension and its meaning in the London suburbs, 1640–1724' in T. Hitchcock, P. King and P. Sharpe (eds.), *Chronicling Poverty: The Voices and Strategies of the English Poor 1640–1840* (Basingstoke, 1997), pp. 34–5. St Martin's orphans wore woollen 'suits' with the letters 'S.M.F.' embroidered on them (F363 (1636–37)).

144 E.g. WAC, F2001, ff. 131A, 145, 163A. In 1608, it was said that those seeking relief at St Martin's normally attended the weekly meeting when the overseers paid the parish pensioners, WAC, F335, n.f.

145 WAC, E145, 1578–79, f. 36v; F356 (1629–30); E20 (1636–38), n.f.

146 See also Hindle, 'Exhortation', pp. 114–17. On reputation more generally see L. Gowing, *Domestic Dangers* (Oxford, 1996), pp. 105–38; C.B. Herrup, 'Law and morality in seventeenth-century England', *P&P* 106 (1985); M. Ingram, *Church Courts, Sex and Marriage in England 1570–1640* (Cambridge, 1987).

147 WAC, F335, n.f.

behaviour of parish officials towards the poor was not a simple matter. Rather, as will be demonstrated, officials' behaviour could vary significantly, and reflected a complex interaction between the changing financial circumstances of the parish, on the one hand, and a mixture of varying attitudes towards the poor, viewed either as a group or as individuals, on the other.

Study of the behaviour of Westminster's parish officials reveals a more general process whereby, as the problem of poverty became more acute, so the parishes adopted a more rigorous attitude towards the criteria for relief. It is possible to map increasing fears of 'vagrancy', and a hardening of the already existing distinctions between the virtuous needy and the idle, vicious poor, which historians have observed in the Tudor period.[148] Such fears, and a desire to restrict the outlay involved, led the Westminster parishes to use residence more systematically as a crucial criterion to determine access to poor relief, and length of residence in particular could determine how far the community felt a responsibility to relieve an individual's poverty.[149] Fears of disorder and pressure on resources also led to a more systematic patrolling of the moral behaviour of the poor who received relief. Nevertheless, as we shall see, individual parish officials regularly deviated from such precisely articulated and restrictive policies, revealing a broader charitable impulse than we might have expected.

While a tightening of the criteria for poor relief is a familiar feature of the history of this period, Westminster is notable in that – just as we have observed in other aspects of parochial development – there would appear to have been something of a time-lag in the experience of the two parishes.[150] In St Margaret's, the pressure on resources and accompanying intensification of control seems to have been most evident in the 1580s. In St Martin's, the same pattern seems to have emerged only some thirty years later, in the 1610s. These patterns tally with what we know of population increase and the pattern of western suburban expansion during this period.

In St Margaret's, the new pressures are evident in a number of developments – from the establishment of the Court of Burgesses in 1585 to the new pewing regulations in the 1590s. They are most evident, however, in concerns about the behaviour of the immigrant poor. Such concerns were not new: as early as 1561 a proposal had been put forward to build a house of correction in Westminster in which the potential occupants – vagabonds and common strumpets – were painted in the blackest terms. The proposal warned that officials would be dealing with 'the most desperatest people of the earth, geuen to all spoyle and robery, and soch as will break from you & steale',

---

148 S. Brigden, 'Religion and social obligation in early sixteenth-century London', *P&P* 103 (1984), pp. 67–112; Slack, *Poverty and Policy*, ch. 2.

149 Parish records make it clear that length of residence was an important consideration in determining who received aid, although it is not known whether the Westminster parishes dictated a minimum period of residency before parishioners qualified for relief, as was the practice in some London parishes.

150 See above, ch. 4.

and therefore stocks and iron shackles would be necessary 'for the tamyng of the wylde and lewde persons'.[151] The preoccupation with specifically immigrant poor was also the main theme of a 1578 survey of inmates. In addition to quantifying the state of the problem, the survey may also have served to establish residency and therefore the right to apply for parish relief.[152]

It was in the 1580s that St Margaret's embarked on a vigorous campaign to expel vagrants from the parish, which resulted in the expulsion of about fifty vagrants per year. Even this was clearly just the tip of the iceberg, since the complicated business of resettlement seems to have only been employed towards a fraction of English migrants during this period.[153] Finally, the Court of Burgesses, established in 1585 largely through the influence of St Margaret's men, spent much of its energies in regulating inmates and taking bonds to ensure that new-comers did not burden the parish.[154]

While St Martin's presumably did expel the occasional vagrant during this period, there seems to have been little of the anxiety evident in St Margaret's parish. It was in the 1610s that concerns about the poor rose dramatically in St Martin's, and here the survival of reasonably full vestry minutes enables us to trace the changing treatment of the poor by parish officials in much more detail than is possible at St Margaret's. Here we see the same concerns over the immigrant poor and vagrants that were acute in St Margaret's in the 1580s. In the early Stuart period we first begin to find references in St Martin's parish records to the expulsion of 'maymed people' and sturdy beggars, and St Martin's undoubtedly experienced its share of the increasing numbers of vagrants in Westminster that were singled out for specific complaint by the Privy Council in the 1610s.[155] But, aside from fears of the immigrant poor, the parish also made a determined attempt to impose greater restrictions on those accredited parishioners who received relief, and to patrol their moral behaviour more strictly.

To begin with, St Martin's parish officials acted to limit the number of commitments that might involve the parish in long-term expenditure. This goal was openly acknowledged in parish records, where officials might emphasize that any sums given in relief were not due to the recipients 'of Right', and that the recipient should therefore promise 'to no more trouble the Vestry'.[156] As we have seen, parishes might also lend money or pay fines in order to pre-empt individuals and their families from

---

151 S.A. Peyton, 'The houses of correction at Maidstone and Westminster', *EHR* 42 (1927), pp. 258, 260. There is no evidence that this house was ever erected, although stocks of flax were retained by the parish to set the poor to work: WAC, E145 (1572–73), f. 8v; E146 (1583–84), f. 35.

152 WAM 25029; cf. Boulton, p. 221 and how the laws of settlement might encourage the poor to conceal themselves when they first came to a parish.

153 Slack, *Poverty and Policy*, p. 92; WAC, E146, 1581 (*sic*).

154 See above, ch. 7.

155 E.g. WAC, F2 vol. 2, ff. 284, 395; WCB1, p. 195; *APC 1615–16*, pp. 210–11, 695–6.

156 E.g. WAC, F2001, f. 163v.

becoming a burden on the local poor rate.[157] The Westminster parishes acted quickly to limit the large expenses imposed by orphans, who normally had all their expenses paid. Officials went to extraordinary lengths to locate next of kin, to apprentice children as soon as possible or to prevent the problem altogether by conveying pregnant women out of the parish, sometimes at night.[158] Parish officials also drew attention to the importance of residential criteria; one tailor received 2s 6d 'in the extremities of sicknes haveinge dwelt 11 yeares in this parishe', while by contrast in 1619 one Widow Spencer was denied 'houseromme' (presumably a place in the almshouses) 'in respect of her long absence out of the parishe'.[159]

Concerns over resources, and the consequent need to tighten the criteria for relief, are particularly evident in the new 'orders' for the poor drawn up by St Martin's vestry in 1622. The vestry formally expressed concern in the minute book over 'the multitude of poore people which daylie increase the charge of the parishe', and the new orders were directed to be painted on boards which were hung prominently in the church (given that many of the poor may not have been able to read, one can only assume that such a gesture was meant to give notice of their serious intent and perhaps to impress existing and future parish officials). The orders aimed to tighten up the procedures governing the distribution of poor relief. Constables were directed to enquire at least once a month 'in their severall wardes of all inmates undersitters and new commers into the parishe . . . to the end such abuses may be reformed and prevented'. Weekly pensions were to be reviewed once every quarter, when it would be decided 'who are fitt to be contynued or discharged', and overseers of the poor were not to increase the number of pensions without the consent of the vestry.[160]

These concerns coincided with renewed worries over the moral behaviour of the poor. Just one year previously, in 1621, St Martin's vestry went so far as to create a committee to watch over the behaviour of the almsfolk, 'examining their Conversations from tyme to tyme and Reforming their disorders'. This was to be accomplished by 'admonition, displacing or otherwise as in their discretions they shall think fitting'.[161] Those censured included Richard Sheppard, one of the beadles, 'for lodging two young

---

157 E.g. WAC, F341, n.f.

158 WAC, F345, 1618–19. Similarly, St Margaret's in 1636–37 paid four porters to carry a heavily pregnant woman out of the George Yard and into St Martin's parish (WAC, E20, 1636–37 payments). At St Margaret's, authorities required the fathers of illegitimate children to pay the lying-in costs of the women concerned and to take a bond to prevent the child from falling upon the parish (e.g. WAC, F343, n.f.; E151 (1619–20), f. 32v). When, in 1617, Thomas Jones, 'sometimes shoppkeeper in Brittaines Burse', secretly fled St Martin's with his new wife, abandoning his five young children, the churchwardens quickly sought out other relatives. The goods left behind by Jones were sold off 'by outcrye to the best values', and the sum passed on to the family in return for a bond to discharge the parish of any responsibility: WAC, F2001, f. 115; F347, n.f.

159 WAC, F341, n.f. See also F6039, f. 3; WAC, F2001, f. 131v.

160 WAC, F2001, ff. 162r–v.

161 *Ibid.*, f. 153; F2002, f. 34.

women in his chamber since his wifes decease'. The committee took away his staff and removed him from the office of beadle, although granting that he might 'redeem' himself in 'the favour of the Burgesses and vestrymen' and so be restored to office 'if it appeare he become a new man'.[162] Just a few years earlier, the parish had also placed stocks at the ends of Drury Lane and Ragged Row, streets where many of the poor lived.[163] Although 'good' behaviour, including following norms of social deference, had doubtless been expected from recipients of poor relief, the establishment of a formal committee to monitor the behaviour of those receiving the greatest benefit the parish had to bestow – a place in the almshouses – seems in keeping with an elite sense of contracting resources and a sterner attitude towards the poor evident from the early 1620s.

The same concerns over tightening the residential criteria for those receiving relief, and patrolling recipients' moral behaviour, are evident in St Margaret's, and also echo attitudes visible in some of the private forms of charity distributed in the parish. Thus, those granted a place in the almshouses established by Lady Dacre were expected to be over the age of fifty, already in receipt of poor relief and to have resided in the parish for at least three years. They were all to be 'honest and Godly poor aged men and women' who must have fallen into poverty 'without there [*sic*] own default', through such traditionally recognized means as illness, robbery or fire.[164] The regulations also sought to ensure the Christian virtue of the almspeople, by stipulating that only those who could say the Lord's Prayer, the Ten Commandments and 'the Articles of the Christian beliefe' were to be admitted. No almsperson was to be an 'enemy' of the gospel or of established religion. The regulations went on the exclude swearers, adulterers, fornicators, thieves, hedge-breakers, scolds and drunkards.[165] Similarly, Lord Keeper Egerton specified that his benevolence of Christmas 1597 should go only to 'poore adged and Impotent housholders' and none to 'any common begger in the streetes nor feildes'.[166] Generally, charitable bequests were organized and distributed by parish officials, and it was they who would decide who were its appropriate recipients, but there seems no reason to doubt that they would have shared the concerns of donors.

The moves in St Martin's resemble strategies employed by parishes in London as early as the 1580s when increasing poverty created more difficult conditions. Their overall significance may rest more in the desire to formalize procedures than in any novelty in attitudes. By the 1630s both St Martin's and St Margaret's can be seen to

---

162 WAC, F2001, ff. 155–156. Sheppard was allowed to retain his pension and lodging 'uppon the tryall of his amendment' (f. 156). The burgesses were probably mentioned in relation to his office as beadle.

163 For the poor in Ragged Row see WAC, F343, n.f.

164 *Parochial Charities*, pp. 63–4.

165 *Ibid.*, p. 64; cf. Boulton, pp. 93, 143–4.

166 Bodl., Rawlinson MS D.406, f. 188v.

be operating tightened-up systems of poor relief, and harsher distinctions between 'deserving' and 'undeserving' poor. By this period both parishes operated workhouses where the moral imperative of work seems to have been as important as any money that these institutions might generate.[167] In the later 1630s St Margaret's spent no less than £242 on a major scheme for setting the 'Towne poore to work', including the purchase of seventeen spinning wheels and reels and nearly 3,000 pounds of hemp.[168] Hundreds of vagrants were also ejected by Westminster JPs in sustained drives in 1631 and 1639.[169]

Despite measures designed to restrict relief and to discipline the poor, by the early Stuart period there is every indication that the problem of poor relief had slipped beyond the authorities' control. It would be easy to represent changes in St Martin's as merely reflecting a mounting burden on the system of relief, but the reality was probably somewhat more complex. Throughout the late 1610s and 1620s, for example, the overseers' accounts always ran a healthy surplus (perhaps prompting the pensioner Thomas Morton's scepticism about what happened to the money). Also, numbers of parish pensioners at St Martin's only doubled during the Jacobean period, even though the population seems to have trebled. It seems likely that parish officials no longer tried to keep pace with the growth in either population or poverty, concentrating instead upon those they could effectively relieve. In a similar fashion, the numbers admitted to London's Bridewell stabilized during the 1610s, not because poverty was less severe but because officials abandoned efforts to keep up with the scale of the problem. Even payments funded from collections at the door of St Martin's church were spread more thinly. In 1616, £10 had been distributed in the form of eighty-four payments to poor individuals. By 1624, £12 14s now sufficed to relieve 220 poor people.[170]

The insistence on residential criteria, concern at incurring future obligations, and the concentration of efforts on those whom the parish felt able to relieve effectively helped to create a strange combination of relatively generous charity and brutal rejection. Thus in the year 1618–19 St Martin's recorded payments for conveying a pregnant woman and orphans out of the parish, while also paying out £55 to approved orphans in the same year.[171]

Despite these observations, it would be a serious distortion to depict the distribution of poor relief in early modern Westminster as being motivated solely by the grudging and coercive instincts of social control, and hostility towards outsiders. On the contrary, it is clear that the parish authorities were still capable of responding charitably towards the needy regardless of their residential status or the state of their

---

167 See WAC, E20 (1636–38), n.f.; F363 (1636–37).

168 WAC, E20 (1636–38), n.f. The poor were also taught how to thread beads: E19 (1634), f. 48.

169 TNA, SP16/189/48, 16/420/17.

170 Slack, *Poverty and Policy*, p. 71; WAC, F2, vol. 2, ff. 264–6, 427. These figures could vary considerably from year to year.

171 WAC, F345 (1618–19).

souls. While the treatment of the poor as a social category could be ruthless, parish officials could also respond directly and sympathetically to cases of individual need. It is St Martin's parish that provides the fullest evidence in this regard. It is striking that, even in a period of belt-tightening, Jacobean St Martin's allocated a portion of its resources to the destitute and homeless, apparently without regard to their parish of origin. By contrast, 'extraordinary', one-off payments at St Margaret's seem to have been restricted to known parishioners, to help them through a temporary crisis such as illness. These individuals would also have received aid at St Martin's. But typical 'extraordinary' expenses at St Martin's always included one-off payments to the destitute, such as on Easter's eve 1617, when the overseers distributed 4s 'to diverse poore people in the streete, being in greate want', while even beggars at the church door sometimes received alms.[172] It may be significant that overseers served in office only for one year. The emotive language used in accounts and occasional tussles with the vestry over expenditure suggest that some overseers may have been less hardened to poverty when personally confronted with it and more open-handed than long-standing parish officials, such as vestrymen.

One-off payments to the destitute are readily apparent, then, and the overseers' accounts often draw particular attention to the evident distress of these recipients, noting if they were 'crynge' or found in ditches. Such descriptions present these poor in a light more pitiable than threatening, appealing to criteria beyond those of the 'idle' and 'undeserving' poor.[173] Such Christian imperatives were reinforced from the parish pulpit. Robert Hill, St Martin's charismatic parish lecturer, composed a catechism in the early Jacobean period dedicated to his St Martin's parishioners, which dealt in some detail with questions of practical piety. Hill not only explained that a portion of an individual's goods should go to the poor, but also emphasized the dignity of the poor: his readers should not 'contemne such as are in povertie' nor should they give 'to the poor with reproching them'. That being said, Hill did seek to convey more subtle distinctions and imperatives. Like many clerics, Hill tried to strike a balance between encouraging charitable giving more generally while also suggesting that those who led Christian lives deserved special consideration. A portion of one's goods should go to the poor, Hill maintained, although one had a particular duty to one's kindred. But God's elect merited special treatment, and parishioners were reminded that 'especially I must give to the godly'. This view was mirrored in discussion of the Sabbath. After attending divine service, the Christian should ideally visit any 'comfortles' and furnish aid where it was needed. But once again Hill returned to provision for the elect, and directed readers to provide 'something which I may distribute to the necessity of the saintes'.[174]

---

172 WAC, F343, n.f.

173 E.g. WAC, F301, f. 14.

174 Hill, 'The Lord's Prayer Expounded' (1606), pp. 27, 33; 'A Christian Directed' (1606), pp. 18–19. Note also the discussion of the 1598 campaign for 'general hospitality', which implicitly disregarded distinctions between 'deserving' and 'undeserving' poor, in S. Hindle, 'Dearth, fasting and alms: the campaign for general hospitality in late Elizabethan England', *P&P* 172 (2001).

A commitment to making particular contributions towards the godly in distress could override the parish's concern to restrict charitable giving to members of their own community. When Hill was acting as St Martin's lecturer, it is striking that, even as the parish's poor relief system came under increasing pressure, it developed a two-tier system of one-off payments that allowed the parish to extend aid to deserving strangers. The collections taken at the church door may have allowed officials and clerics alike to put into practice certain notions about the proper relationship between Christian charity and godliness. The records of how this money was spent consistently emphasize the worthiness of recipients even more than their need. Payments were made to a number of poor scholars and ministers, often at the request or recommendation either of St Martin's curate and later benefactor James Palmer, or the parish lecturer Robert Hill.[175] The parish also sometimes relied on certificates to help select deserving beneficiaries.[176]

These church-door collections are especially interesting in the light of comments made by Hill, which we have quoted earlier. It seems that Hill's views were here being put into practice by St Martin's vestrymen as they disposed of the church-door collections, providing some help for the completely destitute and particular aid to poor 'brethren'.[177] The link between what was preached in the church and donations to the parish is suggested also by the extent of charitable contributions received at sermons and when parishioners took communion. In the City of London it is known that those parishes that supported a popular lecturer tended to record higher collections from communion collections. At St Martin's too, communion collections during the tenure of Robert Hill (1602–13) averaged £16 a year, whereas in the previous decade they had hovered around £5 a year.[178]

---

175 WAC, F2, vol. 1, ff. 146–147, 161, 181. Palmer, the son of a well-to-do Westminster family, later founded almshouses and a free school in Westminster during his own lifetime: see Merritt thesis, p. 358. For Hill see below, ch. 9.

176 For example, the wardens gave 2s 6d to the widow Alice Wiborne, who was a suitor to the Lord Chancellor 'on behalfe of herselfe and 30 widdowes, and 25 fatherless children of the Priory in Norwich'. The wardens also responded to the terrible circumstances endured by one Nicholas Shrewsbury of Rexley, 'who had his house burnt by suddaine Tempest of thunder and lightning, and three children burnt and his wife lunaticke As appeared by certificat': WAC, F2, vol. 1, f. 161. These examples seem to refer to individuals who actually possessed charitable briefs, allowing collections in churches to be held on their behalf.

177 It is notable that another Westminster cleric, Henry Smith, lecturer at St Clement Danes during the 1580s and 1590s, drew attention to the plight of the poor and a new, harder attitude towards them. To those who objected that the poor man that they relieved might be an idler or an 'unthrift', he countered, 'let theyr bad deedes fall on their own necks, for if they perish for want, we are in danger of God's wrath for them'. Although alms-giving that merely permitted 'lewd' persons to continue their evil behaviour was 'very offensive', yet Smith argued that 'every commonwealth that letteth anie member in it to perish for hunger is unnaturall and an uncharitable commonwealth': Henry Smith, *The Poore Mans Teares* (1592), pp. 13–14, 18, 27.

178 Archer, p. 180; WAC, F329–340. Other reasons, such as perception of need and the size of the churchgoing population, may also be at work here.

Elite responses to the poor emerge from this study as anything but faceless and monolithic. They were shifting and multi-faceted, and were often mediated by parish officials who undoubtedly acted in a discriminating manner which could, nevertheless, entail some flexibility. The behaviour and reputation of those seeking relief was subject to careful scrutiny. Yet the changing availability of resources provides a vital chronological background to the interpretation of the behaviour of parish officials. Larger numbers of the poor meant increasing belt-tightening and a more rigorous implementation of residential and moral criteria in the distribution of relief. This was perhaps heightened by fears of disorder generated by the increasing visibility of the poor and destitute. As we shall see, however, by the seventeenth century it was the mounting impact of the plague that imposed the greatest strain on parishes and the poor relief system. It is in Westminster's experience during these crisis years that the politics of communal responsibility, and the values which underlay it, already evident in the organization of poor relief, are still more starkly revealed.

PLAGUE, POVERTY AND THE COMMUNITY

During the plague epidemic of 1625, it fell to Justice James Whitelocke to go to Westminster Hall to adjourn the Michaelmas law term. From his house in Buckinghamshire, where he had safely retired during the worst of the epidemic, he travelled towards the capital, stopping off at Hyde Park Corner. There,

> he and his Retinue dined on the Ground, with such Meat and Drink as they brought in the Coach with them, and afterwards he drove fast through the Streets, which were empty of People, and overgrown with Grass, to Westminster Hall: where . . . the Judge and his Company went straight to the King's Bench, adjourned the Court, returned to his Coach, and drove away presently out of Town.[179]

Whitelocke's account partly recaptures the devastating impact of plague on the locality: the bustling streets now eerily deserted, the flight of the law courts and parliament, and the hasty departure of the privileged elite. But this was no mere ghost town. Off the deserted streets through which Whitelocke rode, local society still struggled to function, even if largely behind closed doors. This included poor men and women who had little choice but to stay, others who weighed up the risks and still remained for business or personal reasons, and finally those who felt obliged to stay to carry out public duties.

THE CROWN AND ELITE RESPONSES TO PLAGUE

One of the themes of this chapter has been the increasingly sharp juxtaposition of Westminster as a courtly enclave and its position as a London suburb with a spiralling, poor

179 Bulstrode Whitelocke, *Memorials of the English Affairs* (1732), p. 2.

population. For this reason, any disease especially associated with the poor was bound to create particular tensions in the area. Contemporaries such as William Bullein, writing in the sixteenth century, had identified plague as a disease of the poor, while others noted its coincidence with the 'sluttish' conditions in which the poor lived and their often 'disordered' mode of life.[180] In reality, because plague was a disease carried by rats and fleas, those most vulnerable were indeed the poor, who lived in crowded tenements and possessed few changes of clothing. In the metropolis, poor immigrants and over-crowded conditions were increasingly found in the capital's expanding suburbs and it was these areas which came to suffer most severely during plague epidemics.[181] Westminster, like other suburban areas, also began to attract the immigrant poor in large numbers, many of whom lived in cramped conditions just streets away from their more fortunate fellow-parishioners.[182] Consequently, the linked problems of poverty and plague increasingly made themselves felt in Westminster, even if the area as a whole still fared better than the desperately poor parishes of London's north-eastern and southern suburbs.[183]

Not surprisingly, Westminster's experience of the plague was characterized by the heavy involvement of the Crown. As early as the Henrician period, the Crown had shown its concern with plague spreading to the royal court, when fear of contagious dead bodies on their way to burial had prompted it to alter parish boundaries near Whitehall.[184] Such sensitivity continued during Elizabeth's reign,[185] with William Cecil ordering the printing of plague regulations specifically for Westminster in March 1564, even though the epidemic of 1563 had been far more virulent in the parishes of the inner City. Over the next forty years, however, the pattern of epidemics reversed itself, with plague becoming most severe in the suburbs and less virulent in the City.[186] There was now even greater reason to fear the spread of the disease in Westminster, and by the early Stuart period these concerns prompted ever more activity on the part of authorities in the town, ranging from the Privy Council down to minor parish officials.

180 A. Wear, *Knowledge and Practice in English Medicine, 1550–1680* (Cambridge, 2000), p. 281.

181 *Ibid.* For other factors affecting mortality rates see J. Champion, 'Epidemics and the built environment in 1665' in J. Champion (ed.), *Epidemic Disease in London* (1993), pp. 35–52.

182 Power, 'The east and the west', pp. 170, 174–5.

183 With a crisis mortality ratio of 3.7 in 1625, the plague raged less fiercely in Westminster than in eastern parishes such as St Botolph Aldgate and St Botolph Bishopsgate, with combined ratios of 6.6. Nevertheless, the crisis mortality ratio for St Margaret's parish alone was 4.08, whereas the figure of 3.7 applied to the Westminster parishes overall: Slack, 'Metropolitan government', p. 63.

184 This follows other measures prompted by the appearance of plague in the capital, such as the introduction of bills of mortality: P. Slack, *The Impact of Plague in Tudor and Stuart England* (1985), pp. 148–9.

185 In 1577, Recorder Fleetwood of London undertook an inspection of the Savoy precinct and also the adjacent Westminster parishes, marching 'twice past with all the Constables between the Bars [i.e. Temple Bar in the Strand] and the Tiltyard in both Liberties, to see the Houses shut in'. The earl of Leicester also seems to have intervened: Strype, II.iv.104–5.

186 *Wyllyam Cecill knight, high steward of the citie of Westminster . . . To the baylyffe* (1564). Slack, 'Metropolitan government', pp. 62–3.

The close proximity of Westminster's plague-ridden poor to courtiers, lawyers and the denizens of fashionable society inevitably generated intense fears and easily exacerbated existing social divisions. Contemporaries assumed an intimate connection between plague, poverty and vagrancy, and thus with broader forms of disorder. Bowling alleys, taverns and poor housing might be associated with disorderly behaviour, but the fact that 'common people' resorted to them also branded them a plague risk.[187] These social tensions were partly obviated by the fact that Westminster's fashionable elite often fled at the first hint of plague. The ethics of flight and the limits of responsibility to friends and neighbours were hotly contested. Few objected to the sensible precaution whereby the schoolboys of Westminster school retired to the dean's house at Chiswick during plague epidemics. But when the dean himself, the famous Lancelot Andrewes, left Westminster during the 1603 plague, he attracted heavy criticism.[188] Wealthy residents were faced with a stark choice of whether to flee, or to restrict their social contacts to an absolute minimum. The gentry anxiously scanned the published bills of mortality, always half-poised to leave, and sizing up the risk involved in remaining in the capital. Once the signs of significant plague infestation were clear, gentry residents tended to leave for the country in large numbers. During the height of the 1636 plague epidemic parish officials remaining in St Martin's desperately petitioned the lord keeper to appoint some new JP to help them in their difficulties, 'the rest of the Justices beeing then out of Towne'.[189]

The Crown was itself concerned by the flight of local officials, not only because it might endanger the stability of the area around the Court but also because it might undermine the enforcement of other royal policies. In the 1630s, for example, the flight of the wealthy left the locality protesting that it was unable to pay Ship Money, while the Privy Council worried that recent orders against illegal building – always difficult to enforce – would more easily be infringed as the building commissioners fled.[190] But just as important was government anxiety that plague regulations might be disregarded – or indeed actively opposed – especially those orders which challenged normal social relations, such as quarantine. This placed a heavy burden on those local officials who remained. To some extent, the initiative of local officials was recognized by the very elite who fled. In the aftermath of the 1625 plague, St Martin's vestry received an official letter of commendation signed by Sir Francis Cottington and Sir Thomas Wilson, two courtly figures who also served as justices of the peace for Westminster.

187 E.g. *HMC Hatfield*, XV, 227–8.

188 Slack, *Impact*, pp. 234–6.

189 J.C. Robertson, 'Reckoning with London: interpreting the bills of mortality before John Graunt', *Urban History*, 23 (1996), pp. 339–42. WAC, F363 (1636–37), n.f. In 1636 the Westminster JP Robert Fenn described how the sessions ended so suddenly that he did not even have time to pass on details of recognizances to the clerk of the peace: LMA, WJ/SR (NS) 46/18.

190 *CSPD 1635–36*, p. 522; *CSPD 1637*, pp. 502, 505.

They acknowledged that during the time of the visitation 'few men of worth or quality were residinge with the saide parishe' and that many more would have died had not officials acted on their own authority, expending every penny of the parish stock – a sum of £560 which was now gradually being repaid. The letter, however, made a special point of praising the resourcefulness of officials in order to 'encourage' them 'if God sends a similar visitation'.[191]

Such praise highlights what was apparently growing concern that local authorities should remain in place to oversee plague measures. The dearth of magistrates in 1636 led the Privy Council to order in 1637 that half of the Westminster burgesses should always reside in the town, and in 1638 the lax enforcement of plague orders in St Margaret's parish led to another stern Privy Council directive requiring the burgesses to execute their offices effectively or be punished.[192]

Throughout this period, then, Westminster's political significance, and the socially elevated character of many of its inhabitants, meant that Westminster was expected to act with especial vigilance towards plague. For this reason, the Westminster parishes were often in the vanguard in introducing policies intended to control the disease, including the use of pesthouses. In addition, the Westminster parishes also made far earlier and more systematic use of special plague rates to fight the disease than was the case in London.[193] In all these cases, the very absence of an overarching Westminster government seems to have prompted the Privy Council to chivvy Westminster's parishes into forms of regulation that were more difficult to compel in London. Nevertheless, these policies were themselves controversial and still remained inadequate to the scale of the problem that plague epidemics represented.

QUARANTINE AND THE COMMUNITY

'O but my friendes will not come at me . . . alas, I shall want my solemne funerall' exclaims a fictitious parishioner in a work composed by St Martin's lecturer Robert Hill, which included a discussion of plague.[194] Hill knew what he was talking about – he had remained in St Martin's during the 1603 plague epidemic, taking refuge in the house of one of its vestrymen. In the catechism that he dedicated to his parishioners in 1606, Hill devoted a portion of the work to the thorny moral questions posed by the

---

191 WAC, F2002, f. 60. This sum represented only a portion of what was spent in plague-related expenses.

192 TNA, PC2/48, p. 123; 2/49, pp. 351–2. The Privy Council was particularly alarmed by the 'want of keepinge Close the Pesthouses, and disposing and distributinge the monies to bee expended amongst the visited, as also by permitting those that are shutt up in theire houses to goe abroade amongst others . . . through the want of watchmen to attend att the severall houses and places infected'.

193 See below. For a more detailed comparison of the response to plague in London and Westminster see Merritt thesis, pp. 311–12.

194 Robert Hill, *The Pathway to Prayer and Pietie* (1613), pp. 146–7.

disease and his publication vividly recaptures the impact of plague upon notions of community and rites of passage.[195]

The issues and moral dilemmas discussed by Hill partly reflect those that we know from other sources worried contemporaries, and it should be emphasized that Hill's views clearly lent support to official regulations surrounding the plague. The question addressed at greatest length was the neighbourly – and indeed Christian – duty of visiting the sick, which plague orders necessarily disrupted. Here Hill set himself to answer a series of questions, which included the observation that 'many escape, who visit their friendes at such a time'. Other questions sought to explain why regulations needed to be followed if God had already determined who should live and who die: 'what needs all this, if you have a particular faith, that you shall not die of the plague: may you visit any for all this?'[196] The attendance of a minister at one's deathbed was another solace that was normally withdrawn at plague time, and Hill tackled this awkward issue in some detail.[197] Indeed plague epidemics posed a range of spiritual dangers, not the least of which were the efforts of Roman Catholic priests to effect conversions among lonely and distraught plague victims, a phenomenon that was reported in St Margaret's parish in the 1630s.[198] As we have seen, plague regulations also restricted normal funerals, but, despite the support for such measures provided by clerics such as Hill, men and women found it very difficult to abandon such important rites of passage. Westminster JPs were still complaining in 1630 of 'such fond persons as . . . would accompanie the Corpes', although they noted that the problem had declined.[199]

If neighbourly conduct was dangerous according to official plague regulations, so was the vein of fatalism that undoubtedly ran through the population at a time of such enormous and apparently arbitrary mortality. As we have seen, the questions which Robert Hill set himself to answer convey something of this simple fatalism, in both its optimistic and pessimistic guises.[200] Yet such fatalism received encouragement from a

---

195 Hill, *A Godly and Learned Exposition or the Commentarie upon the three first Chapters of the Revelation* (1607), ep. ded.; Hill, *Pathway*, ep. ded. The Pathway was originally published in 1606 under the title of *Christs Prayer Expounded*. In 1607, Hill added 'A Direction to Die Well' to this work, which included a discussion of plague. I have quoted from the 1613 edition of the *Pathway*, which is available in a modern facsimile edition.

196 Cf. 'yet for all your saying, my dayes are numbred, my death is appointed: If I shal[l] die of that disease, I cannot flie it by not visiting; if I shall not, I shall not die of it though I visite', Hill, *Pathway* (1613), 'A Direction to Die Well', pp. 142–4.

197 *Ibid.*, pp. 140–2. Hill does, however, make the significant exception that if he knew of a good Christian whose 'love to mee [were] unfained' who could find no comfort but from his presence, then 'using the best preservatives, before and after, which I could', he would visit such a man, though with the proviso that 'this is not an usuall thing' (*ibid.*, p. 142).

198 TNA, SP16/331/93.

199 TNA, SP16/175/3. Cf. Slack, 'Metropolitan', p. 75.

200 For medical optimism on plague as a curable disease see Wear, *Knowledge*, pp. 288–98.

later St Martin's parish lecturer, the radical John Everard, who attacked official prayers against the 1625 epidemic, including prayers for the King, as useless – mere toys for those too weak to accept the strong meat of divine providence.[201]

Behind the fear and fatalism that plague aroused, stood the demands of plague regulations and the most contentious policy of all – that of quarantine. Increasingly, it was in Westminster, more than any other part of the capital, that the imposition of quarantine consistently weighed most heavily. As early as 1564, for example, Westminster's plague orders had stipulated that infected houses should be completely isolated and closed for forty days, even though in adjacent London quarantine periods varied and inmates from infected houses in 1570 were still allowed out if they carried wands.[202] Far more striking, however, was the financial support provided for household isolation from 1603. In this year, both St Margaret's and St Martin's introduced a system of compulsory rates – a rarity in the metropolis where, amazingly, only two other parishes introduced a special plague levy before 1625.[203] In addition, some Westminster households continued to be isolated in the years following 1603, when plague continued at a lower level. Moving into the Caroline period, the sheer scale of measures taken against the plague in Westminster is staggering – and came in the wake of equally enormous numbers of fatalities, comparable to those found in a substantial provincial town. During a single week in August 1625, for example, St Margaret's parish paid pensions to nearly eight hundred individuals confined within their houses.[204] The intensity of these isolation measures seems to have increased steadily over the period, regardless of the actual severity of the outbreak: in St Martin's more people were quarantined in 1636 than in the much worse epidemic of 1625 – over the year as a whole 388 families comprising 1,328 people were incarcerated and supported.[205]

The experience of the poor and infected during plague epidemics was grim. As we shall see, organizing the quarantine system and administering its finances was left to parish officials. But it was poor men and women who filled those lowly and dangerous posts which actually brought them into regular direct contact with plague victims. Payments to searchers of dead bodies, bearers of corpses, waterbearers and gravediggers all marked the presence of plague in a parish. As early as 1603, St Margaret's required

---

201 TNA, SP16/41/73.

202 Slack, *Impact*, pp. 206, 208. Nevertheless, the 1585 Westminster Ordinances now seemed to allow one member of each infected household to leave the house long enough to buy supplies, Manchée, p. 219. For the gradual move towards complete isolation of infected households in London see Slack, 'Metropolitan', p. 66.

203 WAC, E149 (1603–4), ff. 16–21v, 58v, 59v; Kitto, p. 570; Slack, 'Metropolitan', pp. 69–70. More detailed records of plague rate expenditure survive for St Martin's only from 1625. No records survive to show whether a plague rate was imposed in St Clement Danes in 1603, but this seems likely.

204 WAC, E152, 1625–26, ff. 32–5v.

205 Slack, 'Metropolitan', p. 71, citing WAC, 4512, 4514, 4516, ff. 15v, 17.

those who came in regular contact with the infected to live in a special house in Tothill Fields, away from the built-up areas of the town, 'for that theye were allwaies endangered'.[206] Money collected by the parish went primarily to support those not permitted to leave their houses because of plague. Watchmen stood outside infected houses or were posted at the entrance to streets or alleys to prevent their inhabitants from escaping. Stout locks were fitted to doors, which were also to be marked with a red cross and papers bearing the inscription 'Lord have mercy upon us'.[207]

Although most plague victims were shut up within their own houses, from at least 1606 St Margaret's parish maintained a pesthouse in Tothill Fields, which was resurrected during subsequent epidemics.[208] Similarly, St Martin's parish operated pesthouses in the open spaces of Soho. These were not makeshift structures, but were created by converting tenements belonging to Sir Edward Wardour.[209] Pesthouses had long been recommended as the preferred means of isolating the sick. This was particularly urged by the Privy Council to the City and Middlesex in 1630, which proposed a ring of pesthouses to encircle London, stretching from Westminster to Greenwich. Before the 1630s London was served by only a single small pesthouse in St Giles Cripplegate.[210] While it has been observed that in London 'the new policy of pesthouses proved impractical', nevertheless in St Martin's in 1636–37 they seem to have been used fairly systematically, even if alongside, rather than instead of, household isolation. This outbreak was relatively mild, yet up to sixty-six people might be present in the pesthouses at one time – in 1637 this was often around two-thirds of the entire number of people quarantined at any one time.[211] Although pesthouses were probably intended for the poor, those placed there were not simply neglected. While 'the pesthouse' was used as a collective term, it is clear that it in fact consisted of a large number of individual houses built in 'the Pestfield' with chimneys, and supplied with sea-coal. A Book of Common Prayer with the relevant prayers was purchased 'to bee read at the Pesthouse to the poore Visited people'. Several searchers, nurses, bearers and doorkeepers were also based there. It was doubtless the low intensity of the plague outbreak of 1636–37 that made St Martin's use of pesthouses

---

206 WAC, E149 (1603–4), f. 42.

207 *Ibid.* (1603–4), ff. 29v, 55v. By contrast, weekly payments to infected households were rare in the metropolis before 1636, although orders promulgated in London in 1608 allowed for these: Slack, 'Metropolitan', p. 67. WAC, F2002, f. 82; *CSPD 1636–37*, p. 393.

208 WAC, E149 (1606–7), f. 39, (1625), ff. 50v, 53v. A 'matron' of the pesthouse is mentioned in 1625.

209 WAC, F2002, f. 89v.

210 Slack, *Impact*, pp. 214, 218.

211 Slack, *Impact*, pp. 217–18; Slack, 'Metropolitan', p. 71; WAC, F4514. It is difficult to provide accurate figures for the entire period – lists of those resident at the pesthouse date only from late January 1637, although it had clearly been in use for several months previously. It may be significant that one St Martin's resident was the court physician, Sir Theodore de Mayerne, who had urged King Charles in 1631 to avoid household quarantine in favour of a system of pesthouses.

feasible, but this nevertheless represented a significant advance on earlier provision. Men and women regularly survived to come out of the pesthouse, but these institutions clearly inspired fear: the Privy Council ordered that one John Cheek, a shoemaker of St Martin's Lane, was to be forced, if necessary, to leave his house with his wife and children and go the place allocated for them in the 'Pest Field'.[212]

For those who were locked up in what were labelled as infected houses, life could be even more bleak and quarantine difficult to endure. Maintaining quarantine also potentially threatened public order, as seems to have been the case in Westminster in 1603, when it was reported that the 'visited' of the town were increasingly unruly, tearing off the bills set upon their doors, and constraining townsmen 'to force them into their houses, which are infected'. In the circumstances, Westminster's high bailiff suggested to Robert Cecil that a proclamation was needed 'wherein some sharp punishment may be imposed corporally'.[213] In another instance a woman obviously suffering from plague not only broke out of quarantine but also caused consternation when she strode deliberately into Westminster Abbey.[214] Of course, many healthy people objected to a quarantine policy which divided family and friends, left the infected to the mercy of sometimes corrupt officials and shut up the sick with the healthy. Because fear and depression were believed to make individuals more susceptible to plague, the melancholy induced by long days of quarantine was another argument brought against it.[215] Westminster JPs complained of 'reprochfull speeches' and 'unseemelie speeches' used against them by residents when they shut up their neighbours' houses. Some inhabitants went further to defy the quarantine orders, occasionally with the collusion of doorkeepers, as was complained in St Martin's in 1630.[216] Clearly, some people broke out of quarantine during every epidemic.[217] Other inhabitants sought to pre-empt quarantine altogether by offering bribes to prevent the reporting of plague deaths. During the 1636 outbreak, Edith Plase and Frisweed Williams, both sworn searchers for the parish of St Martin's, confessed that they had received 'private rewards' to conceal plague deaths – a temptation that was probably difficult for these very poor women to resist. However, their relatively mild punishment – sitting in the stocks for three hours wearing a paper on their heads describing

212 WAC, F4514; *CSPD 1636–37*, p. 393.

213 *HMC Hatfield*, XIV, 189–90. The next year a parliamentary statute authorized the use of force against plague victims, Slack, *Impact*, p. 211.

214 Slack, 'Metropolitan', p. 73.

215 See A. Wear, 'Fear, anxiety and the plague in early modern England: religious and medical responses' in J. Hinnels, R. Porter and R. Sydney (eds.), *Religion, Health and Suffering* (1999), pp. 339–63.

216 TNA, SP16/175/3.

217 In 1630, St Margaret's officials recorded payments to two journeymen shoemakers living in St Stephen's Alley 'from the time they were shutt upp till they runn awaye', WAC, E153, 1630 plague rate, n.f.

the offence – may well reflect the difficulty of finding people who were willing to undertake the job of examining corpses.[218]

Plague also tipped both the healthy and the sick into poverty. The policy of quarantine bore especially heavily upon the poor, who were also more vulnerable to infection. Given that those who were shut up tended to be poorer to begin with, it is not surprising that the 'poor visited' became increasingly destitute during the period of their quarantine. Over 88 per cent of people quarantined in St Martin's in the week of 11–18 September 1636, for example, were wholly dependent on the parish for sustenance.[219] One attempt to address this problem was made in 1636, however, when St Martin's parish took the unusual step of establishing a scheme whereby 257 of the 'poor visited' were paid to spin flax and hemp 'in the tyme of their great necessity'.[220]

The plague was thus a very regular feature of life in early Stuart Westminster. While it is impossible to assess the degree to which effective quarantine was imposed, nevertheless there does seem to be evidence that it was implemented in a increasingly systematic, regulated and strictly monitored way.[221] Given the social divisiveness of the policy, the absence of significant unrest is all the more remarkable.

Part of the reason for this may lie in the fact that the Westminster authorities confronted directly the need for substantial relief to be provided to the quarantined poor during epidemics. This would, however, place an enormous financial and administrative burden on parishes, as we shall see.

THE FINANCIAL IMPACT OF PLAGUE

Because so much of the surviving material connected to Westminster's experience of the plague was generated by the administrative response to it, it is important to remember the larger context of economic hardship that accompanied plague. Just earning a living became a struggle when so much of the economy was virtually frozen. During plague epidemics all the law courts operating within Westminster Hall moved out of the capital, and with them the many suitors whose money would normally have been spent on food, drink, clothing and all the luxuries sold within the town. Similarly the Court took up residence outside the capital, as did parliament

218 LMA, WS/M/40. St Martin's usually employed a maximum of only three searchers during the outbreak of 1636–37: see WAC, F4514. On women searchers see R. Munkhoff, 'Searchers of the dead: authority, marginality and the interpretation of plague in England 1574–1665', *Gender and History*, 11 (1999), pp. 1–29.

219 WAC, F4514, n.f.

220 WAC, F363 (1636–37), n.f.; F3358. Payments for materials needed for spinning may indicate a similar scheme at St Margaret's in the same year. In the City a work scheme operated at St Andrew by the Wardrobe in 1636: Slack, *Impact*, p. 189.

221 Thanks to conciliar intervention, household quarantine was also enforced more rigorously than before in the City in 1630 and 1636: Slack, *Impact*, p. 219.

if it was in session.[222] Local fairs, such as St James's Fair, were also banned, to prevent the spread of disease.[223] For those near the breadline, the plague regulations could inflict additional hardship even on those who remained uninfected. One Richard Lea admitted that he had broken the order which prohibited the slaughter of animals near St Clement's Well during the epidemic, but pleaded he had acted only to relieve his wife and children.[224] Others risked the consequences of ignoring further restrictions, such as the man prosecuted for crying out pots and glasses in the street 'contrary to Proclamation' and the poor tailor who walked the streets selling the remnants of old cloaks and other clothing.[225]

Plague was also an enormous financial and administrative problem, as well as a human tragedy. The costs associated with plague were enormous, although it is only in the seventeenth century that we begin to be able to evaluate the impact upon local government, which in Westminster meant its individual parishes. There is also reason to think that the burden increased in the early Stuart period. In part, this reflected worsening levels of plague in the area, as well as a more widespread and costly system of quarantine. More surprising, perhaps, is the extent to which the Westminster parishes suffered financially not just during the better known epidemic years (1603, 1625, 1630 and 1636) but also for extended periods of time in between, when plague measures continued to be a drain upon financial resources – and hence upon local ratepayers. For this reason, as we shall see, the plague rate became a staple feature of life for early Stuart residents of the town.

We have already suggested that policy towards the plague was not identical in Westminster and London. The City fathers were slow to impose centralized policies in London, and especially resisted the compulsory taxation needed to meet the costs of plague regulation. Rates met opposition partly on the grounds that it was better to rely upon London's vast charitable resources. It has also been emphasized that the complexity of City government meant that rates faced opposition not only from the powerful lord mayor and aldermen but also from the many layers of its local government.[226] By contrast, the Crown not only had special concerns about the vicinity of the royal court but also seems to have expected to intervene in Westminster affairs, given the weakness of overall local government – and indeed locals periodically asked for assistance in times of crisis.[227] It was this situation, paradoxically, that made it simpler in

222 For the adjournment of the law courts see for example J. Larkin and P. Hughes (eds.), *Stuart Royal Proclamations* (2 vols., 1973–83), I, 56–60, 148–51, 230–2. Nevertheless, restraints placed on using sedan chairs during plague time (TNA, PC2/50, p. 283) suggest that some well-to-do people still remained during lesser outbreaks.

223 E.g. *Stuart Royal Proclamations*, I, 40–1.

224 *CSPD 1636–37*, p. 110.

225 LMA, WJ/SR (NS) 29, ff. 45, 47.

226 Slack, 'Metropolitan', p. 68.

227 *HMC Hatfield*, XV, 189–90, 227–8.

Westminster than in the City to impose the compulsory plague rates that were necessary to achieve the enforcement of plague regulations thought desirable by the Council.

It was in 1603 that the parishes of St Martin's and St Margaret's first took the then highly unusual step of imposing compulsory rates to help them support house-holds quarantined by the plague.[228] Both parishes had already collected money during the 1592–93 plague through a highly systematic form of weekly and monthly 'benevolences'.[229] When plague broke out in 1603, however, St Margaret's parishioners were rated by Westminster burgesses and Middlesex JPs, according to a warrant from the Privy Council dated 19 June. This produced a book of taxation listing those 'thoughte moste able to yeild reliefe to the visited persons', which was sent to the Council. These 176 households represented only a little over half the number that normally paid the poor rate.[230] In addition to a special plague rate, a normal poor rate was also collected for the year 1603–4, while benevolences worth £278 4s 6d were also recorded (an amount larger than that generated by the plague rate). But despite the money collected by poor rates and plague rates, St Margaret's still struggled to meet the costs of isolating infected households, caring for the sick and burying the dead. The flight of wealthier residents was one of many difficulties that impeded the immediate collec-tion of rates. Accordingly, the Privy Council also directed St Margaret's to borrow whatever money it needed to cover its expenses.[231] The years after the 1603 epidemic saw pressure continue on parish finances, since plague remained endemic in the capital as a whole between 1606 and 1610, with mortality rates between ten and twenty per cent above average.[232] In 1603, St Margaret's officials noted that the plague rate would continue 'until it should please God to stay the visitation'.[233] In practice this meant that its ratepayers paid a plague rate on top of a poor rate every year from 1603 to 1610.[234]

---

228 The City authorities resisted the introduction of compulsory plague rates throughout London until 1636. In 1625, it was the House of Lords (probably prompted by the Privy Council) that ordered the doubling of the normal poor rate in London and its suburbs: Slack, 'Metropolitan government', p. 70.

229 WAC, E147 (1593), ff. 7–10; Kitto, p. 583.

230 WAC, E149 (1603–4), ff. 16–17, 58v. This yielded £190 18s 11d. Misleadingly, the receipts are at one point described as 'voluntarily yielded a weekly contribution', but other evidence clearly points to a rate. By contrast, during a lesser outbreak in 1630 (when St Margaret's recorded only thirty plague deaths), the parish imposed a plague rate that included far larger numbers, but at much smaller assessments. Rates from 757 people yielded only about £50, and most of the money went on searchers, bearers and watchmen, with few payments to the infected themselves: WAC, E153 (1630 plague rate), n.f.

231 WAC, E149 (1603–4), f. 59v.

232 Slack, 'Metropolitan', p. 61.

233 WAC, E149 (1603–4), ff. 16, 43.

234 WAC, E149–150 (1603–10). The 1610 plague assessment in St Margaret's raised over £32 (E150, ff. 26–35). St Martin's parish recorded plague-related expenses in 1608–9 (F2, vol. 1, f. 108), although the first decade of the century saw a special plague rate levied only in 1603.

Administration of the plague rate created its own problems. During the plague epidemic of 1603, well-to-do dual residents simply refused to pay rates for the 'poor infected'.[235] The flight of wealthy residents also restricted the number of people available to pay the rate in this and other years. Although the flight of rich inhabitants during epidemics was a more general problem in England, this behaviour compounded what was already perceived to be the tendency of Westminster's gentry residents to avoid their parochial obligations. While St Martin's sought to deal with this problem by rating the inhabitants who had left town at twice the amount of those who remained, such money could not be recouped until well after the crisis was over. Moreover, some of Westminster's inhabitants who remained in the town seem also to have resisted plague rates. In St Martin's in 1625, Sir John Finet, future master of ceremonies to Charles I, paid his assessment, but recorded his protest in his own hand in the collectors' notebook. By the names of other refractory inhabitants, the collectors noted 'he refuseth, he liketh not this taxe'.[236] The motives behind refusal remain unclear – but may have ranged from opposition to the uncharitable policy of quarantine to a concern with the financial precedent.

That plague rates were insufficient to meet the costs of a major outbreak was revealed even more clearly in 1625. This may have reflected not simply the severity of the outbreak but also the fact that household isolation was more stringently enforced in 1625.[237] As the plague raged in the capital, St Martin's was quick to impose the doubling of the poor rate which Parliament itself authorized from its safe haven in Oxford. Yet, as we have seen, many parishioners resisted the rate. Although St Martin's acted to impose the tax far more swiftly than most parishes in the metropolis, their assessments are still dated 15 November, well after the plague had struck and the richer residents had fled. In the meantime, parish officials coped as best they could. The preamble to the written plague assessments justifies the rate, describing how 'the Ancientes' of St Martin's had borrowed and 'engaged themselves in bondes for the sommes of £300 and upwardes, and also for that the stock of the said parish is all expended'. The plague rate itself probably raised about £290, while the amount that the parish received in charitable contributions is impossible to estimate accurately. It seems clear, however, that private charity still played a significant role in parochial finances, and was important in bridging the gap between the decision to levy plague rates and the date of their collection.[238]

---

235 *HMC Hatfield*, XV, 189–90. A reference to collectors for houses visited by plague in the 1608–9 parish accounts may indicate that a plague rate was imposed also during at least part of the period 1606–10, when plague was endemic in the capital: WAC, F335, n.f.; Slack, 'Metropolitan', p. 61.

236 WAC, F3354.

237 WAC, E152 (1625–26), ff. 32–35v. Stricter quarantine was also observed in the City in 1625: Slack, 'Metropolitan', p. 66.

238 WAC, F3354, n.f. The figure for assessments is based on the £211 collected from the 'landside' part of the parish and an estimate for the 'waterside' based on the relative yield of the poor rate in

At St Margaret's, charity played an even more vital role than rates in meeting the needs of plague-stricken parishioners. In 1625 the parish recorded an impressive £663 in benevolences compared to the relatively paltry £121 collected in plague rates. Much of this charity, however, came from sources outside the parish. The Crown donated £100, but the crucial payment was one of £300 from a national collection for the relief of London and the suburbs.[239] This latter payment, however, was obtained only after St Margaret's vestry petitioned the House of Lords to receive some of the £1,000 raised by the nationwide collection, and the sum was given only with the stern proviso that Westminster (meaning St Margaret's) should be 'fully excluded' from any further relief.[240] In these circumstances, it is not surprising that St Margaret's parish still ran short of cash during the height of the epidemic, borrowing at least £117.[241]

The years after 1625 saw plague continuing to undermine parochial finances, even though the Caroline period never witnessed another epidemic as severe as that of 1625. Once again, it seems that rigorous enforcement of quarantine was partly to blame. During the less virulent plague of 1636, St Martin's, as we have seen, quarantined more people than during the more severe epidemic of 1625. At St Margaret's, however, the parish struggled to meet not only the costs of the 1636–37 outbreak but also similar expenses over the next two years.[242] As before, the Crown ultimately stepped in to help – donating £100 each to St Margaret's and St Martin's in December 1636.[243] But this, and other benevolences, were not enough to meet what became serious shortfalls in funding. By 1638–39 nearly £1,200 had been spent by St Margaret's officials 'for the use of the poor visited with the plague' over a period of nineteen months.[244] For St Martin's, the problems of parochial finance seem to have been particularly

---

previous years. Charity must have exceeded £150. Some benevolences are recorded in the church-wardens' accounts, WAC, F3, f. 23. Slack, 'Metropolitan', pp. 70, 72.

239 WAC, E152 (1625–26) ff. 10v–12v. The national collection was authorized by the House of Lords, and the bishop of London then distributed the money. Because collections took time, the Chamber seems to have advanced money to individual parishes: Slack, 'Metropolitan', pp. 70, 72. It was complained in parliament that very little of the money raised by the collection had gone to the suburbs. St Martin's and St Clement Danes were able to secure extra amounts of £20 and £25 16s respectively: *Proceedings in Parliament 1626*, ed. W. Bidwell and M. Jansson (4 vols., New Haven, 1991–96), I, 488.

240 *Proceedings in Parliament 1626*, I, 79, 150, 153–4, 206, 209, 314, 488.

241 WAC, E152 (1625–26 plague account), f. 12v. The parish had also been instructed by the Privy Council to borrow £100 to cover plague expenses in 1603–4: E149 (1603–4), f. 59v.

242 It is worth noting that more people died in St Margaret's during the single month of August 1625 than in the whole of 1636. Parish registers record 449 plague deaths in 1636, but a further 269 in 1637 and 96 in 1638 (45 of whom died in July), during which time the plague regulations had still to be enforced: TNA, PC2/49, pp. 351–2; A.M. Burke (ed.), *Memorials of St Margaret's Church Westminster* (1914), pp. x, 572–88.

243 WAC, E153 (1636–37); F363 (1636–37).

244 Slack, 'Metropolitan', p. 71; WAC, E152 (1625–26), ff. 32–35v. The figure for 1638–39 is noted in J.E. Smith, *A Catalogue of Westminster Records* (1900), p. 104. The relevant plague rate account was destroyed during the Second World War.

severe. Although the parish levied a combined plague and poor rate in 1636–37, yielding £629, its expenses that year totalled a staggering £1,406.[245] This included expenses in caring for poor orphans, the number of whom increased from sixty-four to 122, at a cost of £434 in 1636–37 alone.[246] Once again the parish relied on loans from parish notables: £390 from local residents, none of whom were gentry.[247]

The low background-level plague of the period 1637–39 is seldom noted by historians, but, if actual plague deaths were few, the costs of implementing plague regulations were nevertheless crippling for Westminster's parishes. In addition, the large charitable donations that poured in during major epidemics were not forthcoming in years of low-level plague. While the scale of poverty in Westminster made substantial demands on parishes, it was the occasional incidence of plague, and the threat of plague, which seems to have done the greatest damage to parochial finances. It is against this background, then, that one must understand the tightening controls on poor relief in Westminster, which drew ever larger distinctions between 'local' poor and poor outsiders, who were in any case believed to be major factors in the transmission of plague.

CONCLUSION

Poverty and plague inevitably heightened the questions of belonging and social responsibility, neighbourhood obligation and parochial identity, that always lurked in the background in early modern Westminster. These tensions, as we have seen, resulted from a complex interaction between different elements in Westminster society, from members of the courtly elite and middle-ranking parish officials to increasing numbers of poor men and women.

Westminster was distinctive in this particular concatenation of social groups. Of course, many aspects of its response to the poor were entirely conventional, with criteria such as length of residence and moral probity used to define those sections of the community entitled to aid. Nevertheless, the timing and implementation of such policies was crucially affected by the specific circumstances of the locality. Given contemporary fears of poverty and disease as interlinked threats, and the juxtaposition of rich and poor in the area, we would tend to expect that the local poor would experience a uniformly harsh and bureaucratically anonymous poor relief regime. But the unusually rich records of Westminster reveal significant variations and flexibility (not to say inconsistency) in the treatment of the poor. These variations underline the extent to which relief in this period still encompassed a significant face-to-face element and

---

245 WAC, F3358. In 1635–36, parishioners had paid £326 in poor rate, while expenditure on the poor had totalled around £583: F363, n.f.

246 WAC, F363, n.f.

247 *Ibid.* The lenders included the vestryman Simon Greene.

allowed officials to exercise considerable discretion. There was also a clear expectation that poor relief *should* reflect such face-to-face encounters. Finally, there is no doubt that the special circumstances of Westminster partly explain varying behaviour towards the poor, with elite fears partly balanced by the parishes' potential access to larger reserves of cash, be it from the Crown, aristocracy or middling-rank parish notables.

Provision for the poor of Westminster – especially in difficult years – was crucially dependent on the sometimes erratic contributions of Crown, gentry and aristocracy, contributions that were frequently mediated by parish officials anxious to ensure that these upper ranks of society contributed their share to relieve the local community. The danger lay in attitudes such as those later expressed by Edward Waterhouse in the early Restoration period. Waterhouse claimed that gentry families could live well in the capital, despite the high rents, since they were compensated by 'the little Hospitality' that one was obliged to keep.[248] Clearly some members of the gentry and aristocracy avoided charitable giving, while others may have preferred to dispense their own charity among the local poor, rather than placing money at the disposal of parishes. Of course, during times of plague a sense of fear might encourage gifts to the parish in order to support quarantine. More generally, however, local officials wished to evoke a sense of responsibility for the local poor, channelling charity via the parish, partly to ensure that this was distributed according to their own percep-tions of need. As we have seen, St Margaret's parish – despite the precociousness of its poor rate – ultimately depended on attracting large numbers of bequests as the basis of its income for the poor. By contrast, officials at St Martin's apparently calculated that they could not trust to the spontaneous sense of parochial obligation among its wealthiest parishioners, who might have shallower ties to the parish. Instead, the parish opted for a rigorous rating system, with all the associated struggles over arrears, combined with efforts to tap the charitable impulses of current residents before, rather than after, death. In both cases, there was a struggle to reaffirm a more general sense of communal responsibility and identity which would manifest itself in practical and financial terms. This was a struggle that intensified in the face of ever-increasing demands on paro-chial finances in the 1630s, strongly exacerbated by the costs that a more rigorous quarantine system imposed during plague years.

248 Edward Waterhouse, *The Gentleman's Monitor* (1665), p. 296.

Chapter 9

◆

Religious life and religious politics
c.1558–1640

EARLIER chapters have charted the many long-term changes to the social and cultural life of Westminster. Many of these changes, however, were played out against a background of substantial religious change, especially during the successive Tudor 'reformations'. The Elizabethan settlement marked the end of this series of revolutions in religious legislation, but the working out of its implications for the religious life of the area was to be a drawn-out and ambiguous affair, with very different consequences in the different Westminster parishes.

The accession of Elizabeth ultimately marked the end of established Catholicism in Westminster, symbolized by the final and permanent dissolution of the Abbey, now reconstituted as a collegiate church. The arrival and consolidation of Protestantism brought with it a number of new ideas about how religious life should be organized. These would have important implications for the corporate life and religious experience of Westminster's inhabitants. For many Protestants, the primacy of the Word implied a consequent downgrading of the importance attached to church decoration, rituals and processions in building and sustaining piety. But how far should parishes go in dismantling past structures, and building up new evangelical ones? As we will see, Westminster's parishes offer us examples of two very different responses to the Elizabethan settlement, and to the challenge of building and sustaining a religious community under Protestantism. For this reason, examining religious life in Westminster can help to shed important light more generally on the development of English Protestantism.

This chapter will also explore the interaction of religion with the social and political developments that we have observed in the post-Reformation town. For example, did the increasing gentrification of Westminster have an impact on forms of religious life? Did the church seek to minister to the spiritual needs of the growing numbers of the Westminster poor? And what impact did the Court and Abbey have on religious developments in the town? This chapter will also investigate whether the newly emergent parish oligarchies, who played such a decisive role in local government, also brought a distinctive religious agenda to their management of parochial affairs. And finally, given that the Westminster parishes stood at the heart of English government, we will consider how far religious life there became politicized in the years leading up to the Civil War.

St Martin's and the growth of Protestant lay activism

St Martin's emerged in this period as a parish with a vigorously Protestant evangelizing profile. This is far easier to document for the Jacobean period, but its origins are not difficult to discern even during the early days of Elizabeth. The parish effortlessly passed early tests of Elizabethan conformity, swiftly purchasing the necessary service books, displaying the Ten Commandments and (unlike the neighbouring St Margaret's) purchasing the Bishop's Bible when required.[1] To explain and analyse this development, we will begin by examining the role played by the parish clergy, then the emergence of a small godly elite among the most prominent parishioners, before finally examining the religious experience of the wider body of parishioners.

clergy and laity

Early Elizabethan parishioners at St Martin's would have listened to the sermons of their reinstated vicar, Robert Beste – not a Marian exile as such, but a man deprived for conducting English services during Mary's reign. Beste served St Martin's from 1558 until his death in 1572, and he must have conveyed a more enthusiastic sort of Protestantism than was to be found in many parts of the City of London, where thirty-six Marian priests were still in post at the end of 1560.[2] Certainly by the time of Beste's death there were frequent sermons in the parish, and donations to the poor were regularly made on these occasions.[3] The vicars who succeeded Beste were all university graduates, and by the end of the century these clerics were increasingly well connected to the universities and the Court. Beste's successor, William Welles, for example, was a domestic chaplain to Queen Elizabeth, and, although he stayed at St Martin's only for two years, his appointment suggests that the living of St Martin's was beginning to be seen as one worth obtaining.[4]

Well-educated and committed Protestant clergy undoubtedly were important to religious life in St Martin's, but they received encouragement from godly members of the laity. Many of these were clearly drawn from the middling sort. But it was during

---

1 Kitto, pp. 185, 190, 191, 255, 264, 264 n. 1.

2 Hennessey, p. 294; E. Mullins, 'The effects of the Marian and Elizabethan religious settlements upon the clergy of London 1553–1564' (London M.A., 1948), p. 212.

3 E.g. WAC, F301 et seq.

4 For individual clerics see Merritt thesis, pp. 331–2.

Elizabeth's reign that the parish began to attract increasing numbers of gentry residents, many of whom lent support to an evangelizing Protestantism. Most notable among such residents was that committed but judicious Protestant Sir Nicholas Bacon of Gorhambury, who occupied York House, near Charing Cross. Together with his wife (formerly Anne Cooke, sister-in-law to Lord Burghley) he attended sermons and received communion in St Martin's church, and baptized their son Francis there. Lady Bacon continued to act as one of the chief benefactors of the parish poor well after her husband's death and was widely known as a patron of godly clerics, including those whose zeal landed them in trouble with the authorities.[5] These gentry connections sometimes intersected more directly with parish officialdom, as in the case of William Cooke, who was not only Lady Bacon's brother but also a vestryman of St Martin's. This meant that the parish possessed a vestryman who had been a Marian exile and counted the puritan parliamentarian James Morice among his closest friends. We know little of how Cooke may have influenced parish religious policy, but his godly leanings are suggested in bequests in his will to the firmly Protestant Dutch and French stranger churches of London and his stipulation that his 1589 funeral in St Martin's church should be marked by a sermon from 'some godly learned preacher'.[6]

The desire for ever more godly preaching provides us with the first more explicit evidence of St Martin's Protestant laymen acting collectively. In 1600, a group of St Martin's parishioners, acting on behalf of the parish, wrote to Robert Cecil with a proposal to establish a lectureship. The petition tactfully but pointedly criticized the current vicar, Thomas Knight, whose advancing years and ill-health apparently left him unable to fulfil his duties – especially preaching – to the satisfaction of his more godly parishioners. Knight initially resisted the introduction of a lecturer, whose appointment might reflect on his learning or application, and the matter was a delicate one, given that Knight evidently enjoyed Cecil's patronage. It seems that the removal of Knight may also have been one of the petitioners' aims, and ultimately the old man exchanged his St Martin's living for one in Huntingdonshire 'of little chardge and more quietnesse'. The manner in which these changes took place is particularly interesting, for it highlights the depth of Cecil patronage in the area. Rather than writing to the bishop of London, who controlled the advowson and who might have seemed the natural mediator in such a case, both the petitioners and Knight himself wrote to Cecil, high steward of Westminster. The petitioners were careful to ask that the matter might be settled by three designated individuals – Dr Richard Webster (archdeacon of Middlesex and a Cecil appointee to the neighbouring vicarage of St Clement Danes), Thomas Bellot (former steward to Lord Burghley) and Walter Cope (one of Cecil's closest associates). Significantly, the petitioners emphasized the fitness of these men for the task, 'being persons for their qualities, sowndenes in religion &

---

5 Kitto, p. 190. E.g. WAC, F301 ff. 11, 23; P. Collinson, 'Sir Nicholas Bacon and the Elizabethan via media' in *Godly People: Essays on English Protestantism and Puritanism* (1983), pp. 146–51.

6 Hasler, *House of Commons*, s.n. William Cooke I; TNA, PCC, Prob. 11/74/97.

nearnes in dutie to your honor and your howse such as may (we hope) give best satisfaction to your honour thereof, and mediate a good settlement betweene Mr Knight ourselfes, the reste of the parishe and our desired preacher'.[7]

As a result of these manoeuvrings, St Martin's moved into the Jacobean period with two important clerics at its helm. In 1602, the parish acquired both a new vicar, Thomas Montford, and a lecturer, Robert Hill, who was said to preach 'by the assignment' of Dr Montford, although paid for by a group of parishioners, presumably including the original petitioners.[8] But Hill's talents as a preacher were not intended to prop up those of a dull careerist, for Montford himself was committed to frequent preaching and noted for his accomplished and learned sermons. Together Montford and Hill inaugurated a period of intensive religious mobilization in the parish. Montford's role was the more enduring one in that he served St Martin's parish for thirty years, until his death in 1633, and he played a central role in the religious politics of the parish. His background reveals a scholarly, cultured and urbane figure, but one who was sympathetic towards moderate puritans. With his love of music and impressive library, Montford might well have seemed the ideal cleric for the increasingly gentrified parish of St Martin's. In his cultural erudition he resembles another Westminster cleric of the period, John Layfield, the vicar of St Clement Danes, who translated the early books of the Old Testament for the King James Bible.[9]

It is worth examining Montford more closely, since his blend of solid conformity and sympathy for puritans may partly have protected the more radical puritan preachers who were often appointed to the parish lectureship in the early Stuart period. Montford started his career as a chaplain to Ambrose, earl of Warwick – a well-known patron of the godly – and he soon rose to prebendal stalls at Westminster (1585) and St Paul's Cathedral (1597). At the time of his appointment to St Martin's, Montford stood near the fringes of power, serving as chaplain in ordinary to the Queen, and he was sufficiently trusted by the government to be chosen to attend the imprisoned earl of Essex after his abortive rebellion in 1601, sending back regular reports of Essex's behaviour. Montford's name also appears on a short-list of proposed chaplains for the new monarch, James I, written in Archbishop Whitgift's hand, while he also acted as a licenser for the archbishop and served on High Commission.[10] All this points to

7 Hatfield House, Salisbury MSS, vols. 250/118, 80/26 (italics mine).

8 Robert Hill, *The Pathway to Prayer and Pietie* (1610), Preface. It seems likely that lecturers relied on the donations of wealthy parishioners to make up the largest part of their income. In 1623, for example, the 2nd earl of Salisbury paid £3 a year to 'Mr Andrews' the current St Martin's lecturer: *HMC Hatfield*, XXII, 138. See below for the religious views of individual petitioners.

9 Montford reportedly knew Hebrew, Greek, Latin, French, Italian and Spanish, while he was also said to be thoroughly familiar with ancient history as well as the Fathers: *Alumni Oxoniensis, 1500–1714*, ed. J. Foster (4 vols., Oxford, 1892), s.n. Thomas Montford; Anon., *Two Sermons* [Funeral sermons of Thomas Montford and his wife Elizabeth] (1632), pp. 49–50. *DNB*, s.n. John Layfield.

10 Anon., *Two Sermons*, p. 54; WAM, Muniment Book 15, ff. 4, 6; *HMC Hatfield*, XV, 224; Merritt thesis, pp. 335–6, 383.

Montford's conformity, but other aspects of his background suggest his sympathy with moderate puritanism. For example, he included the godly controversialist Andrew Willet among his friends, and backed the strongly puritan Robert Hill for St Martin's lectureship at a time when the latter had just emerged from a bruising doctrinal conflict with the future dean of St Paul's, the proto-Arminian John Overall. Montford's Calvinist views are also clear: he was the dedicatee of an anti-Arminian sermon preached by Roger Ley in 1619, just after the Synod of Dort.[11] As a man with moderate puritan inclinations but good official contacts and experience, Montford was perfectly placed to ensure that godliness was promoted effectively within the parish, and yet not in a manner that would create either internal division or governmental interference. Records of parish meetings suggest that one of Montford's greatest assets was his tact – probably a necessary virtue in a parish with a sizeable gentry contingent, where disputes over social status were common.[12] It is these qualities that may explain his appointment as acting bishop of London during the long vacancy after the death of Bishop King in 1621.[13]

The arrival of Montford and Hill at St Martin's marked the beginning of a sustained programme of thoroughgoing religious reform in the parish. This new regime was supported by a range of lay activists, in tandem with St Martin's clergy. The parish vestry must clearly have given their support. But, beyond the vestry, there also appears to have been a broader circle of godly laymen in the parish, partly identifiable through their signatures on the petition of 1600. Although these petitioners described themselves as the 'chief parishioners' of St Martin's, they did not consist entirely of parish administrators of the middling sort, nor were they the most prominent gentry residents. The men certainly held some links in common – two of them were parish vestrymen – but it appears that a shared religious vision was the overriding bond between them. Five of the seven signatories have left evidence of advanced Protestant views.[14] Francis Bertie, for example, was a Dutch merchant and veteran of the international Protestant cause who had played a key role in establishing the Protestant stranger churches

---

11 Merritt thesis, pp. 335, 383; Roger Ley, *Two Sermons* (1619), ep. ded., p. 39. On Hill see generally J.F. Merritt, 'The pastoral tight-rope: a puritan pedagogue in early Stuart London' in T. Cogswell, R. Cust and P. Lake (eds.), *Politics, Religion and Popularity* (Cambridge, 2002).

12 Anon., *Two Sermons*, p. 58. For Willet see below. For Montford's tact see *ibid.*, p. 57 and also his conduct at a vestry meeting during the dispute between Sir George Coppin and Raphe Dobbinson described in TNA, STAC 8/101/19.

13 For Montford as acting bishop of London see Bodl., MS Rawlinson MS D.818, ff. 88, 133; GL, 9531/13 pt 2, f. 396r; LMA, DL/C/341 (Vicar General's Book 1616–23), ff. 194r, 195r, 198r–199r, 201r–v. Montford's unusual appointment may have derived from the fact that the archbishop of Canterbury (George Abbot) was at that time suspended from his duties following his accidental killing of a gamekeeper, while there was also a vacancy in the deanery of St Paul's after the death of Valentine Carey in the same year. Montford was presumably appointed because he was the senior prebendary of St Paul's. His tenure as acting bishop has been overlooked by ecclesiastical historians of the period.

14 See also Merritt thesis, pp. 337–42.

during the reign of Edward VI. By the time of his death, his 'lovinge Freindes' included St Martin's lecturer Robert Hill and the young Thomas Gataker, a stalwart of the Protestant cause. While not a vestryman in the parish, Bertie was involved in parish affairs, and his dedication to promoting godly preaching is reflected in moneys left to set up a pulpit in St Martin's new churchyard.[15] Bertie's signature was joined by that of his son-in-law, Arnold Oldisworth, a London lawyer and an important St Martin's vestryman of long standing. Oldisworth moved among a circle of highly committed Protestants, including Alexander Nowell, dean of St Paul's (who had personally supervised his education) and the countess of Warwick, whose legal adviser he became.[16] We know less about the religious views of the other St Martin's vestryman who signed the petition, Chidiock Wardour, although his 1611 will confidently asserted his knowledge that he was one of God's 'elect flocke'.[17] It may be that the gentlemenly status, as well as the religious enthusiasm, of both Wardour and Oldisworth explain why they signed the petition when other parish officials did not. Two other signatories displayed clear godly credentials. Sir William Cooke, a son of the earlier St Martin's vestryman William Cooke, was a patron of the puritan divine Thomas Gataker and remained friends with his father's old associate, the radical James Morice. Sir William also continued his father's involvement in local affairs, representing Westminster in the 1601 parliament, soon after signing the petition.[18] A final signatory of the 1600 petition was William (later Sir William) Lane, whose support in 1605 for nonconforming ministers from his native Northamptonshire resulted in a summons to appear before the Privy Council. Lane, an equerry of the Queen's stables from 1598, may have been the most fiery Protestant of all the petitioners.[19]

The 1600 petition thus affords us a rare glimpse of the role being played in the parish by a group of well-connected godly laymen whose promotion of their own brand of word-centred Protestantism is not directly evident from parish records.[20]

---

15 TNA, PCC, Prob. 11/118/60; A. Pettegree, *Foreign Protestant Communities in Sixteenth-century London* (Oxford, 1986), p. 31.

16 Merritt thesis, pp. 337–8, 384.

17 Hasler, *House of Commons*, s.n. Chidiock Wardour; WAC, F2001 passim; TNA, PCC, Prob. 11/118/75.

18 T. Gataker, *A Discours Apologeticall* (1654), pp. 15–16, 36; Gataker, 'The Spirituall Watch' in *Certaine Sermons* (1637), pp. 57–9; *DNB*, s.n. Thomas Gataker; Hasler, *House of Commons*, s.n. William Cooke II; Merritt thesis, pp. 338–40.

19 While Lane was called before the Privy Council shortly thereafter, his puritan activities may have been viewed in a more positive light. In the aftermath of the Gunpowder Plot, Lane was entrusted with the custody of the earl of Northumberland and ultimately received lands confiscated from the conspirators: Hasler, *House of Commons*, s.n. William Lane; S.B. Babbage, *Puritanism and Richard Bancroft* (1962), pp. 131–43.

20 Another gentleman, Sir John Stanhope, was not a signatory of the petition, but he was also a prominent figure who formed a close bond with the parish's puritan lecturer Robert Hill. Hill praised Stanhope both for his personal favour and for the example that he gave the parish in attending morning and evening prayers and monthly communions: *The workes of . . . Richard Greenham* (5th ed., 1612), pt 4, ep. ded. (by Hill), sig. L13.

A CULTURE OF PREACHING

The determination of some of St Martin's parishioners to found a lectureship reflected their experience of a parish that already supported a range of godly sermons and exercises. Even during Elizabeth's reign it is clear that clergymen other than the vicar preached at St Martin's. These sermons are poorly documented, but the preachers included Gabriel Goodman, dean of Westminster, and William Gravet, vicar of the nearby parish of St Sepulchre's, whom the churchwardens supplied with bread and wine.[21] The fact that sermons preached by strangers were used as opportunities to collect for the poor suggests that they were popular occasions. From the accounting year 1611–12, it was necessary to pay a scrivener to compile what were obviously lengthy lists of 'stranger' preachers.[22] Visiting preachers could be distinguished ones: Tobie Matthew, bishop of Durham and later archbishop of York, regularly preached at St Martin's on his visits to the capital, and twice gave sermons in the parish church on Easter Sunday and once at Pentecost.[23] The vestry were anxious that as many parishioners as possible should benefit from these many sermons, experimenting with the position of the pulpit in 1621 to see 'whether the parish may hear the Preacher better in all partes of the churche'.[24]

Of course, the size of St. Martin's congregation necessarily limited access to sermons. Nevertheless, the Jacobean parish attempted to combat this problem by arranging for sermons to be preached outdoors in its new churchyard. From 1609 a series of sermons was regularly preached in the churchyard during Whitsun week and possibly at other times. On these occasions a portable pulpit, large numbers of forms and a special canopied seat for the privy councillor Lord Stanhope were all brought out into the churchyard. The custom appears to have stemmed from the bequest of the parishioner Nicholas Saunders, a Frenchman in the service of the earl of Bedford.[25] It is not clear how often other preaching was heard out-of-doors, but it is striking that St. Martin's received two separate bequests for special pulpits to be used on such occasions. In 1611 Francis Bertie (one of the petitioners for the lectureship) left money for a pulpit (probably of wood) to be made in the new churchyard, while in his 1625 will the haberdasher Symon Rowlandson arranged for the stonework for an outdoor

---

21 E.g. WAC, F301, f. 11 (1574), F311, n.f. (1584); Kitto, p. 311.

22 WAC, F2 vol. 1, f. 160. Canon 52 of the 1604 Canons required churchwardens to keep a book of stranger preachers, to include the name of the bishop from whom the preacher had obtained his licence.

23 Matthew's preaching diary refers specifically to preaching in St Martin in the Fields on nine occasions between 1603 and 1621 (York Minster Archive, Add. 18, pp. 70, 74, 76, 94, 107, 108, 129), but another twelve references to preaching at 'St Martin's' almost certainly also refer to the Westminster parish (*ibid.*, pp. 21, 76–7, 81, 82, 83, 108). He did also preach three times at St Margaret's, including Christmas Day 1605 (pp. 43, 81) and once in Westminster Abbey (p. 107), but St Martin's was clearly his favoured venue.

24 WAC, F2001, f. 151v.

25 WAC, F2 vol. 1, ff. 126, 176, 194, 235; F2001, f. 57v.

pulpit 'to bee sett up and exercised for and in the service and worshipping of god and such other divine and religious exercises and services as are to bee done'.[26]

A sense of religious commitment prompted local men to ensure that frequent and inspiring preaching was heard from St Martin's pulpit. The appointment of a parish lecturer also meant that laypeople might influence the religious message that parishioners heard. Certainly Robert Hill, St Martin's first lecturer, was keenly aware that his position depended on pleasing those laymen who funded the lectureship. Writing in 1608, Hill assured his parishioners of his devotion to them, but noted that he could not promise to live and die with them 'for no Minister can say it, who dependeth upon voluntarie contribution'.[27] Nevertheless, Hill did seem to please, and he seems to have provided his listeners with vivid but accessible sermons, propounding the sound doctrine that one would expect from a protégé of the godly William Perkins of Cambridge. It also seems likely that Hill was able to command the respect of those hotter puritans left strongly dissatisfied by the Jacobean settlement.[28] As St Martin's parish acquired a larger gentry population, however, the profile of its pulpit also rose, and there was an increasing tendency for local notables to propose their own candidates for the lectureship.

It was after the departure of Hill in 1613 that the character of the lectureship was contested. One Hamlet Marshall now filled the position of parish lecturer, principally on the recommendation of the earl of Suffolk, but presumably with the assent of other parishioners. Nevertheless, Marshall seems to won little support from those who had previously contributed towards Hill's stipend, and he complained about the smallness of his remuneration. This lack of parochial enthusiasm may have stemmed from Marshall's churchmanship, which was apparently of a more conformist tone than that of Hill.[29] Marshall's suggestion that a fixed charge be levied on parishioners to maintain him met with outrage. The suggestion also appears to have sensitized parishioners to the principle of their free choice in the selection of lecturers. In a letter outlining their position, the vestry emphasized the dangerous precedent that a levy would introduce. A lecturer's merit, they asserted, should enable him to survive on voluntary contributions. A rate to support preaching was out of the question, and they explained haughtily that 'we are very well served by our reverend doctor and his Curate a Batchlor in divinitie and divers other worthie men from the universities, besides the Kinge and princes chapleines and others the chapleines of honorable persons who do often desire

---

26 TNA, PCC, Prob. 11/118/60; Prob. 11/98/111.

27 R. Hill, *The Pathway to Prayer and Pietie* (1609), Preface [dated 1608].

28 Merritt, 'Pastoral tight-rope', pp. 145–6, 154–6.

29 It may be significant that in 1606 Marshall was chosen to replace the deprived puritan rector of St Clement East Cheap. At least some of St Martin's parishioners, for example Sir William Lane (one of the petitioners for the lectureship), deeply sympathized with the godly ministers who resisted subscription: Babbage, *Puritanism*, p. 155; E.R. Foster (ed.), *Proceedings in Parliament, 1610* (2 vols., 1966), I, 61.

to preach but cannot be admitted'.[30] That Marshall stayed at St Martin's for only a short time suggests that the parish was ultimately able to resist pressure applied by individual noblemen. Thereafter, St Martin's vestry consistently resisted attempts to transform an expression of voluntary religion into a sinecure for the protégés of local aristocrats. As we will see, similar disputes emerged more than once during the period before the Civil War. The vestry normally lent their support to more radical puritans, and Marshall's replacement by the fiery John Everard indicates how complete was the vestry's rejection of the brand of Protestantism represented by Marshall. Everard would be responsible for a number of highly inflammatory sermons and yet, as we shall see, he always enjoyed strong support from the parish vestry.

CATECHIZING AND COMMUNION

The promotion of sermons at St Martin's was only one of the religious initiatives launched by the parish in this period. Others focused on providing widespread religious instruction and attempting to ensure that all parishioners met the basic standard of yearly attendance at Easter communion. In this St Martin's clergy and vestry may partly have been prompted by the recent Canons of 1604, but the need to enlarge St Martin's church during the same decade may also have focused attention on the difficulties of integrating the swelling numbers of parishioners – who included large numbers of immigrants – into the religious community.[31] It was here that members of St Martin's vestry brought important administrative expertise to this project, and in February 1609 a series of orders relating to religious practice were agreed upon by the vestry.[32]

These orders contained a number of provisions, including a systematic programme to ensure that all parishioners received catechizing. It was ordered that every Sunday, before one o'clock, 'all the children and servantes of the one half of every Constables warde of this parishe, shall attende the Catechising in the church'. This practice was to begin the following Sunday, in the ward of John Skire on the 'landside' and 'so from Constable to Constable every Sunday, throughout the parishe'. There seems no reason to assume that catechizing had not been practised before in the parish.[33] What is particularly intriguing about this order, however, is the way that it emulates other attempts by authorities to make the rapidly growing parish a more administratively manageable unit through the use of the ward, a distinctive subdivision of Westminster parishes.

---

30 WAC, F6036, ff. 1–2, but see F2001, f. 102.

31 Merritt thesis, p. 239.

32 WAC, F2001, f. 56.

33 The publication of Robert Hill's catechism for the parish in 1606 would indicate that the parish catechized at an earlier date, as required by ecclesiastical law. The churchwardens' accounts for 1604–5 refer to the confirmation of parish children at Whitechapel during the bishop of London's visitation, but the level of instruction that was required to participate in this ceremony is not clear: WAC, F2 vol. 1, f. 38. On catechizing in London see Archer, p. 88.

There is also good evidence that such a catechizing programme represented more than mere administrative efficiency. Those responsible for implementing it were notable for their particular interest in religious education. The parish curate from 1606 to 1615, James Palmer, was a local man of puritan inclinations who later became famous for his educational and charitable activities in Westminster (including the foundation of an almshouse with a free school attached), which makes it reasonable to infer an earlier commitment to education.[34] Another cleric who appears to have been involved in this programme is the parish lecturer, Robert Hill. In 1606 Hill had published a catechism 'for the benefit of this parish' of St Martin's, describing it as an 'ocular sermon' and encouraging his readers to think of it as a continuation of the sermons that he had preached to them. It also seems likely that Hill's work was used for formal catechizing within the parish. *The Pathway to Prayer and Pietie*, as it is usually called, went through many editions and followed up Hill's earlier interest in the popular dissemination of religious ideas. The work is especially notable for its readiness to tackle difficult pastoral questions in a practical, down-to-earth and encouraging way. More generally, Hill strongly promoted catechizing, listing it among the chief duties of clerics.[35]

While clerically organized catechizing may have been regarded as crucial, laypeople were also exhorted to help each other independently. Hill stressed the need for individual Christians to help one another to better understanding.[36] Indeed, much of the *Pathway* emphasized the importance of voluntary religion and the continuing religious education that should occur within each household – a vital supplement to church services within a parish where, as Hill remarked, 'your congregation is as the thousands of Israel'.[37] Heads of households were exhorted to bring their families to church with them and to make sure that their servants accompanied them both to and from the church, and to discuss the sermon back at home 'and see that each of my Family have learned somewhat'.[38] Earlier, in 1596, Hill had produced *The Contents of Scripture*, an abridgement of the Bible, 'wherby the yong beginner might get entrance into reading, & the old reader be readied in remembering'. Hill noted that the appendix to this work, a collection of aphorisms derived from Calvin's *Institutes*, 'will serve yong children for a profitable Catechisme, where parents can out of them moove questions to their children and make them answer as it is there set downe'.[39]

---

34 For more on Palmer see Merritt thesis, pp. 337, 356, 358–9.

35 Merritt, 'Pastoral tight-rope'; Robert Hill, *Christs Prayer expounded* (1606), epistle, ii, p. 25.

36 Hill, *Christs Prayer*, ii, 25, 11, 28–9. Hill favoured admittance to first communion on the basis of an initial examination by the minister – a position that was opposed by many bishops, who maintained that confirmation by the local bishop was necessary: Hill, *Pathway to Prayer and Pietie* (1615–16), iii, pp. 7, 10; K. Fincham, *Prelate as Pastor* (Oxford, 1990), pp. 125–6.

37 Hill, *The Pathway to Prayer and Pietie* (1613), 'The Preface of Prayer'.

38 *Ibid.*, ii, 94, 103–4.

39 Robert Hill, *The Contents of Scripture* (1596), sig. a4v.

· Of course, Protestant religious instruction, whether undertaken by the parish or by the householder, tended to presuppose a basic level of literacy. Much writing on popular religious commitment in this period has emphasized the difficulties that Protestantism faced in weaning a largely illiterate population away from Catholicism and in transmitting new religious ideas based on scripture.[40] There is every reason to think that Westminster shared the higher rate of literacy enjoyed by the capital and Middlesex generally – a higher rate which was also found among servants, apprentices and women residents of the area.[41] Nonetheless, St Martin's, like a number of London parishes, seems to have undertaken the basic education of at least some local children. Certainly, orphans supported by the parish were provided with bibles and taught to read. The Jacobean period also witnessed the growth of the parish school, which had operated from at least 1570. A new schoolhouse was built adjoining the church in 1615 and the following year the parish employed an additional schoolmaster, with a third schoolmaster employed in 1622.[42] Some of St Martin's Jacobean schoolmasters were notable figures, including the writer Henry Peacham and the prominent puritan John Davenport.[43] The desire to improve educational standards seems to parallel other parish endeavours, although it is difficult to assess the social background of the children who attended or the character of the teaching provided.[44]

Another initiative at Jacobean St Martin's was a drive to ensure high rates of attendance at communion and to enforce the minimum standard of yearly attendance at an Easter communion. Contemporaries and historians alike have highlighted the difficulties that large, shifting suburban populations posed for parochial authorities seeking to ensure full church attendance and reception of communion. In theory, all souls within a parish were required to attend church and take communion at Easter. In practice, of course, this was hardly possible in the more populous parishes such as St Martin's. In 1609, George Downame specifically named the huge suburban par-

---

40 C. Haigh, 'The Church of England, the Catholics and the people' in C. Haigh (ed.), *The Reign of Elizabeth I* (1984). Assessing the level of religious commitment among the laity in the Elizabethan and early Stuart period has proved a highly controversial topic: see M. Ingram, 'From Reformation to toleration: popular religious culture in England 1540–1690' in T. Harris (ed.), *Popular Culture in England 1500–1850* (1995), pp. 95–123; E. Duffy, 'The godly and the multitude', *The Seventeenth Century* 1 (1986); J. Maltby, ' "By this Book": parishioners, the Prayer Book and the established church' in K. Fincham (ed.), *The Early Stuart Church* (1993); K. Wrightson, *English Society, 1580–1680* (1982), pp. 206–20; J.P. Boulton, 'The limits of formal religion: the administration of holy communion in late Elizabethan and early Stuart London', *London Journal* 10 (1984), p. 135; P. Marshall, *Reformation England 1480–1642* (2003), ch. 6.

41 D. Cressy, *Literacy and the Social Order* (Cambridge, 1980), pp. 72–5, 77, 128–9, 134–5, 149.

42 Kitto, p. 256; WAC, F2001, f. 103; F2 vol. 2, f. 218.

43 WAC, F2001, ff. 148, 156; LMA, DL/C/316, f. 216. Davenport became more radical with age and ultimately emigrated to America: P. Seaver, *The Puritan Lectureships* (Stanford, 1970), pp. 65, 227, 236–7, 241.

44 Several of St Martin's vestrymen aspired rather higher for their children: the tailors Andrew Hacket and Christopher Collard sent their sons to Westminster school.

ishes of St Sepulchre, St Giles Cripplegate, and St Olave and St Saviour, Southwark, where churches were so small and parishioners so numerous that 'it is not possible to assemble all together at one time, though they should be crowded never so much'.[45] The Westminster parishes could easily have been added to the same list. Factors such as increasing population, residential mobility and suburban poverty might suggest that a substantial part of the population had little or no contact with the church.[46] Yet the evidence of parish token books has demonstrated that even large suburban parishes such as St. Botolph Aldgate and St. Saviour Southwark could achieve very high rates of attendance at communion, by dint of a sophisticated administrative system and the co-operation that parishioners gave to local officials in implementing it.[47]

Like other suburban parishes, St Martin's not only held monthly communions but also circumvented the problem of space by organizing a special rota system of staggered 'Easter' communions on the Sundays following Easter. As the population of the parish increased, so the number of Easter communions seems to have steadily risen, from nine in 1594 to eighteen in 1619.[48]

St Martin's had employed a system of communion tokens since the Elizabethan period in order to monitor attendance – and hence conformity to the established church – and to ensure the payment of ecclesiastical duties at Easter. There are signs, however, that this system was under strain by the 1590s.[49] Once again, it seems that the early Jacobean period saw St Martin's parish vestry tackle the difficulty of maintaining religious discipline in an increasingly populous parish. It responded with alacrity to the Canons of 1604, which were specifically referred to in formal parish documents and by 1605 it followed the provisions requiring parishes to make lists of those who attended communion 'so often every year . . . as the laws and our constitutions do require'.[50] The parish clerk and his assistant took several days to collect the names of

---

45 P. Collinson, *The Religion of Protestants* (Oxford, 1982), p. 210; Boulton, 'Limits', p. 135. Clerical complaints bemoaning lay ignorance were commonplace, but may in themselves reflect the higher standards of an increasingly well-educated clergy: see *ibid.*, pp. 200–4; Green, 'For children', p. 143; Duffy, 'The godly and the multitude'; C. Haigh, 'Communion and community: exclusion from communion in post-Reformation England', *JEH* 51 (2000).

46 P. Clark and P. Slack, *English Towns in Transition 1500–1700* (Oxford, 1976), p. 71; C. Hill, *Society and Puritanism in Pre-Revolutionary England* (1964), p. 484.

47 Boulton, 'Limits', pp. 146, 148.

48 WAC, F320, f. 6v; F345, n.f. This practice was followed by many parishes in the capital and elsewhere in England: Boulton, 'Limits', pp. 143, 147–8. Technically, staggering these communions over a period of more than forty days infringed the Canons of 1604, but authorities probably tolerated this because the parishes concerned were acting in the spirit of the canons.

49 Boulton, 'Limits', p. 138; WAC, F2001, f. 19. It is unlikely, however, that the sum paid by each communicant covered the total cost of the communion bread and wine. During the Jacobean period, St Martin's communicants paid only a halfpenny per person in contrast to St Botolph, Aldgate, where each parishioner paid 2d: Boulton, 'Limits', p. 141.

50 *Ibid.*, p. 138. Boulton points out that this requirement was vague and did not specify triannual attendance.

communicants, which were then alphabetized and copied into a book, presumably to help in compiling future lists and so that 'it might easier Appeare who received, and who did not'.[51] In 1609, the vestry issued further orders. Those eligible to receive communion were now required to visit the minister the day before the service, pay their duties and receive a token. At that time they were also meant to give their names. The next day, communicants were to return their tokens and once again give their names to those in attendance.[52] Such a system, coupled with lists of communicants from previous years, should have resulted in quite high rates of attendance.[53] From 1616 the churchwardens' accounts carefully recorded the precise number of Easter communicants. In that year 3,034 communicants came forward to receive Easter communion. By 1625 this number rose to nearly four thousand, a rate of increase that cannot be explained by population growth alone.[54] Unfortunately, we cannot estimate the percentage of the population receiving communion, as we do not possess sufficient information about the age structure of the population. By the 1630s, however, it would appear that the parish was finding it more difficult to enforce attendance: no fewer than eight hundred people were presented for not attending communion in 1634.[55]

Of course, the desire to promote high levels of attendance at St Martin's is not in itself indicative of any particular religious stance. It does suggest that local authorities considered it important to ensure basic conformity and to prevent the development of an urban anonymity which might encourage various forms of unorthodox behaviour and belief. But it also seems clear that some at least of Westminster's ecclesiastical establishment sought to infuse communion attendance with a more evangelical meaning. It is notable that Robert Hill's catechism was one of the first specifically to address the issue of preparation for communion, in a section which was continually expanded in later editions.[56] A desire for plentiful sermons, good catechizing and high attendance levels at communion need not in themselves reflect a puritan agenda – these are not exclusively 'puritan' concerns. However at St Martin's, the very fact that these

51 WAC, F2 vol. 1, f. 55.

52 WAC, F2001, f. 56.

53 Attendance levels would probably not have been as high as those at St Saviour's, with its extraordinary attendance rates of between 80 and 98 per cent, since officials there went from house to house to distribute the tokens. St Martin's 'passive' system may have discouraged poorer parishioners from attending: Boulton, 'Limits', pp. 143, 146–7; Merritt thesis, pp. 378–9.

54 WAC, F2 vol. 2, ff. 228, 414.

55 WAC, F3 (1634–35), n.f. Numbers of communicants seem to have hovered around the four thousand mark in the 1630s, but precise calculations are difficult as from 1635 onwards the vestry directed that a specific sum should be taken as token money, and numbers of communicants were no longer entered (*ibid.*). The parish clearly continued to keep a communion book: the curate thus can be found checking the communion book to confirm that a servant took Easter communion in 1634 and 1635: *CSPD 1635*, p. 465.

56 Green, 'For children', pp. 405–6; Hill, *Christ's Prayer*, iii, 'A Communicant prepared to the Lordes Table'.

activities were presided over by a group of emphatically and self-consciously godly clergy and vestrymen seems likely to have lent them a more evangelical gloss.

It is, of course, impossible to calculate how great an impact St Martin's godly clergy and vestrymen were able to make on their parishioners. The social and occupational structure of Westminster's parishes inevitably created fundamental problems in maintaining religious standards. Social class may not have determined religious commitment, but the church and indeed established religion more generally found their influence weakest among the young, especially servants and the highly mobile.[57] These groups, of course, formed a significant portion of the population in Westminster, with its service-based economy. In particular, a large servant population – many of them employed on a casual basis and dependent on the royal court, law terms and meetings of parliament – must have been difficult to integrate into parish religion. Equally, if immigrants came to the attention of the parish authorities, they were often more eager to move them out of the parish than to inquire into the state of their souls. But those who stayed longer potentially had access to the services and sermons of a parish which considered itself vibrant and evangelizing. Of course the dearth of parochial festivals under Protestantism made it difficult for parishes to use other means to ensure that the wider body of the laity gained some positive contact with the church. One rare survival was perambulation, and it is notable that the strongly Protestant parish of Hill and Montford still maintained a lively Rogationtide procession. By the 1620s though, as we have noted, this became a more exclusive and rationed arrangement, precisely around the same time that escalating population undermined efforts to provide for the parish poor and to regulate attendance at communion.[58]

This rise in population did not lead parish authorities to write off its poorer parishioners, nor did it result in a diminution of evangelical fervour. Indeed as we shall see, the 1620s and 1630s saw St Martin's vestry lend support to a range of extreme puritan preachers. What is most striking is the lengths to which St Martin's parish elite went to provide greater access to church services for the parish's rapidly expanding population. The parish made several attempts to establish chapels of ease for its parishioners, even after the substantial enlargement of St Martin's church in 1606–9. These attempts included the operation of a chapel at Knightsbridge, originally associated with Knightsbridge hospital. By the 1610s, this distant and rural part of the parish was sufficiently well populated for the minister to travel there to administer communion.[59] In the late 1620s a petition in the name of St Martin's inhabitants cited the enormous population of the parish in order to plead for the conversion of a hall in Durham House into a chapel of ease, the parish expressing a

---

57 M. Ingram, *Church Courts, Sex and Marriage in England 1570–1640* (Cambridge, 1987), p. 123.

58 See ch. 6, below.

59 E.g. WAC, F2 vol. 2, ff. 309, 377, 400. The chapel was in a poor state in 1608 (LMA, DL/C/306, f. 379), but enlarged and improved in the late 1620s: WAC F6036; LPL, COMM. XIIa/12/ vol. 12, ff. 389–90.

willingness to pay for the conversion as well as for the services of a minister. The suit failed, despite the parish petitioning a number of noblemen to support it, as did a proposal by the churchwardens in 1619 that the parish acquire a piece of ground around Covent Garden for a chapel of ease.[60] In the event, this latter project would soon be superseded by the earl of Bedford's creation of a new parish in the same area. In the long term it was the creation of new parishes, rather than of chapels of ease, which provided a partial solution to the social and religious problems posed by St Martin's spiralling population.[61]

THE POST-REFORMATION ABBEY AND RELIGIOUS
CONSERVATISM IN ST MARGARET'S

Of Westminster's three post-Reformation parishes, the one that distinguished itself by its conservatism and attachment to ceremony was St Margaret's, where the influence of the Abbey church made itself most felt. The development of parish religion there not only differed from what we have seen at St Martin's, but also, it appears, from the experience of St Clement Danes. At St Clement's, the heavy concentration of lawyers at the Inns of Court supported at least two puritan lecturers – Robert Johnson and the celebrated preacher Henry Smith – who both crossed swords with the Elizabethan ecclesiastical authorities.[62] At St Margaret's, however, there is little evidence of the activities that we have observed at St Martin's – no puritan preachers, no parish lectureship and no elaborate arrangements for catechizing.[63] It may seem particularly puzzling that the spirit of voluntary religion which characterized St Margaret's during the pre-Reformation period seems at first glance to have decayed.

It is not surprising, of course, that a parish which had responded so enthusiastically to Mary's reforms should have been sluggish in its response to the Elizabethan settlement, although after 1562 and the intervention of the archdeacon of Westminster it generally followed the letter of the law.[64] The parish bought the necessary service books, although in 1564 its copy of the *Paraphrases* of Erasmus was described as

---

60 WAC, F2001, f. 133; F3, f. 102; TNA, SP16/44/51.

61 In addition to St Paul Covent Garden, the later seventeenth century saw the new parishes of St Anne Soho and St James Piccadilly created out of St Martin's.

62 A lectureship was first established in 1571. Johnson was imprisoned during a more widespread crackdown on presbyterianism and penned polemic against conservative clerics including Dean Goodman of Westminster: WAC, B19 (1604–5), f. 2; P. Collinson, *The Elizabethan Puritan Movement* (1967), pp. 134, 152. Smith's suspension was lifted only by the intervention of his kinsman Lord Burghley: Seaver, *Puritan Lectureships*, pp. 135–6, 217. Poor parish records prevent a more sustained analysis of St Clement's, but see Merritt thesis, pp. 328–9.

63 For one rare example of a lay bequest see the will of Quentin Sneyton (a servant of Burghley's and usher in the Court of Wards) who left money to St Margaret's in 1575 for two small sermons to be made twice a year: TNA, PCC Prob. 11/57/27.

64 See above, ch. 2.

'defaced'.[65] St Margaret's did not acquire its copy of the new Bishop's Bible (required by the 1571 Convocation) until 1574–75, apparently soon after a visitation by Westminster's archdeacon.[66] In these circumstances, the efforts of local clergy may have been channelled into obtaining a basic conformity to Protestant practice. Lay activity in religious affairs may actually have been discouraged if this was associated with Catholic survivalism and a previously flourishing tradition. Indeed the apparent purging of the parish elite early in Elizabeth's reign may have served to discourage the religiously activist elements in local society. Certainly, those men associated with pre-Reformation guilds appear to have withdrawn from new forms of religious organization in the following period.

This was not, of course, a parish bereft of individuals of emphatic Protestant convictions. Several of its vestrymen left behind wills espousing strong Protestant and anti-Catholic views. William Stanlake's 1628 will expressed his confidence that he would inherit the kingdom that God 'hath purchased for his Elect'.[67] Nevertheless, these beliefs do not seem to have translated into actions which benefited the wider body of parishioners. For example, the parishioner Edmund English left £1,000 to the godly seminary of Emmanuel College but left no religious bequests to his own parish of St Margaret's, while the churchwarden John Bradshawe sent two of his sons to Emmanuel College and left £5 each to ten noted puritan ministers in 1605 (asking them to act as overseers of his will and to ensure that his children would 'walk in the wayes of the lorde') but bequeathed nothing for his own church or local clergy.[68] It seems that zealous Protestants who lived in the parish of St Margaret's chose to deploy their religious energies and money elsewhere.

There are a number of possible reasons behind the parish's failure to emulate the forms of Protestant lay activism evident at the neighbouring St Martin's. One is the lack of obvious clerical leadership. While St Martin's enjoyed the services of its newly reinstated Edwardian vicar until his death in 1572, during the same period at St Margaret's the cure was served by at least four different men, none of whom was a university graduate. At least another nine ministers served the cure during Elizabeth's reign, and they were all similarly obscure individuals.[69] It is remarkable that

---

65 WAC, E4 (1562–64), n.f..

66 Kitto, p. 264, n.1; WAC, E5 (1574–75), n.f.

67 TNA, PCC, Prob. 11/68/57 (John Dodington), Prob. 11/109/25 (John Bradshawe); WAC, PCW, 218 Camden (William Stanlake).

68 Andrew Willet, *Synopsis Papismi* (1634), pp. 1235–6. Bradshawe was churchwarden for 1582–84: TNA, Prob. 11/109/25. The ministers in his will include a number who had recently been suspended for non-subscription, two of whom – Stephen Egerton and Anthony Wotton – were named in 1606 as possible executors of the notorious will of the wealthy London widow Susan Venables, who bequeathed most of her estate to support deprived ministers: N. Tyacke, *The Fortunes of English Puritanism, 1603–1640* (1990), pp. 5–6.

69 The list of curates in Hennessey's *Novum Repertorium Ecclesiasticum Parochiale Londinense* is seriously flawed and unreliable. Analysis of curates' signatures in the churchwardens' accounts gives the following series (the account years signed are placed in parentheses): Thomas Sowdley (1562), Humfrey Fletcher (1564), Robert Danyell (1566, 1568), Edmund Tow (1572), James Johnson

St Margaret's – a parish situated at the heart of Elizabethan government – suffered the indignity of being listed in a 1586 puritan survey among parishes that were served by non-preaching 'dumb dogs'.[70] Matters seem to have improved in the early seventeenth century, when a single minister, William Murrey, served the cure for twenty years, but the relatively low calibre of parochial clergy still contrasts sharply with the experience of other Westminster parishes.[71]

The obscurity of St Margaret's curates ultimately reflected the relatively unrewarding nature of the position. The Abbey controlled the advowson, and fixed the attached stipend at a mere 20 marks a year.[72] But the Abbey also exercised a decisive influence over the parish in other ways. In the years after 1560, St Margaret's was uniquely under the direct control of the dean and chapter, being exempt from the jurisdiction of the bishop of London. Indeed, the dean and chapter's insistence on this jurisdiction led them to clash with the House of Commons in 1621, when the Commons attempted to choose a minister to preach to them at a Commons fast-day service at St Margaret's.[73] Individual prebendaries, acting as the archdeacon of Westminster, conducted regular visitations to ensure that religious standards were maintained within the parish of St Margaret's. These visitations offered one means by which the Abbey's own preferred style of churchmanship might have been transmitted to St Margaret's. The 'ould and auncient custome' whereby clergy from the Abbey

---

(1576, 1578), William Holande (1580), George Tickeridge (1584), Edmund Medowcroft? (1586), John Fennell (1588), Richard Burton (1590), Francis Key (1592), William Farmer (1594, 1596), William Murrey (1602). Murrey may have gone on to a more illustrious career (see below, n. 71).

70 A Peel (ed.), *A Seconde Parte of a Register* (2 vols, Cambridge, 1915), II, p. 184.

71 Merritt thesis, pp. 328–9. Murrey was also a minor canon 1602–3 (WAM 33656, f. 2v) and leased the reserved tithes of the parsonage of St Margaret's and the anchorite's house adjoining the church in 1604 (*Acts*, no. 531 n. 208). The anchorite's house was normally occupied by the parish curate; however it seems that it was was only in 1618, when the lease was renewed, that Murrey received a patent of the curateship of St Margaret's for life (WAM 18135). Murrey is described as an M.A. in WAM Reg. II, ff. 35v–36, but it is not clear whether Murrey can be identified as the later bishop of Llandaff. Later appointments to St Margaret's curateship are Isaac Bargrave (1622), Vincent Peirce (1626) (*pace* Hennessey, see WAM Chapter Act Bk II, f. 40v) and Gilbert Wimberley (1630).

72 This stipend (of £13 6s 8d) was paid by the person leasing the anchorite's house (which abutted the south part of the chancel of the church) from the dean and chapter: the amount does not seem to have changed between 1572 and 1650: compare WAM Reg. VI, ff. 95v–96v; Reg. XIII, f. 104; WAM 36063; LPL, COMM. XIIa/12/ vol. 12, f. 372. The overall income of the curate, however, including tithes, fees and leases, was estimated at around £49 a year (*ibid.*, ff. 373–374). The leasee was also required to provide bread and wine for communions in St Margaret's and to repair the chancel.

73 *CJ* I, pp. 510, 516, 517. The dean and chapter also held the tithes of the parish, although these were usually farmed out: see WAM 38192; *Acts*, nos. 225 n. 133, 279, 374, 508, 531, 533; Chapter Act Bk II, f. 15v; TNA, Prob. 11/94/77. The Abbey also farmed out the tithes of St Martin in the Fields: see TNA, REQ2, 188/41; *Acts*, nos. 261, 491, 508, 531, 539; Chapter Act Bk II, ff. 14v, 35. It should not be implied that St Margaret's always meekly accepted the Abbey's control: see for example their determination to appoint their own parish clerk: *HMC Hatfield*, XI, 587–8.

assisted at Easter communions in St Margaret's may also have provided an opportunity to introduce a little of Abbey colour and ceremonial.[74] Just as the Abbey may have inspired St Margaret's Marian restoration, so it may have reinforced a lack of enthusiasm for more evangelical forms of Protestantism.

St Margaret's records yield little evidence of sermons other than those presumably given by their own minister. Those who are known to have preached at St Margaret's have been almost impossible to identify, although in 1595–96 one John Crevecure, alias Fote, 'a pore scholler borne in this parish' was paid the generous sum of 20s after his sermon. Possibly the preachers were selected on the basis of their local connections rather than their learning or reputation alone.[75] It is possible that the availability of occasional sermons at the Abbey may have discouraged the establishment of a lectureship at St Margaret's.[76] That being said, the Abbey was not a great centre of preaching in the way that St Paul's was in London. In 1591 provisions in the will of the Countess of Sussex (founder of Sidney Sussex College in Cambridge) led to the establishment of a lectureship within the collegiate church. But the funding seems to have been problematic, while those who preached and their intended audience remain obscure: the fact that lectures were limited to the law terms suggests that the lectureship was not specifically targeted at local inhabitants.[77] It is possible that the prebendaries or dean preached at St Margaret's, but there is no record of this and they seem to have found it difficult enough to fulfil their preaching duties in the collegiate church.[78]

Throughout Elizabethan England, cathedral and collegiate churches represented bastions of conservatism within the English church, preserving elaborate music and liturgical practices that later became associated with the Laudian movement.[79] This was particularly true of Westminster Abbey, where Dean Goodman, one of the most conservative churchmen of the Elizabethan period, presided over the collegiate church from 1561 to 1601. While there, he attempted to retain the Abbey's ceremonial richness and musical traditions, while keeping strict control over the Abbey pulpit, introducing requirements which seem designed to prevent more puritan-minded clergy from preaching there. The remarkable length of Goodman's tenure meant that the

---

74 WAM 36063.

75 Hennessey, p. 294; WAC, E6 (1595–96), f. 17. One unusual case is that of the puritan Richard Blincoe, who preached at St Margaret's on 21 August 1608. It seems likely, however, that this was some sort of recantation sermon: see LMA, DL/C/306, ff. 223r, 223v, 307; WAC, E6 (1608–9), f. 12v; Merritt thesis, pp. 354–5.

76 For examples of listings of sermons preached in the Abbey see WAM 9392 (1626), 40732 (1595).

77 *Acts*, nos. 424, 541; Sidney Sussex College, Cambridge, College Muniments Box 19/11. The stipend was £20: e.g. WAM 33241, f. 108.

78 *Acts*, nos. 202, 286, 291.

79 On the position of cathedrals in post-Reformation English Protestantism see D. MacCulloch, 'The myth of the English Reformation', *Journal of British Studies* 30 (1991); MacCulloch, *The Later Reformation 1547–1603* (Basingstoke, 1990), pp. 119–21.

churchmanship of his immediate successors now reflected a new wave of ceremonialism which emerged in the early seventeenth century. Deans such as Lancelot Andrewes (1601–5) and Richard Neile (1605–10) espoused what Peter Lake has dubbed Jacobean 'avant-garde conformity' – a phenomenon which itself foreshadowed the Laudianism of the 1630s.[80] Neile in particular seems to have left his mark on the Abbey. He was a relatively humble native of Westminster who had attended Westminster school and seems to have kept up links (and part-time residence) in the locality even when he moved on to further preferment.[81] During his time as dean, Neile organized funding to encourage music at the Abbey as well as undertaking efforts to beautify the Abbey church itself.[82]

St Margaret's parishioners can hardly have been unaware of developments in the collegiate church, which towered over their own parish church. At least some parishioners occasionally attended services there. The usual weekly congregations at the Abbey may have been limited to Abbey clergy and officials, high-ranking visitors and the social elite of St Margaret's parish, but scattered evidence suggests the attendance of less socially elevated parishioners at evening service.[83] From 1585 the Westminster burgesses were expected to attend services in the Abbey, although they also had a special pew within St Margaret's as well, and it is possible that they attended the Abbey only on major feast days.[84] Such feast days may have attracted a considerable congregation: in 1624, Dean John Williams distributed communion 'to a great multitude' on Christmas Day, the service and subsequent communion lasting more than four hours.[85] A longstanding and possibly inspiring example of elaborate ceremonial thus existed on the doorstep of St Margaret's.

If lay enthusiasm for preaching seems to have been strikingly absent in St Margaret's, then, it may have been the case that parishioners' activism was simply redirected. In contrast to St Martin's, where devotion to the Word was more actively promoted, St Margaret's parish seems to have lavished attention on church ceremony, the provision of sumptuous fittings and elaborate church music. Unlike many London parishes, St Margaret's kept its organ after the accession of Elizabeth and clearly used it during services, while parish clerks were expected to play the instrument in addition to their other duties.[86] In 1595–96 the parish also purchased the organ of the adjacent Abbey, while in 1600–1 it invested considerable

80 J.F. Merritt, 'The cradle of Laudianism? Westminster Abbey 1558–1630', *JEH* 52 (2001), 623–46.

81 WAM 6612; WAM 33659, f. 6; Durham Cathedral Library, Hunter MS 44/17, ff. 216r, 217v, 219r, 220r; WAM 9370.

82 Foster, 'Biography', pp. 26–7, 32–3.

83 E.g. LMA, WJ/SR (NS) 41/3, 4, 4a.

84 WAC, E6, 1604–5, f. 11.

85 John Hacket, *Scrinia Reserata* (1693), i, 211.

86 WAC, E4 (1567–68), n.f.; E6 (1590–91), f. 10, (1606–7), f. 10. In E5 (1577–78), n.f. there is a payment to Richard Baker 'for his Attendance on the Organs in absence of the Clerke'.

sums in the construction of an elaborately decorated organ loft.[87] The parish seems to have retained a taste for music of all kinds. In 1562–63, the churchwardens purchased four 'songe bookes for the servyce of god' and four books of metrical psalms specifically said to be for the choir, while it also paid the parish clerk for copying two books 'with the Te deum laudamus for the quyer', the settings of which could be quite elaborate.[88] The high musical standards which the parish maintained probably owed more to traditional links with the Abbey and the pre-Reformation custom of the Abbey singingmen performing at St Margaret's on holy days, a custom which was revived from at least 1585, if not earlier.[89] By the 1590s, and possibly as early as 1593, St Margaret's parish clerks included William Heather, the noted chorister and friend of William Camden, who went on to found the Heather professorship of music at Oxford. He continued as clerk until at least 1613, shortly afterwards becoming a gentleman of the Chapel Royal.[90] In addition, the singingmen of the Collegiate church participated in services at St Margaret's on 'highe dayes' such as Christmas from at least 1585, and throughout the Jacobean period.[91] It is notable too that St Margaret's parish seems to have spent greater sums of money on items such as surplices and church linen than was the case at St Martin's. In 1608–9 the parish spent over £20 on cloth of gold for cushions and coverings for the communion table and pulpit. It was probably no coincidence that during the same period Dean Richard Neile authorized funds for the beautification of St Margaret's chancel, as well as the Abbey itself.[92]

It would be unfair to conclude from the more elaborate services held at St Margaret's, and the sparser evidence of parochial preaching, that the parish was neglectful of its parishioners. After all, non-preaching clerics could play a useful role in the community, reading homilies, providing pastoral care and catechizing. Such men were also expected to arrange for others to preach quarterly (and later monthly) in their stead, and by the seventeenth century St Margaret's ministers must have been able to preach adequately. While there is no evidence that St Margaret's drew up the elaborate catechizing rota that operated at St Martin's or actively sought outside preachers, nevertheless the parish seems to have arranged for its numerous parishioners to receive communion in an orderly fashion.

Like St Martin's, St Margaret's allowed parishioners to attend a series of

---

87 WAC, E6 (1595–96), f. 18v; (1600–1), f. 9v.

88 WAC, E4 (1562–63), n.f.; N. Temperley, *The Music of the English Parish Church* (2 vols., 1979), I, 18, 43–6.

89 WAC, E5 (1585–86), f. 24. For Goodman see below.

90 WAC, E8 (1612–13), f. 16; S. Sadie (ed.), *The New Grove Dictionary of Music and Musicians* (20 vols., 1980), s.n. William Heyther.

91 E.g. WAC, E5 (1585–86), f. 24; E6 (1594–95), f. 8v; E14 (1624–25), f. 22.

92 WAC, E5 (1586–87), ff. 23–24; E6 (1592–93), f. 21v; (1599–1600), f. 19r–v; (1608–9), f. 14; E8 (1613–14), f. 30v; Foster, 'Biography', pp. 26–7, 32–3.

staggered 'Easter' communions on the Sundays following Easter,[93] and the parish had issued tokens from at least 1562–63.[94] Yet a general slackness on the part of St Margaret's officials is suggested by a process served on its churchwardens in 1607–8 'for not making Presentmentes soe often as the Comissarye requireth'.[95] Unlike at St Martin's, the churchwardens did not record the precise number of communicants at Easter, but it is possible to make some estimates from the amount of token money received. This number, however, varied greatly from year to year: between 1608 and 1609, for example, numbers of communicants would seem to have fallen by more than a thousand.[96] Gradually, however, the system seems to have improved, and changes in token money collected at St Margaret's begin to track population estimates more closely, with fluctuations becoming increasingly rare. In the 1630s, communion numbers of over six thousand are regularly suggested by receipts of token money.[97]

Token money amounts therefore suggest that St Margaret's was increasingly able to secure a reasonably high level of communion attendance. Of course, a conservative religious mentality could be just as anxious to secure a broad attendance at church as an evangelical one. A variety of other factors, beyond the purely religious, may also lie behind this development, which (as we have seen) was not combined with the sort of evangelical initiatives witnessed in St Martin's. One motive – operative in both parishes – would have been the collection of ecclesiastical 'duties' payable at Easter. Securing attendance may also fit into a broader pattern of concern over matters of public order, and the curbing of urban anonymity, which we have noticed in the conduct of St Margaret's officials elsewhere.[98] Parish perambulations, too, seem to have responded to times of social crisis, with larger sums spent in years of particular distress.[99]

---

93 I have assumed the existence of staggered communions at St Margaret's from the numbers receiving at Easter (over two thousand c.1610) and the receipt of token money on more than a single Sunday (e.g. WAC, E5 (1568–69), n.f.).

94 WAC, E4 (1562–63).

95 WAC, E6 (1604–5), f. 11r–v; (1607–8), f. 23.

96 WAC, E6 (1609–10), ff. 11, 26v. Amounts of token money collected were £6 3s 2d in 1608 and £4 in 1609 which, assuming that St. Margaret's parishioners paid a halfpenny each for a token (as they did at St. Martin's), would indicate 2,944 communicants and nearly 1,920 communicants respectively, with a parish population of about 8,200, comprising approximately 2,150 households. The impact of plague (endemic in Westminster between 1603 and 1609) on these figures is difficult to assess, and the population total may be a significant underestimate. The amount of wine consumed also seems to have varied greatly from year to year in the early years of Elizabeth's reign, although this might reflect a conservative reluctance to receive in both kinds. WAC, E4 (1562–63), n.f., (1565–66), n.f., (1570–71), n.f.

97 E.g. WAC, E17, ff. 15v, 28v; E18, ff. 16v, 38v; E19, ff. 18, 43v; E20 (1637–38), n.f.

98 St Margaret's officials were at the forefront of the movement to establish the Court of Burgesses (see above, ch. 3). Note also the sort of fines levied by the archdeacon of Westminster and parish officials for offences such as shopkeeping during time of divine service. These fines were then turned over to the overseers of the poor. From 1568 until about 1615 the overseers regularly recorded fines from the archdeacon's court (WAC, E145–150). On the nature of the offences see Merritt thesis, pp. 367–9, 390.

99 Amounts shot up in 1640–41, for example: see above, ch. 6.

Forms of religious conservatism thus flourished in St Margaret's and there are few signs of an active, evangelizing laity making their presence felt in the parish. It would be unwise, however, to paint too monolithic a picture. After all, even at the neighbouring Abbey there were members of its establishment sympathetic towards advanced Protestantism, including some of Westminster's schoolmasters and preben-daries.[100] Nevertheless, it is very difficult to identify any group of godly laity in St Margaret's who directed their evangelical enthusiasms towards the needs of the parish. Indeed, it was a prebendary of the Abbey, George Darrell, who left money in 1631 to build a chapel of ease by Tothill Fields especially to serve St Margaret's poorer parishioners, his particular concern being to provide 'prayers and Cathechising for the meaner sort of people'.[101] Darrell lamented the state of St Margaret's parishioners in the area concerned, 'nowe utterly unprovided in the necessary groundes of Religion' and therefore in desperate need of 'playne Catechising'. These comments seem to tally with a lack of widespread evangelical commitment among parishioners. Although Darrell's chapel was ultimately completed in 1638, its doors did not open until 1642 because of lack of provision for a minister. By this time, however, it could profit from the attentions of puritan gentry, who by the 1640s had begun to move into the parish in significant numbers and to play a more active role in its affairs.[102]

MAGIC AND PROPHECY IN WESTMINSTER

Much of our discussion has thus far focused on parochial structures and questions of conformity. Yet early modern English culture also embraced a range of irregular views about the supernatural which coexisted rather awkwardly with orthodox Protestantism.[103] Beliefs in magic and witchcraft are often treated as essentially rural phenomena, yet they also appear among Westminster's residents (many of whom must have been rural immigrants in any case). Nor were such beliefs confined to poorer groups in society. 'Cunning folk' and other practitioners of white magic were just as likely to have more socially elevated residents among their clientele.

When in 1610, the St Martin's lecturer, Robert Hill, condemned men and women who sought 'to use the helpe of good Witches, or Cunning men, as they are called', as

---

100 Merritt, 'Cradle of Laudianism', pp. 642–4.

101 WAC, PCW, 175v–177 Camden.

102 P. Guillery, 'The Broadway Chapel, Westminster: a forgotten exemplar', *London Topographical Record* 26 (1990), pp. 107–14. On the later creation of the parish of Christ Church in Tothill Fields and its division from St Margaret's see V.F. Snow and A.S. Young (eds.), *The Private Journals of the Long Parliament 7 March to 1 June 1642* (New Haven, 1987), p. 141. Darrell's hopes for 'preaching if meanes may bee hadd to mayntenne it' were also not fulfilled for some time (WAC, PCW, f. 176v Camden). See also WAC, E21, f. 70. In fairness, it should be noted that St Paul's Covent Garden also ran into problems over the question of who was to pay for its minister.

103 R. Hutton, 'The English Reformation and the evidence of folklore', *P&P* 148 (1995); Ingram, 'From Reformation', pp. 106–8.

representing their going 'from God to the Devill', he was nevertheless forced to admit that 'yet this is the practise of most people'.[104] In 1561 eight men had been set in the pillory at Westminster for 'conjuring', and the demand does not seem to have declined over the years.[105] Finding lost property and telling fortunes seem to have been the services most in demand. Buckingham's confidant, the notorious 'Dr' Lambe, for example, was a Westminster resident who was active in deploying his 'magical' skills in local society. He was examined on a number of charges before the Westminster Sessions in 1627, which included the accusation that he conjured up spirits and forecast storms, and he was crossexamined on his knowledge of astrology and astronomy. While he denied the charge that the children of Westminster School came to him, he did confess to what was clearly his main activity, accepting money in return for 'coniectures' about the location of missing items. Lambe was anxious to emphasize that he would not undertake such work for under 7d, and if his clients had their goods successfully located then they were required to pay him '1os, 20s, or 40s etc. proportionable to the worth of the things that were lost'. His clients were clearly among the wealthier members of society, and Lady Purbeck and others also paid Lambe for physic and surgery (although he confessed that he had no training in either vocation).[106] The self-educated doctor and astrologer Simon Forman also ran a good business among the socially prominent in the capital. Some of Westminster's prominent Protestant patrons were among those seeking his assistance (which may explain Hill's despairing reluctance to discuss the problem in any detail). Both Lady Margaret Hoby and the later Duchess of Richmond and Lennox regularly sought Forman's advice, on questions of sickness and marriage plans respectively. 'Many gentlewomen' also visited the cunning woman Mary Woods, who helped to find lost property and told fortunes during the 1610s. Among her clients was Frances Howard, who invited Woods to visit her at Salisbury House.[107]

Fears of witchcraft also haunted the streets of Westminster as well as rural villages. After her dogs had been secretly poisoned by her servants, Lady Susan Greene leapt to the conclusion that the dogs had been bewitched. She therefore arranged for

---

104 Hill, *Pathway* (1610), 'A direction to die well', p. 138.

105 *The Diary of Henry Machyn*, ed. J.G. Nichols (Camden Society o.s. 42, 1848), p. 261.

106 LMA, WJ/SR (NS) 20/27 (6 December 1627). While he denied that he conjured spirits, Lambe did admit that he used 'his book Cattam'. Another report of this case had it that Lambe was imprisoned for inducing a Westminster scholar 'to give himself to the devil': R.F. Williams (ed.), *The Court and Times of Charles I* (2 vols., 1848), I, 305 (cf. p. 252). The case was examined before Bishop Richard Neile in Durham House, although it was theoretically outside his jurisdiction. This is perhaps to be explained by the fact that Lambe had claimed that Neile had accepted him as a physician. On 18 December Lambe was examined by the Royal College of Physicians at the request of Neile acting on behalf of the King (L.M. Goldstein, 'The Life and Death of John Lambe', *Guildhall Studies in London History* 4, 1 (1979), p. 24).

107 A.L. Rowse, *The Case Books of Simon Forman* (1976), pp. 142, 232–40; A. Somerset, *Unnatural Murder* (1997), pp. 120–1.

an 'old woman' to bring another dog to the house to see whether it too would be infected with the witchcraft.[108] Joan Ellyse, a woman illicitly associated with a Westminster brewer, was ultimately hanged for witchcraft. She faced a series of accusations which included the bewitchment of both people and animals. Four horses were said to have died as a result of her witchcraft, which also caused Edward Williamson of St Margaret's to languish and lay 'wasted and consumed in his body' for three months – a condition which extended also to his cow. Ellyse's efforts were also said to have caused the labourer William Crowche to suffer from a similar wasting condition. These cases may not have been common, but many Westminster inhabitants, including the clergy, were well-primed to such eventualities: indeed the half-brother of Henry Smith, Elizabethan minister at St Clement Danes, had been at the centre of a celebrated witchcraft case in Leicestershire, while St Martin's long-serving vicar Thomas Montford was himself well versed in trials of alleged demonic possession.[109]

For all Westminster's courtly urban sophistication, then, the world of magic and witchcraft was alive and well there. Moreover, while the godly might condemn recourse to cunning men, they also displayed their own predilection for a succession of popular prophets who found their way into the town during this period. Prophets and prophetesses walked the streets – from the man who cried 'Woe to Rome, woe to all Papists' before the gates of Whitehall Palace three times a week throughout 1621, to the 'Prophet Ball', who addressed crowds in St Clement Danes. Such individuals did not necessarily meet with disapproval from local officials. In 1617–18 St Martin's vestry paid one Anne Walker 'a supposed Prophetesse' five shillings – more than three times the amount that they paid the same year to a poor scholar sent to them by the vicar Montford.[110]

BEYOND THE ESTABLISHED CHURCH

Some local inhabitants might stay away from church, from either sheer indifference or perhaps a preference for the rival attractions of the alehouse. Other members of Westminster society, however, felt bound on principle not to attend the services of the established church.

---

108 LMA, WJ/SR (NS) 8/122.

109 *Middlesex County Records*, ed. J.C. Jeaffreson (4 vols., 1886–92), I, 84–5, see also the St Martin's women accused of 'diabolical inchauntementes' (p. 145). J. Nichols, *The History and Antiquities of the County of Leicester* (4 vols., 1795–1815), II, 471. Montford served on the panel of judges in the Denham case described in F.W. Brownlow, *Shakespeare, Harsnett and the Devils of Denham* (Newark, DL, 1993), p. 339.

110 *Historical Notices . . . by Nehemiah Wallington* (2 vols., 1869), I, 12–13; WAC, F2 vol. 2, f. 289. For the Prophet Ball see below. On Protestant attitudes towards prophets see A. Walsham, *Providence in Early Modern England* (Oxford, 1999), pp. 203–18.

CATHOLICS

Early modern Westminster had the reputation of being a haunt of crypto-papists and recusants. Nevertheless, Westminster's parishes do not seem to have played host to unusually high numbers of Catholic residents, compared with the substantial figures in some other London suburbs. Estimating numbers of Catholics in Elizabethan or early Stuart Westminster is fraught with difficulties, not least because Catholics were not necessarily recusants.[111] Nevertheless, Alan Dures has calculated for the period of 1581–1628 a total of 580 recusants in St Andrew Holborn, 204 in St James Clerkenwell and 140 in St Giles in the Fields, contrasting with a mere 60 in St Martin in the Fields and 81 in St Margaret's, despite the vastly greater population in the Westminster parishes.[112] These numbers may constitute only a rough approximation, but they may suggest the relative proportions of Catholics in the different western parishes of the metropolis. Certainly in the 1620s, the ex-Catholic John Gee identified most Catholics as living in Holborn, although he also noted the presence of a Jesuit living in St Martin's Lane and, two secular priests lodging in the Strand, as well as 'a dangerous Jesuite' and another secular priest more vaguely 'lodging about Westminster'.[113] In Westminster itself, reported recusants seem to have been more numerous in the parish of St Clement Danes (perhaps owing to the proximity of the Inns of Court).[114] Certainly, a survey of December 1628 recorded as many confirmed recusants in St Clement's as in the other two Westminster parishes combined.[115]

Indigenous Catholicism seems to have been relatively thin on the ground. Despite the strong support for the revival of Catholicism in Marian St Margaret's, there is little evidence that significant numbers of parishioners deserted their parish church when Protestant services were reintroduced. In the 1580s a London alderman was alerted to the fact that 'there be two houses, joyning upon Tuthill fields, by Westminster, with fore doores one waie and back dores another waye, wherein papistes have bene usually lodged, being very suspicious houses by meanes of the situation of the places, having passages forward and backward'.[116] But overall there is little evidence of Catholic survivalism, at least in the form of recusancy. Some of the most prominent supporters of the Marian restoration at St Margaret's had died before

---

111 See M. Questier, 'Conformity, catholicism and the law' in P. Lake and M. Questier (eds.), *Conformity and Orthodoxy in the English Church, c.1560–1660* (Woodbridge, 2000), pp. 237–61.

112 A. Dures, 'The distribution of Catholic recusants in London and Middlesex c.1580–1629', *Essex Recusant* 10 (1968), p. 78. Cf. J.J. LaRocca (ed.), *Jacobean Recusant Rolls for Middlesex* (Catholic Record Society 76, 1997), p. vii. Dures's conclusion that by 1640 the county of Middlesex was probably 'the least catholic in England' (p. 75) needs to be treated with caution, however.

113 John Gee, *The Foot out of the Snare* (ed. T. Harmsen, Nijmegen, 1992), pp. 253, 255, 261, 269, 271.

114 A total of 112 recusants is recorded for the parish for 1581–1629 in Dures, 'Distribution', p. 78.

115 TNA, SP16/123/12. The totals reported are 11 (St Margaret's), 21 (St Martin's) and 33 (St Clement Danes).

116 *Queen Elizabeth and Her Times*, ed. T. Wright (2 vols., 1838), II, 250n.

Elizabeth succeeded to the throne. One who survived until 1575, Richard Dod, provides a hint of what may have kept conservative Roman Catholics attending St Margaret's church: his will bequests include the gift of a ring to Westminster Abbey's conservative dean, Gabriel Goodman.[117]

The contemporary preoccupation with crypto-popery in Westminster seems to have stemmed primarily from concern over the social importance of the individuals concerned, rather than their numbers. Westminster's increasing attractiveness to gentry and aristocratic visitors, many of whose families counted recusants and church papists among their members, helped to fuel these anxieties, which the presence of Catholics and crypto-Catholics in the House of Lords and at Court can have done little to diminish.[118]

It is certainly true that a throng of prominent recusants and church papists lived at least part of the year in Westminster. During the Jacobean period they included the earls of Northampton and Worcester and the countess of Arundel (all of whom had townhouses in Westminster), the dowager countess of Buckingham, the duchess of Buckingham, Sir George Calvert, Sir John Danvers, Sir Francis Cottington, Sir Henry Jerningham, Sir Thomas Vavasour, Lady Anne Conway, Sir George Cotton, Sir William Harman and Lady Olive Heneage.[119] Catholic gentry and aristocrats might also maintain establishments in which they employed their co-religionists, which in itself could draw other Catholics into the area. This was true not only of the great households but also of lesser gentry such as Lady Anne Waller, who was presented for recusancy in 1622, along with three others 'all of one household' in St Martin's parish.[120]

These Catholic residents do not, however, seem to have experienced rigorous prosecution through systematic enforcement of the recusancy laws. From 1581, laws against recusancy had been introduced by statute and St Martin's parish regularly prepared lists of recusants from this time onwards. Records of the Middlesex Sessions and the London consistory court also confirm the presentment of small numbers of recusants by both St Martin's and St Clement's parishes.[121] But the same handful of names tended to appear on lists year after year.[122] This may reflect the reluctance of

117 WAC, PCW, 120 Elsam. Ludford and Jennyngs had died by August 1558 and Smallwood by January 1558/9.

118 For Catholicism at the early Stuart Court see J.H. Aveling, *The Handle and the Axe* (1976), pp. 122–40. See also R. Clifton, 'Fear of popery' in C. Russell (ed.), *The Origins of the English Civil War* (1973); T. Cogswell, 'England and the Spanish Match' and P. Lake, 'Anti-popery: the structure of a prejudice' in R. Cust and A. Hughes (eds.), *Conflict in Early Stuart England* (1989).

119 Residency has been established primarily through poor-rate listings. For these individuals as Catholics see Aveling, *Handle and Axe*, p. 141 and *passim*.

120 F. Heal, *Hospitality in Early Modern England* (Oxford, 1990), pp. 169–75; LMA, WJ/SR (NS) 6, n.f. April 1622.

121 E.g. Kitto, pp. 330, 384, 394, 396–7; W. Le Hardy (ed.), *Calendar of Middlesex Sessions Records* (n.d.), V, 135; VI, 55; LMA, WJ/SR (NS) 15/101, 7/17.

122 E.g. *Middlesex County Records*, I, 124–9, 133, 140, 144–5, 156–8, 173, 198, 254–5.

local governors to prosecute those of higher social status – a thorny issue more generally in the area. In St Clement Danes, for example, officials noted the absence from church of the Howards of Arundel House, but they preferred to refer this delicate matter to Robert Cecil rather than take further action themselves.[123] Records also hint at deals struck with Catholic gentry. Sir Henry and Francis Jerningham, members of a prominent recusant family, were presented by St Martin's churchwardens in 1608. The ecclesiastical court, however, merely ordered them to certify either that they had attended church and received communion there or that the minister had read public prayers to them at home, in the presence of a 'convenient company'.[124]

In 1605 the uncovering of the Gunpowder Plot shook the nation. But it also revealed a Catholic plan designed to unfold in the very heart of Westminster, and therefore it might have been expected to generate more intense fears in the locality. Certainly, Westminster parishioners were closely involved in the Plot's most dramatic events: Edmund Doubleday (a burgess and St Margaret's vestryman) was the first to discover and grapple with Guy Fawkes, Peter Heywood (later a St Margaret's vestryman, burgess and JP) seized Fawkes's lantern, and Edward Forsett (a St Martin's vestryman) took a prominent part in examining the plotters afterwards.[125] The fact that the plot coupled secrecy with conspirators of high social status would also have fed fears of undetected recusancy as a component of the area's 'gentrification'. St Martin's lecturer Robert Hill composed a bloodcurdling 'prayer of thanksgiving' in which the reader was instructed to pray to God that, if Catholics' children did not reform, He would 'deliver them up to famine, let them drop by the force of the sword, let their wives be robbed of their children, and be widowes, and let their husbands bee put to death'.

Despite such rhetoric, the subsequent imposition of the oath of allegiance seems generally to have been moderate.[126] Edward Forsett composed a justification of the oath of allegiance in which he insisted on the importance of ensuring that Catholics took it.[127] Yet as one of the Middlesex justices enforcing the oath he seems to have exercised some leniency. In June 1612, for example, Forsett, in the company of Sir Walter Cope, examined one Margaret Church of St Clement Danes about her failure to take the oath of allegiance. On this occasion she was authorized to consult with the rector, John Layfield, 'touching the pointes of her religion which she holdeth contrary' to the teachings of the Church of England. In the meantime all proceedings

---

123 *HMC Hatfield*, XVII, 177.

124 LMA, DL/C/306, f. 565. The Jerninghams were a noted Catholic family in Elizabethan Suffolk, with links to the Exchequer: D. MacCulloch, *Suffolk and the Tudors* (Oxford, 1986), pp. 187, 212–14, 235–6, 252–3, 320.

125 Edmund Howes, *The Annales* (1615), p. 878; CUL, Add. MS 40/31; *DNB*, s.n. Edward Forsett.

126 On the oath of allegiance more generally see M.C. Questier, 'Loyalty, religion and state power in early modern England: English Romanism and the Jacobean oath of allegiance', *HJ* 40 (1997), 311–29.

against her were halted. She returned before the authorities late in August, when she and her husband reported that since her previous appearance Dr Layfield had been either out of town or not at leisure to confer with them. Margaret Church then requested that she be allowed additional time to confer, a petition which the bishop's chancellor granted as 'reasonable'. These entries are far from suggesting urgency and may indicate the extent to which the authorities were ready to turn a blind eye, or were at least prepared to be lenient towards those who expressed a willingness to confer about the oath.[128] Indeed, in 1627 St Martin's officials had to be pressured by the bishop's chancellor to make more presentments of recusants.[129]

The godly vicar of St Martin's, Thomas Montford, also exercised notable restraint in December 1618 when preaching the funeral sermon of Lady Cecily Blount, a lifelong Catholic who had converted to Protestantism only during her final illness. Montford did not use the occasion to rail against Catholics or to cast doubt on their loyalties. Although he warned his audience against simply accepting the religion of their ancestors, he granted that the Samarians (whom he compared to Catholics) had not lacked good intentions.[130] Montford's careful handling of the subject may have found some appreciative listeners: the problem of recusant wives was regularly raised in parliament and would have been familiar to many Westminster gentlemen.[131]

Yet for all this restraint shown in dealing with familiar individual local Catholics, St Martin's nevertheless became a notable venue for anti-catholic preaching, as we shall see.

SEPARATISTS AND HETERODOXY

London was a centre of radical puritan activity in the early modern period, and it also seems that Westminster attracted its own share of religious radicals.[132] We have already noted the presence of popular prophets in Westminster. More radical religious ideas were also to be heard. John Hilton reputedly confessed before convocation in

---

127 E. Forsett, *A Defence of the Right of Kings* (1624), pp. 5, 7, 85, 89, 92–3.

128 LMA, DL/C/310, ff. 123, 166. Cf. *Calendar of Middlesex Sessions*, VII, 210.

129 WAC, F3, ff. 99, 100. When they chose, however, Westminster officials could single out individual recusants for more vigorous treatment: e.g. WAC, F2 vol. 2, f. 355.

130 T. Montford, *A Sermon Preached at the Funerall of Lady Blount* (1619), esp. pp. 16, 19, 25, 37. Lady Cecily Blount was the wife of Sir Richard Blount of Mapledurham: see Merritt thesis, pp. 348, 386.

131 W. Notestein, *The House of Commons, 1604–1610* (New Haven and London, 1971), pp. 281, 285; Foster, *Proceedings*, I, 50–1. It was not just wives who could prove an embarrassment. The prominent St Margaret's parishioner William Mann had a Catholic brother Francis, who was seized at a mass in London: Bodl., Rawl. MS D.399, f. 95v. See also A. Milton, 'A qualified intolerance: the limits and ambiguities of early Stuart anti-catholicism' in A. Marotti (ed.), *Catholicism and Anti-Catholicism in Early Modern English Texts* (1999).

132 For recent discussion see P. Lake, *The Boxmaker's Revenge* (Manchester, 2001).

1584 'that he had said in a sermon at St Martin's in the Fields that the Old and New Testaments are but fables, that himself was no Christian but a heathen, and further had blasphemed Christ most horribly'.[133] The same vestry that paid the prophetess Anne Walker also supported the firebrand preacher John Everard, who by 1626 was already straying into antinomian language in a sermon at St Martin's in which he distinguished 'them that are perfect & sublim'd' from 'such as were not yet perfect', and not many years later Everard was to embrace Familism.[134] The parish of St Clement Danes had also played host to a number of prominent Familists with links to the Court in the late Elizabethan period. Most notable of these was Robert Seale, who even served the locality on the prestigious Court of Burgesses.[135]

While Familists still felt able to attend the services of the established church, other Protestants felt compelled to separate from it altogether, and again such groups were to be found in Westminster. In 1568 a group of seventy-two people – members of the so-called 'Plumber's Hall Congregation' – were found together in the house of the goldsmith James Tynne in St Martin's parish, and were subsequently examined by clerics including Dean Goodman. Only three of those taken, however, seem to have been inhabitants of Westminster.[136] The Jacobean period witnessed a new wave of separatist activity in the face of the campaign for clerical subscription that followed the Hampton Court conference.[137] St Martin's lecturer Robert Hill, who had connections with radical non-subscribers such as Samuel Hieron, showed an acute awareness of the danger. His 1606 catechism even directed readers on what to do 'if you be tempted to forsake the church, because of some abuses supposed in the church'.[138] Hill expanded this section of the work in 1610, and particularly addressed arguments put forward by the Brownists, who were being prosecuted in significant numbers at the Middlesex Sessions at this time.[139] Further editions of Hill's work addressed the complaints of those who refused to attend services where set forms of prayer were used

133 E. Cardwell (ed.), *Synodalia* (2 vols., Oxford, 1842), II, 554–5. Hilton's particular errors seem to have concerned the nature of the Trinity, of Christ's substance, and his redemption.

134 TNA, SP16/41/73; T. Wilson Hayes, 'John Everard and the Familist tradition' in M. and J. Jacob (eds.), *The Origins of Anglo-American Radicalism* (1984), pp. 65–7. Cf. Lake, *Boxmaker's Revenge*, pp. 270–6; D. Como and P. Lake, 'Puritans, antinomians and Laudians in Caroline London: the strange case of Peter Shaw in context', *JEH* 50 (1999).

135 TNA, SP12/268/68; Christopher Marsh, *The Family of Love in English Society, 1550–1630* (Cambridge, 1994), pp. 92, 154, 165–6. On Familism in the early Stuart metropolis see Lake, *Boxmaker's Revenge*, pp. 179–83. Seale died in St Clement's in 1606–7.

136 TNA, SP12/46/46, gives the names of those found (transcribed in C. Burrage, *Early English Dissenters* (2 vols., Cambridge, 1912), II, 9–11).

137 P. Milward, *Religious Controversies of the Jacobean Age* (1978), pp. 3–7.

138 The reply explained that a sick child was not abandoned by its parent, nor was a diseased body by its owner: Hill, *Christs Prayer*, i, 66. On Hill's links with Hieron see Merritt, 'Pastoral tight-rope', pp. 157–8.

139 Hill, *Pathway* (1610), i, 76–7; Milward, *Religious Controversies*, pp. 48–53, 58–9; *Calendar of Middlesex Sessions*, VI, 54, 155.

(because they considered them unlawful), and those whose distaste for kneeling at communion could be a forerunner of 'schismaticall separation'.[140] It seems likely that at least some of these ideas were circulating among the St Martin's parishioners to whom Hill dedicated his work, although, unlike areas such as Southwark, Westminster does not seem to have actually fostered separatist congregations.

There is little obvious evidence of separatism in Westminster by the 1630s, but its emergence in the 1640s can have caused few surprises. By 1641 there were reports of lay preachers in Westminster, but even so the heartlands of metropolitan separatism lay elsewhere, and abusive remarks made around this time against ministers during divine service at St Clement Danes, St Margaret's and Westminster Abbey seem to have been the work of Londoners from outside the Westminster parishes.[141]

RELIGIOUS POLITICS IN THE 1620S AND 1630S

It was a feature of English religious life in the 1620s and 1630s that religion became increasingly politicized. Fears of Catholicism were exacerbated by the pro-Spanish policies of the Crown. The initial failure of the government to support the Elector Palatine and the cause of international Protestantism also heightened fears that a crypto-Catholic faction was at work at Court. The presence after 1625 of a Catholic queen, who worshipped in Catholic chapels, did little to dampen such fears. In addition, anti-puritan policies and the promotion of the 'beauty of holiness' in the English church fed fears that the ecclesiastical establishment had itself been taken over by crypto-Catholic forces. These fears circulated in Westminster as much as elsewhere, and played a significant role in religious life in the locality in the 1620s and 1630s.

THE 1620S: ANTI-CATHOLICISM AND PROTESTANT MILITARISM

During these years Westminster – and particularly the parish of St Martin's – emerged as a prominent venue for the expression of anti-Catholic feeling. This was true despite the fact that numbers of indigenous Catholics were low, and their treatment reasonably lenient. Instead, traditional anxieties about crypto-Catholics among the seasonal gentry visitors now extended to include fears of highly placed Catholics at the heart of

---

140 Hill, *Pathway* (1613), 'Christ's Prayer Expounded', p. 119 (cf. pp. 120–37), 'A Communicant Instructed', pp. 30–3.

141 John Taylor, *The Brownists Synagogue* (1641), pp. 2, 4; K. Lindley, *Popular Politics and Religion in Civil War London* (Aldershot, 1997), p. 88. Note also the St Margaret's parishioner among the separatists before High Commission in May 1632: S.R. Gardiner (ed.), *Reports of Cases in the Courts of Star Chamber and High Commission* (Camden Society n.s. 39, 1886), p. 295.

government. In 1612 pews were broken in St Martin's church when crowds flocked to hear Lewis Bayly, chaplain to the late Prince Henry, deliver a notorious sermon in which he condemned Catholic privy councillors who 'tell theyre wives what passes [in Council], and they carie yt to theyre Jesuites and confessors'.[142] The political danger of Catholicism was increasingly emphasized. Preachers such as Hill sought to dissuade their listeners from converting to popery by condemning it as a religion 'where subjects are so freed from allegeance to their soveraigne, that if he be not a Romanist, it shall be meritorious to kill him'.[143]

Controversy surrounding the Spanish Match provided a catalyst for further anti-Catholic preaching. The Spanish Match itself entailed a proposed marriage between the Prince of Wales and the Spanish Infanta and was first widely mooted in 1614. Fears for the state of the monarchy grew as some perceived King James to be favouring Catholics at the expense of the godly. In August 1622, James ordered the suspension of the penal laws against Catholics. This, followed by some dramatic aristocratic conversions to Catholicism, fuelled fears of a threat from within the governing ranks of society.[144] Some of the most virulent anti-Catholic rhetoric heard in the capital came from St Martin's pulpit when Dr John Everard was parish lecturer. This was a period that coincided with revived plans for the Spanish Match, culminating in a trip to Spain by the Prince of Wales in 1623. Everard seems to have been appointed to the lectureship in January 1617 and was selected in preference to one Dr Hammer, the candidate recommended by the earls of Pembroke and Montgomery. Even before his official appointment Everard had preached at St Martin's, at which time the vestry had 'taken a good lyking' to him. Although the vestry passed over the earls' candidate, they noted that their support of Everard was 'not without the like approbacion of diverse gentlemen of learning and Judgement in the parishe'. It seems that Everard may already have obtained the strong backing that would later prove so useful to him.[145] While the outspoken Everard's preaching regularly aroused controversy, it was his sermons at the time of the Spanish Match in 1621–22 which gained him most notoriety, when they led to his imprisonment on six or seven occasions. Everard obviously possessed influential backers, for no sooner did he preach yet another anti-Spanish sermon than 'some

---

142 N.E. McClure (ed.), *The Letters of John Chamberlain* (2 vols., Philadelphia, 1939), I, 392; WAC, F2 vol. 1, f. 179. For another prominent anti-Catholic sermon delivered at St Martin's in the same year see Richard Sheldon, *The First Sermon of R. Sheldon priest, after his Conversion* (1612).

143 Hill, *Christs Prayer*, i, 65–6. Hill expanded this section in the 1610 edition of the same work: i, 75. The 1606 edition (iii, 32–7) also includes a prayer of thanksgiving which deals partly with the Gunpowder Plot, and which was repeated in later editions.

144 Clifton, 'Fear', pp. 157–8, 165; Cogswell, 'England and the Spanish Match', pp. 111, 118; A. Milton and A. Walsham, 'Introduction' to Richard Montagu, 'Concerning recusancie of communion with the Church of England' in S. Taylor (ed.), *From Cranmer to Davidson* (Church of England Record Society 7, 1999), pp. 77–80.

145 WAC, F2 vol. 1, f. 71. Accordingly, Dr Montford and the vestry made choice of Everard 'as much as in them lyeth'. The qualification is interesting, in that it suggests that final approval lay elsewhere, perhaps among those 'diverse gentlemen of learning and Judgement'.

lord or other', it was said, would intervene on his behalf, obtaining a royal pardon for him. The frequency with which this was necessary even provoked King James to quip, 'What is this Dr Ever-out? his name shall be Dr Never-out'.[146]

It remains unclear which noblemen acted to protect Everard.[147] His aristocratic protectors need not necessarily have been St Martin's parishioners: Everard's political outspokenness would have been politically useful to many opposed to the Spanish Match who dared not raise such objections themselves. What is clear, however, is that Everard was not simply supported by aristocrats: the less socially exalted ranks of vestrymen who had first urged his appointment also gave their lecturer strong support during his periods of imprisonment. In March 1621, shortly after his first imprisonment, the churchwardens paid Everard £10 'by order from the Vestry'. Again in 1622 another £10 was paid out to Everard 'to releeve him in prison and helpe to Release him lyeinge in Execution for debt'. The churchwardens were careful once again to note that the payment was made 'by the consent of the Vestreymen and by their appointment'.[148] It is notable that the same vestry had previously authorized a payment to Andrew Willet, another cleric who actively opposed the Spanish Match.[149]

Little is known of the individual religious views of the well-to-do craftsmen, victuallers and tailors who comprised St Martin's vestry in this period.[150] But there is no doubting the strength of the anti-catholic feeling which expressed itself in St Martin's churchwardens' accounts for 1622, when the traditional ringing on the anniversary of the Gunpowder Plot was said to be 'in memorie of that great delivrance from that hellishe Gunnepowder treason which was to have been executed at the Parliament house at Westminster, Contrived by Treacherous Papists, and prevented by Gods

---

146 Everard also attacked the Court of Orphans at a Paul's Cross sermon in 1618, after which the bishop of London compelled him to apologize publicly for slandering the Lord Mayor and aldermen. John Everard, *Some Gospel Treasures Unopened* (1653), preface, sigs. a2v–a3r; *DNB*, s.n. John Everard. Everard also published a providentialist tract in 1622 warning of the influence of Antichrist: Walsham, *Providence*, p. 219 (cf. p. 268).

147 For Everard's links with the earl of Holland, which date from around 1623, see Merritt thesis, pp. 386–7. Everard preached at least once at St Martin's after he had ceased to be lecturer: TNA, SP14/41/73.

148 WAC, F2 vol. 2, ff. 356, 402.

149 WAC, F2001, f. 138; *CSPD 1611–18*, p. 525. Willet enjoyed close relations with Montford and also the vestryman Raphe Dobbinson, whom Willet persuaded to found a hospital in Barley, the town where Willet served as vicar and where Dobbinson had been born: A. Willet, *Sacrorum Emblematum Centuria Una* (?1592), sigs. E1v–E2r; TNA, PCC, Prob. 11/139/61; A. Willet, *Tetrastylon* (appended to *Synopsis Papismi* in 1613) in *Synopsis Papismi* (1634), pp. 1224, 1233.

150 Their wills, however, often contain a longer than average preamble expressing strongly worded but orthodox Protestant beliefs (e.g. Hacket, Greene). Some of those whose wills survive trusted, like William Stacy, to enjoy life everlasting 'amongst other the elect children of god', while others directed that their funerals should eschew 'vayne ostentation' (Dobbinson) and mourning 'blackes' (Waller). Some asked for a sermon at their funeral (Brewer, Waller) or made donations towards a new pulpit (Rowlandson). The surviving wills are: TNA, PCC, Prob. 11/150/143 (Stacy), 11/98/111 (Rowlandson), 11/139/61 (Dobbinson), 11/137/5 (Hacket), 11/139/2 (Waller), 11/184/119 (Brewer).

gratious Goodnes'.[151] It is striking that the same expressions begin to appear with increasingly regularity in the churchwardens' accounts of St Margaret's parish too.[152]

The return of Charles from Spain (without a Catholic bride) clearly delighted many Westminster's residents. Simonds D'Ewes reported the ecstatic response of Westminster to Charles's safe return from Spain without his Spanish bride, remarking that 'ther weere 335 [bonfires] or therabouts between Whitehall and Temple Barre'.[153] But Charles's subsequent Catholic marriage to Henrietta Maria lent any future commemoration of Charles's return an implicitly critical edge. Again, it is noticeable that it was St Margaret's parish that made a point of ringing the church bells on the anniversary of Charles's return from Spain: first in 1630 (after the hasty dissolution of parliament in 1629 and the subsequent peace treaty with Spain) and then every year from 1637 onwards.[154]

Why should the normally conservative St Margaret's have become more prone to expressions of anti-Spanish and anti-Catholic sentiment, and of support for the Protestant cause on the continent, in the 1620s? A significant influence here may have been the minister appointed in 1622, the well-connected Isaac Bargrave, who seems to have gained the position at the same time as his appointment as chaplain to Prince Charles. Bargrave was a strong supporter of the Protestant Elector Palatine: he had urged in a Court sermon in 1621 that his audience should not forget 'the afflictions of our brethren abroad' and should aid them in their hour of need. In a sermon before the Commons in 1624, Bargrave had attacked 'Church Papists' and 'English Pensioners to Forraine States', urging his listeners to remember God's blessings in the defeat of the Armada and Gunpowder Plot, and in Charles's safe return from Spain.[155] His successor, Vincent Peirce, may have shared similar sentiments. Among charitable payments to poor ministers (which themselves are something of a novelty at St Margaret's) we also find payments to 'distressed' Protestant ministers from the Valteline and the Palatinate, and a poor French minister, with one payment specifically made at Peirce's request.[156] Another unusual feature of Westminster life in the 1620s was the almost continuous presence of parliament in the locality. As a result, St Margaret's church, which had held services for the House of Commons from 1614,

---

151 Cogswell, 'England and the Spanish Match', pp. 116–19; WAC, F2 vol. 1, f. 406.

152 In November 1628 St Margaret's churchwardens' accounts for the first time spell out that the bells were rung on the fifth 'in memorie of our deliverance from the Gunpowder treason': WAC, E16, f. 30v. Cf. E17, f. 32.

153 *The Diary of Sir Simonds D'Ewes, 1622–1624*, ed. E. Bourcier (Paris, 1974), pp. 162, 188. The war fever of the succeeding months led to popular riots by the Spanish ambassador's house in the Strand.

154 WAC, E17, f. 32; E20 (1637–38), n.f.; E21, ff. 65, 124; E23 (1640–41), n.f.

155 Isaac Bargrave, *A Sermon against Selfe Policy* (1624), p. 38; Bargrave, *A Sermon preached before the Honourable Assembly* (1624), pp. 23–6, 34; Bodl., MS Rawlinson C. 799, ff. 185v–186.

156 WAC, E15, fol. 43v; E16, f. 31r–v; E17, ff. 31v, 33r–v, 35v, 36.

found itself being used in this manner with greater frequency.[157] It was in St Margaret's church, for example, that the Commons received the sacrament in thanksgiving for the Prince's return from Spain, with Bargrave preaching to them.[158]

St Margaret's parishioners could hardly have been unaware of parliamentary developments, or of the sermons preached and speeches made on religious and political issues. In 1628 bells rang out from the church to celebrate Charles I's acceptance of the Petition of Right, and one of St Margaret's vestrymen, Thomas Morrice, was one of the so-called 'patriots' elected to serve as an MP in the same parliament.[159] Regular parliaments also meant that St Margaret's parishioners as well as those of other metropolitan parishes would have gained from the sudden surge in preaching available from bishops in town for the parliament.[160] That being said, there is little evidence of the major interference by MPs in parish affairs that became a feature of St Margaret's from the early years of the Long Parliament.[161] Clearly, St Margaret's officials must themselves by this time have been more sympathetic towards that support for the 'Protestant Cause' on the continent and antipathy to international Catholicism that Professor Adams has dubbed 'political puritanism', although there are few if any obvious radical puritans joining the vestry in this period.[162] Another factor that may help to explain signs of political puritanism in St Margaret's is the role played by John Williams, the dean of Westminster, who now enjoyed an increasingly strained rela-

---

157 In 1614 the House of Commons had objected to the popish associations of the type of communion bread being used in Westminster Abbey and had switched to St Margaret's: M. Jansson (ed.), *Proceedings in Parliament 1614* (Philadelphia, 1988), pp. 37, 42, 74, 99. These services for parliament did not involve St Margaret's parishioners, who attended church on other days and were forced to observe different fast days from those observed by parliament: e.g. *LJ*, III, p. 711.

158 *The Holles Account of Proceedings in the House of Commons*, ed. C. Thompson (Orsett, 1985), pp. 1, 11; Bargrave, *A sermon preached, passim.*

159 WAC, E16, f. 29; Williams, *Court and Times*, I, 327. Other St Margaret's vestrymen served in 1620s parliaments, but William Mann (1621, 1624 and 1625) and Peter Heywood (1626) were presumably of more conservative sentiments.

160 E.g. Hampshire Record Office, MS 44M69/F6 (Diary of Sir Richard Paulet, 1610). Cf. TNA, SP16/119/33.

161 See J.E. Smith, *Catalogue of Westminster Records* (1900), p. 66.

162 S. Adams, 'The Protestant cause: religious allegiance with the West European Calvinist communities as a political issue in England, 1585–1630' (Oxford D.Phil., 1973). A number of possible supporters of 'political puritanism' can be identified. William Bell, one of the churchwardens for 1628–30 and later a vestryman, was one of Westminster's Long Parliament MPs. Signatories who vetted parish accounts in 1628 included John Brigham (who continued to serve as a Westminster burgess throughout the 1640s), and the MP Thomas Morrice (described at the time as a 'patriot'). The 1630 accounts were signed by Thomas Kirke and John Biscoe, who were both collectors for parliament in August 1642. Biscoe and Edward Martin (who was signing parish accounts by 1638) are described as 'noteworthy radical figures' in Lindley, *Popular Politics*, pp. 146, 220. Biscoe and Martin seem to be the exceptions, however. Certainly figures such as Kirke should not be associated with political radicalism since he, along with a number of collectors for parliament and signatories of the supposedly 'radical' petition of 11 January 1642, was also a signatory of the Westminster peace petition. HLRO, MP 29 August 1642, 20 December 1642 (parchment collection, box 8), 11 January 1644 (*sic, vere* 1642).

tionship with the government. Although the feisty Williams may not necessarily have promoted anti-Catholic and pro-Palatine sentiments in the parish, the lack of a restraining hand from the Abbey may in itself have been significant.[163]

Anti-Catholic attitudes around the 1620s often combined with a bellicose Protestant nationalism. A tailor in St Clement Danes known as 'the Prophet Ball' was reported in 1619 as having created and 'putt forth much mony upon it' a new sect entitled 'Of the beleefe', 'which hold that our Kings Majestie shall in the yeare 1622 be crowned Emperor of Roome [Rome] & putt downe the Pope'.[164] A less eccentric outlet for Protestant militarism came in the form of the Military Company, created in Westminster in 1616. This was founded in emulation of the revived Artillery Company of the City of London, and seems to have been the first of many such imitations that were founded throughout England around this time.[165] These companies acted as a focus for Protestant civic militarism in the wake of the confessional warfare on the continent. Their rationale was the revival of the godly chivalric honour of the past in the face of present-day decadence and corruption: in the words of one of the Military Company's preachers, John Everard, to 'pluck up again, the sunke and drowned honour of our Country'.[166] The most famous puritan preachers of the time were recruited to deliver sermons to such companies, and Westminster's Company was no exception.[167] The Military House which the Company occupied in St Martin's Field was furnished expensively, perhaps to cater to its more wealthy supporters.[168] While the Military Company's symbolic importance is clear, it would, however, be wrong to overemphasize its significance in Westminster society. Its members do not seem to have included parish officials from either St Margaret's or St Martin's.[169] Nor

---

163 There is a reference to a lecturer at St Margaret's, one Mr Harris, who preached to the Commons in the parish church on a fast day in February 1629 (*Commons Debates for 1629*, ed. W. Notestein and F.H. Relf (Minneapolis, 1921), p. 42; A. Searle (ed.), *Barrington Family Letters 1628–32* (Camden Society 4th ser. 28, 1983), p. 53). But this appears to be simply a matter of careless phrasing: Harris does not appear to have had any official or permanent connection with the parish beyond preaching in the church on this occasion, and there is no other evidence of a parish lectureship before the 1640s (for which see LPL, COMM. XIIa/12/ vol. 12, ff. 376–377).

164 BL, Trumbull MS XVIII, no. 41 (18 November 1619). Ball would later be imprisoned for having 'quoted scripture' to the Privy Council 'mightily' when opposing the forced loan: Williams, *Court and Times*, I, 154.

165 W. Hunt, 'Civic chivalry and the English Civil War' in A. Grafton and A. Blair (eds.), *The Transmission of Culture in Early Modern Europe* (Philadelphia, 1990), 204–37 at pp. 215–18.

166 John Everard, *The Arriereban: A Sermon preached to the Company of the Military Yarde* (1618), p. 103.

167 Hunt, 'Civic chivalry', pp. 222–6; Thomas Taylor, 'The Valew of True Valour . . . Discovered in a Sermon preached July 25 before the worthy Gentlemen of the Military Company', pp. 7, 19, 24–5 in his *Two Sermons* (1629).

168 TNA, C5/486/26; SP16/88/35.

169 For example, the Company accounts for the years 1616–18 in TNA, SP16/88/35, do not mention the names of a single vestryman from St Margaret's or St Martin's. One important later exception is the St Martin's parish official and JP George Hulbert, who became President of the Military Company in the 1630s: TNA, SP16/413/129.

did the Company always enjoy harmonious relations with the rest of the community. Indeed, the Company clashed directly and acrimoniously with the same St Martin's vestry that supported John Everard as its lecturer.[170] Nevertheless, whatever the complexities of local allegiances, the 1620s had witnessed a marked raising of the religious and political temperature in both Westminster parishes.

THE 1630S: LAUDIANISM AND CATHOLICISM

If fears for the integrity of English Protestantism were aroused in the 1620s, they were intensified by the ecclesiastical policies pursued in the 1630s and associated with Archbishop Laud. These focused upon restoring 'the beauty of holiness' in parish churches (most notably the railing in of communion tables at the east end of the church) along with the revival of the wealth and independent authority of the church and clergy. These initiatives posed obvious problems for those parishes that had pursued a more word-centred, evangelical piety in which the laity had expected to play an active role. Such parishes were also vulnerable to the increasing drive to prevent unlicensed 'puritanical' preaching which strayed into Calvinist doctrine or implicit criticism of the government.

Westminster was also the setting for the punishment of the most notorious opponents of Laudian policies. It was in New Palace Yard that Burton, Bastwick and Prynne were pilloried (and one St Margaret's parishioner even left £10 in his will to Bastwick while the latter was imprisoned in the Westminster Gatehouse).[171] Other prosecutions struck at the heart of Westminster's establishment. The dean of Westminster, John Williams, was Laud's great enemy, and his prosecution and suspension occurred in front of the whole locality. After Williams had been condemned in the Court of Star Chamber (a short stroll from the Abbey) in 1637, it was ordered that the dean's suspension from all ecclesiastical offices should be publicly announced in Westminster Abbey in the time of divine service, when the greater part of the congregation had assembled. At the same time, Lambert Osbaldeston, the master of Westminster School and an ally of Williams, avoided punishment only by fleeing in disguise. If this was not enough to ensure Laud's interest in Westminster, he was also himself a prebendary of the Abbey, as well as possessing jurisdiction over two of the Westminster parishes as bishop of London (from July 1628) and archbishop of Canterbury (from 1633).[172]

---

170 See above, pp. 206. This should provide a minor corrective to Hunt's elision of the artillery companies with the defence of common fields against enclosure, and his implication that the opponents of the companies were merely recusants and 'the Hispanophile faction at Court' (Hunt, 'Civic chivalry', pp. 215, 226–7). The Westminster Company also seems to have struggled to match the godly prestige of the City of London's Artillery Company: in a sermon delivered to the Military Company in the late 1620s the famous puritan Thomas Taylor berated it for its lack of godly zeal: Taylor, 'The Valew', p. 26.

171 Knowler, II, 85; WAC, PCW, 31 Todd.

172 *CSPD 1637*, p. 326; Hacket, *Scrinia*, ii, 110–37; Knowler, II, 149–50.

We have seen that Reformation legislation (although admittedly more far-reaching) had not been implemented in a uniform fashion in the Westminster parishes. Would Laud's reforms fare any better? At first glance, the Westminster parishes would appear to represent a success story for the Laudian reforms. The churches of St Margaret's and St Martin's appear to have possessed communion rails a good deal earlier than the rest of the metropolis. While we would expect a prompt response from the conservative parish of St Margaret's, it is particularly striking how Laudian innovations seem to have taken hold in the more evangelical parish of St Martin's. The communion table was raised and railed in relatively early (1630), the font coloured, the communion plate consecrated and a position of organist generously funded. So, was St Martin's finally emerging as an unequivocally 'courtly' parish, with royal influence promoting religious practices that closely mirrored those of the church and royal Court? A closer examination reveals a far more complex picture.

For all their apparent capitulation to the Laudian programme, St Martin's vestry had in fact been involved in a series of tense stand-offs with the King and bishop of London during the later 1620s. The first of these occurred in 1627, and concerned that perennial point of controversy, the St Martin's lectureship. On the death of John Andrewes in February 1627, the King attempted to place one of his own chaplains, Humphrey Peake, in the lectureship. The vestry strongly protested, and it was only by the mediation of the second earl of Salisbury that a compromise was reached. Peake in the end was appointed, but only by order of the vestry and 'others of the parish of good sort' who had heard Peake preach, and only after the King had accepted 'that the libertye of the Parish in the free election of the lecturer shall not hereafter by any auchthoritie of his Majestie or any under him bee hindered or infringed'.[173] This point of principle was confirmed in a letter written by Bishop Montaigne to St Martin's vicar Thomas Montford and the vestry. The bishop admitted that he had formerly appointed Peake on the King's command, but that the King had now instructed him to leave the parishioners to a free election. What is particularly striking about this clash, however, is the care that St Martin's vestry took to protect themselves against future royal intervention. A copy of Montaigne's letter was carefully placed in the vestry minutes, and the file in which the original appointment had been made was officially removed from the records of the bishopric to prevent the creation of a precedent. The removal of this file took place formally at the office of the bishop's registrar, in the presence of both Montaigne's and Montford's servants.[174] The ultimate acceptance of Peake, then, seems to have been viewed as a price worth paying to secure a free selection in the future.

---

173 WAC, F2002, f. 51v; Seaver, *Puritan Lectureships*, p. 141. The involvement of the second earl of Salisbury testifies to the continuing importance of Cecil links in St Martin's. These were preserved partly by the second earl's regular payments towards the lecturer's stipend throughout the 1620s. For example, Salisbury paid the lecturer Andrewes a regular allowance of £6 a year (e.g. Hatfield House Accounts, 160/5 (1625), ff. 55, 106). This represented a sizeable advance on his father Robert Cecil's payment of only £2 a year to Robert Hill (*ibid.*, Box G/13, ff. 13, 49v, 80).

174 WAC, F2002, f. 52.

A significant figure in this exchange was probably St Martin's vicar, Thomas Montford. It is tempting to see the hand of Montford – a former acting bishop of London – behind moves to prevent the creation of an ecclesiastical precedent. It is not clear how much the principle of parochial independence meant to Montford, but it seem clear that he was willing to lend his assistance to those who opposed the anti-Calvinist churchmanship of Laud (whom he would have encountered as a fellow pre-bendary at St Paul's and Westminster). The importance of Montford's role is further suggested by the pace of events after his death in 1633. Just over a month later, on the very day of the first recorded vestry meeting after Montford's death (which was hardly a coincidence), the King wrote to Laud recommending a new lecturer for the parish to replace the departing Peake. He briskly stated his expectation that the parishioners would yield to him, 'considering the greatnes of that parishe, and the quality of the Auditors'. Laud passed on Charles's letter, along with one of his own, in time to be read at the vestry's meeting. Laud's letter is more tactfully phrased, stressing that he would not have named anyone to them 'because the maintenance ariseth from the Parishe', but urging them to follow the King's wishes.[175] Under such pressure, the vestry seems to have complied without further incident, and one Alexander Levingston was appointed.[176] But if the acceptance of a royal appointee as lecturer was a striking concession, it was the immediate replacement of Montford by William Bray, one of Laud's own chaplains, that was more significant for St Martin's parish.[177]

Laud's anxiety to place his right-hand man in the parish would have been sharpened not only by the conflict over the appointment of Peake in 1627 but also by a series of problems with lecturers and sermons at St Martin's in the years that had followed Peake's appointment. While evidence is fragmentary, it seems to be the case that, while parishioners acceded to the King's wish to appoint Peake as lecturer, they then simply paid into a further fund to support lecturers who were more to their liking. This meant figures such as the mercurial John Everard (who was still preaching in the parish in December 1626) but also the notorious puritan Thomas Foxley, who seems to have preached a weekly lecture at St Martin's throughout the second half of the 1620s. Indeed his lectures may have started around the same time that Peake became the 'official' lecturer.[178] Thereafter Foxley was briefly suspended by Laud, at

175 WAC, F2002, f. 93; TNA, SP16/236/12.

176 See the references to Levingston as lecturer in WAC, F3, 1633–34, n.f.; GL, MS 9537/14, f. 37v, 9537/15, f. 52r. Information about the St Martin's lectureship is always only fragmentary. The vestry sent a messenger to Bray in Canterbury later in the 1630s concerning the election of the parish lecturer: WAC, F3, 1638–39, n.f.

177 Bray was instituted on 2 March 1633 and 'received into the vestry' ten days later: GL, MS 9531/15, f. 71v; WAC, F3 (1632–33), n.f.

178 HLRO, MP 1640. Formerly or concurrently lecturer at St Antholin's in the 1620s, Foxley had been very closely involved with the Feoffees for Impropriations, and may well have been the appointee that the Feoffees had in mind when they inquired about purchasing the new living of St Paul's Covent Garden from the earl of Bedford: BL, Harl. MS 832, ff. 5v, 28.

which time St Martin's churchwardens were cross-examined about one of his sermons. Parish officials, however, chose a stand-in who proved no less inflammatory. This was Abraham Grymes, lecturer at St Nicholas Acons and St Katherine Cree, who was soon called before Laud himself, about a sermon preached at St Martin's in Foxley's stead. In this sermon Grymes had attacked the practice of bowing at the name of Jesus – a practice that was being revived and vigorously enforced by Laudians. Grymes astutely tailored his sermon to his titled St Martin's audience, arguing for the pre-eminence of the title 'Christ' over the name 'Jesus' by noting that in the same way the titles of lord, duke and countess were more to be esteemed than mere Christian names.[179] Clearly, the popularity of St Martin's pulpit was still as important as it had been in the 1610s, and, while Laud and the King might hope to control the main stipendiary lecturer, they could not ensure that this would clinch control of the parish pulpit. Foxley continued to be a thorn in Laud's side for much of the 1630s: his lectureship was suspended ostensibly because of the plague, and he was finally imprisoned in 1637, but several parishioners petitioned the Long Parliament for his release.[180]

The arrival of Laud's trusted chaplain, Bray, at St Martin's obviously does much to explain the ceremonial innovations that began to be implemented in the parish church. Bray remained with Laud at Lambeth for much of the time (St Martin's churchwardens constantly visited him there, or even at Croydon), but he attended most vestry meetings and was presumably able to exercise a veto on any major religious decision. To Bray we can perhaps attribute innovations that reflected a preoccupation with ceremonial reverence and the sacred character of church furniture and ornaments. These included measures such as the erection of a board which contained an order 'concerning putting off hattes, in time of divine service' and the decision to abandon the normal practice of simply borrowing plate for communion from local vintners, and instead to purchase two 'double guilt' silver chalices for nearly £34 and three silver 'belly Pottes' for £81 10s.[181] Bray was certainly described as having directed the purchase of two damask cloths for the communion table, and may have been behind the acquisition of 'two tables part guilded concerning the relation of the sacrament'.[182]

Nevertheless, some innovations seem to have entered the church independently of direct Laudian influence. The introduction of new communion rails, for example, was under discussion by the vestry as early as 1626, and coloured glass was installed in church windows by 1629. There is no need to see these innovations as prompted by Laudian sentiments: an orderly and attractive church was a fitting receptacle for local

179 WAC, F3 (1630–31); GL, MS 9531/15, ff. 21v–23.

180 HLRO, MP 1640. Signatories of the petition were Anthony Withers, Nicholas Skynner, John Clendon and Samuel Grant. See also *CJ*, VI, 605.

181 WAC, F3 (1634–35), n.f. The engraving and 'colouring' of the chalices is specifically described in the accounts as being by Bray's direction. Note also the two new surplices purchased in 1634.

182 WAC, F2002, f. 105v; F3 (1635–36), n.f.

pride, and even Calvinist bishops such as George Abbot had seen the practical benefits of processing to the altar to receive communion.[183] The railing of the communion table formed only part of a substantial beautification of the chancel, which itself preceded significant work on the west end of the church and the building of a new south gallery.[184] What is striking about the communion rails and stained glass, however, is the fact that, in contrast to all the more substantial work of beautification, the vestry took enormous care that the introduction of these items should not be misinterpreted as indicating 'ceremonialist' sentiments. A special committee was established to enquire about the rails around the communion table, and was exceptionally required to certify to the vicar Dr Montford for further approval and direction. It was only after more than three years of intense and protracted discussion that the rails were ordered to be finished in February 1630 'in such sort as is now agreed'. The vestry seem throughout to have carefully used the word 'frame' rather than 'rail', and the church-wardens' accounts refer painstakingly to the 'rayles and Ballessters (being French Termes) sett upp about the Communion Table' according to a bill 'allowed and signed by divers of the vestry'. Clearly, such matters were deeply controversial and vestrymen appear to have been anxious to patrol the style and even the nomenclature of the communion rails, lest they be glossed in an erroneously crypto-popish fashion.[185] The reglazing of church windows was monitored with equal care, with the stipulation that the great west window was to be glazed 'with white glass only', and coloured glass placed in the east window only 'suitable to that which remayneth'.[186]

Of course, church beautification and even the changes introduced by Bray may have found support among parishioners. Bray may have prompted the purchase of new communion plate, but other parishioners donated communion plate too, and so-called 'benevolences' towards the church fabric (even if many of these were in effect glorified fines) helped to cover the further costs of the plate, whereas the new church of St Paul Covent Garden found it necessary to levy a rate for its own plate.[187] While

---

183 J.F. Merritt, 'Puritans, Laudians and the phenomenon of church building in early Stuart London', *HJ* 41 (1998); G.W.O. Addleshaw and F. Etchells, *The Architectural Setting of Anglican Worship* (1948), p. 123.

184 See especially WAC, F3 (1629–30) (n.f.), which refers to laying 106 feet of black marble and Purbeck 'under the Communion table'.

185 WAC, F2002, ff. 49 (where the word 'rayle' is carefully crossed out and 'frame' inserted), 70, 72, 74v; F3 (1629–30), n.f. Note also the reference in the wardens' accounts to going several times into churches in the City to 'take paterne' of the manner in which the communion table had been railed.

186 WAC, F2002, f. 70r–v. In 1641 glaziers were commissioned to make a 'new glasse window of divers coloured glasse' for Dulwich College chapel 'of the same worke and fashion as the east windowes of the Parishe Churches of St Martin in the fields and St Clement Danes': G.F. Warner, *Catalogue of the Manuscripts and Muniments of Alleyn's College of God's Gift in Dulwich* (1881), p. 148.

187 Mrs Frances Layton paid £10 'in plate' and Mr John Wandrake gave 'one bib'd Flaggon double guilt' weighing 43 oz. to the parish on Good Friday 1637, which was consecrated in March 1638: WAC, F3 (1634–35), n.f.; (1637–38), n.f. Wandrake also lent £100 for use of visited houses in the following year (F3, 1638–39). On Bray providing the ornaments for Covent Garden, and the commission for rating for them: *CSPD 1639*, p. 217; TNA, PC2/51 p. 342; BL, Harl. MS 1831, f. 39.

the employment of an organist was unquestionably a novelty and presumably reflected an intention for the organ to make a more elaborate contribution to services, this too may have met with approval among parishioners.[188] St Martin's parishioners had certainly included some zealous ceremonialists in the recent past, in the shape of Bishop Neile's sister and brother-in-law. The former had her funeral sermon delivered in St Martin's by Neile's protégé, the noted ceremonialist John Cosin, while her husband had presented the parish in 1619 with a new service book 'guilded with his name upon it'.[189] Nevertheless, the decision that the new church plate should be taken over to Lambeth for consecration by Laud is emblematic of the archbishop's concern that the parish and its troublesome vestry should continue to be closely supervised.[190]

Little detailed evidence survives of St Margaret's religious character during the the 1630s or its reaction to the Laudian agenda. Records do not reveal the sort of conflict found at the neighbouring St Martin's. As a historically more conservative parish, we might assume that St Margaret's would have welcomed the Laudian changes. The parish already appears to have had a communion rail, and other elaborate furnishings still survived from earlier periods: the 1630 parish inventory includes 'One cushion for the Communion table with Images, being old'.[191] There were some further developments: the churchwardens' accounts for 1638 record the quite exceptional phenomenon of the font being railed in 'by order of the vestry'. The font was subsequently painted, along with a nearby pillar and the King's arms.[192] But there is no evidence that the parish seized the opportunity of the Laudian reforms to invest more heavily in church ornamentation – there are no references to an enhanced communion table or rails. Instead, it was the font and pulpit that received attention.[193] These innovations in the later 1630s may represent the influence of the committee appointed to oversee the Abbey during Dean Williams's suspension. In 1632, the

---

188 WAC, F3 (1636–37), n.f., (1637–38), n.f.; F2002, f. 106v. The parish had owned an organ for many years. When he first arrived at St Martin's, Montford 'did moove the vestry about the Organs' (Kitto, p. 561), so presumably the old organ was maintained while Montford was vicar.

189 *The Works of John Cosin*, ed. J. Sansom (5 vols., Oxford, 1843–55), I, 24–43; *The Register of St Martin-in-the-Fields 1619–1636*, ed. J.V. Kitto (Harleian Society Registers 36, 1936), p. 179; *Acts*, no. 540; WAC, F2001, f. 133A.

190 WAC, F3 (1634–35; 1635–36).

191 WAC, E17, ff. 44v–46. Matthew Wren urged the example of St Margaret's, as well as St Martin's, as churches which had had a communion rail 'time out of mind': Christopher Wren, *Parentalia* (1750), p. 77 (although if St Martin's had indeed introduced a rail when the church was rebuilt in 1606–9 it is curious that there is no reference to it among the debates on the new rail in 1626–29). I would like to thank Dr Ken Fincham for drawing my attention to Wren's assertion. J. Davies (*The Caroline Captivity of the Church* (Oxford, 1992), pp. 228–9) rather unhelpfully cites 'E17–E23' (accounts for the entire period 1631–42) for evidence of St Margaret's rail; in fact there is no reference to a rail in the accounts.

192 WAC, E21, ff. 65, 66. Accounts also mention the purchase of expensive new surplices (E20 (1637–38), n.f.), and the 'new making' of the pulpit, stairs and reading place (E21 (1638–39), n.f.).

193 For the pulpit see WAC, E21 (1638–39), f. 63.

Abbey appointed one of its own prebendaries, Gilbert Wimberley, as curate of St Margaret's. Despite such preferment, Wimberley remains a shadowy figure, albeit a rare D.D. for St Margaret's. His later willingness to yield up a lecturing position in the parish to the puritan Stephen Marshall in 1642[194] may suggest his weakness in the face of an increasingly active laity.[195]

Fears of Catholic activity in Westminster, and particularly of conversions, were also a notable feature of the 1630s. Anxieties about highly placed Catholics in the area, who might shelter their co-religionists and convert weak-minded individuals were, of course, nothing new. In the Jacobean period Robert Hill had devoted a portion of his catechism to answering the question 'if man tempt you to Popish religion, how must you resist this temptation?'[196] Certainly some local inhabitants did convert to Catholicism, although in the best documented case – that of John Somers of St Martin's – it seems to have been independent reading of works of religious controversy, combined with a distaste for the divisions among Protestants, that swayed his allegiance.[197] By the 1630s, however, there were more open forms of Catholicism visible in Westminster. In 1631 a Catholic priest was seized saying mass in Lady Shrewsbury's house at Piccadilly Hall. Five Catholic priests, described as being of St Margaret's Westminster, were indicted in King's Bench for high treason in 1634. Two more priests were also reportedly active in St Margaret's during the 1636 plague. The 'sub-curate' of the parish, Robert White, complained to Laud that, under pretext of distributing alms from the friars in Somerset House, the priests entered infected houses in order to convert their occupants, bribing the watchers to keep quiet.[198]

Particular concerns were aroused by the availability of Catholic services at Court and in the chapels of foreign ambassadors. These acted as magnets for English Catholics as well as providing lodging for missionaries who could operate in the surrounding area.[199] Conversions were notoriously frequent at Court in the 1630s, and the Queen's new chapels excited particular concern. 'All sorts' of English people attended the

194 A.G. Matthews, *Walker Revised* (Oxford, 1948), s.n. Gilbert Wimberley; Smith, *Catalogue of Westminster Records*, p. 66. The post of 'lecturer' referred to here is unclear, but presumably refers to a small endowed lecture (perhaps that bequeathed by Sneyton – see above, n. 63) rather than an equivalent of the full lectureship operating in St Martin's. This would explain the reference to the curate Wimberley having previously held the post, presumably as a supplement to his meagre curate's stipend.

195 In the early 1640s the parish would be increasingly dominated by more puritanically disposed members of the laity such as Thomas Falconbridge, Emery Hill and Sir Robert Pye.

196 Hill, *Christs Prayer*, i, 65–6.

197 CUL, MS Dd/14/25 (3), pp. 13–17, 28–49.

198 *CSPD 1631–33*, p. 89; *CSPD 1634–35*, p. 160; TNA, SP16/331/93. Worcester House in the Strand has also been identified as 'a center for London Catholics' (C. Hibbard, *Charles I and the Popish Plot* (Chapel Hill, 1983), p. 40). See also the remarks by the Capuchins themselves in Williams, *Court and Times*, II, 310.

199 Hibbard, *Charles I*, pp. 40–2; W.R. Trimble, 'The embassy chapel question, 1625–1660', *Journal of Modern History* 18 (1946).

Queen's chapel at Somerset House, reported the vicar of the nearby St Giles in the Fields, who complained of conversions among his own parishioners in 1637.[200] Reports of a night-time procession on Holy Thursday 1638, moving down Drury Lane between the Spanish ambassador's house and Somerset House, created dismay and supposedly caused the King to investigate the involvement of English people.[201] Back in 1626, a St Martin's resident who attended mass in the French ambassador's chapel at Durham House had been severely punished by Westminster JPs for 'the evil and pernicious example' that he had given to others.[202] Nevertheless, the King periodically intervened to prevent local officials pursuing recusancy proceedings.[203] Even when English Catholics could be prosecuted, officials could do less about Catholic foreigners who had settled in the area: Westminster JPs reported in March 1639 that there were 641 French strangers residing within Westminster.[204]

The calling of the Long Parliament in 1640 did little to quell fears of the presence of Catholics in the area. It was a Westminster MP, John Glynn, who denounced 'the boldnes and impudencie of preists, friers and Jesuites (besides such as attended the Queenes Majestie) walking at noone day' and complained that 'divers went as ordinarilie and frequentlie to masse in Denmark howse and St James and to the Chappels of forraigne Ambassadors as to any church in London'.[205] When the local JP Peter Heywood was stabbed by a deranged Catholic in Westminster Hall 'as he was showing to a friend of his a schedule of such suspected and notorious Papists as were about Westminster', all stereotypes of Catholic bogeymen seemed to be fulfilled.[206] This was a stabbing that provided an eerie echo of the stabbing committed by William Flower at St Margaret's on Easter day 1555. Religious anxieties in Westminster were as heightened in 1640 as they had been when Elizabeth had first succeeded to the throne.

CONCLUSION

Distinctive patterns of religious development are visible in the parishes of St Martin's and St Margaret's, as both struggled with the task of instilling Protestantism into a large suburban population. In neither parish did the church simply focus its energies on influential gentry and the parish elites at the expense of the wider body of parishioners,

---

200 Knowler, I, 246; 2, 57.

201 TNA, C115/N8/8817.

202 LMA, WJ/SR (NS), 16/29, 138, 153.

203 E.g. *Middlesex County Records*, III, 67, 71.

204 *CSPD 1638–39*, p. 563.

205 *The Journal of Sir Simonds D'Ewes from the Beginning of the Long Parliament*, ed. W. Notestein (New Haven, 1923), p. 290.

206 *HMC De l'Isle & Dudley*, VI, 344–5; D'Ewes, *Journal*, p. 53; M. Jansson (ed.), *Two Diaries of the Long Parliament* (New York, 1984), p. 137; BL, Add. MS 38856/5, ff. 18, 37.

but each parish adopted a rather different means of providing for the broader parish community. St Martin's focused on the word preached, with a religious impetus linked in part to the fashionable development of the area, and an alliance of godly gentlemen and middle-ranking vestrymen. St Margaret's, on the other hand, sought to sustain the outward beauty of worship and ceremony. St Margaret's close ties to the Abbey may have helped to reinforce the social and religious conservatism of the parish. St Martin's burgeoning religious activism in part reflected its development as a fashionable neighbourhood and the decisive patronage of some committed gentlemen or aristocrats. But, as we have seen with parish government more generally, religious developments owed much to an informal alliance which appears to have developed between the traditional craftsman members of St. Martin's vestry and those few who could rightly claim gentlemanly status. What is more significant is that St Martin's pulpit did not simply become a mouthpiece either for government policy or for discontented aristocrats, or even a mere vehicle for the exercise of governmental patronage. Rather, the parish often endorsed a religious radicalism which could have overtly political implications. Notable too is how the different Westminster parishes gradually came to resemble one another by the 1630s, exhibiting a similar religious profile. At St Martin's, fashion-conscious residents (along with an intrusive Laudian vicar) pushed the parish towards at least a semblance of that 'beauty of holiness' long evident in St Margaret's, while in the latter parish political and religious developments helped to produce a vestry that was better disposed towards evangelical values and implicit criticism of the government's religious policy. In the end, Westminster's development as a fashionable neighbourhood may have stimulated the growth of a godly political consciousness, but ironically the very proximity of the Court ensured a visible, Catholic aristocratic presence of the sort most likely to antagonize such Protestant convictions.

Conclusion

THE decade of the 1530s was a climacteric in Westminster's history, ushering in dramatic changes that would crucially affect its later development. These years saw the creation of Whitehall Palace as the chief seat of the monarch, with major land exchanges with the Abbey and the extension of royal power into the locality, culminating in the wider changes of the Reformation by the late 1530s, and the dissolution of the monastery.

The story of Westminster in the following century is partly one of the fall-out from these events. The creation of Whitehall Palace is a case in point. In spatial terms, the absorption into the palace of part of the main thoroughfare of King Street, the reorganization of parish boundaries and the acquisition and preservation of large tracts of neighbouring land as royal hunting grounds all powerfully affected the subsequent development of the locality (some of which is still evident today in Hyde Park and St James's Park). The more established royal presence in the area also boosted the local economy, enormously expanding an already existing service sector and encouraging the numbers of luxury retailers. The presence of the royal Court also acted as a magnet for the gentry and the developing fashionable society. The later seventeenth century would see the gradual withdrawal of the royal Court from this heavily urbanized area to the peripheries of the metropolis. But the period between the Reformation and the Civil War was a distinctive phase in the history of the relationship between the Crown and the metropolis. Entrenched in a busy urban centre, the Crown's increasing sensitivities as a Westminster 'householder' led to royal attempts to regulate the disease, new building and pollution that characterized the suburb in which it was located. In this sense, the specific problems that the Westminster location posed for the Crown could act as the catalyst for broader royal policy initiatives.

Nevertheless, for all the prominence of the Crown in Westminster during this period, there were significant limits to its intervention in the locality. After Henry

VIII the Crown never effected such dramatic changes in key local institutions and land usage again, and there is little evidence that later monarchs sought to secure direct royal control over the area. The potential of Westminster to become a royal city seems never to have been systematically pursued by the Crown. Moreover, the relationship between local inhabitants and the domineering presence of the Court was more complex than historians have tended to assume. It hardly needs emphasizing that the prosperity of locals was built primarily upon an economy centred on the royal court and government bureaucracy, and that locals were also susceptible to sustained pressure from the Crown and aristocratic residents (most notably in the period when the Cecils were the dominant source of patronage in the area). Nevertheless, Westminster's non-gentry inhabitants were adept at manipulating these connections to further their own personal, and also communal, ends. Thus they worked to draw members of the nobility into local affairs and to solicit their charity. In the case of the Privy Council, it was not simply a matter of local inhabitants passively receiving orders handed down to them. Indeed it is clear that local officials often drew upon and solicited the Council's authority, especially during times of crisis such as plague, or when the power of parishes did not seem sufficient. The temptation to portray Westminster's inhabitants as mere adherents of the Court should therefore be resisted. As we have seen, the Westminster parliamentary elections of 1628 and 1640 displayed strong local opposition to 'court candidates'.

Early modern Westminster emerged from the traumas of the 1530s as a peculiar mixture of the old and the new. Indeed it is this unusual combination of traditional structures of power and authority and new social forces that typifies Westminster in this period. This patchwork of old and new, continuity and change, was nowhere more evident than in the continuing importance of Westminster Abbey in the area. The Abbey was able to cling on to its remaining powers with remarkable resilience in the century after the Reformation. The dean remained one of the most important men in Westminster – a presiding figure in the Court of Burgesses as well as a justice of the peace – while the Abbey retained ecclesiastical jurisdiction over St Margaret's parish and continued to exercise patronage as a local landlord and employer. Taken together, these features gave Westminster a very distinctive profile within the metropolis – indeed nowhere else in the capital did an ecclesiastical body wield such extensive secular authority after the Reformation. But perhaps most important of all, the Abbey indirectly shaped the future of local government in the metropolis by its resistance to all attempts to achieve a full and separate incorporation for the town, a stance it was ultimately able to maintain through the support of the Crown.

But where some old power structures and patterns of authority survived, new forces were also visible. Most striking was the size of Westminster's population, which increased dramatically in the century following the 1530s. But, as we have seen, Westminster's growth and development pulled in different directions. On the one hand much of its population increase was fuelled by poor immigrants to the capital, many of whom took jobs in the service sector. Yet our period also witnessed the beginnings of a fashionable 'West End'. This was important for many reasons, not the least of which was its impact on the use of space and urban development. The building of new houses suitable for the gentry was one of the most significant developments in early modern Westminster, and the commercial opportunities that fashionable society generated, from house-letting and the shops of Britain's Burse to the gambling at the pleasure gardens of Shaver's Hall, increasingly shaped the character of the town. This was also the period when the notion of a separate residential quarter for aristocrats and royal servants first emerged. By the second half of the seventeenth century, more un-settled areas to the north and west of Westminster's built-up areas would attract the nobility and become the sites of newer fashionable developments. But it is important not to read later seventeenth-century developments back into the earlier period. Rather, pre-1640 Westminster presents us with a distinctive phase in the establishment of a fashionable quarter in the metropolis. At this stage, the tendency was more for fashionable housing to swallow up older tenements and garden plots, or to cluster adjacent to existing built-up areas. The idea of a separate gentry enclave had only begun to emerge, and members of the gentry and aristocracy lived in close proximity to those who serviced their needs, in a more established urban centre. For all the distinctive forms of elite consumerism, gentry residents and visitors did not therefore live cocooned from the society around them, and this is a crucial time for observing how the gentry and aristocracy began to adopt an urban mode of life in the capital and how they defined their place within it. As we have seen, the extent to which these individuals imposed themselves upon the locality, and whether they were integrated within or remained aloof from the parishes in which they resided, was a matter of continual debate and negotiation.

In the period that we have been discussing, ideas of community were necessarily shaped by the unit of the parish. As we have seen, this was especially true in West-minster for historical reasons. The work of Gervase Rosser has demonstrated how the medieval parish of St Margaret and its fraternities allowed inhabitants to express a distinctive communal, urban identity in the absence of other structures. The frater-nities were one of the casualties of the Reformation, but the same drive towards communal organization in Westminster became focused still more firmly on the parish. With the frustration of plans for an incorporated municipal government, the parishes became the foremost organizations in Westminster. Indeed, Westminster's parishes became some of the most populous and powerful in the country. They have emerged from this study as vitally important, both as a unit of administration and also as a focus of local identity.

Parish elites reflected both old and new forces in Westminster. St Margaret's parish officials embodied the older social and economic interests of the medieval 'vill', with those connected to the Abbey, law courts, government bureaucracy and the victualling trade prominent among parish elites. By contrast, St Martin's officials partly reflected newer trends in courtly politics and urban development, with a greater gentry contingent, and an especially prominent body of officials from the King's Works.

But these parish elites were no mere passive reflections of social power in the area, moved around the chessboard of local politics by higher patrons, nor did they reflect a single dominant economic or political interest. Rather, they represented the range of different interest groups active in the area. They were nearly all, however, drawn from the middling groups of society, who felt squeezed between wealthy gentry residents and the large numbers of immigrant poor.

Westminster's parish officials were responsible for an administrative unit whose responsibilities were becoming increasingly complex and burdensome. It was partly in response to practical problems of administration that parish vestries became more oligarchic in character, and in this period lie the roots of Westminster's enormously powerful vestries of later centuries. The period between the Reformation and the Civil War was a time when the Westminster parishes' governing elites became narrower, and the parish community was defined more restrictively, with emphasis upon residential and moral criteria. Nevertheless, parish officials were still careful to emphasize the importance of the parish as a community bound together by mutual ties of interest and obligation. As we have seen, however, the extent of this community and its responsibilities could be defined differently in the light of different circumstances. The idea of the parish community thus continued to be invoked even as it was recast, redefined and appropriated by the parish's self-appointed 'ancients'. For parish officials, the use of the rhetoric of community was an important means by which they could bolster their own authority in the area in the face of aristocrats and the poor alike. But it also enabled them to defend what they perceived to be wider communal interests, such as access to lammas land and rights of way.

The constant attempts to invoke, appropriate and define the membership and interests of the parish community in this period reflect how powerfully social change had affected the locality at both ends of the social scale, but they also suggest the continuing attraction of notions of parish community in the face of such developments.

Finally, the religious life of Westminster's parishes was also expressive of this changing, transitional phase in Westminster's history, with the new and the old often standing in sharp and immediate contrast. Thus St Martin's parish was notable for its devotion to the word preached, with its religious impetus linked partly to the fashionable development of the parish, and an alliance of godly gentlemen and middle-ranking craftsmen on the vestry. By contrast, St Margaret's parish strikingly embodied the more conservative and traditional aspects of the locality. The parish's religious life was marked by an emphasis on ceremonialism, elaborate ritual and continuing close links to the Abbey. Nevertheless, with its increasing use as the parish church of the House of Commons and the involvement of more gentry in the parish, St Margaret's vestry and pulpit began to be more politically engaged from the 1620s onwards.

The result of these many developments was a town of remarkably varied contrasts and multiple identities. In a sense one can identify many different 'Westminsters' in this period – the venue of national institutions, the neighbourhood of the royal court, the domain of Westminster Abbey, the post-medieval suburb, the gentry playground of the emergent West End, the location of a uniquely powerful collection of parishes and the site of an abortive city government. It was also, of course, a locality struggling to meet the challenge of a soaring population, with enormous problems of poverty and plague.

Inevitably, conflicts might take place between the denizens of these different 'Westminsters' – and we have noted how clashes particularly occurred over the use and appropriation of land and space, when different groups sometimes found that their interests conflicted. Some uses of the local environment tended to preclude others – new building by the nobility might block local rights of way, the noxious fumes created by brewing and brickmaking might seem incompatible with the maintenance of a healthy and decorous environment at the royal court, and so on. In addition, different elite groups could find it difficult to maintain their privileges. This was an area not of a single hierarchy but of competing hierarchies, where a visiting nobleman might not command the same local status as an enterprising and public-spirited crafts-man, and where courtiers might find themselves outranked by humbly-born local officials when seats in the church were allocated. Even the process of 'gentrification' was not uniform, with some members of the nobility behaving more as birds of passage, while others chose to play more of a role in the locality, thereby acquiring an enhanced local status. Sorting out how these different claims to social status should be managed was a delicate and sometimes acrimonious business.

Early modern Westminster was thus not a venue of independent and self-sufficient societies and communities that happened to occupy the same space. Rather, it was the interaction of these different groups (whether supportive or conflicting) that made the social world of the town so distinctive. Accordingly, local inhabitants became adept at invoking the authority of more powerful interests to further their own goals. In the struggles over common lands, enclosers and lammas-day protesters alike sought to invoke the Queen's interests in the area as a local inhabitant, while locals inconvenienced by traders' stalls in King Street emphasized the special dignity of the area as the venue of parliament and the law courts in order to sway the Privy Council in their favour.

But for all the varied facets of Westminster society – the different 'Westminsters' one can evoke – there was an overarching urban identity which strained to express itself and which saw itself as distinct from London. This identity is partly revealed in the Court of Burgesses (even if in an emasculated form) as inhabitants sought full corporate status for what was clearly a city in name only. Three times in fifty years there were attempts to incorporate Westminster, and there would be at least two further attempts in the period after 1640. Although it is the failure of these bids for incorporation that has been one of this period's most long-term legacies, it is vital to remember that this was a time when the creation of an independent city could still be envisaged.

This study has sought to build Westminster into our picture of the early modern metropolis. This has been achieved partly by exploring Westminster's distinctiveness, and contrasting its government, administration and social structure with that of London. But this is not to deny that Westminster's experience was intimately connected to that of London. Both confronted massive population increase, poverty, plague and the expansion of built-up areas. Westminster was also necessarily connected to the larger metropolitan economy, and social and cultural developments in one area inevitably had an impact on the other. Nevertheless, many new developments in housing, urban planning, patterns of consumption and leisure and even certain forms of religious piety were especially evident, and found their most prominent early examples, in Westminster. And crucial to our understanding of these trends is a properly integrated sense of the distinctive Westminster context in which they emerged, and by which they were shaped. The history of early modern Westminster should therefore stand as an important chapter, not just in the history of London but also in the history of England.

Bibliography of selected primary sources

MANUSCRIPTS

BODLEIAN LIBRARY, OXFORD

Ashmole MSS
Bankes MSS
Rawlinson MS A.169   Papers on Marshalsea Court
Rawlinson MS D.818   Miscellaneous papers relating to see of London

BRITISH LIBRARY

Lansdowne MSS
5/30   Instructions for erecting a house of correction in Westminster, c.1563
7/21   Orders for Westminster in the time of plague, 1563
10/26   Contributors to the building of a market house in St Margaret, Westminster, 1568
14/36   Provision for the poor in St Martin's, St Clement Danes, Savoy and Westminster, 1572
16/74   Account of collections for the poor in Westminster, 1573
21/30   Petition of shoemakers of Westminster, 1575
26/66   Shoemakers of Westminster to Lord Burghley, 1578
35/32   Account of inmates within Westminster, 1582
43/74   Observations on parliamentary bill concerning Westminster, 1585
44/48   Names of headboroughs and boundaries of their wards in Westminster (wrongly identified in catalogue as London), c.1585

Harleian MSS
832   Collection of papers relating to the creation of St Paul Covent Garden
1831   Register book made by the burgesses and assistants of Westminster, c.1660

Cotton MSS
Julius C, III   Letter of Dean Williams of Westminster to Sir Robert Cotton, 1628

Trumbull MSS

CAMBRIDGE UNIVERSITY LIBRARY

Dd.14.25   Diary of John Somers

CHATSWORTH HOUSE, DERBYSHIRE

Bolton MSS   Accounts of the earls of Cumberland

DURHAM CATHEDRAL ARCHIVES

Hunter MS 44 Memorials of the almanac books of William Neile, 1593–1624

GUILDHALL LIBRARY, LONDON

MS 9531/12, 13, 15 Registers of Bishop of London
MS 9537/14, 15 Visitation Call Books, 1636–37
MS 15201/2 Vintners' Company Court Minutes

HAMPSHIRE RECORD OFFICE

MS 44M69/F6 Diary of Sir Richard Paulet, 1610

HATFIELD HOUSE, HERTFORDSHIRE

Correspondence, household cash books and miscellaneous bills
Accts 160/5 Household accounts of the second earl of Salisbury, 1621–25

HOUSE OF LORDS RECORD OFFICE

Draft bill 27 Eliz. I c. 47
Main Papers 1625, 1640, 1641, 1642

LAMBETH PALACE LIBRARY

MS658 Richard Webster to the earl of Essex, 1596
Shrewsbury MS 709 Petition of Westminster inhabitants for the suspension of the 1585 Act
Carte Misc. 7/79/5 Return of St Martin's vestry, 1635/6
COMM XIIa/12 Interregnum valuations of clerical stipends

LONDON METROPOLITAN ARCHIVES

Consistory Court of London
DL/C/300 Office Act Book, Jul. 1583–Mar. 1583/84
DL/C/306 Office Act Book, Nov. 1607–June 1609
DL/C/308 Office Act Book, May 1609–Oct. 1611
DL/C/310 Office Act Book, Nov. 1611–Oct. 1613
DL/C/312 Office Act Book, Nov. 1612–Oct. 1615
DL/C/313 Office Act Book, Nov. 1615–Mar. 1616/17
DL/C/315 Office Act Book, Nov. 1619–May 1621
DL/C/316 Office Act Book, Oct. 1620–June 1624
DL/C/617 Vicar General's Book 1616–23

Middlesex Sessions
MJ/SBR Sessions of the peace registers, 1608–67
WJ/SR (NS) 1–5 Westminster sessions of the peace rolls, 1620–1844

Bibliography

THE NATIONAL ARCHIVES, LONDON (FORMERLY PUBLIC
RECORD OFFICE)

C2   Chancery Proceedings
C3   Chancery Proceedings
C5   Chancery Proceedings
C66   Chancery, Patent Rolls
C115 Chancery, Masters' Exhibits
C181 Chancery, Crown Office, Entry Books of Commissioners
E36   Exchequer, Treasury of the Receipt, Miscellaneous Books
E101 Exchequer, King's Remembrancer, Miscellanea
E124 Exchequer, King's Remembrancer, Entry Books of Orders
E135 Exchequer, Miscellaneous Ecclesiastical Documents
E163 Exchequer, King's Remembrancer, Miscellanea of the Exchequer
E178 Exchequer, King's Remembrancer, Special Commissions of Inquiry
E179 Exchequer, King's Remembrancer, Lay Subsidies (assessments, certificates, etc.)
E215 Exchequer, King's Remembrancer, Commissions on Fees
E351 Exchequer, Various Accounts
PC2/41–52 Privy Council Registers (June 1631–September 1640)
PCC/Prob. 11 Prerogative Court of Canterbury, Will Registers
REQ2 Court of Requests, Proceedings
SO3   Signet Office Docquet Books
SP12 State Papers Domestic, Elizabeth I
SP14 State Papers Domestic, James I
SP16 State Papers Domestic, Charles I
STAC5 Star Chamber Proceedings, Elizabeth I
STAC8 Star Chamber Proceedings, James I

SHEFFIELD CITY ARCHIVES

Strafford Papers, Wentworth Woodhouse Muniments, vols 6, 12
Elmhirst Pye Papers MS 1287(c)

SIDNEY SUSSEX COLLEGE, CAMBRIDGE

Muniments Box 19/11   Will of the Countess of Sussex

SURREY HISTORY CENTRE

MS LM/1989   Loseley MSS, Petition concerning disputed parliamentary election in Westminster,
      1621
MS LM/1331/27   Further petition concerning the 1621 election

WESTMINSTER ABBEY MUNIMENTS

Accounts, Fraternity of the Virgin's Assumption (1515–21) and St Mary Rounceval (1520–24,
      1538–40) bound in a single volume with earlier guild accounts
Chapter Act Book, vol. II, 1609–42

Muniment Book 7 (the Dean's Book)
Muniment Book 15
Register books II, VI, XIII
WAM 5299A   Account of the 'bounds' of the 'Cittie of Westminster and the liberties thereof', temp. James I
WAM 6557   Precis of contents of proposed incorporation of Westminster, 1607
WAM 6558   Details of New Incorporation
WAM 6559   Dean and chapter's objections to proposed New Incorporation of the Suburbs, 1630s
WAM 6560   Further objections of dean and chapter to New Incorporation, 1630s
WAM 6561   Copy of proposed incorporation of Westminster, 1633, with comments of Dean Williams, and copy of WAM 6587
WAM 6562   Petition for separate Westminster sessions, pre-1618
WAM 6586   Draft charter of incorporation for Westminster, 1607
WAM 6587   Collated objections of dean and chapter to draft charter of incorporation
WAM 9340   Order and rules for house lately built for the poor of St Margaret's, temp. Elizabeth I
WAM 9353   List of poor inhabitants in the ward of Maurice Pickering, 1595
WAM 9628   Bond of William Jeve, as bailiff of Westminster, 1618
WAM 9629   Indenture of 1620 parliamentary election in Westminster
WAM 9631   Draft letter from the dean and chapter making void the appointment of James Lowman as bailiff and escheator, 1622
WAM 9886   Letters patent for the appointment of the earl of Buckingham as high steward, 1618
WAM 17212   Inquisition into the Lammas grounds in St Martin in the Fields held in common with St Margaret Westminster, 1592
WAM 25029   View of poor and impotent in St Margaret's, 1578
WAM 25095   Dean Williams's defence against charges, 1630s
WAM 25109   Memorandum of royal commission for visitation of Westminster college, January 1637
WAM 37252   Easter book, St Margaret Westminster, 1549
WAM 37494–37547   List of those receiving alms from Abbey, mid-Tudor
WAM 37550   Easter book, St Margaret Westminster, 1554
WAM 38126   Renunciation of churchwardens of St Margaret Westminster and appointment of successors, 1562
WAM 57269   Petition from vicar of St Martin in the Fields concerning a church rate, 1608

WESTMINSTER ARCHIVES CENTRE

St Clement Danes
Parish registers, I (1558–1644)
B1   Accounts, Surveyors of the highways 1581–1621
B9   Accounts of church building expenses 1575
B19   Accounts, overseers for the poor 1604–11
B21   Accounts, overseers for the poor 1617–18

St Margaret Westminster
E2–6   Churchwardens' accounts 1510–1610
E8   Churchwardens' accounts 1612–13
E13–21   Churchwardens' accounts 1622–40
E22   Relief of poor visited with plague, 1638–39
E23   Churchwardens' accounts 1640–42
E144   Accounts, collectors for the poor, 1561–62, 1565–71
E145–148   Accounts, collectors for the poor, 1572–99

Bibliography

E149–151   Accounts, overseers for the poor, 1600–24

E152–154   Accounts, overseers for the poor, 1624–40, including 'special account' for relief of plague victims, 1625

E2413   Vestry minutes, 1591/2–1661/2

St Martin in the Fields

F2   Churchwardens' accounts 1604–24

F3   Churchwardens' accounts 1624–47

F301   Accounts, collectors for the poor, 1574–75

F304–311   Accounts, collectors for the poor, 1577–84

F312–317   Accounts, collectors for the poor, 1585–91

F319–324   Accounts, collectors for the poor, 1592–98

F325–352   Accounts, overseers for the poor, 1598–1626

F353–360   Accounts, overseers for the poor, 1626–34

F361–368   Accounts, overseers for the poor, 1635–42

F2001   Vestry minutes 1574–1623

F2002   Vestry minutes 1624–52

F3354   Rate for the visited poor, collector's book, Landside, 1625

F3355   Rate for the poor visited, 1630

F3356   Names and assessments of those out of town (incomplete), 1636

F4511–4512   Accounts, Examiners for visited houses, 1625

F4514   Subscription for relief of plague sufferers, list of premises shut by plague, 1636–38

F4515   Churchwardens' disbursements for poor visited, 1631

F4516   Accounts, collectors for poor visited, 1636–37

F6036   Certificate of churchwardens and vestry to Thomas, earl of Suffolk, concerning a lecturer recommended by him, 1615

F6039   Survey of the poor, 1602/3

PCW   Peculiar Court of Westminster, wills, registers and act books, 1504–1858

WCB1   Minutes, Westminster Court of Burgesses 1610–13

WCB2   Minutes, Westminster Court of Burgesses 1613–16

1656/1   Minute Book of the Court of Governors, St Margaret's Hospital, 1641–1737

YORK MINSTER ARCHIVE

Add 18   Archbishop Matthew's preaching diary

Printed primary sources

Place of publication is London, unless otherwise stated.

The Account Books of St Bartholomew Exchange, ed. E. Freshfield (1895)

Acts of the Dean and Chapter of Westminster, 1543–1609, ed. C.S. Knighton (Westminster Abbey Record Series, I–II, 1997–99)

Acts of the Privy Council of England, ed. J.R. Dasent (32 vols., 1890–1907)

Hugh Alleys' Caveat: The Markets of London in 1598, ed. I. Archer, C. Barron and V. Harding (London Topographical Society, 137, 1988)

Anon., *Two Sermons* [funeral sermon of Thomas Montfort] (1632)

The Arraignment of John Selman (1612)

Bargrave, Isaac, *A Sermon against Selfe Policy* (1624)

—— *A Sermon preached before the Honourable Assembly* (1624)

Barrington Family Letters 1628–32, ed. A. Searle (Camden Society, 4th ser., 28, 1983)

Cabala (1654)

Calendar of the Correspondence of the Smyth Family of Ashton Court 1548–1642, ed. J.H. Bettey (Bristol Record Society 35, 1982)

Calendar of the Patent Rolls, Edward VI, Philip and Mary, Elizabeth (1924–86)

Calendar of State Papers, Domestic

Calendar of State Papers, Venetian

Calendar of Wynn of Gwydir Papers 1515–1690 (Aberystwyth, 1926)

Records of the Worshipful Company of Carpenters, ed. B. Marsh, J. Ainsworth and A.M. Millard (7 vols., 1914–68)

A Catalogue of Westminster Records, ed. J.E. Smith (1900)

Wyllyam Cecill knight, high steward of the citie of Westminster . . . to the Baylyffe (1564)

The Letters of John Chamberlain, ed. N.E. McClure (2 vols., Philadelphia, 1939)

The Diaries of Lady Anne Clifford, ed. D.J.H. Clifford (Stroud, 1990)

Commons Debates in 1621, ed. W. Notestein, F. Relf and H. Simpson (7 vols., New Haven, 1935)

Commons Debates for 1629, ed. W. Notestein and F.H. Relf (Minneapolis, 1921)

The Works of John Cosin, ed. J. Sansom (5 vols., Oxford, 1843–55)

Private Correspondence of Lady Jane Cornwallis, ed. Lord Braybrooke (1842)

The Court and Times of Charles I, ed. R.F. Williams (2 vols., 1848)

Cyvile and Uncyvile Life: a discourse where is disputed, what order of Lyfe best beseemeth a Gentleman (1579) – another issue reprinted in W.C. Hazlitt (ed.), *Inedited Tracts* (1868)

Dekker, Thomas, *The Dead Terme. Or Westminsters Complaint for Long Vacations* (1608)

The Diary of Sir Simonds D'Ewes, ed. E. Bourcier (Paris, 1974)

The Journal of Sir Simonds D'Ewes from the Beginning of the Long Parliament, ed. W. Notestein (New Haven, 1923)

A Deep Sigh Breath'd through the lodgings at Whitehall (1642)

Two Diaries of the Long Parliament, ed. M. Jansson (New York, 1984)

A Discourse of the Common Weal, ed. E. Lamond (Cambridge, 1893)

Documentary Annals of the Reformation, ed. E. Cardwell (2 vols., Oxford, 1844)

The Complete English Poems of John Donne, ed. C.A. Patrides (1985, reprt, 1990)

Egerton Papers, ed. J. Payne Collier (Camden Society 12, 1840)

Everard, John, *The Arriereban* (1618)

—— *Some Gospel Treasures Unopened* (1653)

Featley, Daniel, *Clavis Mystica* (1636)

Ceremonies of Charles I: the Note Books of John Finet, 1628–1641, ed. A.J. Loomie (New York, 1987)

Bibliography

Fisher, William, *A Sermon Preached at Paules Crosse* (1580)

Forsett, Edward, *A Defence of the Right of Kings* (1624)

Foxe, John, *Acts and Monuments*, ed. S.R. Catley (8 vols., 1838)

Fuller, Thomas, *History of the Worthies of England* (1662)

Gataker, Thomas, *Certaine Sermons* (1637)

—— *A Discours Apologeticall* (1654)

The workes of . . . Richard Greenham (5th ed., 1612)

Hacket, John, *Scrinia reserata* (1693)

The Autobiography of Lady Anne Halkett, ed. J.G. Nichols (Camden Society, n.s. 13, 1875)

Harrison's Description of England, ed. F.J. Furnivall (4 parts, 1877–1908)

Hill, Robert, *The Contents of Scripture* (1596)

—— *Christs Prayer Expounded A Christian Directed A Communicant Prepared* (1606)

—— *A Godly and Learned Exposition or the Commentarie upon the three first Chapters of the Revelation* (1607)

—— *The Pathway to Prayer and Pietie* (1613)

Historical Manuscripts Commission:

—— *Cowper II*

—— *De l'Isle and Dudley VI*

—— *Downshire VI*

—— *Hastings*

—— *Hatfield House/Salisbury* (24 vols., 1883–1976)

—— *Seventh Report*

The Diary of Lady Margaret Hoby, ed. D.M. Meads (1930)

Letters of John Holles 1587–1637, ed. P.R. Seddon (Thoroton Society, 31, 35–6, 1975–86)

The Holles Account of Proceedings in the House of Commons, ed. C. Thompson (Orsett, 1985)

Howes, Edmund, *Annales* (1631)

Howell, James, *Epistolae Ho-Elianae* (5th ed., 1678)

—— *Londinopolis* (1657)

The Political Works of James I, ed. C. McIlwain (Cambridge, Mass., 1918)

James, Richard, *Marmora Arundeliana* (1628)

The Works of Ben Jonson, ed. C.H. Herford, P. Simpson and E.M.S. Simpson (11 vols., Oxford, 1925–52)

Journals of the House of Commons

Journals of the House of Lords

The Journals of Two Travellers in Elizabethan and Early Stuart England, ed. P. Razzell (1995)

Household Accounts and Disbursement Books of Robert Dudley, Earl of Leicester, ed. S. Adams (Camden Society, 5th ser., 6, 1995)

Letters and Memorials of State, ed. A. Collins (2 vols., 1746)

Letters and Papers, Foreign and Domestic, of the reign of Henry VIII, ed. J.S. Brewer, J. Gairdner and R.H. Brodie (1862–1932)

'William Latymer's Cronickille of Ane Bulleyne', ed. M. Dowling, *Camden Miscellany XXX* (Camden Society, 4th ser., 1990)

Ley, Roger, *Two Sermons* (1619)

London and Middlesex Chantry Certificate, 1548, ed. C.J. Kitching (London Record Society, 16, 1980)

The Diary of Henry Machyn, Citizen and Merchant-Taylor of London, 1550–1563, ed. J.G. Nichols (Camden Society 42, 1848)

Memorials of St Margaret's Church Westminster: The Parish Registers, 1539–1600, ed. A.M. Burke (1914).

Middlesex County Records, ed. J.C. Jeaffreson (4 vols., 1886–92)

Calendar of Middlesex Sessions Records, ed. W. Le Hardy (4 vols., 1935–41)

Minutes of Parliament of the Middle Temple, ed. C.T. Martin (3 vols., 1904)

Montford, Thomas, *A Sermon Preached at the Funeral of Lady Blount* (1619)

Moryson, Fynes, *An Itinerary Containing His Ten Yeeres Travell* (4 vols., 1907–8)

Narratives of the Days of the Reformation, ed. J.G. Nichols (Camden Society, 77, 1859)

'The undergraduate account book of John and Richard Newdigate, 1618–21', ed. V. Larminie, *Camden Miscellany 30* (Camden Society, 4th ser., 39, 1990)

Norden, John, *Speculum Britanniae, Description of Middlesex* (1593)

The Norwich Census of the Poor, 1570, ed. J.F. Pound (Norfolk Record Society 40, 1971)

The Order of the Communion, 1548, ed. H.A. Wilson (1908)

The Oxinden Letters 1607 to 1642, ed. D. Gardiner (1933)

The Parochial Charities of Westminster, First Report of the Trustees (Westminster, 1890)

Peacham, Henry, *Coach and Sedan* (1636)

——— *The Art of Living in London* (1642), ed. V. Heltzel (Cornell, N.Y., 1962)

——— *The Gentlemens Exercise* (1612)

A Petition of the Citie of Westminster (1643)

Thomas Platter's Travels in England in 1599, ed. C. Williams (1937)

Poor Relief in Elizabethan Ipswich, ed. J. Webb (Suffolk Records Society 9, 1966)

Poverty in Early Stuart Salisbury, ed. P. Slack (Wiltshire Record Society 31, Devizes, 1975)

The Private Journals of the Long Parliament 7 March to 1 June 1642, ed. V.F. Snow and A.S. Young (New Haven, 1987)

Proceedings in the Parliaments of Elizabeth I, ed. T.E. Hartley (3 vols., Leicester, 1981–95)

Proceedings in Parliament, 1610, ed. E.R. Foster (2 vols., 1966)

Proceedings in Parliament 1626, ed. W. Bidwell and M. Jansson (4 vols., New Haven, 1991–96)

Queen Elizabeth and Her Times, ed. T. Wright (2 vols., 1838)

Jacobean Recusant Rolls for Middlesex, ed. J.J. LaRocca (Catholic Record Society 76, 1997)

A Register of Baptisms, Marriages, and Burials in the Parish of St. Martin-in-the-Fields . . . from 1550 to 1619, ed. T Mason (Harleian Society Registers, 25, 1898)

Bibliography

The Register of St Martin-in-the-Fields 1619–1636, ed. J.V. Kitto (Harleian Society Registers, 36, 1936)

A Transcript of the Registers of the Company of Stationers, 1554–1640, ed. E.A. Arber (5 vols., London and Birmingham, 1875–94)

Les Reportes del Cases in Camera Stellata 1593–1609, ed. W. Baildon (1894)

Reports of Cases in the Courts of Star Chamber and High Commission, ed. S.R. Gardiner (Camden Society, n.s. 39, 1886)

St Martin-in-the-Fields. The Accounts of the Churchwardens, 1525–1603, ed. J.V. Kitto (1901)

The Seconde Parte of a Register, ed. A. Peel (2 vols., Cambridge, 1915)

Sheldon, Richard, *The First Sermon of R. Sheldon priest, after his Conversion* (1612)

Shirley, James, *The Lady of Pleasure*, ed. R. Huebert (Manchester, 1986)

Stow, John, *A Survey of London*, ed. C.L. Kingsford (2 vols., Oxford, 1908)

The Earle of Strafforde's Letters and Despatches, ed. W. Knowler (2 vols., 1739)

Strype, John, *A Survey of the Cities of London and Westminster* (2 vols., 1720)

—— *Ecclesiastical Memorials* (6 vols., 1822)

—— *Memorials of Thomas Cranmer* (2 vols., 1840)

Stuart Royal Proclamations, ed. J. Larkin and P. Hughes (2 vols., 1973–83)

Synodalia, ed. E. Cardwell (Oxford, 1842)

Taylor, John, *The Brownists Synagogue* (1641)

The Book of Architecture of John Thorpe, ed. J. Summerson (Walpole Society 40, 1966)

The London Surveys of Ralph Treswell, ed. J. Schofield (London Topographical Society, 135, 1987)

Tudor Royal Proclamations, ed. P.L. Hughes and J.F. Larkin (3 vols., New Haven, 1964–69)

The Vestry Minute Book of the Parish of St Bartholomew Exchange in the City of London, 1567–1676, ed. E. Freshfield (1890)

Visitation Articles and Injunctions of the Early Stuart Church, ed. K. Fincham (2 vols., Church of England Record Society 1, 5, 1994–98)

Visitation Articles and Injunctions of the Period of the Reformation, ed. W.H. Frere and W.P. Kennedy (3 vols., 1910)

The Diary of Baron Waldstein, ed. G.W. Groos (1981)

Historical Notices . . . by Nehemiah Wallington (2 vols., 1869)

Walsingham, Francis, *A Search Made into Matters of Religion* (St Omer, 1609)

Waterhouse, Edward, *The Gentleman's Monitor* (1665)

Whitelocke, Bulstrode, *Memorials of the English Affairs* (1732)

The Diary of William Whiteway, ed. D. Underdown (Dorset Record Society 12, 1991)

Willet, Andrew, *Sacrorum Emblematum Centuria Una* (?1592)

—— *Synopsis Papismi* (1634)

Wren, Christopher, *Parentalia* (1750)

Wriothesley, C., *A Chronicle of England During the Reigns of the Tudors*, ed. W.D. Hamilton (2 vols., Camden Society, n.s., 11, 20, 1875–77)

Index

Lightning Source UK Ltd.
Milton Keynes UK
UKOW030703250712

196520UK00001B/1/P